Introduction to

MICROECONOMICS

EDWIN G. DOLAN
Ph.D. Yale University

DAVID E. LINDSEY
Ph.D. University of Chicago

Best Value Textbooks

EDITOR: Kristin Van Gaasbeck

TEXT DESIGN AND COMPOSITION: Archetype Book Composition

COVER DESIGN: Walker Printing

ISBN: 1-932856-02-1

TABLE OF CONTENTS

PREFACE

THE MOST RELIABLE constant of life in a market economy is constant change. Sitting down to work on this new edition of this textbook has brought many changes to my attention.

Some of them are trivial. One chapter mentioned some authors who were on the best-seller list at the time of the last edition—good books they wrote, but just as the market economy is in constant change, so is the publishing industry. Out they go, to be replaced by J.K. Rowling and Dan Brown.

Other changes are much more fundamental, such as the trend toward globalization of both the macro- and micro-economy. Professional economists will know that this trend is not really new. If one looks at the data, trends in imports and exports, integration of labor and financial markets, and global brand penetration started long ago. Yet, although statistically well established, these trends have clearly hit a new threshold of public awareness in the first decade of the 21st century. For that reason alone, a modern textbook must reflect the global nature of the economy.

One of the signs of its increased global outlook is the disappearance of a separate chapter on foreign exchange markets and international monetary policy. Because these topics are more important than ever, it is no longer appropriate to isolate them in the last chapter of the macroeconomics course, too easily skipped in the rush toward final exams. Instead, topics like the effects of exchange rates on aggregate demand and the relationship between price stability and exchange rate policy are now integrated directly into the various macro chapters that deal with related issues for the domestic economy. The result is a book that is both more up-to-date and more streamlined. Numerous globally-oriented cases and topics appear in the micro chapters as well.

One final change is in the textbook market itself. Earlier editions of this book reflected the college publishing world of the past: Fat, heavy volumes with fat, heavy price tags that, over time, came to be one of the most resented financial burdens of a college education. And students didn't even get their money's worth from those texts of an earlier era. The technology of the day meant long lead times and the sheer costs of production meant substantial intervals between revisions, so that textbooks were often several years out of date before they hit the classroom. Things were even worse for students who, because of financial pressure, depended on lower-cost used copies of earlier editions. Happily, that model of publishing is now in retreat.

It is a great pleasure to me to see this new edition come out through Best Value Textbooks at a price that offers a fair value to students. The advantages of working with a publisher who uses the latest technology to bring the book to market just a few months after final revisions are made makes the pleasure all the greater. I hope you, as a user of the book, will complete the cycle by providing me, as author, with your feedback so that your suggested changes can be quickly incorporated in future editions.

Acknowledgments

My first thanks must go to my long-time co-author, David E. Lindsey, with whom I worked on earlier editions of this text over a period of many years. During his years as Deputy Director of the Division of Monetary Affairs of the Board of Governors of the Federal Reserve System, David was able to find the ideal balance between the theory and practice of economics. Although he did not contribute directly to preparation of this new edition, his strong influence can still be seen in both the macroeconomic and microeconomic chapters.

Second, I would like to thank Kristin van Gaasbeck, Ph.D for her innovative work in updating data sources, news items, and many other elements for the new edition. Her work has made a big difference in keeping the content of the book fresh and up to date, and in bringing it to market faster than could ever have been done without her able contribution.

Finally, I thank the entire publishing and editorial staff of Best Value Textbooks for introducing me to this great new concept in college publishing. I hope you, the user, benefit as much as I have.

EDWIN G. DOLAN
Lopez Island, Washington

Features of This Edition

- *State of the art pedagogy*. An abundance of case studies introduce and illustrate the subject matter of every chapter.
- *Integrated international economics*. As the world economy itself comes closer together, international economics must be more closely integrated into the principles course. Accordingly, topics in international economic theory and policy, ranging from balance of payments accounts to the foreign exchange operations of the Fed, are introduced in the chapters in which they occur naturally, rather than presented separately in a single chapter.

Supplements

Test Bank

The accompanying Test Bank contains over 2,000 questions in a variety of formats including multiple choice, true/false, and essay questions..

Instructor's Manual

The expanded Instructor's Manual contains material which can be easily included in lectures. The manual also includes all of its traditional elements, including instructional objectives, lecture notes, and suggestions.

Study Guide

The Study Guide has hands-on applications and self-testing programs. It is available in two versions, *Macroeconomics*, and *Microeconomics*. Students can gain an advantage by reinforcing their reading and lecture notes with the following study guide features:

- *Where You're Going*. The objectives and terms for each chapter are recapped to tie concepts together.
- *Walking Tour.* The "Walking Tour" section provides a narrative summary of the chapter and incorporates questions on key points. Answers are given in the margin.
- *Hands On*. Geographical and numerical exercises clarify concepts and better prepare students for tests and quizzes.
- *Economics in the News*. A news item illustrates how concepts covered in the chapter can appear in the real world. Questions and answers reinforce the concepts.
- *Questions for Review.* These questions and answers follow the key chapter concepts, preparing students for the self-test.
- *Self-Test*. Extra test preparation increases a student's understanding and ability to succeed.
- *Careers in Economics*. Formerly an appendix in the text, this material provides students with an understanding of where the study of economics could lead them.

Best Value Textbooks Online Student Tutorial

Created to support and enhance the student's comprehension of the economic principles discussed in the textbook. The online tutorial includes chapters objectives and study questions. To access the tutorial please visit our Students section on our Web site www.bestvaluetextbooks.com. Username: Economics Password: DolanLindsey

Best Value Textbooks Economic PowerPoint Transparencies

This PowerPoint slide set combines graphics and text to further illustrate the economic principles discussed in the text.

Best Value Textbooks Transparencies

Graphs, charts, and illustrations from the text creates additional in-class support for the instructor and students.

About the Authors

EDWIN G. DOLAN was born in Oklahoma and grew up in a small town in Oregon. He attended Earlham College and Indiana University, where he majored in Russian Studies and received the Certificate of Indiana University's famed Russian and East-European Institute. After earning a doctorate in economics from Yale University, he taught at Dartmouth College, the University of Chicago, George Mason University and Gettysburg College. In 1990, he began teaching in Moscow, Russia, where he and his wife founded the American Institute of Business and Economics, an independent, not-for-profit MBA program. Since retiring as President of that institution in 2001, he has lectured on global macroeconomics and managerial economics in Riga, Latvia; Budapest, Hungary; and Zagreb, Croatia. When not lecturing abroad, he makes his home in Washington's San Juan Islands.

DAVID E. LINDSEY comes from the university town of West Lafayette, Indiana. He received his B.A. from Earlham College, where he and Dolan were roommates. He then earned a Ph.D. from the University of Chicago under the direction of Milton Friedman. Lindsey taught economics for several years at the Ohio State University and Macalester College. From 1974 to 2003, he was on the staff of the Board of Governors of the Federal Reserve System, where he served for many years as Deputy Director of the Division of Monetary Affairs and Associate Economist for the Federal Open Market Committee.

PART I

Overview of Economics

CHAPTER 1

The Economic Way of Thinking

After reading this chapter, you will understand:

1. The subject matter of economics
2. The considerations underlying four fundamental economic choices:
   - What an economy will produce
   - How goods and services will be produced
   - Who will produce which goods and services
   - For whom goods will be produced
   - How to coordinate economic choices
3. How economists use theory, graphs, and evidence in their work

CASE STUDY: LAND MANAGEMENT AND WILDFIRE

In autumn of 2003, wildfires spread through Southern California, closing schools, businesses, and freeways in San Diego and Los Angeles. The growing population in this region has created pressure to erect homes closer to forests and canyons, exposing more people to the threat of fire. Such wildfires not only damage buildings, but also destroy trees and wildlife. As metropolitan areas have spread closer to forests (8 million people live in wildland areas), the demand for fire protection has grown.

However, in working to prevent fire, these communities actually increase the chances of wildfire. California's climate and topography create ideal natural conditions for wildfire. To combat destructive wildfires, the California

Department of Forestry and Fire Protection (CDF) uses prescribed burning. Isolated forest fires occur naturally and serve many purposes. They cleanse the forest floor, removing brush and debris. This exposes the soil to essential sunlight, fostering the growth of healthier trees, grasses, and plants that provide wildlife habitat. The CDF hopes to recreate this process by igniting controlled fires in state parks. Prescribed burning not only serves an important purpose to support natural growth in forests, but reduces the chances of a devastating wildfire. By consuming brush, diseased trees, and other debris, forest fires consume fuel. Without fire, this debris builds up over time, making wildfires more of a threat.

In addition to prescribed burning, the CDF wants to establish larger Wildfire Protection Zones to buffer communities from forests and canyons. These zones would institute an area between wildland and development. This will prove more difficult as the pressures of a growing population create the need for more housing.

Source: California Fire Plan, California Board of Forestry, May 2000.

Scarcity

A situation in which there is not enough of a resource to meet all of everyone's wants.

Economics

The social science that seeks to understand the choices people make in using scarce resources to meet their wants.

THE DIFFICULTY OF land management is an example of **scarcity**—a situation in which there is not enough of something to meet everyone's wants. Scarcity and the way people deal with it are the central topics of **economics**, which can be defined as the social science that seeks to understand the choices people make in using scarce resources to meet their wants.

Economics, as the definition makes clear, is a study not of things or money or wealth but of *people*. Economics is about people because scarcity itself is a human phenomenon. Although Southern California encompasses a certain amount of land, land became scarce when it became the object of human wants. The same is true of all other scarce resources—mozzarella cheese is scarce because people want pizzas, Manhattan real estate is scarce because people want to live and do business on that crowded island, and time is scarce because people have many things they want to do each day.

A second reason that economics is about people is that the choices it studies are made in a social context. That is why economics is considered a social science rather than a branch of operations management, engineering, or mathematics. Take, for example, the social context of decisions regarding the use of land and prescribed burning. People want to prevent fire because they want to protect their homes. The decision to use resources to build homes closer to forests reflects a judgment about which human wants should be given priority over others that the same resources could be used to satisfy. The California Department of Forestry and Fire Protection's desire to create Wildfire Protection Zones reflects the debate about how to allocate the world's scarce resources.

Economic choices are being made every day. You make economic choices when you buy clothes or groceries, when you work at a job—even when you choose to fill one of the scarce slots in your class schedule with a course in economics rather than with one in environmental toxicology. Economic choices are made everywhere: in the factory that made the computer this book was typed on, in the government offices that oversee affirmative-action policies, in nonprofit organizations such as churches and student clubs, and in just about any other situation you can think of.

Microeconomics

The branch of economics that studies the choices of individuals, including households, business firms, and government agencies.

All the examples just given come from the branch of economics known as **microeconomics**. The prefix *micro,* meaning "small," indicates that this branch of economics deals with the choices of small economic units such as households, firms, and government agencies. Although microeconomics studies individual behavior, its scope can be worldwide. For example, households, firms, and government agencies conduct worldwide trade in such goods as cars, chemicals, and crude oil. That trade and the policies regulating it fall within the scope of microeconomics.

Macroeconomics

The branch of economics that studies large-scale economic phenomena, particularly inflation, unemployment, and economic growth.

Economics also has another branch, known as **macroeconomics.** The prefix *macro,* meaning "large," indicates that this branch deals with larger-scale economic phenomena. Typical problems in macroeconomics include how to maintain conditions in which people who want jobs can find them, how to protect the economy against the distortions caused by the widespread price increases called inflation, and how to provide for a continued increase in living standards over time. Government policies concerning taxes, expenditures, budget deficits, and the financial system are central concerns of macroeconomics. However, inasmuch as macroeconomic phenomena, such as inflation, represent the summation of millions of individual choices regarding the prices of particular goods and services, macroeconomics rests on a microeconomic foundation. Both microeconomics and macroeconomics study the problem of scarcity. While microeconomics focuses on individual choices, macroeconomics examines how society as a whole behaves.

Whether one is dealing with microeconomics or macroeconomics, with domestic or international economic relationships, all economic analysis comes down to a special way of thinking about how people choose to use scarce resources.

WHAT? HOW? WHO? FOR WHOM?

In every economy certain basic choices must be made. Among these, the most important are *what* goods will be produced, *how* they will be produced, *who* will do which jobs, and *for whom* the results of economic activity will be made available. Each of these choices is made necessary because of scarcity, and each can be used to introduce key elements of the economic way of thinking.

Deciding What to Produce: Opportunity Cost

Factors of production

The basic inputs of labor, capital, and natural resources used in producing all goods and services.

Labor

The contributions to production made by people working with their minds and muscles.

Capital

All means of production that are created by people, including tools, industrial equipment, and structures.

Natural resources

Anything that can be used as a productive input in its natural state, such as farmland, building sites, forests, and mineral deposits.

Opportunity cost

The cost of a good or service measured in terms of the forgone opportunity to pursue the best possible alternative activity with the same time or resources.

The first basic choice is that of what goods to produce. In any real economy the number of goods and services that could be produced is immense. The essential features of the choice of what goods to produce, however, can be illustrated using an economy in which as few as two alternative goods exist—for example, cars and education. For many students, going without a car (or driving an older, used car instead of a new one) is a sacrifice that must be made in order to get a college education. The same trade-off that is faced by an individual student is also faced by the economy as a whole: Not enough cars and education can be produced to satisfy everyone's wants. Someone must choose how much of each good to produce.

The impossibility of producing as much of everything as people want reflects a scarcity of the productive resources that are used to make all goods. Many scarce productive resources must be combined to make even the simplest of goods. For example, making a table requires lumber, nails, glue, a hammer, a saw, the work of a carpenter, that of a painter, and so on. For convenience, productive resources are often grouped into three basic categories, called **factors of production**: labor, capital, and natural resources. **Labor** includes all of the productive contributions made by people working with their minds and muscles. **Capital** includes all the productive inputs created by people, including tools, machinery, buildings, and intangible items, such as computer programs. **Natural resources** include anything that can be used as a productive input in its natural state—for example, farmland, building sites, forests, and mineral deposits.

Productive resources that are used to satisfy one want cannot be used to satisfy another at the same time. Steel, concrete, and building sites used for automobile factories cannot also be used for classrooms. People who are employed as teachers cannot spend the same time working on an automobile assembly line. Even the time students spend in class and studying for tests represents use of a factor of production that could otherwise be used as labor in an auto plant. Because production uses inputs that could be used elsewhere, the production of any good entails forgoing the opportunity to produce something else instead. In economic terms, everything has an **opportunity cost**. The opportunity cost of a good or service is its cost in terms of the forgone opportunity to pursue the best possible alternative activity with the same time or resources.

Let's go back to the example of an economy that has only two goods, cars and education. In such an economy, the opportunity cost of producing a college graduate can be stated in terms of the number of cars that could have been produced by using the same labor, capital, and natural resources. For example, the opportunity cost of educating a college graduate might be four Ford Mustangs. Such a ratio (graduates per car or cars per graduate) is a useful way to express opportunity cost when only two goods are involved. More typically, though, we deal with situations in which there are many goods. Having more of one means giving up a little bit of many others.

In an economy with many goods, opportunity costs can be expressed in terms of a common unit of measurement, money. For example, rather than saying that a college education is worth four Mustangs or that a Mustang is worth one-fourth of a college education, we could say that the opportunity cost of a car is $20,000 and that of a college education is $80,000.

Useful as it is to have a common unit of measurement, great care must be taken when opportunity costs are expressed in terms of money, because not all out-of-pocket money expenditures represent the sacrifice of opportunities to do something else. At the same time, not all sacrificed opportunities take the form of money spent. *Applying Economic Ideas 1.1*, which analyzes both the out-of-pocket expenditures and the opportunity costs of a college education, shows why.

The importance of opportunity cost will be stressed again and again in this book. The habit of looking for opportunity costs is one of the distinguishing features of the economic way of thinking.

Deciding How to Produce: Efficiency and Entrepreneurship

A second basic economic choice is that of how to produce. There is more than one way to produce almost any good or service. Cars, for example, can be made in highly automated factories using a lot of capital equipment and relatively little labor, or they can be built one by one in small shops, using a lot of labor and only a few general-purpose machines. Ford Mustangs are built the first way, Mercedes and BMWs the second way. The same kind of thing could be said about education. Economics can be taught in a small classroom with one teacher and a blackboard serving 20 students, or it can be taught in a large lecture hall in which the teacher uses projectors, computers, and TV monitors to serve hundreds of students.

Economic efficiency

A state of affairs in which it is impossible to make any change that satisfies one person's wants more fully without causing some other person's wants to be satisfied less fully.

Efficiency in production

A situation in which it is not possible, given available knowledge and productive resources, to produce more of one good without forgoing the opportunity to produce some of another good.

EFFICIENCY Efficiency is a key consideration in deciding how to produce. In everyday speech, *efficiency* means producing with a minimum of expense, effort, and waste. Economists use a more precise definition. **Economic efficiency**, they say, refers to a state of affairs in which it is impossible to make any change that satisfies one person's wants more fully without causing some other person's wants to be satisfied less fully.[1]

Although the definition of economic efficiency may be unfamiliar, it is actually closely related to the everyday notion of efficiency. If there is some way to make you better off without making me worse off, it is wasteful (*inefficient*) to pass up the opportunity. If I have a red pen that I am not using, and you need one just for a minute, it would be wasteful for you to buy a red pen of your own. It is more efficient for me to lend you my pen; it makes you better off and me no worse off. If there is a way to make us both better off, it would be all the more wasteful not to take advantage of the opportunity. You lend me your bicycle for the afternoon and I will lend you my volleyball. If I do not ride a bicycle very often and you do not play volleyball very often, it would be inefficient for us both to own one of each item.

The concept of economic efficiency has a variety of applications: one such application centers on the question of *how* to produce. **Efficiency in production** refers to a

APPLYING ECONOMIC IDEAS 1.1

THE OPPORTUNITY COST OF A COLLEGE EDUCATION

How much does it cost you to go to college? If you are a resident student at a typical four-year private college in the United States, you can answer this question by making up a budget like the one shown in Figure A. This can be called a budget of out-of-pocket costs, because it includes all the items—and only those items—that you or your parents must actually pay for in a year.

Your own out-of-pocket costs may be much higher or lower than these averages. Chances are, though, that these are the items that come to mind when you think about the costs of college. As you begin to think like an economist, you may find it useful to recast your college budget in terms of opportunity costs. Which of the items in Figure A represent opportunities that you have forgone in order to go to college? Are any forgone opportunities missing? To answer these questions, compare Figure A with Figure B, which shows a budget of opportunity costs.

Some items are both opportunity costs and out-of-pocket costs. The first three items in Figure A show up again in Figure B. To spend $14,000 on tuition and fees and $1,200 on books and supplies, you must give up the opportunity to buy other goods and services—to buy a car or rent a ski condo, for instance. To spend $1,100 getting to and from school, you must pass up the opportunity to travel somewhere else or to spend the money on something other than travel. Not all out-of-pocket costs are also opportunity costs, however. Consider the last two items in the out-of-pocket budget. By spending $7,000 a year on room, board, and personal expenses during the year, you are not really giving up the opportunity to do something else. Whether or not you were going to college, you would have to eat, live somewhere, and buy clothes. Because these are expenses that you would have in any case, they do not count as opportunity costs of going to college.

Finally, there are some items that are opportunity costs without being out-of-pocket costs. Think about what you would be doing if you were not going to college. If you were not going to college, you probably would have taken a job and started earning money soon after leaving high school. As a high-school graduate, your earnings would be about $16,000 during the nine months of the school year. (You can work during the summer even if you are attending college.) Because this potential income is something that you must forgo for the sake of college, it is an opportunity cost even though it does not involve an outlay of money.

Which budget you use depends on the kind of decision you are making. If you have already decided to go to college and are doing your financial planning, the out-of-pocket budget will tell you how much you will have to raise from savings, a job, parents' contributions, and scholarships to make ends meet. But if you are making the more basic choice between going to college and pursuing a career that does not require a college degree, the opportunity cost of college is what counts.

Figure A	Budget of Out-of-Pocket Costs	Figure B	Budget of Opportunity Costs
Tuition and fees	$14,000	Tuition and fees	$14,000
Books and supplies	1,200	Books and supplies	1,200
Transportation to and from home	1,100	Transportation to and from home	1,000
Room and board	7,000	Forgone income	16,000
Personal expenses	1,400		
Total out-of-pocket costs	**$24,700**	**Total opportunity costs**	**$32,200**

situation in which it is not possible, given available productive resources and existing knowledge, to produce more of one good without forgoing the opportunity to produce some of another good. The concept of efficiency in production, like the broader concept of economic efficiency, includes the everyday notion of avoiding waste. For example, a grower of apples finds that beyond some certain quantity, using more fertilizer per tree does not increase the yield of apples. To use more than that amount would be wasteful. Better to transfer the extra fertilizer to the production of, say, peaches. That way more peaches can be grown without any reduction in the apple crop.

The economist's definition also includes more subtle possibilities for improving the efficiency of production in cases where the waste of resources is less obvious. For example, it is possible to grow apples in Georgia. It is also possible, by selecting the right tree varieties and using winter protection, to grow peaches in Vermont. Some hobbyists do grow both fruits in both states. However, it would be inefficient to do so on a commercial scale even if growers in both states followed the most careful cultivation practices and avoided any obvious "waste." To see why, suppose that initially apple and peach trees were planted in equal numbers in the two states. Then compare this with a situation in which 500 fewer struggling peach trees had been planted in Vermont, and 500 thriving apple trees had been planted instead. At the same time, suppose 500 fewer heat-stressed apple trees had been planted in Georgia, and their place had been taken by peaches. Clearly, the second alternative would increase the output of both fruits without increasing the total land, labor, and capital used in fruit production. This shows that the original distribution of trees was inefficient.

HOW TO INCREASE PRODUCTION POTENTIAL Once efficiency has been achieved, more of one good can be produced only by forgoing the opportunity to produce something else, assuming that productive resources and knowledge are held constant. But over time, production potential can be expanded by accumulating more resources and finding new ways of putting them to work.

In the past, discovery of new supplies of natural resources has been an important way of increasing production potential. Population growth has always been, and still is, another source. However, as the most easily tapped supplies of natural resources are depleted and as population growth slows in the most developed countries, capital will increasingly be the factor of production that contributes most to the expansion of production potential.

Investment

The act of increasing the economy's stock of capital—that is, its supply of means of production made by people.

The act of increasing the economy's stock of capital—that is, its supply of productive inputs made by people—is known as **investment**. Investment involves a trade-off of present consumption for future consumption. To build more factories, roads, and computers, we have to divert resources from the production of bread, movies, haircuts, and other things that satisfy immediate wants. In return, we put ourselves in a better position to satisfy our future wants.

Entrepreneurship

The process of looking for new possibilities—making use of new ways of doing things, being alert to new opportunities, and overcoming old limits.

Increased availability of productive resources is not the only source of economic growth, however. Even more important are improvements in human knowledge—the invention of new technology, new forms of organization, new ways of satisfying wants. The process of looking for new possibilities—making use of new ways of doing things, being alert to new opportunities, and overcoming old limits—is called **entrepreneurship**. It is a dynamic process that breaks down the constraints imposed by existing knowledge and limited supplies of factors of production.

Entrepreneurship does not have to mean inventing something or starting a new business, although it sometimes does. It may mean finding a new market for an existing product—for example, convincing people in New England that tacos, long popular in the Southwest, make a quick and tasty lunch. It may mean taking advantage of price differences between one market and another—for example, buying hay at a low price in Pennsylvania, where growing conditions have been good in the past year, and reselling it in Virginia, where the weather has been too dry.

Households can be entrepreneurs, too. They do not simply repeat the same patterns of work and leisure every day. They seek variety—new jobs, new foods, new places to visit. Each time you try something new, you are taking a step into the unknown. In this sense you are an entrepreneur.

Entrepreneurship is sometimes called the fourth factor of production. However, entrepreneurship differs from the three classical factors of production in important ways. Unlike labor, capital, and natural resources, entrepreneurship is intangible and difficult to measure. Although entrepreneurs earn incomes reflecting the value that the market places on their accomplishments, we cannot speak of a price per unit of entrepreneurship; there are no such units. Also, unlike human resources (which grow old), machines (which wear out), and natural resources (which can be used up), the inventions and discoveries of entrepreneurs are not depleted as they are used. Once a new product or concept, such as the transistor, the toothpaste pump, or the limited-partnership form of business, has been invented, the required knowledge does not have to be created again (although, of course, it may be supplanted by even better ideas). All in all, it is more helpful to think of entrepreneurship as a process of learning better ways of using the three basic factors of production than as a separate factor of production in itself.

Deciding Who Will Do Which Work: The Division of Labor

The questions of what will be produced and how to produce it would exist even for a person living in isolation. Even the fictional castaway Robinson Crusoe had to decide whether to fish or hunt birds, and if he decided to fish, he had to decide whether to do so with a net or with a hook and line. In contrast, the economic questions of who will do which work and for whom output will be produced exist only for people living in a human society—another reason economics is considered one of the social sciences.

The question of who will do which work is a matter of organizing the social division of labor. Will everyone do everything independently—be a farmer in the morning, a tailor in the afternoon, and a poet in the evening? Or will people cooperate—work together, trade goods and services, and specialize in one particular job? Economists answer these questions by pointing out that it is more efficient to cooperate. Doing so allows a given number of people to produce more than they could if each of them worked alone. Three things make cooperation worthwhile: teamwork, learning by doing, and comparative advantage.

First consider *teamwork*. In a classic paper on this subject, Armen Alchian and Harold Demsetz use the example of workers unloading bulky crates from a truck.[2] The crates are so large that one worker alone can barely drag them along or cannot move them at all without unpacking them. Two people working independently would take hours to unload the truck. If they work as a team, however, they can easily pick up the crates and stack them on the loading dock. This example shows that even when everyone is doing the same work and little skill is involved, teamwork pays.

A second reason for cooperation applies when there are different jobs to be done and different skills to be learned. In a furniture plant, for example, some workers operate production equipment, others use office equipment, and still others buy materials. Even if all the workers start out with equal abilities, each gets better at a particular job by doing it repeatedly. *Learning by doing* thus turns workers of average productivity into specialists, thereby creating an even more productive team.

A third reason for cooperation comes into play after the process of learning by doing has developed different skills and also applies when workers start out with different talents and abilities. It is the principle of division of labor according to *comparative advantage*. **Comparative advantage** is the ability to do a job or produce a good at a relatively lower opportunity cost than someone else.

Comparative advantage

The ability to produce a good or service at a relatively lower opportunity cost than someone else.

An example will illustrate the principle of comparative advantage. Suppose two clerical workers, Bill and Jim, are assigned the job of getting out a batch of letters. Jim is a whiz. He can type a letter in 5 minutes and stuff it into an envelope in 1 minute. Working alone, he can finish ten letters in an hour. Bill is clumsy. It takes him 10 minutes to type a letter and 5 minutes to stuff it into the envelope. Alone, he can do only four letters an hour. In summary form:

Jim: Type 1 letter 5 min.
Stuff 1 envelope 1 min.

Bill: Type 1 letter 10 min.
Stuff 1 envelope 5 min.

Without cooperation, the two workers' limit is 14 letters per hour between them. Could they do better by cooperating? It depends on who does which job. One idea might be for Jim to do all the typing while Bill does all the stuffing, because that way they can just keep up with each other. But at 5 minutes per letter, that kind of cooperation cuts their combined output to twelve letters per hour. It is worse than not cooperating at all.

Instead, they should divide the work according to the principle of comparative advantage. Even though Bill is the slower typist, he has a *comparative advantage* in typing because the opportunity cost of typing is lower for him: The 10 minutes he takes to type a letter is equal to the time he needs to stuff two envelopes. For Jim, the 5 minutes he takes to type a letter could be used to stuff five envelopes. Thus, for Bill the opportunity cost of typing one letter is to forgo stuffing *two* envelopes, whereas for Jim the opportunity cost of typing one letter is to forgo stuffing *five* envelopes.

Because Bill gives up fewer stuffed envelopes per letter than Jim, the principle of comparative advantage says that Bill should spend all his time typing. If he does, he can produce six letters per hour. Meanwhile Jim can spend 45 minutes of each hour typing nine letters, and the last 15 minutes of each hour stuffing all 15 envelopes. By specializing according to comparative advantage, the two workers can increase their total output to 15 letters per hour, their highest possible joint productivity.

In this example the principle of comparative advantage points the way toward an efficient division of labor between two people working side by side. But the principle also has broader implications. It can apply to a division of labor between individuals or business firms working far apart—even in different countries. In fact, the earliest application of the principle was to international trade (see *Who Said It? Who Did It? 1.1*). Today comparative advantage remains one of the primary motivations for mutually beneficial cooperation, whether on the scale of the workplace or on that of the world as a whole.

Whatever the scale, the principle of comparative advantage is easy to apply provided one remembers that it is rooted in the concept of opportunity cost. Suppose there are two tasks, A and B, and two parties (individuals, firms, agencies, or countries), X and Y, each capable of doing both tasks, but not equally well. First ask what is the opportunity cost for X of doing a unit of task A, measured in terms of how many units of task B could be done with the same time or resources (the opportunity

WHO SAID IT? WHO DID IT? 1.1

DAVID RICARDO AND THE THEORY OF COMPARATIVE ADVANTAGE

David Ricardo was born in London in 1772, the son of an immigrant who was a member of the London stock exchange. Ricardo's education was rather haphazard, and he entered his father's business at the age of 14. In 1793, he married and went into business on his own. These were years of war and financial turmoil. The young Ricardo developed a reputation for remarkable astuteness and quickly made a large fortune.

In 1799, Ricardo read Adam Smith's *The Wealth of Nations* and developed an interest in political economy (as economics was then called). In 1809, his first writings on economics appeared. These were a series of newspaper articles on "The High Price of Bullion," which appeared during the following year as a pamphlet. Several other short works added to his reputation in this area. In 1814, he retired from business to devote all his time to political economy.

Ricardo's major work was *Principles of Political Economy and Taxation*, first published in 1817. This work contains, among other things, a pioneering statement of the principle of comparative advantage as applied to international trade. Using a lucid numerical example, Ricardo showed why it was to the advantage of both countries for England to export wool to Portugal and to import wine in return, even though both products could be produced with less labor in Portugal, as long as wool can be produced relatively less expensively in England.

But international trade is only a sideline of Ricardo's *Principles*. The book covers the whole field of economics as it then existed, beginning with value theory and progressing to a theory of economic growth and evolution. Ricardo held that the economy was growing toward a future "steady state." At that point economic growth would come to a halt and the wage rate would be reduced to the subsistence level. This gloomy view and the equally pessimistic views of Ricardo's contemporary, Thomas Malthus, gave political economy a reputation as "the dismal science."

Ricardo's book was extremely influential. For more than half a century thereafter, much of the writing on economic theory published in England consisted of expansions and commentaries on Ricardo's work. Economists as different as Karl Marx, the revolutionary socialist, and John Stuart Mill, a defender of liberal capitalism, took Ricardo's theories as their starting point. Even today there are "neo-Ricardian" and "new classicist" economists who look to Ricardo's works for inspiration.

cost). Then ask the same question for Y. The party with the lower opportunity cost for doing a unit of task A has the comparative advantage in doing that task. To check, ask what is the opportunity cost for each party of doing a unit of task B, measured in terms how many units of task A could be done with the same time or resources. The party with the lower opportunity cost for doing a unit of task B has the comparative advantage in doing that task.

Deciding for Whom Goods Will Be Produced: Positive and Normative Economics

Together, the advantages of team production, learning by doing, and comparative advantage mean that people can produce more efficiently by cooperating than they could if each worked in isolation. But cooperation raises yet another issue: For whom will goods be produced? The question of the distribution of output among members of society has implications in terms of both efficiency and fairness.

EFFICIENCY IN DISTRIBUTION Consider first a situation in which production has already taken place and the supply of goods is fixed. Suppose, for example, that 30 students get on a bus to go to a football game. Bag lunches are handed out. Half the bags contain a ham sandwich and a root beer; the other half contain a tuna sandwich and a cola. What happens when the students open their bags? They do not just eat whatever they find—they start trading. Some swap sandwiches; others swap drinks. Maybe there is not enough of everything to give each person his or her first choice. Nevertheless, the trading makes at least some people better off than they were when they started. Moreover, no one ends up worse off. If some of the students do not want to trade, they can always eat what was given to them in the first place.

This example shows one sense in which the "for whom" question is partly about efficiency: Starting from any given quantity of goods, the allocation can be improved through trades that result in better satisfaction of some people's preferences. As long as it is possible to trade existing supplies of goods in a way that permits some people to satisfy their wants more fully without making others worse off, **efficiency in distribution** can be improved even while the total quantity of goods remains fixed.

Efficiency in distribution

A situation in which it is not possible, by redistributing existing supplies of goods, to satisfy one person's wants more fully without causing some other person's wants to be satisfied less fully.

Efficiency in distribution and efficiency in production are two aspects of the general concept of economic efficiency. When both aspects are taken into account, the relationship between distribution and efficiency is not restricted to situations in which the total amount of goods is fixed in advance. That is so because the rules for distribution affect the patterns of production. For example, the rules for distribution affect the supply of productive resources, because most people earn their incomes by providing labor to business firms, and the amount they supply is affected by the wages they are promised. Another reason is that rules for distribution affect incentives for entrepreneurship. Some people may work hard to discover new ways of doing things even if they expect no material reward, but that is not true of everyone.

FAIRNESS IN DISTRIBUTION Efficiency is not the whole story when it comes to the question of for whom goods will be produced. One can also ask whether a given distribution is fair. Questions of fairness often dominate discussions of distribution.

One widely held view judges fairness in distribution in terms of equality. This concept of fairness is based on the idea that all people, by virtue of their shared humanity, deserve a portion of the goods and services turned out by the economy. There are many versions of this concept. Some people think that all income and wealth should be distributed equally. Others think that people have an equal right to a "safety net" level of income but that inequality in distributing any surplus beyond that level is not necessarily unfair. Still others think that certain goods, such as health care, food, and education, should be distributed equally but that it is fair for other goods to be distributed less equally.

An alternative view, which also has many adherents, judges fairness primarily in terms of the procedures through which a given distribution is carried out. In this view, fairness requires that certain rules and procedures be observed, such as respect for private property or nondiscrimination on grounds of race and gender. As long as those rules are followed, any resulting distribution of income is viewed as acceptable. In this view, equality of opportunity is emphasized more than equality of outcome.

POSITIVE AND NORMATIVE ECONOMICS Many economists make a sharp distinction between the question of efficiency and that of fairness. Discussions of efficiency are seen as part of **positive economics**, the area of economics that is concerned with facts and the relationships among them. Discussions of fairness, in contrast, are seen as part of **normative economics**, the area of economics that is devoted to judgments about whether particular economic policies and conditions are good or bad.

Positive economics

The area of economics that is concerned with facts and the relationships among them.

Normative economics

The area of economics that is devoted to judgments about whether economic policies or conditions are good or bad.

Normative economics extends beyond the question of fairness in the distribution of output. Value judgments also arise about the fairness of the other three basic choices faced by every economy. In choosing what will be produced, is it fair to permit production of alcohol and tobacco but to outlaw production of marijuana and cocaine? In choosing how to produce, is it fair to allow people to work under dangerous or unhealthy conditions, or should work under such conditions be prohibited? In choosing who does which work, is it fair to limit access to specific jobs according to age, gender, race, or union membership? As you can see, normative issues extend to every corner of economics.

Positive economics, rather than offering value judgments about outcomes, focuses on understanding the processes by which the four basic economic questions are or could be answered. It analyzes the way economies operate, or would operate if certain institutions or policies were changed. It traces relationships between facts, often looking for measurable regularities in economic observations.

Most economists consider positive economics their primary area of expertise, but normative considerations influence the conduct of positive economics in several ways. The most significant of those influences is the selection of topics to investigate. An economist who sees excessive unemployment as a glaring injustice may study that problem; one who sympathizes with victims of job discrimination may take up a different line of research. Also, normative views are likely to affect the ways in which data are collected, ideas about which facts can be considered true, and so on.

At one time it was thought that a purely positive economics could be developed, untouched by normative considerations of values and fairness. Within its framework, all disputes could be resolved by reference to objective facts. Today that notion is less widely held. Nevertheless, it remains important to be aware that most major economic controversies, especially those that have to do with government policy, have normative as well as positive components, and to be aware of the way each component shapes the way we think about those controversies.

COORDINATING ECONOMIC CHOICES

To function effectively, an economy must have some way of coordinating the choices of millions of individuals regarding what to produce, how to produce it, who will do each job, and for whom the output will be produced. This section discusses how people, businesses, and the government interact in the coordination of economic choices.

A Noneconomic Example

Everyone has had the experience of shopping at a supermarket where there are several long checkout lines. In such a situation, you and other shoppers want to get through the checkout process as fast as possible. How can the store avoid the frustrating situation in which some lines have a long wait for service while the cashiers in other lines stand idle for lack of customers?

One way would be for the store to direct certain customers to certain lines. The store could use a standard rule, such as customers with names starting with A–D go to line 1, E–H go to line 2, and so on. Or the store could hire an employee to sit in a special booth and direct shoppers to one line or another.

But supermarkets do not work that way. Instead, they leave shoppers to decide for themselves what line to join, based on information from their own observations. As you approach the checkout area, you first look to see which lines are the shortest. You then make allowance for the possibility that some shoppers may have carts that are heaped full, while others have only a few items. Using your own judgment, you head for the line you think will be fastest.

Market

Any arrangement people have for trading with one another.

The Importance of Markets

In economics, the the coordination of decisions occurs through market activities. A **market** is any arrangement people have for trading with one another. Some markets have formal rules and carry out exchanges at a single location, such as the New York Stock Exchange. Other markets are more informal, such as the word-of-mouth networks through which teenage babysitters get in touch with people who need their services. Despite the wide variety of forms that markets take, they all have one thing in common: They provide the information and incentives people need to coordinate their decisions.

Just as shoppers need information about the length of checkout lines to coordinate their efforts, participants in markets need information about the scarcity and opportunity costs of various goods and factors of production. Markets rely primarily on prices to transmit this information. If a good or factor of production becomes more scarce, its price is bid up. The increase in the price tells people it is worth more and signals producers to make greater efforts to increase supplies. For example, when platinum first began to be used in catalytic converters to reduce pollution from automobile exhaust, this brought buyers into the market. With the discovery of its new use, platinum becomes more difficult to acquire because of the newly increased desire to use it. Competition for available supplies then bids up the price of platinum. This sends a message to buyers of its increased value. The producers learn that, where possible, they should increase the quantity of platinum mined.

Instead, suppose a new technology reduces the cost of producing platinum, for example, by allowing extraction of platinum from mine wastes that were previously discarded. Information about the reduced cost is transmitted by markets in the form of a lower price. People can then consider increasing the quantity of platinum they use.

In addition to knowing the best use for resources, people must also have incentives to act on that information. Markets provide incentives to sell goods and productive resources where they will bring the highest prices and to buy them where they can be obtained at the lowest prices. Profits motivate business managers to improve production methods and to design goods that match consumer needs. Workers who stay alert to opportunities and work where they are most productive receive the highest wages.

Adam Smith, often considered the father of economics, saw the achievement of coordination through markets as the foundation of prosperity and progress. In a famous passage in *The Wealth of Nations,* he called markets an "invisible hand" that nudges people into the economic roles they can play best (see *Who Said It? Who Did It? 1.2*). To this day, an appreciation of markets as a means of coordinating choices remains a central feature of the economic way of thinking.

The Role of the Government

Important as markets are, they are not the only means of achieving economic coordination. Some decisions are guided by direct authority within organizations. The most important example is decisions made by government agencies. Government decisions are made not through the spontaneous choices of individuals, but via directives issued by a central authority.

WHO SAID IT? WHO DID IT? 1.2

ADAM SMITH ON THE INVISIBLE HAND

Adam Smith is considered to have been the founder of economics as a distinct field of study, even though he wrote only one book on the subject: *The Wealth of Nations*, published in 1776. Smith was 53 years old at the time. His friend David Hume found the book such hard going that he doubted that many people would read it. But Hume was wrong—people have been reading it for more than 200 years.

The wealth of a nation, in Smith's view, was not a result of the accumulation of gold or silver in its treasury, as many contemporary theorists believed. Rather, it was the outcome of the activities of ordinary people working and trading in free markets. To Smith, the remarkable thing about the wealth produced by a market economy is that it is not a result of any organized plan, but rather the unintended outcome of the actions of many people, each of whom is pursuing the incentives the market offers with his or her own interests in mind. As he put it:

> It is not from the benevolence of the butcher, the brewer, or the baker that we expect our dinner, but from their regard to their own interest. . . . Every individual is continually exerting himself to find out the most advantageous employment for whatever capital he can command. . . . By directing that industry in such a manner as its produce may be of the greatest value, he intends only his own gain, and he is in this, as in many other cases, led by an invisible hand to promote an end which was no part of his intention.*

Much of the discipline of economics as it has developed over the past two centuries consists of elaborations on ideas found in Smith's work. The idea of the "invisible hand" of market incentives that channels people's efforts in directions that are beneficial to their neighbors remains the most durable of Smith's contributions to economics.

*Adam Smith, *The Wealth of Nations* (1776), Book 1, Chapter 2.

Individuals and the government deal with one another through markets. Markets and the government thus play complementary roles in achieving economic coordination. Some economies rely more on markets, others on government planning. At one extreme, the centrally-planned economy of North Korea places heavy emphasis on government authority. Market economics, such as that of the United States, make greater use of markets. But no economy uses one means of coordination to the exclusion of the other. Government regulatory agencies in the United States establish laws to control pollution or protect worker safety; on the other hand, North Korea uses small-scale markets to distribute some goods. Likewise, in the United States, the government fosters coordination in markets by enforcing laws and providing national security. This protects an individual's right to property, encouraging market interaction.

In short, wherever one turns in economics, the question of coordination arises. Understanding economic coordination means understanding the complementary roles of markets and the government.

ECONOMIC METHOD

The economic way of thinking is a very broad concept; economic method is a somewhat narrower idea having to do with the way economists go about their work. The chapter would be incomplete without a few comments about method.

Theories and Models

At the beginning of the chapter we defined economics as the social science that seeks to understand the choices people make in using scarce resources to meet their wants. Later, in discussing positive economics, we noted that understanding something means discovering how its parts are related to one another. In economics, we want to know how each of the four basic types of choices are related to the context in which they are made, and how outcomes are related to those choices.

Theory

A representation of the way in which facts are related to one another.

Model

A synonym for theory; in economics, often applied to theories that are stated in graphical or mathematical form.

Any representation of the way in which facts are related can be called a **theory** or a **model**. The terms are synonyms, although economists tend to use the term *theory* to refer to more general statements about economic relationships and the term *model* to refer to more particular statements, especially those that take the form of graphs or mathematical equations.

Economics needs theories and models because facts do not speak for themselves. Take, for example, the fact that between 1979 and 1981, U.S. motorists cut their use of gasoline by more than 10 percent, from 80.2 billion to 71.7 billion gallons per year. Why did they do that? Economists have a theory. They relate the drop in gasoline consumption to another fact: the 50 percent rise in the retail price of gasoline, from $.86 per gallon to $1.31 per gallon, over the same period. The relationship between the price and consumption of gasoline is seen as a particular instance of a broader theory according to which an increase in the price of any good, other things being equal, tends to decrease the quantity of that good that consumers buy.

The theory as stated is a simple one. It relates quantity purchased to just one other fact, the price of the good. A more complete theory would bring in other factors that influence consumer choice, such as the prices of goods other than gasoline, consumers' incomes, changes in the average fuel economy of cars, and so on. Where does one draw the line? How much detail does it take to make a good theory?

There is no simple answer to this question, because adding detail to a theory involves a trade-off. On the one hand, if essential details are left out, the theory may fail altogether to fit the facts. On the other hand, adding too much detail defeats the purpose of understanding because key relationships may become lost in a cloud of complexity. The only real guideline is that a theory should be just detailed enough to suit the purpose for which it is intended, and no more.

By analogy, consider the models that aircraft designers use. The wind tunnel models made to test the aerodynamics of a new design need to represent the shapes of the wings, fuselage, and control surfaces accurately, but they do not need to include tiny seats with tiny tables and magazine racks. On the other hand, a full-scale model built for the purpose of training flight attendants to work on the new plane would need seats and magazine racks, but it would not need wings.

In much the same way, the theories and models presented in this book are designed to highlight a few key economic relationships. They are helpful in understanding economics in the same way that playing a flight simulation game on a computer is helpful in understanding the basics of flying. Professional economists use more detailed models, just as professional pilots train with complex flight simulators rather than with simple computer games. Nevertheless, the basic principles learned from the simple models do not contradict those that apply to the more complex ones. In the simple games, just as in the complex simulators, adjusting the rudder makes the plane turn and adjusting the elevators makes it climb or dive.

The Use of Graphs[3]

The theories introduced so far have been stated in words. Words are a powerful tool for developing understanding, but they are even more powerful when they are supplemented by pictures. Economists support their words with pictures called graphs. An example will illustrate how economists use graphs to represent theories.

THE PRODUCTION POSSIBILITY FRONTIER Recall our earlier discussion of the trade-off between education and cars. Figure 1.1 shows the trade-off in graphical form for an economy in which only those two goods are produced. The horizontal axis measures the quantity of education in terms of the number of college graduates produced per year; the vertical axis measures the production of cars. Any combination of education and cars can be shown as a point in the space between the two axes. For example, production of 10 million graduates and 5 million cars in a given year would be represented by point E.

In drawing this graph, supplies of productive resources and the state of knowledge are assumed to remain constant. Even if all available resources are devoted to education, there is a limit to the number of graduates that can be produced in a year: 20 million. The extreme possibility of producing 20 million graduates and no cars is shown by point A. Likewise, the maximum number of cars that would be produced if no resources were put into education is 18 million cars, shown by point B. Between those two extremes is a whole range of possible combinations of education and cars. Those intermediate possibilities are shown by points such as C and D, which fall along a smooth curve. The curve is known as a **production possibility frontier**.

Production possibility frontier

A graph that shows possible combinations of goods that can be produced by an economy given available knowledge and factors of production.

EFFICIENCY AND ECONOMIC GROWTH The production possibility frontier is a boundary between the combinations of education and cars that can be produced and those that cannot, using given knowledge and productive resources. As such, it serves nicely to illustrate the concept of efficiency in production. Points inside the frontier, such as point E, represent inefficient production. Beginning from such a point, more cars can be made without cutting the output of education (shown by a vertical move toward the frontier); more education can be produced without cutting the output of cars (a horizontal move toward the frontier); or the output of both goods can be increased (a move up and to the right toward the frontier).

Points such as A, B, C, and D that are on the frontier represent efficient production. Starting from any of those points, it is not possible to produce more of one good

FIGURE 1.1 PRODUCTION POSSIBILITY FRONTIER

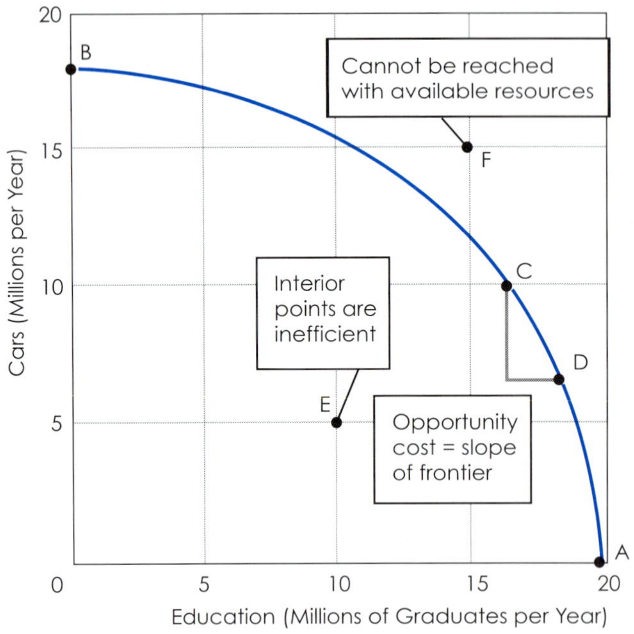

This figure shows combinations of cars and education that can be produced in a simple economy in which they are the only two products. Quantities of available factors of production and the state of existing knowledge are assumed to be fixed. If all factors are devoted to education, 20 million college graduates can be produced each year (point A). If all factors are devoted to making cars, 18 million cars can be produced each year (point B). Other combinations of the two goods that can be produced using available factors efficiently, such as those represented by points C and D, lie along a curve called a production possibility frontier. The slope of the frontier indicates the opportunity cost of education in terms of cars. Interior points, such as E, represent inefficient use of resources. Beginning from such a point, more of one good can be produced without producing less of the other. Points outside the frontier, such as F, cannot be reached using available factors of production and knowledge.

without producing less of the other. For example, in moving from C to D, output of education is increased but output of cars falls. Points such as F that lie outside the frontier cannot be reached even when the currently available knowledge and factors of production are used efficiently.

Over time, however, economic growth can stretch the production possibility frontier outward so that points such as F become possible. As mentioned earlier, the discovery of new ways of using available factors of production is one source of growth. So are additions to the total stock of factors of production—for example, through growth of the labor force. The case under discussion points to still yet another source of growth: Over time, the educational process itself improves the quality of the labor force, thus making a given number of people capable of producing more.

OPPORTUNITY COST AND COMPARATIVE ADVANTAGE The production possibility frontier can also be used to represent the concept of opportunity cost. As we have seen, once the economy is producing efficiently at a point on the frontier, choosing to make more of one good means making less of the other. For example, suppose we start at point C, where 16 million students graduate each year and 10 million cars are being made. If we want to increase the output of graduates to 18 million per year, we must give up some cars and use the labor, capital, and natural resources freed in this way to build and staff classrooms. In moving from point C to point D, we trade off production of 4 million cars for the extra 2 million graduates. Over that range of the frontier, the opportunity cost of each extra graduate is about two cars. The opportunity cost of graduates, measured in terms of cars, is shown by the slope of the frontier.

As more graduates are produced, and the economy moves down and to the right along the frontier, the frontier becomes steeper and the opportunity cost of producing graduates increases. A major reason is that not all factors of production—especially not all workers—are alike. Suppose we start all the way up at point B, where no education is produced, and transfer enough resources to education to open one small college. The first people we would pull off the assembly line to staff the classrooms would be those who have a comparative advantage in teaching. By the time enough resources have been transferred to education from the auto industry to reach point D, the most suitable recruits for academic life have already been used. Increasingly, to produce still more education we have to take some of the best production workers with no assurance that they will be good teachers. The opportunity cost of increasing the output of education (shown by the slope of the frontier) is correspondingly greater.

Theory and Evidence

Empirical

Based on experience or observation.

Theories are of no use in explaining relationships among facts unless they fit those facts. Theory building is a matter of constantly comparing proposed explanations with evidence gleaned from observations of the actual choices people make—that is, with **empirical** evidence. When empirical evidence is consistent with the relationships proposed in a theory, confidence in the validity of the theory is increased. When evidence is not consistent with the theory, the theory needs to be reexamined. The relationships proposed in it may be invalid, or they may be valid only under circumstances different from those that prevailed when the observations were made. The theory then needs to be modified by changing the proposed relationships or adding detail.

For example, earlier we noted that the drop in gasoline usage between 1979 and 1981 was consistent with the theory that people will buy less of something when its price goes up, other things being equal. But what about the fact that from 1976 to 1978 gasoline usage rose by 8 percent even though the price of gasoline rose by 11 percent? In seeking an explanation of this observation, an economist would first suggest that probably some of the "other things" were not equal after all. A more detailed theory that considers some of those other things is called for.

In the case of gasoline usage, such a line of inquiry proves fruitful. In the period from 1976 to 1978, two factors offset the tendency of a rising price to depress gasoline sales. First, the prices of goods and services other than gasoline rose even faster, so that gasoline actually became cheaper relative to the other things consumers bought. Second, consumer incomes rose by a strong 8 percent from 1976 to 1978, which would tend to make people buy more of many goods and services, including gasoline.

From 1979 to 1981, neither of those factors was present. During that period, gasoline prices rose twice as fast as the prices of other goods, and consumer incomes were stagnant, rising less than 1 percent. Thus, both the 1976–1978 and 1979–1981 observations are consistent with a more complete theory that takes gasoline prices, other prices, and consumer incomes into account.

Government agencies and private firms generate mountains of empirical data on economic activity. Economists constantly examine those data in an effort to confirm theories or find inconsistencies that point the way to better theories. Statistical analysis of empirical economic data is known as **econometrics**—literally, the science of economic measurement.

Econometrics

The statistical analysis of empirical economic data.

Theories and Forecasts

Economic theories can help us understand things that happened in the past—trends in gasoline consumption in the 1970s, the effects of the tax reforms of the 1980s, and so on. But understanding the past is not always enough. People also want forecasts of future economic events.

Within limits, economic theory can be useful here, too. Any theory that purports to explain a relationship between past events provides a basis for predicting what will happen under similar circumstances in the future. To put it more precisely, economic theory can be used to make **conditional forecasts** of the form "If A, then B, other things being equal." Thus, an economist might say, "If gasoline prices rise, and if at the same time consumer incomes and the prices of other goods do not change, gasoline purchases will fall."

Conditional forecast

A prediction of future economic events in the form "If A, then B, other things being equal."

Thousands of economists make a living from forecasting. Decision-makers in business and government use economic forecasts extensively. Forecasts are not perfect, however, and forecasters sometimes make conspicuous mistakes. There are at least three reasons for the mistakes.

First, insufficient attention is sometimes paid to the conditional nature of forecasts. The news might report, for example, that "economists predict an upturn in inflation," yet inflation might not increase after all. In such a case the news report may have failed to note the forecasters' precautionary comments. The forecasters may have said that the rate of inflation would rise only if bank loans continued to expand as they had in the immediate past, but loans may not have increased after all.

Second, a forecast may be invalid because the theory on which it is based is incorrect or incomplete. Economists do not always agree on what theory best fits the facts. Some theories give more weight to one fact, others to different facts. The competing theories may imply conflicting forecasts under some conditions. At least one of the forecasts will then turn out to be wrong. Finding out which theories yield better forecasts than others is an important part of the process through which valid theories are distinguished from inadequate ones.

Third, economic forecasts can go wrong because some of the things that business managers and government officials most want to know are among the hardest to predict. For example, a competent economist could produce a fairly accurate forecast of gasoline sales, making certain assumptions about incomes and the prices of gasoline and other goods, but only a few specialists would be interested. In contrast, millions of people—including bankers, bond market traders, and families planning to buy homes—would like accurate forecasts of interest rates. Interest rates, however, happen to be among the hardest economic variables to forecast accurately.

This does not mean that economists do not try to forecast interest rates. They do try; they just do not succeed very well. Forecasts of certain other major macroeconomic variables, such as unemployment, inflation, and growth of the nation's total output, do a little better than forecasts of interest rates, but their accuracy remains low relative to the publicity they get.

Most economists take the view that well-founded conditional forecasts, for all their limitations, are a better basis for business and public policy decisions than whims and guesswork. Still, they caution against relying too heavily on forecasts. For example, in the 1970s many forecasters projected higher energy prices right through the rest of the century. When energy prices fell in the 1980s, oil companies, bankers, and even national governments that had relied on the forecasts were in trouble.

Theory and Policy

Economists are often asked to use their theories to analyze the effects of public policies and forecast the effects of policy changes. The government may, for example, be considering new measures to aid unemployed workers, new approaches to improving air quality, or new measures to regulate international trade. How will the effects of such policies be spread through the economy? How will they affect people's lives?

Economists have their own characteristic way of thinking about public policy, just as they have their own way of thinking about other topics. In particular, economists are concerned with identifying both the direct and indirect effects of policy, as well as any indirect or unintended consequences. They are also constantly alert to both the long-run and short-term effects of policy.

- Unemployment compensation has the intended effect of aiding unemployed workers, but it also has the unintended effect of increasing the number of workers who are unemployed, because workers receiving compensation can afford to take their time finding just the right new job.
- Regulations intended to improve the fuel efficiency of automobiles encourage production of cars that weigh less, but the lighter cars are somewhat less safe.

Increased highway deaths among drivers of the lighter cars may thus be an unintended consequence of efforts to save fuel.

- Beginning in the 1930s, the federal government began to insure consumer deposits in savings and loan associations and banks. The intent was to stabilize the banking system by convincing consumers that their savings were protected. As a consequence, consumers were more willing to place funds in risky, poorly managed banks that offered high interest rates on insured deposits. This effect contributed to the massive banking crisis of the 1980s.

While policies may have unintended consequences, public policy still plays an important role in the economy. It would be wrong to conclude that the government should never act simply because its actions may do some harm as well as some good. Rather, economists simply urge that policy makers look at the whole picture, not just part of it, before they make a decision. As Henry Hazlitt once put it, the whole of economics can be reduced to a single lesson:

> *The art of economics consists in looking not merely at the immediate but at the longer effects of any act or policy; it consists in tracing the consequences of that policy not merely for one group but for all groups.*[4]

SUMMARY

1. **What is the subject matter of economics?** *Economics* is the social science that seeks to understand the choices people make in using scarce resources to meet their wants. *Scarcity* is a situation in which there is not enough of something to meet everyone's wants. *Microeconomics* is the branch of economics that studies choices that involve individual households, firms, and markets. *Macroeconomics* is the branch of economics that deals with large-scale economic phenomena, such as inflation, unemployment, and economic growth.

2. **What considerations underlie the choice of what an economy will produce?** Producing more of one good requires producing less of something else because productive resources that are used to produce one good cannot be used to produce another at the same time. Productive resources are traditionally classified into three groups, called *factors of production*. *Labor* consists of the productive contributions made by people working with their hands and minds. *Capital* consists of all the productive inputs created by people. *Natural resources* include anything that can be used as a productive input in its natural state. The *opportunity cost* of a good or service is its cost in terms of the forgone opportunity to pursue the best possible alternative activity with the same time or resources.

3. **What considerations underlie the choice of how to produce?** Goods and services can be produced in many different ways, some of which are more efficient than others. *Economic efficiency* refers to a state of affairs in which it is impossible to make any change that satisfies one person's wants more fully without causing some other person's wants to be satisfied less fully. *Efficiency in production* refers

to a situation in which it is not possible, given the available productive resources and existing knowledge, to produce more of one good or service without forgoing the opportunity to produce some of another good or service. Once efficiency has been achieved, production potential can be expanded by increasing the availability of resources or by improving knowledge. The process of increasing the economy's stock of capital is known as *investment.* The process of looking for new possibilities—making use of new ways of doing things, being alert to new opportunities, and overcoming old limits—is known as *entrepreneurship.*

4. **What considerations underlie the choice of who will do which work?** Although a person can survive apart from all human contact, economic efficiency is greatly enhanced by cooperation with others. Three things make cooperation worthwhile: teamwork, learning by doing, and comparative advantage. Teamwork can enhance productivity even when there is no specialization. Learning by doing improves productivity even when all workers start with equal talents and abilities. Comparative advantage comes into play when people have different innate abilities or, after learning by doing, have developed specialized skills. Having a *comparative advantage* in producing a particular good or service means being able to produce it at a relatively lower opportunity cost than someone else.

5. **What considerations underlie the choice of for whom goods will be produced?** In part, deciding for whom goods will be produced revolves around issues of efficiency. *Efficiency in distribution* refers to a state of affairs in which, with a given quantity of goods and services, it is impossible to satisfy one person's wants more fully without satisfying someone else's less fully. Efficiency is part of *positive economics,* the area of economics that is concerned with facts and the relationships among them. *Normative economics* is the area of economics that is devoted to judgments about which economic conditions and policies are good or bad.

6. **What mechanisms are used to coordinate economic choices?** The most important mechanism for achieving coordination occurs through the interaction of individuals in *markets.* Markets describe arrangements people have for trading with one another. The government plays a role in economic coordination through legislation, law enforcement, and national security. The relative importance of markets and the government in achieving coordination differs across countries.

7. **How do economists use theory, graphs, and evidence in their work?** A *theory* or *model* is a representation of the ways in which facts are related to one another. Economists use graphs to display data and make visual representations of theories and models. For example, a *production possibility frontier* is a graph that shows the boundary between combinations of goods that can be produced and those that cannot, using available factors of production and knowledge. Economists refine theories in the light of *empirical* evidence, that is, evidence gleaned from observation of actual economic decisions. The economic analysis of empirical evidence is known as *econometrics.* Economic models are often used to make *conditional forecasts* of the form "If A, then B, other things being equal."

KEY TERMS

Scarcity
Economics
Microeconomics
Macroeconomics
Factors of production
Labor
Capital
Natural resources
Opportunity cost
Economic efficiency

Efficiency in production	Market
Investment	Theory
Entrepreneurship	Model
Comparative advantage	Production possibility frontier
Efficiency in distribution	Empirical
Positive economics	Econometrics
Normative economics	Conditional forecast

PROBLEMS AND TOPICS FOR DISCUSSION

1. **Opportunity cost.** Gasoline, insurance, depreciation, and repairs are all costs of owning a car. Which of these can be considered opportunity costs in the context of each of the following decisions?
   a. You own a car and are deciding whether to drive 100 miles for a weekend visit to a friend at another university.
   b. You do not own a car but are considering buying one so that you can get a part-time job located 5 miles from where you live.

   In general, why does the context in which you decide to do something affect the opportunity cost of doing it?

2. **Comparative advantage in international trade.** Suppose that in the United States a car can be produced with 200 labor hours, while a ton of rice requires 20 labor hours. In Japan, it takes 150 labor hours to make a car and 50 labor hours to grow a ton of rice. What is the opportunity cost of producing rice in each country, stated in terms of cars? What is the opportunity cost of cars, stated in terms of rice? Which country has a comparative advantage in cars? Which in rice?

3. **Efficiency in distribution and the food stamp program.** The federal food stamp program could have been designed so that every low-income family would receive a book of coupons containing so many bread coupons, so many milk coupons, and so on. Instead, it gives the family a book of coupons that can be spent on any kind of food the family prefers. For a given cost to the federal government, which plan do you think would better serve the goal of efficiency in distribution? Why?

   Now consider a program that would allow families to trade their food stamps for cash (some such trading does occur, but it is restricted by law) or one in which poor families are given cash, with which they can buy whatever they want. Compare these alternatives with the existing food stamp program in terms of both positive and normative economics.

4. **Spontaneous order in the cafeteria.** Suppose that your college cafeteria does not have enough room for all the students to sit down to eat at once, so it stays open for lunch from 11:30 A.M. to 1:30 P.M. Consider the following three methods of distributing diners over the two-hour lunch period in such a way that everyone can have a seat.
   a. The administration sets a rule: Freshmen must eat between 11:30 and 12:00, sophomores between 12:00 and 12:30, and so on for juniors and seniors.
   b. The lunch period is broken up into half-hour segments, with green tickets for the first shift, blue tickets for the second, and so on. An equal number of tickets of each color is printed. At the beginning of each semester an auction is held in which students bid for the ticket color of their choice.
   c. Students can come to the cafeteria whenever they want. If there are no empty seats, they have to stand in line.

   Compare the three schemes in terms of the concepts of (i) spontaneous order and hierarchy; (ii) information and incentives; and (iii) efficiency.

5. **A production possibility frontier.** Bill Swartz has four fields spread out over a hillside. He can grow either wheat or potatoes in any of the fields, but the low fields are better for potatoes and the high ones are better for wheat. Here are some combinations of wheat and potatoes that he could produce:

Number of Fields Used for Potatoes	Total Tons of Potatoes	Total Tons of Wheat
All 4	1,000	0
Lowest 3	900	400
Lowest 2	600	700
Lowest 1	300	900
None	0	1,000

Use these data to draw a production possibility frontier for wheat and potatoes. What is the opportunity cost of wheat, stated in terms of potatoes, when the farmer converts the highest field to wheat production? What happens to the opportunity cost of wheat as more and more fields are switched to wheat?

CASE FOR DISCUSSION

Zimbabwe's Land Questions

HARARE, November 2003—President Mugabe continued seizure of primarily white-owned land in urban areas. The country's white farmers own much of the country's best agricultural land; according to government figures, 4,400 whites owned 32% of Zimbabwe's agricultural land, while about one million black peasant families farmed 38%. Furthermore, whites own a disproportionate share of the country's most fertile land. The situation was created in colonial times when blacks were forced off their ancestral lands. "The land question" was the source of discontent among the majority of Zimbabweans and a major cause of the guerrilla war that led to Zimbabwe's independence in 1980. When Mugabe came to power in 1980, he promised to balance the scales for black farmers through land reform.

Land reform and redistribution is expensive. Not only does the government need to compensate farmers giving up their property, but it also needs to provide infrastructure—such as roads, schools, and hospitals—for land redistribution to be beneficial. There is also the difficulty of taking large, sophisticated farms and then subdividing them into plots to give to people without the means to farm them effectively.

President Mugabe says Britain should pay because the British government colonized the region, seizing land from African farmers in the late 19th century. While the U.K. and others have provided some aid to help the government purchase land from "willing" white farmers, donors have refused further support unless President Mugabe's land program is more clearly defined.

The white farmers themselves do not see why they should have to pay because of what happened in the past. Many say they bought their farms at market rates since Zimbabwe's independence and reject arguments rooted in colonization. While Zimbabwe's government has paid some farmers, a new law requires farmers to leave their farms before receiving compensation.

Despite promises to target the seizure of the least-productive farms, many of those on the so-called "hit-list" have been the most efficient growers of tobacco. President Mugabe's opponents accuse him of exploiting the land question to win support amid Zimbabwe's current economic crisis.

The threat of land seizures has led to a steep decline in agricultural production on white-owned farms, exacerbating food shortages and unemployment in Zimbabwe. This coupled with two years of drought threaten a famine in which up to six million of Zimbabwe's citizens could go hungry. Aid agencies estimate over one-third of the population will be unable to feed themselves by the end of the year.

Consider the following hypothetical situations involving individuals and the government in Zimbabwe:

- Shekan currently owns 100 hectares of land that he uses for tobacco farming. On this land he has hired several hands to assist in harvesting and curing the tobacco leaves. He owns capital equipment to assist in curing the tobacco leaves. Shekan pays his workers 5 Zimbabwean dollars per pound of tobacco. Shekan then sells tobacco at the market price of 7 Zimbabwean dollars per pound.
- Amadika is a middle-aged woman who works on Shekan's farm. Using Shekan's curing equipment, she gathers and cures 50 pounds of tobacco each year.
- Tatenda is a young woman who was able to gather and cure 60 pounds of tobacco on Shekan's farm. She has decided to leave the farm and attend college in the United States. Tatenda has received a full scholarship and financing from the school to cover her expenses.
- Dakarai is a young man who currently works on Shekan's farm. He is able to gather and cure 75 pounds of tobacco each year using the available capital equipment. Instead of giving all 75 pounds to Shekan, he sells 25 pounds of tobacco illegally to a cigarette manufacturer for 6 Zimbabwean dollars per pound.

QUESTIONS

1. What might explain why Shekan pays his workers 5 Zimbabwean dollars per pound of cured tobacco while he sells it for 7 Zimbabwean dollars? What is Shekan's contribution to the tobacco production process?
2. Under President Mugabe's land management plan, Amadika is to receive 10 hectares of Shekan's property, but she receives none of the capital equipment she currently uses on Shekan's farm. When Amadika receives 10 hectares of land from Shekan's farm, will she be able to gather and cure the same amount of tobacco? Why or why not?
3. In terms of Zimbabwean dollars, what is Tatenda's opportunity cost of attending college? Why is there still a cost, even though Tatenda receives a scholarship? If she were to receive land under President Mugabe's plan, how might this affect her decision to attend school?
4. Assume that a gallon of milk costs 2 Zimbabwean dollars. What is the cost of a gallon of milk in terms of pounds of tobacco?
5. Suppose Zimbabwe's government decides that 2 dollars is too expensive for milk, and imposes a law that sets the price of milk at 1 Zimbabwean dollar per gallon. How will this affect the availability of milk in Zimbabwe?
6. Why might Dakarai sell some of his tobacco crop to Shekan at 5 Zimbabwean dollars per pound, when he can receive 6 dollars from an illegal trader?
7. President Mugabe recently denounced people, such as Dakarai, who engage in illegal trade. The government, and many Zimbabweans, see people like Dakarai as an exploiter who robs from Shekan. Discuss this issue in terms of fairness and efficiency.

END NOTES

1. Efficiency, defined this way, is sometimes called *Pareto efficiency* after the Italian economist Vilfredo Pareto.
2. Armen A. Alchian and Harold Demsetz, "Production, Information Cost, and Economic Organization," *American Economic Review* (December 1972): 777–795.
3. Some basic graphical concepts—axes, points and number pairs, slopes, and tangencies—are discussed in the appendix to this chapter.
4. Henry Hazlitt, *Economics in One Lesson* (New York: Arlington House, 1979), 17.

Appendix to Chapter 1

WORKING WITH GRAPHS

Graphs are an invaluable aid in learning economics precisely because they make use of these three special abilities of the human brain. Graphs are not used to make economics harder, but to make it easier. All it takes to use graphs effectively as a learning tool is the inborn human skill in working with pictures plus knowledge of a few simple rules for extracting the information that graphs contain. This appendix outlines those rules in brief. Additional details and exercises can be found in the *Study Guide* that accompanies this textbook.

Pairs of Numbers and Points

The first thing to master is how to use points on a graph to represent pairs of numbers. The table in Figure lA.1 presents five pairs of numbers. The two columns are labeled "x" and "y." The first number in each pair is called the *x value* and the second the *y value*. Each pair of numbers is labeled with a capital letter. Pair A has an *x* value of 2 and a *y* value of 3; pair B has an *x* value of 4 and a *y* value of 4; and so on.

The diagram in Figure lA.1 contains two lines that meet at the lower left-hand corner; they are called *coordinate axes*. The horizontal axis is marked off into units representing the *x* value and the vertical axis into unit representing the *y* value. In the space between the axes,

FIGURE 1A.1 NUMBER PAIRS AND POINTS

	x	y
A	2	3
B	4	4
C	6	5
D	8	6
E	10	7

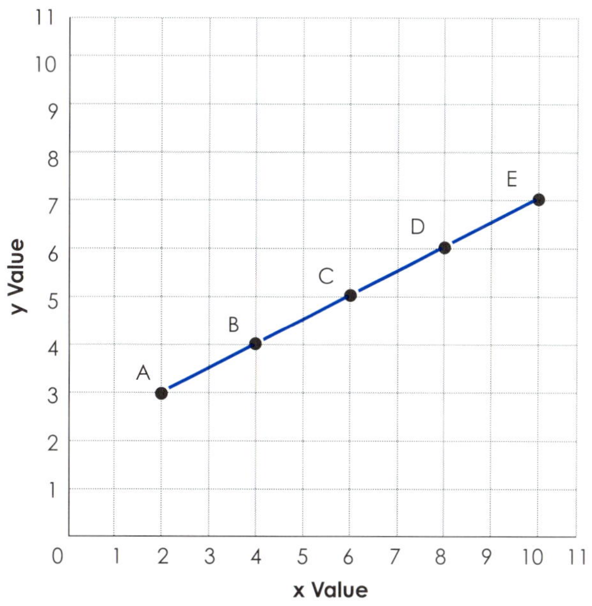

Each lettered pair of numbers in the table corresponds to a lettered point on the graph. The x value of each point corresponds to the horizontal distance of the point from the vertical axis; the *y* value corresponds to its vertical distance from the horizontal axis.

FIGURE 1A.2 SLOPES OF LINES

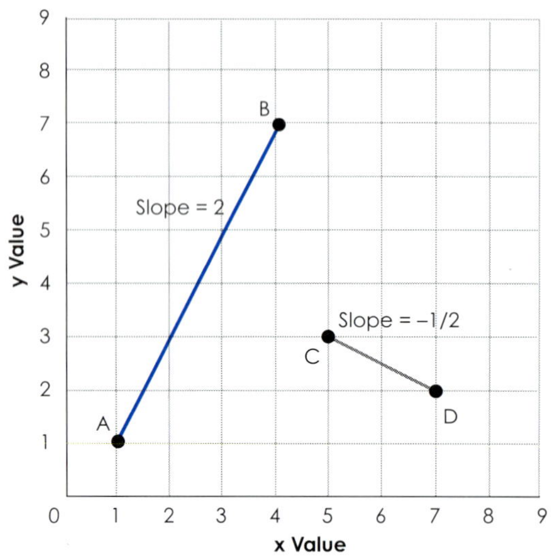

The slope of a straight line drawn between two points is defined as the ratio of the change in the y value to the change in the x value as one moves from one point to the other. For example, the line between points A and B in this Figure has a slope of +2, whereas the line between points C and D has a slope of −1/2.

Slope

For a straight line, the ratio of the change in the *y value* to the change in the *x value* between any two points on the line.

each pair of numbers from the table can be shown as a point. For example, point A is found by going two units to the right along the horizontal axis and then three units straight up, parallel to the vertical axis. That point represents the *x* value of 2 and the *y* value of 3. The other points are located in the same way.

The visual effect of a graph usually can be improved by connecting the points with a line or a curve. By doing so, the relationship between *x* values and *y* values can be seen at a glance: as the *x* value increases, the *y* value also increases.

Slopes and Tangencies

The lines or curves used in graphs are described in terms of their slopes. The **slope** of a straight line between two points is defined as the ratio of the change in the *y* value to the change in the *x* value between the two points. In Figure lA.2, for example, the slope of the line between points A and B is 2. The *y* value changes by six units between these two points, whereas the *x* value changes by only three units. The slope is the ratio 6/3 = 2.

Positive slope

A slope having a value greater than zero.

Direct relationship

A relationship between two variables in which an increase in the value of one variable is associated with an increase in the value of the other.

The slope of a line between the points (x_1, y_1) and (x_2, y_2) can be expressed in terms of a simple formula that is derived from the definition just given:

$$\text{Slope} = (y_2 - y_1)/(x_2 - x_1)$$

Applied to the line between points A and B in Figure 1A.2, the formula gives the following result:

$$\text{Slope} = (7 - 1)/(4 - 1) = 6/3 = 2$$

A line such as that between A and B in Figure 1A.2 is said to have a **positive slope**, because the value of its slope is a positive number. A positively sloped line represents a **direct relationship** between the variable represented on the *x* axis and that represented on the *y* axis—that is, a relationship in which an increase in one variable is associated with an increase in the other. The relationship of the age of a tree to its height is an example of a direct relationship. An example from economics is the relationship between family income and expenditures on housing.

When a line slants downward, such as the one between points C and D in Figure 1A.2, the *x* and *y* values change in opposite directions. Going from point C to point D, the *y* value changes by –1 (that is, decreases by one unit) and the *x* value changes by +2 (that is, increases by two units). The slope of this line is the ratio –1/2.

When the slope of a line is given by a negative number, the line is said to have a **negative slope**. Such a line represents an **inverse relationship** between the *x* variable and the *y* variable—that is, a relationship in which an increase in the value of one variable is associated with a decrease in the value of the other variable. The relationship between the temperature in the room and the time it takes the ice in your lemonade to melt is an example of an inverse relationship. To give an economic example, the relationship between the price of gasoline and the quantity consumers purchase, other things being equal, is an inverse relationship.

The concepts of positive and negative slopes, and of direct and inverse relationships, apply to curves as well as to straight lines. However, the slope of a curve, unlike that of a straight line, varies from one point to the next.[1] We cannot speak of the slope of a curve in general, but only of its slope at a given point. The slope of a curve at any given point is defined as the slope of a straight line drawn tangent to the curve at that point. (A **tangent** line is one that just touches the curve without crossing it.) In Figure 1A.3, the slope of the curve at point A is 1 and the slope at point B is –2.

Negative slope

A slope having a value less than zero.

Inverse relationship

A relationship between two variables in which an increase in the value of one variable is associated with a decrease in the value of the other.

Tangent

A straight line that touches a curve at a given point without intersecting it.

[1]Economists try to be consistent, but in talking about lines and curves, they fail. They have no qualms about calling something a "curve" that is a straight line. For example, later we will encounter "demand curves" that are as straight as a stretched string. Less frequently, they may call something a line that is curved.

FIGURE 1A.3 SLOPES OF CURVES

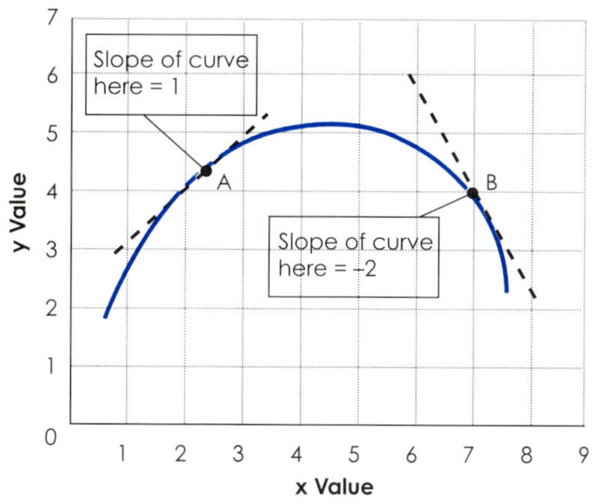

The slope of a curve at any point is defined as the slope of a straight line drawn tangent to the curve at that point. A tangent line is one that just touches the curve without crossing it. In this figure, the slope of the curve at point A is 1 and the slope at point B is –2.

Using Graphs to Display Data

Graphs are used in economics for two primary purposes: for visual display of quantitative data and for visual representation of economic relationships. Some graphs are primarily designed to serve one purpose, some the other, and some a little of both. We begin with some common kinds of graphs whose primary purpose is to display data.

Figure 1A.4 shows three kinds of graphs often used to display data. Part (a) is *pie chart*. Pie charts are used to show the relative size of various quantities that add up to a total of 100 percent. In this case, the quantities displayed are the percentages of U.S. foreign trade accounted for by various trading partners. In the original source, the graph was drawn as part of a discussion of U.S. trade with Canada, Japan, and Western Europe. The author wanted to make the point that trade with these countries is very important. Note how the graph highlights Canadian, Japanese, and Western European trade with the U.S., and at the same time omits details not relevant to the discussion by lumping together the rest of Europe, Africa, the rest of Asia, and many other countries under the heading "rest of the world." In reading graphs, do not just look at the numbers, but ask yourself, "What point is the graph trying to make?"

Part (b) of Figure lA.4 is a *bar chart*. Bar charts, like pie charts, are used to display numerical data (in this case, unemployment rates) in relationship to some nonnumerical classification of cases (in this case, educational attainment). Bar charts are not subject to the restriction that data displayed must total 100 percent. What point do you think the author of this graph was trying to make?

Part (c) of Figure lA.4 is an example of a data display graph very common in economics—the *time-series graph*. A time-series graph shows the values of one or more economic quantities on the vertical axis and time (years, months, or whatever) on the horizontal axis. This graph shows the ups and downs of the U.S. unemployment rate by month over the period 1980 through 1991.

Note one feature of this time-series graph: the scale on the vertical axis begins from 3 percent rather than from 0. By spreading out the data points in the range 3 to 11 percent, one can show the trend of unemployment in greater detail. The advantage of greater detail has an offsetting danger, however. Careless reading of the graph could cause one to exaggerate the amount by which unemployment rises during a recession. For example, the unemployment line is more than three times higher above the horizontal axis in December 1991 than in March 1989. However, careful reading of the graph shows that the unemployment rate in December 1991 was actually only about 1.4 times as high as in March 1989. The moral of the story: Always examine the vertical and horizontal axes of a graph carefully.

Using Graphs to Display Relationships

Some graphs, rather than simply recording observed facts, attempt to represent theories and models—that is, to show the relationships among facts. Figure 1A.5 shows two typical graphs whose primary purpose is to display relationships.

Part (a) of Figure 1A.5 is the production possibility frontier that we encountered in Chapter 1. The graph represents the inverse relationship between the quantity of cars that can be produced and the quantity of education that can be produced, given available knowledge and productive resources.

Figure 1A.4 Using Graphs to Display Data

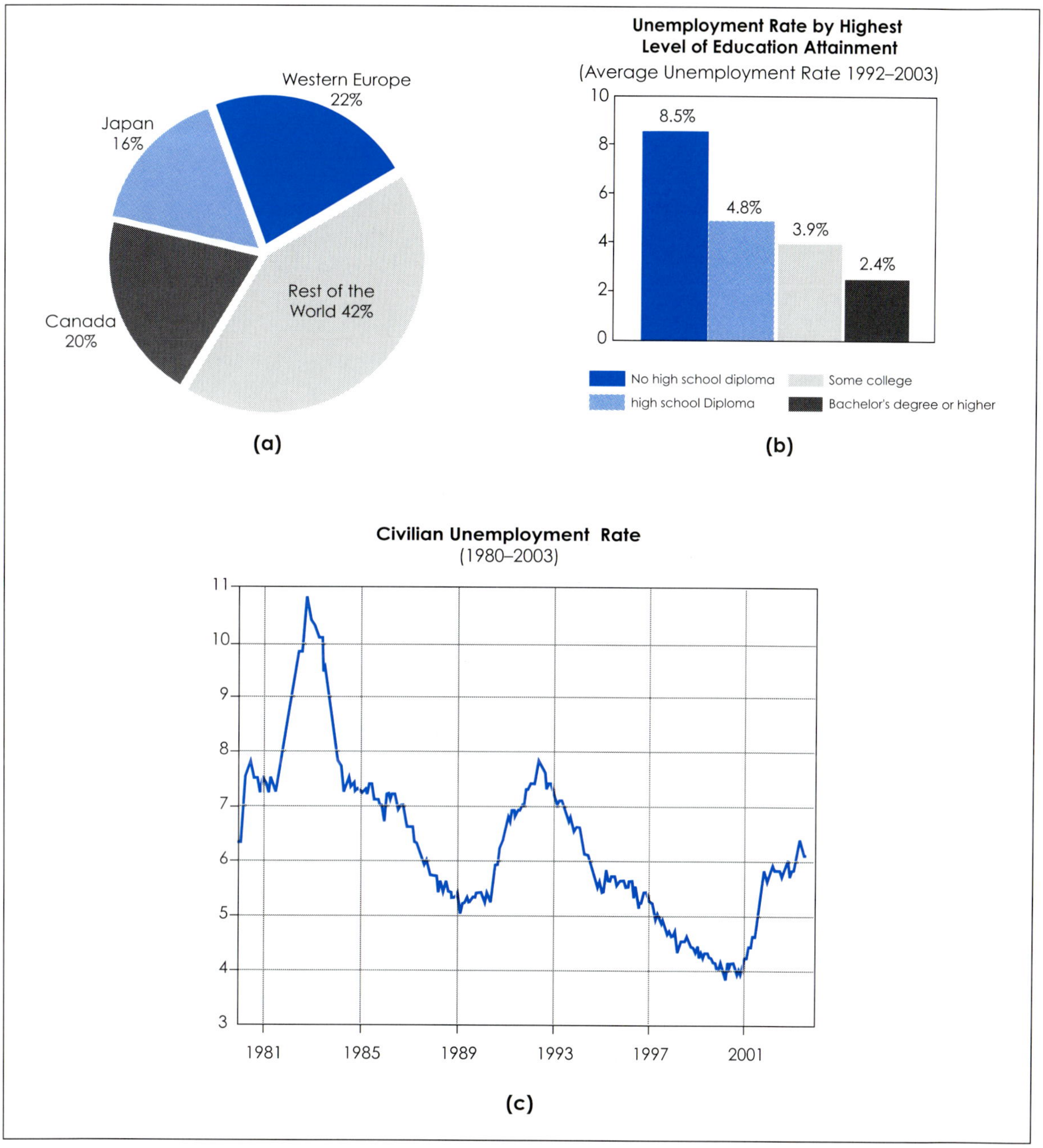

This figure shows three common kinds of data display graphs. The *pie chart* in part (a) is used when the data items sum to 100 percent. The *bar chart* in part (b), like the pie chart, is used when reporting numerical data that are associated with nonnumerical categories (in this case educational attainment). The bar chart does not require data items to sum to 100 percent. The *time-series graph* in part (c) shows the values of one or more economic quantities on the vertical axis and time on the horizontal axis.

Source: Part (a), U.S. Council of Economic Advisers, *Economic Report of the President* (Washington, D.C.: Government Printing Office, 2002), Table B-105, 397; part (b), Bureau of Labor Statistics, *Current Population Survey*; and part (c), Bureau of Labor Statistics, *The Employment Situation*.

FIGURE 1A.5 USING GRAPHS TO SHOW RELATIONSHIPS

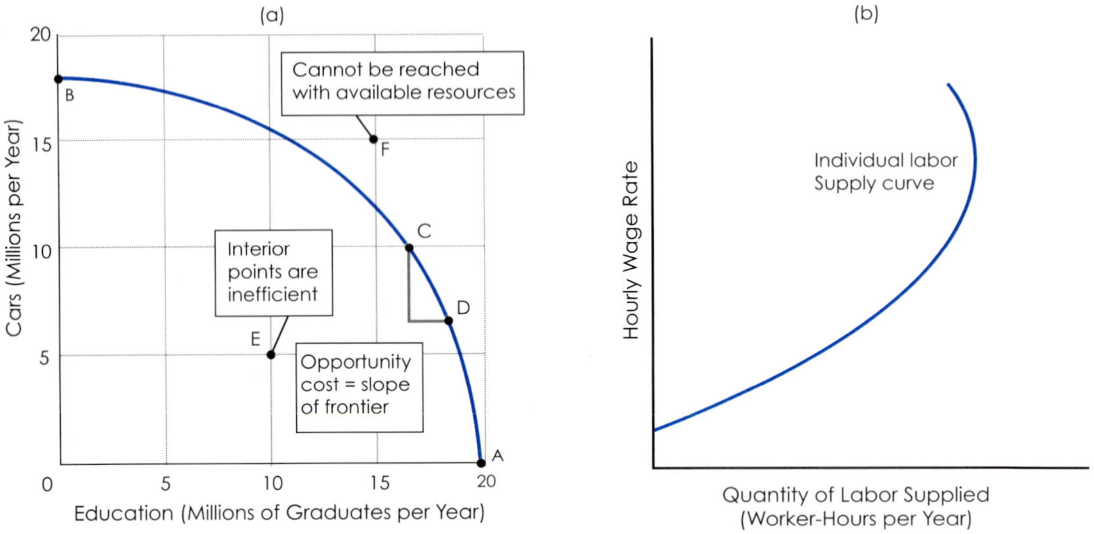

Relational graphs are visual representations of theories, that is, of relationships among facts. Two typical relational graphs are shown here. Part (a) is the production possibility frontier discussed in Chapter 1. It relates quantities of cars to quantities of education that can be produced with given factors of production and knowledge. Part (b) represents a theory of individual labor supply, according to which an increase in the hourly wage rate, after a point, will cause a person to reduce the quantity of labor supplied. Part (b) is an abstract graph in that it shows only the general nature of the relationship, with no numbers on either axis.

Part (b) of Figure lA.5 represents a relationship between the quantity of labor that a person is willing to supply (measured in worker-hours per year) and the wage rate per hour the person is paid. According to the theory portrayed by the graph, raising the wage rate will, up to a point, induce a person to work more hours. But beyond a certain point (according to the theory), a further increase in the wage will actually cause the person to work fewer hours. Why? Because the person is so well off, he or she prefers the luxury of more leisure time to the reward of more material goods.

Note one distinctive feature of this graph: There are no numbers on the axes. It is an abstract graph that represents only the qualitative relationships between the hours of labor supplied per year and the wage rate. It makes no quantitative statements regarding how much the number of hours worked will change as a result of any given change in wage rate. Abstract graphs are often used when the point to be made is a general one that applies to many cases, regardless of quantitative differences from one case to another.

Packing Three Variables into Two Dimensions

Anything drawn on a flat piece of paper is limited to two dimensions. The relationships discussed so far fit a two-dimensional framework easily, because they involve just two variables. In the case of the production possibility frontier, the two are the quantity of education (horizontal axis) and the quantity of cars (vertical axis). In the case of the labor supply, they are hours worked per year (horizontal axis) and wage rate per hour (vertical axis). But reality does not always cooperate with geometry. Often one must take three or more variables into account in order to understand relationships among facts.

A number of methods have been devised to represent relationships involving three or more variables. For example, a map of the United States might use coordinates of latitude and longitude to indicate position, contour lines to indicate altitude, and shadings of various colors to indicate vegetation. An architect might use a perspective drawing to give the illusion of three dimensions—height, width, and depth—on a flat piece of paper. This section deals with one simple method of packing three variables into two dimensions. Although the method is a favorite of economists—it will be used in dozens of graphs in this book—we will show its generality by beginning with a noneconomic example.

A NONECONOMIC EXAMPLE The example concerns heart disease, the leading cause of death in the United States. In recent years, medical researchers have discovered that the risk of heart disease is closely linked to the quantity of cholesterol in a person's blood. Studies have indicated, for example, that a 25 percent reduction in cholesterol can cut the risk of death from heart attack by nearly 50 percent. Knowing this, millions of people have had their cholesterol levels tested, and if they were found to be high, have undertaken programs of diet, exercise, or drug therapy to reduce their risk of heart disease.

Important though cholesterol is, however, just knowing your cholesterol level is not enough to tell you your risk of dying of a heart attack in the coming year. Other variables also enter into the risk of heart disease. One of the most important of these variables is age. For example, for men aged 20 with average cholesterol levels, the mortality rate from heart disease is only about 3 per 100,000. For men aged 60, the mortality rate rises to over 500 per 100,000, still assuming average cholesterol. We thus have three variables to deal with: mortality, cholesterol, and age. How can we represent these three variables using only two-dimensional graphs?

A possible approach would be to draw two separate graphs. One would show the relationship between age and heart disease for the male population as a whole, without regard to differences in cholesterol counts. The other would show the relationship between cholesterol and heart disease for the male population as a whole, without regard to age. By looking from one diagram to the other, we could get an idea of the three-variable relationship as a whole.

However, such a side-by-side pair of graphs would be clumsy. There must be a better way to represent the three variables in two dimensions. The better way, shown in Figure lA.6, is to use cholesterol and mortality as the *x* and *y* axes, and to take age into account by plotting separate lines for men of various ages. That chart is far easier to interpret than the side-by-side pair would be. If you are a man and know your age and cholesterol count, you just pick out the appropriate line and read off your risk of mortality. If you do not like what you see, you go on a diet.[2]

The multi-curve graph is a lovely invention. One of the great things about it is that it works for more than three variables. For example, we could add a fourth variable, gender, to the graph by drawing a new set of lines in a different color to show mortality rates for women

[2]We could instead have started with the age-mortality chart and drawn separate lines for men with different cholesterol levels. Such a chart would show exactly the same information. We could even draw a chart with cholesterol and age on the axes, and separate contour lines to represent various levels of mortality. The choice often depends on what one wants to emphasize. Here, we emphasize the cholesterol-mortality relationship because cholesterol is something you can do something about. You cannot do anything about your age, so we give age slightly less emphasis by not placing it on one of the two axes.

FIGURE 1A.6 THREE VARIABLES IN TWO DIMENSIONS

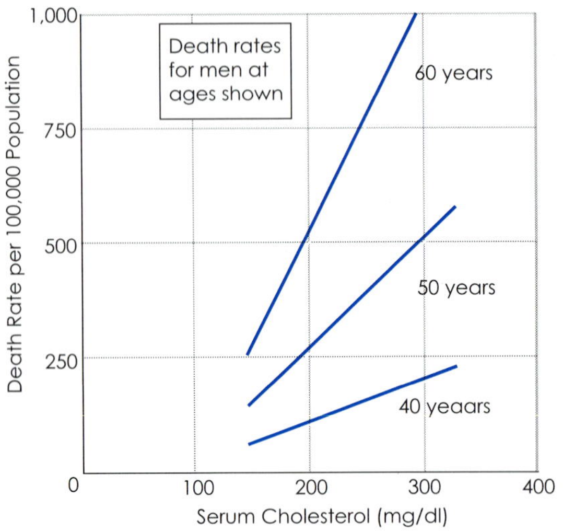

This graph shows a common way of representing a three-variable relationship on a two-dimensional graph. The three variables in this case are serum cholesterol (a measure of the amount of cholesterol in the blood), age, and death rate from heart disease for the U.S. male population. The relationship among the three variables is most easily interpreted, if all three variables are included in one graph, by drawing separate cholesterol-death rate lines for each age group. As a man ages, his cholesterol-death rate line shifts upward.

of various ages. Each line for women would have a positive slope similar to the men's lines, but would lie somewhat below the corresponding line for men of the same age, because women, other things being equal, experience lower mortality from heart disease.

SHIFTS IN CURVES AND MOVEMENTS ALONG CURVES Economists use three-variable, multi-curve graphs often enough that it is worth giving some attention to the terminology used in discussing them. How can we best describe what happens to a man as he ages, given the relationship shown in Figure 1A.6?

One way to describe the effects of aging would be to say, "As a man ages, he moves from one curve to the next higher one on the chart." There is nothing at all wrong with saying that, but an economist would tend to phrase it a bit differently, saying "As a man ages, his cholesterol-mortality curve shifts upward." The two ways of expressing the effects of aging have exactly the same meaning. Preferring one or the other is just a matter of habit.

If we express the effects of aging in terms of a shift of the cholesterol-mortality curve, how should we express the effects of a reduction in cholesterol for a man of a given age? An economist would say it this way: "Cutting a man's cholesterol count through diet or exercise will move him down along his cholesterol-mortality curve."

Before you finish this book, you will see the phrases "shift in a curve" and "movement along a curve" a great many times. How can you keep them straight? Nothing could be easier.

- If you are talking about the effect of a change in a variable that is shown on one of the coordinate axes of the diagram, the effect will be shown as a movement along one of the curves.

- If you are talking about the effect of a change in a variable that is not shown on one of the coordinate axes of the diagram, the effect will be shown by a shift in one of the curves.

Study Hints

So much for the basic rules of graphics. Once you master them, how should you study a chapter that is full of graphs?

The first—and most important—rule is to avoid trying to memorize graphs as patterns of lines. In every economics course, at least one student comes to the instructor after failing an exam and exclaims, "But I learned every one of those graphs! What happened?" The reply is that the student should have learned economics instead of memorizing graphs. Following are some hints for working with graphs.

After reading through a chapter that contains several graphs, go back through the graphs one at a time. Cover the caption accompanying each graph, and try to express the graph's "picture" in words. If you cannot say as much about the graph as the caption does, reread the text. Once you can translate the graph into words, you have won half the battle.

Next, cover each graph and use the caption as a guide. Try to sketch the graph on a piece of scratch paper. How are the graph's axes labeled? How are the curves labeled? What are the slopes of various curves? Are there important points of intersection or tangencies? If you can go back and forth between the caption and the graph, you will find that the two together are much easier to remember than either one separately.

Finally, try going beyond the graph that is shown in the book. If the graph illustrates the effect of an increase in the price of butter, try sketching a similar diagram that shows the effect of a decrease in the price of butter. If the graph shows what happens to the economy during a period of rising unemployment, try drawing a similar graph that shows what happens during a period of falling unemployment. This is a good practice that may give you an edge on your next exam.

MAKING YOUR OWN GRAPHS For some students, the hardest test questions to answer are ones that require original graphs as part of an essay. Suppose the question is, "How does a change in the number of students attending a university affect the cost per student of providing an education?" Here are some hints for making your own graph.

1. Write down the answer to the question in words. If you cannot, you might as well skip to the next question. Underline the most important quantities in your answer, such as "The larger the *number of students* who attend a college, the lower the *cost per student* of providing them with an education, because fixed facilities, such as libraries, do not have to be duplicated."

2. Decide how you want to label the axes. In our example, the vertical axis could be labeled "cost per student" and the horizontal axis "number of students."

3. Do you have specific numbers to work with? If so, the next step is to construct a table showing what you know and use it to sketch your graph. If you have no numbers, you must draw an abstract graph. In this case, all you know is that the cost per student goes down when the number of students goes up. Your graph would thus be a negatively sloped line.

4. If your graph involves more than one relationship between quantities, repeat steps 1 through 3 for each relationship you wish to show. When constructing a graph with more than one curve, pay special attention to points at which you think the curves should intersect.

(Intersections occur whenever both the x and y values of the two relationships are equal.) Also note the points at which you think two curves ought to be tangent (which requires that their slopes be equal), the points of maximum or minimum value, if any, and so on.

5. When your graph is finished, try to translate it back into words. Does it really say what you want it to?

A REMINDER As you read this book and encounter various kinds of graphs, turn back to this appendix now and then. Do not memorize graphs as meaningless pictures; if you do, you will get lost. If you can alternate between graphs and words, the underlying point will be clearer than if you rely on either one alone. Keep in mind that the primary focus of economics is not graphs; it is people and the ways in which they deal with the challenge of scarcity.

CHAPTER 2

Supply and Demand: The Basics

After reading this chapter, you will understand:

1. How the price of a good or service affects the quantity demanded by buyers
2. How other market conditions affect demand
3. How the price of a good affects the quantity supplied by sellers
4. How other market conditions affect supply
5. How supply and demand interact to determine the market price of a good or service
6. Why market prices and quantities change in response to changes in market conditions
7. How price supports and price ceilings affect the operations of markets

Before reading this chapter, make sure you know the meaning of:

1. Spontaneous order
2. Markets
3. Opportunity cost
4. Law of unintended consequences

PORSCHE FACES HARD TIMES IN THE 1990S

During the boom years of the 1980s, few status symbols could outclass a new Porsche in the driveway of a young, upwardly mobile lawyer or stockbroker. Not even German rivals Mercedes or BMW could match Porsche's flashy, sporty image, or its rocket-like performance.

But Porsche ran into trouble during the 1990s. By 1992, the German automaker's sales in the United States, its biggest single market, had fallen some 85 percent from their 1986 peak.

Chairman Arno Bohn of the Stuttgart-based company told *The Wall Street Journal* that Porsche had no intention of abandoning the U.S. market. Considering that nearly half of all Porsches in existence are on U.S. roads, to do so would be unthinkable. But even as Bohn was insisting that many people still dreamed of owning a Porsche, layoff notices were going out to Porsche employees both in Europe and North America. What caused all of Porsche's trouble? Certainly not any fault of its vaunted engineering staff. The latest Porsches are the fastest, most stylish ever. But car sales are influenced as much by economics as by engineering, and economic changes have worked against the company.

Price is a major factor. Between 1984 and 1991, the price of a Porsche in the United States doubled. In part, this reflected the fact that German industrial workers have become the world's most highly paid. And, in part, the rising value of the German mark on foreign exchange markets meant that U.S. consumers had to pay more dollars for a car, even if the cost of building it in Germany remained constant.

The competitive environment was changing, too. In the late 1980s, Japanese automakers introduced high performance sports cars of their own at prices lower than those of European models.

At the same time, the U.S. economy was hit hard by recession. And there was a new element in the recession of the early 1990s: In the past, high-paid white-collar workers—Porsche's core customer base—often rode out business downturns unscathed. This time, many of them lost their jobs. Not a good time to spend $95,000 on a new mechanical toy. Finally, tastes seemed to be changing, too. In the 1980s, the attitude among many wealthy Americans was, "If you've got it, flaunt it." By the early 1990s, even people whose incomes were untouched by recession were less eager to make a public statement of the fact by buying the most expensive car they could find.

Porsche remains a profitable, debt-free company insistent on maintaining its independence. Fortunately for Porsche, the extended economic expansion of the 1990s, coupled with its business strategies, helped Porsche turn things around, fueling a turnaround for luxury vehicles and sports cars.

Source: Based in part on Krystal Miller and Terence Roth, "Porsche, a Favorite in Times of Plenty, Struggles to Survive in a More Frugal Era," *The Wall Street Journal*, Jan. 27, 1992, B1.

LUXURY CARS ARE just one category among millions of goods and services for which prices, quantities sold, and other market conditions vary from day to day and from year to year. Whether they are goods that we ourselves buy and sell, or goods that our employers, neighbors, or family members buy and sell, the changing market conditions affect our lives in many ways. The factors determining market prices and quantities are thus a good starting point for any discussion of economics.

This chapter outlines a model of price determination in a market economy, the supply-and-demand model. Economists use the term **supply** to refer to sellers' willingness and ability to provide goods for sale in a market. **Demand** refers to buyers' willingness and ability to purchase goods.

Supply

The willingness and ability of sellers to provide goods for sale in a market.

Demand

The willingness and ability of buyers to purchase goods.

Law of demand

The principle that an inverse relationship exists between the price of a good and the quantity of that good that buyers demand, other things being equal.

DEMAND

The fact that sales of Porsches fell as their price increased is an example of the law of demand in action. The **law of demand** can be stated formally as follows: In any market, other things being equal, an inverse relationship exists between the price of a good and the quantity of the good that buyers demand—that is, the amount they are willing and able to buy. Thus, the quantity demanded tends to rise as the price falls and to fall as the price rises.

We expect this to happen for two reasons. First, if the price of one good falls while the prices of other goods stay the same, people are likely to substitute the cheaper good. Second, when the price of one good falls while incomes and other prices stay the same, people feel a little richer. They use their added buying power to buy a bit more of many things, including, in most cases, a little more of the good whose price went down.

The terms *demand* and *quantity demanded,* as used in economics, are not the same as *want* or *need.* They combine the notion of willingness with that of ability to buy. I might want a Porsche, but I do not have that kind of money. Even if I did, there are other things I want more. Thus, the quantity of Porsches I demand at the going price is zero, just as it would be if I were prepared to spend $95,000 on a car but wanted a Lotus rather than a Porsche.

On the other hand, I might *need* dental surgery to avoid losing my teeth. But suppose I am poor. If I cannot pay for the surgery or find someone to pay for it on my behalf, I am out of luck. The quantity of dental surgery I demand, therefore, is zero, however, great my need for that service.

The Demand Curve

The law of demand states a relationship between the quantity of a good that people are willing and able to buy, other things being equal, and the price of that good. Figure 2.1 represents this one-to-one relationship for a familiar consumer good, chicken.

The figure shows the demand relationship in two different ways. First look at part (a). The first row of the table shows that when the price of chicken is $3.00 a pound, the quantity demanded per year is 1 billion pounds. Reading down the table, we see that as the price falls, the quantity demanded rises. At $2.50 per pound, buyers are willing and able to purchase 1.5 billion pounds per year; at $1.50, 2.5 billion pounds; and so on.

Demand curve

A graphical representation of the relationship between the price of a good and the quantity of that good that buyers demand.

Part (b) of Figure 2.1 presents the same information in graphical form. The graph is called a **demand curve** for chicken. Suppose we want to use the demand curve to find out what quantity of chicken will be demanded at a price of $2.00 per pound. Starting at $2.00 on the vertical axis, we move across, as shown by the arrow, until we reach the demand curve at point A. Continuing to follow the arrow, we drop down to the horizontal axis. Reading from the scale on that axis, we see that the quantity demanded at a price of $2.00 per pound is 2 billion pounds per year. That is the quantity demanded in row A of the table in part (a).

The effect of a change in the price of chicken, other things being equal, can be shown as a movement from one point to another along the demand curve for chicken. Suppose that the price drops from $2.00 to $1.00 per pound. In the process, the quantity that buyers plan to buy rises. The point corresponding to the quantity demanded at the new, lower price is point B (which corresponds to row B of the table). Because of the inverse relationship between price and quantity demanded, the demand curve has a negative slope.

FIGURE 2.1 A DEMAND CURVE FOR CHICKEN

(a)

	Price of Chicken (Dollars per Pound)	Quantity of Chicken Demanded (Billions of Pounds per Year)
	$3.50	0.5
	$3.00	1
	$2.50	1.5
A	$2.00	2
	$1.50	2.5
B	$1.00	3
	$0.50	3.5

(b)

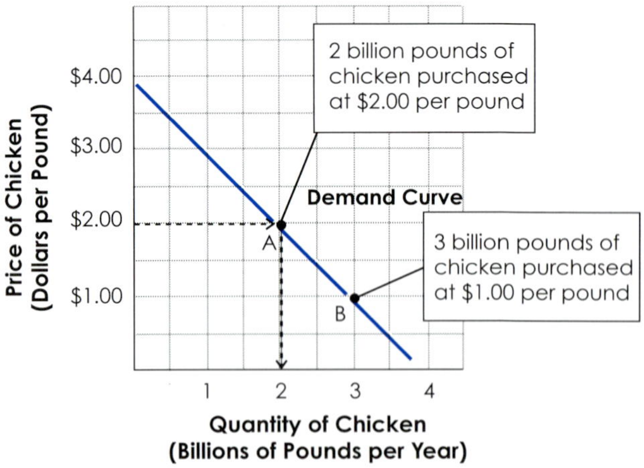

Both the table and the chart show the quantity of chicken demanded at various prices. For example, at a price of $2.00 per pound, buyers are willing and able to purchase 2 billion pounds of chicken per year. This price-quantity combination is shown by row A in part (a) and point A in part (b).

Change in quantity demanded

A change in the quantity of a good that buyers are willing and able to purchase that results from a change in the good's price, other things being equal; shown by a movement from one point to another along a demand curve.

Economists speak of a movement along a demand curve as a **change in quantity demanded**. Such a movement represents buyers' reaction to a change in the price of the good in question, other things being equal.

Shifts in the Demand Curve[1]

The demand curve in Figure 2.1 represents a relationship between two variables: the price of chicken and the quantity of chicken demanded. But changes in other variables can also affect people's purchases of chicken. In the case of chicken, the prices of beef and pork would affect demand. Consumer incomes are a second variable that can affect demand. Changes in expectations about the future are a third, and changes in consumer tastes, such as an increasing preference for foods with a low saturated-fat content, are a fourth. The list could go on and on—the demand for ice is affected by the weather; the demand for diapers is affected by the birthrate; the demand for baseball tickets is affected by the won-lost record of the home team; and so on.

How are all these other variables handled when drawing a demand curve? In brief, two rules applу:

1. When drawing a single demand curve for a good, such as the one in Figure 2.1, all other conditions that affect demand are considered to be fixed or constant under the "other things being equal" clause of the law of demand. As long as that clause is in force, the only two variables at work are quantity demanded (on the horizontal axis) and price (on the vertical axis). The effect of a change in price on quantity demanded thus is shown by a *movement along* the demand curve.

2. When we look beyond the "other things being equal" clause and find that there is a change in a variable that is not represented on one of the axes, such as the price of another good or the level of consumer income, the effect is shown as a *shift* in the demand curve. In its new position, the demand curve still represents a two-variable price-quantity relationship, but it is a slightly different relationship than before because one of the "other things" has changed.

These two rules for graphical representation of demand relationships are crucial to understanding the theory of supply and demand as a whole. It will be worthwhile to expand on them through a series of examples.

CHANGES IN THE PRICE OF ANOTHER GOOD We have already noted that the demand for chicken depends on what happens to the price of beef, as well as what happens to the price of chicken. Figure 2.2, which shows demand curves for both goods, provides a closer look at this relationship.

Suppose that the price of beef is initially \$3.00 per pound and then increases to \$4.50 per pound. The effect of this change on the quantity of beef demanded is shown in part (a) of Figure 2.2 as a movement along the beef demand curve from point A to point B. Part (b) of the figure shows the effect on the demand for chicken. With the price of beef higher than before, consumers will tend to buy more chicken *even if the price of chicken does not change.* Suppose the price of chicken is $2.00 per pound. When beef was selling at $3.00 a pound, consumers bought 2 billion pounds of chicken a year (point A′ on demand curve D_1). After the price of beef goes up to $4.50 a pound, they will buy 3.5 billion pounds of chicken a year, assuming that the price of chicken does not change (point B′ on demand curve D_2).

A rise in the price of beef would cause consumers to buy more chicken regardless of the initial price of chicken. If the price of chicken had started out at $3.00 a pound and remained there while the price of beef went up, consumers would have increased their chicken consumption from 1 billion pounds a year to 2.5 billion pounds a year. At a price of $1.00 a pound for chicken, the quantity would have risen from 3 billion pounds to 4.5 billion pounds, and so on. We see, then, that a change in the price of beef causes the entire demand curve for chicken to shift. The "other things being equal" clause of the new demand curve, D_2, incorporates a price of $4.50 a pound for beef, rather than the price of $3.00 a pound assumed in demand curve D_1.

Change in demand

A change in the quantity of a good that buyers are willing and able to purchase that results from a change in some condition other than the price of that good; shown by a shift in the demand curve.

Earlier we explained that economists refer to a movement along a demand curve as a "change in quantity demanded." The corresponding term for a shift in a demand curve is a **change in demand**. A change in quantity demanded (a movement along the curve) is caused by a change in the price of the good in question (the variable on the vertical axis). In contrast, a change in demand (a shift in the demand curve) is caused

FIGURE 2.2 EFFECTS OF AN INCREASE IN THE PRICE OF BEEF ON THE DEMAND FOR CHICKEN

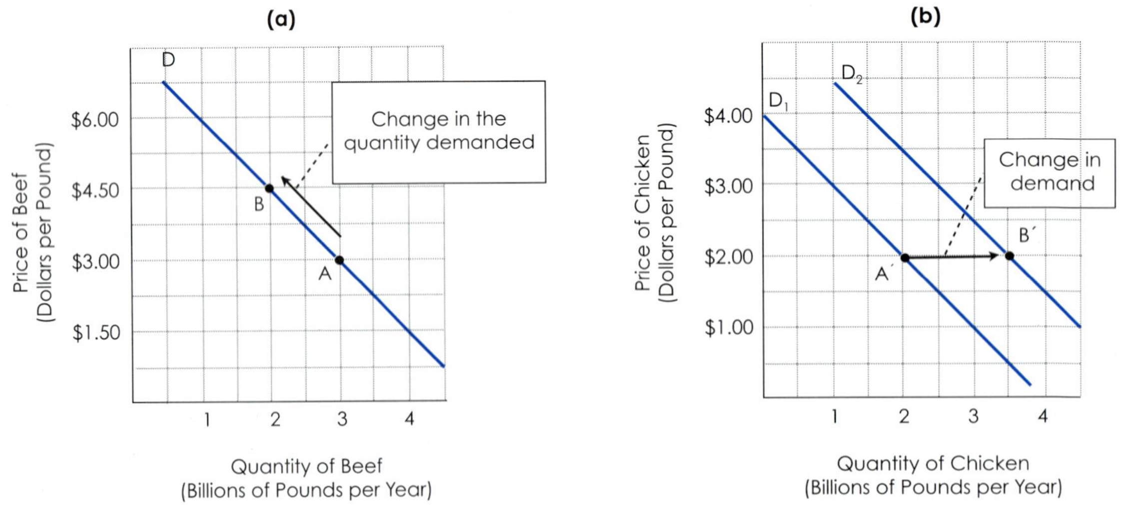

An increase in the price of beef from $3.00 to $4.50 per pound, other things being equal, causes a movement from point A to point B on the beef demand curve—a decrease in the quantity of beef demanded. With the price of chicken unchanged at $2.00 per pound, consumers will substitute chicken for beef. That will cause an increase in the demand for chicken, which is shown as a shift in the chicken demand curve from D_1 to D_2.

by a change in some variable other than the price of the good in question (one that does not appear on either axis).

Substitute goods

A pair of goods for which an increase in the price of one causes an increase in demand for the other.

Complementary goods

A pair of goods for which an increase in the price of one results in a decrease in demand for the other.

In the example in Figure 2.2, people bought more chicken when the price of beef went up, replacing one meat with the other in their dinners. Economists call such pairs of goods **substitutes**, because an increase in the price of one causes an increase in the demand for the other—a rightward shift in the demand curve.

Consumers react differently to price changes when two goods tend to be used together. One example is tires and gasoline. When the price of gasoline goes up, people drive less; therefore, they buy fewer tires even if there is no change in their price. An increase in the price of gasoline thus causes a movement upward along the gasoline demand curve and a *leftward* shift in the demand curve for tires. Pairs of goods that are related in this way are known as **complements**.

Whether a given pair of goods are substitutes or complements depends on buyers' attitudes toward those goods; these terms do not refer to properties of the goods themselves. Some people might regard cheese and beef as substitute sources of protein in their diets; others, who like cheeseburgers, might regard them as complements.

One more point regarding the effects of changes in the prices of other goods is also worth noting: In stating the law of demand, it is the price of a good *relative to those of other goods* that counts. During periods of inflation, when the average level of all prices rises, distinguishing between changes in *relative prices* and changes in *nominal prices*—the number of dollars actually paid per unit of a good—is especially important. When the economy experiences inflation, a good can become relatively less expensive even though its nominal price rises, provided that the prices of other goods rise even faster.

Consider chicken, for example. Between 1950 and 2003 the average retail price of a broiler rose by almost 40 percent, from $.59 per pound to $1.05 per pound. Over the same period, however, the average price of all goods and services that consumers bought rose by 600 percent. The relative price of chicken thus fell during the period even though its nominal price rose. The drop in the relative price of chicken had a lot to do with its growing popularity on the dinner table.

CHANGES IN CONSUMER INCOMES The demand for a good can also be affected by changes in consumer incomes. When their incomes rise, people tend to buy larger quantities of many goods, assuming that the prices of those goods do not change.

Figure 2.3 shows the effect of an increase in consumer incomes on the demand for chicken. Demand curve D_1 is the same as the curve shown in Figure 2.1. Suppose now that consumer incomes rise. With higher incomes, people become choosier about what they eat. They do not just want calories, they want high-quality calories from foods that are tasty, fashionable, and healthful. These considerations have made chicken increasingly popular as consumer incomes have risen.

More specifically, suppose that after their incomes rise, consumers are willing to buy 2.5 billion pounds of chicken instead of 1 billion pounds at a price of $3.00 per

FIGURE 2.3 EFFECTS OF AN INCREASE IN CONSUMER INCOME ON THE DEMAND FOR CHICKEN

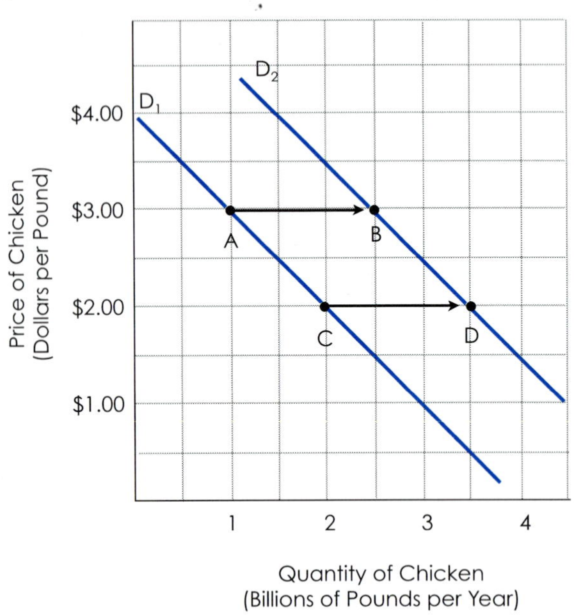

Demand curve D_1 assumes a given level of consumer income. If their incomes increase, consumers will want to buy more chicken at any given price, other things being equal. That will shift the demand curve rightward to, say, D_2. If the prevailing market price at the time of the demand shift is $3.00 per pound, the quantity demanded increases to 2.5 billion pounds (B) from 1 billion (A); if the prevailing price is $2.00 per pound, the quantity demanded will increase to 2 billion pounds (D) from 3.5 billion (C); and so on.

pound. The change is shown as an arrow drawn from point A to point B in Figure 2.3. If the initial price of chicken had been $2.00 per pound, even more chicken would be bought at the new, higher level of income. At the original income level and a price of $2.00, the amount purchased would be 2 billion pounds, as shown by point C. After the increase in incomes, buyers would plan to purchase 3.5 billion pounds, shown by the arrow from point C to point D.

Whatever the initial price of chicken, the effect of an increase in consumer incomes is shown by a shift to a point on the new demand curve, D_2. The increase in demand for chicken that results from the rise in consumer incomes thus is shown as a shift in the entire demand curve. If consumer incomes remain at the new, higher level, the effects of any changes in the price of chicken will be shown as movements along the new demand curve. There is, in other words, a chicken demand curve for every possible income level. Each represents a one-to-one relationship between price and quantity demanded, given the assumed income level.

Normal good

A good for which an increase in consumer incomes results in an increase in demand.

In the example just given, we assumed that an increase in income would cause an increase in the demand for chicken. Experience shows that this is what normally happens. Economists therefore call chicken a **normal good**, meaning that when consumer incomes rise, other things being equal, people will buy more of it.

There are some goods, however, that people will buy less of when their incomes rise, other things being equal. For example, among your classmates, those with higher incomes are likely to go out for pizza more often than those with lower incomes. On nights when they eat pizza, they do not eat in the cafeteria, so the demand for cafeteria food falls as income rises. Similarly, when their incomes rise, people tend to buy less flour for baking at home and to buy more baked goods instead. People tend to buy fewer shoe repair services when their incomes rise; instead, they buy new shoes. Goods such as cafeteria food, flour, and shoe repair services are termed **inferior goods**. When consumer incomes rise, the demand curve for an inferior good shifts to the left instead of to the right. As in the case of substitutes and complements, the notions of inferiority and normality arise from consumer choices; they are not inherent properties of the goods themselves.

Inferior good

A good for which an increase in consumer incomes results in a decrease in demand.

CHANGES IN EXPECTATIONS Changes in buyers' expectations are a third factor that can shift demand curves. If people expect the price of a particular good to rise relative to the prices of other goods, or expect something other than a price increase to raise the opportunity cost of acquiring the good, they will step up their rate of purchase before the change takes place.

For example, suppose that in May, consumers rushed to buy airline tickets in response to a series of news reports indicating that prices would be raised for tickets ordered after June 5. The people who bought their tickets in May included many who were planning to travel late in the summer and ordinarily would have waited several more weeks before making their purchase. Thus, many more tickets were sold in May than would have been sold at the same price if consumers had not anticipated the June price rise. We can interpret the surge in ticket sales in May as a temporary rightward shift in the demand curve.

CHANGES IN TASTES Changes in tastes are a fourth source of changes in demand. Sometimes these changes occur rapidly, as can be seen, for example, in such areas as popular music, clothing styles, and fast foods. The demand curves for these goods and services shift often. In other cases, changes in tastes take longer to occur but are more permanent. For example, in recent years consumers have been more health conscious than they were in the past. The result has been reduced demand for cigarettes and high-cholesterol foods, along with increased demand for fish, chicken, and exercise equipment.

SUPPLY

The Supply Curve

We now turn from the demand side of the market to the supply side. As in the case of demand, we begin by constructing a one-to-one relationship between the price of a good and the quantity that sellers intend to offer for sale. Figure 2.4 shows such a relationship for chicken.

Supply curve

A graphical representation of the relationship between the price of a good and the quantity of that good that sellers are willing to supply.

The positively sloped curve in Figure 2.4 is called a **supply curve** for chicken. Like demand curves, supply curves are based on an "other things being equal" condition. The supply curve for chicken shows how sellers change their plans in response to a change in the price of chicken, assuming that there are no changes in other conditions—the prices of other goods, production techniques, input prices, expectations, or any other relevant condition.

Why does the supply curve have a positive slope? Why do sellers, other things being equal, plan to supply more chicken when the prevailing market price is higher than they plan to supply when the price is lower? Without going too deeply into a discussion of microeconomic theory, we can consider some common-sense explanations here.

One explanation is that the positive slope of the supply curve represents *producers' response to market incentives.* When the price of chicken goes up, farmers have an incentive to devote more time and resources to raising chickens. Farmers who raise chickens as a sideline may decide to make chickens their main business. Some people may enter the market for the first time. The same reasoning applies in every market.

FIGURE 2.4 A SUPPLY CURVE FOR CHICKEN

(a)

	Price of Chicken (Dollars per Pound)	Quantity of Chicken Demanded (Billions of Pounds per Year)
	$4.00	4
	$3.50	3.5
A	$3.00	3
	$2.50	2.5
B	$2.00	2
	$1.50	1.5
	$1.00	1

(b)

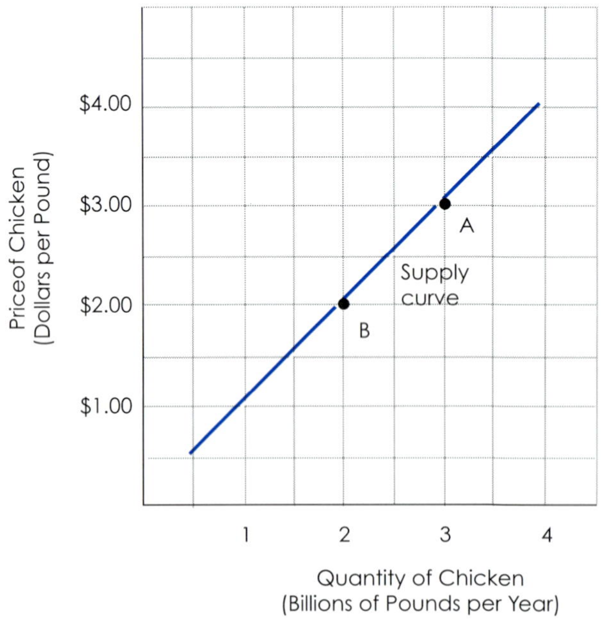

Parts (a) and (b) of this figure show the quantity of chicken supplied at various prices. As the price rises, the quantity supplied increases, other things being equal. The higher price gives farmers an incentive to raise more chickens, but the rising opportunity cost of doing so limits the supply produced in response to any given price increase.

If parents are finding it hard to get babysitters, what do they do? They offer to pay more. If a sawmill cannot buy enough timber, it raises the price it offers to loggers, and so on. Exceptions to this general rule are rare.

Another explanation is that the positive slope of the supply curve reflects *the rising cost of producing additional output in facilities of a fixed size.* A furniture factory with a fixed amount of machinery might be able to produce more chairs only by paying workers at overtime rates to run the machinery for more hours. A farmer who is trying to grow more wheat on a fixed amount of land could do so by increasing the input of fertilizer and pesticides per acre, but beyond a certain point each unit of added chemicals yields less additional output.

Finally, the positive slope of the supply curve can be explained in terms of *comparative advantage and opportunity cost.* Figure 2.5a shows a production possibility frontier for an economy in which there are only two goods, tomatoes and chicken. Farmers can choose which product they will specialize in, but some farmers have a comparative advantage in growing tomatoes, others in raising chickens. Beginning

FIGURE 2.5 THE PRODUCTION POSSIBILITY CURVE AND THE SUPPLY CURVE

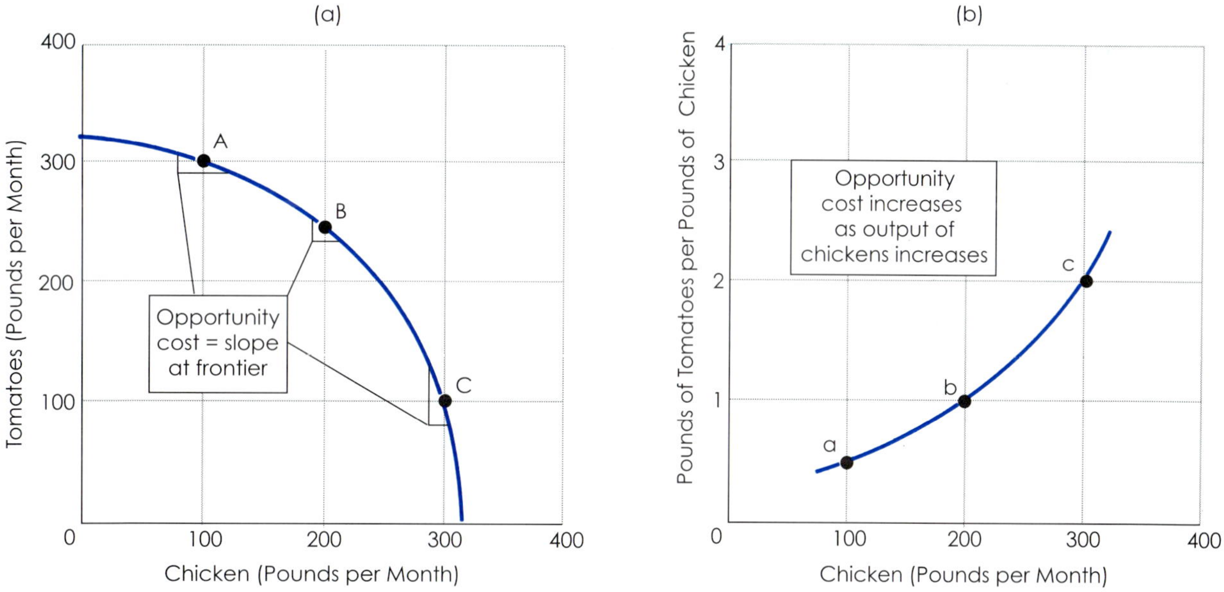

This figure offers an interpretation of the supply curve in terms of the production possibility frontier for an economy in which two goods are produced, tomatoes and chicken. Part (a) shows a production possibility frontier. The slope of the frontier at any point shows the opportunity cost of producing an additional pound of chicken measured in terms of the quantity of tomatoes that could have been produced using the same factors of production. The frontier curves because some operators have a comparative advantage in producing tomatoes and others have a comparative advantage in producing chicken. As more chicken is produced, those with the greatest comparative advantage in producing chicken are the first to stop producing tomatoes. Because the frontier gets steeper as more chicken is produced, the opportunity cost rises, as shown in part (b). The curve in part (b) can be interpreted as a supply curve, in the sense that an incentive, in the form of a higher price, will cause factors of production to be shifted from tomatoes to chicken despite the rising opportunity cost of producing chicken.

from a situation in which only tomatoes are produced, farmers with the strongest comparative advantage in raising chickens—that is, those who are able to produce chicken at relatively the lowest opportunity cost—will switch from tomatoes to chicken even if the price of chicken is low. As the point of production moves along the frontier, the price of chicken must rise to induce farmers with relatively higher opportunity costs to make the switch. The slope of the frontier at any point represents the opportunity cost of producing more chicken for a farmer who finds it worthwhile to switch from tomatoes to chicken just at that point.

In Figure 2.5 the slopes at points A, B, and C in part (a) are graphed on a new set of axes in part (b). The graph can be interpreted as a supply curve if it is noted that the price of chicken must rise relative to the price of tomatoes to induce more farmers to switch to chicken as the opportunity cost rises.

Each of these common-sense explanations fits certain circumstances. Together, they provide an intuitive basis for the positive slope of the supply curve.

Shifts in the Supply Curve

Change in quantity supplied

A change in the quantity of a good that suppliers are willing and able to sell that results from a change in the good's price, other things being equal; shown by a movement along a supply curve.

Change in supply

A change in the quantity of a good that suppliers are willing and able to sell that results from a change in some condition other than the good's price; shown by a shift in the supply curve.

As in the case of demand, the effects of a change in the price of chicken, other things being equal, can be shown as a movement along the supply curve for chicken. Such a movement is called a **change in quantity supplied**. A change in a condition other than the price of chicken can be shown as a shift in the supply curve. Such a shift is referred to as a **change in supply**. Four sources of change in supply are worth noting. Each is related to the notion that the supply curve reflects the opportunity cost of producing the good or service in question.

CHANGES IN TECHNOLOGY A supply curve is drawn on the basis of a particular production technique. When entrepreneurs reduce the opportunity costs of production by introducing more efficient techniques, it becomes worthwhile to sell more of the good than before at any given price. Figure 2.6 shows how an improvement in production technology affects the supply curve for chicken.

Supply curve S_1 is the same as the one shown in Figure 2.4. It indicates that farmers will plan to supply 3 billion pounds of chicken per year at a price of $3.00 per pound (point A). Now suppose that the development of a faster-growing bird reduces the amount of feed used in raising chickens. With lower costs per unit, farmers will be willing to supply more chicken than before at any given price. They may, for example, be willing to supply 4 billion pounds of chicken at $3.00 per pound (point B). The move from A to B is part of a shift in the entire supply curve from S_1 to S_2. Once the new techniques are established, an increase or decrease in the price of chicken, other things being equal, will result in a movement along the new supply curve.

CHANGES IN INPUT PRICES Changes in input prices are a second item that can cause supply curves to shift. An increase in input prices, other things being equal, increases the opportunity cost of producing the good in question, and hence it tends to reduce the quantity of a good that producers plan to supply at a given price. Refer again to Figure 2.6. Suppose that starting from point A on supply curve S_1, the price of chicken feed increases and no offsetting changes occur. Now, instead of supplying 3 billion pounds of chicken at $3.00 per pound, farmers will supply, say, just 2 billion pounds at that price (point C). The move from A to C is part of a leftward shift in the supply curve, from S_1 to S_3.

If the price of feed remains at the new level, changes in the price of chicken will cause movements along the new supply curve. For example, farmers could be induced to supply the original quantity of chicken—3 billion pounds—if the price of chicken rose enough to cover the increased cost of feed. As you can see in Figure 2.6, that would require a price of $4.00 per pound for chicken (point D).

CHANGES IN THE PRICES OF OTHER GOODS Changes in the prices of other goods that could be produced using the same factors of production can also produce

FIGURE 2.6 SHIFTS IN THE SUPPLY CURVE FOR CHICKEN

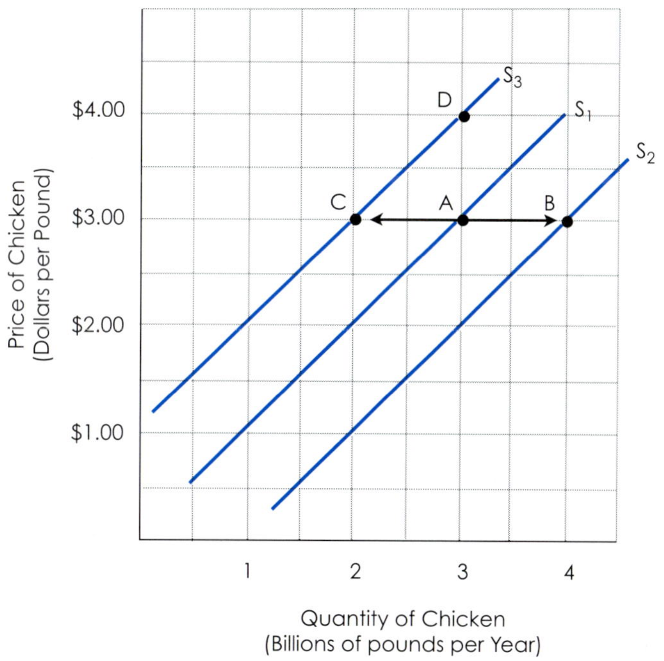

Several kinds of changes can cause the supply of chicken to increase or decrease. For example, a new production method that lowers costs will shift the curve to the *right*, from S_1 to S_2. The shift is to the right because, taking into account the new, lower cost of production per unit, producers will be willing to supply more chicken at any given price. An increase in the price of inputs, other things being equal, will shift the curve to the *left*, from S_1 to S_3. The shift is to the left because, taking into account the new, higher price of inputs, producers will be willing to supply less chicken at any given price. Changes in sellers' expectations or in the prices of competing goods can also cause the supply curve to shift.

a shift in the chicken supply curve. In our earlier example, farmers could use available resources to produce either chickens or tomatoes. Suppose that the price of tomatoes rises while the price of chicken stays at $3.00. The rise in the price of tomatoes gives some farmers who would otherwise have produced chickens an incentive to shift the use of their labor, land, and capital to the production of tomatoes. Thus, the effect of an increase in the price of tomatoes can be shown as a leftward shift in the chicken supply curve.

CHANGES IN EXPECTATIONS Changes in expectations can cause supply curves to shift in much the same way that they cause demand curves to shift. Again, we can use farming as an example. At planting time, a farmer's selection of crops is influenced not so much by current prices as by the prices expected at harvest time. Expectations over a time horizon longer than one growing season also affect supply. Each crop requires special equipment and know-how. We have just seen that an increase in the price of tomatoes gives farmers an incentive to shift from chicken to tomatoes. The incentive will be stronger if the price of tomatoes is expected to remain at the higher level. If it is, farmers are more likely to buy the special equipment needed for that crop and to learn the necessary production techniques.

THE INTERACTION OF SUPPLY AND DEMAND

Markets transmit information, in the form of prices, to people who buy and sell goods and services. Taking these prices into account, along with other knowledge they may have, buyers and sellers make their plans.[2] As shown by the demand and supply curves, buyers and sellers plan to buy or sell certain quantities of a good at any given price.

Each market has many buyers and sellers, each making plans independently. When they meet to trade, some of them may be unable to carry out their plans on the terms they expected. Perhaps the total quantity of a good that buyers plan to purchase is greater than the total quantity that suppliers are willing to sell at the given price. In that case, some of the would-be buyers must change their plans. Or, perhaps planned sales exceed planned purchases at the given price. In that case, some would-be sellers will be unable to carry out their plans.

Market Equilibrium

Equilibrium

A condition in which buyers' and sellers' plans exactly mesh in the marketplace, so that the quantity supplied exactly equals the quantity demanded at a given price.

Sometimes no one is surprised: The total quantity of a good that buyers plan to purchase exactly matches the total quantity that producers plan to sell. When buyers' and sellers' plans mesh when they meet in the marketplace, no buyers or sellers need to change their plans. Under these conditions, the market is said to be in **equilibrium**.

Supply and demand curves, which reflect the plans of sellers and buyers, can be used to give a graphical demonstration of market equilibrium. Figure 2.7 uses the same supply and demand curves as before, but this time both curves are drawn on the same diagram. If the quantity of planned sales at each price is compared with the quantity of planned purchases at that price (either the table or the graph can be used to make this comparison), it can be seen that there is only one price at which the two sets of plans mesh. That price—$2.00 per pound—is the equilibrium price. If all buyers and sellers make their plans with the expectation of a price of $2.00, no one will be surprised and no plans will have to be changed.

Shortages

But what will happen if for some reason people base their plans for buying or selling chicken on a price other than $2.00 a pound?[3] Suppose, for example, that they base their plans on a price of $1.00. Figure 2.7 shows that at that price buyers will plan to purchase chicken at a rate of 3 billion pounds per year, but farmers will plan to supply only 1 billion pounds. When the quantity demanded exceeds the quantity supplied, as in this example, the difference is an **excess quantity demanded** or, more simply, a **shortage.** In Figure 2.7 the shortage is 2 billion pounds of chicken per year when the price is $1.00 per pound.

Excess quantity demanded (shortage)

A condition in which the quantity of a good demanded at a given price exceeds the quantity supplied.

Inventory

A stock of a finished good awaiting sale or use.

In most markets the first sign of a shortage is a drop in the **inventory**, that is, in the stock of the good in question that has been produced and is waiting to be sold or used. Sellers plan to hold a certain quantity of goods in inventory to allow for minor changes in demand. When they see inventories dropping below the planned level, they change their plans. Some may try to rebuild their inventories by increasing their output, if they produce the good themselves; or, if they do not make it themselves, they may order more from the producer. Some sellers may take advantage of the strong demand for their product to raise the price, knowing that buyers will be willing to pay more. Many sellers will do a little of both. If sellers do not take the initiative, buyers will—they will offer to pay more if sellers will supply more. Whatever the details, the result will be an upward movement along the supply curve as both price and quantity increase.

As the shortage puts upward pressure on price, buyers will change their plans too. Moving up and to the left along their demand curve, they will cut back on their planned purchases. As both buyers and sellers change their plans, the market will move toward equilibrium. When the price reaches $2.00 per pound, both the shortage and the pressure to change buying and selling plans will disappear.

In the markets for most goods, sellers have inventories of goods ready to be sold. There are exceptions, however. Inventories are not possible in markets for services—haircuts, tax preparation, lawn care, and the like. Also, some goods, such as custom-built houses and machine tools that are designed for a specialized need, are not held in inventories. Sellers in these markets do not begin production until they have a contract with a buyer.

In markets in which there are no inventories, the sign of a shortage is a queue of buyers. The queue may take the form of a line of people waiting to be served or a list of names in an order book. The queue is a sign that, given the prevailing price, buyers

FIGURE 2.7 EQUILIBRIUM IN THE CHICKEN MARKET

(a)

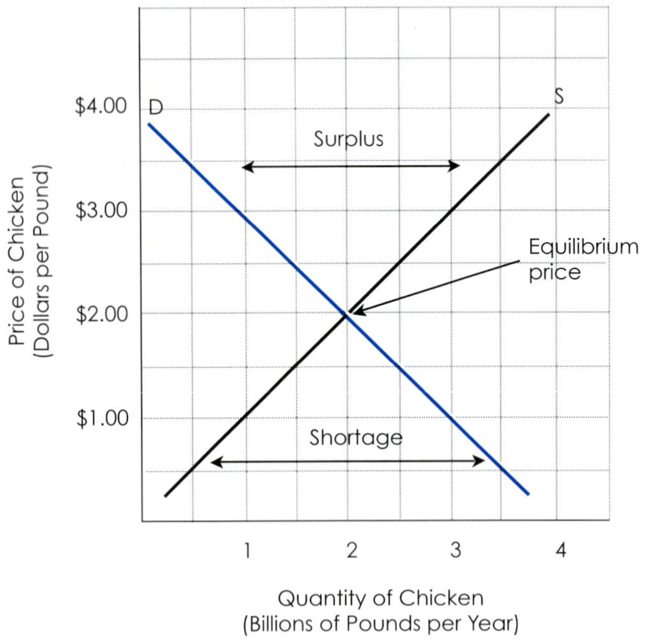

(b)

Price (per Pound)	Quantity Demanded (Billions of Pounds)	Quantity Supplied (Billions of Pounds)	Shortage (Billions of Pounds)	Surplus (Billions of Pounds)	Direction of Pressure on Price
$3.50	0.5	3.5	—	3	Downward
$3.00	1	3	—	2	Downward
$2.50	1.5	2.5	—	1	Downward
$2.00	2	2	—	—	Equilibrium
$1.50	2.5	1.5	1	—	Upward
$1.00	3	1	2	—	Upward
$0.50	3.5	0.5	3	—	Upward

This figure shows the supply and demand curves for chicken presented earlier in graphical and numerical form. The demand curve shows how much buyers plan to purchase at a given price. The supply curve shows how much producers plan to sell at a given price. At only one price—$2.00 per pound—do buyers' and sellers' plans exactly match. That is the equilibrium price. A higher price causes a surplus of chicken and puts downward pressure on price. A lower price causes a shortage and puts upward pressure on price.

would like to purchase the good at a faster rate than that at which producers have planned to supply it. However, some plans cannot be carried out—at least not right away. Buyers are served on a first-come, first-served basis.

The formation of a queue of buyers has much the same effect on the market as a decrease in inventories. Sellers react by increasing their rate of output, raising their prices, or both. Buyers react by reducing the quantity they plan to purchase. The result is a movement up and to the right along the supply curve and, at the same time, up and to the left along the demand curve until equilibrium is reached.

Surpluses

Having considered what happens when buyers and sellers initially expect a price below the equilibrium price, we now turn to the opposite case. Suppose that for some reason buyers and sellers of chicken expect a price that is higher than the equilibrium price—say, $2.50 per pound—and make their plans accordingly. Figure 2.7 shows that farmers will plan to supply 2.5 billion pounds of chicken per year at $2.50, but their customers will plan to buy only 1.5 billion pounds. When the quantity supplied exceeds the quantity demanded, there is an **excess quantity supplied**, or a **surplus**. As Figure 2.7 shows, the surplus of chicken at a price of $2.50 per pound is 1 billion pounds per year.

Excess quantity supplied (surplus)

A condition in which the quantity of a good supplied at a given price exceeds the quantity demanded.

When there is a surplus of a product, sellers will be unable to sell all that they had hoped to sell at the planned price. As a result, their inventories will begin to grow beyond the level they had planned to hold in preparation for normal changes in demand.

Sellers will react to the inventory buildup by changing their plans. Some will cut back their output. Others will lower their prices to induce consumers to buy more and thus reduce their extra stock. Still others will do a little of both. The result of these changes in plans will be a movement down and to the left along the supply curve.

As unplanned inventory buildup puts downward pressure on the price of chicken, buyers change their plans too. Finding that chicken costs less than they had expected, they buy more of it. In graphical terms, they move down and to the right along the demand curve. As that happens, the market is restored to equilibrium.

In markets in which there are no inventories, surpluses lead to the formation of queues of sellers looking for customers. Taxi queues at airports are a case in point. At some times of the day the fare for taxi service from the airport to downtown is more than high enough to attract a number of taxis that is equal to the demand. A queue of cabs waiting for passengers then forms. In some cities drivers who are far back in the queue try to attract riders by offering cut-rate fares. Often, though, there are rules against fare cutting. The queue then grows until the next peak period, when a surge in demand shortens it.

Changes in Market Conditions

On a graph, finding the equilibrium point looks easy. In real life, though, it is a moving target. Market conditions—all the items that lie behind the "other things being equal" clause—change frequently. When they do, both buyers and sellers revise their plans and the point of equilibrium shifts.

RESPONSE TO A SHIFT IN DEMAND We will first consider a market's response to a shift in demand. The decline in demand for beef caused by consumers' avoidance of high-cholesterol foods provides a good example. Part (a) of Figure 2.8 interprets this case in terms of the supply-and-demand model.

As the figure is drawn, the market is initially in equilibrium at E_1. There the price is \$3.00 per pound and the quantity produced is 2 billion pounds per year. Now the changed dietary habits of U.S. consumers cause the demand curve to shift to the left, from D_1 to D_2. (There is a shift in the demand curve rather than a movement along it, because a change in tastes is not one of the items represented by the axes of the diagram.) What will happen next?

At the original price of \$3.00 per pound, there will be a surplus of beef. The supply curve shows that at that price ranchers will plan to produce 2 billion pounds per year. However, according to the new demand curve, D_2, consumers will no longer buy that much beef at \$3.00 per pound. Instead, given their new tastes, they will buy only 1billion pounds at that price.

But the price does not stay at \$3.00 for long. As soon as the demand curve begins to shift and the surplus begins to develop, beef inventories rise above their planned levels, putting downward pressure on the price. As the price falls, ranchers revise their plans. They move down and to the left along their supply curve, reducing the quantity supplied as the price drops. (There is a movement along the supply curve, not a shift in the curve, because the ranchers are responding to a change in the price of beef, the variable shown on the vertical axis. Nothing has happened to change the "other things being equal" condition, such as technology, input prices, and so on, which could cause the supply curve to shift.)

As ranchers move downward along their supply curve in the direction shown by the arrow in part (a) of Figure 2.8, they eventually reach point E_2, where their plans again mesh with those of consumers. At that point the price has fallen to \$2.25 per pound and production to 1.5 billion pounds. Although health-conscious consumers would not have bought that much beef at the old price, they will do so at the new, lower price. E_2 thus is the new equilibrium point.

RESPONSE TO A SHIFT IN SUPPLY The original equilibrium might be disrupted by a change in supply rather than by a change in demand. For example, beginning from a condition of equilibrium, a drought in the corn belt might result in a higher price for grain for cattle feed. That would shift the supply curve to the left while the demand curve remained unchanged, as shown in part (b) of Figure 2.8.

Given the new supply curve, there will be a shortage of beef at the original price. Inventories will decline and the prices will rise in response. As the price increases, producers will move upward and to the right along their new supply curve, S_2, and consumers will move upward and to the left along their demand curve, D_1, which remains in its original position. A new equilibrium is established when the price reaches \$4.50 per pound.

FIGURE 2.8 EFFECTS OF CHANGING CONDITIONS IN THE BEEF MARKET

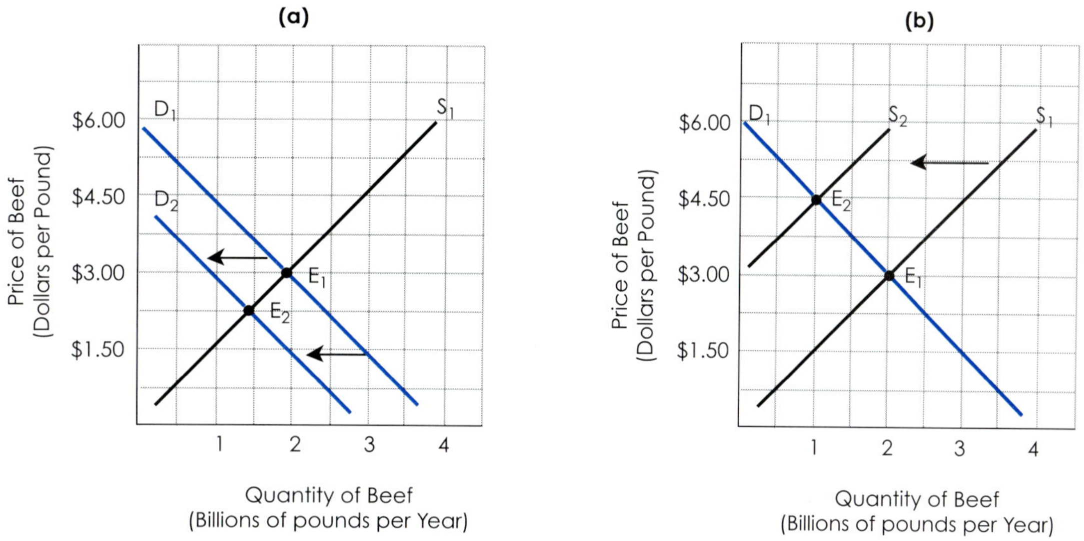

Part (a) of this figure shows the effects of a decrease in demand for beef caused by a shift in tastes away from high-cholesterol foods. Initially the market is in equilibrium at E_1. The change in tastes causes a shift in the demand curve. At the original equilibrium price of $3.00 per pound, there is a temporary surplus of beef. This causes inventories to start to rise and puts downward pressure on the price. As the price falls, producers move down along their supply curve to a new equilibrium at E_2. There both the price and quantity of beef are lower than before the shift in demand. Part (b) shows the effects of a decrease in supply caused by a drought, which raises the price of corn used to feed cattle. The shift in the supply curve causes a shortage at the initial price of $3.00 per pound. The shortage puts upward pressure on price. As the price rises, buyers move up and to the left along the demand curve until a new equilibrium is reached at E_2. In each case, note that only one curve needs to shift to bring about the new equilibrium.

One of the most frequent mistakes people make in learning the supply-and-demand model is to think that *both* curves must shift in order to restore equilibrium. The examples given in Figure 2.8 show clearly that this is not the case. In part (a), after the demand curve shifts, a movement along the supply curve is enough to establish the new equilibrium. No shift in the supply curve is needed. Similarly, in part (b), after the supply curve shifts, the demand curve does not need to shift to reach the new equilibrium.

In the turmoil of real-world markets, cases can be found in which both curves shift at once, but that happens only when two separate changes in conditions occur at the same time, one acting on the supply curve and the other on the demand curve. An example would be a drought that shifted the supply curve just as the market was already in the process of adjusting to a shift in the demand curve caused by changing tastes.

Equilibrium as Spontaneous Order

The ability of markets to move toward a new equilibrium following a disturbance is an example of economic coordination through spontaneous order. In the case we have been following, the disturbance began either with a change in health consciousness among consumers or with a change in the weather. The challenge: How to coordinate the decisions of thousands of farmers, wholesalers, retailers—the whole chain of supply—to serve consumers wants under changing conditions.

No central planning agency or regulatory bureaucracy is required to accomplish the needed shift in the use of scarce resources. It is all brought about through information and incentives transmitted in the form of changing market prices. To take a real example, in 1988, as the demand for beef lagged and the drought raised the price of feed grains, ranchers culled their herds to 98 million head, down 26 percent from their peak. Meanwhile, labor, capital, natural resources, and entrepreneurial energy flowed into chicken production, where demand was booming.

The process was remarkably smooth for so vast a shift in resource use. Behind the scenes, surpluses and shortages nudged choices in the needed directions, but at no time did shortages occur in the acute form of empty meat coolers at the supermarket or lines of chicken-hungry consumers stretching down city streets. Similarly, surpluses of beef caused ranchers to cut back their herds, but they did not take the form of mountains of rotting beef that had to be dumped into landfills.

No one *intended* this process of adjustment. Equilibrium is not a compromise that must be negotiated by a committee of consumers and producers. Just as shoppers manage to equalize the length of supermarket checkout lines without the guidance of a central authority, markets move toward equilibrium spontaneously, through the small, local adjustments that people make in their efforts to serve their own interests. As Adam Smith might have put it, we have not the benevolence of Frank Perdue or the Beef Industry Council to thank for our dinner; instead it is their self-interest that puts the right food on our table.

Market Adjustment and Entrepreneurship

The supply-and-demand model provides a clear and time-tested account of the process through which markets adjust to equilibrium in response to a change in conditions, yet in an important sense the model is incomplete. The behavior of consumers and producers as represented by demand and supply curves is overly mechanical. In the real world, people do not react so passively. As *Economics in the News 2.1* relates, they fight back when their interests are threatened. The examples cited—Rhonda Miller's better steak, Excel's vacuum-wrapped roasts, and Kroger's oven-ready meat loaves—are entrepreneurial responses to the decline in demand for beef. They show that beef producers do not just accept the shift in the demand curve and respond by sliding down the supply curve. Instead, they grab onto the demand curve and try to pull it back.

Taking entrepreneurship into account does not mean that the supply-and-demand model has to be discarded. In fact, the model provides just the framework we need to talk about what entrepreneurs are trying to do. Rhonda Miller's efforts to make a better steak have the effect of nudging the demand curve for beef to the right. Some other en-

ECONOMICS IN THE NEWS 2.1

BEEF PRICES UP; FAST FOOD CHAINS SWITCH TO CHICKEN

Stock up the freezer if you like steak because beef prices at the supermarket are on their way up. And they're likely to stay there for a while.

U.S. cattle prices are at a record high, say economists with the U.S. Department of Agriculture . They've increased 34% since July, and this month the benchmark price of Nebraska choice steers went from $90 to $116 per 100 pounds. A year ago, the price per 100 pounds was $64.

"We've seen increases in the last 10 days," said Jim Robb, director of the Livestock Marketing Information Center in Denver. "Choice T-bone steak and New York strip steak, those prices are double what they were three weeks ago."

"Those prices will ease off a little bit but not much," said David Kay of *Cattle Buyers Weekly*. "We look as if we're going to have even tighter cattle supplies for slaughter in 2004 and even into 2005."

Prices are up because of a set of circumstances that Robb calls "completely unprecedented." First, consumer demand for beef has increased nearly 10% since 1998 after declining for 20 years.

Recent increases in consumption may be due in part because of the increasing popularity of high-protein diets, such as this summer's blockbuster South Beach diet, and the venerable Atkins diet.

Second, as Wayne Purcell of the Research Institute on Livestock Pricing at Virginia Tech points out, the U.S. banned imports of Canadian cattle and beef five months ago. The ban was imposed because of the discovery of a case of mad cow disease there last spring and reduced cattle and meat imports to the USA by 9%.

Consumers already may be feeling the impact, whether they're eating out or at home. U.S. restaurant chains such as McDonald's and Wendy's have been hyping salads and lean chicken pieces lately, and industry observers say it's no coincidence that the switch coincides with rising beef prices. Experts expect cost-cutting by other restaurant companies to offset rising food prices.

It is not clear how long it will take for the impact of the price increases to be felt at local meat counters. Retail beef prices typically trail the price paid at the stockyard anywhere from two weeks to two months. So last week's increase will not show up at supermarkets until the first weeks of November or until Christmas.

If grocers think the price hike is temporary, they may eat the difference rather than risk aggravating customers.But if grocers do raise prices, "they'll raise their everyday prices only a little, but they will keep them up for a year or so. And we just won't see beef featured in sales very much," Kay said.

Source: Elizabeth Weise, "Beef Prices On the Way Up," *USA Today*, October 24, 2003.

trepreneur might be trying to save on feed costs by developing a genetically engineered steer. If successful, the project would give the supply curve for beef a rightward shove.

PRICE FLOORS AND CEILINGS: AN APPLICATION

Economics—both macro and micro—encompasses a great many applications of the concepts of supply and demand. Although each situation is unique, each to some extent draws on ideas developed in this chapter. This section, which uses the model to analyze the effects of government-imposed price floors and ceilings, provides some examples. Many more will be added in later chapters.

Price Supports: The Market for Milk

In our earlier example of the market for beef, a decrease in demand caused a surplus, which in turn caused the price to decrease until the surplus was eliminated. Markets are not always free to respond by adjusting prices, however. The market for milk is a case in point.

Figure 2.9 shows the market for milk in terms of supply and demand curves. Suppose that initially the market is in equilibrium at point E_1. The wholesale price of milk is $13 per hundredweight, and 110 million hundredweight is produced per year. A trend in taste away from high-cholesterol foods—the same trend that hit the market for beef—shifts the demand curve for milk to the left. As in the case of beef, the result is a surplus, as shown by the arrow in Figure 2.9.

Here the similarity between the beef and milk markets ends. In the beef market prices are free to fall in response to a surplus, but in the milk market they are not. Instead, an elaborate set of government-imposed controls and subsidies puts a floor under the price of milk. In the figure, the government agrees to pay $13 per hundredweight for all milk that cannot be sold at that price on the open market.

With the demand curve in position D_1, there is no surplus; thus, the government need not buy any milk. But with the demand curve in position D_2, there is a surplus of 40 million hundredweight per year. Under the price support law the government

FIGURE 2.9 PRICE SUPPORTS FOR MILK

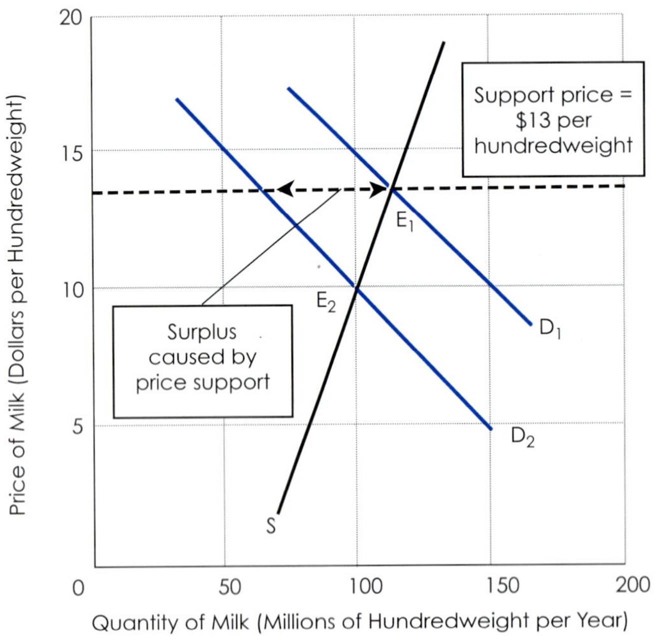

Suppose that initially the market for milk is in equilibrium at E_1. A shift in tastes away from high-cholesterol foods then shifts the demand curve to D_2. If the price were free to fall, there would be a temporary surplus that would push the price down to a new equilibrium at $10 per hundredweight. Instead, the government maintains a support price for milk at a level shown here as $13 per hundredweight. The government buys the surplus milk and stores it in the form of butter and cheese to keep the price from falling.

must buy this surplus and store it in the form of cheese, butter, and other products with long shelf lives. Since 1980, the combined costs of the support law to consumers and taxpayers has been estimated at more than $1,000 per family—enough to buy each family its own cow.

Without price supports, the shift in demand would cause the price of milk to fall to the new equilibrium price of $10 per hundredweight. When price supports are applied to a product at a level higher than the equilibrium price, however, the result is a lasting surplus condition. This happens because the support price sends misleading messages to consumers and producers. To consumers, the price of $13 says, "Milk is scarce. Its opportunity cost is high. Hold your consumption down." To producers, it says, "All is well. Incentives are unchanged. Feel free to continue using scarce resources to produce milk."

A drop in the price to $10 would send a different set of messages. Consumers would hear: "Milk is cheaper and more abundant. Although it is not cholesterol free, give in to temptation! Drink more of it!" But producers would hear: "The milk market is not what it once was. Look at your opportunity costs. Is there perhaps some better use for your labor, capital, and natural resources?"

From time to time the government has tried to eliminate the milk surplus by shifting the supply curve to the left so that it would intersect the demand curve near the support price. Under one recent program, for example, farmers were encouraged to sell their cows to be slaughtered for their meat, thereby reducing the size of dairy herds. But such programs have failed to eliminate the milk surplus. The chief reason is the dairy farmers' entrepreneurial response to the high price of milk. The government's efforts to cut the size of herds have been largely offset by increased output per cow as a result of genetic improvements and better farm management practices. For example, some dairy farms in California now have 3,000 and even 4,000 cows, compared with 50 or so on a traditional dairy farm. The cows never see a pasture—they spend their days in a pen munching high-protein alfalfa. Whereas the average Mississippi Delta cow gives 13,000 pounds of milk a year (a marvel to farmers in much of the world), its Pacific cousin yields over 21,000 pounds a year. To add insult to injury, the alfalfa they eat is grown in fields that are irrigated with government-subsidized water. Meanwhile, the government's vast inventories of butter and cheese continue to grow.

Price Ceilings: The Case of Rent Control

In the milk market, the government maintains a support price that is above the equilibrium price. In certain other markets, a price ceiling below the equilibrium price is imposed. An example of the latter situation is rent control in housing markets.

Rent control in one form or another exists in several major U.S. cities, including New York, Washington, D.C., San Francisco, and Los Angeles. The controls vary from one city to another, but in all cases maximum rents, at least for some categories of apartments, are established by law. The purpose of rent control is to aid tenants by preventing landlords from charging "unreasonably high" rents. What is unreasonably high is determined by the relative political strength of landlords and tenants rather than by the forces of supply and demand.

INTENDED EFFECTS Figure 2.10 interprets the effects of rent control in terms of supply and demand. For the sake of simplicity it is assumed that the supply of rental housing consists of units of equal size and rental value. Part (a) of the figure shows the effects of rent control in the short run. Here the short run means a period that is too short to permit significant increases or decreases in the supply of rental housing. (The short-run supply curve, which is drawn as a vertical line, indicates that a change in price will not result in any change in the quantity of apartments supplied in the short run.[4])

Under the conditions shown, the equilibrium rent per standard housing unit is $1,250 per month for each of the 200,000 units in the city. Now suppose that a rent ceiling of $500 is imposed. The result is a gain to tenants of $750 per unit per month. The total sum transferred to tenants (that is, the benefit to them from below-

FIGURE 2.10 EFFECTS OF RENT CONTROL

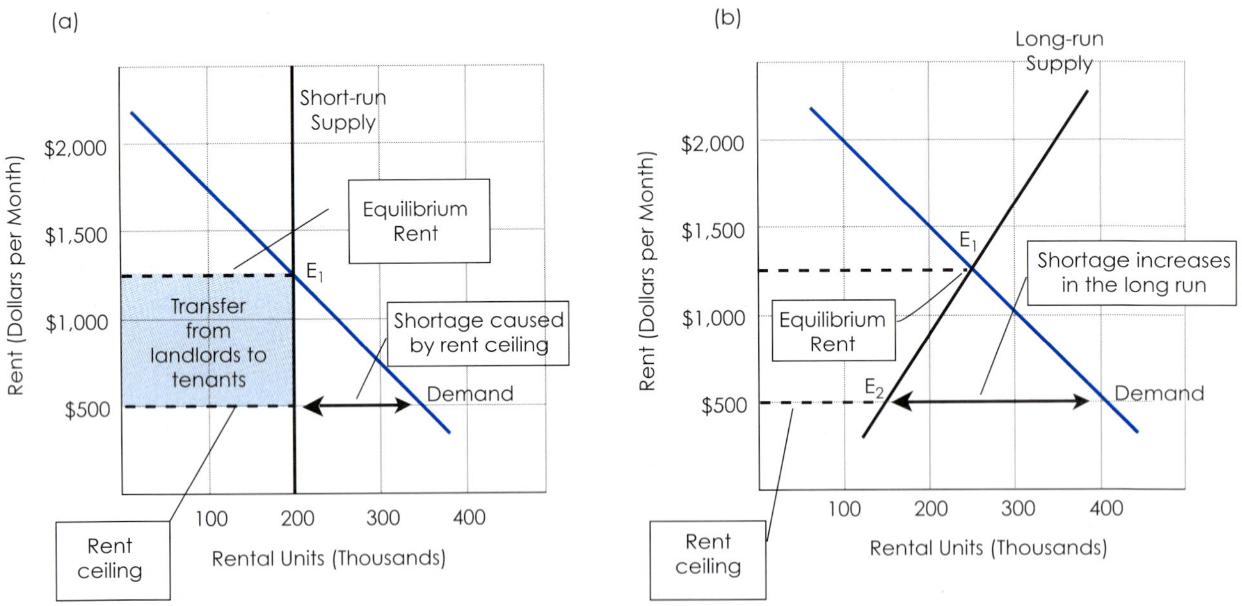

Part (a) shows the short-run effects of rent control. In the short run, the supply of rental apartments is considered to be fixed. The equilibrium rent is $1,250 per month. A rent ceiling of $500 per month is then put into effect. One possible outcome is that landlords will charge disguised rent increases, which will bring the true price back to $1,250 per month. If such disguised increases are prohibited, there will be a shortage of 350,000 units at the ceiling price. Part (b) shows the long-run effects when there is time to adjust the number of units in response to the price. If the ceiling price is enforced, landlords move down their supply curve to E_2. The shortage then becomes even more severe than in the short run.

market rents) is $750 per unit times 200,000 units, or $150 million, in all. In graphical terms, that sum is equal to the area of the shaded rectangle in Figure 2.10. The benefit to tenants at the expense of landlords is the principal intended effect of rent control.

UNINTENDED EFFECTS The policy of rent control, which does accomplish its goal of benefiting tenants at the expense of landlords, provides a classic illustration of the law of unintended consequences. In the short run, when the stock of apartments is fixed, the unintended consequences stem from the apartment shortage created by the controls. The shortage occurs because the quantity demanded is greater at the lower ceiling price than at the higher equilibrium price.

ECONOMICS IN THE NEWS 2.2
RENT CONTROLS IN NEW YORK

Robert L. Bartley, "Rent Control: New York's Self-Destruction," Thinking Things Over, *The Wall Street Journal*, May 19, 2003.

Advocates of rent control view these responses as cheating and often try to outlaw them. If prohibitions are enforced, the landlord will find that there are many applicants for each vacant apartment. In that case, the landlord must decide to whom to rent the apartment. The result will often be discrimination against renters who are from minority groups, who have children, or who have unconventional lifestyles.

In the long run, rent control has other unintended effects. The long run in this case means enough time for the number of rental units to grow through construction of new units or shrink through abandonment of old ones (or their conversion to condominiums). Other things being equal, the higher the rent, the greater the rate of construction, and the lower the rent, the greater the rate of abandonment or conversion. This is reflected in the positively sloped long-run supply curve in part (b) of Figure 2.10.

If rent controls are enforced in such a way that there are no disguised charges by landlords, the number of rental units shrinks and the market moves from E_1 to E_2. At E_2, the unintended effects that appeared in the short run become more pronounced. The intensity of housing discrimination increases relative to the short-run case, because the difference between the number of units available and the number sought by renters increases. Graphically, that difference is shown by the horizontal gap between the supply and demand curves at the ceiling price. In the short run, there is a shortage of 50,000 units; in the long run, the shortage increases to 75,000 units.

Rent controls are often defended as being beneficial to the poor. But when all of the unintended effects of rent control are taken into account, one may question whether poor families really benefit. In cases in which disguised rent increases are possible, the true cost of rental housing is not really decreased. Further, it is hard to believe that landlords' tendency to discriminate against minority group members, single-parent families, and tenants with irregular work histories will benefit the poor. The most likely beneficiaries of rent control are stable, middle-class families who work at the same jobs and live in the same apartments for long periods.

Given the many unintended consequences of rent controls, one might legitimately wonder why the policy retains its popularity in many large cities. Why not replace rent control with some other form of housing assistance for the poor—for example, direct subsidies that would allow poor families to rent apartments at market-determined prices, as is already done in some cities? Some economists explain the popularity of rent control in terms of the political power of the middle-class tenants who are most likely to benefit from rent controls and who see helping the poor as nothing more than a convenient cover for simple self-interest. Some explain their popularity in terms of the short time horizon of government officials: The adverse effect on tenants of ending rent control would appear very quickly, whereas such benefits as increased construction of new apartments would materialize only long after the next election. And some attribute the popularity of rent control to the simple fact that many voters do not give much thought to the policy's unintended consequences.

The greater quantity demanded has several sources. First, people who would otherwise own a house or condominium may now want to rent. Second, people who would otherwise live in non–rent-controlled suburbs may now seek rent-controlled units in the city. Third, each tenant may want more space, which results in a demand for more of the standardized units shown in Figure 2.10.

The shortage creates a problem for both landlords and tenants: How will the limited supply of apartments be rationed among those who want them? Both landlords and tenants devise a number of creative responses—*entrepreneurial* responses, as an economist would say.

One response on the part of landlords is to seek disguised rent increases. These may take the form of large, nonrefundable "key deposits" or security deposits. As an alternative, they may sell old, used furniture or drapes at inflated prices as a condition for renting the apartment. Finally, the costs of certain maintenance or security services that the landlord might otherwise have paid for may be transferred to tenants.

Tenants too may get into the act. When they decide to move, they may sublet their apartments to other tenants rather than give up their leases. Now it is the tenant who collects the key money or sells the old drapes to the subtenant. The original tenant may have moved to a distant city but maintains a bank account and a post office box for use in paying the rent. The subtenant is instructed to play the role of a "guest" if the landlord telephones. This charade may become quite elaborate and can go on for decades in cities such as New York, where rent control is long established, as illustrated by *Economics in the News 2.2*.

THIS CHAPTER HAS covered the basics of the supply-and-demand model and described a few applications of that model. There are many more applications in both macro- and microeconomics. In macroeconomics, the supply-and-demand model can be applied to financial markets, labor markets, and the problem of determining the rate of inflation and real output for the economy as a whole. In microeconomics, the model can be applied to product markets, markets for productive resources, and policy issues ranging from pollution to farm policy to international trade, to name just a few. As the great economist Alfred Marshall once put it, nearly all of the major problems of economics have a "kernel" that reflects the workings of supply and demand (see *Who Said It? Who Did It? 2.1*).

When one takes a detailed look at the underpinnings of the model, it appears to fit some kinds of markets more closely than others. The fit is best for markets in which there are many producers and many customers, the goods sold by one producer are much like those sold by others, and all sellers and buyers have good information on market conditions. Markets for farm commodities, such as wheat and corn, and financial markets, such as the New York Stock Exchange, meet these standards reasonably well.

WHO SAID IT? WHO DID IT? 2.1

ALFRED MARSHALL ON SUPPLY AND DEMAND

Alfred Marshall, often considered to have been the greatest economist of his day, was born in London in 1842. His father was a Bank of England cashier who hoped the boy would enter the ministry. Young Marshall had other ideas, however. He turned down a theological scholarship at Oxford to study mathematics, receiving his M.A. from Cambridge in 1865.

While at Cambridge, Marshall joined a philosophical discussion group. There he became interested in promoting the broad development of the human mind. He was soon told, however, that the harsh realities of economics would prevent his ideas from being carried out. Britain's economic potential as a country, it was said, could never allow the masses sufficient leisure for education. This disillusioning episode appears to have triggered Marshall's fascination with economics.

At the time, British economics was dominated by the classical school founded by Adam Smith and David Ricardo. Marshall had great respect for the classical writers. Initially he saw his own work as simply applying his mathematical training to strengthen and systematize the classical system. Before long, however, he was breaking new ground and developing a system of his own. By 1890, when he brought out his famous *Principles of Economics,* he had laid the foundation of what we now call the neoclassical school.

In an attempt to explain the essence of his approach, Marshall included the following passage in the second edition of his *Principles:*

> In spite of a great variety in detail, nearly all the chief problems of economics agree in that they have a kernel of the same kind. This kernel is an inquiry as to the balancing of two opposed classes of motives, the one consisting of desires to acquire certain new goods, and thus satisfy wants; while the other consists of desires to avoid certain efforts or retain certain immediate enjoyment . . . in other words, it is an inquiry into the balancing of the forces of demand and supply.

Marshall's influence on economics—at least in the English-speaking world—was enormous. His *Principles* was the leading economics text for several decades, and modern students can still learn much from it. As a professor at Cambridge, Marshall taught a great many of the next generation's leading economists. Today his neoclassical school continues to dominate the profession. It has received many challenges, but so far it has weathered them all.

However, even in markets that do not display all of these features, the fit is often close enough so that the supply-and-demand model provides useful insights into what is going on. The rental housing market is an example: Not all rental units are, in fact, alike, even when measurement is standardized for objective characteristics such as floor space. Nevertheless, most economists would agree that valid conclusions about the effects of rent control can be arrived at by applying the supply-and-demand model to that market. Thus, the supply-and-demand model serves a precise analytical function in some cases and a broader, more metaphorical function in others. That flexibility makes the model one of the most useful items in the economist's tool kit.

SUMMARY

1. **How does the price of a good or service affect the quantity of it that buyers demand?** Economists use the term *demand* to refer to the willingness and ability of buyers to purchase goods and services. According to the *law of demand*, there is an inverse relationship between the price of a good and the quantity of it that buyers demand. The *quantity demanded* is the quantity that buyers are willing and able to pay for. The law of demand can be represented graphically by a negatively sloped *demand curve*. A change in the quantity demanded is shown by a movement along the demand curve.

2. **How do other market conditions affect demand?** A change in any of the variables covered by the "other things being equal" clause of the law of demand causes a shift in the demand curve; this is known as a *change in demand*. Examples include changes in the prices of goods that are *substitutes* or *complements* of the good in question as well as changes in consumer incomes, expectations, and tastes.

3. **How does the price of a good affect the quantity supplied by sellers?** *Supply* refers to sellers' willingness and ability to offer products for sale in a market. In most markets an increase in the price of a good will increase the quantity of the good that sellers are willing to supply. This relationship can be shown as a positively sloped *supply curve*. The higher price gives producers an incentive to supply more, but rising opportunity costs set a limit on the amount they will supply at any given price.

4. **How do changes in other market conditions affect supply?** A change in any of the items covered by the "other things being equal" clause of the supply curve will shift the curve. Examples include changes in technology, changes in the prices of inputs, changes in the prices of other goods that could be produced with the same resources, and changes in expectations.

5. **How do supply and demand interact to determine the market price of a good or service?** In a market with a positively-sloped supply curve and a negatively-sloped demand curve, there is only one price at which the quantity of a good that sellers plan to supply will exactly match the quantity that buyers plan to purchase. That is known as the *equilibrium* price. At any higher price there will be a *surplus*, and at any lower price there will be a *shortage*.

6. **Why do market prices and quantities change in response to changes in market conditions?** A change in any market condition that shifts the supply or demand curve will change the equilibrium price and quantity in a market. For example, the demand curve may shift to the right as a result of a change in consumer incomes. This causes a shortage at the old price, and the price begins to rise. As the price rises, suppliers move up along the supply curve to a new equilibrium. No shift in the supply curve is required. On the other hand, better technology may shift the supply curve to the right. In that case, there is a surplus at the old price, and the price will fall. As the price decreases, buyers will move down along their demand curve to a new equilibrium. No shift in the demand curve is required.

7. **How do price supports and price ceilings affect the operation of markets?** A price support prevents the market price from falling when the demand curve shifts to the left or the supply curve shifts to the right. The result may be a lasting surplus. A price ceiling prevents the price from rising to its equilibrium level. The result may be a permanent shortage. The total quantity supplied may then be less than the quantity that buyers would like to purchase at the ceiling price or even at the equilibrium price.

KEY TERMS

Supply
Demand
Law of demand
Demand curve
Change in quantity demanded
Change in demand
Substitute goods
Complementary goods
Normal good
Inferior good
Supply curve
Change in quantity supplied
Change in supply
Equilibrium
Excess quantity demanded (shortage)
Inventory
Excess quantity supplied (surplus)

PROBLEMS AND TOPICS FOR DISCUSSION

1. **Examining the lead-off case.** On the basis of information given in the case, analyze the decline in the quantity of Porsches sold in terms of shifts in versus movements along the demand curve for this luxury car. Specifically, how was the market for Porsches affected by the U.S. recession? By changing consumer tastes? By rising wages of German autoworkers? By the rising foreign exchange value of the German mark?

2. **A shifting demand curve.** A vending machine company has studied the demand for soft drinks sold in cans from machines. On a 70-degree day consumers in the firm's territory will buy about 2,000 cans at a price of $0.75. For each $.05 rise in price, the quantity sold falls by 200 cans per day; for each 5-degree rise in the temperature, the quantity sold rises by 150 cans per day. The same relationships hold for decreases in price or temperature. Using this information, draw a set of curves showing the demand for soft drinks on days when the temperature is 60, 70, and 85 degrees. Then draw a separate diagram with temperature on the vertical axis and quantity on the horizontal axis. Draw a line representing the relationship between temperature and quantity when the price is $0.75. Next draw additional temperature-quantity lines for prices of $0.50 and $1.00. Do the two diagrams give the same information? Discuss. (Note: If you have any trouble with this exercise, review the appendix to Chapter 1, "Working with Graphs," especially the section entitled "Packing Three Variables into Two Dimensions.")

3. **Demand and the relative price of motor fuel.** In 1979 and 1980 the nominal price of motor fuel rose much more rapidly than the general price level, pushing up the relative price of motor fuel. As we would expect, the quantity sold decreased. In 1981 and 1982 the relative price leveled off and then began to fall, but the quantity sold continued to fall. Which one or more of the following hypotheses do you think best explains the behavior of motor fuel sales in 1981 and 1982? Illustrate each hypothesis with supply and demand curves.

   a. In the 1970s the demand curve had the usual negative slope. However, in 1981 and 1982 the demand curve shifted to an unusual positively sloped position.

   b. The demand curve had a negative slope throughout the period. However, the recession of 1981 and 1982 reduced consumers' real incomes and thus shifted the demand curve.

   c. The demand curve has a negative slope at all times, but the shape depends partly on how much time consumers have to adjust to a change in prices. Over a short period, the demand curve is fairly steep because few adjustments can be made. Over the long term, it has a somewhat flatter slope because further adjustments, such as buying more fuel-efficient cars or moving closer to the job, can be made.

Thus, the decreases in fuel sales in 1981 and 1982 were delayed reactions to the price increases that occurred in 1979 and 1980.

4. **Shortages, price controls, and queues.** In 1974 and again in 1979, a decrease in worldwide oil supplies caused long lines of motorists to form at gas stations in the United States but not in European countries. Do you think the lines had anything to do with the fact that the United States had price controls that kept the price at the pump below a dollar a gallon, whereas European countries had no controls, so that prices at the pump rose the equivalent of two dollars a gallon, and even higher? Back up your reasoning with supply and demand curves.

5. **Eliminating queues through flexible pricing.** You are a member of the Metropolitan Taxi Commission, which sets taxi fares for your city. You have been told that long lines of taxis form at the airport during off-peak hours. At peak hours, on the other hand, few taxis are available and there are long lines of passengers waiting for cabs. It is proposed that taxi fares from the airport to downtown be cut by 10 percent during off-peak hours and raised by 10 percent during peak hours. How do you think these changes would affect the queueing patterns of taxis and passengers? Do you think the proposal is a good one from the passengers' point of view? From the cabbies' point of view? From the standpoint of economic efficiency? Discuss.

6. **Rent control.** Turn to part (b) of Figure 2.10, which shows the long-run effects of rent control. If the controls are enforced and there are no disguised rent charges, landlords move down the supply curve to E_2. Buildings are abandoned or converted because of the low rent they bring in. Now consider some alternative possibilities.

   a. Suppose that the controls are poorly enforced so that landlords, through key deposits, furniture sales, or some other means, are able to charge as much as the market will bear. What will the resulting equilibrium price and quantity be, taking both open and disguised rental charges into account?

   b. Now suppose that the controls are enforced so that landlords really cannot collect more than $500 per month. However, the controls are not enforced against tenants who sublet. What will the equilibrium quantity and price be, including both the rent paid to landlords and the disguised rental payments made by subtenants to their subleasors?

CASE FOR DISCUSSION

Supply and Demand for Recycled Materials

A group of visitors to the Port of Providence, Rhode Island, were recently witnesses to one of America's export success stories: A huge freighter being loaded, not with aircraft parts, not with computers or specialty chemicals, but with tons of waste paper bound for China.

In the 1990s, the United States became for waste paper what Saudi Arabia is for oil. Much the same goes for scrap aluminum, old bottles, and other products of the rapidly spreading recycling movement. Recycling, a strictly voluntary activity until a few years ago, has now become mandatory in many cities. Already one-half of all U.S. households are served by curbside recycling programs. But recycling is not always entirely successful.

The case of aluminum cans represents recycling at its best. Mote than two-thirds of all cans are now recycled, one of the highest rates for any material. Making a new can from an old one saves up to 85 percent of the energy required to make a new can from bauxite ore. As a result, aluminum recycling has long been profitable and continues to be so.

Recycling of other materials presents greater problems. Take glass, for example. Making a new bottle from an old one, instead of from sand, saves as little as 10 percent of the energy required. The margin for profit in recycling glass therefore is very narrow. Clear glass, which is most in demand, commands a market price of $40–$45 a ton. But green, brown, and mixed glass are virtually worthless in many regions.

Even newsprint presents problems. Newsprint, like aluminum, has long been a profitable commodity for commercial recyclers. But the introduction of curbside programs can sometimes swamp local markets. Take the case of Babylon, N.Y.: Beginning in 1990, paper started coming in faster than it could be shipped to markets such as China, South Korea, and Taiwan. The town rapidly accumulated 1,200 tons of yellowing paper in an old aircraft hangar. Instead of selling the paper to dealers, the town had to pay the dealers $35 a ton to haul it away. But by 1992, market conditions had improved, and the town was again selling its newsprint for a few dollars a ton.

Critics of across-the-board recycling say that programs should be fine-tuned to market conditions. Energy and other scarce resources are wasted, they say, in costly efforts to collect and sort materials that have no economic value. Proponents of recycling, on the other hand, put their faith in the growth of demand. Several huge de-inking plants currently under construction will boost the demand for waste newsprint. And new uses for other materials, such as "glassphalt" pavement for roads, will soon absorb piles of scrap for which there have been few uses in the past.

Source: Based in part on Frank Edward Allen, "As Recycling Surges, Market for Materials Is Slow to Develop," *The Wall Street Journal*, January 17, 1992, A1.

QUESTIONS

1. Draw supply and demand curves to illustrate the markets for clear glass and for green glass. How would these markets be affected by the growth of demand for glass to be used in "glassphalt" paving material, assuming color makes no difference for that particular use?
2. Draw supply and demand curves to illustrate the market for waste newsprint in Babylon, N.Y., (a) before 1990, showing an equilibrium price of $5 per ton; (b) in 1990–1991, when the town had to pay $35 per ton to have the paper hauled away; and (c) in 1992, when growth of demand again made it possible to sell the paper.
3. Do you think recycling should be pursued as a goal of public policy only when recycled materials can be sold profitably, or even when they cannot be sold profitably? Discuss.

END NOTES

1. Before continuing, the reader may want to review the Chapter 1 appendix "Working with Graphs," especially the section entitled "Packing Three Variables into Two Dimensions."
2. The "plans" referred to need not be formal or thought out in detail, and are subject to change. A consumer might, for example, make out a shopping list for the supermarket based on the usual prices for various foods, but then revise it to take into account unexpected price increases or sales on certain items. On specific occasions, consumer decisions may even be completely impulsive, with little basis in rational calculation. The model of supply and demand does not require that every decision be based on precise analysis, but only that consumer intentions, on the average, are influenced by prices and other economic considerations.
3. Why might buyers and sellers enter the market expecting a price other than the one that permits equilibrium? It may be, for example, that market conditions have caused the supply or demand curve to shift unexpectedly, so that a price that formerly permitted equilibrium no longer does so. It may be that buyers or sellers expect conditions to change, but they do not change after all. Or, it may be that government policy has established a legal maximum or minimum price that differs

from the equilibrium price. Later sections of the chapter will explore some of these possibilities.

4. This is a fairly restrictive assumption. In practice, a small number of housing units can move into or out of the rental market quickly in response to changing conditions. "Mother-in-law apartments" in private homes are an example. If conditions in the rental market are unfavorable, the owners of such units may simply leave them vacant. Allowing for such fast-reaction units means that the short-run supply curve, while still quite steep, would not be vertical. However, a vertical short-run curve simplifies the geometry while capturing the essential features of the situation.

CHAPTER 3

Supply, Demand, and Elasticity

After reading this chapter, you will understand:

1. How the responsiveness of quantity demanded to a price change can be expressed in terms of elasticity
2. How elasticity applies to situations other than the responsiveness of the quantity of a good demanded to a change in its price
3. How elasticity is useful in interpreting issues of taxation and other public policies

Before reading this chapter, make sure you know the meaning of:

1. Supply and demand
2. Demand, quantity demanded
3. Supply, quantity supplied
4. Substitutes and complements
5. Normal and inferior goods

A BUG IN THE SALAD BOWL

There was a time when lettuce was a seasonal food for consumers on the east coast. The transcontinental railroads and refrigerated freight cars changed all this. Produce from California and Arizona, where lettuce can be grown year round, became a standard item in supermarkets throughout the country. During the winter months, farmers in these states ship some 10,000 tons of lettuce to market every day. Densely packed and long-lasting varieties like iceberg are especially popular.

Despite the best efforts of agricultural science, however, the lettuce supply is not immune to disruption. In one recent January, an outbreak of a virus carried by the sweet potato white fly cut production by 25 percent, causing lettuce prices to rise by 300 percent. Consumers were shocked by prices of as much as $2 a head.

Paradoxically, however, the virus outbreak worked to the benefit of many farmers. Not those who lost their entire crops, of course. But many farmers who were able to ship at least some lettuce to market actually came out ahead. "Most growers have come out okay because the prices were up so much," said Wade Whitfield, president of the California Iceberg Lettuce Commission.

Although the virus outbreak caught farmers unprepared, a search for countermeasures was quickly launched. Department of Agriculture scientists searched their collections of wild lettuce strains for those that were resistant to the virus. Over time, through selective breeding and gene splicing, it should be possible to develop tasty but virus-resistant commercial varieties. Such measures take time, however, and do nothing to lessen the short-term impact on the consumer's pocketbook.

Source: Based on Ward Sinclair, "Virus Eats into Lettuce Production: Price Soars," *The Washington Post*, January 6, 1988, A7.

IN THE PRECEDING chapter we saw many examples of supply and demand in action. In this chapter we will shift our focus. Instead of looking only at the direction of changes that result from changing supply and demand conditions, we will stress the size of the changes.

As the case of the lettuce virus shows, the size of the price change associated with a given change in quantity demanded is crucial. We know that a reduction in supply will cause a rise in price as consumers move up along their demand curve. But how much of a hardship will the poor crop cause for farmers? If the price rises only a little, farmers will be hit hard. But if, as in the case just described, the price rises sharply enough, the greater price per unit will more than compensate farmers as a group for the reduction in the overall size of the crop. This chapter provides a framework for approaching such questions. The methods introduced here have many applications in both macro- and microeconomics.

ELASTICITY

The responsiveness of one economic variable to a change in another can be expressed in many ways, depending on the units of measurement that are chosen. Take the quantity of lettuce demanded by consumers. We could say that each $1 increase in the price *per carton* would reduce the quantity demanded by 100,000, 50-pound *cartons per day*. Or we could say that each $1 increase in the price *per ton* would reduce quantity demanded by 437.5 *tons per week*. Although it takes a few minutes with a calculator to verify the fact, these two statements are equivalent; only the units differ.

To avoid confusion arising from the choice of different units of measurement, it is useful to standardize. One common way of doing so is to express all changes as percentages. For example, the news item reports that a 25 percent reduction in quantity was associated with a 300 percent increase in price. These percentages would stay the same regardless of whether the original data were stated in dollars per ton, crates per week, or any other measurement.

The use of percentages to express the response of one variable to a change in another is widespread in economics. The term **elasticity** is used to refer to relationships expressed in percentages. Like equilibrium, elasticity is a metaphor borrowed from physics. Much as equilibrium calls to mind a pendulum that has come to rest hanging straight down, elasticity conjures up the image of a rubber band that stretches by a certain proportion of its length when the force applied to it is increased by a given percentage. This chapter introduces several applications of elasticity in economics.

Elasticity

A measure of the response of one variable to a change in another, stated as a ratio of the percentage change in one variable to the associated percentage change in another variable.

Price elasticity of demand

The ratio of the percentage change in the quantity of a good demanded to a given percentage change in its price, other things being equal.

Revenue

Price times quantity sold.

Elastic demand

A situation in which quantity demanded changes by a larger percentage than price, so that total revenue increases as price decreases.

Price Elasticity of Demand

We begin with the relationship between price and quantity demanded. The **price elasticity of demand** is the ratio of the percentage change in the quantity of a good demanded to a given percentage change in its price. Figure 3.1 presents five demand curves showing different degrees of price elasticity of demand. In part (a), the quantity demanded is relatively responsive to a change in price. In this case, a decrease in price from $5 to $3 causes the quantity demanded to increase from three units to six. Because the percentage change in quantity demanded is greater than the percentage change in price, the drop in price causes total revenue from sales of the good to increase. **Revenue** is the price times the quantity sold. On a supply-and-demand diagram, revenue can be shown as the area of a rectangle drawn under the demand curve, with a height equal to price and a width equal to quantity demanded. In this case comparison of the shaded rectangles representing revenue before the price reduction ($5 per unit × 3 units = $15) and afterward ($3 per unit × 6 units = $18) shows that revenue is greater after the price has been reduced. When the quantity demanded changes by a greater percentage than price, so that a price decrease causes total revenue to increase, demand is said to be **elastic**.

FIGURE 3.1 PRICE ELASTICITY OF DEMAND

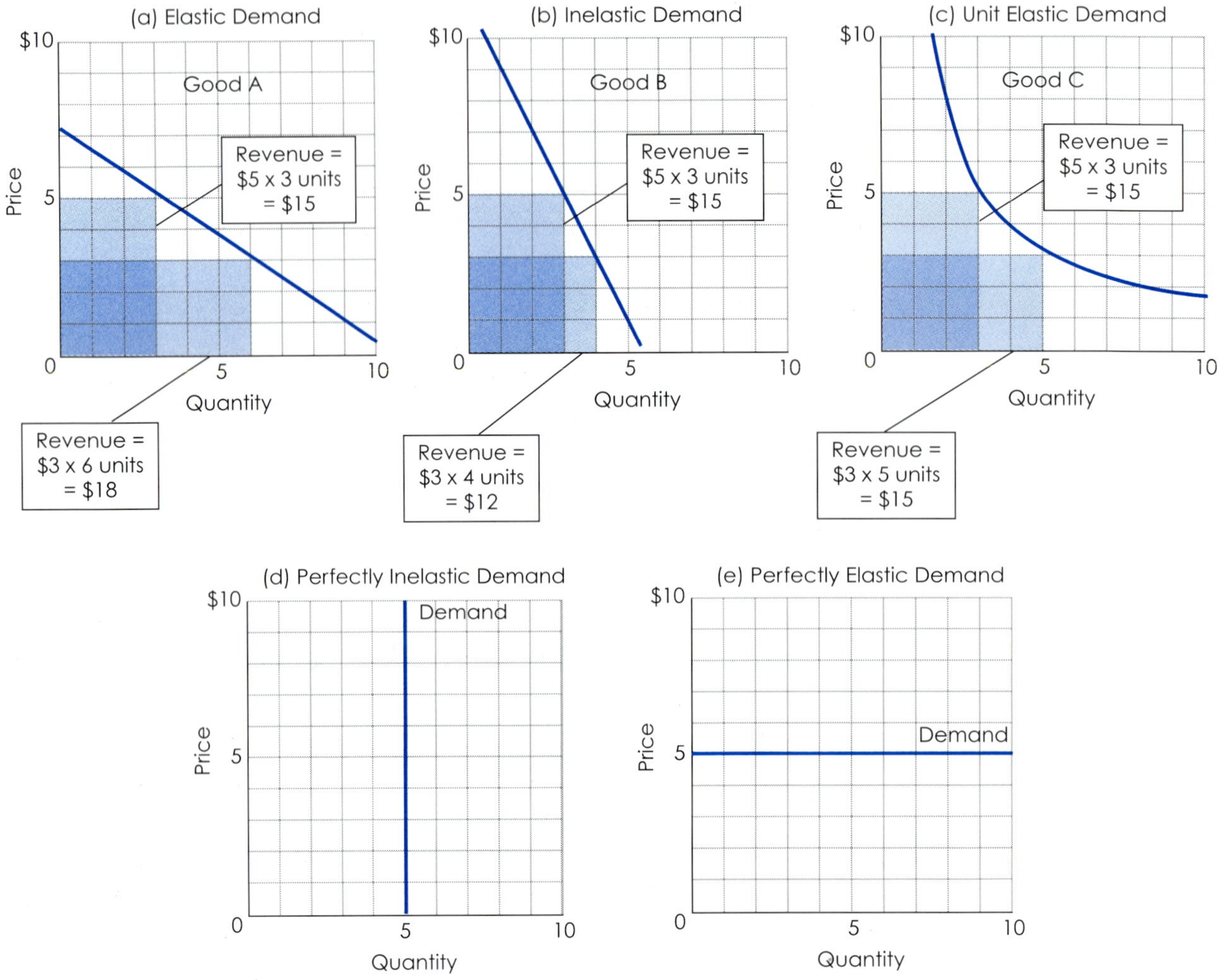

This figure shows five examples of demand curves with various degrees of elasticity over the indicated range of variation of price and quantity. The examples illustrate elastic, inelastic, unit elastic, perfectly inelastic, and perfectly elastic demand. For the first three cases, the revenue change associated with a change in price is shown. When demand is elastic, a price decrease causes revenue to increase. When demand is inelastic, a price decrease causes revenue to decrease. When demand is unit elastic, revenue does not change when price changes.

Inelastic demand

A situation in which quantity demanded changes by a smaller percentage than price, so that total revenue decreases as price decreases.

Part (b) of Figure 3.1 shows a case in which the quantity demanded is relatively unresponsive to a change in price. Here, a $2 decrease in price, from $5 to $3 per unit, causes the quantity demanded to increase by just one unit—from three to four. This time the percentage change in quantity demanded is less than that in price. As a result, the decrease in price causes total revenue to fall (again note the shaded rectangles). In such a case demand is said to be **inelastic**.

Part (c) shows a case in which a change in price causes an exactly proportional change in quantity demanded, so that total revenue does not change at all. When the

Unit elastic demand

A situation in which price and quantity demanded change by the same percentage, so that total revenue remains unchanged as price changes.

Perfectly inelastic demand

A situation in which the demand curve is a vertical line.

Perfectly elastic demand

A situation in which the demand curve is a horizontal line.

percentage change in quantity demanded equals the percentage change in price, demand is said to be **unit elastic**.

The final two parts of Figure 3.1 show two extreme cases. Part (d) shows a vertical demand curve. Regardless of the price, the quantity demanded is five units—no more, no less. Such a demand curve is said to be **perfectly inelastic**. Part (e) shows a demand curve that is perfectly horizontal. Above a price of $5, no units of the good can be sold; but as soon as the price drops to $5, there is no limit on how much can be sold. A horizontal demand curve like this one is described as **perfectly elastic**. The law of demand, which describes an inverse relationship between price and quantity, does not encompass the cases of perfectly elastic and inelastic demand, and we do not expect market demand curves for ordinary goods and services to fit these extremes. Nevertheless, we will see that perfectly elastic and inelastic curves sometimes provide useful reference points for theory building, even though they do not resemble real-world market demand curves.

Calculating Elasticity of Demand

In speaking of elasticity of demand, it is often enough to say that demand is elastic or inelastic, without being more precise. At other times, though, it is useful to attach numerical values to elasticity. This section introduces the most common method used to calculate a numerical value for elasticity of demand.

The first step in turning the general definition of elasticity into a numerical formula is to develop a way to measure percentage changes. The everyday method for calculating a percentage change is to use the initial value of the variable as the denominator and the change in the value as the numerator. For example, if the quantity of California lettuce demanded in the national market is initially 10,000 tons per week and then decreases by 2,500 tons per week, we say that there has been a 25 percent change (2,500/10,000 = .25). The trouble with this convention is that the same change in the opposite direction gives a different percentage. By everyday reasoning, an increase in the quantity of lettuce demanded from 7,500 tons per week to 10,000 tons per week is a 33 percent increase (2,500/7,500 = .33).

Decades ago the eminent mathematical economist R. G. D. Allen proposed an unambiguous measure of percentage changes that uses the midpoint of the range over which change takes place as the denominator. Allen's formula is not the only possible one, but it caught on and remains the most popular.

To find the midpoint of the range over which a change takes place, we take the sum of the initial value and the final value and divide by 2. In our example, the midpoint of the quantity range is (7,500 + 10,000)/2 = 8,750. When this is used as the denominator, a change of 2,500 units becomes (approximately) a 28.6 percent change (2,500/8,750 = .286). Using Q_1 to represent the quantity before the change and Q_2 to represent the quantity after the change, the midpoint formula for the percentage change in quantity is

$$\text{Percentage change in quantity} = \frac{Q_2 - Q_1}{(Q_1 + Q_2)/2}$$

The same approach can be used to define the percentage change in price. In our case, the price of lettuce increased from about \$250 per ton to about \$1,000 per ton. Using the midpoint of the range, or \$625, as the denominator [(\$250 + \$1,000)/2 = \$625], we conclude that the \$750 increase in price is a 120 percent increase (\$750/\$625 = 1.2). The midpoint formula for the percentage change in price is

$$\text{Percentage change in price} = \frac{P_2 - P_1}{(P_1 + P_2)/2}$$

THE MIDPOINT FORMULA FOR ELASTICITY Defining percentage changes in this way allows us to write a useful formula for calculating elasticities. With P_1 and Q_1 representing price and quantity before a change, and P_2 and Q_2 representing price and quantity after the change, the midpoint formula for elasticity is

$$\text{Price elasticity of demand} = \frac{(Q_2 - Q_1)/(Q_1 + Q_2)}{(P_2 - P_1)/(P_1 + P_2)} = \frac{\text{Percentage change in quantity}}{\text{Percentage change in price}}$$

Here is the complete calculation for the elasticity of demand for lettuce when an increase in price from \$250 per ton to \$1,000 per ton causes the quantity demanded to fall from 10,000 tons per day to 7,500 tons per day:

P_1 = price before change = \$250
P_2 = price after change = \$1,000
Q_1 = quantity before change = 10,000
Q_2 = quantity after change = 7,500

$$\text{Elasticity} = \frac{(7{,}500 - 10{,}000)/(7{,}500 + 10{,}000)}{(\$1{,}000 - \$250)/(\$1{,}000 + \$250)}$$

$$= \frac{-2{,}500/17{,}500}{\$750/\$1{,}250}$$

$$= \frac{-.142}{.6}$$

$$= -.24$$

Because demand curves have negative slopes, this formula yields a negative value for elasticity. The reason is that the quantity demanded changes in the direction opposite to that of the price change. When the price decreases, $(P_2 - P_1)$, which appears in the denominator of the formula, is negative, whereas $(Q_2 - Q_1)$, which appears in the numerator, is positive. When the price increases, the numerator is negative and the denominator is positive. However, in this book we follow the widely used practice of dropping the minus sign when discussing price elasticity of demand. Thus, the elasticity of demand for lettuce would be stated as approximately .24 over the range studied.

A numerical elasticity value such as .24 can be related to the basic definition of elasticity in a simple way. That definition stated that price elasticity of demand is the ratio of the percentage change in quantity demanded to a given percentage change in price. Thus, an elasticity of .24 means that the quantity demanded will increase by .24 percent for each 1 percent change in price. An elasticity of 3 would mean that quantity demanded would change by 3 percent for each 1 percent change in price, and so on.[1]

ELASTICITY VALUES AND TERMINOLOGY Earlier in the chapter we defined *elastic, inelastic, unit elastic, perfectly elastic,* and *perfectly inelastic* demand. Each of these terms corresponds to a numerical value or range of values of elasticity. A perfectly inelastic demand curve has a numerical value of 0, since any change in price produces no change in quantity demanded. The term *inelastic* (but not perfectly inelastic) *demand* applies to numerical values from 0 up to, but not including, 1. *Unit elasticity,* as the name implies, means a numerical value of exactly 1. *Elastic demand* means any value for elasticity that is greater than 1. *Perfectly elastic* demand, represented by a horizontal demand curve, is not defined numerically; as the demand curve becomes horizontal, the denominator of the elasticity formula approaches 0 and the numerical value of elasticity increases without limit.

Varying- and Constant-Elasticity Demand Curves

The midpoint formula shows elasticity of demand over a certain range of prices and quantities. Measured over some other range, the elasticity of demand for the same good may be the same or different, depending on the shape of the demand curve, as shown in Figure 3.2.

Part (a) of Figure 3.2 shows a demand curve that, like most of those in this book, is a straight line. The elasticity of demand is not constant for all ranges of price and quantity along this curve. For example, when measured over the price range $8 to $9, the elasticity of demand is 5.66; when measured over the range $2 to $3, it is .33. (The calculations are shown in the figure.)

The calculations illustrate the general rule that elasticity declines as one moves downward along a straight-line demand curve. It is easy to see why. With such a demand curve, a $1 reduction in price always causes the same absolute increase in quantity demanded. At the upper end of the demand curve, a $1 change is a small percentage of the relatively high price, while the change in quantity is a large percentage of the relatively low quantity demanded at that price. At the lower end of the curve, however, the situation is reversed: A $1 change is now a large percentage of the relatively low price, while the increase in quantity is smaller in relation to the

FIGURE 3.2 ELASTICITY AT VARIOUS POINTS ALONG A DEMAND CURVE

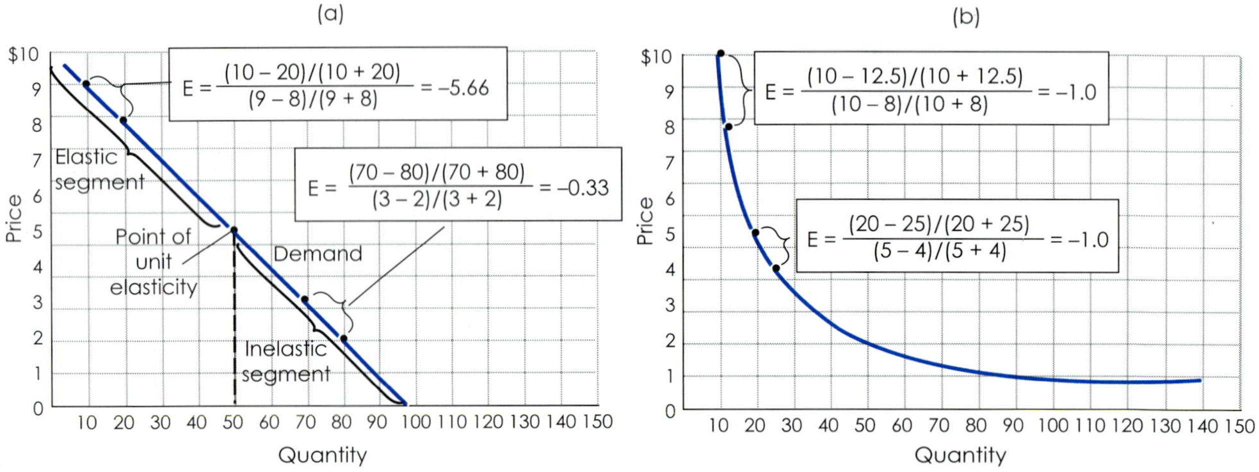

Elasticity varies along a straight-line demand curve, as part (a) of this figure illustrates. At the upper end of the curve, where the price is relatively high, a $1 change in price is a relatively small percentage change, and, because the quantity demanded is low, the corresponding change in quantity is relatively large in percentage terms. Demand is thus elastic near the top of the demand curve. At the lower end of the curve, the situation is reversed: a $1 change in price is now a relatively large change in percentage terms, whereas the corresponding change in quantity is smaller in percentage terms. Thus demand is inelastic. As part (b) shows, a curved demand curve can be drawn such that elasticity is constant for all ranges of price and quantity change.

relatively larger quantity demanded. Because it is percentages, not absolute amounts, that matter in elasticity calculations, a linear demand curve is less elastic near the bottom than near the top.

If the demand curve is not a straight line, other results are possible. There is an important special case in which the demand curve has just the curvature needed to keep elasticity constant over its entire length. Such a curve is shown in part (b) of Figure 3.2. As can be seen from the calculations in the figure, elasticity is 1.0 at every point on that curve. It is possible to construct demand curves with constant elasticities of any value. Econometric studies of demand elasticity often look for the constant-elasticity demand curve that most closely approximates buyers' average sensitivity to price changes as revealed by market data over time.

Determinants of Elasticity of Demand

The fact that elasticity often varies along the demand curve means that care must be taken in making statements about *the* elasticity of demand for a good. In practice, what such statements usually refer to is the elasticity, measured by the midpoint formula or some alternative method, over the range of price variation that is commonly observed in the market for that good. With this understanding, we can make some generalizations about what makes the demand for some goods relatively elastic and the demand for others relatively inelastic.

SUBSTITUTES, COMPLEMENTS, AND ELASTICITY One important determinant of elasticity of demand is the availability of substitutes. When a good has close substitutes, the demand for that good tends to be relatively elastic, because people willingly switch to the substitutes when the price of the good goes up. Thus, for example, the demand for corn oil is relatively elastic, because other cooking oils can usually be substituted for it. On the other hand, the demand for cigarettes is relatively inelastic, because for a habitual smoker there is no good substitute.

This principle has two corollaries. One is that the demand for a good tends to be more elastic the more narrowly the good is defined. For example, the demand for lettuce in the numerical example given earlier was relatively inelastic. This could be because many people are in the habit of eating a salad with dinner and do not think of spinach or coleslaw as completely satisfactory substitutes. At the same time, however, it could be that the demand for any particular variety of lettuce is relatively elastic. If the price of Boston lettuce rises while the prices of iceberg, romaine, and red-leaf lettuce remain unchanged, many people will readily switch to one of the other varieties, which they see as close substitutes.

The other corollary is that demand for the product of a single firm tends to be more elastic than the demand for the output of all producers operating in the market. As one example, the demand for cigarettes as a whole will be less elastic than the demand for any particular brand, such as Viceroy or Winston. The reason is that one brand can be substituted for another when the price of a brand changes.

The complements of a good can also play a role in determining its elasticity. If something is a minor complement to an important good (that is, one that accounts for a large share of consumers' budgets), demand for it tends to be relatively inelastic. For example, the demand for motor oil tends to be relatively inelastic, because it is a complement to a more important good, gasoline. The price of gasoline has a greater effect on the amount of driving a person does than the price of motor oil.

TIME HORIZON AND ELASTICITY One of the most important considerations determining the price elasticity of demand is the time horizon within which the decision to buy is made. For several reasons, demand is often less elastic in the short run than in the long run.

One reason is that full adjustment to a change in the price of a good may require changes in the kind or quantity of many other goods that a consumer buys. Gasoline provides a classic example. When the price of gasoline jumped in the 1970s, many people's initial reaction was to cut out some nonessential driving; the quantity of gasoline demanded fell only a little. As time went by, though, consumers adjusted in many ways. One important adjustment was to buy more fuel-efficient cars. Another was to base the choice of where to live partly on the length of the drive to work or the availability of public transportation. Gradually, as such adjustments were made, the quantity of gasoline demanded fell more than it had at first.

Another reason elasticity tends to be greater in the long run than in the short run is that an increase in the price of one good encourages entrepreneurs to develop substitutes—which, as we have seen, can be an important determinant of elasticity. To take an example from history, consider the response to what has been called America's first energy crisis, a sharp increase in the price of whale oil, which was used as lamp fuel in the early nineteenth century. At first candles were the only substitute for whale-oil lamps, and not a very satisfactory one. People therefore cut their use of whale oil only a little when the price began to rise. But the high price of whale oil spurred entrepreneurs to develop a better substitute, kerosene. Once kerosene came onto the market, the quantity of whale oil demanded for use as lamp fuel dropped to zero.

A final reason for greater elasticity of demand in the long run than in the short run is the slow adjustment of consumer tastes. The case of beef and chicken, featured in the preceding chapter, provides an example. Chicken, originally the more expensive meat, achieved a price advantage over beef many years ago, but eating lots of beef was a habit. Gradually, though, chicken developed an image as a healthy, stylish, versatile food, and finally it overtook beef as the number-one meat.

Income Elasticity of Demand

Determining the response of quantity demanded to a change in price is the most common application of the concept of elasticity, but it is by no means the only one. Elasticity can also be used to express the response of demand to any of the conditions covered by the "other things being equal" assumption on which a given demand curve is based. As we saw in the preceding chapter, one of those conditions is consumer incomes.

Income elasticity of demand

The ratio of the percentage change in the quantity of a good demanded to a given percentage change in consumer incomes, other things being equal.

The **income elasticity of demand** for a good is defined as the ratio of the percentage change in the quantity of that good demanded to a percentage change in income. In measuring income elasticity, it is assumed that the good's price does not change. Using Q_1 and Q_2 to represent quantities before and after the change in income, and y_1 and y_2 to represent income before and after the change, the midpoint formula for income elasticity of demand can be written as follows:

$$\text{Income elasticity of demand} = \frac{(Q_2 - Q_1)/(Q_1 + Q_2)}{(y_2 - y_1)/(y_1 + y_2)} = \frac{\text{Percentage change in quantity}}{\text{Percentage change in income}}$$

For a normal good, an increase in income causes demand to rise. Because income and demand change in the same direction, the income elasticity of demand for a normal good is positive. For an inferior good, an increase in income causes demand to decrease. Because income and demand change in opposite directions, the income elasticity of demand for an inferior good is negative.

Some of the considerations that determine price elasticity also affect income elasticity. In particular, whether a good is considered to be normal or inferior depends on how narrowly it is defined and on the availability of substitutes. For example, a study by Jonq-Ying Lee, Mark G. Brown, and Brooke Schwartz of the University of Florida looked at the demand for frozen orange juice.[2] Orange juice considered as a broad category is a normal good; people tend to consume more of it as their income rises. However, when the definition is narrowed so that house-brand and national-brand frozen orange juice are treated as separate products, the house-brand product turns out to be an inferior good. As their incomes rise, consumers substitute the higher-quality national brands, which have a positive income elasticity of demand.

Cross-Elasticity of Demand

Another condition that can cause a change in the demand for a good is a change in the price of some other good. The demand for chicken is affected by changes in the price of beef, the demand for motor oil by changes in the price of gasoline, and so on. Such relationships can be expressed as elasticities: The **cross-elasticity of demand** for a good is defined as the ratio of the percentage change in the quantity of that good demanded to a given percentage change in the price of another good. The midpoint formula for cross-elasticity of demand looks just like the one for price elasticity of demand, except that the numerator shows the percentage change in the quantity of one good while the denominator shows the percentage change in the price of some other good.

Cross-elasticity of demand

The ratio of the percentage change in the quantity of a good demanded to a given percentage change in the price of some other good, other things being equal.

Cross-elasticity of demand is related to the concepts of substitutes and complements. Because lettuce and cabbage are substitutes, an increase in the price of cabbage causes an increase in the quantity of lettuce demanded; the cross-elasticity of demand is positive. Because motor oil and gasoline are complements, an increase in the price of gasoline causes a decrease in the quantity of motor oil demanded; the cross-elasticity of demand is negative. The previously mentioned study of frozen orange juice found a positive cross-elasticity of demand between house-brand and national-brand juices, indicating that the two are substitutes.

Price Elasticity of Supply

Price elasticity of supply

The ratio of the percentage change in the quantity of a good supplied to a given percentage change in its price, other things being equal.

Elasticity is not confined to demand; it can also be used to indicate the response of quantity supplied to a change in price. Formally, the **price elasticity of supply** of a good is defined as the percentage change in the quantity of the good supplied divided by the percentage change in its price. The midpoint formula for calculating price elasticity of supply looks like the one for determining price elasticity of demand, but the Qs in the numerator of the formula now refer to quantity *supplied* rather than

FIGURE 3.3 CALCULATING PRICE ELASTICITY OF SUPPLY

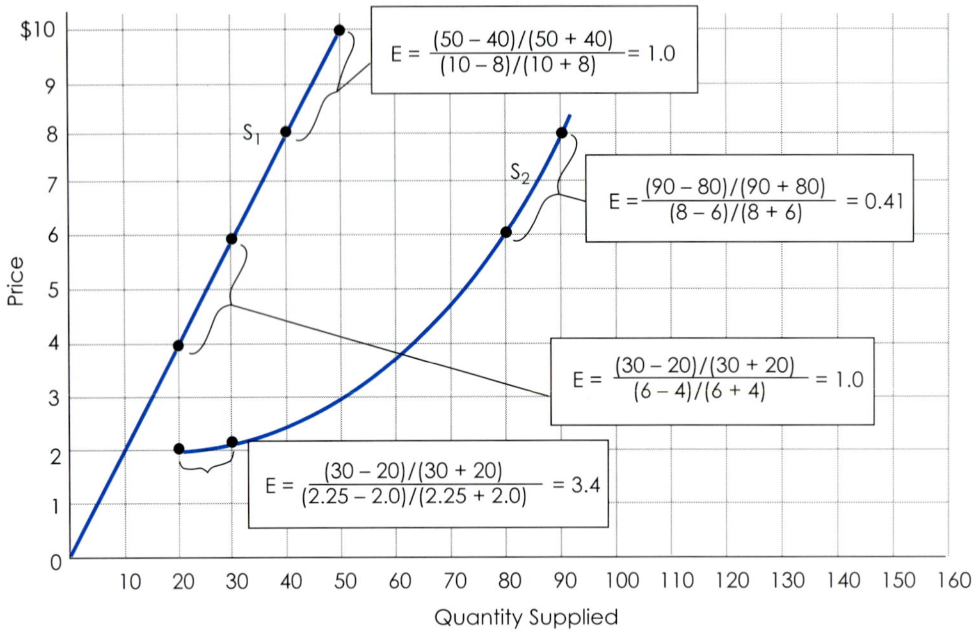

This figure gives four examples of the way price elasticity of supply is calculated. Price elasticity of supply is shown for two ranges on each of the two supply curves. Supply curve S_1 which is a straight line passing through the origin, has a constant elasticity of 1.0. Supply curve S_2, which is curved, is elastic for small quantities and inelastic for larger ones.

quantity *demanded*. Because price and quantity change in the same direction along a positively sloped supply curve, the formula gives a positive value for the elasticity of supply. Figure 3.3 applies the elasticity formula to two supply curves, one with constant elasticity and the other with variable elasticity.

In later chapters we will look in detail at the considerations that determine the elasticity of supply for various products. Two of those considered are especially important, however, and deserve some discussion here.

One determinant of the elasticity of supply of a good is the mobility of the factors of production used to produce it. As used here, *mobility* means the ease with which factors can be attracted away from some other use, as well as the ease with which they can be reconverted to their original use. The trucking industry provides a classic example of mobile resources. As a crop such as lettuce or watermelons comes to harvest in a particular region of a country, hundreds of trucks are needed to haul it to market. Shippers compete for available trucks, driving up the price paid to truckers in the local market. Independent truckers throughout the country learn—from their own experience, from trucking brokers, and from CB radios—where they can earn the best rates for hauling produce. It takes only a modest rise in the price for hauling a load of Georgia watermelons to attract enough truckers to Georgia to haul the crop to market. When the harvest is over, the truckers will move elsewhere to haul peaches, tomatoes, or whatever.

In contrast, other products are produced with much less mobile resources. Petroleum provides a good example. In the 1970s, when oil prices rose, producers had an incentive to drill more wells. However, given limited numbers of drilling rigs and other highly specialized equipment, not to mention limited numbers of sites worth exploring, the tenfold increase in oil prices during the decade caused only a slight increase in oil output. Factor mobility in this industry is limited in the other direction, too. Once a well has been drilled, the investment cannot be converted to a different use. Thus, in the 1980s, when oil prices fell again, production dropped by a much smaller percentage than price.

A second determinant of elasticity of supply is time. As in the case of demand, price elasticity of supply tends to be greater in the long run than in the short run. In part, the reason for this is connected with mobility of resources. In the short run, the output of many products can be increased by using more of the most flexible inputs—for example, by adding workers at a plant or extending the hours of work. Such short-run measures often mean higher costs per unit for the added output, however, because workers added without comparable additions in other inputs (such as equipment) tend to be less productive. If a firm expects market conditions to warrant an increase of supply in the long run, it will be worthwhile to invest in additional quantities of less mobile inputs such as specialized plants and equipment. Once those investments have been made, the firm will find it worthwhile to supply the greater quantity of output at a lower price than in the short-run case because its costs per unit supplied will be lower.

APPLICATIONS OF ELASTICITY

Elasticity has many applications in both macro- and microeconomics. In macroeconomics, it can be applied to money markets, to the aggregate supply and demand for all goods and services, and to foreign-exchange markets, to name just a few. In microeconomics, elasticity plays a role in discussions of consumer behavior, the profit-maximizing behavior of business firms, governments' regulatory and labor policies, and many other areas. To further illustrate elasticity, we conclude this chapter with applications featuring the problems of tax incidence and drug policy.

Elasticity and Tax Incidence

Who pays taxes? One way to answer this question is in terms of *assessments*—the issue of who bears the legal responsibility to make tax payments to the government. A study of assessments would show that property owners pay property taxes, gasoline companies pay gasoline taxes, and so on. However, looking at assessments does not always settle the issue of who bears the economic burden of a tax—or, to use the economist's term, the issue of **tax incidence**.

Tax incidence

The distribution of the economic burden of a tax.

The incidence of a tax does not always coincide with the way the tax is assessed, because the economic burden of the tax, in whole or in part, often can be passed along to someone else. The degree to which the burden of a tax may be passed along depends on the elasticities of supply and demand. Let's consider some examples.

INCIDENCE OF A GASOLINE TAX First consider the familiar example of a gasoline tax. Specifically, suppose that the state of Virginia decides to impose a tax of $.50 per gallon on gasoline beginning from a situation in which there is no tax. The tax is assessed against sellers of gasoline, who add the tax into the price paid by consumers at the pump.

Figure 3.4 uses the supply-and-demand model to show the effects of the tax. Initially, the demand curve intersects supply curve S_1 at E_1, resulting in a price of $1 per gallon. The supply curve is elastic in the region of the initial equilibrium. The elasticity of supply reflects the fact that we are dealing with the gasoline market in just one state; only a slight rise in the price in Virginia is needed to divert additional quantities

FIGURE 3.4 INCIDENCE OF A TAX ON GASOLINE

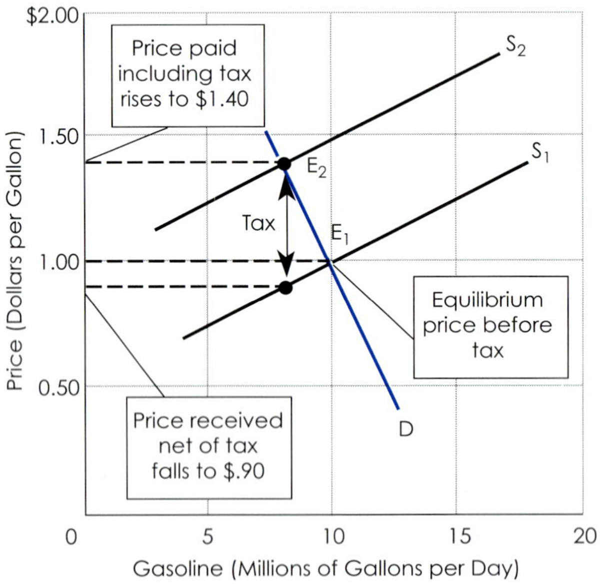

S_1 and D are the supply and demand curves before imposition of the tax. The initial equilibrium price is $1 per gallon. A tax of $.50 per gallon shifts the supply curve to S_2. To induce sellers to supply the same quantity as before, the price would have to rise to $1.50. However, as the price rises, buyers reduce the quantity demanded, moving up and to the left along the demand curve. In the new equilibrium at E_2, the price rises only to $1.40. After the tax is paid, sellers receive only $.90 per gallon. Thus, buyers bear $.40 of the tax on each gallon and sellers the remaining $.10. Buyers bear the larger share of the tax because demand, in this case, is less elastic than supply.

of gasoline from elsewhere in the nation. The demand for gasoline is less elastic than the supply in the region of the initial equilibrium.

The effect of the tax is to shift the supply curve to the left until each point on the new supply curve is exactly $.50 higher than the point for the corresponding quantity on the old supply curve. (We could instead say that the supply curve shifts *upward* by $.50.) Because sellers must now turn over $.50 to the state government for each gallon of gas sold, they would have to get $1.50 per gallon to be willing to sell the same quantity (10 million gallons per day) as initially. However, when sellers attempt to pass the tax on to motorists, motorists respond by reducing the amount of gas they buy. As the quantity sold falls, sellers move down and to the left along supply curve S_2 to a new equilibrium at E_2.

In the new equilibrium, the price is $1.40 per gallon—just $.40 higher than the original price. The new price includes the $.50 tax, which sellers add to their net price of $.90 per gallon—a net price that is $.10 less than before. The amount of the tax—$.50 per gallon—is shown by the vertical gap between the supply and demand curves. The economic burden of the tax is divided between buyers and sellers, but in this case it falls more heavily on the buyers.

INCIDENCE OF A TAX ON APARTMENT RENTS In the preceding example, the incidence of the gasoline tax falls more heavily on buyers than on sellers because demand is less elastic than supply. If the elasticities are reversed, the results will also be reversed, as can be seen in the case of a tax on apartment rents.

In Figure 3.5, the market for rental apartments in Ogden, Utah (a small city) is initially in equilibrium at $500 per month. The supply of rental apartments is inelastic. An increase in rents will cause a few new apartments to be built, whereas a reduction will cause a few to be torn down, but in either case the response will be moderate. On the other hand, demand is fairly elastic, because potential renters consider houses or condominiums a fairly close substitute for rental apartments.

Given this situation, suppose that the local government decides to impose a tax of $250 per month on all apartments rented in Ogden, UT. This tax, like the gasoline tax, is assessed against landlords, who include the tax payment in the monthly rental they charge to tenants. As in the previous example, the tax shifts the supply curve to the left until each point on the new supply curve lies above the corresponding point on the old supply curve by the amount of the tax. (Again, we could instead say the supply curve shifts upward by the amount of the tax.) After the shift, the market reaches a new equilibrium at E_2. There the rental price paid by tenants rises to only $550 per month, as indicated by the intersection of the new supply and demand curves. Landlords succeed in passing only $50 of the $250 monthly tax along to tenants. Their net rental income, after turning over the tax receipts to the town government, is now just $300, down from $500 before imposition of the tax. In this case, because supply is inelastic and demand is elastic, suppliers bear most of the incidence of the tax and buyers only a little.

FIGURE 3.5 INCIDENCE OF A TAX ON APARTMENT RENTS

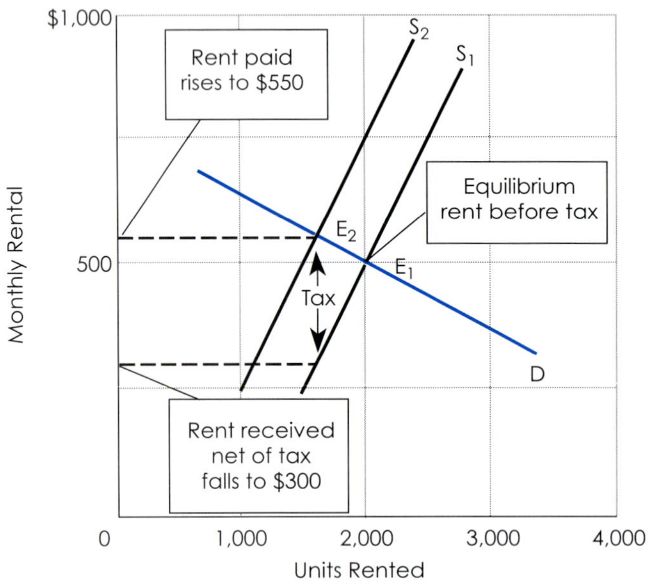

This figure shows the incidence of a tax imposed in a market in which supply is less elastic than demand. Initially, the equilibrium rent is $500 per month. A $250-per-month tax on apartment rents shifts the supply curve to S_2. The new equilibrium is at E_2. Landlords end up absorbing all but $50 of the tax. If they tried to pass more of the tax on to renters, more renters would switch to owner-occupied housing, and the vacancy rate on rental apartments would rise.

INCIDENCE AND TAX REVENUE When the government considers imposing a tax on gasoline, cigarettes, apartments, or any other item, the price elasticity of demand and supply is important not only for how the burden is shared between buyers and sellers, but also for how much tax revenue the government collects. When buyers and/or sellers are more responsive to changes in price (when demand and /or supply is more elastic), a tax will generate less revenue for the government.

Figure 3.6 compares the markets for two items: milk and pork. The price elasticities of supply for these two goods are relatively similar, but the price elasticities of demand differ. Pork is a meat that has several substitutes, such as beef, chicken, and fish. Milk, however, has few substitutes, so its demand is inelastic relative to pork. The markets for milk and pork are shown in Figure 3.6. The equilibrium price of milk is $0.50 per gallon and 12 million gallons are sold each year at this price. The milk market equilibrium is point E_1 on the left panel of Figure 3.6. The equilibrium (shown by the point E_1 on the right panel of Figure 3.6) is $0.75 per pound and 12 million pounds are sold each year.

Suppose the government is considering imposing a $1.00 tax on milk or pork. The diagrams show the effects of this tax in each market. In the milk market, the $1.00 tax leads to a small decrease in the quantity from 12 to 10 million gallons

FIGURE 3.6

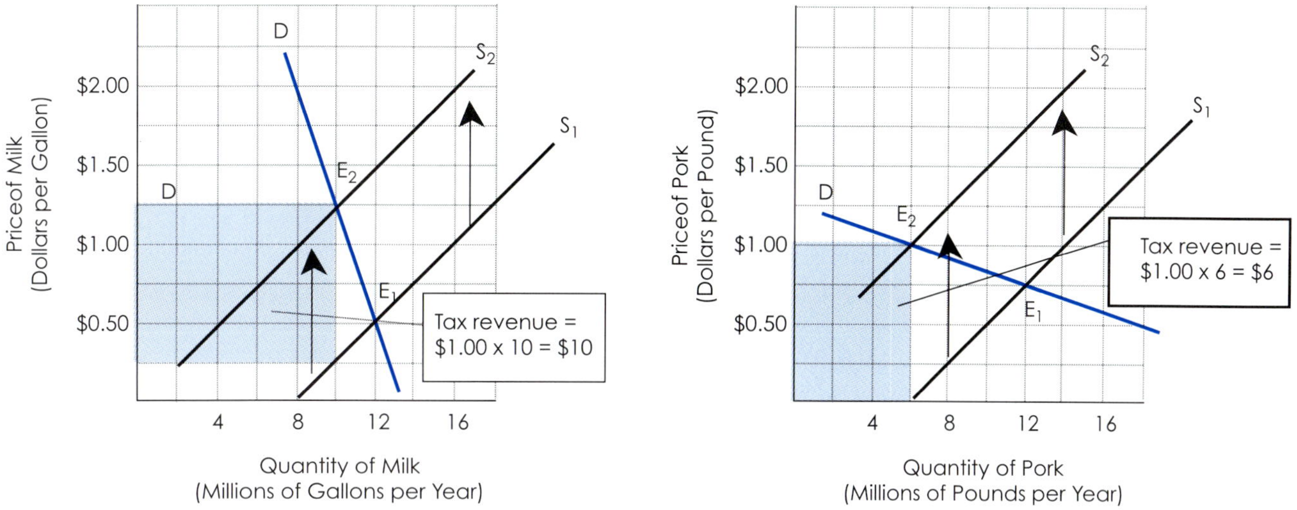

A tax imposed on a good that has an inelastic demand will generate more tax revenue. The diagrams above compare the effects of a $1.00 tax on the markets for milk (inelastic demand) and pork (elastic demand). In the market for milk, the tax reduces the equilibrium quantity by 2 million gallons, from point E_1 (12 million gallons) to E_2 (10 million gallons). Therefore, the government collects a total of $10 million from the milk tax. The same tax in pork has a very different result. In the pork market, the $1.00 tax causes a large reduction in the quantity sold, from 12 million pounds (point E_1) to 6 million pounds (point E_2). This means the government will only collect $6 million, as only 6 million pounds of pork are sold at the new equilibrium.

because demand is relatively inelastic. People buying milk are not very responsive to the change in price in terms of how much milk they buy. The government collects $1.00 on each gallon of milk sold, generating a tax revenue of $10 million from this tax because 10 million gallons are sold. In the market for pork, the tax leads to a large reduction in the quantity people buy from 12 to 6 million pounds. This reflects that the demand for pork is highly elastic. The government will collect a total of $6 million from the tax on pork, collecting $1.00 on each of the 6 million pounds sold. When comparing the two possible taxes, the government collects more revenue from the tax on milk because people don't reduce the amount of milk they buy very much.

Elasticity and Prohibition

In the case of gasoline and apartment rents, a tax led to a reduction in the quantity consumed, which we characterized as an unintended consequence of the tax. In a few cases, the reduction in quantity consumed may be an *intended* consequence of the tax. Taxes on tobacco products are one example: because tobacco is regarded as harmful, a reduction in quantity consumed is seen as desirable. Proposals to tax environmentally harmful products, such as the chemicals thought to be responsible for ozone depletion, are another example.

ECONOMICS IN THE NEWS 3.1

GOVERNOR SCHWARZENEGGER AND THE VEHICLE LICENSE TAX

Drivers in California must pay a Vehicle License Fee (VLF) to register and legally drive their cars once each year. In 2002, a state budget crisis left the then Governor Gray Davis in a difficult situation. Republicans in the state legislature refused to raise state income or business taxes, while Democrats refused to cut high spending in social services and education. This left the state with a projected budget shortfall of $38.2 billion. Governor Davis decided to make up for part of this shortfall by raising the VLF, doubling or tripling the fee depending the type of vehicle. Because the demand for vehicles is inelastic, people were not expected to respond to the higher registration fees by purchasing fewer cars. The result would have been an estimated $4 billion in extra state tax revenue to help fill the 38.2 billion budget shortfall. This provided the governor with a way to raise significant tax revenues without approval from the state legislature.

The VLF hikes were very unpopular for an already unpopular Governor Davis. Eventually, Governor Davis was recalled by the people of California in October 2003, and replaced with Arnold Schwarzenegger. One of Governor Schwarzenegger's first acts in office was to repeal the fee increase. How the state will address the budget crisis, and the missing $4 billion that was supposed to be generated from VLF increase, is unresolved. It is likely California will have to borrow from outside sources to make up for the shortfall and cut funding to higher education.

Prohibition is a more extreme policy aimed at reducing the quantity of a product consumed. For example, alcoholic beverages were subject to prohibition in the United States during the 1920s, and substances such a marijuana, heroin, and cocaine are subject to prohibition today. Prohibition is a common method of environmental regulation as well, with the pesticide DDT and lead additives for gasoline serving as examples.

On the surface, a policy of prohibition may seem very different from a tax, since unlike a tax, prohibition raises no tax revenue for the government. However, if we use economic analysis to look below the surface, we see some similarities as well as differences between taxation and prohibition.

First, passage of a law prohibiting production and sale of a good does not make it impossible to supply the good, but simply more expensive. After the prohibition is in effect, the supplier must consider not only the direct costs of production, but the extra costs of covert transportation and distribution systems, the risk of fines or jail terms, the costs of hiring armed gangsters to protect illegal laboratories, and so on. If the price rises by enough to cover all of these costs, the good will still be supplied. Thus, the effect of prohibition of a good is to shift its supply curve to the left until each point on the new supply curve lies above the corresponding point on the old curve by a distance equal to the extra costs associated with evading the prohibition.

Second, the effects of the prohibition, like those of a tax, depend on the elasticity of demand relative to the elasticity of supply. This is illustrated in Figure 3.7, which compares the effects of prohibition on the market for DDT and on the market for cocaine. The demand for DDT is shown as relatively elastic, because fairly effective substitutes are available at a price only a little higher than the banned pesticide. The demand for cocaine is shown as relatively inelastic, in part because once people become addicted, they will be very reluctant to curtail their use of the drug even if its price rises sharply.

In the case of elastic demand for DDT (Figure 3.7a), even a weakly enforced prohibition, represented by a shift in the supply curve from S_1 to S_2, will sharply reduce the quantity sold. A more vigorously enforced prohibition, as represented by supply curve S_3, may very well eliminate use of the product altogether. In either case, the amount of revenue received by suppliers is reduced. The weak prohibition cuts total revenue from $14,000 per week to $8,500 per week. The strict prohibition cuts revenue to zero.

In the case of inelastic demand for cocaine (Figure 3.7b), even a strongly enforced prohibition, represented by a shift in the supply curve to S_2, has relatively little effect on quantity demanded. Total revenue from the sale of cocaine rises substantially, however, from $130,000 per week at equilibrium E_1 to $300,000 per week at equilibrium E_2. As long as demand is inelastic, increasing strictness of enforcement, which drives the supply curve still higher, will also cause total revenue to increase still further.

FIGURE 3.7 ELASTICITY AND THE EFFECTS OF PROHIBITION

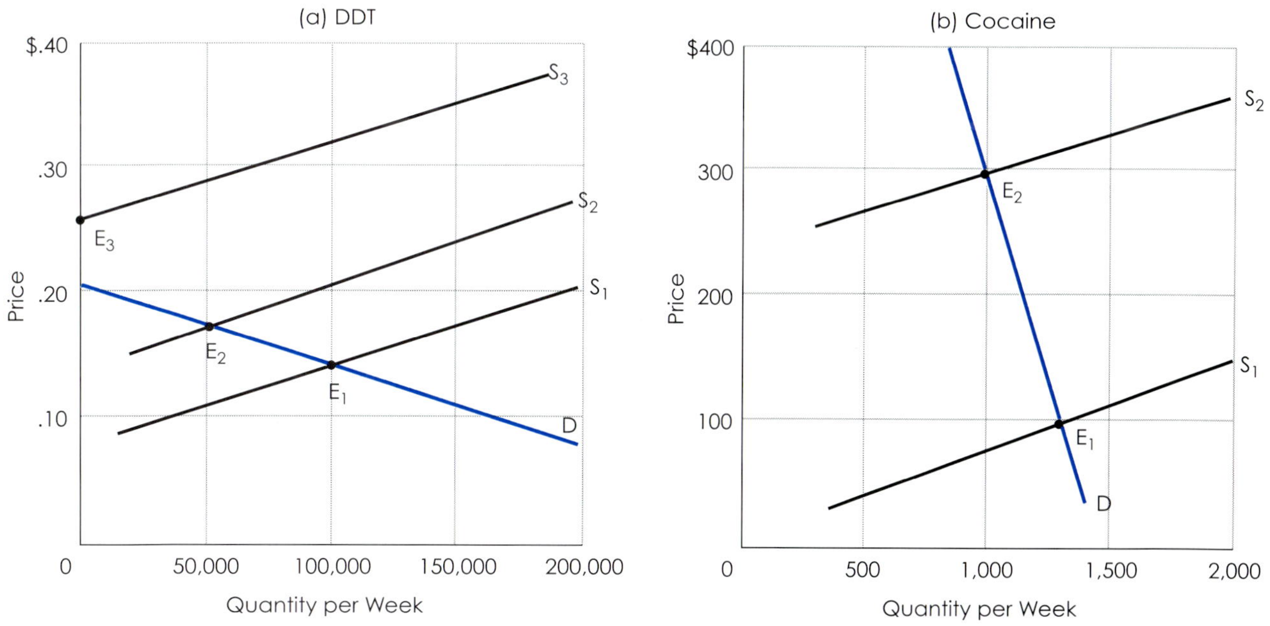

A law prohibiting production and sale of a good, like a tax on the good, shifts its supply curve to the left. The new supply curve will lie above the old supply curve at any given quantity by a distance equal to the cost of evading the prohibition. The effects on price, quantity, and revenue depend on the elasticity of demand. Part (a) uses DDT to illustrate prohibition of a good with elastic demand. A wealthy enforced prohibition (S_2) raises the price, reduces the quantity, and reduces total revenue. A strongly enforced prohibition reduces quantity and revenue to zero (S_3). Part (b) uses cocaine to illustrate prohibition of a good with inelastic demand. In this case, prohibition results in increased total revenue and expenditure on the good.

These simple conclusions based on elasticity of demand are important in understanding the intended and unintended consequences of prohibition. The intended consequence, of course, is to reduce or eliminate use of the product. As we see, the more elastic the demand for the product, the more successful is the policy of prohibition in achieving its intended effects. The unintended effects of prohibition are those associated with the change in revenue that the policy produces. These are very different in the case of elastic and inelastic demand.

Where demand is elastic, the unintended consequences are loss of profit by DDT producers, and a small rise in the cost of growing crops as farmers switch to more expensive pesticides. Neither has major social consequences. The loss of profit from producing DDT will be offset by profits from producing substitutes—very likely by the same companies. And the increased cost of growing crops is offset by the benefits of a cleaner environment.

On the other hand, where demand is inelastic, prohibition increases total expenditure on the banned product. The social consequences of this are severe. First, users of cocaine must spend more to sustain their habit. At best this means impoverishing themselves and their families; at worst it means an increase in muggings and armed robberies by users desperate for cash. Second, the impact of the prohibition on suppliers must be considered as well. For suppliers, the increase in revenue does not mean an increase in profit, but rather, an increase in expenditures to evade the prohibition. In part, the result is simply wasteful, as when drug suppliers buy an airplane to make a single one-way flight rather than using normal transportation methods. Worse, another part of suppliers' increased expenditures take the form of hiring armies of thugs to battle the police and other suppliers, further raising the level of violence on city streets.

The issue of drug prohibition, of course, involves many normative issues that reach far beyond the concept of elasticity. One such issue is people's right to harm themselves through consumption of substances such as tobacco, alcohol, or cocaine. Another concerns the relative emphasis that should be placed on prohibition versus treatment in allocating resources to reduce drug use. The analysis given here cannot answer such questions. However, it does suggest that the law of unintended consequences applies in the area of drug policy as elsewhere, and that elasticity of demand is important in determining the nature and severity of those consequences.

SUMMARY

1. **How can the responsiveness of quantity demanded to a price change be expressed in terms of elasticity?** *Elasticity* is the responsiveness of quantity demanded or supplied to changes in the price of a good (or changes in other factors), measured as a ratio of the percentage change in quantity to the percentage change in price (or other factor causing the change in quantity). The *price elasticity of demand* between two points on a demand curve is computed as the percentage change in quantity demanded divided by the percentage change in the good's price.

2. **How is the elasticity of demand for a good related to the revenue earned by its seller?** If the demand for a good is elastic, a decrease in its price will increase total revenue. If it is inelastic, an increase in its price will increase total revenue. When the demand for a good is unit elastic, revenue will remain constant as the price varies.

3. **How can elasticity be applied to situations other than the responsiveness of the quantity of a good demanded to a change in its price?** The concept of elasticity can be applied to many situations besides movements along demand curves. The *income elasticity of demand* for a good is the ratio of the percentage change in quantity demanded to a given percentage change in income. The *cross-elasticity of demand* between goods A and B is the ratio of the percentage change in the quantity of good A demanded to a given percentage change in the price of good B. The *price elasticity of supply* is the ratio of the percentage change in the quantity of a good supplied to a given change in its price.

4. **What determines the distribution of the economic burden of a tax?** The way in which the economic burden of a tax is distributed is known as the *incidence* of the tax. The incidence depends on the relative elasticities of supply and demand. If supply is relatively more elastic than demand, buyers will bear the larger share of the tax burden. If demand is relatively more elastic than supply, the larger share of the burden will fall on sellers. If the good is subject to prohibition rather than to a tax, elasticity of demand will determine how many resources are likely to be devoted to enforcement and evasion of the prohibition.

KEY TERMS

Elasticity
Price elasticity of demand
Revenue
Elastic demand
Inelastic demand
Unit elastic demand
Perfectly inelastic demand
Perfectly elastic demand
Income elasticity of demand
Cross-elasticity of demand
Price elasticity of supply
Tax incidence

PROBLEMS AND TOPICS FOR DISCUSSION

1. **Examining the lead-off case.** Consider three time horizons: (a) The "very short" run means a period that is too short to allow farmers to change the amount of lettuce that has been planted. No matter what happens to the price, the quantity supplied will be the amount already planted, less the amount destroyed by the virus. (b) The "intermediate" run means a period that is long enough to allow farmers to plant more fields in lettuce, but not long enough to permit them to develop new varieties of lettuce, introduce new methods of cultivation, or acquire new specialized equipment.

(c) The "long" run means a period that is long enough to allow farmers to develop new varieties and improve cultivation techniques. Discuss these three time horizons in terms of the price elasticity of supply. Sketch a figure showing supply curves for each of the time horizons. Which time horizon or horizons are relevant to the story at the beginning of the chapter?

2. **Calculating elasticity.** Draw a set of coordinate axes on a piece of graph paper. Label the horizontal axis from 0 to 50 units and the vertical axis from $0 to $20 per unit. Draw a demand curve that intersects the vertical axis at $10 and the horizontal axis at 40 units. Draw a supply curve that intersects the vertical axis at $4 and has a slope of 1. Make the following calculations for these curves, using the midpoint formula:
   a. What is the price elasticity of demand over the price range $5 to $7?
   b. What is the price elasticity of demand over the price range $1 to $3?
   c. What is the price elasticity of supply over the price range $10 to $15?
   d. What is the price elasticity of supply over the price range $15 to $17?

3. **Elasticity and revenue.** Look at the demand curve given in Figure 2.1. Make a third column in the table that gives revenue for each price-quantity combination shown. Draw a set of axes on a piece of graph paper. Label the horizontal axis as in Figure 2.1, and label the vertical axis from 0 to $1 billion of revenue in increments of $100 million. Graph the relationship between quantity and revenue using the column you added to the table. (You may want to extend the table to show the following additional points: 1 billion units at a price of $.80; 0.5 billion units at a price of $1.00.) Discuss the relationship of your revenue graph to the demand curve, keeping in mind what you know about elasticity and revenue and about variation in elasticity along the demand curve.

4. **Elasticity of demand and revenue.** Assume that you are an officer of your campus film club. You are at a meeting at which ticket prices are being discussed. One member says, "What I hate to see most of all is empty seats in the theater. We sell out every weekend showing, but there are always empty seats on Wednesdays. If we cut our Wednesday night prices by enough to fill up the theater, we'd bring in more money." Would this tactic really bring in more revenue? What would you need to know in order to be sure? Draw diagrams to illustrate some of the possibilities.

5. **Cross-elasticity of demand.** Between 1979 and 1981 the price of heating oil rose by 104 percent. Over the same period, use of fuel oil fell slightly while use of LP gas, another heating fuel, rose. Assuming that there was no change in the price of LP gas, what does this suggest about the cross-elasticity of demand for LP gas with respect to the price of fuel oil? Draw a pair of diagrams to illustrate these events. (Suggestion: Draw upward-sloping supply curves for both fuels. Then assume that the supply curve for heating oil shifts upward while the supply curve for LP gas stays the same.)

CASE FOR DISCUSSION

A Novel Sales Ploy: Cut Prices

General Motors Corp. came up with a plan that might keep its 10-year-old Chevrolet Chevette alive a bit longer.

The plan was simple: cut the price.

To producers of things other than cars, that might seem a fairly obvious task. But in the auto industry, it was novel, even outlandish.

Chrysler Corporation had tried it in the spring of 1986 with its Omni/Horizon models, eight-year-old subcompacts that compete with Chevette. And it worked.

Chrysler knocked $710 off the base price of the Omni/Horizon, added some equipment and the "America" name to the car line, and offered the package for $5,499. The result was a 26.2 percent increase in sales of cars that were on Chrysler's scrap list. The company sold 165,300 Omni/Horizon models in the first nine months of 1986, compared with 130,968 during the same period in the previous year.

General Motors (GM) took the same approach with the pricing of its Chevettes for the coming year. GM trimmed nearly $800 from the price of these rear-wheel-drive, four-cylinder autos, and made standard some formerly optional equipment. The base price was $4,995.

"The car is continuing to sell fairly well, particularly in fleet sales," said Ralph Kramer, Chevrolet's director of public relations. Fleet buyers accounted for about 65 percent of the 75,761 Chevettes sold in 1985, industry analysts say.

Still, the days of the oft-maligned, oft-praised Chevette were numbered.

The level of sales was well below the minimum 100,000 per year needed to make it worthwhile to produce a line of cars. While the strategy did not, in the end, save either of these models (Chevette or Omni/Horizon), the auto industry has since made periodic use of substantial rebates to spur sales without having to cut the manufacturer's suggested retail price (MSRP).

Source: Warren Brown, "Chevette Sales Ploy: Cut Prices," *The Washington Post,* October 15, 1986, Fl.

QUESTIONS

1. Using the data provided in the article, estimate the price elasticity of demand for Chrysler's Omni/Horizon. (Throughout this problem, assume that the changes in sales volume indicate movements along demand curves resulting from the change in price.)
2. If Chevette sales were to increase to 100,000 units in the year following the price cut, what would be the price elasticity of demand for the car?
3. Suppose that demand for the Chevette is elastic, so that the firm's revenues will increase if the price is cut. Does that automatically mean that the firm's profit will increase?

END NOTES

1. As we have said, the midpoint formula (also sometimes called *arc-elasticity*) is not the only one for calculating elasticity. A drawback of this formula is that it can give misleading elasticity values if applied over too wide a variation in price or quantity. Because of this limitation, it is often suggested that the midpoint formula be used only over fairly small ranges of variation in price or quantity. Following this reasoning to its logical conclusion, there is an alternative formula for calculating elasticity for a single point on the demand curve. For a linear demand curve having the formula $q = a - bp$ (with q representing quantity demanded, p the price, and a and b being constants), the *point formula* for elasticity of demand (stated, as elsewhere, as a positive number) is

   $$\text{Elasticity} = bp/(a - bp).$$

   This formula allows you to compute the elasticity at a particular point. The drawback of this approach is that it will give you two different answers, depending on whether you consider an increase in price versus a decrease in price.
2. Jonq-Ying Lee, Mark G. Brown, and Brooke Schwartz, "The Demand for National Brand and Private Label Frozen Concentrated Orange Juice: A Switching Regression Analysis," *Western Journal of Agricultural Economics* (July 1986): 1–7.

PART II

The Basic Theory of Prices and Markets

CHAPTER 4

Economic Theory, Markets, and Government

After reading this chapter, you will understand:

1. The basic structure of economic theory
2. Why rationality is of central importance in economics
3. The meaning of market performance and market failure
4. Some alternative theories of the economic role of government

Before reading this chapter, make sure you know the meaning of:

1. Positive and normative economics
2. Entrepreneurship
3. Law of unintended consequences
4. Supply and demand

WILL COAL BE KING AGAIN?

In the nineteenth century, coal was king. It powered the industrial revolution. It was burned in factories, steamboats, railway locomotives, and parlor stoves. The steamboats, locomotives, and parlor stoves are long gone now, and except for a few basic processes like steelmaking, most of industry has long since converted to cleaner fuels. Yet late in the twentieth century, king coal seemed to be regaining its crown, this time as the nation's leading fuel for generating electricity.

In 1991, coal accounted for 54 percent of electricity generation in the United States, up from 45 percent in 1970. Oil, natural gas, and hydroelectric energy all lost ground over that period. Nuclear energy's share of the market is up compared with 1970, but it has passed its peak and is declining again. By 2002, the picture looked somewhat different. Only 50 percent of electricity generation derived from coal, while gas and hydroelectric power gained some ground.

Market forces explain much of coal's success. In contrast to its dwindling oil supplies, the United States has enough coal to last for centuries. Abundance translates into low prices: As of 2002, coal was selling for $1.26 per million British thermal units (Btu), compared to $3.33 for natural gas having the same energy value.

But coal has its enemies. Environmentalists consider it the dirtiest of fuels. Mining coal makes a mess locally. Burning it spews out sulfur compounds, which are thought to cause acid rain, and carbon dioxide, believed in turn to cause global warming. Coal is cheap enough that utilities can afford to invest in minimizing the mining and acid rain problems. But the only way to solve the carbon dioxide problem associated with coal is to stop burning it.

To win the environmental battle as well as the economic one, coal counts on powerful friends in Washington. It helps that Senator Robert Byrd, chairman of the Senate Appropriations Committee, is from West Virginia, a major coal-producing state. Coal proponents defuse environmental worries by seeking generous research grants to study how to burn coal more cleanly.

Looking further into this century, no one expects the return of coal-fired trains or cars. But they do expect an increasing share of transportation to switch to electric power. And more demand for electricity will probably mean more demand for coal.

Source: Based in part on Robert Johnson and Caleb Solomon, "Coal Quietly Regains a Dominant Chunk of Generating Market," *The Wall Street Journal*, August 20, 1992, A1. 2002 data obtained from the Energy Information Administration, U.S. Department of Energy.

THE COMPETITION BETWEEN coal and natural gas for a larger share of the energy markets is a typical example of economic choice. Markets are the stage on which much of this action takes place. Prices play a central role in market choices, but other considerations matter, too. In the case of coal, financial risk and environmental hazards interact with price per Btu in determining the choice of a fuel.

To make matters more complex still, buyers and sellers are not the only ones involved in market choices; government plays a role as well. The fact that a coal-rich West Virginia is represented on a key committee, rather than oil- and gas-rich Texas, plays a crucial role.

Given the way the world works, the challenge for economists is to recognize simple patterns in complex events and to identify common elements in seemingly dissimilar situations. The chief tool for doing so is economic theory. This chapter opens by expanding on the general comments made earlier on the structure of economic theory, with special attention to aspects of theory that are important for microeconomics. It continues with a discussion of market performance and market failure, and concludes with a look at the economic role of government.

THE STRUCTURE OF ECONOMIC THEORY

To *analyze* something means to break it down into its component parts. A literary critic might analyze a novel in terms of such basic components as plot, character, and dialog. A detective might analyze a murder in terms of motive, means, and opportunity. Similarly, economists look for certain common elements when they analyze the choices people make in using scarce resources to meet their wants.

Objectives, Constraints, and Choices

The elements of which every economic theory is composed are three types of statements: statements about objectives, statements about constraints on opportunities, and statements about choices.

STATEMENTS ABOUT OBJECTIVES An *objective* is anything people want to achieve. A business owner may have the objective of earning the greatest possible profit. A consumer may strive for the greatest possible material satisfaction with a given income. People in any situation may blend their pursuit of narrowly "economic" objectives with family values, social responsibilities, and so on. Terms such as *aims*, *goals*, and *preferences* are interchangeable with *objectives*.

STATEMENTS ABOUT CONSTRAINTS ON OPPORTUNITIES A key part of every economic theory is a statement of the constraints on the set of opportunities that are available to choose among in a given situation. In a world of scarcity, alternatives are never unlimited, and constraints are universal. Some constraints relate to what is physically possible, given available resources and knowledge. Only so many bales of hay can be loaded into a truck that can hold 1,000 cubic feet of cargo. Only so many pounds of iron can be smelted from a ton of ore of a given quality.

Other constraints take the form not of physical limits but of opportunity costs, often defined in terms of prices. For example, there is no physical limit to the number of pairs of shoes a person can own, but if shoes cost $60 a pair and sweaters cost $30 apiece, each pair of shoes purchased means forgoing the opportunity to buy two sweaters (or something else of equal value).

Property rights

Legal rules that establish what things a person may use or control, and the conditions under which such use or control may be exercised.

Still other constraints take the form of legal rules. For example, it may be physically possible and worthwhile, in terms of costs and benefits, for a farmer to control insect pests by spraying DDT; however, it is illegal to do so. A particularly important set of legal constraints are those that define *property rights*. **Property rights** are legal rules that establish what things a person may use or control and the conditions under which that use or control may be exercised. In short, they establish what a person *owns*.

As an everyday example, consider the property rights that establish a person's ownership of a house. Those rights include the right to live in the house, to modify its structure, and to control the arrangement of furniture in its rooms. In some communities, ownership may include the right to park a boat trailer in the driveway and to have a swing set on the front lawn. In others, those particular rights may be limited by zoning laws or restrictive covenants.

Property rights extend to more abstract relationships as well. For example, ownership of a share of common stock in ConocoPhillips Corporation gives the stockholder a complex package of rights, including the rights to vote on issues affecting the firm and to share in the firm's profits. As another example, a software firm's copyright on a program it has produced gives it control over the conditions under which the program may be licensed for use by others.

STATEMENTS ABOUT CHOICES The final component of an economic theory is a statement of the choice that is most likely to be made, given particular objectives and constraints on opportunities. For example, the next chapter will look at the choices that underlie the law of demand. There, consumers will be seen as having the objective of obtaining the greatest possible satisfaction, given the constraints placed on their opportunities by their budgets, the range of goods available, and the prices of those goods. Given those objectives and constraints, the law of demand states that people can be expected to choose to increase their purchases of a good when its price is reduced, other things being equal.

Economic Theory and Rationality

Although all economic theories contain the three types of statements just listed, a successful theory is more than just a list—its elements need to form a coherent whole. Our understanding of the structure of economic theory would be incomplete without a discussion of a key assumption that serves to hold the three elements of a theory together: the assumption that people choose the *best* way of accomplishing their objectives, given the constraints they face. In other words, people are *rational.*

Rationality

Acting purposefully to achieve an objective, given constraints on the opportunities that are available.

Rationality means acting purposefully to achieve an objective, given constraints on available opportunities. The concept of rationality is built into the definition of economics given at the beginning of this book, which speaks of choosing the best way to use scarce resources to meet human wants. To say that some ways of using scarce resources are better than others, and that those are the ones people tend to choose, is to express the essence of rationality.

The assumption of rationality, so central to economics, is sometimes misunderstood as a psychological or philosophical assertion about human nature—an assertion that people are always coolly calculating, not emotional or impulsive. A critic once ridiculed economists for seeing the human individual as a "lightning calculator of pleasures and pains, who oscillates like a homogeneous globule of desire under the impulse of stimuli . . . [who] spins symmetrically about his own spiritual axis until the parallelogram of forces bears down upon him, whereupon he follows the line of the resultant."[1] But as used in economics, the rationality assumption has nothing to do with that sort of caricature of "economic man."

The rationality assumption, properly understood, is simply a tool for giving structure to theories about the choices people make. Economists then fill in the specifics of the structure by observing what people do in various situations, that is, what choices they make when faced with certain opportunities.

Consider a very simple example. Suppose Bundy Hall, a dormitory, and Carpenter Hall, where economics classes are held, are located at opposite corners of a grassy quadrangle in the middle of a college campus. Across the diagonal of the quad between Bundy and Carpenter, a well-worn path has been beaten into the grass. Why is the path there, even though there are perfectly good sidewalks around all four sides of the quad?

If you ask an economist that question, the answer you get will probably be something like this: "The student's objective is to minimize the time it takes to get to class so that they can sleep as late as possible. Of the alternative routes to class, the diagonal path is the shortest one, so that's the path they choose to take."

Ockham's razor

The principle that simpler theories are to be preferred to more complex ones when both are consistent with given observations.

Most people would probably accept that theory as a reasonable explanation of the path across the quad. Why? First and most important, because it is consistent with the observation that the path is there and students use it. Second, adding to its appeal, the theory corresponds with our intuition about what we would do in the given situation. Although economists are wary of relying too heavily on their own experience to verify their theories, in practice introspection plays a significant role. Finally, our theory about the path across the quad is likely to be accepted partly because it is simple. Economists, like their colleagues in other social and natural sciences, tend to prefer simple theories to complex ones when both are consistent with given observations. (The preference for simple theories over complex ones is known as **Ockham's razor**, after a fourteenth-century philosopher who urged its use to "shave away" unnecessary theoretical complexities.)

So far, so good. But suppose now that a transfer student arrives from another campus and says, "At Treelined University there is a big quad just like this one, and there is no diagonal path across it. Here's a picture to prove it. What do you say to that, O Wise Economist?"

This is not a far-fetched possibility. Observations that are inconsistent with previously accepted theories cross economists' desks frequently. When that happens, they look for a way to modify the theory so that it provides a rational basis for the new observation. Given the structure of economic theory, we can expect the search to take one of two directions.

First, closer investigation will often show that the original theory failed to allow for some *constraint* on the opportunities available to people in the situation under study. For example, it might be that the campus police at Treelined University have a nasty practice of slapping a $20 fine on any student caught walking on the grass. A modified theory is then formulated that takes this constraint into account: "Even when the shortest distance to class is a diagonal across the quad, a fine for walking on the grass will induce a certain percentage of students to take the sidewalk. The percentage taking the sidewalk will increase as the fine increases, so that with a sufficiently large fine, not enough students will take the shortcut to wear a path in the grass." This more general theory is consistent with observations made on both campuses.

Second, if closer investigation fails to turn up some previously unnoticed constraint on opportunities, it may turn out that the original theory was based on a mistaken understanding of the *objectives* of the people involved. In the case under discussion, it was assumed that students on both campuses placed a high priority on getting to class on time. However, perhaps the students of Treelined University take great pride in the appearance of their campus. They would rather be late to class than trample on the grass. Thus, there is a path on one campus and not on the other because students at the two schools rank their objectives differently.

Clearly differing choices can sometimes properly be attributed to differing objectives. For example, if Marcia buys pistachio ice cream while Mark buys chocolate ice cream, and the two flavors cost the same, we are comfortable concluding that their choices differ because their preferences do. However, as a rule, economists like first to see whether an explanation of different choices can be framed in terms of differing constraints on opportunities—prices, regulations, climate, and so on. If constraints are not checked first, explaining things in terms of differing preferences is simply too easy. Take, for example, the fact that people in the United States drive larger cars, on average, than people in Italy. Who would be satisfied just to say that Italians prefer little cars, without noting that drivers in Italy face different constraints—narrower streets, more expensive gasoline, and so on?

Something similar can be said about the rationality assumption. If economists are wary of relying too much on differences in preferences to explain choices, they are even more wary of explaining choices in nonrational terms. Suppose, for example, that an economist sees a student, obviously late for class, who, instead of cutting across the quad or even hurrying around by the sidewalk, is walking slowly in circles in the middle of the grass. The economist questions the student, seeking a rational explanation. "Have you lost a contact lens? Are you exercising?" If an explanation cannot be found in terms of constraints and the rational pursuit of objectives, the economist will conclude that it is time to call in some other specialist, perhaps a psychotherapist.

Economics, then, does not deny that people sometimes behave in ways that cannot be explained rationally. It is just that such behavior is usually considered to lie outside the domain of economics.[2] Consider, for example, the economics of crime—a field of study that attempts to analyze the choice between legitimate and criminal activity in terms of people's objectives and the constraints on their opportunities. Researchers in this field have found evidence that the choice between criminal and legitimate activity is, at least in part, a rational one. But although differences in crime rates can be explained to some degree by such factors as differences in probability of punishment and the influence of job availability on the opportunity to earn legitimate income, few people would expect the economic approach to crime to tell the whole story.

Instead, there is always a large unexplained residual in economic studies of criminal behavior. To some extent, the residual may stem from inadequacies in available data on the risks and rewards of crime as seen by criminals. But it is also likely that crime is only partly rational, only partly based on a balancing of the risks and rewards of alternative courses of action. Other factors also play a role—association with criminal neighbors or relatives, abuse in childhood, and so on. To say that crime is not entirely rational does not mean that the economic approach to crime is a failure—just that it has its limits. Ludwig von Mises put it this way: "The most popular objection raised against economics is that it neglects the irrationality of life and reality and tries to press into dry rational schemes and bloodless abstractions the infinite variety of phenomena. No censure could be more absurd. Like every branch of knowledge, economics goes as far as it can be carried by rational methods. Then it stops by establishing the fact that it is faced with an ultimate given, i.e., a phenomenon which cannot—at least in the present state of knowledge—be further analyzed."[3]

Full rationality

The assumption that people make full use of all available information in calculating how best to meet their objectives.

Bounded rationality

The assumption that people intend to make choices that best serve their objectives, but have limited ability to acquire and process information.

Full and Bounded Rationality

Although rational pursuit of objectives in the face of limited opportunities lies at the heart of economics, some economic theories are based on a stricter notion of rationality than others. Two important versions of the rationality assumption are full rationality and bounded rationality.

Theories based on **full rationality** assume that people make full use of all available information in calculating how best to meet their objectives. The cost of making decisions, the possibility of error, and often, the cost of acquiring information are put to one side in theories based on full rationality.

On the other hand, some theories assume *bounded* rather than full rationality. To assume **bounded rationality** means to assume that people *intend* to make choices that best serve their objectives, but that they have limited ability to acquire and process information. They typically have to rely on partial information and use rules of thumb that do not make full use of the information they have.

For example, consider the task of choosing which university to attend. If college applicants strictly followed the assumption of full rationality, they would make full use of all sources of information available. They would carefully study the information on the Web site of every college in the country. On the basis of the information, they would outline preferred four-year programs of study at each school. They would systematically interview people who had attended all of the schools that rated near the top of their list and would perhaps visit those schools. Only when all information was in hand would they make a choice; in doing so, they might weigh such factors as the probable grades they would earn at each school, the influence of grades and choice of school on their lifetime incomes, and so on.

On the other hand, if applicants followed the assumptions of bounded rationality, they would conduct a more limited search. Perhaps they would arbitrarily limit their search in advance to schools from a certain region. They would listen to what friends and relatives said about schools they had attended and perhaps visit the nearest schools. Their final choice might be based more on advice from people they trusted and less on systematic balancing of objective information.

In the chapters that follow, we will encounter examples of theories based both on full and on bounded rationality. The neoclassical school of economics, which traces its roots to the work of Alfred Marshall a century ago, traditionally employs the full rationality assumption.

MARKET PERFORMANCE AND MARKET FAILURE

Economic choices are not made in a vacuum. They are made within the context of a set of institutions, of which markets and government are two of the most important. This section offers a preview of what coming chapters will have to say about markets, especially the key concepts of *market performance* and *market failure*. The next section will preview the role of government in the economy.

Market Performance

Market performance
The degree to which markets work efficiently in providing arrangements for mutually beneficial trade.

Earlier, we defined a *market* as any arrangement that people have for trading with one another. When economists speak of **market performance**, then, they are referring to how efficiently markets do their job of providing arrangements for mutually beneficial trade.

Ideally, markets would make it possible to carry out every exchange that is to the mutual benefit of the parties involved. Suppose we are talking about the market for peaches. The parties to peach trading are farmers and consumers. An exchange will benefit consumers if the satisfaction they get from a peach is at least as great as the satisfaction they would get from spending the same amount on the next most attractive good (say, an apple). The exchange will benefit producers if the price paid for a peach is at least high enough to cover the opportunity cost of producing it. If there is a price that makes the trade beneficial both to consumers and to producers, then carrying out the trade will be *efficient* inasmuch as it will leave at least one party better off and neither worse off.

Although the details will require several chapters to work out, a simple diagram can give an intuitive idea of efficient market performance. Figure 4.1 shows two curves that represent the market for peaches. The demand curve represents the benefit of peaches to consumers as reflected by their willingness to buy peaches, given the price of peaches, the prices of alternative goods, and so on. The supply curve represents the opportunity costs of producing an additional peach as reflected by the willingness of farmers to produce and sell the product under given conditions.

FIGURE 4.1 PERFORMANCE OF THE MARKET FOR PEACHES

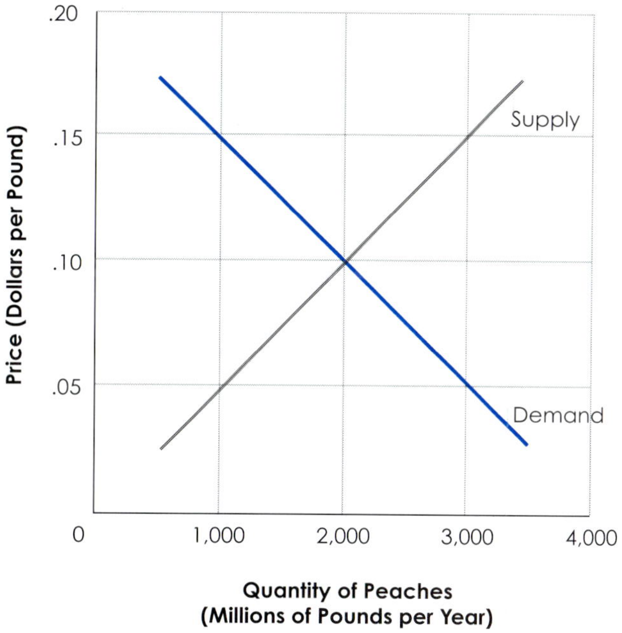

This exhibit shows hypothetical supply and demand curves for peaches. The demand curve reflects the willingness of consumers to buy peaches, given the price of peaches and the prices of alternative goods. The supply curve represents the willingness of farmers to sell peaches, given the price of peaches and the opportunity costs of production. At any point to the left of the intersection of the curves, the price that consumers would willingly pay for a peach (as indicated by the height of the demand curve) is greater than the minimum needed to cover farmers' costs (as indicated by the height of the supply curve). Thus, up to that point, exchanges carried out at a price between the two curves are mutually beneficial to consumers and producers. At any point to the right of the intersection, the maximum amount that consumers would be willing to pay for still more peaches is less than the amount needed to cover farmers' costs. Thus, production beyond the intersection point would not be efficient. It follows, then, that a market in which production is carried out just up to but not beyond the intersection point performs efficiently.

At any point to the left of the intersection of the two curves, the price consumers would willingly pay for a peach (as indicated by the height of the demand curve) is greater than the minimum needed to cover farmers' costs (as indicated by the height of the supply curve). Thus, to the left of the intersection, trades carried out at any price between the two curves are mutually beneficial to consumers and producers. However, to the right of the intersection, the maximum consumers would find it worthwhile to pay for still more peaches is less than what is needed to cover farmers' costs. There is no price at which further trades would benefit both parties, and therefore production beyond the intersection point would not be efficient.

It follows, then, that a market in which production is carried out just up to but not beyond the intersection point performs efficiently. At a lower quantity, some mutually beneficial exchanges would not occur. At a higher quantity, no price could be found that would benefit both parties. Not only is the quantity indicated by the intersection of the two curves just right, but the price is, too. Any higher price would lead to a wasteful surplus of peaches, whereas any lower price would lead to a shortage in which some consumers' wants would not be satisfied.

It is hard to exaggerate the enthusiasm that economists have for markets that generate such efficient outcomes. From those pursuing economic reform in the nations of the former Soviet Union to candidates touting new solutions to problems of American capitalism, there is widespread agreement that within large areas of economic life, markets can be an efficient means of solving basic economic problems. Yet even the most enthusiastic fans of markets recognize that they do not always function perfectly. Several conditions must be met before markets reach a stable equilibrium exactly at the intersection of the supply and demand curves. Let's look briefly at some of the situations in which market performance falls short of the ideal, again leaving details to later chapters.

Market Failure

Market failure

A situation in which a market fails to coordinate choices in a way that achieves efficient use of resources.

A **market failure** is a situation in which a market fails to coordinate choices in a way that achieves efficient use of resources. Of the many possible sources of market failure, three deserve special attention. We will discuss them under the headings of *externalities*, *public goods*, and *insufficient competition*. Other sources of market failure will be mentioned more briefly.

EXTERNALITIES One type of market failure is failure to transmit information about scarcity in the form of prices. For markets to perform their job efficiently, prices should reflect the opportunity costs of producing the goods or services in question. Ordinarily, market prices do reflect at least a reasonable approximation of opportunity costs. However, situations arise in which producers' (and consumers') actions have effects on third parties, that is, people other than the buyer and seller who carry out a transaction. These third-party effects, which are not reflected in

Externalities

The effects of producing or consuming a good whose impact on third parties other than buyers and sellers of the good is not reflected in the good's price.

prices, are known as **externalities**. When externalities are present, the price system does not transmit accurate information about opportunity costs.

The classic example of an externality is pollution. Suppose a utility burns coal in its boilers to generate electricity. The costs of fuel, capital, and labor come to $.05 per kilowatt hour of electricity produced. They are called *internal costs* because they are borne by the utility itself. Those costs are reflected in market transactions—payments to coal producers, workers, stockholders and bondholders, and so on. Internal costs are part of the opportunity cost of making electricity because they represent the forgone opportunities of using the same natural resources, capital, and labor in some other industry. To stay in business, the utility must receive a price of at least $.05 per kilowatt hour, that is, a price at least equal to the internal opportunity costs.

But the internal costs are not the only costs of making electricity, as we saw in the case study at the beginning of the chapter. In the process of burning coal, the utility spews out clouds of sulfur dioxide, soot, and other pollutants. The pollution damages health, kills trees, and corrodes buildings in areas downwind from the plant. Those effects are referred to as *external costs* of generating electricity because they are borne by third parties—people who are neither buyers nor sellers of electricity or any of the inputs used in making it. From the viewpoint of the economy as a whole, external costs are also part of the opportunity cost of generating power. They represent the value of the factors of production that are destroyed by the pollution (such as dead trees or workers in other firms taking extended sick leave) or required in order to repair its effects (repainting houses, treating pollution-related diseases).

Suppose that pollution damage of all kinds comes to $.02 per kilowatt hour of power produced. Added to the $.05 in internal costs, the $.02 of external costs brings the overall opportunity cost of steel to $.07 per kilowatt hour. This figure reflects the value of the factors of production used directly by the utility plus those that are destroyed or diverted from other uses by the pollution.

If the price of electric power is set by supply and demand, its equilibrium value will tend toward the level of $.05 per kilowatt hour that just covers internal costs. But this sends a false signal to users of electricity: It tells them that producing a kilowatt hour puts a smaller drain on the economy's scarce factors of production than is really the case. Thus, electricity users will use more power than they should. They will be less inclined to buy new, more efficient machinery, to design products so as to use less electricity, to shift to cleaner natural gas, and so on. In short, the market will fail to achieve efficient resource allocation because prices will have sent users the wrong information.

In a later chapter, in which we return to the economics of pollution, we will see that externalities can be interpreted as defects in the economy's system of property rights. For example, air pollution arises because no one has clear ownership rights to air. If landowners had the right to control the use of air above their property, they could, in principle, prevent utilities and other pollution sources from using their airspace to dispose of wastes unless they were paid appropriate compensation. Following this reasoning, some economists advocate restructuring property rights to control pollution.

Public goods

Goods that (1) cannot be provided for one person without also being provided for others and (2) when provided for one person can be provided for others at zero additional sum.

PUBLIC GOODS The goods and services discussed in all the examples used to this point—chicken, cars, apartments, and so on—share two characteristics or *properties:* (1) The supplier can decide to supply the good to some people and to exclude others; this is termed the *property of exclusion.* (2) Use of a unit of the good by one person limits the possibility of use of that unit by other people; this is termed the *property of rivalry.* Some goods do not possess the properties of exclusion and rivalry, however. These are known as **public goods**. Lacking the property of exclusion, they cannot be provided for one person without also being provided for others. Lacking the property of rivalry, once they are provided for one person, they can be provided for others at no extra cost. Public goods, like externalities, are a potential source of market failure.

Perhaps the closest thing to a pure public good is national defense. One person cannot be protected against nuclear attack or invasion without the protection being extended to everyone. Also, it costs no more to protect a single resident of an area than to safeguard an entire city or region. Although pure public goods are rare, other goods may lack the properties of exclusion or rivalry to some extent. These can be called impure public goods. Police protection provides one example: In their functions of promoting public safety in general and deterring street crime, the police are providing a public good. But in their function of solving an individual crime, such as a burglary, they are providing a private good to the person who hopes to recover the stolen property. Maintenance of urban streets, the provision of parks, even the space program have been cited as examples of goods that are neither purely public nor purely private.

Private firms have difficulty making a profit selling products that, once they are provided to one customer, become available to others at no additional cost. To see why the market may fail in such cases, imagine that someone tries to set up a private missile defense system—call it Star Wars, Inc.—to be paid for by selling subscriptions to people who want protection from a nuclear attack. There are two reasons I might choose not to subscribe. First, I know that if my neighbors subscribed and got their homes protected, my home would be protected too, even if I did not pay; I could take a *free ride* on a public good paid for by others. Second, I might be willing to contribute if I had *assurance* that at least, say, 1,000 of my neighbors did so. That would raise enough money to buy at least one missile. But I would not contribute without the assurance that this minimum would be met. Contributing along with just 500 neighbors would buy only half a missile, which would be useless, and my contribution would be completely wasted.

Economists have long argued that the *free-rider problem* and the *assurance problem,* which make people reluctant to contribute voluntarily to the support of public goods, mean that government may have to provide those goods if they are to be provided at all. (We say *may* because, as *Applying Economic Ideas 4.1* illustrates, some things that have the characteristics of public goods are provided by private firms.) However, many goods and services that are provided at public expense are public goods only to a small extent, if at all. Take education, for example. The primary beneficiaries of public education are students. It is not impossible to exclude students from the schools. Only a few schools, public or private, operate on an "open admission" basis. Others select their students according to neighborhood, ability to pay, or scholastic achievement. Moreover, education clearly has the property of rivalry in consumption. Students cannot be added to a school without some additional expense. The more students a school admits, the more teachers, classrooms, laboratories, and other facilities it must provide. Thus, education fits the definition of a public good, if at all, only to the extent that it has some overall benefit such as promoting good citizenship.

INSUFFICIENT COMPETITION A third source of market failure is insufficient competition. As we have seen, market prices should reflect opportunity costs if they are to guide resource allocation efficiently. In the case of harmful externalities, market failure occurs because prices fall below opportunity costs. Where competition is insufficient, however, market failure can occur because prices are too high.

Monopoly

A situation in which there is only a single seller of a good or service.

As an extreme case, consider a market in which there is only a single seller of a good or service; such a market is termed a **monopoly**. Residential electric service is a frequently cited example. Suppose that Metropolitan Electric can generate power at an opportunity cost of $10 per kilowatt hour. Selling electric power at that price would guide customers in choosing between electricity and other energy sources, such as oil or coal, and in undertaking energy-saving investments, such as home insulation and high-efficiency lighting.

If homeowners could buy electricity from anyone they chose the way they buy eggs or gasoline, the forces of competition, acting through supply and demand, would push the market price toward the level of opportunity costs. The utility would not sell power at a price below opportunity costs because doing so would put it out of business. Further, in a competitive market any seller that tried to raise prices much above opportunity costs would be undercut by others.

However, utilities do not compete in selling to residential customers. Every home, after all, is connected to only one set of power lines. In this case, if not restrained by government regulation, a utility could substantially increase its profits by charging a price higher than opportunity costs. Of course, raising the price would mean that less power would be sold as customers moved up and to the left along their demand curves. But up to a point, the greater profit per kilowatt hour sold would more than outweigh the effects of the reduction in quantity demanded.

If too high a price is charged, homeowners will get a false message regarding the opportunity cost of electricity. They may make substitutions that are not economically

APPLYING ECONOMIC IDEAS 4.1

PRIVATE PROVISION OF PUBLIC GOODS

Many economists argue that private firms cannot supply public goods because of the assurance and free rider problems that arise whenever goods have the properties of nonexclusion and nonrivalry. In practice, however, private firms and voluntary organizations often do find methods of providing goods that have these properties. Examples include broadcast radio and television, computer software, and amenities like streets and parks in residential neighborhoods.

In some cases private firms simply alter the product in a way that makes it possible to exclude free riders. Thus, television signals can be scrambled so that they can be received only by subscribers who rent a decoder; computer software can be copy protected so that the original purchasers cannot make free copies for their friends; and streets can be equipped with toll booths. In this case, the good ceases to be a public good, even though it continues to have the property of nonrivalry.

Exclusion has its disadvantages, however. The necessary technology may be expensive and less than fully reliable, and the attempt to exclude may be offensive to customers the firm would like to attract. To avoid these disadvantages, private firms and voluntary organizations often use other techniques to provide public goods.

- One approach is to link the public good to an ordinary good, offering the two as a package deal. Thus, public radio stations send their contributors magazines with movie reviews and program guides; computer software companies provide advice via telephone to legitimate registered purchasers; and real estate developers find it worthwhile to build residential streets as part of a package included with the sale of private homes.
- Another approach is to build on the psychological satisfaction of contributing to a good cause or the psychological discomfort of being recognized as a free rider. This works best in small communities where everyone knows everyone else. But organizations like public radio stations can achieve something of the same effect by publicly thanking contributors over the air.
- Still another device is the "assurance contract." Sometimes people hesitate to contribute to a good cause because they fear their contribution will be in vain unless others join them. In such a case, the provider can accept pledges of support that will be activated only if an agreed minimum of support is received. Thus, families might be asked to contribute checks to a fund to build a neighborhood playground on the understanding that the checks will be returned uncashed if the necessary minimum is not raised.

As these examples show, the economic category of "public good" does not always mean a good that must be provided by the government.

justified. For example, they may switch from electricity to oil for heat even in regions where cheap hydroelectric power is available, or from electric air conditioning to gas air conditioning even in areas where the opportunity cost of electricity is below that of gas.

Market failures due to insufficient competition are not necessarily limited to the extreme case of monopoly. Under some circumstances, competition among a small number of firms may also lead to prices that are above opportunity costs, especially if the firms engage in collusion. The circumstances under which competition is or is not sufficient to ensure the efficient operation of markets is the subject of an enormous body of economic research and of more than a few controversies, as we will see in coming chapters.

OTHER MARKET FAILURES Some economists would list other sources of market failure in addition to the three just discussed. For example, the macroeconomic phenomena of inflation and cyclical unemployment are sometimes considered to be market failures. Certainly, an economy that is subject to excessive inflation and unemployment provides a poor environment in which to coordinate the actions of buyers and sellers of individual goods and factor services. However, the effects of inflation and unemployment, together with policies intended to keep them under control, lie outside the scope of the microeconomics course.

As we have defined it, market failure means failure to achieve an *efficient* allocation of scarce resources. In addition, the market may or may not achieve an *equitable* allocation of resources. Whether unfairness, inequality, and economic injustice in a market economy should be given the label *market failure* is more a matter of terminology than of substance. In this book, market failure is defined in a way that makes it an issue of efficiency alone. But this definition is not meant to deny the importance of issues of economic justice. Such issues will be discussed extensively at several points in the following chapters, although not under the heading of market failure.

THE ECONOMIC ROLE OF GOVERNMENT

Although markets play an enormous role in answering the key questions of who, what, how, and for whom, not all economic decisions are made in markets. Some important economic decisions are made in hierarchies. Allocation of resources within a business firm is one example of hierarchical decision making; we will focus on that later. Here we are concerned with the role of government, the other major example of hierarchy in economics.

If we want to understand the microeconomic role of government, a good place to begin is by asking, Why does government play any role in the economy at all? Why, that is, cannot all decisions be made by households and private firms coordinating their actions through markets? Economists offer two answers, one based on the notion of market failure, the other on that of *rent seeking*. The answers are partly contradictory and partly complementary. Each will figure prominently in coming chapters, and each deserves a brief preview here.

The Market Failure Theory of Government

According to the market failure theory of government, the principal economic role of government is to step in where markets fail to allocate resources efficiently and fairly. Each type of market failure calls for a particular type of governmental intervention.

Take the case of pollution. Earlier we gave the example of a utility whose contribution to air pollution caused \$.02 worth of damage for every kilowatt hour of electricity. Government can do a number of things to correct the resulting market failure, for example, it can require the utility to install pollution control equipment that will prevent poisonous gas from escaping into the atmosphere.

When markets fail to supply public goods, government also is called in. Often, as in the case of national defense, the government simply becomes the producer of the public good. In other cases, such as education, which some economists consider to be in part a public good, the government need not be the sole producer. Private schools and colleges are encouraged with subsidies and tax benefits to add to the supply of education produced by public institutions.

Government has attempted to remedy market failures arising from insufficient competition in a variety of ways. In some cases government uses *antitrust laws* to preserve competition by preventing mergers of competing firms, or even by breaking large firms up into a number of smaller ones. In other cases, such as the electric power industry, *regulation* is used to control prices charged by a monopoly firm. In a few cases, such as the Tennessee Valley Authority's electric power facilities, the government itself may become a monopoly producer of a good or service.

The Public Choice Theory of Government

The market failure theory of government is sometimes criticized for being more of a theory about what the government ought to do than about what it actually does. The problem, say the critics, is that too many government programs, rather than correcting market failures, seem to promote inefficiency or inequality in markets that would function well without government intervention. Price supports for milk are an example. That program holds the price of milk above its equilibrium level, thus causing persistent surpluses. That is hardly efficient. Further, although some benefits go to farmers who are in financial difficulty, thus serving the goal of fairness, many of the subsidies go to farmers who are financially well off.

Critics of the market failure theory maintain that government policies should be understood not in terms of broad social goals like efficiency and fairness but in terms of how people use the institutions of government to pursue their own self-interest. This approach to policy analysis is known as **public choice theory**.

Public choice theory

The branch of economics that studies how people use the institutions of government in pursuit of their own interests.

Economic rent

Any payment to a factor of production in excess of its opportunity cost.

RENTS AND RENT SEEKING One of the key concepts of public choice theory is *economic rent*. In everyday language, a *rent* is simply a payment made for the use of something, say, an apartment or a car. Public choice theorists use the term in a more specialized sense, however. An **economic rent** is any payment to a factor of production in excess of its opportunity cost. An example is the huge income a popular author like J. K. Rowling or Dan Brown earns from a new novel—an income much higher than the author could earn working the same amount time in any other line of work.

When rents are earned through competition in markets, they are called *pure economic profits*. Entrepreneurs are always on the lookout for earning such profits, for example, by introducing a new product superior to that of rival firms, or by being the first to implement a cost-saving production method. When they are successful, the income they earn may be substantially higher than what others are able to earn by employing similar factors of production in less imaginative ways.

Pure economic profit that entrepreneurs earn through private market activity is not the only category of economic rents, however. Firms, workers, and resource owners often turn to government in search of rents, rather than trying to outwit their rivals in the marketplace. A dollar earned through a government program that raises the price at which a firm sells its output or lowers the prices at which it buys its inputs is worth just as much as a dollar of profit earned through purely private efforts at innovation. In some cases it may even be better. Profits earned from innovation in a competitive market may be short lived because rivals will soon come out with an even better product or introduce an even cheaper production method. However, government regulations can not only create opportunities to earn rents but also shield those opportunities from competitors. Obtaining and defending rents through government action is known as **political rent seeking**, or often simply as **rent seeking**, with the political aspect implied.[4]

Political rent seeking (rent seeking)

The process of seeking and defending economic rents through the political process.

Consider the case of milk price supports, which, as we saw earlier, are hard to explain in terms of the market failure theory of government. Public choice theorists see this policy as a classic case of *political rent seeking*. Because a large portion of the benefits of price supports go to farmers who are not in trouble, broad-ranging programs generating rents for all farmers will draw much wider political support than programs more narrowly targeted only on needy farmers. Without the political support of the relatively prosperous farmers who draw the bulk of the subsidies, say public choice theorists, programs for farmers in trouble would not get the votes they need in Congress.

Government restrictions on competition are another way of generating rents. For example, tariffs and import quotas on clothing, cars, sugar, steel, and other products shield domestic firms and their employees from foreign competition. The firms thus are able to earn rents by raising prices above the competitive market level, and the employees are able to earn rents in the form of higher wages. Examples of government restrictions on competition can be found within the domestic economy as well. For example, licensing fees and examinations restrict the number of competitors who can enter such professions as law and medicine and often even such occupations as manicuring and hair styling.

FROM THE LAW OF UNINTENDED CONSEQUENCES TO GOVERNMENT FAILURE The notion that government policies do not always promote efficiency and equity is not new. Economists have long been aware of the law of unintended consequences—the tendency of government policies to have effects other than those desired by their proponents. But public choice theory goes beyond the notion of unintended consequences, which could be traced simply to incomplete analysis on the part of policy makers. Rather, the element of rent seeking in the formulation of government policy suggests that there is a systematic tendency for government programs to cause rather than to cure economic inefficiencies—a tendency, that is, toward **government failure**.

Government failure

A situation in which a government policy causes inefficient use of resources.

In introducing the notion of government failure, public choice theorists do not intend to imply that government always makes a mess of things or that the market always functions perfectly; rather, they demonstrate that both the market and government are imperfect institutions. In deciding whether a given function is better performed by government or the market, the possibilities of government failure must be weighed against those of market failure.

Looking Ahead

This chapter has provided an overview of microeconomics in terms of theory and institutions. All economic theory has a common core: the analysis of rational choice given certain objectives and constraints. The great variety within economics comes in large part from the wide range of institutional settings within which these common elements of theory are applied.

Looking ahead, the chapters that follow focus almost exclusively on market institutions. The topics covered in those chapters constitute the core of neoclassical economics and serve as a reference point for all further developments in economic theory. In keeping with the neoclassical tradition, the models presented in those chapters are kept simple through the use of several assumptions:

1. An assumption of full rationality. Decision makers are seen as having well-defined objectives (for example, profit maximization) and as being competent to make use of all available information in choosing how best to pursue those objectives.
2. An emphasis on the price system as the economy's key mechanism for transmitting information. The prices of all goods and services are typically assumed to be public information available free to all households and firms. For the most part, costs of acquiring information are ignored.
3. An emphasis on formal models of economic behavior that can be stated in graphical or mathematical terms, and a focus on conditions of equilibrium. Comparatively little attention is paid to disequilibrium, change, and innovation, especially when formulating formal models.
4. Treatment of households, firms, and where considered, government agencies as "black boxes." The main focus is on the interactions of these units in the marketplace. Relatively little attention is paid to the workings of their internal hierarchies.

The very restrictiveness of these assumptions is the source of much of the success of neoclassical theory. Neoclassical economics is like a searchlight that is able to illuminate objects brightly precisely because it is focused narrowly. In the following chapters, we will encounter one situation after another, ranging from highway safety to negotiations among OPEC oil ministers, where neoclassical economics provides insights of striking clarity and predictions that stand up remarkably well to the test of experience.

Despite the century-old success of neoclassical microeconomics, in recent decades economists have become interested in a number of problems that its narrowly focused searchlight cannot adequately illuminate. The chapters in Parts III and IV take up a number of extensions of neoclassical theory, and, in some cases, challenges to it. In these chapters, many of the simplifying assumptions of the neoclassical tradition are modified.

Chapter 12 begins by lifting the lid of the business firm to look at the economic relationships inside. In the process, the costs of carrying out agreements and enforcing their terms—so-called transaction costs—become a central issue. Also, to explain some features of the firm's organization, it becomes useful to assume bounded rather than full rationality. Among the questions explored in Chapter 12: Why do firms exist at all? Why do they take on so many forms—proprietorships, partnerships, corporations, cooperatives? Why do managers acting as the agent of stockholders control most firms, rather than workers?

Chapter 13 gathers together several strands of thought that constitute the field of information economics. In this field, the price system, although still occupying a very important place, is seen as just one among many sources of information. Moreover, information is treated as costly to acquire and unevenly distributed. Applications in this chapter range from insurance to the difficulty of buying a good used car.

Chapter 14 takes up the topic of economic change. A central focus of the chapter is entrepreneurship, through which firms and households challenge old constraints with new products, new production methods, and new forms of organization. Among the views considered in this chapter are those of the Austrian school, which has a hundred-year history of its own and sees itself as a rival to neoclassical economics.

Chapter 15 rounds out Part III with a survey of public choice theory. Part IV then applies both traditional neoclassical tools and their more recent extensions to five areas of government policy—antitrust and regulation, externalities and environmental policy, labor policy, poverty and income distribution, and international trade.

SUMMARY

1. **What is the basic structure of economic theory?** Economic theories are constructed from statements about people's objectives, aims, and preferences; statements about the constraints on available opportunities; and statements about how people choose among the available opportunities so as to best meet their objectives.

2. **Why is rationality of central importance to economics?** To be rational means to act purposefully to achieve one's objectives, given the available opportunities. In some cases, economists assume *full rationality,* which means that they assume that people make full use of all available information in calculating how best to meet their objectives. In other cases, they assume *bounded rationality,* which means that they assume that people intend to

make the choices that best serve their objectives, but have limited ability to acquire and process information.

3. **What is the meaning of market performance and market failure?** *Market performance* refers to how efficiently markets do their job of providing arrangements for mutually beneficial trade. Ideally, markets would make it possible to carry out every possible mutually beneficial trade, in which case they would operate perfectly efficiently. Sometimes, however, *market failure* occurs, in which case markets fail to carry out their job efficiently. *Externalities, public goods,* and insufficient competition (leading to *monopoly*) are among the most widely discussed sources of market failure.

4. **What are some alternative theories of the economic role of government?** According to the market failure theory of government, everything that markets can do efficiently should be left to them. Government should intervene only to correct market failures, whether narrowly or broadly defined. Another theory maintains that many government policies are not efforts to correct market failure but, instead, result from *political rent seeking.* Rent seeking refers to the process of seeking payments in excess of opportunity costs.

KEY TERMS

Property rights
Rationality
Ockham's razor
Full rationality
Bounded rationality
Market performance
Market failure
Externalities
Public goods
Monopoly
Public choice theory
Economic rent
Political rent seeking (rent seeking)
Government failure

PROBLEMS AND TOPICS FOR DISCUSSION

1. **Examining the lead-off case.** Discuss possible market failures in the market for electric power. Is electricity a public good? Why or why not? Might there be problems of insufficient competition in some markets for electricity? If so, what would be the consequences for the price of electricity? Under what conditions would pollution cause a market failure in this market? What are possible remedies? Would action by government to correct market failure necessarily result in an efficient equilibrium? Why or why not?

2. **Alternative path theories.** The chapter proposes a simple theory to explain the existence of a path across a grassy area on a certain college campus. Here is another theory that might also explain the path: "Economics lectures are so boring that students prefer to be late to them. However, near the sidewalk on one side of the quad there is a beehive, and many students have suffered stings; and on the other side of the quad is the chemistry building, which smells bad when the wind blows a certain way. Sometimes if you cut across the middle of the quad, you find four-leaf clovers that give you good luck on your exams. Those are the reasons that there is a path across the quad." Applying the principle of Ockham's razor, which theory do you think is better? Why? Would you reject the more complex theory out of hand, or would you first want to make some observations? What observations would you make?

3. **Italians in America.** According to a theory suggested in the chapter, people drive smaller cars in Italy than in the United States not because of different preferences but because they face different constraints on their opportunities—higher gasoline prices, narrower streets, and so on. On the basis of that theory, what prediction would you

make about the cars driven by Italians who move to the United States? What kind of observations would you suggest to test whether preferences or constraints are the key factor in the choice of car size?

4. **An alternate definition of economics.** David Friedman has said that economics can be defined as "that way of understanding behavior that assumes that people are rational." Compare Friedman's definition with the one presented in Chapter 1 of this book. What similarities or differences do you see?

5. **The economics of voting.** Did you vote in the most recent state or national election? If so, how was your choice of a candidate influenced by your objectives and constraints? If you did not vote, was your decision not to vote influenced by objectives and constraints? Do you think your choice of a candidate (or your choice not to vote) was a rational one? Discuss.

6. **Government failure versus market failure.** When the possibilities of both government failure and market failure are taken into account, does the fact that a government policy causes inefficiency necessarily mean that abolishing the policy would result in greater efficiency? Does the fact that a certain market fails to work efficiently necessarily mean that intervention by government would improve the situation? Discuss.

CASE FOR DISCUSSION

A Price That's Too Good to Be Bad

Almost any aisle of any supermarket is a battleground in the never-ending war between house brands and national brands. The weapons of the national brands are advertising, reputation, and brand recognition. The big gun on the side of the house brands is price. One day recently, for example, shoppers at a Virginia Safeway store could take their choice of Johnson & Johnson baby powder for $3.29 or a can of Safeway brand at $2.59; of Kellogg's cornflakes at $1.97 per box or the house brand at $1.59; of Wesson vegetable oil at $4.59 per bottle or Safeway's product at $3.39 per bottle; or of Heinz distilled vinegar at $1.93 per quart or Safeway's Townhouse brand at $1.23.

What logic lies behind this competition? One's first thought might be that it all depends on the law of demand. If so, one would think, the lower the price of the house brand, the higher its sales relative to the national brand. But marketers of consumer products have found that the law of demand applies only up to a point in the competition between house brands and national brands. Paradoxically, a price that is *too* low can actually hurt the sales of the house brand.

Consider the case of Pathmark supermarkets' Premium All Purpose cleaner. This house brand product was designed to compete head-to-head with Fantastik, the leading national brand. The two products were chemically identical. The house brand's packaging mimicked that of the national brand. And Pathmark's product was priced at just $.89, versus $1.79 for Fantastik.

Yet, from its first introduction, Premium All Purpose cleaner was a slow seller. Frustrated Pathmark marketers even added a sticker to the label that said, "If you like Fantastik, try me!" But the sticker did not help. Finally Pathmark decided to drop the product.

What went wrong? Interviewed by *The Wall Street Journal,* Robert Wunderle, a spokesman for Supermarket General Corporation, Pathmark's corporate parent, blamed the failure on a price "so low that it discredited the intrinsic value of the product."

Many retailers consider it risky to price their house brands more than 20 to 25 percent below the national brand. But there are exceptions. If the product is so simple and familiar that consumers believe there can be no quality difference, it is safe to establish a bigger discount. Thus, for example, Safeway puts a bigger discount on its house brand vinegar and vegetable oil than on its house brand baby powder or cornflakes.

Peter Schwartz, president of Daymon Associates, Inc., a private-label research and marketing firm, explains the problem this way: "The further the distance from the national brand, the higher the credibility problem for consumers. Once you get outside the customer's comfort zone, the consumer psychology becomes, 'Gee, they must have taken it out in quality.' "

Source: Based in part on Alix M. Freedman, "A Price That's Too Good May Be Bad," *The Wall Street Journal,* November 15, 1988, B1.

QUESTIONS

1. Would you characterize the behavior of consumers who buy Fantastik brand cleaner instead of Pathmark's Premium All-Purpose cleaner as full rationality, irrationality, or bounded rationality? Explain.
2. The case suggests that in choosing among alternative brands of goods, consumers sometimes rely on the rule of thumb that higher prices tend to be associated with higher quality. From your own experience as a shopper, do you think that this rule of thumb is valid on the average? Valid always? Rarely valid? Give examples.
3. A consumer who followed the assumptions of bounded rationality would be most likely to apply the preceding rule of thumb, rather than seeking independent information on product quality, in purchasing which kinds of goods?
   a. Major purchases such as automobiles.
   b. Goods that are purchased frequently and can easily be inspected, such as clothing.
   c. Goods like household cleaners that are purchased infrequently constitute a small part of the consumer's budget and cannot easily be inspected or tested before purchase. Discuss why the rule of thumb is more reasonable in some cases than others, and give additional examples of each case.

END NOTES

1. Thorstein Veblen, "In Dispraise of Economists," in *The Portable Veblen,* ed. Max Lerner (New York: Viking Press, 1958), 232–233.
2. Economist Robert H. Frank of Cornell University argues that some emotional behavior associated with feelings such as rage, guilt, or shame can be understood in terms of economics even though they are not "rational" in the sense of serving the immediate practical goals of the individual on a situation-by-situation basis. As an example, he cites the case of a person who, because of feelings of guilt or pride, would not steal from her employer even if certain not to be detected. A person known to have such "irrational" feelings would have an advantage in seeking promotion to a position of trust in the firm, and the presence of many such individuals would make the firm as a whole function more smoothly. In this and other cases cited by Frank, the expectation that people will respond to situations in emotional rather than in narrowly rational terms facilitates economic coordination. See *Passions within Reason* (New York: W. W. Norton, 1989) and "Beyond Self-Interest," *Challenge* (March–April 1989), 4–13.
3. Ludwig von Mises, *Human Action,* 3rd ed. (Chicago: Henry Regnery, 1966), 21.
4. For a representative collection of papers on the theory of rent seeking, see James M. Buchanan, Robert D. Tollison, and Gordon Tullock, eds., *Toward a Theory of the Rent-Seeking Society* (College Station: Texas A&M Press, 1980).

CHAPTER 5

Consumer Choice

After reading this chapter, you will understand:

1. The elements involved in consumers' rational choices
2. How consumers balance their choices of goods and services to achieve an equilibrium
3. What lies behind the effect of a price change on the quantity of a good demanded
4. Why demand curves have negative slopes
5. Why both consumers and producers gain from exchanges
6. Why the burden of a tax exceeds the revenue raised by government

Before reading this chapter, make sure you know the meaning of:

1. Substitutes and complements
2. Normal and inferior goods
3. Incidence of a tax

DANGER: CHILDREN AND PEDESTRIANS!

Can government regulations requiring the use of seat belts or air bags in cars endanger bicyclists and pedestrians? Can government regulations requiring safety caps on aspirin bottles endanger children? What about motorcyclists wearing helmets? Strange as it may seem, some economists think they can.

Economist Sam Peltzman started the controversy over seat belts with a study that found when people felt their cars to be safer, they reacted by driving faster and less cautiously. The increase in the number of pedestrians and bicyclists mowed down offset the decrease in the number of drivers and passengers who were killed in accidents. Other studies challenge the finding of no net gain in safety from seat belts and air bags, but many of these also found that safer cars result in some increase in danger to pedestrians.

A similar effect may apply to safety caps on aspirin bottles. A study by W. Kip Viscusi found that the safety-cap regulation did not reduce the rate of aspirin poisoning among children. In fact, the proportion of poisonings linked to safety-capped aspirin bottles is greater than the proportion of aspirin sales accounted for by bottles with safety caps. The reason may be that the caps are hard even for adults to use—especially those with fingers stiffened by arthritis who take aspirin for pain relief. To save themselves trouble, many leave the caps off the bottles. Children then find the open bottles and poison themselves.

Are these findings evidence of human stupidity? Of irrationality? Of evil intent? Economists think not; rather, they are simply an outcome of the logic of consumer choice—a logic that government regulators do not always take into account.

Sources: Sam Peltzman, "The Effects of Automobile Safety Regulation," *Journal of Political Economy* 83 (August 1975): 677–725; Robert W. Crandall and John D. Graham, "Automobile Safety Regulation and Offsetting Behavior: Some New Empirical Estimates," *American Economic Review* 74 (May 1984): 328–331; and W. Kip Viscusi, "The Lulling Effect: The Impact of Child-Resistant Packaging on Aspirin and Analgesic Ingestions," *American Economic Review* 74 (May 1984): 324–327.

A CHAPTER TITLE LIKE "Consumer Choice" may evoke an image of people filling their shopping carts in a supermarket, and the economic theory of consumer behavior does apply in a supermarket. But its uses extend much further, as the cases of seat belts and aspirin bottle safety caps suggest. As we will see in this chapter, it applies to any scenario in which people make choices so as to obtain the most satisfaction they can in a situation of scarcity, given the alternatives and opportunity costs that they face. This chapter begins by outlining a theory of rational choice by consumers. Later, it will explore a number of applications of the theory, some of them quite ordinary, others more surprising.

UTILITY AND THE RATIONAL CONSUMER

Economic theories have a typical structure that can be described in terms of statements about objectives, constraints, and choices. Theories of consumer choice fit this pattern. The study of consumer choice thus gives us a chance to fill in the general structure of economic theory with some specific content.

Utility

We begin with the question of consumer *objectives*—why is it that people consume goods and services at all? The answer that people usually give when they think about their own motivations is that consumption of goods and services is a source of pleasure and satisfaction. A loaf of bread to eat, a warm bed to sleep in, a book to read—each serves a particular consumer want or need.

Utility

The pleasure, satisfaction, or need fulfillment that people obtain from the consumption of goods and services.

Economists use the term **utility** to refer to the pleasure or satisfaction people get from the consumption of goods and services. The term goes back some 200 years to the work of the eccentric English social philosopher Jeremy Bentham (1748–1832). Bentham, who studied English law and came to hate it, was obsessed with reforming the law in a way consistent with the principle of the "greatest good for the greatest number." He thought ordinary words such as *pleasure, satisfaction,* or *happiness* were too weak to convey the power of his vision of maximum bliss, so he coined the new word *utility* and established a quasi-religious movement called utilitarianism to promote the idea. Over the centuries, the term *utility* has lost the mystical overtones that it had for Bentham and his followers, but economists still use it in preference to its more ordinary synonyms when they refer to the objective that consumers pursue when choosing among goods and services.

Constraints on Opportunities

Having established utility as the objective, the next step in constructing the theory of consumer choice is to find a way of describing the constraints on the set of opportunities available to consumers. Those constraints encompass all the circumstances that, in a world of scarcity, prevent people from consuming all they want of everything they want.

The most important constraints are limits on the types of goods available, the prices of those goods, and the size of the consumer's budget. A restaurant menu provides a classic example of a constrained opportunity set. You may want tofu salad for lunch, but it is not on the menu. Among the dishes that are on the menu, your favorite might be the filet mignon, but the filet is $18 a serving, and your budget constrains you to spend no more than $5 on lunch. In the end, you settle for a cheeseburger.

To be sure, there are situations in which constraints other than budgets and market prices may be the most important ones. In choosing how fast to drive your car, the "price" (opportunity cost) of greater safety may be taking more time to get where you are going. In choosing a spouse, one constraint is the law that says you can be married to only one person at a time. Later in the chapter, we will look at some examples of nonmarket choices, but choices made in markets remain the central focus of consumer theory.

In constructing a theory of the choices consumers make to maximize utility within their budget constraints, we will proceed in two steps. First, we look at a traditional version of the theory based directly on the notion of utility; then we look at a more modern version in which utility plays a less explicit role.

Diminishing Marginal Utility and Consumer Choice

Jeremy Bentham's notion of "the greatest good for the greatest number" was anything but scientific. In the late nineteenth century, William Stanley Jevons and other economists, working independently, took a major step forward in their understanding of rational choice by consumers when they developed the principle of diminishing marginal utility (see *Who Said It? Who Did It? 5.1*). That step was based on the insight that most of the choices consumers make are not all-or-nothing matters (such as whether to take up smoking or to swear off smoking forever); instead, they are incremental decisions (such as whether to eat chicken one more time a month). Whenever economists refer to the effects of doing a little more or a little less of something, they apply the adjective *marginal*. Thus, the **marginal utility** of a good is the amount of added utility that a consumer gains from consuming one more unit of that good, other things being equal.

Marginal utility

The amount of added utility gained from a one-unit increase in consumption of a good, other things being equal.

The most important principle arrived at by Jevons and others is that of **diminishing marginal utility**. According to this principle, the greater the quantity of any good consumed, the less the marginal utility derived from consuming one more unit of that good.

Principle of diminishing marginal utility

The principle that the greater the consumption of some good, the smaller the increase in utility from a one-unit increase in consumption of that good.

Let us look at how the principle of diminishing marginal utility can be applied to an everyday situation. Assume that you are seated at a lunch counter where pizza is being sold at a price of $2 for a rather skimpy slice and lemonade is being sold at a price of $1 for a small glass. You have $10 to spend on lunch. What will you order?

Your objective is to choose a lunch that will give you the greatest possible utility. Will you spend all your money to buy five pieces of pizza? Probably not. However much you like pizza, you will not get as much satisfaction out of the fifth piece as the first—at least not according to the principle of diminishing marginal utility. Probably you will be willing to pass up the fifth piece of pizza to have a couple of glasses of lemonade with which to wash the first four down. Doing so will increase your total utility, because the first two lemonades will give you a lot of satisfaction and the last piece of pizza only a little. How about the fourth piece of pizza? Maybe you will be willing to give up half of it for one more glass of lemonade. As you cut back on pizza and increase your consumption of lemonade, the marginal utility of pizza rises and that of lemonade falls. Finally you get to the point at which you cannot increase your utility by spending less on one good and more on the other within a given budget. You have reached a point of **consumer equilibrium**.

Consumer equilibrium

A state of affairs in which a consumer cannot increase the total utility gained from a given budget by spending less on one good and more on another.

You reach consumer equilibrium when the marginal utility you get from a dollar's worth of one good equals the marginal utility you get from a dollar's worth of the other. Another way to state this is that the ratio of the marginal utility of a good to its price must be the same for all goods. Thus:

$$\frac{\text{Marginal utility of good A}}{\text{Price of good A}} = \frac{\text{Marginal utility of good B}}{\text{Price of good B}}$$

This formula can be applied using an imaginary unit of utility, the "util." Suppose, for example, that you have adjusted the quantities of pizza and lemonade you buy so that you get 10 utils from another slice of pizza at a price of $2 per slice and 5 utils from another glass of lemonade at a price of $1 per glass. At these ratios, you get no more added satisfaction from an extra dollar's worth (one half-slice) of pizza than from an extra dollar's worth (one glass) of lemonade. It is not worthwhile to trade off some of either good for some of the other. You are in consumer equilibrium.

On the other hand, suppose you get 18 utils from another slice of pizza (9 utils per half-slice) and 4 from another glass of lemonade, still given the same prices. Now you are not in consumer equilibrium. Cutting back by one lemonade would lose you

WHO SAID IT? WHO DID IT? 5.1

WILLIAM STANLEY JEVONS AND MARGINAL UTILITY THEORY

The English economist William Stanley Jevons is credited with the first systematic statement of the theory of marginal utility. Jevons was trained in mathematics and chemistry. With this background, it is not surprising that when his interest turned to economics he tried to restate economic theories in mathematical terms. It was this effort that led him to the theory of marginal utility.

In his *Theory of Political Economy*, published in 1871, Jevons set forth the principle of diminishing marginal utility:

> *Let us imagine the whole quantity of food which a person consumes on an average during twenty-four hours to be divided into ten equal parts. If his food be reduced by the last part, he will suffer but little; if a second tenth part be deficient, he will feel the want distinctly; the subtraction of the third part will be decidedly injurious; with every subsequent subtraction of a tenth part his sufferings will be more and more serious until at length he will be upon the verge of starvation. Now, if we call each of the tenth parts an increment, the meaning of these facts is, that each increment of food is less necessary, or possesses less utility, than the previous one.*

Jevons was the first economist to put the new theory into print, but he shares credit for the "marginal revolution" with at least three others who were working along the same lines simultaneously. The Austrian economist Carl Menger also published his version of marginal utility theory in 1871. Three years later, the Swiss economist Leon Walras, who was not aware of Jevons's or Menger's work, came out with still another version. Finally, Alfred Marshall worked out the basics of marginal utility theory at about the same time in his lectures at Cambridge, although he did not publish his version until 1890.

just 4 utils. You could then use the dollar you saved to buy another half-slice of pizza, thereby gaining 9 utils. By making this adjustment in your consumption pattern, you would not only gain total utility, but also move closer to consumer equilibrium, because the marginal utility you would get from pizza would fall slightly as you consumed more and the marginal utility you would get from lemonade would rise a little as you consumed less.

Attaching numbers to things in this way helps explain the principle involved. Remember, though, that in practice consumer choice is a much more subjective process. Some people count calories when they sit down to lunch; some count the pennies in their pockets; but no one counts "utils"—they cannot really be counted. Utility is something we feel, not something we think about. Because some people feel differently about what they eat than others do, they make different choices. Perhaps you would rather have a cold squid salad and a glass of iced coffee than either pizza or lemonade. Although your choice might differ from someone else's, the logic of the decision—the calculation of utility, the concept of equilibrium—is the same.

From Consumer Equilibrium to the Law of Demand

The concepts of consumer equilibrium and diminishing marginal utility can be combined to give an explanation of the law of demand. The explanation, which is useful even though it is not entirely precise, goes as follows: Suppose you have adjusted your pattern of consumption until you have reached an equilibrium in which, among other things,

$$\frac{\text{MU of pizza}}{\$2} = \frac{\text{MU of lemonade}}{\$1}$$

As long as this equality holds, you will not benefit from increasing your consumption of pizza; doing so would soon push down the marginal utility of pizza. The marginal utility per dollar's worth of pizza would drop below the marginal utility per dollar's worth of lemonade, making you better off if you switched back to more lemonade.

But what if the price of pizza were to drop to, say, $1.50 per slice, upsetting the equality just given? To make the two ratios equal again, given the new price of pizza, either the marginal utility of lemonade would have to rise or that of pizza would have to fall. According to the principle of diminishing marginal utility, one way to get the marginal utility of pizza to fall is to consume more pizza, and one way to get the marginal utility of lemonade to rise is to consume less lemonade. Perhaps you would do a little of both—that is, cut back a little on lemonade and consume a little more pizza. In so doing, you would be acting just as the law of demand would predict: A decrease in the price of pizza would have caused you to buy more pizza.

This line of reasoning connects the law of demand with the principle of diminishing marginal utility in a way that appeals to common sense. However, that is not good enough for all economists. In the next section, we will look at an alternative line of reasoning.

SUBSTITUTION AND INCOME EFFECTS

In the view of some economists, the whole concept of utility is suspect because of its subjective, unmeasurable nature. Instead, they favor an explanation of the law of demand based on the concepts of substitution and income effects of a change in price. The two approaches to demand are, in a broad sense, consistent, but the explanation based on income and substitution effects avoids direct dependence on marginal utility and the measurement of utility.

The Substitution Effect

One reason people buy more of a good whose price falls is that they tend to substitute a good with a lower price for other goods that are relatively expensive. In our earlier example, we looked at the effects of a drop in the price of pizza. The change in price will cause people to substitute pizza for other foods that they might otherwise have eaten—hamburgers, nachos, whatever. Broader substitutions are also possible. With the price of pizza lower than before, people may substitute eating out for eating at home or a pizza party for an evening at the movies. The portion of the increase in the quantity demanded of a good whose price has fallen that is caused by the substitution of that good for other goods, which are now relatively more costly, is known as the **substitution effect** of a change in price.

Substitution effect

The part of the increase in quantity demanded of a good whose price has fallen that is caused by substitution of that good for others that are now relatively more costly.

The Income Effect

A second reason that the change in a good's price will cause a change in the quantity demanded has to do with the effect of price changes on real income.

In economics, the term *nominal* is used to refer to quantities measured in the ordinary way, in terms of the dollar prices at which transactions actually take place. The term *real* is used to indicate quantities that have been adjusted to take into account the effects of price changes. The distinction between real and nominal income is a typical application of these terms: If your monthly paycheck is $1,000, that is your nominal income—the number of dollars you earn. If your nominal income stays at $1,000 while inflation doubles the average prices of all goods and services, your *real* income—your ability to buy things taking price changes into account—will fall by half. If your nominal income stays at $1,000 while the average prices of goods and services drop by half, your real income will double.

In macroeconomics the distinction between real and nominal income is widely used in connection with inflation, which involves changes in the prices of many goods at once. But the distinction can also be applied in microeconomics, which tends to emphasize the effects of price changes for one good at a time. The reason is that if the price of even one good changes while the prices of other goods remain constant, there will be some effect on the average price level and, hence, on real income.

With this in mind, let us return to our example. Again suppose that the price of pizza falls while your nominal income and the prices of all other goods and services remain the same. Although pizza occupies only a small place in your budget, a fall in its price means a slight fall in the average level of all prices and, hence, a slight increase in your real income. If you continued to buy the same quantity of pizza and other goods and services as before, you would have a little money left over. For example, if the price of pizza goes down by $.50 a slice and you usually buy ten slices a month, you would have $5 left over after making your usual purchases. That is as much of an increase in your real income as you would get if your paycheck were increased by $5 and all prices remained constant.

The question now is: What will you spend the $5 on? The answer: You will use it to buy more of things that are normal goods. If pizza is a normal good, one of the things you will buy with your increased real income is more pizza. The portion of the change in quantity demanded of a good whose price has fallen that is caused by the increase in real income resulting from the drop in price is known as the **income effect** of the price change.

Income effect
The part of the change in quantity demanded of a good whose price has fallen that is caused by the increase in real income resulting from the price change.

Income and Substitution Effects and the Demand Curve

In the case of a normal good, the income effect is an additional reason for buying more of a good when its price falls. With both the income and substitution effects causing the quantity demanded to increase when the price falls, the demand curve for a normal good will have a negative slope. We can reach this conclusion with no reference to the awkward concept of utility. So far, so good.

If we are dealing with an inferior good, however, the situation is a little different. Let us say that hot dogs are an inferior good for you. You eat them if you are hungry and they are all you can afford, but if your income goes up enough to buy pizza, you phase out hot dogs. Now what will happen if the price of hot dogs goes down while the prices of all other goods and services remain constant?

First, there will be a substitution effect. Hot dogs now are relatively cheaper compared with lemonade, pizza, pretzels, haircuts, or whatever. Taken by itself, the substitution effect will cause you to buy more hot dogs. Other things (including real income) being equal, the rational consumer will always buy more rather than less of something when its opportunity cost (in this case, its price relative to other goods) goes down. But here other things are not equal. At the same time that the fall in the price of hot dogs tempts you to substitute hot dogs for other things, it also raises your real income slightly. Taken by itself, the increase in your real income would cause you to buy fewer hot dogs because hot dogs are an inferior good for you. Thus, in the case of an inferior good, the substitution and income effects work at cross-purposes when the price changes.

What, then, is the net effect of a decrease in the price of hot dogs? Will you buy more or fewer of them than before? In the case of a good that makes up only a small part of your budget, such as hot dogs, it is safe to assume that a fall in price will cause you to buy more and a rise in price to buy less. The reason is that a change in the price of something of which you buy only a little anyway will have only a miniscule income effect, which will be outweighed by the substitution effect. Thus, when the substitution effect is larger than the income effect, the demand curve for an inferior good will still have a negative slope.

However, there is a theoretical possibility that the demand curve for an inferior good might have a positive slope. For this to be the case, the good would have to make up a large part of a person's budget so that the income effect would be large. Imagine, for example, a family that is so poor that they spend almost all of their income on food, and almost the only foods they can afford to buy are bread and oatmeal. They eat bread as a special treat on Sunday, but the rest of the week they must make do with inferior-tasting but cheaper oatmeal. One day the price of oatmeal goes up, although not by enough to make it more expensive than bread. The rise in the price of oatmeal is devastating to the family's budget. They are forced to cut out their one remaining luxury: The Sunday loaf of bread disappears and is replaced by oatmeal. The paradoxical conclusion, then, is that a rise in the price of oatmeal causes this family to buy more, not less, oatmeal. The family's demand curve for oatmeal has a positive slope. A good that has a positively sloped demand curve for such reasons is called a **Giffen good** after a nineteenth-century English writer, Robert Giffen, who supposedly mentioned the possibility.[1]

Giffen good

An inferior good accounting for a large share of a consumer's budget that has a positively sloped demand curve because the income effect of a price change outweighs the substitution effect.

The conditions required for a positively sloped demand curve—an inferior good that makes up a large portion of the consumer's budget—are very special. Such conditions are unlikely to be encountered in the markets in which people usually conduct transactions. If you are in the pizza business—or even in the oatmeal business—you can be virtually certain that, taking the world as it really is, raising the price of any good or service will cause people to buy less of it and cutting the price will cause them to buy more of it. The Giffen-good phenomenon has been demonstrated under carefully controlled experimental circumstances, however, as reported in *Applying Economic Ideas 5.1*. And nothing in the pure logic of rational choice disproves the possibility of such a situation occurring in an actual market situation.

Applications of Income and Substitution Effects

The law of demand and the concepts of income and substitution effects can be applied to any situation in which a consumer seeks to maximize utility in the face of established alternatives and constraints, even when the "goods" in question are not "for sale," and even when constraints and the opportunity costs of the available alternatives

APPLYING ECONOMIC IDEAS 5.1

TESTING CONSUMER DEMAND THEORY WITH WHITE RATS

Traditionally, most empirical work in economics uses observation of actual market behavior as its data source. In recent years, however, a growing number of economists have engaged in laboratory experimentation. Many of the experiments involve students as their subjects. For example, a group of students might simulate the operation of a stock exchange, with shares of stocks exchanged for tokens or pennies.

The use of human subjects in economic experiments has its limitations, however. For one thing, it is hard to get subjects to agree to participate in long-term experiments that might change their whole way of life. Moreover, human subjects inevitably are aware that they are participating in an experiment. This awareness might affect their behavior. To get around these drawbacks, economists John Kagel of the University of Houston and Ray Battalio of Texas A&M have used animal subjects in economic experiments for several years. These experiments have borne out many of the predictions of consumer choice theory in the laboratory.

For example, in one experiment, two white male rats were placed in standard laboratory cages, with food and water freely available. At one end of each cage were two levers that activated dipper cups. One dipper cup provided a measured quantity of root beer when its lever was depressed; the other provided a measured quantity of nonalcoholic Collins mix. Previous experimentation had shown that rats prefer these beverages to water.

Within this setup, each rat could be given a fixed "income" of so many pushes on the levers per day. The pushes could be distributed in any way between the two levers. Experimenters could also control the "price" of root beet and Collins mix by determining the number of pushes the rat had to "spend" to obtain one milliliter of liquid.

In an initial experimental run lasting two weeks, the rats were given an income of 300 pushes per day, and both beverages were priced at 20 pushes per milliliter. Under those conditions, rat 1 settled down to a pattern of drinking about 11 milliliters of root beer per day and about 4 milliliters of Collins mix. Rat 2 preferred a diet of almost all root beer, averaging less than one milliliter of Collins mix per day.

Once the initial conditions were established, the experimenters were ready to see how the rats would respond to changes in prices and incomes. First, the price (in pushes per milliliter) of root beer was doubled and the price of Collins mix was cut in half. At the same time, each subject's total income of pushes was adjusted to make it possible for each to afford to continue the previous consumption pattern if it were chosen. (That adjustment in total income was made in order to eliminate any possible income effect of the price change and to concentrate solely on the substitution effect.) Economic theory predicts that under the new conditions the rats would choose to consume more Collins mix and less root beer than before, even though their income would be sufficient to maintain the original pattern of consumption if they chose to do so.

The rats' behavior exactly fitted these predictions. In two weeks of living under the new conditions, rat 1 settled down to a new consumption pattern of about 8 milliliters of root beet and 17 milliliters of Collins mix per day. Rat 2, which had chosen root beer almost exclusively before, switched over to about 9 milliliters of root beer and 25 milliliters of Collins mix.

Another experiment focused on income effects. In this case, the two liquids chosen were root beer, which rats love, and quinine water, which they are more reluctant to drink. At the beginning of the experiment, the price of root beer was set at twice the price of quinine water. If the rats' income of pushes per day was kept low, they would drink some of the relatively cheap quinine water along with some of the more expensive root beer. As their income was raised, they would switch away from quinine water toward more root beer. The conclusion: For rats, root beer is a normal good and quinine water an inferior good.

Having established that quinine water was an inferior good, Kagel and Battalio set out to see if they could demonstrate the Giffen-good effect. That effect requires an inferior good that also accounts for a large part of the subject's total expenditures. To produce these conditions, the rats were kept in "poverty." Their budget was kept so low that without drinking a fair amount of quinine, they would become dehydrated.

Without changing the total budget of pushes, the price of quinine water was then reduced. If they maintained their previous consumption pattern, the rats would have pushes left over. What would they spend the extra pushes on? Root beer, of course. Being able to afford more root beer, the rats could now cut back on their consumption of quinine without risking dehydration. The net result: Cutting the price of quinine with no change in nominal income (pushes per day) caused the rats to drink less quinine. For impoverished rats, quinine water is a true Giffen good.

Sources: The root beer–Collins mix experiment is reported in John H. Kagel and Raymond C. Battalio, "Experimental Studies of Consumer Demand Behavior," *Economic Inquiry* 8 (March 1975): 22–38, Journal of the Western Economic Association. Reprinted with permission. Kagel and Battalio's root beer–quinine experiment is summarized in Timothy Tregarthen, "Found! A Giffen Good," *The Margin* (October 1987): 8–10.

are not stated in money. This section will look at some of the wider applications of the theory of consumer choice.

The Demand for Safety

Let us look first at the studies of safety regulations featured at the beginning of this chapter, starting with the case of automobile safety equipment. When you get into a car to go somewhere, you face a trade-off between travel time and safety. A quick trip is good, but so is a safe one. Making the trip safer by driving more slowly, stopping for yellow lights, and so on has an opportunity cost in terms of time. Cutting travel time by driving faster and going through yellow lights has an opportunity cost in terms of safety.

If the opportunity costs change, the choices drivers make also tend to change. For example, suppose there is snow on the road; that makes the road less safe and raises the opportunity cost of speed. When it snows, then, drivers slow down and shift their choices away from speed in the interest of safety, just as the substitution effect would predict.

A change in the design of cars to make them safer also changes the opportunity cost of speed relative to that of safety. Cutting travel time by speeding up and running yellow lights entails giving up less safety in a car with seat belts or air bags than in one without those devices. Because the opportunity cost of speed is lower in a safer car, logically the substitution effect would cause people to drive faster and less carefully. A side effect of this choice would be more deaths of pedestrians and bicyclists. This is the result found by the studies cited earlier. The studies disagree on the size of the effect, but not on its direction.

Some of the studies have found an income effect as well as a substitution effect on driving behavior. The studies by Crandall and Graham indicate that safety is an inferior good. It seems that as people's incomes go up, they begin to feel that their time is too valuable to spend in a car. Perhaps they speed up so they can get to their high-paying jobs or fashionable parties more quickly. If they decide to run a greater risk of killing themselves and others along the way—well, that is part of the logic of consumer choice. Maybe people with less exciting destinations have less reason to be in a hurry.

The case of aspirin bottle caps can also be explained in terms of the logic of consumer choice. Putting the cap back on the aspirin bottle has a benefit: It decreases the chance that young children will poison themselves. If the cap is a safety cap, the benefit is greater still because it is even less likely that a young child will open the bottle. However, putting the cap back on the bottle also has an opportunity cost: It will be harder to grab an aspirin the next time you have a headache. If the cap is a safety cap, the opportunity cost will be greater, because safety caps are often hard even for adults to remove. Thus, fitting aspirin bottles with safety caps increases both the benefit in terms of safety and the cost in terms of convenience. If the increase in cost is greater than the increase in benefit, putting a safety cap on the bottle raises the net opportunity cost of safety. Following the logic of the substitution effect, people shift their behavior away from safety and toward convenience. The result, Viscusi found, is that 73 percent of all aspirin poisonings involve bottles with safety caps, even though only half of all aspirin bottles sold have such caps. Further, half of all the poisonings involve bottles that were left open. The law of unintended consequences strikes again!

Children as Durable Consumer Goods

University of Chicago economist Gary Becker, winner of the 1992 Nobel Memorial Prize for economics, has made his reputation by applying economic reasoning to areas of choice that many people think of as noneconomic. Some of his best-known research concerns choices made within the family. As an example, consider Becker's analysis of the number of children a family chooses to have.

Children, in Becker's view, are durable consumer goods. They return benefits to parents over many years in such forms as love, family pride, and mowing the lawn. But there are opportunity costs associated with having children. Those costs include the goods and services forgone to pay the extra grocery bills, clothing bills, and doctors' bills for the children. But in Becker's view, the biggest opportunity cost of having children is the time parents spend caring for them. That time, too, has an opportunity cost. Time not spent caring for children could be spent working to earn income. Thus the higher the parents' earning power, the greater the opportunity cost of having children.

What does this imply about the number of children a family chooses to have? It has been widely observed in many societies that as family income rises, the number of children per family tends to fall. Does this mean that children are inferior goods? Not at all, says Becker. Children are normal goods; other things being equal, the income effect would cause a family to want more children as its income increases. But other things are not equal. As Becker notes, there is also a substitution effect because, if the higher income reflects a higher hourly wage, it increases the opportunity cost of each hour spent caring for children. On the average, the substitution effect outweighs the income effect, so higher-income families end up having fewer children.

As confirmation of his analysis, Becker notes that the income and substitution effects can be partially distinguished by looking separately at the effects of changes in men's and women's incomes. Traditionally, women perform a greater proportion of child care than men. In a family where this is the case, an increase in a woman's income would have a stronger substitution effect than an increase in a man's income. The reason is that, in such a family, a woman with a high income would encounter a high opportunity cost for each hour taken off from work to devote to child care, whereas, by assumption, the man would take few hours off for child care regardless of his income. Empirical data in fact reveal such a pattern to be prevalent: Birth rates tend to vary directly with incomes earned by men because the income effect outweighs the relatively weak substitution effect. But birth rates vary inversely with incomes earned by women, who experience a relatively stronger substitution effect.

And what is it that parents substitute for a greater quantity of children when their incomes rise? Some, no doubt, substitute vacations at Club Med, BMWs, and other luxuries. But, Becker notes, they have another reaction as well, one that is consistent with the theory of consumer choice. In place of a greater number of children, he says, upper-income families substitute investment in higher-quality children: piano lessons from the age of five; tutors to help cram for SAT exams; tuition payments to Yale Law School. It's all so *rational*, says Becker.

CONSUMER SURPLUS

This chapter has related consumer choice to the demand curve from two perspectives—that of utility theory and that of income and substitution effects. In both cases, the demand curve was viewed as answering the question, How much of a good will consumers wish to purchase at any given price? In this section, we turn to a different question to which the demand curve also can provide an answer: How much will consumers be willing to pay for an additional unit of a good given the quantity they already have?

The Demand Curve as Willingness to Pay

Figure 5.1 shows a demand curve for apples for a college student, Hannah Lee. Lee stocks up on snack foods at a local supermarket and often includes apples in her purchases. The demand curve given in the figure shows that the number of apples she eats each month depends on their price. Currently the price of an apple is \$.40. At this price, she buys ten per month. On other days she substitutes an orange or a banana.

The demand curve indicates that \$.40 is the maximum that Lee would be willing to pay for the tenth apple. If the price rose to \$.45, she would substitute some other fruit for the tenth apple. However, she would not cut out apples altogether. Although \$.40 is the maximum she is willing to pay for the tenth apple, she would not give up the ninth apple unless the price rose above \$.45. Similarly, she would be willing to pay up to \$.50 before giving up the eighth apple, up to \$.55 before giving up the seventh, and so on. The height of the demand curve at each point (emphasized here by a vertical bar) shows the maximum that she would willingly pay for each unit consumed. That maximum decreases as the quantity consumed increases, in accordance with the principle of diminishing marginal utility.

Measuring the Surplus

Figure 5.1 shows the maximum that Lee is willing to pay for various quantities of apples, but it also shows that she need not actually pay this amount. At the going price

FIGURE 5.1 CONSUMER SURPLUS

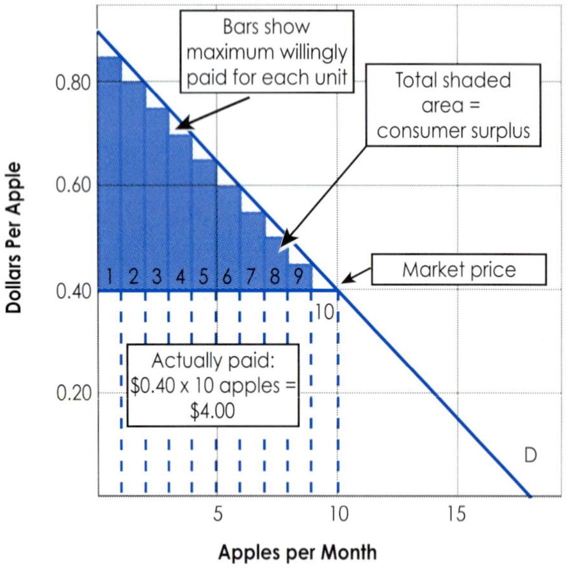

The height of a demand curve shows the maximum that this consumer would be willing to pay for an additional unit of a good. For example, she would be willing to pay up to $.85 for the first apple bought each month but only $.55 for the seventh. The maximum she would willingly pay for each unit is shown by a vertical bar. In this case, the market price is $.40; thus, she buys 10 apples a month, paying a total of $4.00. The difference between what she actually pays at the market price and the maximum she would have been willing to pay, shown by the shaded area, is called consumer surplus.

Consumer surplus

The difference between the maximum that a consumer would be willing to pay for a unit of a good and the amount that he or she actually pays.

of $.40, she pays only a total of $4 for the ten apples she buys each month. Except in the case of the last unit purchased, she gets each unit for less than what she would willingly have paid for it. The difference between what she would willingly have paid for each unit and the amount actually paid at the market is called the **consumer surplus** for that unit. The consumer surplus on each unit is shown by the shaded portion of the corresponding vertical bar. For example, the surplus on the first apple, for which Lee would have willingly paid $.85 if necessary, is $.45, because she actually paid only $.40. The total consumer surplus on all units purchased is shown by the sum of the shaded portions of the bars. The area of the triangle between the demand curve and the market price is an approximate measure of consumer surplus.[2]

Consumer Surplus, Producer Surplus, and Gains from Exchange

The reasoning behind the notion of consumer surplus can be extended to the producers' side of the market as well. Consider Figure 5.2, which shows a typical market operating according to principles of supply and demand. The equilibrium market price is established at the point where the supply and demand curves cross. The demand curve, as we have seen, measures the maximum amount that consumers would be willing to pay for each unit sold; for example, they will pay no more than $1.50 for the one thousandth unit. Consumer surplus is a measure of the difference between the maximum that consumers would have been willing to pay and what they actually pay at the market price.

Now turn to the supply curve. The height of the supply curve at any point represents the minimum that producers would willingly accept for the unit. For example, producers would be unwilling to accept less than $.75 for the one thousandth unit sold. If they could not get at least that much, the producers would divert their resources to an alternative use rather than produce the one thousandth unit of this product.

Producer surplus

The difference between what producers receive for a unit of a good and the minimum they would be willing to accept.

However, as the figure is drawn, producers receive the market price of $1 per unit for all units sold, including the one thousandth. On that unit, they earn a producer surplus of $.25. The **producer surplus** earned on each unit is the difference between the market price and the minimum that the producers would have been willing to accept in exchange for that unit—the difference between $1 and $.75 for the one

FIGURE 5.2 GAINS FROM EXCHANGE

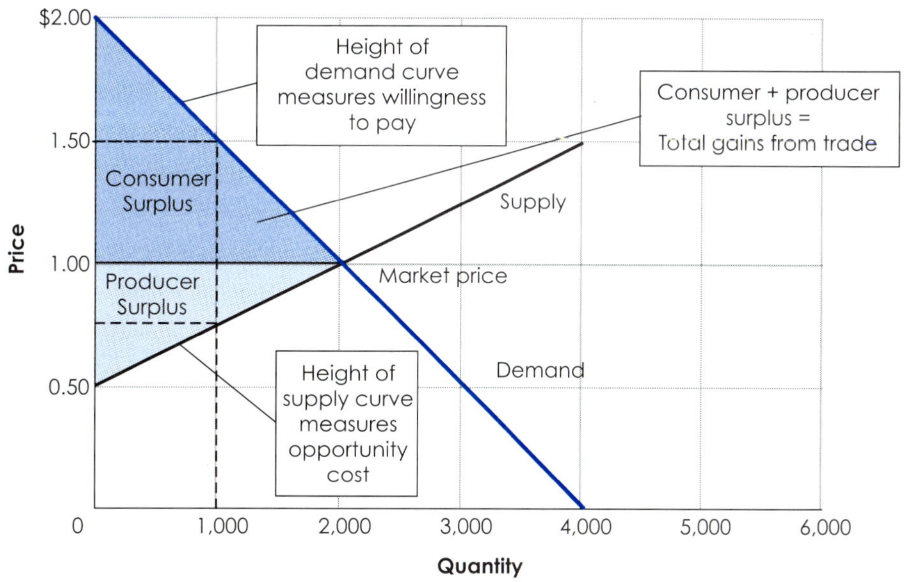

This figure shows that both consumers and producers gain from exchange. Here the equilibrium market price is $1 per unit. The demand curve shows the maximum that consumers would willingly pay for each unit. Consumers' gain from exchange takes the form of consumer surplus, shown by the area between the demand curve and the market price. The supply curve shows the minimum that producers would willingly accept rather than put their resources to work elsewhere. Producers earn a surplus equal to the difference between what they actually receive at the market price and the minimum they would have been willing to accept. The producer surplus is shown by the area between the supply curve and the market price. Assuming an equilibrium is reached at the point of intersection of the two curves, total gains from exchange are thus the entire area between them up to the intersection.

thousandth unit in our example. The total producer surplus earned on all units is shown by the area between the supply curve and the market price.

We see, then, that the concept of surplus in the market is symmetrical. Consumers buy the goods, except for the very last unit, for less than the maximum amount they would have been willing to pay, and producers sell the goods, except for the very last unit, for more than the minimum amount they would have been willing to accept. Thus, *both buyers and sellers gain from exchange*. That is why markets exist. As long as participation is voluntary, they make everyone who buys and sells in them better off than they would be if they did not participate. Assuming an equilibrium at the intersection of the supply and demand curves, as in Figure 5.2, the total of the mutual gains from exchange—consumer surplus plus producer surplus—is equal to the entire shaded triangle between the supply and demand curves to the left of their intersection point.

Application: The Excess Burden of a Tax

Figure 5.3 provides an application of the concepts of consumer and producer surplus to the effects of a price of a tax on gasoline. Imposing a \$.50-per-gallon tax on gasoline shifts the supply curve upward by that amount and raises the equilibrium price, including tax, from \$1 to \$1.40 per gallon. The price received by sellers, after tax, falls from \$1 to \$.90 per gallon.

The concepts of consumer and producer surplus offer additional insight into the issue of tax incidence beyond those we gain by looking at price changes alone. Figure 5.3 shows that the tax brings in \$4 million per day in revenue to the government. This equals the after-tax quantity Q_2, which is 8 million gallons, times the amount of the tax, which is \$.50 per gallon. Part of that revenue is paid by consumers at the expense of the consumer surplus they otherwise would have earned by being able to buy 8 million gallons at \$1 rather than at \$1.40. Part is paid by suppliers at the expense of the producer surplus they would have earned by being able to sell 8 million gallons at \$1 rather than at \$.90. The sum of that part of the consumers' burden and that part of the producers' burden is equal to the tax revenue collected by the government.

Excess burden of the tax

The part of the economic burden of a tax that takes the form of consumer and producer surplus that is lost because the tax reduces the equilibrium quantity sold.

However, there is an additional burden on consumers and producers that is not reflected in the government's revenue from the tax. That burden is associated with the reduction in quantity purchased from 10 million to 8 million gallons per day because of the tax. Consumers would have enjoyed a surplus on the extra 2 million gallons equal to the triangle above the pretax price of \$1 between Q_1 and Q_2; producers would have enjoyed a surplus equal to the triangle below the pretax price between Q_1 and Q_2. The lost consumer-plus-producer surplus is called the **excess burden of the tax**.

The common sense behind this is that the tax imposes a burden on consumers and producers that is larger than the amount the government takes in as revenue. It does so

FIGURE 5.3 EXCESS BURDEN OF A TAX

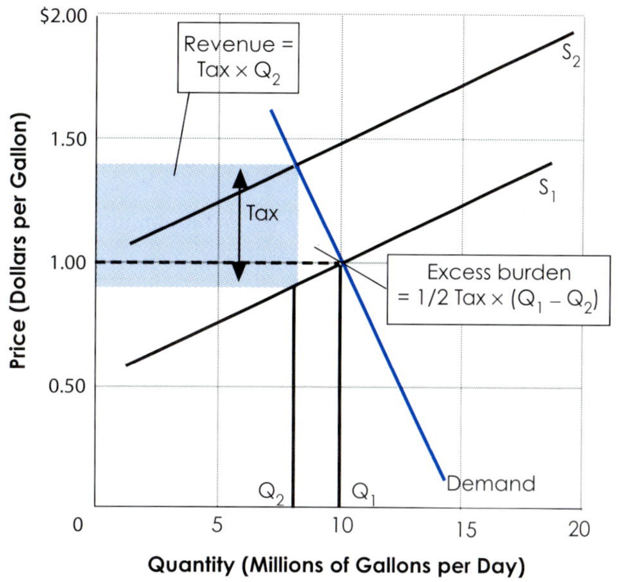

Imposition of a tax of $.50 per gallon on gasoline raises the equilibrium price from $1 to $1.40 per gallon. The price that sellers receive after the tax is paid falls to $.90. Revenue collected by the government equals the tax times Q_2, the equilibrium quantity after tax. The economic burden of the revenue is divided between consumers and sellers. There is also an *excess burden*, which takes the form of the consumer and producer surpluses that would be realized from the sale of the additional quantity that would have been sold without the tax. This is shown by the area of the triangle between the supply and demand curves and between the pretax quantity, Q_1, and the after-tax quantity, Q_2.

because the tax discourages buyers and sellers from doing as much business as they would have done without the tax. The potential mutual gain from pushing exchange in the gasoline market all the way out to 10 million gallons per day is lost. In geometric terms, the size of the excess burden can be calculated by applying the rule that the area of a triangle equals one-half of its height times its base. The height is the tax ($.50), and the base is $Q_1 - Q_2$ (2 million gallons). Thus, the excess burden is $500,000 per day. The total burden on consumers plus producers equals the $4 million collected by the government plus this $500,000 excess burden, or $4.5 million.

The example can be generalized to all taxes because virtually any tax causes firms or individuals to change their behavior by engaging in less of the taxed activity. For instance, income taxes have an excess burden related to their reduction of incentives to work and save. Similarly, tariffs (taxes on imports) have an excess burden related to the fact that they discourage international trade. The excess burden of taxes is just as much a part of the opportunity cost of the services that the government supplies as are the taxes actually collected by the government.

SUMMARY

1. **What elements are involved in consumers' rational choices?** Objectives and constraints on opportunities provide the setting for rational choice by consumers. Consumers choose rationally when they set goals and make systematic efforts to achieve them. The objective of consumer choice is *utility*—the pleasure and satisfaction that people get from goods and services. The added utility obtained from a one-unit increase in consumption of a good or service is its *marginal utility*. The greater the rate of consumption of a good, the smaller the increase in utility from an additional unit consumed.

2. **How do consumers balance their choices of goods and services to achieve an equilibrium?** *Consumer equilibrium* is said to occur when the total utility obtained from a given budget cannot be increased by shifting spending from one good to another. In equilibrium, the marginal utility of a dollar's worth of one good must equal the marginal utility of a dollar's worth of any other good.

3. **What lies behind the effect of a price change on the quantity of a good demanded?** The change in quantity demanded that results from a change in a good's price, other things being equal, can be separated into two parts. The part that comes from the tendency to substitute cheaper goods for more costly ones is the *substitution effect*. The part that comes from the increase in real income that results from a decrease in the price of the good, other things being equal, is the *income effect*.

4. **Why do demand curves have negative slopes?** For a normal good, the substitution and income effects work in the same direction. The demand curves for normal goods therefore have negative slopes. For inferior goods, the income effect and the substitution effect work in opposite directions. For inferior goods, therefore, the demand curve will have a negative slope only if the substitution effect outweighs the income effect. In practice, this is virtually always the case, although *Giffen goods* with positively sloped demand curves are a theoretical possibility.

5. **Why do both consumers and producers gain from exchange?** When consumers buy a product at a given market price, they pay the same amount for each unit purchased. However, because of the *principle of diminishing marginal utility,* the first units purchased are worth more to them than the last ones purchased. The difference between what consumers actually pay for a unit of a good and the maximum they would be willing to pay is the *consumer surplus* gained on that unit of the good. Similarly, the difference between what sellers actually receive for a good and the minimum they would have accepted is known as *producer surplus*.

6. **Why does the burden of a tax exceed the revenue raised by government?** When a tax is imposed on a good or service, the equilibrium price including the tax rises while the equilibrium price net of the tax falls. As a result, the equilibrium quantity falls, making both consumers and producers forgo some surplus. The forgone surplus is not captured in the form of tax revenue and is called the *excess burden of the tax*. It is a burden on consumers and producers over and above the sum that the government collects as tax revenue.

KEY TERMS

Utility
Marginal utility
Principle of diminishing utility
Consumer equilibrium
Substitution effect
Income effect
Giffen good
Consumer surplus
Producer surplus
Excess burden of the tax

PROBLEMS AND TOPICS FOR DISCUSSION

1. **Examining the lead-off case.** The increase in deaths of pedestrians and bicyclists resulting from drivers' use of seat belts or air bags is an example of an externality. What could the government do to prevent this externality while still achieving the goal of increased driver safety? Bonus question: If you complete the appendix to this chapter, analyze the trade-off between speed and safety using an indifference curve diagram. How does the installation of seat belts in a car change the budget line?

2. **Can there be increasing marginal utility?** Can there be increasing marginal utility in some cases? For example, suppose it would take eight rolls of wallpaper to decorate your kitchen. If someone gave you seven rolls of wallpaper, you would get only limited utility from them. An eighth roll, however, would give you great utility. Do you think this is a valid exception to the principle of diminishing marginal utility?

3. **Consumer equilibrium, marginal utility, and prices.** Martha Smith consumes two pounds of pork and five pounds of beef per month. She pays $1.50 a pound for the pork and $2 per pound for the beef. What can you say about the ratio of the marginal utility of pork to the marginal utility of beef, assuming that this pattern represents a state of consumer equilibrium for Smith? Is the ratio 3/4, 4/3, 5/2, 2/5, or none of these?

4. **A Giffen good.** A family living in Minnesota vacations in Florida each January. One year the price of home heating fuel goes up sharply. The family turns the thermostat down a little, but even so the heating bills go up so much that the family cannot afford to go to Florida that year. Staying home in January means that the house must be kept heated during that month. The extra fuel burned during January is more than what the family has been able to save by lowering the thermostat setting in other months. Thus, the total quantity of fuel burned in the winter rises as a result of the increase in the price of heating fuel. Analyze this case in terms of the income and substitution effects. Is home heating fuel a Giffen good for this family? (Hint: Winter vacations in Minnesota are an inferior good for this family. Heating fuel is a complement to winter vacations in Minnesota and hence is also an inferior good.)

5. **Excess burden of a tax.** Figure 3.5 in Chapter 3 demonstrates the incidence of a tax on apartment rents. Using the approach outlined in this chapter, calculate the revenue raised by this tax and the excess burden of the tax. How much of the excess burden is borne by landlords? How much by tenants?

CASE FOR DISCUSSION

Retailing Revolution on the Banks of the Danube

Riding the Metro to the Budapest's sleek new West End shopping mall produces a strange sense of time warp. The Metro, Budapest's fast, reliable underground transit system, is an exact copy of its big brother in Moscow, which first went into service in the 1930s. It has all the features of the Communist-era planned economy: carbon-copy sameness from one country to another, no-frills functionality, and barely adequate spending on maintenance. The West End mall, on the other hand, highlights the characteristics of the modern, consumer-oriented market system. It has spacious, well-lighted public areas, one featuring a three-story indoor waterfall. It has brightly decorated, well-stocked shops selling Italian shoes, Korean electronics, and, of course, local Hungarian brands as well. Yet the West End mall is not a carbon copy of its cousins in Chicago or Seattle. It has many adaptations to suit local shopping habits. For example, its single largest store is a supermarket. Most mall developers in the United States have found that supermarkets don't mix well in shopping malls. American consumers want to be able to load groceries directly into their cars. Central European shoppers shop more often and buy smaller quantities. They seem to find it no great inconvenience to leave the mall with a bag of groceries in one hand and a purchase of new clothing in the other.

But despite a degree of success that is obvious from the crowds, the mall has not completely conquered the Budapest shopping world. Right across the street from the West End mall is a district full of smaller, more traditional shops. Located right on street level of the four- and five-story apartment buildings where most Budapest residents live, these shops carry much smaller selections, but they offer other things of great value: convenience and service. Forget a loaf of bread, a carton of milk, a can of pet food? No need to take the time to head for the mall. Your nearest shop is never more than a block away. Also, many Hungarians prefer to talk over the cut of a piece of meat with a trusted neighborhood butcher rather than buy a pre-wrapped cut in a supermarket. And by keeping overhead low—no waterfalls!—the local merchants manage to compete on price, despite a scale of operation that seems inefficiently small.

One thing is certain: As Hungary has made its transition from a planned economy to membership in the European Union, the consumer has become the driving force of change. Whether catering to teens in the mall's Diesel shop or to pensioners at the local butcher shop, the new Budapest retail world strives to give people what they want. And this strong consumer orientation means that there will be more changes in the years ahead. In a market economy, change is the only constant.

QUESTIONS

1. What opportunity costs must a consumer consider in deciding whether to shop in the West End mall or a traditional small shop?
2. Why would someone prefer to wait in line at a traditional butcher shop to buy custom-cut meat rather than buy a pre-cut roast in a supermarket? Could you use the theory of consumer equilibrium to describe the tradeoff between convenience and quality that is involved in such a decision?
3. The planned economy delivered a limited selection of goods to consumers, but basic goods carried very low prices. Do you think all consumers gain from the transition to a market economy where there is a larger selection of goods but basic goods cost more? Why or why not? Discuss.

END NOTES

1. The positive slope of the demand curve for a Giffen good does not depend on an assumption of bounded rationality. A fully rational consumer would have a negatively sloped demand curve for house-brand cleaner.
2. An intermediate-level microeconomics course would explain that for reasons associated with the income effect, the triangle dues not provide a precise measure of consumer surplus. However, the approximation is close for goods that make up only a small part of consumers' total expenditures.

Appendix to Chapter 5
INDIFFERENCE CURVES

This chapter described two versions of the theory of consumer choice—one based on marginal utility and the other on income and substitution effects. This appendix gives a third version that can be related to the other two, using what are known as *indifference curves.* Indifference curves are not featured in this book, but they are often used in intermediate- and advanced-level economic writings. Many students and instructors find it worthwhile to study them, even if briefly, as part of an introductory course. This appendix will serve their needs.

Constructing an Indifference Curve

Begin by supposing that I am an experimenter and you are my subject. I want to find out how you feel about consuming various quantities of meat and cheese. It would be convenient if I had a utility meter, but I do not. Therefore, to find out your attitudes toward the consumption of these goods, I offer you a number of baskets (two at a time) containing varying amounts of meat and cheese.

As I offer each pair of baskets, I ask: "Would you prefer the one on the left to the one on the right? Would you prefer the one on the right to the one on the left? Or are you indifferent between the two?" In this way, I hope to get a meaningful answer from you. I know I have a better chance of getting such an answer this way than I would if I asked you how many utils you would get from each basket.

At some point in the experiment, I offer you basket A, which contains eight pounds of meat and three pounds of cheese, and basket B, which contains six pounds of meat and four pounds of cheese. I ask you the usual questions, and you answer that you are indifferent between the two baskets. You feel that the extra pound of cheese in basket B just makes up for the fact that it has two pounds less meat than basket A. This gives me a useful bit of information: It tells me that for you baskets A and B belong to an **indifference set**—a set of consumption choices each of which yields the same amount of satisfaction such that no member of the set is preferred to any other. Exploring the matter further, I find that two other baskets, C and D, also belong to the same indifference set, which now has the following four members:

Indifference set

A set of consumption choices, each of which yields the same utility so that no member of the set is preferred to any other.

Basket	Meat (Pounds)	Cheese (Pounds)
A	8	3
B	6	4
C	5	5
D	4	7

Having thanked you for taking part in my experiment, I get out a piece of graph paper. First I draw a pair of axes, as in Figure 5A.1. Pounds of meat are measured on the horizontal axis and pounds of cheese on the vertical axis. Each basket of goods can be shown as a point in the area between the two axes. The points representing baskets A and D are shown in their

Indifference curve

A graphical representation of an indifference set.

proper places on the graph. These points and all those between them that lie on the smooth curve joining them are members of the same indifference set. The curve itself is an **indifference curve**—a curve composed of points that are all members of the same indifference set.

Some Characteristics of Indifference Curves

Indifference curves have characteristics that reflect certain regularities in patterns of consumer preferences. Five of these are of interest to us:

1. *Indifference curves normally have negative slopes.* For example, the curve in Figure 5A.2 is not possible if both meat and cheese are desired goods—that is, if the consumer prefers more to less, other things being equal. The basket shown by point A contains more of both goods than that shown by point B. This implies that if greater amounts of meat and cheese give greater satisfaction, A must be preferred to B; it cannot be a member of the same indifference set as B.

2. *The absolute value of the slope of an indifference curve at any point is the ratio of the marginal utility of the good on the horizontal axis to the marginal utility of the good on the vertical axis.* For example, look at Figure 5A.1. Between D and C, the slope of the curve is approximately –2 (or simply 2 when the minus sign is removed to give the absolute value). This shows that the marginal utility of meat is approximately twice that of cheese when the

FIGURE 5A.1 AN INDIFFERENCE CURVE

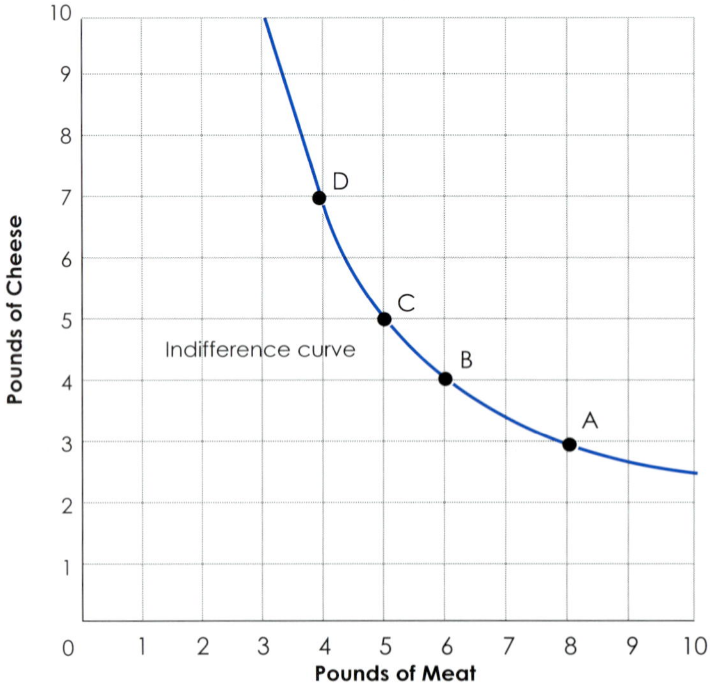

Each point in this diagram stands for a basket of meat and cheese. A, B, C, and D are baskets among which a certain consumer is indifferent. All give equal utility. Those points and all the others on a smooth curve connecting them form an indifference set. An indifference curve is a graphical representation of an indifference set.

amounts consumed are in the region of baskets C and D. Because the marginal utility of meat is twice that of cheese in this region, the consumer will feel neither a gain nor a loss in total utility in trading basket D for basket C, that is, in giving up two pounds of cheese for one extra pound of meat. Because it shows the rate at which meat can be substituted for cheese without a gain or loss in satisfaction, the slope of the indifference curve is called the **marginal rate of substitution** of meat for cheese.

Marginal rate of substitution

The rate at which one good can be substituted for another with no gain or loss in satisfaction.

3. *Indifference curves are convex; their slopes decrease as one moves downward and to the right along them.* This implies that the ratio of the marginal utility of meat to the marginal utility of cheese (or the marginal rate of substitution of meat for cheese) decreases as one moves downward and to the right along the curve. Look once more at Figure 5A.1. In the region between D and C the slope of the curve is approximately –2, indicating that the ratio of the marginal utility of meat to that of cheese is approximately 2:1. By comparison, in the region between B and A the slope is only about –1/2. The substitution of meat for cheese has caused the ratio of the marginal utility of meat to the marginal utility of cheese to fall to approximately 1:2.

4. *An indifference curve can be drawn through the point that represents* any *basket of goods.* Figure 5A.3 shows the same indifference curve as in Figure 5A.1, but here the curve is labeled I_1. Point E, which represents a basket containing seven pounds of meat and five pounds of cheese, is not a member of the indifference set represented by this curve. Because it lies above and to the right of point B and has more of both products than B, it must be preferred to B. Other points, such as F and G, have more cheese and less meat than E and, on balance, give the same satisfaction as E. The consumer is indifferent among E, F, G, and all other points on curve I_2 and prefers all of these points to any of those on I_1.

FIGURE 5A.2 INDIFFERENCE CURVES HAVE NEGATIVE SLOPES

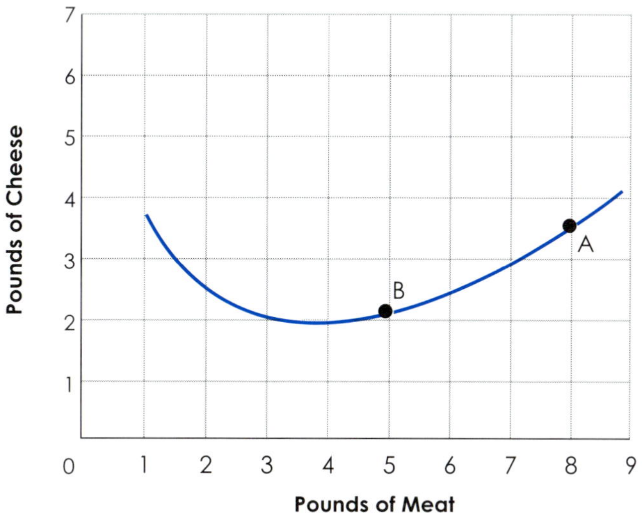

Indifference curves normally have negative slopes. The positively sloped portion of the indifference curve shown here is impossible if both goods give increased satisfaction with increased quantity. A has more of both goods than B. Therefore, point A should be preferred to point B and, hence, could not lie on the same indifference curve.

Any point taken at random, along with the other points that happen to give the same amount of satisfaction, can form an indifference curve. Several other (unlabeled) curves are sketched in Figure 5A.3. Were all possible curves drawn in, they would be so close together that the lines would run into a solid sheet, completely filling the space between the axes. A selection of indifference curves showing their general pattern but leaving enough space to make the graph easy to read is called an **indifference map**.

Indifference map

A selection of indifference curves for a single consumer and pair of goods.

Transitivity

The principle that if A is preferred to B and B is preferred to C, A must be preferred to C.

Indifference curves do not cross. Consumer preferences have **transitivity**, meaning that if you prefer A to B and B to C, you will prefer A to C. Looking at Figure 5A.4, you can see that crossed indifference curves are not possible. Consider points A, B, and C. A and B lie on the same indifference curve, I_1; hence, the consumer is indifferent between them. A and C both lie on I_2; thus, the consumer is indifferent between them, too. Because consumer preferences are transitive, if B is as good as A and A is as good as C, C is as good as B. But C lies above and to the right of B. It represents a mix of goods that contains more of both meat and cheese. If more is better, the consumer must prefer C to B. Because crossed indifference curves imply a contradictory set of preferences, we must conclude that they cannot cross.

The Budget Line

The range of choices open to a consumer with a given budget and with given prices can be shown on the same kind of graph we have used for indifference curves. Figure 5A.5 shows how this can be done. Suppose you have a food budget of \$10 per week, the price of meat is

FIGURE 5A.3 MULTIPLE INDIFFERENCE CURVES

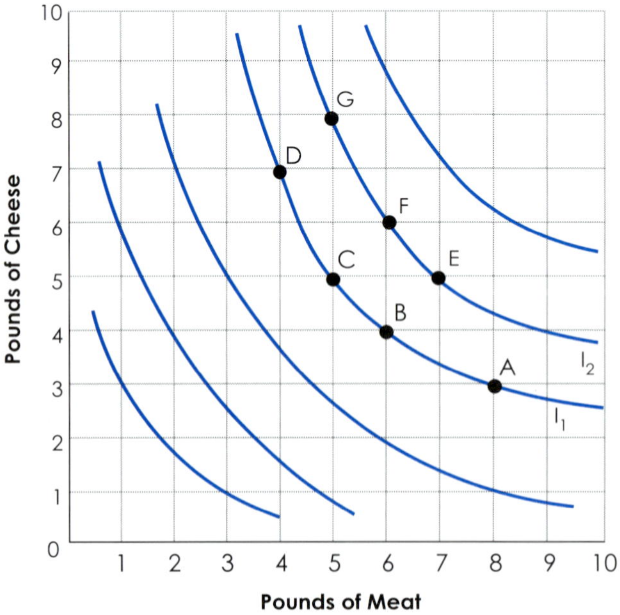

An indifference curve can be drawn through any point. Here curve I_1 represents an indifference set containing points A, B, C, and D, and I_2 represents a set including points E, F, and G. All points on I_2 are preferred to all points on I_1. A representative set of indifference curves like the one shown here can be called an *indifference map*.

FIGURE 5A.4 INDIFFERENCE CURVES CANNOT CROSS

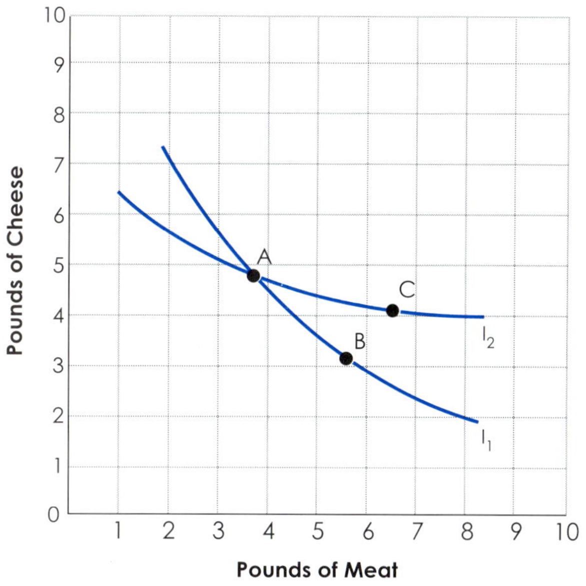

Because consumer preferences are transitive, indifference curves cannot cross. The impossible curves shown here represent contradictory preferences. A and B are both on I_1; therefore, the consumer must be indifferent between them. A and C are both on I_2; hence, the consumer must be indifferent between them as well. Transitivity implies that the consumer is indifferent between B and C, but this is impossible because C contains more of both goods than B does.

$2 a pound, and the price of cheese is $1 a pound. If you spend all your money on meat, you can have up to five pounds of meat; if you spend all your money on cheese, you can have up to ten pounds of cheese. Combinations such as two pounds of meat and six of cheese or four pounds of meat and two of cheese are also possible. Taking into account the possibility of buying a fraction of a pound of meat or cheese, these choices can be shown on the graph as a diagonal line running from 10 on the cheese axis to 5 on the meat axis. Such a line is called a **budget line**.

Budget line

A line showing the various combinations of goods and services that can be purchased at given prices with a given budget.

Using m to stand for amount of meat and c for amount of cheese, the equation for the budget line can be written as

$$2m + 1c = 10.$$

This equation simply says that the number of pounds of meat bought times the price of meat plus the number of pounds of cheese bought times the price of cheese must add up to the total budget if all the money is spent. In more general terms, the equation for a budget line for goods *x* and *y*—with P_x the price of x, P_y the price of y, and B the consumer's total budget is

$$P_xX + P_yY = B.$$

The slope of such a budget line is $-P_x/P_y$. In the case shown in Figure 5A.5, where the price of meat is $2 a pound and the price of cheese is $1 a pound, the slope of the budget line is –2.

A Graphic Representation of Consumer Equilibrium

Indifference curves and the budget line can be used to give a graphic representation of consumer equilibrium. Figure 5A.6 shows the budget line from Figure 5A.5 superimposed on an indifference map like the one shown in Figure 5A.3. In this way, we can easily compare consumer preferences and consumption choices. For example, point B is preferred to point A because it lies on a "higher" indifference curve (one that at some point, such as C, passes above and to the right of A). By similar reasoning, point B is preferred to point D. Of all the points on or below the budget line, it is clear that point E, which represents two and a half pounds of meat and five pounds of cheese, is the most preferred, because all the other points on it lie on lower indifference curves. Every point that is better (like F) lies outside the range of consumption choices.

Because E is the point that gives the greatest possible satisfaction, it is the point of consumer equilibrium. At E, the relevant indifference curve is just tangent to the budget line; this means that the slopes of the curve and the budget line are the same at that point. The slope of the indifference curve, as shown earlier, equals the ratio of the marginal utility of meat to the marginal utility of cheese. The slope of the budget line equals the ratio of the price of meat to the price of cheese. Thus, it follows that in consumer equilibrium,

FIGURE 5A.5 THE BUDGET LINE

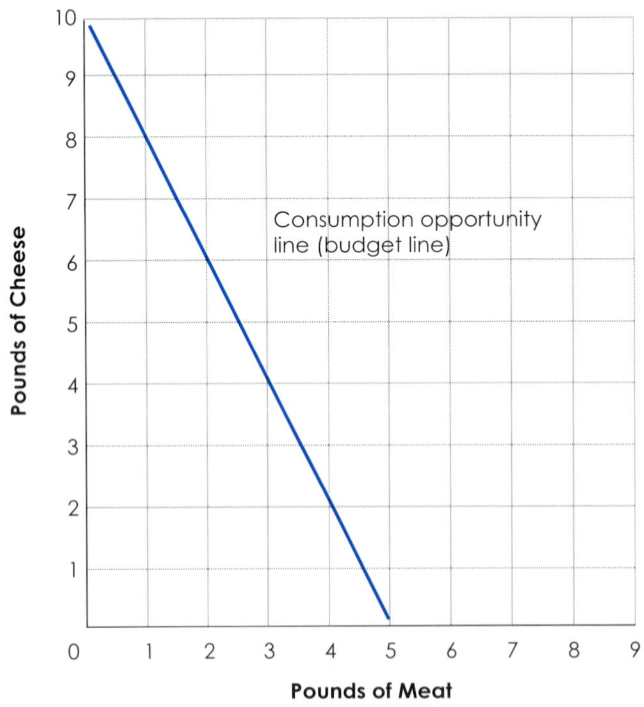

Suppose you have a food budget of $10 per week. You can spend your money on meat at $2 a pound, on cheese at $1 a pound, or on some mix of the two. The consumption opportunity line (budget line) shows all the possible combinations given these prices and your budget.

FIGURE 5A.6 CONSUMER EQUILIBRIUM

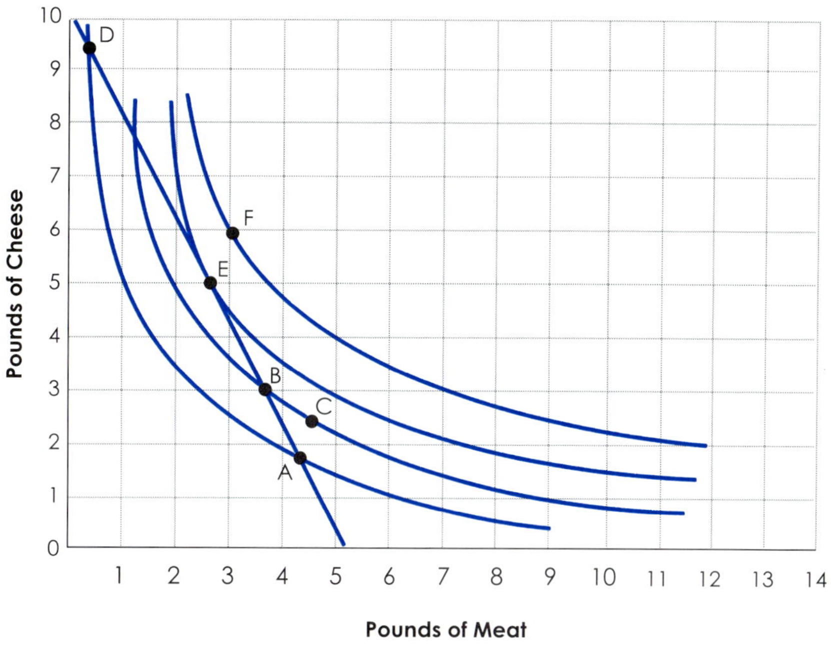

E is the point of consumer equilibrium given the indifference curves and budget line shown. All points that are better than E (such as F) lie outside the budget line. All other points for goods that the consumer can afford to buy (such as A and D) lie on lower indifference curves than E and hence are less preferred.

$$\frac{\text{Marginal utility of meat}}{\text{Marginal utility of cheese}} = \frac{\text{Price of meat}}{\text{Price of cheese}}$$

This is a restatement of the condition for consumer equilibrium given in this chapter.

Derivation of the Demand Curve

This appendix concludes with Figure 5A.7, which shows how a demand curve for meat can be derived from a set of indifference curves. Along with the curves, Figure 5A.7 shows a set of budget lines. Each line is based on the assumption that the price of cheese is $1 a pound and the consumer's budget is $10, as before. Now, however, each budget line assumes a different price, P_m, of meat. The budget line running from 10 on the vertical axis to 2.5 on the horizontal axis assumes that P_m = $4. The budget line running from 10 on the vertical axis to 5 on the horizontal axis assumes that P_m = $2. (This is the same budget line as the one in Figures 5A.5 and 5A.6.) The other two budget lines assume that P_m = $1.50 and P_m = $1, respectively.

The equilibrium pattern of consumption differs for each price of meat, other things being equal. When P_m = $4, point A, which represents six pounds of cheese and one pound of meat, is the best the consumer can do; when P_m = $2, B is the most preferred point.

Given this information, it is a simple matter to draw the consumer's demand curve for meat. Part (b) of Figure 5A.7 shows a new set of axes, with the quantity of meat on the horizontal axis

FIGURE 5A.7 DERIVATION OF A DEMAND CURVE

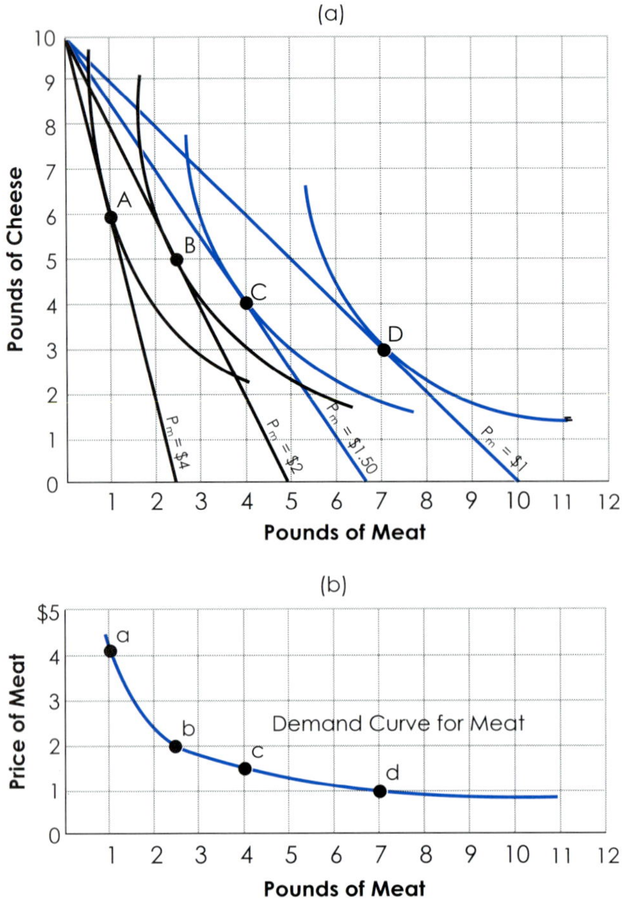

Part (a) of this figure shows a consumer's indifference map for meat and cheese and a set of budget lines. Each budget line corresponds to a different price, P_m, of meat. All four budget lines assume the price of cheese to be $1 and the total budget to be $10. Points A, B, C, and D in part (a) show the choices the consumer makes at meat prices of $4, $2, $1.50, and $1. In part (b), the data on meat consumption at the various prices is plotted on a new set of axes. The smooth line connecting points a, b, c, and d is the consumer's demand curve for meat.

as before but the price of meat on the vertical axis. From part (a) of Figure 5A.7 when P_m = $4 the consumer chooses combination A, which includes one pound of meat. In part (b), therefore, point a is marked as the quantity of meat demanded at a price of $4; then point b, which corresponds to point B in part (a), is added; and so on. Drawing a smooth line through points a, b, c, and d gives the consumer's demand curve for meat. As expected, it has the downward slope predicted by the law of demand.

CHAPTER 6

Production and Cost

After reading this chapter, you will understand:

1. How economists view the concepts of cost and profit
2. The distinction between short-run and long-run time horizons
3. How costs vary in response to changes in the quantity of a variable input
4. How a firm's cost structure can be represented in geometric terms
5. The choices a firm faces in the course of long-run expansion

Before reading this chapter, make sure you know the meaning of:

1. Opportunity cost
2. Entrepreneurship
3. Economic rent

SHARING A DREAM

Andrea and Ralph Martin shared a dream with millions of Americans: to have a business of their own. For some, that dream means a hamburger franchise, a dry-cleaning shop, or a few hundred acres of soybeans. The Martins were more ambitious: they dreamed of having their own company selling their own brand of personal digital assistants (PDAs).

The Martins had no illusions about the entrepreneurial life. They knew that starting their own firm would take hard work and sacrifice. Both were engineers with high-paying jobs at large corporations. On their combined income of $160,000 a year, they could have lived the good life—a house in the suburbs, a Mercedes in the driveway, a condominium in the Virgin Islands. Instead, they lived in a small apartment and saved every dollar they could to build a nest egg with which to start their firm.

The Martins knew they couldn't take on the Palm Pilot in hand-to-hand combat. They needed to find a corner of the PDA market where they could start small and offer customers something new. Ralph's job with ExxonMobil gave him an idea. A year or so before, his company had sent him on an assignment to a new oil development project in Chad. As was his habit, he took along his PDA with which to record data and make on-the-spot computations. But like all the PDAs on the market, his was designed for use in offices. Out in the heat and dust of the Central African desert, it often broke down, causing him a lot of extra work to recreate lost data. Talking about the incident with other field engineers, Ralph became convinced there would be a market for a more ruggedly built device for use throughout the world under field conditions. Andrea was sure she could design one.

The design for the new PDA took shape on paper. The company, Fieldcom Inc., took shape on paper, too. Then one day it was time to take the plunge. The Martins quit their jobs, hired two technicians and an office manager, and went into production. Their factory was an abandoned service station that was available at a rock-bottom rent. Within a month the first of their new products, the Fieldcom I, rolled off the assembly line.

BUSINESS FIRMS LIKE Fieldcom are one of the basic units of microeconomic analysis. They can be studied from many perspectives: as expressions of their owners' personalities, as social systems within which owners and workers interact, as organizations with complex communication structures, as systems of contracts and property rights. Volumes have been written on each of these aspects. In this chapter, however, we will look at firms from a more mundane point of view: as mechanisms for transforming inputs of labor, capital, and natural resources into outputs of goods and services to meet human needs. The firm as a production organization is a key element of the neoclassical tradition in microeconomics. Understanding the firm as a user of inputs to produce outputs will provide a foundation for exploring other perspectives on the firm in later chapters.

COSTS AND PROFITS

As in our discussion of consumer choice, we can begin by looking at the firm's objectives and constraints. Our theory will assume that the principal objective of a private firm like Fieldcom is to maximize its profit. The principal constraints on its opportunities are, first, its costs of production, and second, the demand for its output. We will bring demand into the picture beginning in the next chapter. In this one we will explore costs and their relationship to profit.

The Profit Motive

The assumption that profit is the principal objective of the business firm often meets an objection similar to that raised against the assumption of rationality: It implies too narrow a view of human nature. To be sure, critics say, profit is important, but it is hardly the only thing businesses are interested in. Some firms spend large amounts on supporting the arts or aiding the homeless without calculating the effect such spending might have on profit. Other firms are led by egotists who will risk all in pursuit of building a personal empire. Still others are run by people who prefer to take Wednesday afternoons off for golf as long as their firms earn a minimum level of profit.

Economists' replies to these objections are similar to those given in defense of the rationality assumption. First, the assumption of profit maximization is not intended to serve as a comprehensive description of the motives behind business decisions. Rather, it is a simplification whose purpose is to give a sharper structure to theories about the way decisions are affected by changes in costs or demand. A simple theory should be discarded for a more complex one only if it fails to explain behavior observed in the real world. In practice, theories based on the assumption of profit maximization are able to explain a great deal of what firms are observed to do. In later chapters we will encounter some special situations in which theories can be improved by taking into account objectives other than profit. But such situations are few.

A second defense of the profit maximization assumption is the so-called survivorship principle. To understand this principle, imagine that ownership of firms is at first distributed randomly among people who are inclined to pursue the objective of profit and others who favor the objectives of charity, ego satisfaction, or the easy life. Over time, the firms that maximized profit would increase their capital and grow steadily through investment or acquisition. Those that pursued other objectives would at best have fewer profits to invest in expansion and at worst might be forced out of business by losses. As time went on, then, the survivors of the competitive process would tend to be the profit maximizers.

The Nature of Costs

Because of scarcity, no production can take place without an opportunity cost. There are never enough resources to satisfy all wants, and therefore the decision to produce any one thing implies the need to forgo using the same resources to produce something else. The opportunity costs of production are a fundamental constraint on a firm's ability to maximize its profits. In this section, we will explore several aspects of production costs and explain their relationship to one another.

Explicit costs

Opportunity costs that take the form of explicit payments to suppliers of factors of production and intermediate goods.

Implicit costs

Opportunity costs of using resources contributed by the firm's owners (or owned by the firm itself as a legal entity) that are not obtained in exchange for explicit payments.

Pure economic profit

The sum that remains when both explicit and implicit costs are subtracted from total revenue.

Accounting profit

Total revenue minus explicit costs.

IMPLICIT AND EXPLICIT COSTS The opportunity costs that a firm such as Fieldcom faces include the compensation it must pay to workers, investors, and owners of natural resources in order to attract factors of production away from alternative uses, as well as the payments it must make to other firms that supply it with intermediate goods, such as parts, semifinished materials, and business services. Those costs can be classified in several ways. We begin with the distinction between *explicit* and *implicit* costs.

Explicit costs are opportunity costs that take the form of explicit payments to suppliers of factors of production and intermediate goods. They include workers' wages, managers' salaries, salespeople's commissions, payments to banks and other suppliers of financial services, fees for legal advice, transportation charges, and many other things.

Long as this list is, explicit costs do not include all of the opportunity costs that a firm bears when it engages in production. There are also **implicit costs**—opportunity costs of using resources contributed by the firm's owners (or owned by the firm itself as a legal entity) that are not obtained under contracts calling for explicit payments. For example, if the proprietor of a small firm works along with the firm's hired employees without receiving a salary, he or she gives up the opportunity to earn a salary by working for someone else. As another example, when a firm uses a building that it owns, it need not make a payment to anyone, but it gives up the opportunity to receive payments from someone else to whom it could rent the building. Firms normally do not record implicit costs in their accounts, but this does not make those costs any less real.

COSTS AND PROFITS The distinction between explicit and implicit costs is important in understanding what economists mean by profit—the firm's chief objective. Economists use the term *profit* to mean the difference between a firm's total revenues and its costs, including both explicit and implicit costs. To distinguish this meaning from other possible meanings, we will call it **pure economic profit**. Special care must be taken to distinguish economic profit from two other uses of the term *profit*.

First, in the business world, *profit* is often used to mean revenue minus explicit costs only, without giving consideration to implicit costs. Economists call this concept **accounting profit** because it considers only the explicit payments that appear in the firm's written accounts. The relationship between accounting profit and pure economic profit is as follows

$$\text{Pure economic profit} = \text{Accounting profit} - \text{Implicit costs}$$

or alternatively

$$\text{Accounting profit} = \text{Pure economic profit} + \text{Implicit costs.}$$

Normal profit (normal return on capital)

The implicit opportunity cost of capital contributed by the firm's owners (equity capital).

Second, pure economic profit needs to be distinguished from so-called **normal profit**, a term that is sometimes used to refer to the opportunity cost of capital contributed by the firm's owners (*equity capital,* in financial terminology). Normal **return on capital** is an equivalent term. Let us say, for example, that the Martins use $200,000 of their own savings as capital for their new business. They could instead have invested in securities that paid a 10 percent rate of return, or $20,000 per year. That $20,000 would be the opportunity cost of capital. It represents the return the owners' funds would have earned in their best alternative use.

To understand how the opportunity cost of owners' capital comes to be called *normal profit,* consider a firm that has no other implicit costs. In order for such a firm to earn zero economic profit, its accounting profit would have to be equal to its implicit opportunity cost of capital. Such a rate of accounting profit could be called "normal" in the sense that it is just enough to make it worthwhile for owners to invest their capital in this firm, rather than in the best alternative line of business available. Firms that earned more than this (that is, a positive pure economic profit), would be perceived as "abnormally" profitable, and would swiftly attract new investors and competitors. Firms that earned less would be perceived as less than "normally" profitable, and would tend to shrink as investors channeled their capital elsewhere.

If a firm has other implicit costs in addition to those of owners' capital, its accounting profit must be sufficient to cover them, too, in order to earn zero economic profit. This idea can be expressed in terms of any of the following equations, all of which are equivalent:

Accounting profit = Pure economic profit + Implicit costs
= Pure economic profit + Implicit cost of capital + Other implicit costs
= Pure economic profit + Normal profit + Other implicit costs.

Figure 6.1 uses Fieldcom, Inc., to illustrate the concepts of pure economic profit, accounting profit, and normal profit. The figure shows Fieldcom as having earned total revenues of $600,000. Explicit costs—salaries paid to employees and materials purchased—came to $400,000. That left an accounting profit of $200,000. The explicit costs do not include all of the firm's opportunity costs, however. Both Andrea and Ralph Martin gave up high-paying jobs to start the firm. Their combined former income of $160,000 is listed in Figure 6.1 as an implicit cost of production. Also listed as an implicit cost is $20,000 of forgone income that the Martins could have earned on their $200,000 if they had invested it elsewhere. This is the firm's opportunity cost of capital—the normal profit or normal return on capital required to attract capital to this use rather than to the best alternative use. When both explicit and implicit costs (including normal profit) are subtracted from revenue, the firm is left with a pure economic profit of $20,000.

COSTS ARE SUBJECTIVE A final word is in order regarding the nature of costs. In turning from the theory of consumption set forth in the previous chapter to the

FIGURE 6.1 ACCOUNTS OF FIELDCOM, INC.

Total Revenue	$600,000
Less explicit costs:	
Wages and salaries	300,000
Materials and other	100,000
Equals accounting profit	$200,000
Less implicit costs:	
Forgone salary, Andrea Martin	80,000
Forgone salary, Ralph Martin	80,000
Opportunity cost of capital	20,000
Equals pure economic profit	$ 20,000

This figure shows the implicit and explicit costs of the Martins' firm, Fieldcom, Inc. Total revenue minus explicit costs equals accounting profit. Subtracting implicit costs from this quantity yields pure economic profit. The opportunity cost of capital contributed by the Martins is sometimes referred to as normal profit.

theory of production costs, it may at first appear that we are moving from an area of economics governed by *subjective* valuations to one of *objective* valuations. But this is true only in part, if at all.

It is true that business managers and their accountants do make serious efforts to record costs in numerical form, and in doing so, to apply consistent, rational methods that are as free as possible from wishful thinking and intentional bias. In this sense, the process of cost accounting is objective.

In a deeper sense, however, the theory of cost is just as much rooted in subjective judgments as is the theory of consumer choice. That is because all costs, as explained above, are *opportunity costs*. Opportunity costs reflect the value that would have been produced by resources in the best alternative use. But opinions can differ as to what the best alternative is, and what its value is. For example, what really is the opportunity cost to the Martins of investing their $200,000 savings in their computer firm? Ralph might think that the best alternative use would have been to purchase long-term corporate bonds paying a 10 percent rate of return. Andrea might think the best alternative use would have been to buy common stocks of companies located in rapidly-growing Asian economies, a riskier use of the funds, but one yielding an expected return of 11 percent. Who is to say which one is right? Which alternative use of the $200,000 is best depends not only on subjective estimates of the likely return from alternative investments, but also on the subjective attitude toward risk of the person making the investment.

The same is true of the opportunity costs of resources other than capital. For example, an assessment of the opportunity cost of assigning a talented worker to one task must take into account not just what the worker is paid, but also what he or she could have contributed elsewhere in the firm. It will rarely be possible to measure the worker's productivity objectively in both tasks, so the decision will usually be made on the basis of a manager's subjective judgment. In short, because choices are subjective, costs are subjective, too.

Profit, Rents, and Entrepreneurship

Pure economic profit, as we have defined it, is the difference between what a firm receives for the products it sells and the opportunity cost of producing those products. Previously we encountered the notion of payments in excess of opportunity costs, where we called them *economic rents*. Pure economic profit, then, is a type of economic rent. Nevertheless, the two terms are not fully interchangeable.

For one thing, economic rent is a broader notion than profit. *Profit* is usually used in connection with the activities of a business firm, whereas *rents* can be said to be earned by any factor of production. Consider, for example, the income of rock stars, sports professionals, and other people with exceptional talents in a certain line of work. Their opportunity cost of pursuing their chosen line of work may be low, in the sense that their income from their most attractive alternative occupation (say, selling insurance or working as a lifeguard) may be far lower than what they actually earn. The amount by which their extraordinary income as a rock star, sports professional, or whatever exceeds their income from their best alternative occupation can properly be called economic rent, but that income would not be called profit.

A distinction is also sometimes made between *profit seeking* and *rent seeking*. Profit seeking is commonly associated with the activity of entrepreneurship. Entrepreneurs seek profits by finding ways to use factors of production, purchased at market prices, to create goods and services of greater value or at a lower cost compared with their competitors. The Martins are an example of entrepreneurs seeking profits by finding a new way to satisfy customer needs. Thus, *profit seeking* means finding ways to create new value.

However, some firms seek to increase their revenues not through innovation and cost reduction but by seeking restrictions on competition. For example, the Martins might try to boost their firm's earnings by persuading Congress to ban imports of similar PDAs made in China and Korea. This is an example not of entrepreneurship but of political rent seeking.[1]

The distinction between profits earned by entrepreneurs and rents earned by rent seekers is certainly not watertight. In both cases, we are dealing with revenues that exceed opportunity costs. Data like those presented in Figure 6.1 do not tell us all we might want to know about the origin of the $20,000 of pure economic profit. Was that

$20,000 earned by entrepreneurial creation of a new product superior to the products of competitors, or was it earned by rent seeking—say, as a result of import restrictions that drove the superior products of foreign competitors out of the market? The issues raised by this kind of question go beyond the cost and revenue data that we deal with in this chapter and the next one, but we will return to them in later chapters.

Fixed Costs, Variable Costs, and Sunk Costs

Fixed inputs
Inputs that cannot be increased or decreased in a short time in order to increase or decrease output.

Fixed costs
The explicit and implicit opportunity costs associated with providing fixed inputs.

Variable inputs
Inputs that can be varied within a short time in order to increase or decrease output.

Variable costs
The explicit and implicit costs of providing variable inputs.

Short run
A time horizon within which output can be adjusted only by changing the amounts of variable inputs used while fixed inputs remain unchanged.

Long run
A time horizon that is long enough to permit changes in both fixed and variable inputs.

The implicit-explicit distinction provides one way to classify costs, but it is not the only one. Another important classification of costs is based on the time horizon within which production decisions are made.

The amounts of the inputs a firm uses vary as the amounts of output change. The amounts of some inputs used can be adjusted quickly; for example, the amount of electricity used can be increased just by turning on a switch. Quantities of other inputs take longer to adjust; for example, constructing a new office building takes many months. In general, inputs that take longer to adjust can be thought of as those that define the size of the firm's plant, such as the physical size of structures and the production capacity of machinery. They are known as **fixed inputs**. The costs of providing fixed inputs are called **fixed costs**.

In addition to fixed inputs, the firm uses **variable inputs** that can be adjusted quickly and easily within a plant of a given size as output changes. The costs of providing variable inputs are called **variable costs**. Raw materials, energy, and hourly labor are variable inputs for most firms. However, which inputs are fixed and which are variable depends on the situation. For example, a firm that hires workers on an hourly basis may treat wages as a variable cost. Another firm that hires workers on a yearly contract, subject to a "no layoff" agreement, would treat wages as a fixed cost, at least within the time limits of the contract.

The difference between fixed and variable inputs is the basis for the distinction between two time horizons: the short run and the long run. The **short run** is a length of time in which output can be changed by changing the quantity of variable inputs used, but that is too short to permit changes in the size of a firm's plant (that is, fixed inputs). For example, an automaker can vary output from month to month by adding extra shifts of workers without installing additional equipment or building new factories. The **long run** is a length of time that is long enough to permit changes in the amounts of fixed inputs. For example, an automaker can increase capacity to meet expected growth of demand over a period of a few years by building new plants, as well as by adding extra shifts of workers within its old plants.

IMPLICIT AND EXPLICIT FIXED COSTS In all cases, *cost* means *opportunity cost* and therefore includes both implicit and explicit costs. Particular attention must be paid to this fact in dealing with fixed costs.

Fixed costs are "fixed" in the sense that they do not vary with the firm's rate of output. However, they are ongoing costs that must be borne by the firm each day it continues to lease or own the facilities it needs in order to stay in business. If those ongoing costs take the form of periodic payments, they are explicit fixed costs. If they reflect the opportunity cost of ownership of facilities that have been purchased by the firm, they are implicit costs.

As an example, consider a trucking firm. One of the facilities it needs is a warehouse. The warehouse is a fixed cost in that it is a cost that the firm incurs regardless of how much freight is hauled in a given month, but this cost might take either an explicit or an implicit form. The firm might, for example, lease the warehouse for an annual payment of $12,000 in installments of $1,000 per month. That would make the warehouse an explicit cost. But the firm might instead choose to buy the warehouse for a price of $120,000. The $120,000 in cash used to buy the warehouse could have been used for some other purpose—say, to buy government bonds yielding 10 percent interest. The income ($12,000 a year or $1,000 a month) that could have been earned with these funds if they had not been used to buy the warehouse is an opportunity cost of owning the warehouse—an implicit fixed cost. The cost continues as long as the firm keeps the warehouse, even if it goes a month without carrying any freight at all. But if the firm decides to quit the trucking business, it can sell the warehouse and recover the $120,000 for use elsewhere. In that case it would cease to bear the $1,000-a-month fixed cost of the facility.

Sunk costs

Once-and-for-all costs that, once incurred, cannot be recovered.

SUNK COSTS Fixed costs, especially implicit fixed costs, should not be confused with sunk costs. **Sunk costs** are once-and-for-all costs that, once made, cannot be recovered even if the firm leaves its line of business. For example, the trucking firm just mentioned may have paid $1,000 to have "Taylor Trucking" painted on the wall of its warehouse. That is a sunk cost. If the firm sells the warehouse (or terminates its lease), the sign becomes worthless. There is no way to recover the $1,000 that was paid for it, because the next owner or tenant will want a different sign.

If a firm is planning to enter a new line of business or to expand its operations, the sunk costs of doing so are an opportunity cost associated with entry into the new venture. Thus, in considering serving a new city, the trucking firm must think, "$120,000 to buy the warehouse plus $1,000 to paint the sign." But because they cannot be recovered, sunk costs, unlike fixed and variable costs, are *not* counted as part of the firm's ongoing costs of doing business. Once the commitment has been made, the sunk cost is no longer an opportunity cost to the firm because the firm has, once and for all, lost the opportunity to do anything else with the funds in question. In deciding whether to remain in business, the firm should think only, "We could get $120,000 by selling the warehouse." The $1,000 paid for the sign would not enter into the decision at all. In business, the irrelevance of sunk costs to ongoing operations is often expressed in the phrase "bygones are bygones."

The remainder of this chapter will be concerned only with firms' ongoing fixed and variable costs of doing business; sunk costs will not enter into the picture. In later chapters we will return to the subject of sunk costs when discussing the processes through which firms enter and leave particular markets.

PRODUCTION AND COSTS IN THE SHORT RUN

Now that we have pinned down the meaning of cost, our next task is to build a theory to explain how a firm's costs vary with its level of output. The cost that a firm must bear to produce a given level of output is, as we have said, one of the basic constraints that shape a firm's decisions. Our discussion of cost theory will be divided into two parts, corresponding to the time horizons that we have called the short run and the long run.

Production with One Variable Input in the Short Run

Although most firms have several inputs that can be varied even in the short run, it will simplify matters to begin with a case in which only one input—the quantity of labor employed—can be varied. Let us turn once again to Fieldcom for an example.

Total physical product

The total output of a firm, measured in physical units.

Figure 6.2 shows what happens to the daily production rate measured in physical terms, or **total physical product**, as the number of workers is varied from zero to eight. If no workers are employed, no production can take place. In this firm, one worker alone cannot produce anything either—some parts of the job require a minimum of two people working together. Two workers can get production moving, but because they use a lot of time setting up jobs and changing from one job to another, they are able to produce at a rate of only one PDA per day. When a third worker is added, some degree of specialization becomes possible, and production increases to three units per day. A fourth worker gets things moving really smoothly, and production rises to seven units per day. Adding workers five, six, and seven boosts the plant's output to its maximum of thirteen PDAs per day. At that point it does no good to add more workers; all the tools and equipment are in use, and the extra workers would have to stand around waiting for a turn to use them.

Of course, output could be increased by adding *other* inputs in addition to workers—more assembly tables, more testing equipment, and so on. But for the moment we are looking at the effects of increasing just one variable input, other things being equal.

Marginal physical product

The increase in output, expressed in physical units, produced by each added unit of one variable input, other things being equal.

MARGINAL PHYSICAL PRODUCT The chart in part (b) and columns 1 and 2 in part (a) of Figure 6.2 show the relationship between labor inputs and daily output. In the range of one to seven workers, output rises as labor input increases, but not at a constant rate. Column 3 of the table and the chart in part (c) of the figure show how much output changes for each successive worker. The amount by which output changes in each instance is called the **marginal physical product** of the variable input.

FIGURE 6.2 RESPONSE OF OUTPUT TO CHANGES IN ONE VARIABLE INPUT

(a)

(1) Input (Workers per Day)	(2) Total Physical Product (Units per Day)	(3) Marginal Physical Product (Units per Worker)
0	0	
1	0	0
2	1	1
3	3	2
4	7	4
5	10	3
6	12	2
7	13	1
8	13	0

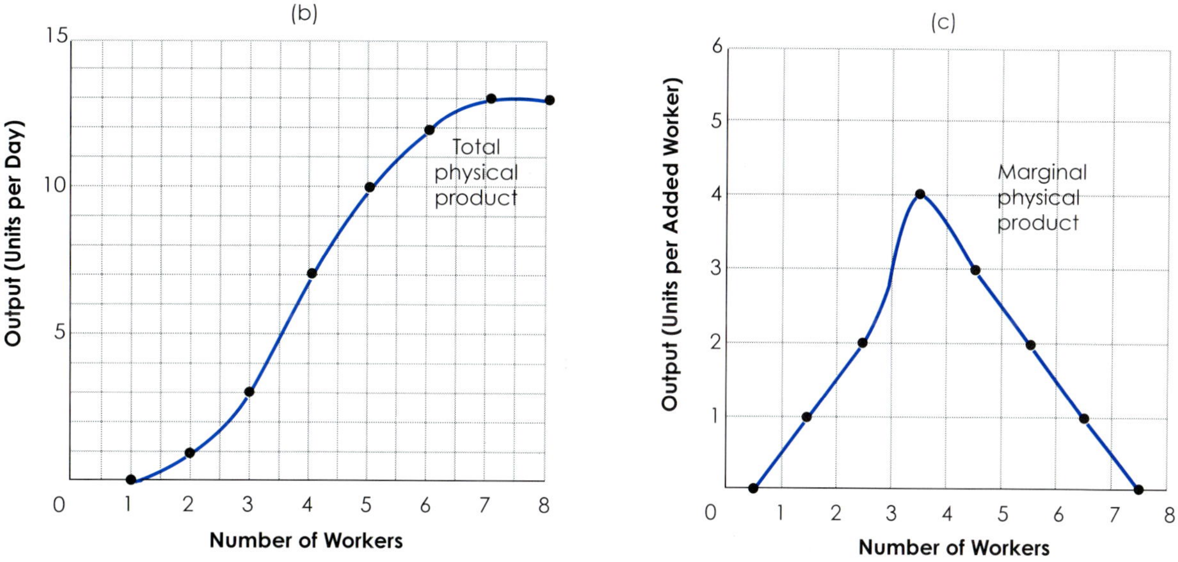

This figure shows how the output of PDAs at Fieldcom, Inc., responds to changes in one variable input—labor. All other inputs remain constant while the number of workers is varied. One worker can produce nothing, since some equipment takes a minimum of two employees to operate. Output increases—at first rapidly, then more slowly—as more workers are used. After seven workers are on the job, all equipment is in use; thus additional workers add nothing more to output. Column 3 of part (a) and the chart in part (c) show the amount of added output that results from each added worker. This is known as the *marginal physical product* of the variable input.

(As elsewhere, the adjective *marginal* refers to the effect of a small change in a quantity—here, the quantity of a variable input.) Adding one full-time worker at a time, as in the table, gives the progression of marginal physical products shown in part (c).

At Fieldcom, as the input of labor is increased from one worker to two, the marginal physical product is one unit of output; as it is stepped up from two to three workers, marginal physical product rises to two units; and so on. The step from three workers to four gives the greatest boost to output. After that, output increases at a diminishing rate with each added worker. Once the staff reaches seven workers, the marginal physical product drops to zero.

THE LAW OF DIMINISHING RETURNS The example just given shows a pattern that economists consider typical for the marginal product of a single variable input such as labor. At first, as workers are added, marginal product increases. Increasing marginal product reflects the advantages of cooperation: the superiority of team production and the benefits of specialization by comparative advantage. After a point, however, as more workers are added, marginal product stops rising and begins to fall. In the case of a single variable input, the principal reason for the eventual decline in marginal physical product is the overcrowding of complementary fixed inputs—in our example, such things as work space, tools, and testing equipment.

Part (c) of Figure 6.2 shows the relationship of marginal physical product to the number of workers in the form of a graph called the *marginal physical product curve.* The part of the curve with a negative slope illustrates a principle known as the **law of diminishing returns**. According to this principle, as the amount of one variable input is increased while the amounts of all other inputs remain fixed, a point will be reached beyond which the marginal physical product of the input will decrease.

Law of diminishing returns

The principle that as one variable input is increased while all others remain fixed, a point will be reached beyond which the marginal physical product of the variable input will begin to decrease.

The law of diminishing returns applies to all production processes and to all variable inputs. The example just given is drawn from manufacturing, but the law could be demonstrated just as well with an example from, say, farming, with fertilizer as the variable input: As more fertilizer is added to a field, output increases, but beyond some point the gain in output brought about by an additional ton of fertilizer tapers off. (In fact, too much fertilizer could poison the plants, in which case marginal physical product would become negative.) Oil refineries, power plants, barber shops, government bureaus—indeed, *any* production process—could be used to illustrate the law of diminishing returns. There can be no exceptions.

From Marginal Physical Product to Marginal Costs

The relationship between inputs and output in terms of physical units is an important constraint on a firm's profit-maximizing activities. However, most business decisions are not made in terms of physical units but in terms of money. Our next step, then, is to restate the constraint implied by the marginal physical product curve in money terms, that is, to ask how much each added unit of output *costs.*

The change in cost associated with a one-unit change in output is called **marginal cost**. To make the conversion from marginal physical product to marginal cost, we proceed as follows, again using Fieldcom as an example.

Marginal cost

The increase in cost required to raise the output of some good or service by one unit.

The first step is to rearrange the data given in Figure 6.2 in terms of input per unit of output. This is done in Figure 6.3. The table in part (a) of the figure reverses the order of the first two columns. Also, the charts in parts (b) and (c) are flipped so that units of output, rather than units of labor input occupy the horizontal axis.

The next step is to convert physical units of input into costs stated in dollars. To do so, we need to know the cost per unit of input. To keep things simple, this example assumes that the variable input, labor, carries an explicit price of $100 per day. Multiplying the labor inputs in column 2 of the figure by the $100-per-day wage

FIGURE 6.3 COST AND OUTPUT WITH ONE VARIABLE INPUT

(a)

(1) Output (Units per Day)	(2) Labor Input	(3) Total Labor Cost (Dollars per Day)	(4) Marginal Cost (Dollars per Unit)
0	0	0	
			200
1	2	200	
			50
3	3	300	
			25
7	4	400	
			33
10	5	500	
			50
12	6	600	
			100
13	7	700	

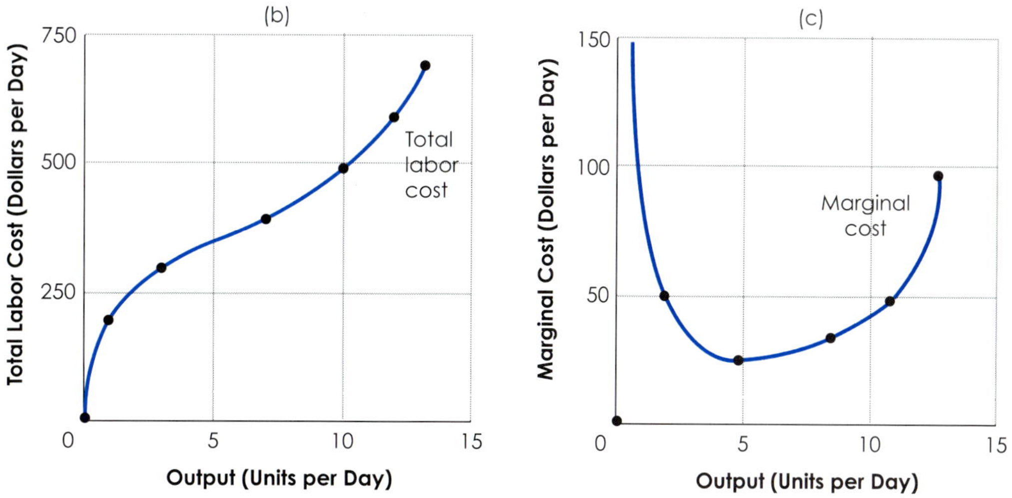

This figure shows how the cost of production at Fieldcom, Inc., changes as output varies. The table and graphs are based on the data used in Figure 6.2, but here they are recast to stress cost assuming a daily wage of $100 per worker. Column 3 of the table and the chart in part (b) show total labor cost for various output levels. Column 4 of the table and the chart in part (c) show marginal cost—the amount by which cost increases per added unit of output. For example, increasing the number of workers from three to four raises output by four units, from three to seven PDAs per day. Over this range, then, the cost of each added PDA is one-quarter of a day's wage, or $25.

yields total labor costs, which are shown in column 3. Those data are used to plot a total labor cost curve in part (b) of the figure. Taking the rearrangement of the axes and the change in units into account, that curve can be recognized as the mirror image of the total physical product curve shown in Figure 6.2.

Finally, column 4 of the table in Figure 6.3 is filled in to show marginal cost, that is, the change in cost, stated in dollars per unit change in output. Increasing output from zero to one requires adding two workers, so the added cost per unit in that range is $200; increasing output by two more units (from one to three) requires one more worker at $100 per day, so the cost per added unit of output in that range is $50; and so on. The marginal cost curve shown in part (c) of the figure is plotted from columns 1 and 4 of the table. As in the case of marginal product, the effect of adding one full-time worker at a time becomes a smooth curve if smaller increments are considered. Again considering the change in units and rearrangement of the axes, part (c) of Figure 6.3 is the approximate mirror image of the marginal physical product curve shown in part (c) of Figure 6.2.

More than One Variable Input

The Fieldcom example assumes that only one input is varied. In practice, short-run increases or decreases in Fieldcom's output would require changes in many—though not all—of its inputs. For example, if the firm wanted to raise its output, in addition to hiring more workers it might burn more fuel to keep the shop heated longer each day and double the rate at which it orders parts.

The appendix to this chapter outlines a way of analyzing changes in two or more variable inputs. Without going into detail, it can be stated that as long as at least some inputs remain fixed, the law of diminishing returns continues to apply. Also, a region of increasing marginal physical product will probably exist at low levels of output. When such a relationship between variable inputs and physical product is combined with a constant price for each input, the result is a total cost curve with a reverse-S shape and a U-shaped marginal cost curve, as in the case of a single variable input.

A Set of Short-Run Cost Curves

Variable cost and marginal cost curves with the shapes just described are shown in Figure 6.4. Those curves are the basis of a whole set of short-run cost curves that can be constructed for an enterprise such as Fieldcom. The figure gives the full set of curves in both graphical and tabular form and also contains some often-used formulas and abbreviations that pertain to cost curves.

Total variable cost is shown graphically in part (a) of Figure 6.4 and numerically in column 2 of part (c). The total variable costs in this example are analogous to the costs shown in the preceding example, except that these allow for more than one variable input. In addition to variable costs, *total fixed costs* (office staff, testing equipment, rent, and so on), which are assumed to be $2,000 per day, are shown in column 3 of part (c). Adding columns 2 and 3 gives short-run *total cost* (variable plus fixed costs), which is shown in column 4. The total fixed cost and total cost curves are plotted together with the total variable cost curve in part (a). Because by definition total fixed cost does not vary as output changes, the total fixed cost curve is a horizontal line $2,000 above the horizontal axis. Total fixed cost is the amount by which total cost exceeds total variable cost, so the total cost curve parallels the total variable cost curve at a higher level. The vertical distance between the total cost and total variable cost curves equals total fixed cost.

The next column in part (c) of Figure 6.4 is marginal cost. Marginal cost data appear on lines between the total cost entries in order to stress that marginal cost shows how total cost changes as the level of output varies. The marginal cost curve is plotted in part (b) of the figure.

All of the cost concepts shown in total terms in part (a) of the figure can also be expressed on a per-unit basis. This is done in the last three columns in the table and the chart in part (b) of Figure 6.4. *Average variable cost* equals total variable cost divided by quantity of output; *average fixed cost* equals total fixed cost divided by output; and *average total cost* equals total cost divided by output. The three average cost curves are drawn together with the marginal cost curve in part (b) of the figure.

Some Geometric Relationships

Parts (a) and (b) of Figure 6.4 demonstrate some important geometric relationships among the cost curves. First, compare the marginal cost curve with the total variable cost curve. The bottom of the U-shaped marginal cost curve lies at exactly the level of output at which the slope of the reverse-S-shaped total variable cost curve stops flattening out and starts getting steeper. (In the language of geometry, this is the *inflection point* of the total variable cost curve.) This relationship holds because the slope of the total variable cost curve shows the rate at which total variable cost changes as output changes, and that is the definition of marginal cost. In graphical terms, then, the *height* of the marginal cost curve always equals the *slope* of the total variable cost curve.

A second feature of the cost curves in Figure 6.4 also deserves comment. The marginal cost curve intersects both the average variable cost and the average total cost curves at their lowest points. This is not a coincidence; it is a result of a relationship that can be called the **marginal-average rule**, which can be explained as follows: Beginning at any given point, ask what the cost of making one more unit of output will be. The answer is given by marginal cost. Then ask whether that cost is more or

Marginal-average rule

The rule that marginal cost must equal average cost when average cost is at its minimum.

FIGURE 6.4 A SET OF SHORT-RUN COST CURVES

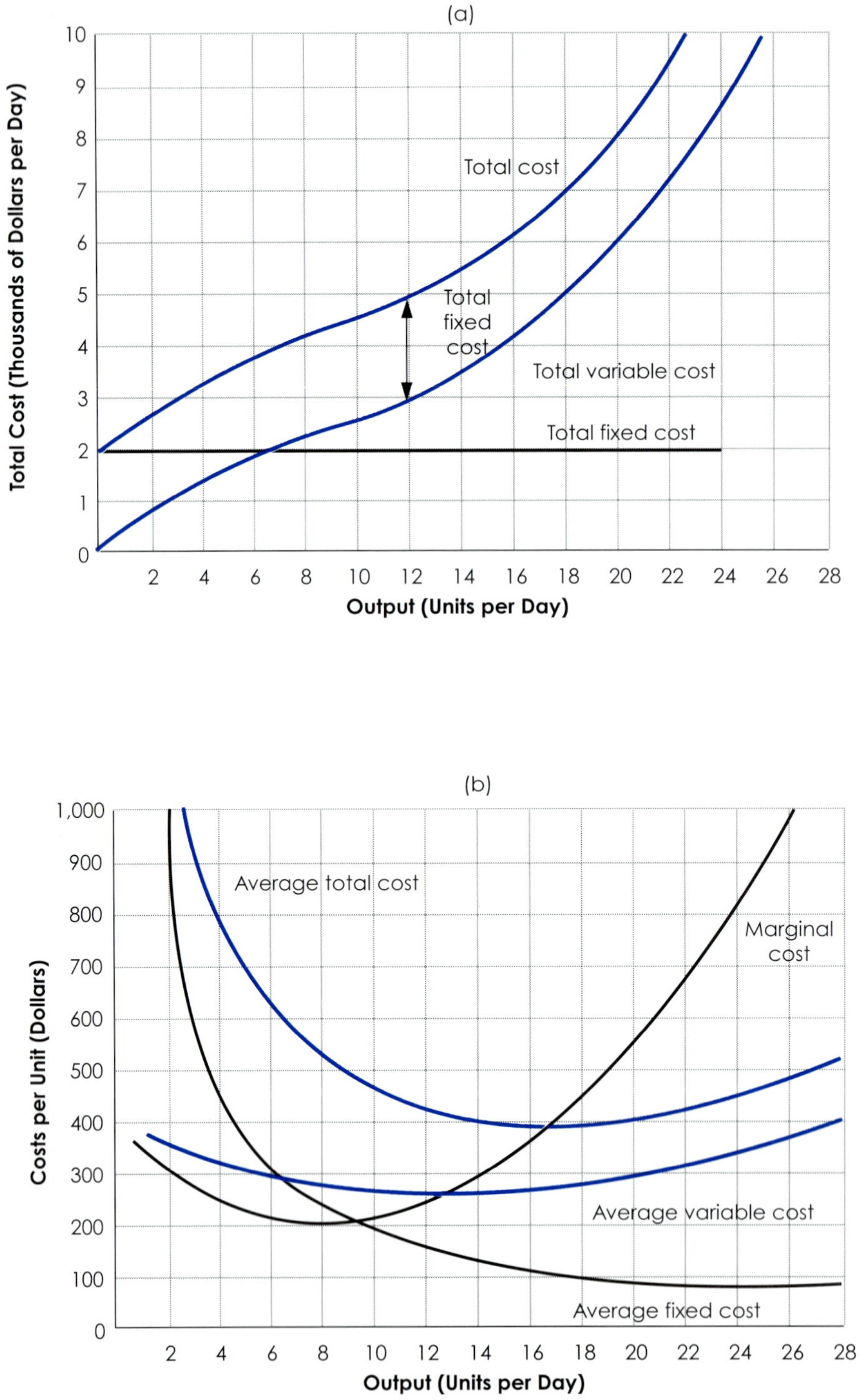

(continues)

FIGURE 6.4 A SET OF SHORT-RUN COST CURVES, CONTINUED

(c)

Quantity of Output (Units per Day) (1)	Total Variable Cost (Dollars per Day) (2)	Total Fixed Cost (Dollars per Day) (3)	Total Cost (Dollars per Day) (4)	Marginal Cost (Dollars per Unit) (5)	Average Variable Cost (Dollars per Unit) (6)	Average Fixed Cost (Dollars per Unit) (7)	Average Total Cost (Dollars per Unit) (8)
0	$ 0	$2,000	$ 2,000		—	—	—
1	380	2,000	2,380	$380	$380	$2,000	$2,380
2	720	2,000	2,720	340	360	1,000	1,360
3	1,025	2,000	3,025	305	342	667	1,009
4	1,300	2,000	3,300	275	325	500	825
5	1,550	2,000	3,550	250	310	400	710
6	1,780	2,000	3,780	230	296	333	629
7	1,995	2,000	3,995	215	285	286	571
8	2,200	2,000	4,200	205	275	250	525
9	2,400	2,000	4,400	200	266	222	488
10	2,605	2,000	4,605	205	260	200	460
11	2,820	2,000	4,820	215	256	181	437
12	3,050	2,000	5,050	230	254	169	421
13	3,300	2,000	5,300	250	254	154	408
14	3,575	2,000	5,575	275	255	143	398
15	3,880	2,000	5,880	305	259	133	392
16	4,220	2,000	6,220	340	264	125	389
17	4,600	2,000	6,600	380	271	118	389
18	5,025	2,000	7,025	425	279	111	390
19	5,500	2,000	7,500	475	289	105	394
20	6,030	2,000	8,030	530	302	100	402
21	6,620	2,000	8,620	590	315	95	410
22	7,275	2,000	9,275	655	331	91	422
23	8,000	2,000	10,000	725	348	87	435
24	8,800	2,000	10,800	800	367	83	450

(d)

Common abbreviations

Q	Quantity of output
TC	Total cost
TFC	Total fixed cost
TVC	Total variable cost
MC	Marginal cost
AVC	Average variable cost
AFC	Average fixed cost
ATC	Average total cost

Useful formulas:

$$TC = TFC + TVC$$

$$MC = \frac{\text{Change in TC}}{\text{Change in Q}} = \frac{\text{Change in TVC}}{\text{Change in Q}}$$

$$AVC = \frac{TVC}{Q}$$

$$AFC = \frac{TFC}{Q}$$

$$ATC = \frac{TC}{Q}$$

A whole set of short-run cost curves can be derived from data on fixed and variable costs, as this figure shows. The data are presented in the form of a table and a pair of graphs. The figure also lists a number of useful abbreviations and formulas.

FIGURE 6.5 SHORT- AND LONG-RUN AVERAGE COST CURVES

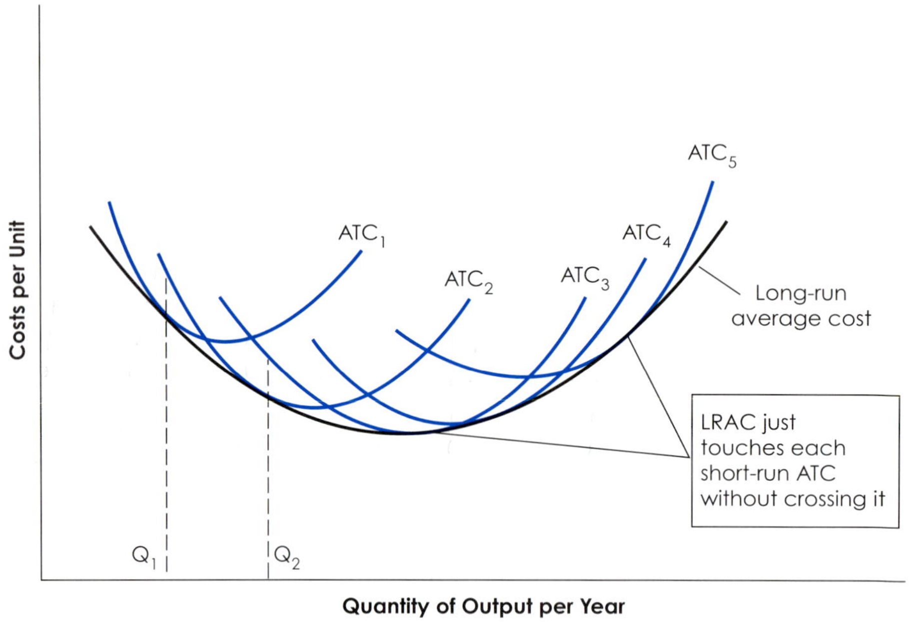

The position of the short-run average total cost curve for a firm depends on the size of the plant. In the long run, the firm has a choice of operating with any size of plant it chooses. Each plant size can be represented by a U-shaped short-run average total cost curve. Five such curves are shown in this graph. A new firm might begin with a plant that can be represented by a short-run average total cost curve such as ATC_1. Then, as demand for its product expands, it might move to one of those farther to the right. The firm's long-run average cost curve is the "envelope" of these and other possible short-run average total cost curves; that is, it is a smooth curve drawn so that it just touches the short-run curves without intersecting any of them.

used to its designed capacity. On the other hand, the larger plant represented by ATC_2 is the best plant size for output Q_2. That larger output could be produced in the smaller plant, but only by running it at a rate higher than the one for which it is designed. The penalty, in terms of unit cost, is shown by the fact that ATC_1 lies above ATC_2 at the output level Q_2.

If a firm wants to produce at an unusually high or low rate for a short time, it may make sense to do so by moving along the short-run average total cost curve corresponding to its present plant size. An example would be a firm that decides to run overtime to fill an exceptionally large order, or one that cuts back to half-shifts to weather a temporary business downturn. But when sustained increases in output level are under consideration, costs are minimized by building a larger plant, as a young firm such as Fieldcom will do when it expands. Likewise, a firm that is planning to reduce its output permanently will eliminate some plant rather than keep production facilities operating at lower levels of output than those for which they

APPLYING ECONOMIC IDEAS 6.1

SONY CORPORATION FACES COSTS AND OPPORTUNITIES

Akio Morita is chairman of the Japanese electronics giant, Sony Corporation. His firm, like most others, started small. Here he recalls an episode from Sony's early days.

Our first transistor radio of 1955 was small and practical—not as small as some of our later efforts, but we were very proud of it. I saw the United States as a natural market. I took my little $29.95 radio to New York and made the rounds of possible retailers.

While making the rounds, I came across an American buyer who looked at the radio and said he liked it very much. He said his chain, which had about 150 stores, would need large quantities. He asked me to give him a price quotation only on quantities of 5,000, 10,000; 30,000, 50,000 and 100,000 radios. What an invitation!

But back in my hotel room, I began pondering the possible impact of such grand orders on our small facilities in Tokyo. We had expanded our plant a lot since we outgrew the unpainted, leaky shack on Gotenyama [a hill on the southern edge of Tokyo]. We had moved into bigger, sturdier buildings adjacent to the original site and had our eye on some more property, but we did not have the capacity to produce 100,000 transistor radios a year and also make the other things in our small product line. Our capacity was less than 10,000 radios a month. If we got an order for 100,000, we would have to hire and train new employees and expand our facilities even more. This would mean a major investment, a major expansion and a gamble.

I was inexperienced and still a little naive, but I had my wits about me. I considered all the consequences I could think of, and then I sat down and drew a curve that looked something like a lopsided letter U. The price for 5,000 would be our regular price. That would be the beginning of the curve. For 10,000 there would be a discount, and that was at the bottom of the curve. For 30,000 the price would begin to climb. For 50,000 the price per unit would be higher than for 5,000, and for l00,000 units the price would have to be much more per unit than for the first 5,000.

My reasoning was this: If we had to double our production capacity to complete an order for 100,000 and if we could not get a repeat order the following year we would be in big trouble, perhaps bankrupt, because how in that case could we employ all the added staff and pay for the new and unused facilities?... In Japan, we cannot just hire people and fire them whenever our orders go up or down. We have a long-term commitment to our employees and they have a commitment to us.

I returned the next day with my quotation. The buyer looked at it and blinked as though he couldn't believe his eyes. He put down the paper and said, patiently, "Mr. Morita, I have been working as a purchasing agent for nearly thirty years and you are the first person who has ever come in here and told me that the more I buy the higher the unit price will be. It's illogical!" I explained my reasoning to him and he listened carefully to what I had to say. When he got over his shock, he paused for a moment, smiled, and then placed an order for 10,000 radios—at the 10,000 unit price—which was just right for him and for us.

Source: Akio Morita, "When Sony Was an Up and Comer," *Forbes*, October 6, 1986, 98–102. Adapted from *Made in Japan: Akio Morita and Sony* by Akio Morita with Edwin M. Reingold and Mitsuko Shimomura. Copyright 1986 by E. P. Dutton, a division of NAL Penguin, Inc. Reprinted by permission of the publisher, E. P. Dutton.

were designed. Decisions of that kind represent movements out or back along the firm's long-run average cost curve.

Economies of Scale

Economies of scale

A situation in which long-run average cost decreases as output increases.

Movements along a firm's long-run average cost curve, during which the firm is free to adjust quantities of all the inputs it uses, are referred to as changes in the *scale* of production. Some special terminology is used to describe the way long-run average cost changes as the scale of production changes. In any output range in which long-run average cost *decreases* as output increases, the firm is said to experience **economies of scale**. In any output range in which long-run average cost *increases*, the

Diseconomies of scale

A situation in which long-run average cost increases as output increases.

Constant returns to scale

A situation in which there are neither economies nor diseconomies of scale.

Minimum efficient scale

The output level at which economies of scale cease.

firm is said to experience **diseconomies of scale**. Finally, if there is any range of output for which long-run average cost does not change as output varies, the firm is said to experience **constant returns to scale** in that range.

The long-run average cost curve in Figure 6.5 is smoothly U-shaped, so there is no range of constant returns to scale. However, empirical studies suggest that the long-run cost curves of actual firms may have long flat sections in the middle over which average cost changes relatively little as output changes. Economies of scale for such a firm appear only over a range of rather low output levels, and diseconomies appear only over a range of very high output levels. For a firm with such a long-run average cost curve, the level of output at which economies of scale end and constant returns to scale begin can be called the firm's **minimum efficient scale**.

SOURCES OF ECONOMIES OF SCALE Where do economies of scale come from? If firms grew simply by increasing fixed and variable inputs in exact proportion, so that a large plant amounted to nothing more than a lot of small plants built side by side, one might expect changes in scale to have no effect at all on average cost. But that is not the way firms expand. As they grow, they tend to change the technologies they use and their methods of internal organization to take advantage of new opportunities offered by the higher output level. Those changes give rise to economies of scale.

In part, economies of scale stem from the human factors mentioned before—the advantages of team production and specialization according to comparative advantage. A firm can get very large before it completely exhausts the possibilities for cooperation and specialization. In a small firm, for example, the marketing function may be something the owner does from 3:00 P.M. to 4:00 P.M. after touring the plant floor and perhaps taking a turn running a machine. A somewhat larger firm can afford to hire a marketing manager who devotes full time to the job. In a still larger firm, subspecialties develop—a sales manager, a director of product development, an advertising specialist, all under the direction of the marketing manager.

Other economies of scale have origins in technology. In many lines of production, for example, a machine that is capable of doing twice the work of a smaller one costs less than twice as much to build and operate. A pizza oven that is big enough to bake 60 pizzas an hour costs less than twice as much as a 30-pizza-per-hour model. A tractor that can plow 50 acres a day costs less than twice as much as one that can plow only 25 acres, and the large model still requires only one driver. For a firm that is too small to utilize a large piece of equipment fully, the smaller model can still be the appropriate choice. But as the firm grows, technological economies lower its average costs.

What is more, growth of a firm does not just mean constant expansion of a single plant. Operation of multiple plants can yield further economies of scale even after each plant reaches the minimum efficient scale at which technical economies are exhausted. The McDonald's hamburger chain provides a good example. The minimum efficient scale for a single plant (restaurant) is very small in the fast-food industry. Yet McDonald's gains some important economies by running a large number of restaurants as a system. Some of these are production economies: Individual food items and ingredients can be made in central kitchens; managers can be trained at "Hamburger University"; and so on. A multiplant firm such as McDonald's also realizes economies of scale in such areas as finance and marketing.

SOURCES OF DISECONOMIES OF SCALE Although there are many sources of economies of scale, they are not limitless. As a firm expands, it encounters diseconomies of scale as well as economies. Technological sources of diseconomies can often be avoided. For example, as an airline grows, at first it may buy larger and larger planes, but rather than keep this up until its planes get so big that they cannot fly, it starts buying more and more planes of optimal size. In other lines of business, firms can avoid potential technical diseconomies by building multiple plants of optimal size.

The most important diseconomies are organizational. As a firm grows, it finds itself depending more and more on hierarchical means of coordinating its employees' activities. As a hierarchy grows, the cost of channeling information to key decision makers tends to rise. Moreover, individual incentives tend to get diluted in a large hierarchical organization. More and more managerial skill has to be devoted to maintaining employee loyalty and motivation. There is an increasing risk that departments and divisions will pursue parochial interests that diverge from those of the firm as a whole.

In some lines of business, firms can grow to a very large size before the diseconomies start to outweigh the economies. Huge firms, such as General Motors, AT&T, and IBM, successfully manage hierarchies that are bigger than the governments of all but a handful of countries. But the very mention of such corporate giants calls to mind their vulnerability to smaller, more aggressive rivals. All three of the companies just listed have lost sales in recent years to smaller competitors in important product lines.

In other lines of business, comparatively small firms seem to have the edge. In farming, services, and retail trade, small units predominate. In still other industries, franchising is used to combine economies of scale in a few functions such as marketing and product development with the production advantages of small-unit operation.

SUMMARY

1. **How do economists view the concepts of cost and profit?** *Explicit costs* are opportunity costs that take the form of explicit payments to suppliers of factors of production and intermediate goods. *Implicit costs* are the opportunity costs associated with using resources contributed by the firm's owners (or owned by the firm itself as a legal entity) that are not obtained under contracts calling for explicit payments. Implicit costs include the opportunity cost of capital needed to attract owners' capital to the firm. If only explicit

costs are subtracted from revenue, the result is *accounting profit*. Revenue minus all costs, both implicit and explicit, is *pure economic profit*.

2. **What is the distinction between short-run and long-run time horizons?** *Fixed inputs* cannot be increased or decreased in a short time; they are linked with the size of the firm's plant. The costs of such inputs are termed *fixed costs*. *Variable inputs* can be varied quickly in order to increase or decrease output; they include hourly labor, energy, and raw materials. The costs of those inputs are termed *variable costs*. *Sunk costs* are once-and-for-all expenditures that cannot be recovered once they have been made. The *short run* is a period within which only variable inputs can be adjusted. In the *long run* changes can be made in fixed inputs, including plant size.

3. **How do costs vary in response to changes in the quantity of a variable input?** As the amount of one input to a production process increases while the amounts of all other inputs remain fixed, output will increase, at least over some range. The amount of output added by each one-unit increase in the variable input is known as the *marginal physical product* of that input. According to the *law of diminishing returns*, as the amount of one variable input used in a production process increases (with the amounts of all other inputs remaining fixed), a point will be reached beyond which the amount of output added per unit of added variable input (that is, the marginal physical product of the variable input) will begin to decrease. The principle applies to all production processes.

4. **How can a firm's cost structure be represented in geometric terms?** A whole set of cost curves can be constructed for a firm, given data on its fixed and variable costs. The most commonly used cost curves are total cost, total fixed cost, total variable cost, average fixed cost, average variable cost, average total cost, and marginal cost. According to the *marginal-average rule*, the marginal cost curve intersects the average variable cost and average total cost curves at their lowest points.

5. **What choices does a firm face in the course of long-run expansion?** In the long run a firm can adjust the amounts of fixed inputs that it uses by expanding or reducing its plant. Each possible plant size has a U-shaped short-run average total cost curve. The firm's long-run average cost curve is a shallower U-shaped curve based on a set of short-run curves. When long-run average cost decreases as output increases, the firm is said to experience *economies of scale*. When long-run average cost increases as output increases, the firm is said to experience *diseconomies of scale*. If there are neither economies nor diseconomies of scale, the firm is said to experience *constant returns to scale*.

KEY TERMS

Explicit costs
Implicit costs
Pure economic profit
Accounting profit
Normal profit (normal return on capital)
Fixed inputs
Fixed costs
Variable inputs
Variable costs
Short run
Long run
Sunk costs
Total physical product
Marginal physical product
Law of diminishing returns
Marginal cost
Marginal-average rule
Economies of scale
Diseconomies of scale
Constant returns to scale
Minimum efficient scale

PROBLEMS AND TOPICS FOR DISCUSSION

1. **Examining the lead-off case.** One of the opportunity costs borne by the Martins is that of exchanging the secure life of employees of large

firms for the risky life of entrepreneurs. Do you think they would be willing to do this if they expected to earn no more than their previous salaries plus a "normal profit" on the capital they invested in the firm? Do you think that pure economic profit can be viewed as compensation to entrepreneurs for the risk they bear? Discuss.

2. **Implicit and explicit costs.** List the basic costs of owning and operating an automobile. Which are explicit costs? Which are implicit costs? Does driving an automobile impose any external opportunity costs on the economy as a whole that do not show up on your list as either implicit or explicit costs? If so, what are they?

3. **Fixed and variable costs.** Divide the costs of owning and operating an automobile into fixed and variable costs. Suppose that you were deciding whether to drive to a football game at a nearby college or to take the bus instead. Would you take both fixed and variable costs into account? Suppose that you were deciding whether to buy a house in a neighborhood where you could walk to work or a house in a neighborhood where you would have to buy a second car to drive to work every day. Would you take both fixed and variable costs into account? Explain the difference between the two situations.

4. **Economies and diseconomies of scale.** Do you think the business of running a college is subject to economies or diseconomies of scale? Which parts of the college's operation (such as library, dormitories, faculty salaries, moving students between classes, and so on) are subject to economies of scale, diseconomies of scale, or constant returns to scale?

5. **Total cost curves.** Draw a set of coordinate axes on a piece of graph paper. Label the x axis "Output" (0 to 20 units) and the y axis "Cost" (0 to 20 units). Plot the following (x, y) points on your graph: (0, 4); (2, 6); (4, 7); (7, 8); (9, 9); (11, 11); (13, 14). Connect these points with a smooth curve and label it "total cost." Working from this curve, construct a total fixed cost curve and a total variable cost curve for the same firm.

6. **Marginal and average cost curves.** Draw a second set of coordinate axes on another piece of graph paper. Label the horizontal axis "Output" (0 to 20 units) and the vertical axis "Cost per Unit" (0 to 2 units, in tenths of a unit). Using as a basis the total cost, total variable cost, and total fixed cost curves you drew for problem 5, construct the following curves on your new graph: marginal cost, average total cost, average variable cost, and average fixed cost.

7. **Relating the long- and short-run cost curves.** Turn to Figure 6.5 and copy the diagram onto a sheet of graph paper, drawing the long-run average total cost curve and one of the short-run average total cost curves. Use these curves to construct the corresponding long- and short-run total cost curves. Both total cost curves should be reverse-S shaped and tangent to each other at the same output level for which the average total cost curves are tangent.

8. **Diminishing returns.** Suppose that you examine the relationship between the amount of coal burned per week in a certain power plant and the amount of electricity generated per week. You find that for small amounts of coal—too small even to bring the boiler up to the temperature needed to make steam—no electricity can be produced. After a certain minimum amount of coal is burned, the plant begins to operate. From that point on, the added amount of electricity generated per added ton of coal burned is constant over a wide range. Then a point is reached beyond which burning more coal produces no more electricity. Sketch the total physical product curve for this plant, and draw a graph showing how marginal physical product varies as output changes. Does this production process obey the law of diminishing returns?

9. **More on diminishing returns.** It has been said that were it not for the law of diminishing returns, all the food that the world needs could be grown in a flowerpot. Discuss this statement. (Suggestion: Think of land as the only fixed factor and fertilizer as the only variable factor. How much food could be grown in the flowerpot if the marginal physical product of fertilizer were constant regardless of the amount used per unit of land?)

CASE FOR DISCUSSION

Tennis at the Olympia

The Olympia Sport and Health Club is a large, modern facility in the suburbs of Washington, D.C. The club offers many activities, including swimming, weight training, and aerobics, but its leading attraction is excellent indoor tennis courts. Members may play on clay or two types of hard-surface courts. To add to members' enjoy-ment of the sport, the club offers private and group lessons; tournament, ladder, and team competitions; and numerous social events.

To join the club, a single individual pays a $1,000 nonrefundable initiation fee. In addition, there is an $88 monthly membership charge, which must be paid whether or not the member uses the facilities. Those two fees cover most of the club's costs, so it is able to keep the charge for actual playing time quite low. The fee for an hour's use of a court is only $2.

At first the low hourly court fee created a problem for the club. The fee was so low that members would not bother to call to cancel a court reservation if they changed their minds about playing. Other members would then be told that no reservations were available, when in fact the courts stood empty.

To overcome this problem, the club introduced a new rule: Members who make reservations and use the court pay the usual $2 per hour. But a member who makes a reservation and does *not* show up pays a penalty rate of $10 per hour for the unused time. A reservation can be canceled nine hours or more in advance with no charge at all. This rule has proved successful in reducing abuses of the reservation system and making court time more readily available to all members.

QUESTIONS

1. Classify the costs of membership in the Olympia as fixed, variable, and sunk.
2. Suppose that you are thinking about joining the Olympia to play indoor tennis. Which of the costs are opportunity costs that would be relevant to your decision?
3. Suppose you are a member of the Olympia but are considering dropping your membership so that you can afford to do other things, such as traveling. Which of the costs of the club are opportunity costs that would be relevant to your decision?
4. Suppose that you are a member of the club and are deciding whether to spend next Saturday afternoon playing tennis there. Which of the costs are opportunity costs that would be relevant to your decision?
5. Suppose that it is noon on Saturday. You have made a reservation for an hour of court time at 5:00 P.M. A friend asks you to join a pickup basketball game at that time instead. What is the opportunity cost associated with abandoning the tennis reservation to join the basketball game?

END NOTES

1. See James M. Buchanan, "Rent Seeking and Profit Seeking," in *Toward a Theory of the Rent-Seeking Society,* eds. James M. Buchanan, Robert D. Tollison, and Gordon Tullock (College Station: Texas A&M University Press, 1980), 3–15.

Appendix to Chapter 6
COST AND OUTPUT WITH TWO VARIABLE INPUTS

In this chapter we looked at the relationship between cost and output when just one input is varied and all other inputs are kept constant. In this appendix, we extend the theory of cost to the case in which more than one input is varied.

Substitution of Inputs

The main new feature of situations in which more than one input is varied is the possibility of substituting one input for another. Consider the case of Henry Hathaway, a farmer who grows corn. Hathaway spends all his time working on his farm and does not hire anyone to help him. For him, the amount of labor used in growing corn is a fixed input. In addition to fixed amounts of labor and machinery, he uses two variable inputs: land and fertilizer.

Hathaway can grow a given quantity of corn—say, 200 bushels—in many different ways. Some of the possibilities are shown in Figure 6A.1. One way to grow 200 bushels of corn is to use 2.5 tons of fertilizer and 10 acres of land. This is represented by point P on the graph. If Hathaway wants to grow the same amount of corn on less land, he can substitute fertilizer for land. For example, at point Q he can grow 200 bushels of corn on 5 acres by using 5 tons of

FIGURE 6A.1 AN ISOQUANTITY LINE

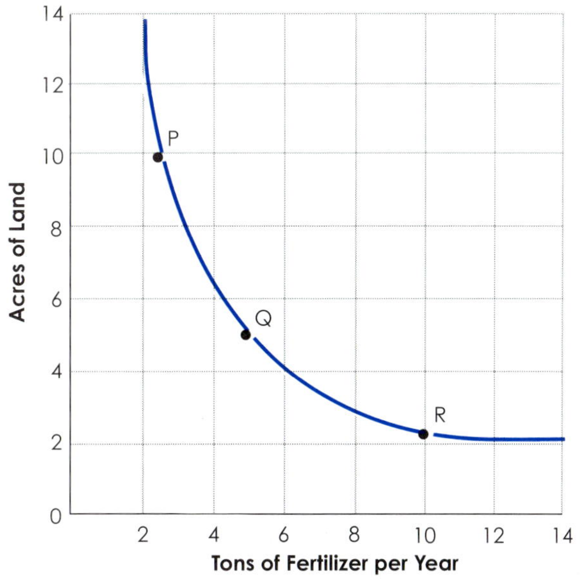

This graph shows an isoquantity line, or isoquant, for the production of 200 bushels of corn. The variable inputs are land and fertilizer; the other inputs, labor and machinery, are assumed to be fixed. Points P, Q, and R represent various ways of growing the given quantity of corn. A movement downward along the isoquant represents the substitution of fertilizer for land while output is maintained at 200 bushels per year. As more and more fertilizer is substituted for land, the isoquant becomes flatter because of diminishing returns.

fertilizer. By substituting still more fertilizer for land, he can move to point R, where the 200 bushels are grown on just 2.5 acres using 10 tons of fertilizer.

Diminishing Returns in Substitutions

In this chapter, we defined the law of diminishing returns as it applies to a situation in which one input is varied while all others remain constant. In that situation, after a certain point the amount of the variable input needed to make an extra unit of output increases. (This is another way of saying that the marginal physical product of the variable input decreases.) A similar principle applies when one input is substituted for another in such a way as to keep output at a constant level: As the amount of input x is increased, the amount of x needed to replace one unit of y increases.

The example in Figure 6A.1 illustrates this principle. In moving from point P to point Q, 2.5 tons of fertilizer replace 5 acres of land while output stays constant at 200 bushels. But in moving from point Q to point R, 5 more tons of fertilizer are needed to replace just 2.5 acres of land.

As a result of the law of diminishing returns in substituting one input for another, a curve connecting points P, Q, and R becomes flatter as one moves downward and to the right along it. This reflects the decreasing ratio of the marginal physical product of fertilizer to the marginal physical product of land as more fertilizer is substituted for land.

Choosing the Least-Cost Production Method

Isoquantity line (isoquant)

A line showing the various combinations of inputs with which a given quantity of output can be produced.

The line connecting points P, Q, and R in Figure 6A.1 is called an **isoquantity line** or **isoquant**, because it shows the combinations of inputs that can be used to produce a given amount of output. (The prefix *iso* comes from a Greek word meaning "equal.") Although all the points on the isoquant are equal in terms of output, they are not equal in terms of cost. To see how a producer can choose the least-cost method of producing a given level of output, we need to know the prices of the inputs.

In the appendix to Chapter 5, we used budget lines as a graphical device to represent the prices of consumer goods. As Figure 6A.2 shows, the same technique can be used to represent the prices of inputs. The graph assumes a cost of $50 a ton for fertilizer and a rental price of $50 per year for land. The sum of $400 can buy 8 tons of fertilizer and no land, 8 acres of land with no fertilizer, or any of the other points on line A; the sum of $500 will buy 10 tons of fertilizer, 10 acres of land, or any of the other points on line B; and so on.

When the isoquant for 200 bushels of corn is drawn on top of a set of budget lines for the inputs, it is easy to see the least-cost method of producing that output level: It is the method that uses 5 tons of fertilizer and 5 acres of land. This corresponds to point Q on the graph, where the isoquant just touches budget line B. Points P and R are possible ways of growing 200 bushels of corn, but they lie on budget line C, which corresponds to a cost of $625. Note also that a budget of less than $500 (say, $400, as shown by budget line A) is not enough to reach the 200-bushel isoquant no matter how it is split between fertilizer and land.

Responses to Changes in Input Prices

If input prices change, the least-cost combination of inputs is likely to change as well. Suppose that the suburbs begin to expand in the direction of Hathaway's farm, driving up the price of land. Now land that used to rent for $50 per acre per year rents for $200 per acre. The price of fertilizer remains unchanged at $50 a ton.

FIGURE 6A.2 FINDING THE LEAST-COST PRODUCTION METHOD

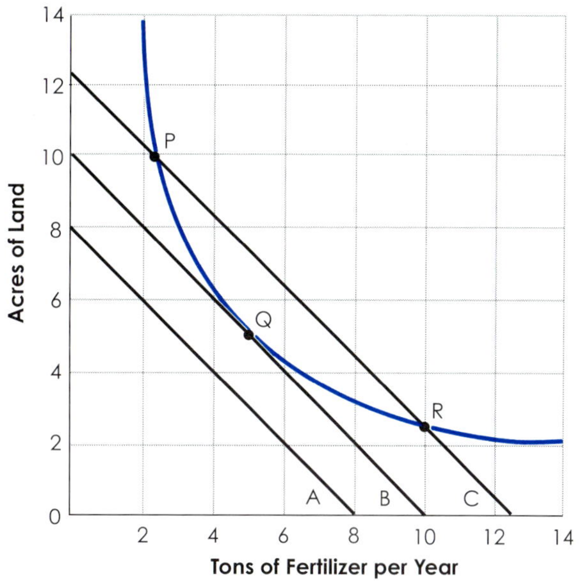

This graph shows how the least-cost method of production can be found from among the points on an isoquant given the prices of the variable inputs. Here the price of fertilizer is assumed to be $50 a ton and the rental price of land $50 per year. A set of budget lines is drawn to represent various levels of spending on inputs. Line A, which corresponds to a total variable cost of $400, does not provide enough inputs to produce 200 bushels of corn. Line C, which corresponds to a total variable cost of $625, provides enough inputs to grow 200 bushels of corn using methods P or R. Line B, which corresponds to a total variable cost of $500, permits the 200 bushels to be grown using method Q, which is the least-cost method given these input prices.

The results of the increase in the price of land are shown in Figure 6A.3. Now $500 will not be enough to buy the combinations of inputs that fall along budget line B. Even if all the money were spent on land, only 2.5 acres could be rented. The new $500 budget line is C, which does not reach the 200-bushel isoquant at any point.

To grow 200 bushels, Hathaway must now spend more than $500. As he increases his budget for land and fertilizer, the budget line shifts upward but stays parallel to C. When the budget line reaches D, which corresponds to spending $1,000 on inputs, it just touches the isoquant at R. We see that now $1,000 is the lowest cost at which 200 bushels of corn can be grown, given a price of $50 a ton for fertilizer and $200 an acre for land. With those prices, R is the least-cost combination of inputs.

In this case, the effect of an increase in the price of an input is typical. Less of the input whose price has gone up is used, and the other input, which has become relatively less costly, is substituted for it. We will return to this topic in later chapters, where we discuss the markets for productive resources.

Varying Output

The isoquant technique can also be used to analyze variations in output with two variable inputs. Part (a) of Figure 6A.4 shows an isoquant "map" with three sets of points that correspond to

FIGURE 6A.3 EFFECTS OF A CHANGE IN INPUT PRICES

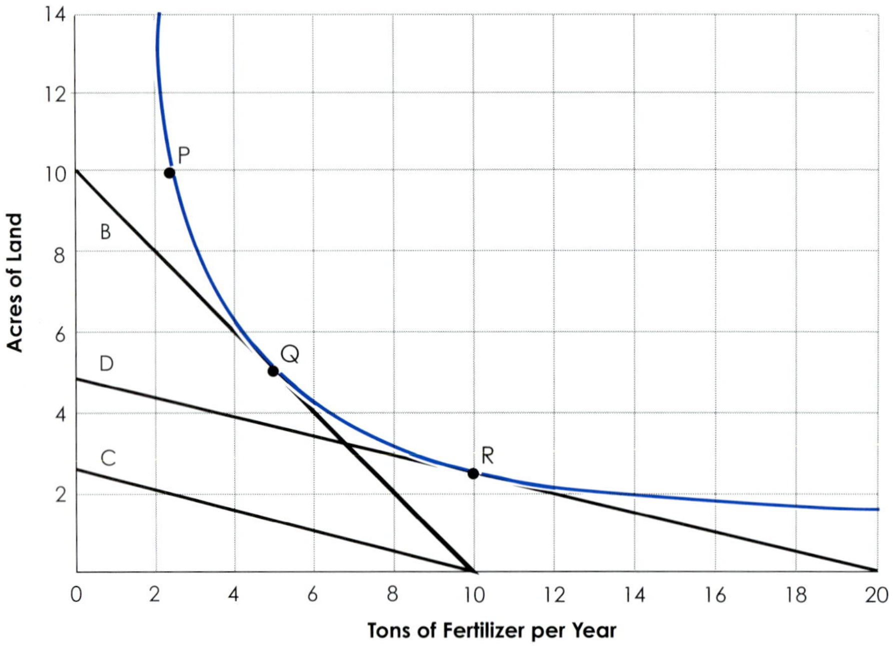

If the rental price of land increases from $50 to $200 per year while the price of fertilizer remains fixed at $50 a ton, 200 bushels of corn can no longer be produced for $500. The $500 budget line shifts from position B to position C and now falls short of the 200-bushel isoquant. Increasing the amount spent on variable inputs to $1,000 shifts the budget line up to position D, where it just touches the isoquant at point R. The increase in the price of land thus not only raises the total variable cost of growing 200 bushels of corn but also causes fertilizer to be substituted for land, which is now relatively more costly.

three output levels. As before, P, Q, and R represent three ways of growing 200 bushels of corn. Points S, T, and U represent three ways of growing 100 bushels, and points V, W, and X are three ways of growing 300 bushels. An isoquant has been drawn through each set of points.

In this figure, we return to the assumption that land costs $50 an acre and fertilizer $50 a ton. Using these prices, a set of budget lines has been drawn, each corresponding to a different total variable cost, $300, $500, and $1,000.

As the graph clearly shows, there is a least-cost method for producing each output level given these prices. Point T is the best way to produce 100 bushels; Q is best for 200 bushels; and W is best for 300 bushels. Other output levels would be possible as well; these would lie along the line drawn from the origin through points T, Q, and W. This line is called the firm's **expansion path**. As the firm moves along its expansion path, more of both the variable inputs, land and fertilizer, is used. Meanwhile, the fixed inputs—labor and machinery, in Hathaway's case—remain constant.

Expansion path

A line on an isoquant diagram showing the least-cost combinations of inputs used to produce various levels of output, for given input prices.

Deriving a Cost Curve from the Isoquant Map

Once the expansion path has been identified, we can easily construct a total variable cost curve. All we need do is construct a graph that links each output point on the expansion path

FIGURE 6A.4 EXPANSION OF OUTPUT AND TOTAL VARIABLE COSTS

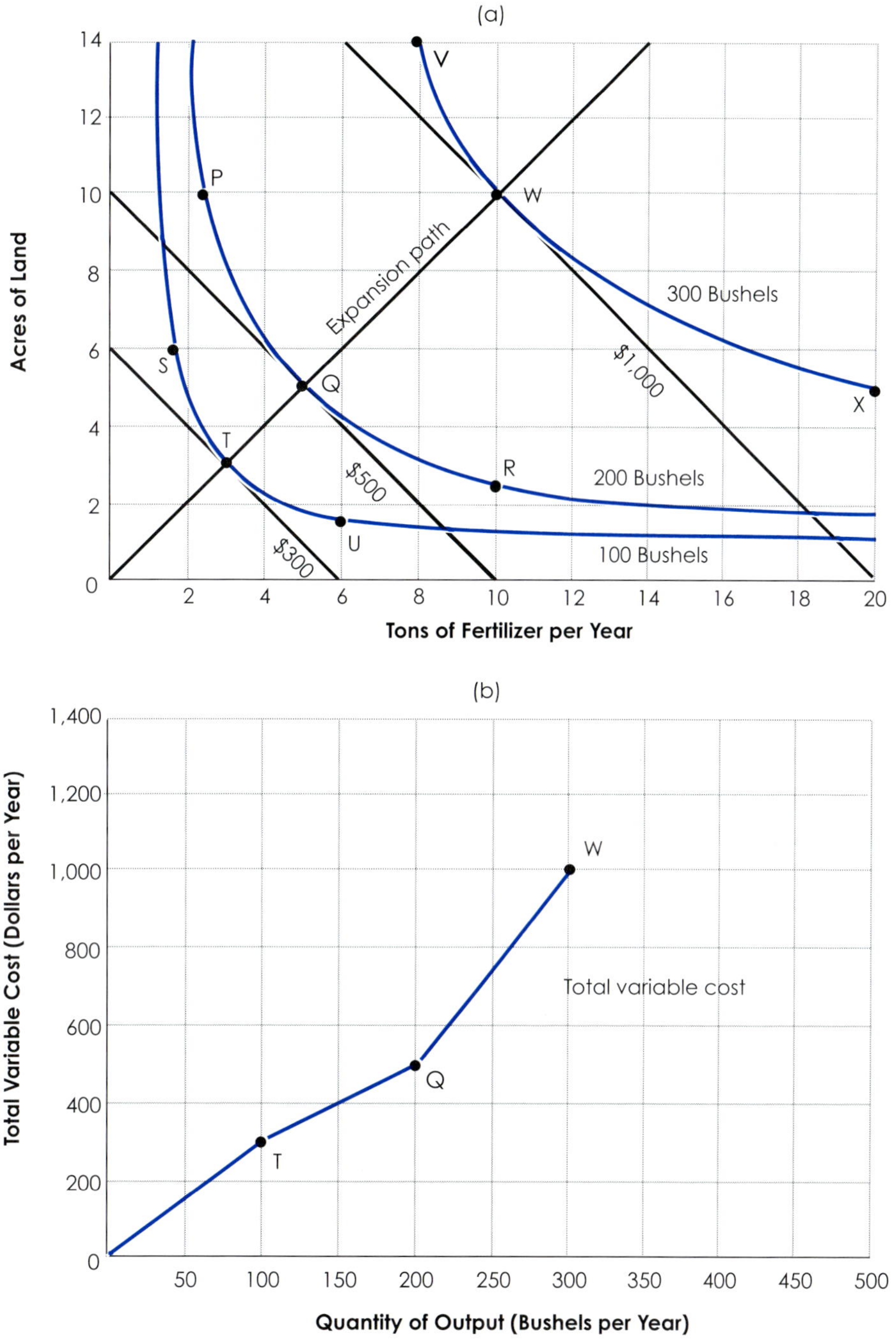

Part (a) of this figure shows three isoquants for the production of corn corresponding to outputs of 100, 200, and 300 bushels per year. Assuming input prices of $50 an acre for land and $50 a ton for fertilizer, budget lines can be drawn to show the minimum total variable cost for each output level. As output expands, the firm will move from T to Q and then to W along the expansion path. Part (b) of the figure plots the amount of output and the total variable cost for each of these points. The result is a reverse-S-shaped total variable cost curve that shows the effects of diminishing returns for output levels above 200 bushels per year.

with the variable cost level of the corresponding budget line. This is done in part (b) of Figure 6A.4. At the origin, both output and total variable cost are zero. At point T, output is 100 bushels per year and total variable cost is $300 per year; at Q, we have 200 bushels and $500; and at W, 300 bushels and $1,000. Plotting these points and connecting them give the firm's total variable cost curve.

This curve has the same reverse-S shape as the cost curve of Fieldcom, Inc., discussed earlier in this chapter. This shape results from the law of diminishing returns, here applied to the case in which two inputs vary while all others remain fixed. Beyond point Q, the amounts of inputs needed to produce each added unit of output begin to rise, just as they did when only one input was allowed to vary. Only if all inputs are allowed to vary and none is allowed to remain fixed can a firm escape the effects of the law of diminishing returns.

CHAPTER 7

Supply Under Perfect Conditions

After reading this chapter, you will understand:

1. The elements involved in consumers' rational choices
2. What characteristics define the structure of a market
3. What determines the profit-maximizing output level in the short run for a perfectly competitive firm
4. Under what conditions a firm will continue to operate even if it sustains a loss
5. How a firm's short-run supply curve is related to its cost curves
6. The conditions for long-run equilibrium in a perfectly competitive industry
7. What determines the shape of the long-run supply curve for a perfectly competitive industry
8. How efficiently markets perform under perfect competition

Before reading this chapter, make sure you know the meaning of:

1. Entrepreneurship
2. Efficiency
3. Theories and models
4. Perfectly elastic demand
5. Objectives, constraints, and choices
6. Market performance
7. Monopoly
8. Short- and long-run costs

THE WORLD BY THE TAIL

When Ralph and Andrea Martin started Fieldcom, Inc., they thought they had the world by the tail. Their rugged personal digital assistant (PDA), the first one designed for use under hot and dusty field conditions, would be a sure source of profits. With only a small investment, they quickly got their firm off the ground and their PDA into production. No one had a product that would come close to what theirs would do.

Then the structure of the market began to change. What the Martins had not take into account was that the very factors that made the PDA market easy for them to enter would make it easy for everyone else to enter, too. As soon as their machine proved that there was a market for rugged PDAs, copies sprang up on all sides.

Makers of office-type PDAs beefed up their carrying cases and shock-mounted their components. Other start-up firms brought out machines that, from the user's point of view, were just as good as Fieldcom's. Equipment supply dealers contracted with little-known electronics firms in the Far East to produce rugged PDAs for sale under the dealers' own brand names. In the office computer market, "clones" of the famous Palm Pilot PDA, had made personal digital assistants a "commodity"—a good that consumers saw as very much the same from one brand to another and bought only if the price was the lowest available. Now clones of Fieldcom's rugged PDA were doing the same thing to its market.

Within a year, many similar products were available, none of which was able to capture a dominant share of the growing market. The pressure to trim prices was relentless. At the end of their second year in business, the Martins were working hard just to break even when the full opportunity costs of their firm were taken into account.

IN THE LAST chapter we looked at Fieldcom by itself. However, in the real world firms like the Martins' do not operate alone; they face competition. Competition may take the form of giants such as General Motors and Toyota struggling to dominate a market, or advertising campaigns by rivals wooing fickle consumers. Sometimes it takes the form of rapid increases in the number of brands and styles, as in markets for breakfast cereal and clothing. Sometimes, as in Fieldcom's case, it takes the form of many small firms selling essentially identical products in a market in which entry and exit are easy. In this chapter, we take a first look at the phenomenon of competition.

Market structure

The key traits of a market, including the number and size of firms, the extent to which the products of various firms are different or similar, ease of entry and exit, and availability of information.

Economists refer to the conditions under which competition occurs in a market as **market structure.** Market structure is defined in terms of the number and size of firms, the nature of the product, ease of entry and exit, and availability of information.

Perfect competition

A market structure that is characterized by a large number of small firms, a homogeneous product, freedom of entry and exit, and equal access to information.

In this book we will look at four market structures. The first, to which this chapter is devoted, is **perfect competition**. The defining characteristics of perfect competition are the presence of many firms, none with a significant share of the market; a product that is homogeneous; easy entry into the industry and exit from it; and equal access to information by buyers and sellers. By a "significant" share of the market, we mean a share that is large enough so that the actions of a single firm are enough to noticeably affect the market price. By a "homogeneous product," we mean that the various firms' products are alike in all important respects. By "ease of entry," we mean that firms that are just starting to produce the product can do so on an equal footing with existing firms in terms of the prices paid for inputs, access to government permits or licenses, and so on. By "ease of exit," we mean that firms face no legal barriers to leaving the market and are able to find buyers or other uses for their fixed inputs. Finally, by "equal access to information," we mean that all buyers and sellers have complete information about the price of the product and of the inputs used to produce it, that buyers know all they need to know about product characteristics, and that all producers have equal knowledge of production techniques.

Oligopoly

A market structure in which there are a few firms, at least some of which are large in relation to the size of the market.

Monopolistic competition

A market structure in which there are many small firms, a differentiated product, and easy entry and exit.

A second market structure, *monopoly,* is at the opposite extreme from perfect competition. A monopoly, as defined in Chapter 4, is a market in which a single firm accounts for 100 percent of sales of a product that has no close substitutes. Monopoly will be examined in detail in the next chapter. The third market structure, known as **oligopoly**, is a market with a few firms, at least some of which have a significant share of the market. The product may be either homogeneous or differentiated; there may or may not be significant barriers to entry; and buyers and sellers need not have equal access to all kinds of information. The fourth market structure that we will look at is **monopolistic competition**. It resembles perfect competition in that there are many small firms and easy entry and exit, but under monopolistic competition the various firms' products are differentiated from one another. Oligopoly and monopolistic competition will be discussed in a future chapter.

The characteristics of the four market structures are summarized in Table 7.1.

PERFECT COMPETITION AND SUPPLY IN THE SHORT RUN

In building a model to fit the market structure of perfect competition, our objectives are (1) to show how the profit-maximizing decisions of individual firms determine

TABLE 7.1 MARKET STRUCTURES

	Number and Size of Firms	Nature of Product	Entry and Exit Conditions	Information Availability
Perfect Competition	Many firms, all small	Homogenous	Easy	Equal access to all information
Monopolistic Competition	Many firms, all small	Differentiated	Easy	Some restrictions
Oligopoly	Few firms, at least some of them large	Differentiated or homogeneous	May be some barriers to entry	Some restrictions
Monopoly	One firm	Unique product	Barriers to entry are common	Some restrictions

The structure of a market refers to the conditions under which firms compete in it—the number and size of firms, the nature of the product, the ease of entry and exit, and the availability of information. Perfect competition and monopoly are "ideal" types of structures. Few—if any—markers fit their definitions perfectly. Monopolistic competition and oligopoly are descriptive of most markets in the U.S. economy.

the quantity they will supply at various prices and (2) to show how individual firms' decisions generate market supply curves. We will look first at the short run and then at the long run.

The Constraints

With a few brief exceptions (discussed in a later chapter), all models considered in this book assume that, regardless of market structure, the firm's objective is to maximize profit. That means that differences in the choices that firms make under various market structures must be traced to differences in the constraints they face rather than to differences in objectives.

COST CONSTRAINTS One set of constraints, those imposed by costs, was discussed in the preceding chapter. In the case of perfect competition, we make three special assumptions regarding costs:

1. All firms in the market have access to the same technology and know where to buy inputs at the same prices. These conditions are implied by the assumptions of a homogeneous product and equal access to information by all firms. As a result, all firms have identical long- and short-run cost curves.

2. Economies of scale are exhausted at a small level of output relative to the quantity demanded in the market at the prevailing price so that there is room for many firms producing at the minimum long-run average cost. Without this assumption, it would not be possible to maintain many firms, each small relative to the market, as is required in this market structure.

3. There are no sunk costs. Firms that leave the market are able to recover implicit fixed costs by selling their plant and equipment to other firms. This is part of the requirement of free entry and exit.

DEMAND CONSTRAINTS: THE FIRM AS PRICE TAKER The other principal constraint on the choices made by a profit-maximizing firm is the demand for the product that the firm produces. The perfectly competitive market structure imposes a very special demand constraint on the firm: Because all firms in such an industry are small and have homogeneous products, each firm is a **price taker**. This means that the price at which each firm sells its output is determined by forces beyond the firm's control, namely, supply and demand conditions in the market as a whole. Demand conditions under perfect competition for the individual firm and for the market as a whole are illustrated in Figure 7.1.

Price taker

A firm that sells its output at prices that are determined by forces beyond its control.

Part (a) of Figure 7.1 shows the supply and demand curves for the market for chicken as given in earlier chapters. The equilibrium price is $2.00 per pound, and the equilibrium quantity is 2 billion pounds per year. Part (b) shows how the market looks from the viewpoint of an individual producer. The range of possible outputs is measured in terms of thousands rather than billions of pounds. The range of choice over which any one firm can vary its output is so small relative to the total quantity demanded that the market price will not be perceptibly affected whether the firm produces 10,000, 20,000, or 40,000 pounds of chicken a year. A 10,000-pound movement is too small even to see on the scale of the market supply and demand curves. As far as the individual firm is concerned, then, the demand curve it faces appears to be perfectly elastic (horizontal) at the market price, even though, when viewed from the perspective of the market as a whole, the demand curve has the usual negative slope.

Previously we introduced the term *marginal cost* to refer to the amount by which total cost changes when output changes by one unit. Now we can introduce a similar term, **marginal revenue**, to refer to the amount by which total revenue changes as a result of a one-unit change in output. Recall that *revenue* means price times quantity sold. For a firm with a perfectly elastic demand curve, marginal revenue simply equals price. For example, if the price of chicken is $2 per pound, the firm will receive a revenue of $200 from the sale of 100 pounds of chicken and a revenue of $202 from the sale of 101 pounds. A 1-pound increase in output yields a $2 increase in revenue, that is, an increase in revenue equal to the product's price. Under perfect competition, then, marginal revenue and price are equal for the individual firm. (In

Marginal revenue

The amount by which total revenue changes as a result of a one-unit increase in quantity sold.

FIGURE 7.1 MARKET DEMAND AND DEMAND FOR THE PERFECTLY COMPETITIVE FIRM

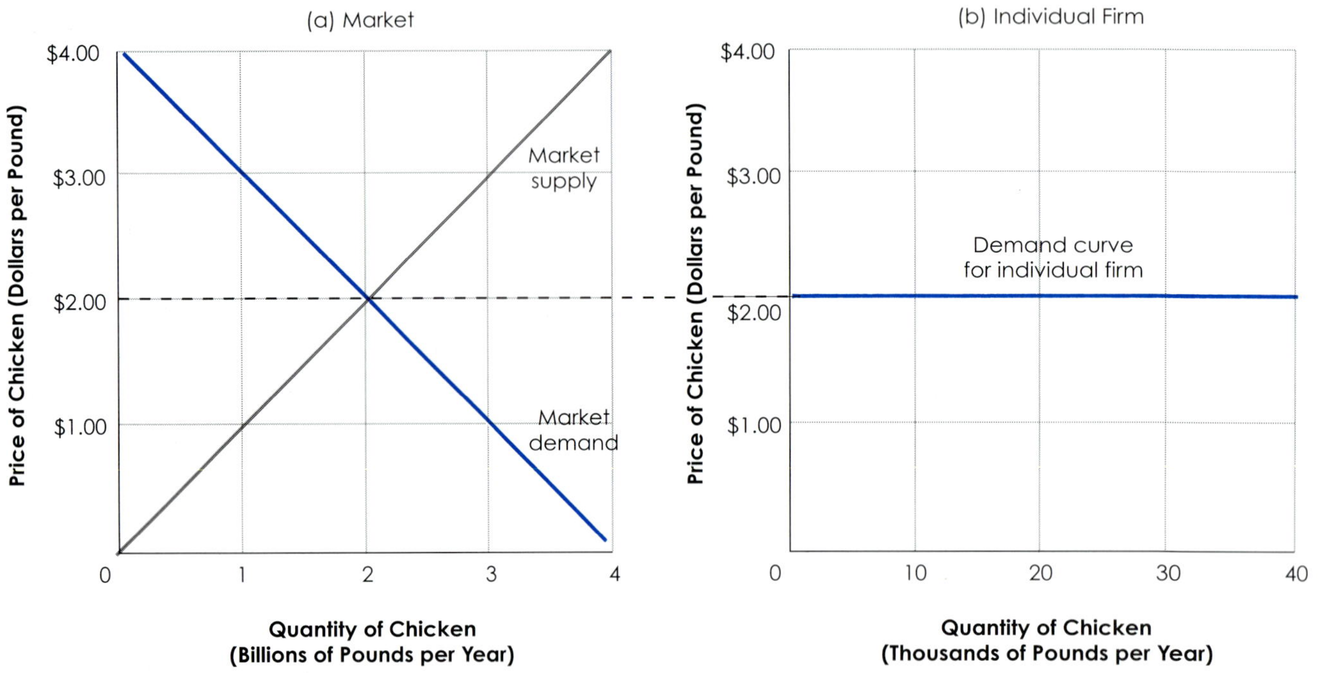

The perfectly competitive firm is a price taker. It is so small relative to the market as a whole that its decisions do not significantly affect the market price. In this example, the market equilibrium price is $2.00 per pound. The price will not be much affected if the individual firm shown in part (b) produces 20,000 rather than 40,000 pounds out of the billions of pounds produced in the market as a whole. Because the individual competitive firm is a price taker, the demand curve it faces is perfectly elastic. As a result, revenue equals price for a perfectly competitive firm.

the next chapter, we will see that marginal revenue and price are not equal in market structures where the firm's demand curve is not perfectly elastic.)

Short-Run Profit Maximization for the Firm

Now that we have introduced some basic concepts, we can apply them to the problem of how an individual firm chooses a level of output that results in maximum profit, given the constraints imposed by its cost and demand curves. In doing so, it will be convenient to refer to a specific numerical example. Our example will be based on the computer firm Fieldcom featured in this chapter and the preceding one. Bear in mind, however, that neither this nor any other real-world firm exactly fits the ideal type.

Part (a) of Figure 7.2 shows short-run cost data for Fieldcom as given in the last chapter. It also shows the revenue Fieldcom earns from the sale of each quantity of output, assuming a market price of $500 per unit.

Subtracting total cost in column 3 from total revenue in column 2 yields the total profit the firm earns at each output level. The maximum is reached at 19 units per day, where a profit of $2,000 per day is earned. The profit-maximizing output level is shown graphically in part (b) of Figure 7.2. There the firm's total profit is indicated by the distance between the total revenue and total cost curves. That distance is greatest at 19 units of output.

Instead of comparing total cost and total revenue, we can find the profit-maximizing output level by comparing marginal cost and marginal revenue. Look first at columns 5 and 6 of part (a) of Figure 7.2. Column 5 gives data on marginal cost. (As before, the data are printed on lines between the entries in the first four columns to show that marginal cost is the change in cost as output moves from one level to another.) Column 6 shows marginal revenue, which, as explained, is equal to the product's price. Each PDA that Fieldcom sells adds $500 to its total revenue.

As the table shows, both total cost and total revenue rise as output increases. If the increase in revenue exceeds the increase in cost (that is, if marginal revenue is greater than marginal cost), boosting output by one unit increases total profit. If the increase in cost exceeds the increase in revenue (that is, if marginal cost is greater than marginal revenue), raising output by one unit reduces total profit. Therefore, to maximize profit a firm should expand its output as long as marginal revenue exceeds marginal cost and should stop as soon as rising marginal cost begins to exceed marginal revenue. A comparison of columns 5 and 6 of Figure 7.2 shows that for Fieldcom this means producing 19 units of output per day—the same number we arrive at when we compare total cost and total revenue.

The marginal approach to short-run profit maximization is shown graphically in part (c) of Figure 7.2. At up to about 19 units of output, the marginal cost curve lies below the marginal revenue curve, so each added unit of output increases profit. (The graph, unlike the table, pictures output as a continuous quantity so that profit maximization need not occur exactly at an even number of units.) Beyond that point, the marginal cost curve rises above the marginal revenue curve so each added unit of output reduces profit. The point of profit maximization—the point at which the rising section of the marginal cost curve intersects the marginal revenue curve—matches the point in part (b) at which the spread between total revenue and total cost is greatest.

In part (c), the vertical distance between the demand curve, which shows price, and the average total cost curve represents the profit per unit. Profit per unit multiplied by the number of units gives total profit. Thus, from the standpoint of part (c), total profit equals the area of the shaded rectangle.

Minimizing Short-Run Losses

In the example just given, Fieldcom was able to make a profit at a price of $500. However, market conditions might not always be so favorable. Suppose, for example, that the market price drops to $300. A lower market price means a downward shift in the firm's perfectly elastic demand curve. Being a price taker, the firm can do nothing

FIGURE 7.2 SHORT-RUN PROFIT MAXIMIZATION UNDER PERFECT COMPETITION

(a)

Quantity of Output (1)	Total Revenue (2)	Total Cost (3)	Total Profit (2) – (3) (4)	Marginal Cost (5)	Marginal Revenue (6)
0	$ 0	$2,000	–$2,000		
1	500	2,380	–1,880	$380	$500
2	1,000	2,720	–1,720	340	500
3	1,500	3,025	–1,525	305	500
4	2,000	3,300	–1,300	275	500
5	2,500	3,550	–1,000	250	500
6	3,000	3,780	–780	230	500
7	3,500	3,955	–495	215	500
8	4,000	4,200	–200	205	500
9	4,500	4,400	100	200	500
10	5,000	4,605	395	205	500
11	5,500	4,820	680	215	500
12	6,000	5,050	950	230	500
13	6,500	5,300	1,200	250	500
14	7,000	5,575	1,425	275	500
15	7,500	5,880	1,620	305	500
16	8,000	6,220	1,780	340	500
17	8,500	6,600	1,900	380	500
18	9,000	7,025	1,975	425	500
19	9,500	7,500	2,000	475	500
20	10,000	8,030	1,970	530	500
21	10,500	8,620	1,880	590	500
22	11,000	9,275	1,725	655	500
23	11,500	10,000	1,500	725	500
24	12,000	10,800	1,200	800	500

(continues)

This figure shows the profit-maximizing level of output chosen by a perfectly competitive firm, Fieldcom, Inc., given a market price of $500 per unit. That level of output can be found by comparing total cost and total revenue, as shown in parts (a) and (b). It can also be found by comparing marginal cost and marginal revenue. (Because the firm is a price taker, marginal revenue is equal to price.) Profit increases up to the point at which rising marginal cost begins to exceed marginal revenue; after that point, it declines. Regardless of the approach used, the profit-maximizing output is 19 units per day and the maximum profit per day is $2,000.

about the price and will have to adjust its output as best it can to meet the new situation. The required adjustments are shown in Figure 7.3.

There is no output level at which the firm can earn a profit given a price of $300. Unable to earn a profit, the firm must focus on keeping its losses to a minimum. With a price of $300 per unit, the minimum loss occurs at 14 units of output. As in the

FIGURE 7.2 SHORT-RUN PROFIT MAXIMIZATION UNDER PERFECT COMPETITION, CONTINUED

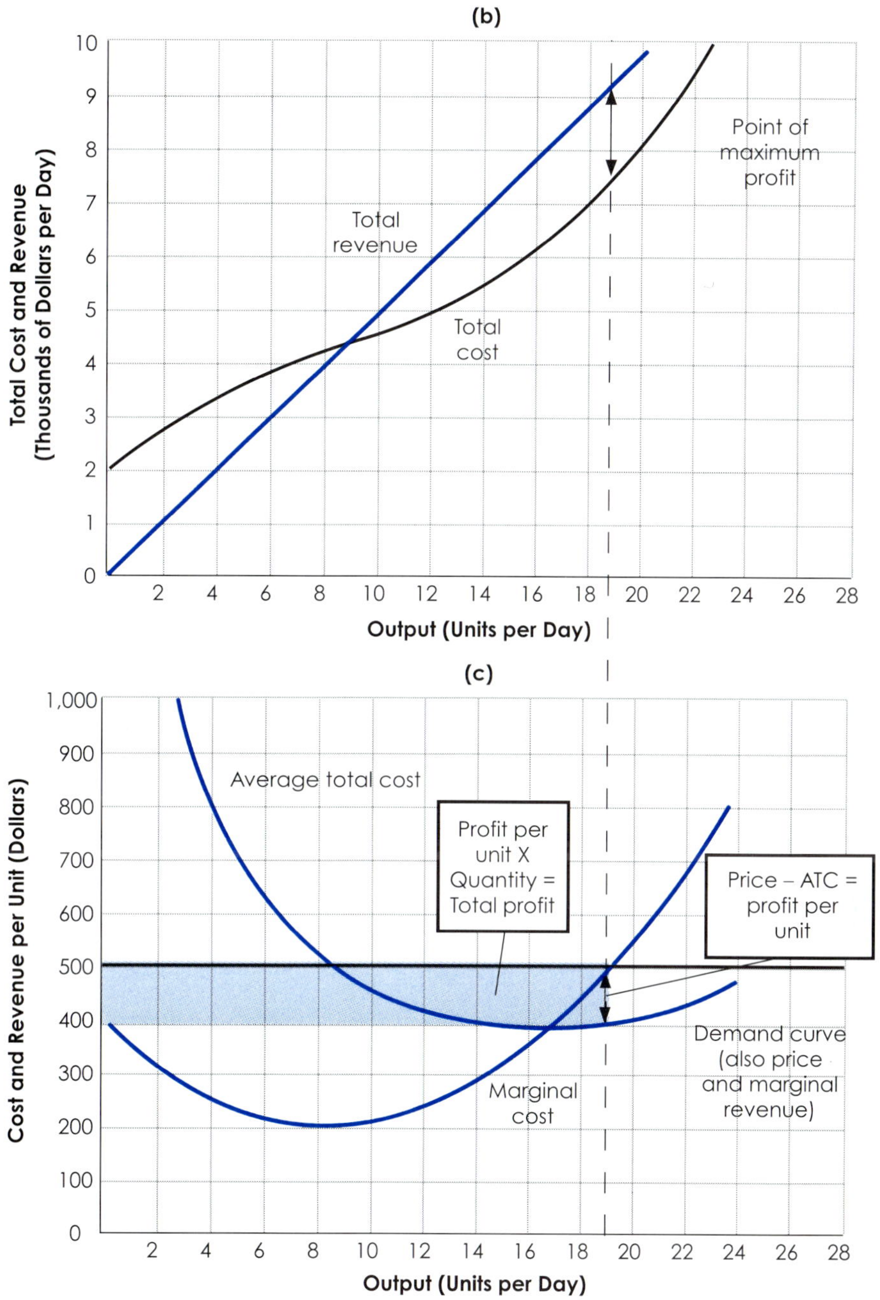

previous case, that is the output level beyond which marginal cost begins to exceed the product's price.

In graphical terms, we note that the point at which the rising section of the marginal cost curve intersects the marginal revenue curve lies between the average total cost and average variable cost curves.[1] Because the demand curve is below the average total cost curve, there is a loss on each unit sold. The total loss is equal to the shaded rectangle (loss per unit times quantity of output). However, the demand curve lies above the average variable cost curve. This means that revenue per unit is more than enough to cover variable cost and, hence, that each unit sold makes at least some contribution to covering fixed cost. Thus, losses are smaller than they would be if no output were produced, assuming that fixed costs must be paid even when output drops to zero.

As an aid to understanding the logic of the loss-minimizing decision, suppose for a moment that wages are the firm's only variable cost and that rent on its building is its only fixed cost. At the point shown, the firm is bringing in more than enough revenue to pay its wage bill (variable costs); the remainder will help pay the rent. If the firm shuts down temporarily, it will have to pay the rent with no help at all from current revenue. That would mean a loss equal to fixed cost—even more of a loss than at 14 units of output per day.

The logic of continuing operations in order to minimize losses applies only in the short run, when the costs of fixed inputs must be borne regardless of how much output is produced. A firm would not continue to operate indefinitely with the price below average total cost as shown in Figure 7.3. In the long run, a firm can free itself

FIGURE 7.3 MINIMIZING SHORT-RUN LOSSES UNDER PERFECT COMPETITION

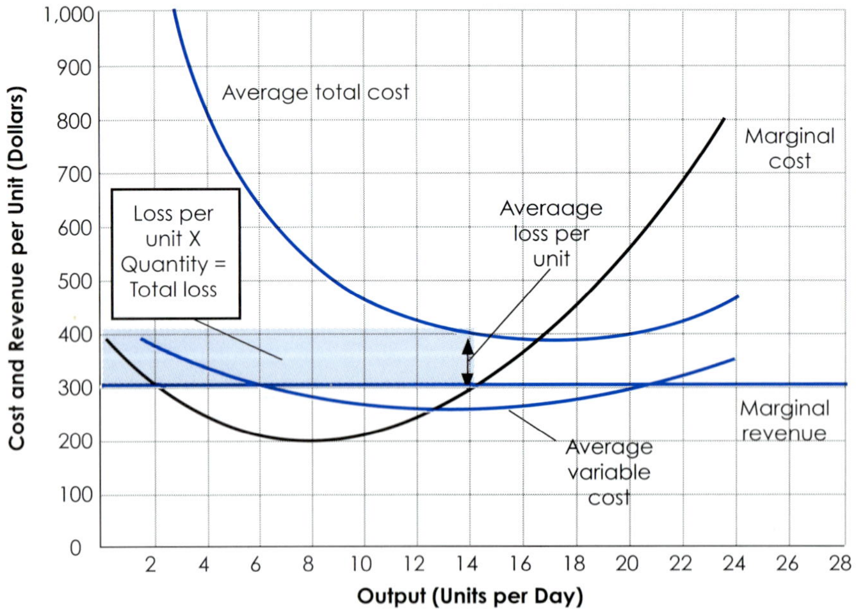

If the product's market price is too low to permit earning a profit, the firm must try to keep its losses to a minimum. For Fieldcom, Inc., given a price of $300 per unit, the point of minimum loss is 14 units of output per day. The marginal cost curve intersects the marginal revenue curve at a point higher than average variable cost but lower than average total cost. Each unit of output sold earns more than its share of variable cost but not enough to pay for its share of total cost when its share of fixed cost is included.

of fixed costs by selling its equipment, allowing long-term leases to expire, and so on. We will return to the conditions under which firms will leave the industry later in the chapter.

Shutting Down to Cut Short-Run Losses

What would happen if the price of PDAs dropped even lower than $300? Would it then still be worthwhile for the firm to keep making them even though it was losing money? The answer, as shown in Figure 7.4, is no.

The figure assumes a price of $225 per unit. With such a low price the firm cannot make a profit at any output level. But this time the best thing for the firm to do in the short run is to shut down. As illustrated by *Economics in the News 7.1*, brief shutdowns are a normal way of adjusting inventories to changing supply and demand conditions. The example illustrates the point that shutting down is not at all the same as going out of business. Provided that the outlook for the future is good, it makes sense for a firm to keep its plant intact, pay its rent, and even continue some benefits for employees to ensure that they will be ready to come back when called.

FIGURE 7.4 SHUTTING DOWN TO MINIMIZE SHORT-RUN LOSS

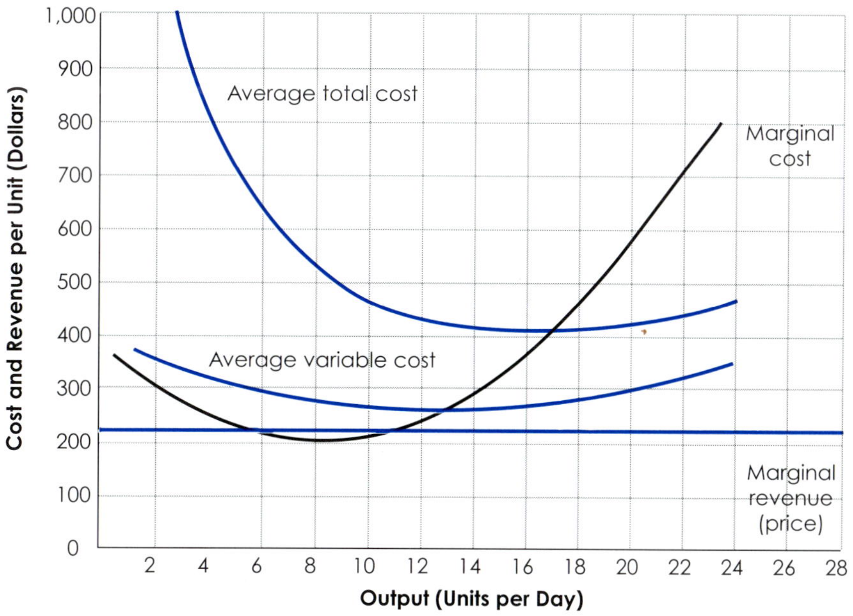

The price of a firm's output may drop so low that the firm must shut down in order to keep short-run losses to a minimum. As illustrated here, such a situation occurs for Fieldcom at a price of $225 per unit. Marginal cost rises above marginal revenue at about 11 units of output. That output yields a smaller loss ($2,345) than those slightly greater or lower. However, the loss can be reduced to just $2,000 a day if the firm shuts down. The marginal cost curve in this case intersects the marginal revenue curve at a point below average variable cost. That is the signal to shut down.

APPLYING ECONOMIC IDEAS 7.1

CHANGING WITH THE SEASONS

Croatia is a small, newly independent country that must make the most of its resources as it hurries to catch up to the living standards of the rest of Europe. Luckily it has one big asset: its stunning Adriatic coast line with brilliant sun, sparkling clear water, and hundreds of islands, perfect for get-away weekends by Parisians or Berliners.

In some people's opinion, the crown jewel among the Coastian islands is Hvar. The tiny port of Hvar Town is a tourist paradise of ancient red-roofed houses cascading down a steep hill from an old fort at the top to a quaint fishing harbor below. Taking advantage of some fine, clear weather in mid-March, a recent visitor found the streets of Hvar Town lined with hotels, restaurants, and souvenir shops—all of them closed! Although it has facilities to serve thousands of tourists in the summer, all but one hotel and all but three or four restaurants close for the season each winter, to open again in the late spring.

At first it seems like such a waste. All that natural beauty is still there, and the water is just as clear even if the air is a few degrees cooler. Why don't the hotels and restaurants just offer low, off-season rates in order to stay busy all winter? With a little thought, though, the economic logic of the decision to shut down becomes clear. Hotel and restaurant owners have to take a close look at their costs when deciding whether to operate on a year-round or seasonal basis. Some costs, like property taxes and interest on bank loans can't be avoided by shutting down, but others, especially labor costs for clerks and kitchen staff can be eliminated when the establishment is closed. To a certain point, it pays to stay open by offering lower, off-season rates, but when those rates fall so low that they don't even cover the wages of the cooks and cleaners, it is time to put up the shutters and wait for spring.

And what about the one hotel that stays open in the winter? Is the owner just ignorant of economics? No, there's an economic logic behind this hold-out strategy, too. If just one hotel stays open while all others shut, the small number of visitors to the town are enough to push its revenues above the break-even point. It's all an example of competition in action.

The firm therefore does not escape its fixed costs. When market conditions improve, inventories are brought into line with demand, and as the market price rises again, the firm can resume operations. Only if market conditions are never expected to improve will the firm consider winding up its affairs and going out of business.

In the case of a temporary shutdown, it can be misleading to follow the rule of expanding output until marginal cost begins to exceed marginal revenue. With the price at $225, such a point is reached at about 11 units of output per day. That output level does give the firm a lower loss than a level slightly higher or slightly lower. But in this case the firm takes an even smaller loss by not producing at all.

The reason 11 units of output does not minimize loss is that the demand curve lies below the average variable cost curve at that point. Suppose again that wages are the firm's only variable cost and rent is its only fixed cost. At 11 units of output, revenue is not enough even to meet the firm's payroll. The firm will do better to send its workers home and save the cost of wages, even though when it does this the owners will have to pay the entire rent from reserves, without any help from current sales revenue.

The Firm's Short-Run Supply Curve

The examples just given provide the information needed to draw a short-run supply curve for a perfectly competitive firm. Let's work through an example like the one shown in Figure 7.5 starting with a price of $500. As we saw earlier, Fieldcom will turn out 19 devices a day at that price. Point E_1 of the firm's short-run marginal cost curve thus is a point on its supply curve.

Now suppose that the demand for PDAs slackens and the market price begins to fall. As it does so, the point at which marginal revenue equals marginal cost moves downward along the firm's marginal cost curve. Soon point E_2 is reached—the point at which marginal cost and average total cost are equal. This occurs at an output of about 17 units and a price of about \$385. At that price, the best the firm can do is break even; either a greater or a smaller output will result in a loss.

If the price falls still lower, the firm's objective becomes one of keeping its loss to a minimum. At a price of \$300, for example, the firm minimizes its loss by making 14 units (point E_3). In the range of prices between minimum average total cost and minimum average variable cost, the supply curve continues to follow the marginal cost curve.

At about \$250 the price reaches the lowest point on the average variable cost curve. There the firm is just on the edge of shutting down—it is covering its variable costs with nothing to spare. Its loss is equal to its fixed costs. At any lower price the firm will minimize its losses by shutting down. Thus, point E_4 is the lowest point on the marginal cost curve that can be considered part of the firm's supply curve.

FIGURE 7.5 DERIVATION OF THE SHORT-RUN SUPPLY CURVE

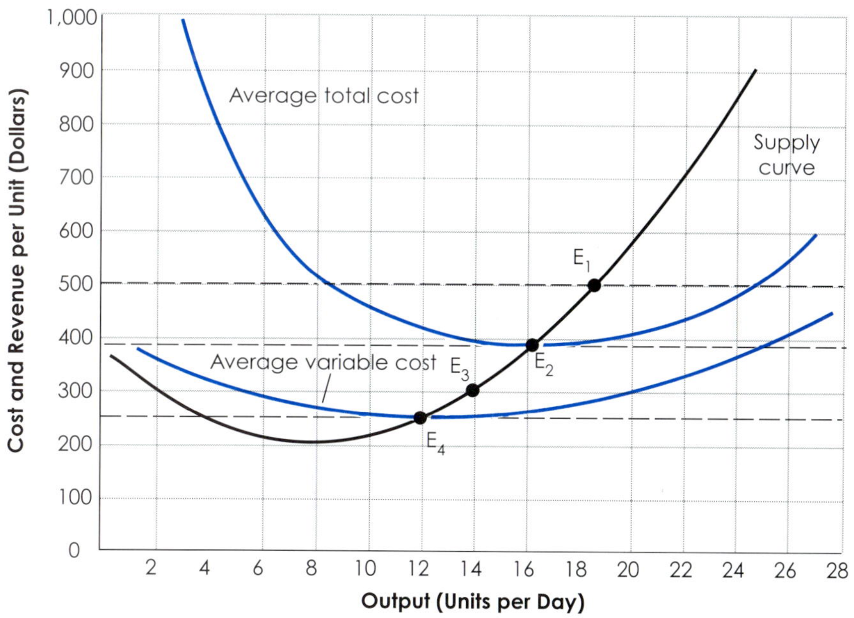

This graph shows how a short-run supply curve for Fieldcom, Inc. can be derived from its cost curves. When the price and marginal revenue is \$500, the firm will produce at point E_1. As the price falls the firm will move downward along its short run marginal cost curve as shown by points E_2 and E_3. The firm will continue to produce at the point at which price equals marginal cost until marginal cost falls below average variable cost. E_4 thus is the lowest point on the firm's supply curve. Below that price the firm will shut down.

The preceding discussion of the firm's short-run supply decision can be summed up as follows: *The short-run supply curve of a profit-maximizing firm operating in a perfectly competitive market coincides with the upward sloping part of the marginal cost curve lying above its intersection with the average variable cost curve.*

The Industry's Short-Run Supply Curve

Once we have a supply curve for each firm in an industry, we can add them together to construct a supply curve for the industry as a whole. Figure 7.6 shows how this can be done, beginning with the supply curves for three firms. To get the total supply of the three firms at each price, the quantities supplied by each firm are added together. In graphical terms this means adding the supply curves horizontally. To generalize the process to an industry with many firms, the individual supply curves of the remaining firms in the industry would be added to the three shown.

In adding the firms' supply curves together, we assumed that input prices did not change as output expanded. For a small firm in a perfectly competitive industry, this is a realistic assumption. However, if all firms in an industry try to grow at the same time, the assumption may not hold. In fact, input prices will rise unless a greater quantity of inputs can be purchased without paying higher prices, that is, unless the short-run supply curves for inputs to the industry are perfectly elastic. If input prices rise as the industry's total output grows, each firm's cost curves will shift upward as the output of all firms increases. That will make the short-run industry supply curve somewhat steeper than the sum of the individual supply curves.

FIGURE 7.6 DERIVATION OF A SHORT-RUN INDUSTRY SUPPLY CURVE

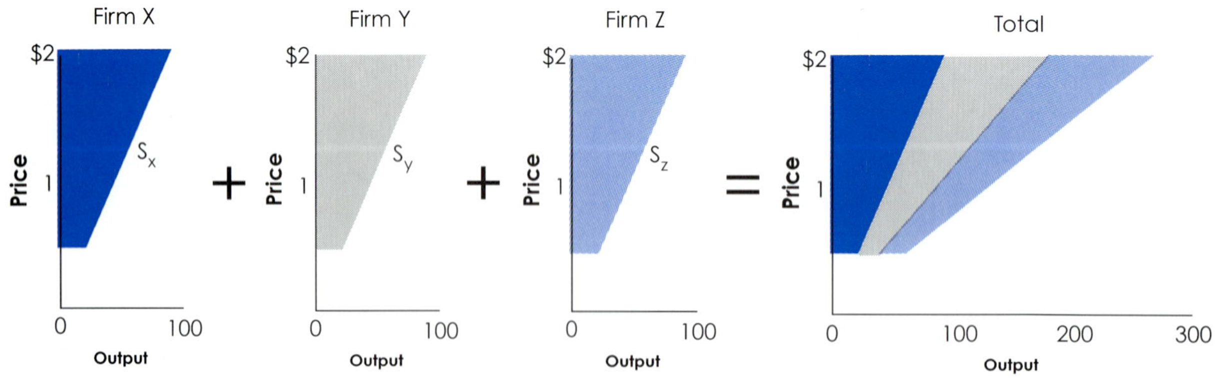

A short-run industry supply curve can be obtained by summing the supply curves of individual firms. Here this method is shown for the first three firms in an industry. The supply curves of additional firms would be added in the same way. If the prices of inputs change as industry output varies, the industry supply curve will need to be adjusted.

LONG-RUN EQUILIBRIUM UNDER PERFECT COMPETITION

Up to this point we have considered changes in industry output that result from firms' decisions to produce more or less as the market price changes. In doing so, however, we have neglected an important part of a competitive industry's response to changes in demand: the processes of entry and exit.

Consideration of entry and exit moves us from the short run to the long run. In the last chapter we distinguished between the long run, when all inputs can be varied, and the short run, when some inputs are fixed. The ability to vary all inputs in the long run—even durable ones such as land, structures, and major pieces of equipment—allows firms to enter a market for the first time, starting with a new plant and work force. It also means that they can leave a market for good, releasing all their employees and selling their plant and equipment. (Sometimes firms leave peacefully, with the owners selling the firm's assets and dividing up the proceeds. Other times they leave the market only when forced to do so, such as when creditors resort to a bankruptcy court to force a sale of the firm's assets in order to pay its debts.) Typically, as an industry expands and contracts, many firms enter and leave it.

Free entry and exit of firms is one of the basic traits of a perfectly competitive market. Free entry does not mean that firms can enter at no cost. They may have to pay a great deal to purchase equipment, hire key employees, and so on. Free entry simply means that if they are willing to make the necessary investment, new firms are free to compete with existing ones on a level playing field. They are not kept out by patents or licensing requirements, trade secrets, collusion by firms already in the industry, or lack of raw materials. Likewise, free exit means that firms face no legal barriers to shutting down or moving if they find that they cannot make a profit. Strictly interpreted, free exit also means that firms have no sunk costs. When they leave the industry, they can put fixed assets to other uses or find buyers for them.

Free entry and exit did not play a direct role in our discussion of a firm's short-run supply decision. However, as we will now see, it is crucial to understanding how a competitive market works in the long run.

Long-Run Equilibrium for a Competitive Firm

At numerous points we have used the term *equilibrium* to refer to a state of affairs in which economic decision makers have no incentive to change their plans. Three conditions are required for a perfectly competitive firm to be in equilibrium in the long run:

1. The firm must have no incentive to produce a larger or smaller output given the size of its plant (that is, the amount of fixed inputs it uses). That requires

that short-run marginal cost be equal to short-run marginal revenue, which means that the short-run equilibrium condition is also a condition for long-run equilibrium.

2. Each firm must have no incentive to change the size of its current plant (that is, with the amount of fixed inputs it uses).

3. There must be no incentive for new firms to enter the industry or for existing firms to leave it.

Figure 7.7 shows a perfectly competitive firm for which these three requirements are met. First, short-run marginal cost equals price at 25 units of output per day, which is the level of output the firm will choose in order to make the maximum profit. Second, the firm has a plant that is just the right size to make short-run average total cost equal to the lowest possible long-run average cost at the chosen output level. The short-run average total cost curve for a plant of any other size would give a higher average total cost for the chosen output. Third, both long-run average cost and short-run average total cost are equal to price at the equilibrium level of output. This guarantees that there is no incentive for entry or exit. As always, average total

FIGURE 7.7 A PERFECTLY COMPETITIVE FIRM IN LONG-RUN EQUILIBRIUM

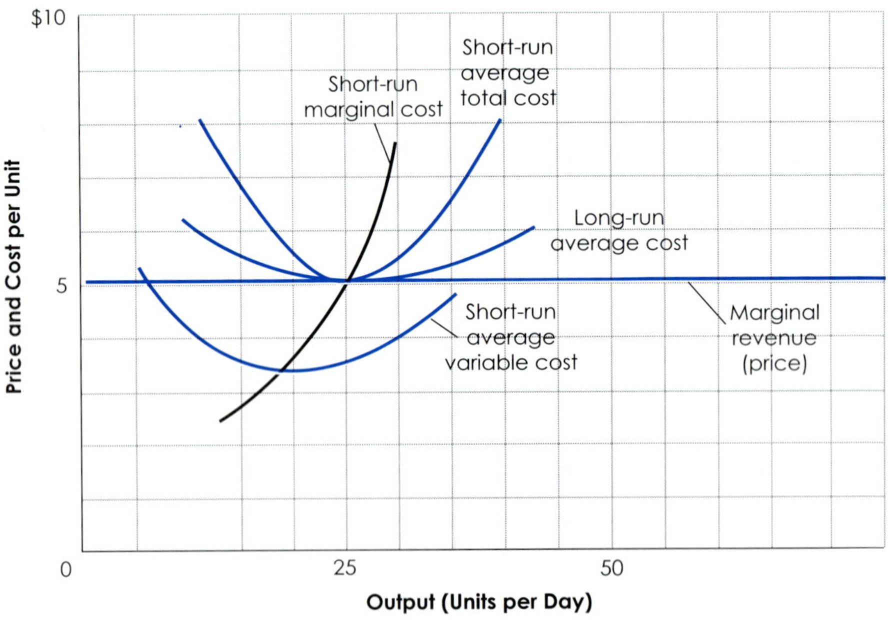

Long-run equilibrium in a perfectly competitive industry requires that the typical firm (1) have no short-run incentive to change the level of its output; (2) have no long-run incentive to change the size of the plant used to produce its output; and (3) have no long-run incentive to enter or leave the industry. This requires that price, short-run marginal cost, short-run average total cost, and long-run average cost all have the same value in equilibrium as shown here.

cost comprises both explicit and implicit costs, including the opportunity cost of capital, or "normal profit." When price equals average total cost, then, firms are earning zero economic profit. Any positive economic profit would attract new firms into the industry, whereas negative economic profits (economic losses) would cause firms to leave the industry.

The three conditions for long-run equilibrium are summarized in the following equation.

Price = Marginal cost = Short-run average total cost = Long-run average cost

If any part of this equation does not hold, firms will have a reason to change their plans. If price does not equal short-run marginal cost, they will have an incentive to change their output levels by changing the quantity of variable inputs used, even if they cannot, in the short run, change the size of their plants. If short-run average total cost does not equal long-run average cost, their current plant is too large or too small to produce their current level of output at the least possible cost. They will want to change the size of the plants they are using, so their plant will be the ideal size to produce their current output. And if price is lower than long-run average cost, firms in the industry will want to leave it; if price is above long-run average total cost, firms outside the industry will want to enter it.

Industry Adjustment to Falling Demand

A state of long-run equilibrium, such as that shown in Figure 7.7, exists only as long as outside conditions do not change. Suppose, though, that those conditions do change—for example, there is a long-run decrease in the market demand for the firm's product. Figure 7.8 shows what will happen.

Part (a) of Figure 7.8 shows a set of cost curves for a typical firm. Part (b) is a supply-and-demand diagram for the market as a whole. The short-run industry supply curves shown are built up from those of the individual firms in the market (see Figure 7.6). The demand curves in part (b) are market demand curves.

Suppose that initially the short-run market supply and demand curves are in the positions S_1 and D_1. The equilibrium price is \$5. Each firm takes this price as given and adjusts its output on that basis, producing 25 units. At that price and output, a typical firm would just break even. (Remember, though, that "breaking even" in the economic sense means earning enough to cover all costs, including the opportunity cost of capital.)

Now something happens—say, a change in consumer tastes or incomes—that shifts the demand curve to a new position, D_2. The short-run result is a drop in the market price, to \$4. Each firm, being a price taker, will view the decline in price as beyond its control and will adjust to it as best it can. As shown in part (a) of Figure 7.8, this means cutting back output slightly in order to keep losses to a minimum,

FIGURE 7.8 LONG-RUN ADJUSTMENT TO DECLINING DEMAND

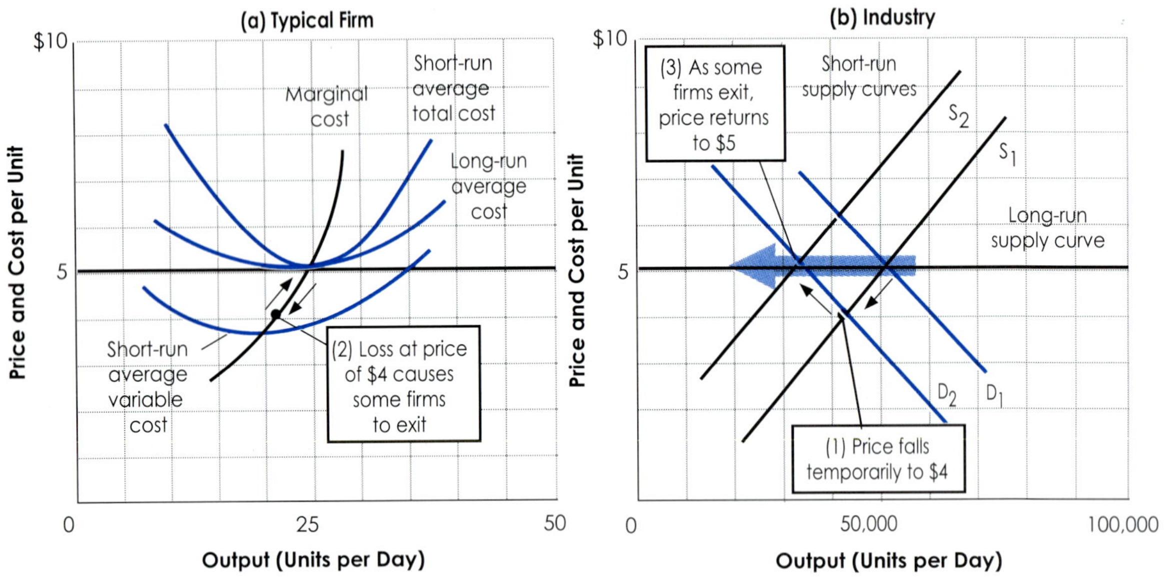

Part (a) represents a typical firm in a perfectly competitive industry; part (b) represents the industry as a whole. At first, both the firm and the industry are in long-run equilibrium at a price of $5. Then something happens to shift the market demand curve leftward from D_1 to D_2. In the short run, the price falls to $4 at the intersection of D_2 and S_1. The firm's short-run response is to move downward along its marginal cost curve. Because the price is still above average variable cost, the firm does not shut down. After a while, some firms (not the one shown) get tired of taking losses and leave the industry. This causes the market supply curve to shift toward S_2 and the market price to recover. The typical firm returns to the break-even point. The market has traced out part of its long-run supply curve as shown by the large arrow.

but not shutting down completely. Each firm's movement downward along its short-run marginal cost curve is what causes the movement of the market as a whole downward and to the left along the short-run supply curve.

However, the new situation cannot be a long-run equilibrium, because each firm is operating at a loss. The firms' owners are not earning a normal rate of return, that is, they are not earning enough to cover the opportunity costs of keeping their capital invested in the industry. If the market demand curve shows no hope of shifting back to the right, some owners will pull their capital out of the industry. They may go bankrupt, abandoning their fixed assets to their creditors. They may sell their plant and equipment and get out while they can. Or they may keep their firms running but convert their plants to make goods for other, more profitable markets.[2]

For the sake of the example, suppose that the typical firm shown in Figure 7.8 is not one of the first to leave. As some other firms withdraw, industry output falls by the amount of their output. The short-run market supply curve, which now comprises fewer individual supply curves, shifts to the left toward S_2. As it does so, the market price begins to move upward along demand curve D_2. When the price gets all the way back to \$5, the firms remaining in the industry will no longer be losing money. Firms will stop leaving the industry, and the market will have reached a new long-run equilibrium. At the new equilibrium price, short-run marginal cost, short-run average total cost, and long-run average cost will once again be equal.

This sequence of events has traced out a portion of the industry's *long-run supply curve,* as shown by the large horizontal arrow. A long-run supply curve for an industry shows the path along which equilibrium price and quantity move when there is a lasting change in demand. Movement along this curve requires enough time for firms to adjust the sizes of their plants or enter or leave the market.

Industry Adjustment to Rising Demand

When there is a long-run increase in demand, freedom of entry plays the same role that freedom of exit plays when demand falls. Such a case is shown in Figure 7.9. The starting position in this figure is the same as that in Figure 7.8. Short-run supply curve S_1 and demand curve D_1 result in an equilibrium price of \$5. The individual firm breaks even at an output of 25 units. Now watch what happens as the demand curve shifts to the right, to D_2. The short-run result is an increase in the market price, to \$6. The typical firm adjusts to the new price by moving up along its short-run marginal cost curve. As all firms do this, the market moves up and to the right along short-run supply curve S_1.

But again the short-run position is not the new long-run equilibrium, because now all firms are making an economic profit. Entrepreneurs will soon spot this healthy, growing market as a good one in which to invest. Some of them may start new firms in this market; others may shift plant and equipment from making something else to making goods for this industry. Whether the entry is by new firms or by existing ones that are producing for this market for the first time, new entries will cause the supply curve to shift to the right, toward S_2.

As the short-run market supply curve shifts to the right, the price falls. It does not fall far enough to drive the new entrants out of the market, but it does fall far enough to drive pure economic profits back to zero. Entry of firms into the market will stop, and the market will reach a new long-run equilibrium at the intersection of S_2 and D_2.

Once again a portion of the long-run supply curve for the industry has been traced out, as shown by the large horizontal arrow in Figure 7.9. This long-run supply curve again is perfectly elastic. A rightward shift in the demand curve has, in the long run, produced an increase in quantity supplied but no rise in price.

As a final detail, note the importance of the assumption that there are no sunk costs in the industry. If entering the industry required specialized investments that could not be recovered later, firms would view them as opportunity costs when deciding whether to enter the market. They would not enter unless the price was high enough (and was expected to stay high enough) to give them a normal rate of

FIGURE 7.9 LONG-RUN ADJUSTMENT TO AN INCREASE IN DEMAND

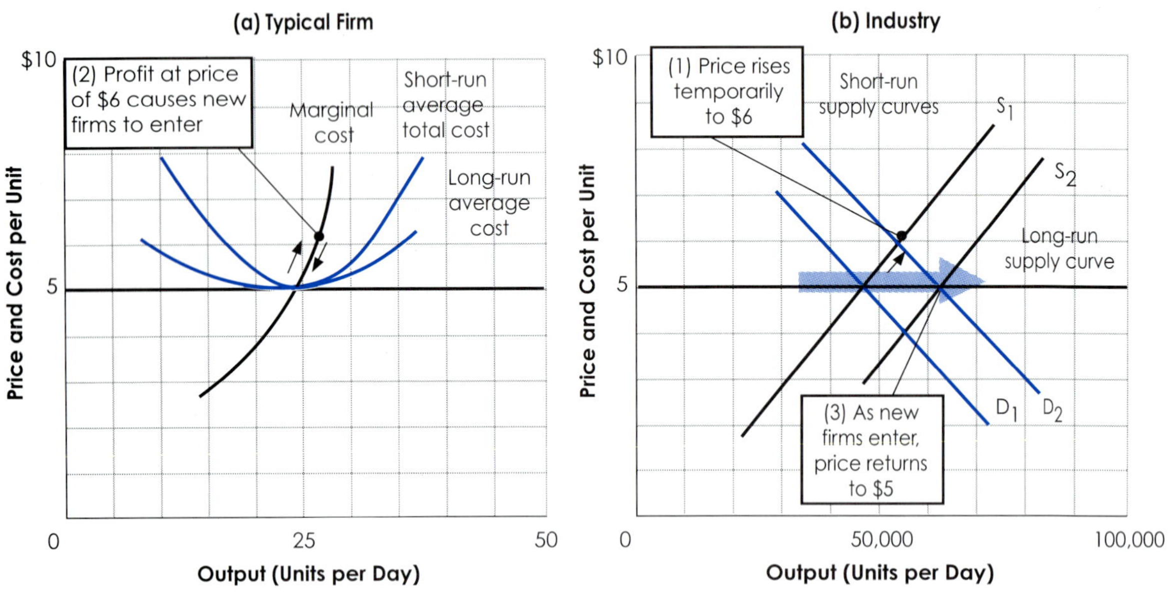

In this figure, both the firm and the industry start out in equilibrium at a price of $5. Then something happens to shift the market demand curve rightward to D_2. In the short run, the price rises to $6 at the intersection of D_2 and S_1. The firm's short-run response is to move upward along its marginal cost curve, earning better-than-normal profits. After a while, the high profits attract new firms into the industry. As those firms enter, the market supply curve shifts toward S_2. Profits for the typical firm return to zero, and new firms stop entering the industry. Again the market has traced out part of its long-run supply curve as shown by the large arrow.

return on the nonrecoverable investments. Once in the industry, however, those sunk costs would no longer affect decisions, according to the "bygones are bygones" principle. They would not count as part of the fixed (but not sunk) costs that must be covered by revenue for continued operation to be worthwhile. Thus, existing firms may *stay* in business indefinitely even if the price falls somewhat below what would be needed to attract new firms. When sunk costs are present, then, the industry supply curve is no longer a two-way street. Such an industry would, in effect, follow one supply curve when expanding and a different, lower one when contracting.

Although the theoretical model of perfect competition does not allow for sunk costs, such costs are common in the real world. Consider drive-in theaters. In the early years after World War II, drive-in theaters were a growing business. With demand high, many entrepreneurs entered the industry. Later, demand for this form of entertainment declined. But even when market demand dropped well below the level needed to make it worthwhile to construct new drive-ins, existing operators stayed in business. They did so even though they were no longer earning enough to cover the original sunk cost of their screens and projection houses because those facilities could neither be moved nor converted to any other use. Only when demand fell still lower, so that revenues no longer covered recoverable fixed costs (such as the cost of land) and variable costs (such as wages, electricity, and film rentals) did drive-in theater operators finally leave the market.

The Elasticity of Long-Run Supply

The long-run industry supply curve in Figures 7.8 and 7.9 is perfectly elastic. Given such a curve, a change in demand affects only the equilibrium quantity, not the price, in the long run. However, that is not the only possible case. Supply curves that are positively sloped, negatively sloped, and U-shaped are also possible.

The shape of the long-run industry supply curve depends mainly on what happens to the industry's input prices in the long run as output expands. If the long-run supply curves for all inputs to the industry are perfectly elastic, the prices of those inputs will not change as the quantities of them demanded by the industry increase. It may also be that the industry uses such a small part of the total supply of each input that any change in input prices that does occur will be slight. For example, cookie stores use such a small part of the total supply of flour and eggs that expansion or contraction of such stores will have no perceptible effect on the market prices of those inputs. Industry output can therefore expand without affecting the costs of the individual firms, and the supply curve will be perfectly elastic.

Suppose, however, that the industry is a heavy user of relatively specialized inputs whose outputs can be boosted only at an increasing cost. For example, consider the home construction business, which uses a substantial portion of all the lumber produced in the country. An expansion of the construction industry will cause lumber suppliers to exhaust the lowest-cost stands of trees and begin harvesting higher-cost timber. The home construction industry also employs a significant proportion of all carpenters in the country. If the industry expands, carpenters' wages may have to rise relative to those of, say, auto mechanics in order to attract additional workers into the occupation.

Figure 7.10 shows what happens in such an industry as a permanent increase in demand causes output to expand. As in the preceding case, the shift in demand first pushes up price along the short-run supply curve. New firms enter the market. However, the expansion of the industry raises input prices. Each firm's short-run marginal cost and average total cost curves are shifted upward from MC_1 to MC_2 and from ATC_1 to ATC_2 as shown. As a result, the new long-run equilibrium is at a higher price than the initial equilibrium. The long-run industry supply curve, drawn through the two points of short-run equilibrium, therefore has a positive slope.

It is also possible for the price of an input to decrease as the industry's total output increases. For example, as sales of electronic equipment expand, the firms that make components for such equipment may be able to use cheaper production methods. If that occurs, the short-run cost curves for all firms will drift downward as new firms enter the industry. The long-run supply curve then will be negatively sloped.

FIGURE 7.10 A POSITIVELY SLOPED LONG-RUN INDUSTRY SUPPLY CURVE

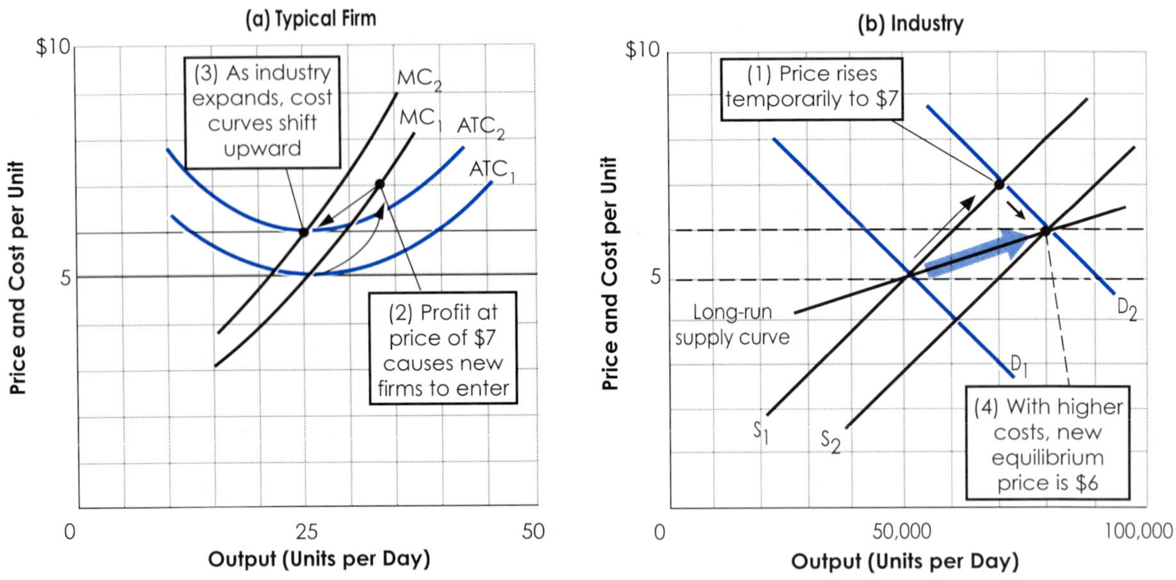

In Figures 7.8 and 7.9, it was assumed that input prices do not change as industry output expands. This pair of diagrams shows what happens if industry expansion causes input prices to rise. As output expands, rising input prices push up the firm's marginal cost curve from MC_1 to MC_2 and its average total cost from ATC_1 to ATC_2. The result is a new long-run equilibrium price that is higher than the initial price. The long-run industry supply curve thus has a positive slope.

Finally, it is possible for these various forces to operate together. At first long-run supply is influenced by the falling price of one special input, but beyond a certain point some other special input becomes a limiting factor that causes the long-run supply curve to bend upward. The long-run industry supply curve then becomes U-shaped.

As we have seen, many variations are possible. Only through direct observation of the industry in question can we tell which possibility applies.

MARKET PERFORMANCE UNDER PERFECT COMPETITION

Earlier in the text we introduced the notion of *market performance* in reference to how efficiently exchanges within markets resolve the basic economic questions of what, how, who, and for whom. Perfectly competitive markets have long earned high marks for several aspects of performance. In this section we look at market performance under perfect competition as it relates to the questions of *what* should be produced and *how* it should be produced.

What Should Be Produced

When the concept of market performance was introduced, we used a diagram similar to Figure 7.11 to show the quantity of a good (peaches, in this case) that must be produced for a market to perform efficiently. The demand curve, we said, represents the amount consumers are willing to pay for an additional pound of peaches, given any level of output. That amount reflects the benefit of the marginal pound as perceived by consumers. The supply curve represents the amount suppliers require if they are to produce an additional pound of peaches. That amount corresponds to the opportunity cost to producers of supplying the marginal pound. As long as the demand curve is higher than the supply curve, trade at a price between the two curves can potentially benefit both parties. Accordingly, opportunities for mutually beneficial trades are exhausted (and efficiency is achieved) only if production is carried out to the point of intersection between the supply and demand curves, but not beyond that point.

In this chapter we have shown that the supply curve in a perfectly competitive market is the summation of the marginal cost curves of the individual firms. At any

FIGURE 7.11 EFFICIENT OUTPUT UNDER PERFECT COMPETITION

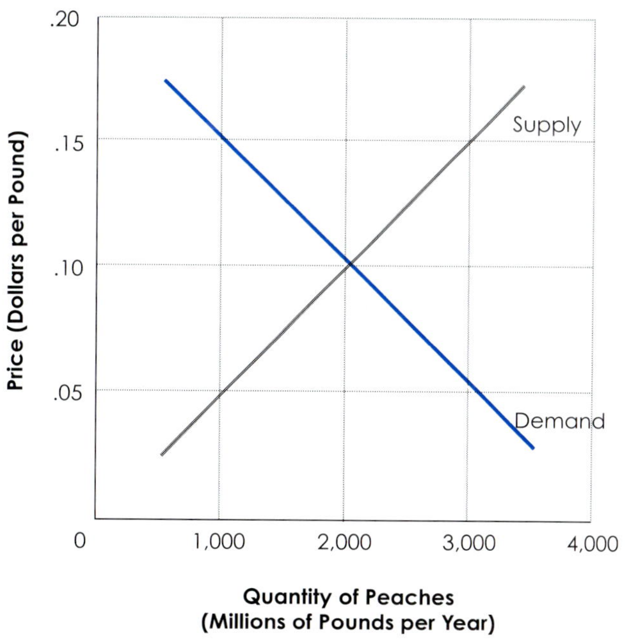

This figure shows supply and demand curves for a perfectly competitive market for peaches. Under perfect competition, each firm's efforts to keep marginal cost equal to marginal revenue ensure that the industry will produce at some point on the supply curve. Equilibrium for the market as a whole can occur only at the point where the supply and demand curves intersect. That represents an efficient resolution to the question, What should be produced?

given market price, producers will supply the quantity that makes marginal cost equal to marginal revenue, which in turn is equal to the market price. Thus, the price-quantity combination at which transactions take place in a competitive market will be some point on the supply curve.

For the market to end up at the right point on the supply curve, the market price must correspond to the intersection of the supply curve with the demand curve. To see why this will happen in a competitive market, we can put Chapter 2's analysis of market equilibrium together with this chapter's conclusions regarding perfect competition. From Chapter 2, we know that a price that is higher than the intersection of the supply and demand curves results in a surplus. Unplanned accumulation of inventory causes the price to fall. As the price falls, firms move down along the supply curve so as to keep marginal cost equal to marginal revenue. Similarly, a price that is lower than the intersection of the supply and demand curves results in a shortage. Depletion of inventories causes the market price to rise. Firms move up along the supply curve to keep marginal cost and marginal revenue equal. Thus, in a perfectly competitive market the equilibrium point will correspond to the intersection of the supply and demand curves. That is the efficient outcome.

Generalizing from these conclusions, we can see that in an economy in which all markets were perfectly competitive and in which there were no externalities the efficient quantity of every good would be produced. That would represent an efficient solution to the overall question of what should be produced—how many peaches, apples, tomatoes, and so on. Beginning from a situation in which the competitive markets for all products were in equilibrium, it would not be possible to substitute any one good for another (say, by producing more peaches at the expense of using fewer resources to produce apples) in a way that would make any person better off without making at least one other person worse off.

How to Produce

The preceding conclusion about what should be produced holds in both short- and long-run equilibrium. In addition, in the long run only, perfectly competitive markets ensure that each good is produced at the lowest possible cost—a key aspect of how goods should be produced.

To understand why goods are produced at the lowest cost in a situation of long-run competitive equilibrium, review Figures 7.8 and 7.9. In those figures the point of long-run equilibrium is shown to occur at the point where the typical firm operates at the minimum point of both the short-run average total cost curve and the long-run average cost curve.

Starting from such a point, a decrease in demand causes the market price to fall. In response, each firm reduces its output to the point where short-run marginal cost equals the new price. Although short-run marginal cost is lower at that output, short-run average total cost is higher because the firm moves up and to the left along the average total cost curve as output falls. Thus, at this point in the adjustment to falling demand, the given level of output is not being produced at the lowest possible cost. That is inefficient.

However, the inefficient situation does not last. Because short-run average total cost exceeds the market price, the firms suffer an economic loss, and some of them will leave the industry. Assuming no further change in demand, as the number of firms in the industry decreases, each firm is able to increase its output and move back toward its point of least-cost production. Similar reasoning applies to the expansion of industry output in response to an increase in demand.

Under perfect competition, firms are led not only to produce at the lowest possible short-run average total cost, given the size of their plants, but also to select the correct plant size to minimize average cost in the long run. To see why, suppose that one firm had a plant that was not the optimal size. As we saw in the last chapter, the short-run average total cost curve for such a firm would be tangent to its long-run average cost curve at a point above and to the right of the point of long-run minimum cost (if the plant were too large) or above it and to the left (if the plant were too small). The firm with the wrong size plant would thus be at a cost disadvantage relative to its competitors. As competition drove the market price toward a level equal to minimum long-run average cost, the firm would either adjust the size of its plant to the cost-minimizing level or leave the industry because of economic losses.

Other Aspects of Market Performance

The tendency of perfectly competitive markets to produce the efficient quantity of each good and to produce those quantities at the lowest cost are important strengths of this market structure. In a future chapter we will extend the analysis of perfect competition to factor markets. In doing so, we will see that perfectly competitive markets perform efficiently with regard to the questions of *who* and *for whom* as well as those of *what* and *how.* In these respects, long-run equilibrium in perfectly competitive markets sets a standard against which the performance of other market structures can be judged.

Nevertheless, it would be claiming far too much to say that perfect competition is the ultimate in market performance under all conditions. It would be premature to condemn every respect in which real-world markets depart from the structural characteristics of perfect competition. Before we write off all markets that are not made up exclusively of small firms, all markets in which products are not homogeneous, all markets in which newly entering firms encounter entry barriers or incur sunk costs, or all markets in which some participants know things that others do not, many questions must be asked. Among them are the following:

- Are there conditions in which other market structures equal or at least approximate the efficiency of perfect competition?

- How do alternative market structures perform when attention is focused on innovation and entrepreneurship rather than on equilibrium under conditions where technology and product characteristics are assumed to be unchanging?

- When markets fail to perform efficiently, what public-policy options are available? How should the dangers of government failure be weighed against the dangers of market failure?

Only when these additional aspects of the problem have been explored will we be in a position to make a balanced judgment of market performance under various market structures.

SUMMARY

1. **What characteristics define the structure of a market?** A *market structure* is defined in terms of the number and size of firms in the market, the nature of the product, ease of entry and exit, and availability of information. A *perfectly competitive market* has the following traits: (1) There are many buyers and sellers, each of which is small compared with the market as a whole; (2) the product is homogeneous; (3) it is easy to enter or leave the market; and (4) all buyers and sellers have equal access to information. Other market structures to be studied in this course include *monopoly, oligopoly,* and *monopolistic competition.*

2. **What determines the profit-maximizing output level in the short run for a perfectly competitive firm?** In the short run the relationship between marginal cost and *marginal revenue* (price) determines the profit-maximizing output level for a perfectly competitive firm. The firm should expand output up to, but not beyond, the point at which marginal cost rises to the level of marginal revenue, provided that marginal revenue is at least equal to average variable cost at that point.

3. **Under what conditions will a firm continue to operate even if it sustains a loss?** If marginal revenue is below average total cost at the point at which marginal cost and marginal revenue are equal, the firm cannot earn a profit. It will minimize loss in the short run by staying open if marginal revenue is above average variable cost. If marginal revenue is below average variable cost at the same point, the firm will minimize loss by shutting down.

4. **How is a firm's short-run supply curve related to its cost curves?** The short-run supply curve for a perfectly competitive firm is the upward-sloping part of the marginal cost curve lying above its intersection with the average variable cost curve.

5. **What are the conditions for long-run equilibrium in a perfectly competitive industry?** Long-run equilibrium in a perfectly competitive industry requires (1) that price be equal to short-run marginal cost so that each firm is content with the level of output it is producing; (2) that short-run average total cost be equal to long-run average cost so that firms are satisfied with the size of their plants, given their output rate; and

(3) that price be equal to long-run average cost so that there is no incentive for new firms to enter the industry or for existing firms to leave it.

6. **What determines the shape of the long-run supply curve for a perfectly competitive industry?** A perfectly competitive industry adjusts to long-run changes in demand through exit of firms (in the case of a drop in market demand) or entry of new firms (in the case of a rise in market demand). If input prices do not change as the industry's output changes, the industry's long-run supply curve will be perfectly elastic. If input prices rise, the long-run supply curve will have a positive slope; if they fall, it will have a negative slope.
7. **How efficiently do markets perform under perfect competition?** Under conditions of equilibrium, a perfectly competitive market produces a quantity of output that corresponds to the intersection of the market's supply and demand curves. In an economy in which all markets are in perfectly competitive equilibrium and there are no externalities, the question of what to produce is thus resolved efficiently. Also, in a situation of long-run equilibrium the output of a perfectly competitive market is produced at the lowest possible cost. This means that the question of how to produce is also resolved efficiently.

KEY TERMS

Market structure	Monopolistic competition
Perfect competition	Price taker
Oligopoly	Marginal revenue

PROBLEMS AND TOPICS FOR DISCUSSION

1. **Examining the lead-off case.** What assumptions are made about the market in which Fieldcom operates that cause that market to approximate perfect competition? In what respects does the PDA market in the real world meet these conditions? Does it matter what kind of PDAs you consider—color display, personal computer, and high-memory PDAs? Discuss.
2. **Market structures.** Give examples (other than those presented in the text) of industries that fit, or approximate, the market structures of perfect competition, monopoly, oligopoly, and monopolistic competition.
3. **Buyers as price takers.** The concept of price taking can apply to buyers as well as to sellers. A price-taking buyer cannot influence prices by changing the amount purchased. Are you a price taker for the goods you buy? Can you give an example of a firm that might not be a price taker in the market in which it buys one or more of its inputs?
4. **Changes in fixed cost and the supply curve.** Fieldcom buys some automated equipment to speed up production of its PDAs. The equipment adds $500 per day to the firm's fixed costs, but it saves $50 per unit in variable costs. Rework the graph in Figure 7.5 to show how the new equipment affects Fieldcom's supply curve. (You may want to rework part (a) of Figure 7.2 as a basis for the new supply curve.) What is the minimum price the firm must now charge to continue operating in the short run? What is the lowest price at which it can break even?
5. **Long- and short-run elasticity of supply.** In Chapter 3 it was asserted that, other things being equal, the elasticity of supply of a good tends to be greater the more time firms have to adjust to new market conditions. Using the theory of perfect competition as presented in this chapter, explain the basis for that assertion.
6. **Long-run supply with falling input prices.** Figure 7.10 shows the long-run adjustment of a

competitive industry to an increase in demand in the case in which input prices rise as industry output increases. Assume instead that input prices fall as output rises. Draw a new set of diagrams to show how a typical firm and the industry as a whole would respond to an increase in demand.

CASE FOR DISCUSSION

Independent Truckers as a Perfectly Competitive Industry

The next time you are out on the highway, take a look at the trucks that are passing you. You will see many that belong to large firms, such as Yellow Freight, that haul large numbers of small shipments all over the country on regular schedules. You will also see trucks that bear the names of companies such as Sears or Sun Oil, for which transportation is a sideline.

If you look closely, though, you will see that about one truck in four looks a little different. The tractors, many of which are brightly painted and highly chromed, often have sleepers attached to them. The trailers, often refrigerated, are likely to be filled with farm produce moving to market. These are the trucks of independent owner-operators, who move much of the nation's output of farm goods and some manufactured goods.

Each firm in this market consists of a person who owns and drives just one truck. There are many such firms—as many as 35,000, by some estimates.

From the shipper's point of view, one refrigerated truck is about as good as another as long as it is headed in the right direction. And most independent truckers will go wherever their loads take them.

Entry into the market is easy. Some people go into business with a used truck and as little as $5,000. Most operators buy their trucks on credit. Exit is also easy—too easy, some say. Many independent truckers go broke every year, and the number of firms rises and falls with the state of the economy.

People who run the giant trucking companies that haul manufactured goods often look down their noses at the independent truckers with their loads of apples and potatoes. They call them gypsies or worse. But this system succeeds in putting fresh produce on dinner tables in every town every day.

QUESTIONS

1. In what ways does the independent trucking industry approximate the requirements of perfect competition? Are there any ways in which it does not meet those requirements?
2. On the average, the firms in a perfectly competitive industry earn no pure economic profits. However, average conditions do not always apply. What would you expect to happen to the profits of independent truckers when the economy enters a recession? When it enters a period of prosperity? What do you think would happen to the number of firms in the industry at such times?
3. Diesel fuel is a major input for independent truckers. What would you expect to happen to the profits of independent truckers and the number of firms in the industry as the price of fuel rises and falls? Outline the sequence of events in each case. (Drawing a graph may help.)

END NOTES

1. This graph shows why we emphasize that profit maximization occurs where the *rising* section of the marginal cost curve intersects the marginal revenue curve. There is sometimes also an intersection of the *falling* section of the marginal cost curve with the marginal revenue curve, as is the case at about 3 units of output in Figure 7.3. That intersection is *not* a point of profit maximization, but rather, one of loss maximization.
2. The discussion of exit from a perfectly competitive market seems to pose a paradox: If all firms are *exactly* alike, why don't they all stay in the market as long as conditions are favorable, and then all leave the market at the same instant when conditions become unfavorable? However, real-world markets only approximate the conditions of perfect competition. In such markets, small differences in firms' circumstances of cost or demand, or in the temperaments of their owners, will cause some to leave the market before others do.

CHAPTER 8

The Theory of Monopoly

After reading this chapter, you will understand:

1. The circumstances in which monopoly can exist
2. How the profit-maximizing price and output for a monopoly are determined
3. How long-run equilibrium is achieved under monopoly
4. Why monopolies and other price-searching firms sometimes engage in price discrimination
5. How monopoly affects market performance

Before reading this chapter, make sure you know the meaning of:

1. Market performance and market failure
2. Rent seeking
3. Consumer and producer surplus
4. Market structure

A CAVIAR MONOPOLY FALLS ON HARD TIMES

Back in the days of the Cold War, Soviet cartoonists regularly drew caricatures of fat, sneering oppressors of the working class, adding the label "monopoly" to their top hats, just in case anyone might miss the point. Meanwhile, behind the scenes, Communist bureaucrats were happy to do business with Western monopolists whenever they saw a chance to make a profit by doing so.

One of the coziest arrangements was that between the Soviet Ministry of Fisheries and Paris-based Petrosian S.A. The Petrosian brothers had been born in Iran of Armenian ancestry, had been educated in Russia, and had subsequently emigrated to France. Soon after the revolution, they struck a deal to bring caviar to the West. The family business has been doing so ever since.

The key to Petrosian's success was always scarcity. Good caviar is naturally scarce. Fisheries in the Caspian Sea near the mouth of the Volga are the source of most of the world's top quality supplies, about 2,000 tons a year. (Some caviar is also harvested in Iranian waters along the southern shores of the Caspian, and a tiny amount comes from the Hudson River.) But natural scarcity was not enough for the caviar monopolists. They found that by limiting exports to a paltry 150 tons, they could push prices to fantastic heights—as much as $1,000 a pound for some varieties. This meant a steady flow of hard currency for the Soviet authorities and handsome profits for Petrosian. The remaining 1,850 tons of caviar stayed in the Soviet Union to be consumed at official banquets or distributed at give-away prices in special stores for the Communist party elite.

Then came the fall of the Soviet Union. Suddenly there were three new countries bordering the Caspian Sea—the former Soviet republics of Kazakhstan, Azerbaijan, and Turkmenistan. Each wanted a cut of the caviar harvest. On top of that, a general breakdown of authority caused the Ministry of Fisheries to lose control over the harvest even within Russia. Poaching became widespread, new export deals were struck by independent operators who bypassed the ministry, and the world was threatened by a caviar glut.

But nature came to the rescue of caviar prices in a way caviar lovers—and conservationists—hardly found pleasing. Overfishing by poachers and worsening pollution of the Volga has now made the salty black delicacy as scarce as the official export monopoly did in the past. Furthermore, many Western countries, concerned with the effect of poaching on the sturgeon population, have strictly limited imports from all but the most reliable sources. So don't expect fish eggs to replace hen's eggs on Egg McMuffins any time soon.

Source: Based in part on Jane Mayer, "Horrors! Fine Caviar Now Could Become Cheap as Fish Eggs," *The Wall Street Journal,* November 18, 1991, A1, and Michael Dobbs, "The Coming Caviar Crisis," *The Washington Post,* May 30, 1992, A1.

As defined earlier in the text, a monopoly is a market structure in which a single firm is the sole supplier of a product that has no close substitute. Petrosian's 60-year partnership with the Soviet Ministry of Fisheries came about as close to this market structure as any real-world market can. This chapter presents a model of profit maximization under monopoly and also discusses the reasons why few monopolies last forever.

VARIETIES OF MONOPOLY

We can begin by distinguishing among three types of circumstances in which a single firm can occupy the position of sole supplier to a market.

Closed monopoly
A monopoly that is protected by legal restrictions on competition.

Natural monopoly
An industry in which long-run average cost is minimized when only one firm serves the market.

Open monopoly
A monopoly in which one firm is, at least for a time, the sole supplier of a product but has no special protection from competition.

1. A **closed monopoly** is protected by legal restrictions on competition. The caviar monopoly mentioned in the opening case is one example. Patents and copyrights give rise to other cases of closed monopoly.
2. A **natural monopoly** is an industry in which long-run average cost is minimized when just one firm serves the entire market. Distribution of natural gas to residential customers is an example. In such an industry the minimum efficient scale of production for a good is close to (or even larger than) the quantity that is demanded at any price high enough to cover per-unit production costs. Thus, dividing production between two or more firms would result in an inefficiently small scale of production for each. Closely related to natural monopolies based on economies of scale are monopolies based on ownership of a unique natural resource. For example, for many years ownership of a uniquely productive mine in Utah gave the Brush Wellman company a virtual monopoly over production of beryllium, an ultra-light metal used in aerospace applications.
3. An **open monopoly** is a case in which a firm becomes, at least for a time, the sole supplier of a product without the special protection against competition that is enjoyed by a closed or natural monopoly. The first firm to venture into the market for a new product often finds itself in such a position, although other competitors may enter later. An example is Sony's first home video cassette recorder, which reached the market before similar machines later produced by its competitors.

The classification of monopolies into these three categories is a loose one. Some firms may belong to more than one category. For example, local utilities such as electric and gas companies may be both natural monopolies (because of economies of scale) and closed monopolies (because of regulatory barriers to competition). Also, the classification may depend on the time horizon in question. For example, patent protection may give a firm a closed monopoly in the short run, but the monopoly may be open in the long run, not only because patents eventually expire but also because competitors are able to invent new products or processes that circumvent them. Patented pharmaceuticals frequently illustrate this phenomenon.

Ultimately, all monopolies can probably be considered open. The legal restrictions that protect closed monopolies from competition are subject to challenge in legislatures and courtrooms. (For example, many trucking companies lost monopoly rights to haul freight on certain routes when Congress deregulated the industry in 1980.) The cost advantages enjoyed by natural monopolists may be eroded by changes in technology. (Long-distance telephone service, on which AT&T once held a monopoly, is a case in point.) And all monopolists face competition by substitutes for the products they produce. (Beryllium, despite its unique chemical and physical properties, faces competition from titanium, carbon-fiber composites, and other lightweight structural materials.) Later in the chapter we will return to the tendency of monopolies to attract competitors; first we will develop a formal model of this market structure.

SIMPLE MONOPOLY

Like the model of perfect competition presented in the preceding chapter, the model of monopoly aims to explain the operation of markets in terms of the firm's objectives and constraints. For monopoly, as for perfect competition, standard neoclassical models assume that profit maximization is the firm's objective. The differences in market outcomes between the two cases, then, stem from differences in the constraints that are assumed to define the set of opportunities open to the firm.

Constraints Faced by Monopoly

The monopolist's ability to earn a profit, like that of other firms, is constrained in part by its production costs. The model presented here is based on the theory of cost presented in an earlier chapter. The special restrictions imposed in perfect competition (a minimum efficient scale that is small relative to the size of the market and no sunk costs) do not apply to monopoly.

The other principal constraint on the monopolist's profit-making opportunities is the demand for its product. Because a monopolist is by definition the only firm in its market, the demand curve faced by the firm is the same as the market demand curve for the product. The monopolist's demand curve, then, is negatively sloped—the quantity of output that can be sold increases as the price decreases.

The monopolist is assumed to know, at least roughly, the characteristics of the demand curve for its product, whether from econometric studies, trial and error, or simple intuition. Because both price and quantity vary along the negatively sloped demand curve, the monopolist, unlike a perfectly competitive firm, is not a price taker. Instead, its demand curve represents a menu of possible price-quantity combinations, from which it selects the combination that will yield the maximum profit.

Price searcher

Any firm that faces a negatively sloped demand curve for its product.

Simple monopoly

A monopoly that, at any given time, sells its product at a single price that is uniform for all customers.

Because it searches for the most profitable price in a range of possible prices, a monopolist can be called a **price searcher**.

The model of monopoly presented in this section incorporates one additional constraint: At any given time the monopolist must sell all of its output at a single price that is uniform for all customers. A monopoly in which the same price is charged for all units sold is termed a **simple monopoly**. The case of price discrimination, in which some units are sold at a different price than others, will be discussed later in the chapter.

Output, Price, and Marginal Revenue Under Simple Monopoly

We first noted the relationship between price and total revenue along the demand curve earlier in this book, when the concept of elasticity was introduced. There we showed that when demand is *elastic* a drop in price causes total revenue to rise. (The reason is that in percentage terms the quantity sold rises by more than the price falls; thus, the product of price times quantity, which equals revenue, increases.) In contrast, when demand is *inelastic* revenue falls when the price drops. (This occurs because with inelastic demand the percentage increase in quantity is less than the percentage decrease in price.) With a straight-line demand curve, such as the one in part (b) of Figure 8.1, the upper half is elastic and the lower half inelastic. That accounts for the shape of the "revenue hill" in part (c).

Earlier we defined *marginal revenue* as the change in total revenue that results from a one-unit increase in a firm's output. Column 4 in part (a) of Figure 8.1 presents data on marginal revenue for the firm in this example. The figures in the column are the differences between the entries in column 3. Part (b) of the exhibit shows the firm's marginal revenue curve. The marginal revenue curve is above the horizontal axis when total revenue is increasing (elastic demand) and below it when total revenue is decreasing (inelastic demand). It intersects the horizontal axis at the point of maximum total revenue.

An easy rule can be used to sketch the marginal revenue curve corresponding to any straight-line demand curve: *The marginal revenue curve for a straight-line demand curve always cuts the horizontal distance from the demand curve to the vertical axis exactly in half.* Following this rule, the point where the marginal revenue curve intersects the horizontal axis can be placed halfway between the origin and the horizontal intercept of the demand curve (that is, the point where the demand curve intersects the horizontal axis). (In Figure 8.1 the marginal revenue curve cuts the horizontal axis at 17.5, half of 35.) The vertical intercept of the marginal revenue curve is the same as that of the straight-line demand curve. (The vertical intercept is at $10 in Figure 8.1.) (This rule does not apply to curved demand curves, but the examples in this book are kept simple.)

The marginal revenue curve is always below the demand curve. For a simple monopolist, the marginal revenue that the firm gets from the sale of one additional unit

FIGURE 8.1 DEMAND, TOTAL REVENUE, AND MARGINAL REVENUE UNDER SIMPLE MONOPOLY

(a)

Quantity of Output (1)	Price (2)	Total Revenue (3)	Marginal Revenue (4)
1	$10.00	$10.00	
2	9.70	19.40	$9.40
3	9.40	28.20	8.80
4	9.10	36.40	8.20
16	5.50	88.00	
17	5.20	88.40	.40
18	4.90	88.20	–.20
33	.40	13.20	
34	.10	3.40	–9.80
35	.00	.00	–3.40

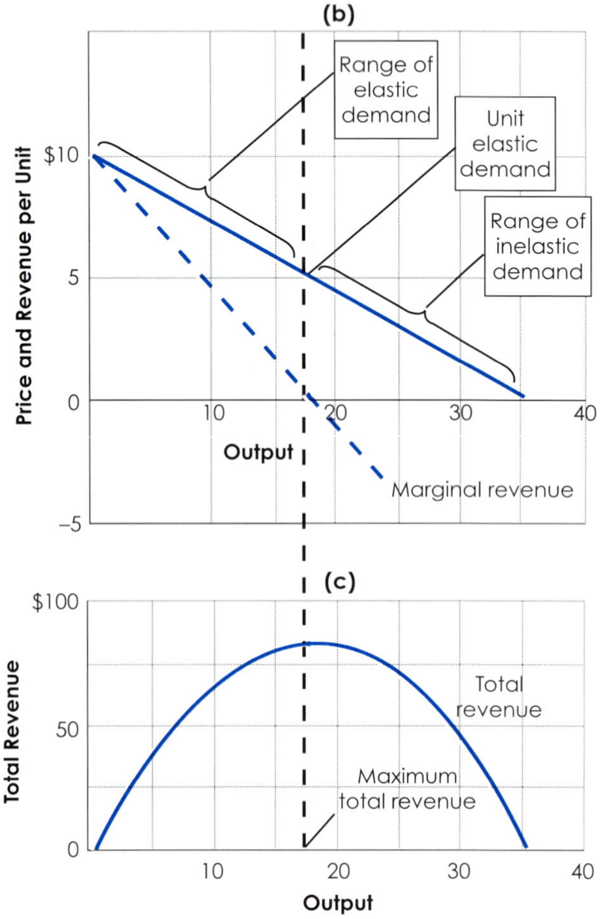

This figure shows how demand, total revenue, and marginal revenue are related under simple monopoly. Total revenue is found by multiplying price by output at each point on the demand curve. Marginal revenue is the increase in total revenue that results from a one-unit increase in output. When demand is elastic, marginal revenue is more than zero and total revenue is increasing. When demand is inelastic, marginal revenue is less than zero and total revenue is decreasing. Marginal revenue is less than price at all levels of output.

is *less* than the price at which the unit is sold, not equal to the price as in a perfectly competitive firm. The gap between price and marginal revenue stems from the fact that the firm sells all units supplied in a given period at the same price. This means that it must cut the price on all units sold per period, not just on the last one, in order to increase the quantity sold. For example, if our monopolist wants to increase sales from 10 units per period to 11 units per period, it must cut the price on all 11 units from $7.30 to $7. Although the firm gains $7 in revenue from the sale of the eleventh unit, its total revenue increases by only $4, from $73 to $77. The added revenue from the eleventh unit is partly offset by a $3 reduction ($.30 per unit) in total revenue from the other 10 units.

The fact that the marginal revenue curve for a monopolist lies below its demand curve illustrates the marginal-average rule discussed in the preceding chapter. The average revenue realized by the simple monopolist, as represented by the height of the demand curve for any given level of output, must be falling if marginal revenue is less than average revenue.

Finding the Point of Maximum Profit

Figure 8.2 adds the monopolist's cost curves to its demand and marginal revenue curves. The data presented there can be used to identify the price-quantity combination that will yield the maximum profit. As in the preceding chapter, this can be done either by comparing total cost with total revenue or by taking a marginal approach.

A monopolist maximizes profits by producing the quantity of output for which marginal cost equals marginal revenue. The price it charges for the product is determined by the height of the demand curve (rather than the height of the marginal revenue curve) at the profit-maximizing output. Note that maximizing profit is not the same as maximizing revenue. Beyond 13 units of output (the profit-maximizing level in this case), total revenue continues to rise for a while, but profit falls because total cost rises even more rapidly.

Total cost for the firm at various output levels is given in column 6 of part (c) of Figure 8.2. Subtracting total cost from total revenue (column 3) gives total profit (column 7). A glance at column 7 shows that the profit-maximizing output level is 13 units. The total revenue–total cost approach to profit maximization is shown graphically in part (a) of the exhibit. Total profit equals the vertical gap between the total cost and total revenue curves. It reaches a maximum at about 13 units of output, where the two curves are farthest apart. (As in the preceding chapter, the graphs, unlike the tables, are continuous, so maximums and minimums need not occur exactly at whole-number quantities of output.) Note that maximizing profit is not the same as maximizing revenue. Between 13 and 17 units of output, total revenue continues to rise. But because total cost rises even more rapidly, profit falls.

The marginal approach to profit maximization is illustrated by the data in columns 4 and 5 in part (c) of Figure 8.2. Marginal revenue is the amount by which total revenue increases when output is increased by one unit; marginal cost is the amount by which total cost increases. It follows that as long as marginal revenue exceeds marginal cost, adding one more unit of output adds more to total revenue than to total cost and hence adds to total profit. Beyond 13 units of output, marginal revenue falls below marginal cost; therefore, any further expansion of output reduces total profit. The logic here is exactly the same as for a perfectly competitive firm, except that now marginal revenue is variable rather than constant.

Part (b) of Figure 8.2 compares marginal revenue and marginal cost in graphical terms. The profit-maximizing output is found at the point where the positively sloped section of the marginal cost curve intersects the marginal revenue curve; that

FIGURE 8.2 PROFIT MAXIMIZATION FOR A MONOPOLIST

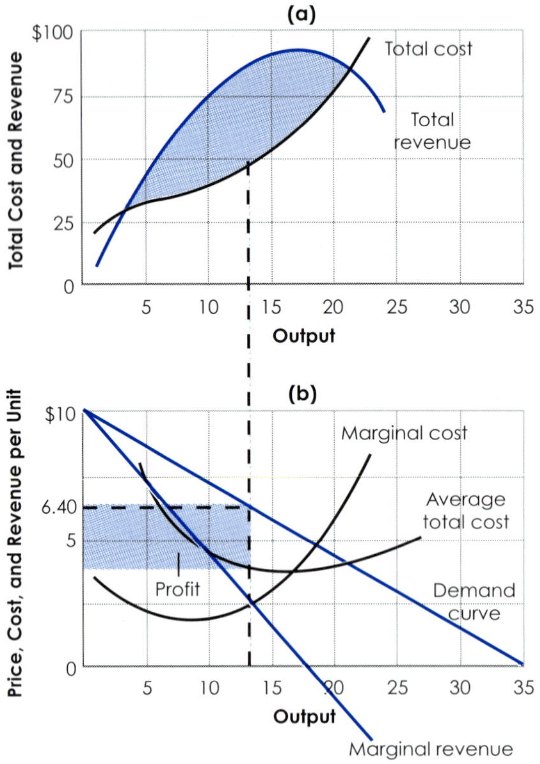

(c)

Quantity of Output (1)	Price (2)	Total Revenue (3)	Marginal Revenue (4)	Marginal Cost (5)	Total Cost (6)	Total Profit (7)
1	$10.00	$10.00			$23.80	–$13.80
2	9.70	19.40	$9.40	$3.40	27.20	–7.80
3	9.40	28.20	8.80	3.05	30.25	2.05
4	9.10	36.40	8.20	2.75	33.00	3.40
5	8.80	44.00	7.60	2.50	35.50	8.50
6	8.50	51.00	7.00	2.30	37.80	13.20
7	8.20	57.40	6.40	2.15	39.95	17.45
8	7.90	63.20	5.80	2.05	42.00	21.20
9	7.60	68.40	5.20	2.00	44.00	24.40
10	7.30	73.00	4.60	2.05	46.05	26.95
11	7.00	77.00	4.00	2.15	48.20	28.80
12	6.70	80.40	3.40	2.30	50.50	29.90
13	**6.40**	**83.20**	**2.80**	**2.50**	**53.00**	**30.20**
14	6.10	85.40	**2.20**	**2.75**	55.75	29.65
15	5.80	87.00	1.60	3.05	58.80	28.20
16	5.50	88.00	1.00	3.40	62.20	25.80
17	5.20	88.40	.40	3.80	66.00	22.40

A monopolist maximizes profits by producing the quantity of output for which marginal cost equals marginal revenue. The price it charges for the product is determined by the height of the demand curve (rather than the height of the marginal revenue curve) at the profit-maximizing output. Beyond 13 units of output (the profit-maximizing level in this case), total revenue continues to rise for a while, but profit falls because total cost rises even more rapidly.

is, at about 13 units of output. Profit per unit at that output is equal to the vertical gap between the demand curve (which shows the price at which the product is sold) and the average total cost curve. Profit per unit times quantity of output equals total profit, as shown by the shaded rectangle.

The intersection of the marginal cost and marginal revenue curves in Figure 8.2 gives the profit-maximizing *output* for the firm, but the profit-maximizing *price* is given by the height of the demand curve for that level of output. For a monopolist, that price is always above marginal cost when profit is being maximized. For the firm in our example, marginal cost at 13 units of output is $2.50 per unit, but according to the demand curve consumers are willing to buy 13 units at a price as high as $6.40 per unit. Therefore, $6.40, not $2.50, is what the monopolist will charge for the 13 units of output in order to earn the maximum profit.

Profit Maximization or Loss Minimization?

If market conditions are unfavorable, a monopolist, like a perfectly competitive firm, may be unable to earn a profit in the short run. (Think of a firm that has a monopoly on the sale of peanuts at the local baseball stadium; such a firm might well suffer losses during a season when the home team is playing badly and attendance is low.) In such a case, it will aim to minimize losses. Whether a profit is possible depends on the position of the demand curve relative to the firm's average total cost curve.

The possibility of a loss is shown in Figure 8.3. The demand curve lies below the average total cost curve at all points. The monopolist might find itself in such a position during a recession, when a drop in consumer income temporarily shifts the demand curve to the left. Following the usual rule, the profit-maximizing (or loss-minimizing) level of output is found at the point where the marginal cost and marginal revenue curves intersect, that is, at about 10 units. According to the demand curve, that much output cannot be sold for more than $4 per unit, even though average total cost at 10 units of output is $4.60. At a price of $4 per unit, then, the firm will lose $.60 on each unit sold. The total loss is shown by the shaded rectangle.

Although the firm suffers a loss at 10 units of output, no other output level will yield a smaller loss. In Figure 8.3, the price of $4 per unit is more than enough to cover average variable costs. A monopolist, like a perfect competitor, is better off staying in business in the short run, even at a loss, as long as the price at which it can sell its output is greater than the average variable cost. But if the demand curve shifts so far to the left that it falls below the average variable cost curve at all points, the firm will minimize its short-run losses by shutting down.

We see, then, that being a monopolist does not guarantee that a firm will be able to earn a profit. It can do so only if demand conditions allow the product to be sold at a price that exceeds the cost of producing it. The situation shown in Figure 8.3 was assumed to be only temporary, in which case the firm would ride it out, waiting for better times to return. Sometimes, however, a monopolist faces a permanent decline

FIGURE 8.3 A MONOPOLIST SUFFERING A SHORT-RUN LOSS

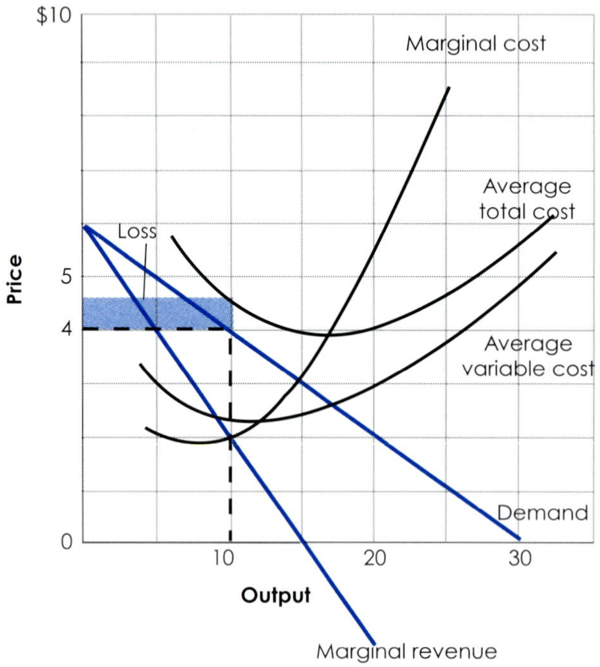

Sometimes demand may not be high enough to allow a monopolist to earn a profit. In this graph, for example, the demand curve lies below the average total cost curve at all points. The best the monopolist can do in the short run is cut losses by producing at the point at which marginal cost equals marginal revenue. If the demand curve were to shift downward even further, preventing the firm from obtaining a price that would cover average variable cost, the short-run loss-minimizing strategy would be to shut down.

in demand. A privately owned, profit-maximizing monopolist will then leave the industry, freeing itself of its fixed costs by selling its assets, terminating its long-term leases, and so on. *Applying Economic Ideas 8.1* illustrates this possibility with the case of urban mass transit systems, which, in many cities, formerly operated as privately owned closed monopolies. When the demand for mass transit services fell, the systems could no longer operate at a profit and might have disappeared entirely but for public subsidies.

PROFIT MAXIMIZATION IN THE LONG RUN

In presenting the model of perfect competition, we distinguished between two time horizons. In the short run, each firm had a plant of fixed size, and the number of firms in the industry was also fixed. In the long run, each firm was free to adjust the size of its plant, and firms were free to enter or leave the industry. Each case gave rise to a clearly defined equilibrium. The simple model of monopoly presented in the preceding section is oriented toward the short run. The issues raised by consideration of the long run under monopoly conditions are more complex. Not all of them can be resolved in terms of simple equilibrium solutions. Nevertheless, some of the issues are worth considering.

Long-Run Equilibrium Without Threat of Entry

The simplest situation is that of a monopolist that faces no threat of entry into its market by competitors. For such a firm, a graph such as Figure 8.2 can represent long-run as well as short-run profit maximization. Only the interpretation of the curves changes. The curve that is labeled average total cost in Figure 8.2 would now be interpreted as the firm's long-run average cost curve, allowing for free adjustment of fixed inputs as in the long-run competitive case. The marginal cost curve would be the corresponding long-run marginal cost curve, and the demand curve would be the long-run demand curve. The long-run equilibrium would occur at the output where long-run marginal cost equals long-run marginal revenue, and the long-run equilibrium price would be given by the height of the long-run demand curve at that point. Beyond what has already been said about the short run, three things are worth noting about such a long-run equilibrium.

1. The firm must at least break even in the long-run equilibrium. The loss-minimizing situation shown in Figure 8.3 cannot be a long-run equilibrium because the firm would leave the market if it could not at least recover its long-run average cost.

2. Unlike the case of perfect competition, long-run equilibrium under monopoly need not occur at the minimum point on the firm's long-run total cost curve. It could occur at an output below minimum long-run average cost (as shown in Figure 8.2), or at an output greater than minimum long-run average cost (as would be the case if the demand curve in Figure 8.2 were to shift strongly to the right). Whatever its long-run equilibrium output, the monopolist will select the size of plant that is best suited to that level of output. In graphical terms, this would mean a short-run average total cost curve tangent to the long-run average cost curve at the equilibrium output.

3. The price that will maximize long-run profit for the firm will be lower than the price that will maximize short-run profit if, as is usually the case, demand is more elastic in the long run than in the short run. Beginning from a point of long-run equilibrium, a monopolist could temporarily increase its profit by raising its price and cutting output to move up along its less elastic short-run demand curve. But, given that higher price, customers would make long-run adjustments in their consumption patterns, reducing the quantity demanded until they were back on the long-run demand curve at a correspondingly lower level of output. The monopolist's profit at the higher price would then be less than at the original long-run equilibrium price.

APPLYING ECONOMIC IDEAS 8.1

SUBSIDIZED MONOPOLY: THE CASE OF MASS TRANSIT

To many people, monopoly is synonymous with vast profits. Not all monopolies are profitable however. A case in point is the mass transit systems of most large U.S. cities.

Until the 1960s, the majority of urban bus lines in the United States were privately owned. Often there was more than one transit firm in a city—Chicago had more than thirty at one point. But the city government granted each firm a closed monopoly over the routes it operated. Thus, people were often unable to choose among transit systems to get to any given destination.

In 1950 this largely private transit system carried some 17 billion passengers. Gradually, however, more and more commuters and shoppers begin to travel by car. By 1970 ridership on urban mass transit systems had fallen to just 7 billion. Along the way, the business became unprofitable for most private firms, despite their monopoly status. In 1963, for the first time, urban mass transit as a whole experienced an operating loss. Since that date it has never regained profitability.

City governments could simply have let the private transit systems go out of business. In some cases, especially trolley systems, they did so. However, all subway and most urban bus systems were gradually transferred to city ownership where they remain to this day.

These government-owned monopoly transit systems like their private predecessors, must decide how to price their product. One possible rule would be to equate marginal cost and marginal revenue in order to minimize losses and keep subsidies for the system to a minimum. However, several considerations suggest a lower fare and a larger subsidy than would result from a simple loss-minimization strategy.

One such consideration is efficiency. It could be argued that for commuters to choose efficiently between mass transit and driving their own cars, the transit fare should be equal to the marginal cost of providing an additional ride on the public transit system A subsidy-minimizing price would be higher than marginal cost and, thus, higher than the efficient level.

Second, it can be argued that a further adjustment of the fare should be made to allow for traffic congestion, a form of negative externality that in itself results in inefficient use of transportation resources. A low fare that causes people to choose mass transit rather than travel by car can be defended as a means of offsetting the adverse effects of traffic congestion.

Finally, low transit fares are often defended as a means of benefiting low income households, which tend to be heavy users of public transportation. Without affordable public transportation as a means of getting to work, it is argued, some lower-income people would not be able to keep their jobs and instead would have to depend on the assistance of public welfare payments.

In practice, then, most mass transit systems do not set fares to minimize subsidies. To do so would require operating at a point at which marginal revenue is positive, indicating that the system is operating on the elastic part of its demand circle. However, fare increases on most systems result in higher revenues, showing that they are on the inelastic portion of the demand curve. As a rule, city governments leave transit fares low until taxpayers start complaining about the size of the necessary subsidies. Then they raise fares to the point at which the strength of the marginal complaint from transit riders balances that of the marginal complaint from taxpayers.

Open Monopoly, Entrepreneurship, and Limit Pricing

In the case just examined it is easy to identify an equilibrium point, but only because the case excludes an essential element of reality: entrepreneurship. It treats short- and long-run demand curves as given, whereas in practice any firm that earns a pure economic profit for any length of time is sure to attract the attention of entrepreneurs eager to get a piece of the action. They will have their own ideas about what is given and what is subject to change.

Consider long-run equilibrium for an open monopolist. Such a firm is currently the sole supplier of its product but is not protected by the decisive cost advantages of a natural monopoly or the legal barriers to entry of a closed monopoly. With little or no built-in protection from would-be rivals, what options does it have?

One option is to push the price all the way up to the short-run profit-maximizing level, enjoy pure economic profits while they last, and accept the fact that sooner or later other firms will enter the market and take away part or all of those profits. In many cases that is just what firms do. The consumer electronics industry provides many familiar examples. The first firm to reach the market with a stereo TV, compact disk player, or digital audiotape machine typically sets a high initial price. Soon other firms enter with products that closely imitate the original one. The market then becomes an oligopoly in which the first firm may still hold a significant market share, but at a much lower price level. With luck, by the time pure economic profits disappear entirely, the firm's research department will come up with a new product from which the firm can again reap temporary monopoly profits. Often the hope of even short-lived monopoly profits is a strong spur to innovation.

But there is a second option available to an open monopolist. Instead of setting the price at the short-run profit-maximizing level, it may set a somewhat lower price, one that gives it a moderate profit but at the same time makes the market a less attractive target for would-be competitors. Such a strategy is called **limit pricing** because it limits short-run profits in the hope of limiting entry.

Limit pricing

A strategy in which the dominant firm in a market charges less than the short-run profit-maximizing price in order to limit the likelihood of entry by new competitors.

The analysis of limit pricing quickly becomes complicated.[1] In general terms, a limit pricing strategy tends to be more attractive if the monopolist enjoys any cost advantage, even a small one, over potential entrants. For example, a new entrant may need to incur sunk costs, say, to recruit a network of dealers or acquaint consumers with a new brand name. Or perhaps through "learning by doing" the first firm in the market has achieved lower production costs than another firm can achieve when it first enters the market. Given such a cost advantage, the first firm may be able to earn a pure economic profit at a price that is still low enough to deter other entrants.

There need not be an all-or-nothing choice between short-run profit maximization and limit pricing. A firm may set an intermediate price that merely slows entry without entirely preventing it. It may introduce its product at a high price and then "slide down the demand curve" as other firms enter. The variations are endless. As the firm's attention turns away from the marginal cost–marginal revenue calculus of the simple monopolist to strategic moves and countermoves against actual and potential rivals, the market structure that we have called open monopoly shades into oligopoly. And that is a subject for another chapter.

Closed Monopoly and Rent Seeking

Let us turn now to the implications of entrepreneurship for a closed monopoly—one that is protected by a legal barrier, such as a government permit or a patent. If the market is truly closed to competition in any form, there is nothing to add beyond what was said earlier in the section on long-run equilibrium without threat of entry. However, few if any monopolies are closed that tightly. Instead, they face threats to their profits on two fronts: (1) the development of substitute products and (2) challenges to the legal barriers that close the market to competition.

First consider substitute products. Although the market structure of monopoly assumes that the product has no "close" substitutes, closeness is clearly a matter of degree. There is no such thing as a product with no substitutes at all. Moreover, a monopolist must consider not only existing substitutes, but also the development of new ones. If one firm has a monopoly on a patented drug, rival researchers will strive to develop alternate therapies for the condition. If a railroad charges a monopoly price on a route that has no competing rail service, it will encourage competition from pipelines, barges, and trucks.

Over time, then, the higher the price set by the monopolist and the longer that price is maintained, the more rival entrepreneurs will attempt to supply varied and attractive substitutes. As they do so, the monopolist's demand curve will gradually be pushed to the left.

Meanwhile, the same or other rivals will be at work on another front. The closed monopolist's hold on the market may be protected by law, but lobbyists can persuade legislatures to change laws, and lawyers can find loopholes in them. If the closed monopoly is earning pure economic profits, lawyers and lobbyists become attractive investments for potential rivals. To combat them, the monopolist will have to invest in lawyers and lobbyists of its own.

The efforts of firms to break into or protect closed monopolies are examples of rent seeking. The "rents" being sought in this case are the pure economic profits that the monopolist earns over and above the opportunity costs of producing its product. But rent seeking and defenses against rent seeking are costly. They require a firm to hire lawyers, lobbyists, and researchers, and divert the time of its managers from other tasks. These costs must be added to production costs when computing profit. In terms of our model, expenditures that arise from rent seeking and defenses against it push a firm's cost curves upward.

Rent seeking need not be limited to rivals that seek to enter the firm's market. The firm's own employees may get in on the act. Monopoly profits earned by a protected employer—say, a municipal transit company or a firm with a monopoly contract to collect a city's garbage—are an attractive target for unions. Unions do not always depend only on their own bargaining power; sometimes they may seek legislative intervention in labor disputes. Rent seeking by a monopolist's suppliers and even by its customers may also occur.

The closed monopolist thus is caught in a vise. Entrepreneurs developing substitute products push its demand curve to the left, and at the same time the need to defend itself against rent seekers pushes its costs upward. Even if no rivals enter the monopolist's market directly, it will gradually be forced toward the position shown in Figure 8.4, where it just breaks even. When it reaches a situation of zero economic profit, an equilibrium will finally be established in which the rate of introduction of substitutes and the level of rent-seeking expenditures stop increasing.

FIGURE 8.4 THE BREAKEVEN POSITION FOR A MONOPOLIST

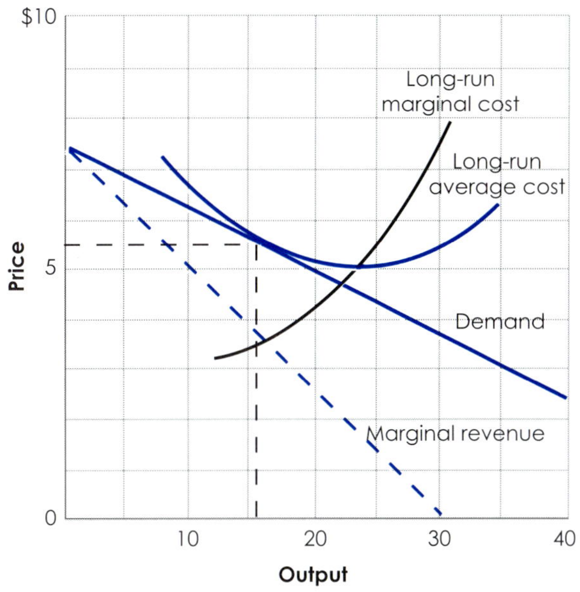

This exhibit shows a monopolist that is just breaking even. The firm earns enough revenue to cover all costs, including the opportunity cost of capital, but not enough to permit an economic profit. A closed monopoly could be driven to this position in the long run through erosion of demand as substitutes are developed or by the costs of defending its monopoly position against rent seekers.

As an example of a monopolist caught in such a squeeze, consider the U.S. Postal Service. For two centuries it has fought for and held on to its closed monopoly on delivery of first-class mail. Yet the postal service, far from being richly profitable, is lucky if it breaks even. A large part of the explanation is found in the vigorous expansion of substitutes (UPS, Federal Express, electronic transmission of documents via fax or Internet), and the highly successful rent-seeking activities of postal employee unions.

To summarize, the life of a monopolist is not a bed of roses. True, extraordinary short-run profit opportunities may arise, but a monopolist must not be overly aggressive in exploiting them. New substitute products, newly entering firms, and rent-seeking all pose threats. In real life, being a monopolist is a lot more work than finding the point where a couple of lines cross on a graph.

PRICE DISCRIMINATION

The model of simple monopoly assumes that all units sold in a given period must be sold at the same price. Some firms, however, charge different prices to different buyers for the same product. When the prices charged to different buyers do not simply reflect differences in the costs of serving them, the firm is said to practice **price discrimination**. Thus, a theater that charges adults $8 for a seat and children just $6 is practicing price discrimination; the cost of providing a seat to a child and to an adult is the same. However, a gas station that charges $.04 per gallon less for cash purchases than for credit card purchases is not practicing price discrimination. It is simply passing along the lower cost of cash transactions to its cash customers.

Price discrimination
The practice of charging different prices for various units of a single product when the price differences are not justified by differences in cost.

Conditions Required for Price Discrimination

Two conditions must be met for a price searcher to engage in price discrimination. First, it must be impossible or at least inconvenient for buyers to resell the product. For example, it is unlikely that your campus bookstore (a monopoly on many campuses) could get away with selling economics texts at list price to seniors and at a 25 percent discount to everyone else. If it tried to do so, some clever sophomore would soon go into business buying books for resale to seniors at a split-the-difference price. The bookstore's list-price sales would soon fall to zero. Second, the seller must be able to classify buyers into groups on the basis of the elasticity of their demand for the good. Those with highly inelastic demand can then be charged high prices and those with more elastic demand can be charged lower prices.

Although it is convenient to discuss price discrimination in conjunction with monopoly, the practice may appear in other market structures, as well. Consider, for example, price discrimination by colleges and universities, which are certainly not monopolies. First, the school's business office sets tuition and fees at a level that it thinks is about as high as anyone would be willing to pay. Next, the admissions office gives its approval to a certain number of qualified applicants. Finally, the financial aid office gives selective price rebates, called scholarships, to students who would be unwilling or unable to attend if they were charged the full tuition.

A college or university is in an ideal position to practice price discrimination. For one thing, the product cannot be resold. If you are admitted to both Harvard and Dartmouth, you cannot sell your Dartmouth admission to someone who did not get into either place. Also, the school insists that applicants supply a great deal of information on families' willingness and ability to pay. Because the demand for a good tends to be less elastic the smaller the share of income a family spends on it, rich families are likely to have less elastic demand for college education than poor families. Finally, an applicant's high-school grades and test scores also help in estimating his or her elasticity of demand. A student with relatively high grades probably has many alternatives and, hence, relatively elastic demand. A student with lower grades may be lucky to get into just one school.

In this case, as in others where markets can be divided into separate submarkets with distinct demand curves, the firm sets marginal cost equal to marginal revenue in each market. The result is a higher equilibrium price for customers whose demand is less elastic.

Fairness and Price Discrimination

Price discrimination is often viewed as unfair, especially by those who pay the higher prices. Many people, for example, are annoyed if they learn that the person sitting next to them on an airplane paid less than they did for a ticket on the same flight. In fact, many people think it is unfair for a firm to charge different prices to different customers even when the difference is justified by considerations of cost and does not count as price discrimination in the economic sense. An example is the practice of charging young men more than young women for automobile insurance. Insurance companies insist that the different rates are justified by the fact that men are involved in more accidents, but this does not end the perception that the difference in rates is unfair.

Economists, on the other hand, tend to look more kindly on price discrimination. They not only see it as a practice that promotes efficiency, but, properly understood, as one that often promotes fairness, as well. The example of college scholarships illustrates some of the reasons that price discrimination can be beneficial. This form of price discrimination makes it possible for some students to attend colleges that they otherwise could not afford, while shifting part of the cost, in the form of high tuition, to the students who can most afford to pay. Similarly, price discrimination makes it easier for parents to take young children to the movies. It makes it possible for students who are willing to buy tickets in advance and stay at their destinations over a Saturday night to fill airline seats that business travelers would leave empty.

These examples emphasize that price discrimination may, in some circumstances, be beneficial in terms of fairness. Later in the chapter we will see that it can also allow markets to perform more efficiently. For these reasons, although price discrimination will always have its critics, economists often rise to its defense.

MARKET PERFORMANCE UNDER MONOPOLY

In the last chapter we looked at market performance under perfect competition. That market structure received high marks for two aspects of market performance. First, we noted that in competitive equilibrium marginal cost is equal to market price. Production thus proceeds to the point at which no further mutual gains for buyers and sellers are possible. In that sense an economy of competitive markets provides an efficient solution to the question of what to produce. Second, we noted that in long-run equilibrium a perfectly competitive firm produces at the lowest point on its long-run average cost curve. This is a key aspect of efficiency in the choice of how to produce.

In this section we look at market performance under monopoly. First, we compare simple monopoly with perfect competition in terms of the questions of what and how to produce. We then look briefly at the question of for whom goods are produced. Finally, we explore some unresolved issues.

What to Produce: Consumer and Producer Surplus

The concepts of consumer and producer surplus, which were introduced in a previous chapter, provide a useful tool for analyzing market performance with regard to the quantity of each good that is produced. Figure 8.5 makes the comparison between perfect competition and simple monopoly.

Part (a) of the exhibit shows a perfectly competitive market. As we saw in Chapter 5, the height of the demand curve measures the maximum amount that consumers would willingly pay for a given quantity of output. The height of the supply curve measures the minimum amount that suppliers would willingly accept for a given output. Because the supply curve is based on the marginal cost curves of individual firms, it reflects the opportunity cost of producing each additional unit. The equilibrium price is $20 and the equilibrium quantity 200 units. Consumers, who would be willing to pay more than $20 for all but the two hundredth unit, earn a consumer surplus equal to the area beneath the demand curve but above the market price. Producers, who produce all but the two hundredth unit at an opportunity cost of less than $20, earn a producer surplus equal to the area above the supply curve but

FIGURE 8.5 MARKET PERFORMANCE UNDER MONOPOLY AND COMPETITION

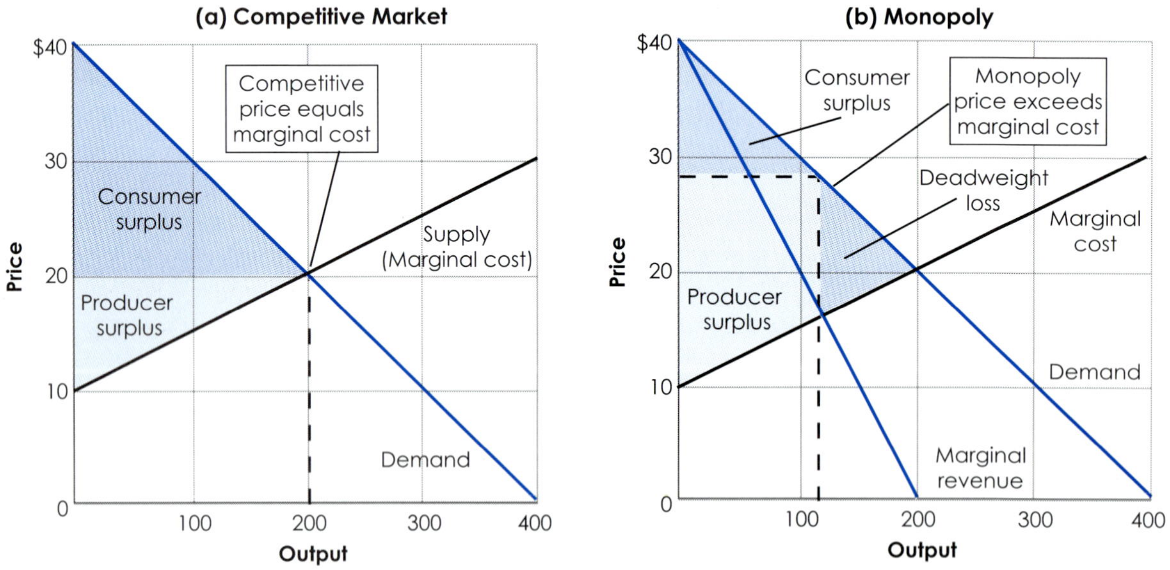

Under perfect competition, shown in part (a), production is carried out to the point at which the price consumers are willing to pay for the last unit produced just equals the opportunity cost of producing it. All possible gains from trade are realized in the form of producer and consumer surplus. Under monopoly, production stops short of that point. Consumer surplus is smaller and producer surplus larger than under competition, but the total of the two is smaller. Some potential gains from trade go unrealized. This deadweight loss is the reason monopoly is considered a form of market failure.

beneath the market price. These surpluses represent consumers' and producers' mutual gains from exchange.

Under competitive conditions production is carried to the point at which all potential gains from exchange are exhausted. Nothing would be gained from producing beyond the 200-unit mark. From the 201st unit on, the opportunity cost of the unit to producers as measured by the supply curve would exceed its value to consumers as measured by the demand curve.

Now consider the situation under monopoly, as shown in part (b) of the exhibit. To make the comparison easy, the demand and marginal cost curves for the monopolist in question are assumed to be the same as the market demand and supply curves for the competitive industry.

To maximize its profits, the monopolist limits production to 120 units and charges a price of $28 per unit. Even at that price, consumers are better off than they would be if the good were entirely unavailable. They realize a surplus equal to the area beneath the demand curve but above the $28 price. The monopolist, on the other hand, realizes a substantial producer surplus. The 120th unit, which is sold for $28, costs only $16 to produce, yielding a producer surplus of $12. Surpluses on earlier units, which are produced at a lower opportunity cost, are correspondingly greater. The total producer surplus equals the shaded area above the marginal cost curve but below the $28 price, bordered on the left by the vertical axis and on the right by the profit-maximizing quantity.

Comparison of the competitive case with the monopoly case reveals these three differences.

1. Consumer surplus is smaller under monopoly.
2. Producer surplus is larger under monopoly.
3. The total of producer and consumer surpluses is smaller under monopoly.

The third difference reveals the inefficiency of monopoly. It indicates that some potential gains from exchange are not realized. Other things being equal, production of units 121 through 200 would provide benefits to consumers that exceed their costs. This would make both producers and consumers better off. The potential gains from trade that are "wasted" are shown by the triangle lying between the supply and demand curves and bordered on the left by the monopolist's profit-maximizing quantity. That area represents a **deadweight loss**—a term that is often used to refer to any benefit that is lost by one party but not gained by another. The excess burden of a tax, illustrated in Chapter 5, is another example of a deadweight loss.

Deadweight loss

A loss of consumer or producer surplus that is not balanced by a gain to someone else.

If producing another 80 units of output would make both producers and consumers better off, one might ask why this is not done. The answer lies in the assumption that a simple monopolist offers a single price per unit to all buyers. We have already seen one alternative pricing strategy that would make a monopolized market more efficient. If the monopolist could hold the price of the first 120 units at $28 while selling units 121 through 200 at a price of $20, both the firm and its customers would benefit. The deadweight loss would then be recaptured. A simple monopolist, on the other hand, must sell all units at a uniform price. Such a firm cannot cut the price on units 121 through 200 without also cutting the price on units 1 through 120. The intersection of the marginal cost and marginal revenue curves marks the limit of the simple monopolist's willingness to produce.

Another common pricing strategy practiced by monopolists and firms in other market structures as well is to set a price equal to or close to marginal cost, and then to collect extra revenue in the form of some kind of "access fee." Well known examples include night clubs that require a "cover charge" for people who enter regardless of how much food or drink they order, cell phone companies that charge a fixed monthly fee plus a fee for each call, and golf clubs that have a monthly membership fee plus a "greens fee" each time a member plays. All of these strategies keep the price of the last unit sold close to marginal cost and thereby limit deadweight loss.

To summarize, the fact that a simple monopoly's price exceeds its marginal cost in a situation of equilibrium means that too little of the good is produced to realize all potential gains from trade. Simple monopoly therefore distorts the choice of what to produce. Compared with perfectly competitive industries, simple monopolies produce goods in inefficiently small quantities. However, in the real world, monopolies, monopolistic competitors, and oligopolists often use more complex pricing strategies that keep prices closer to marginal cost and thus experience less of a deadweight loss.

How to Produce: Average Total Cost in Monopoly Equilibrium

A second favorable trait of perfect competition, as we saw in the preceding chapter, is the fact that its equilibrium output is produced at the least possible long-run average cost. This trait is not shared by monopoly. As we saw earlier in this chapter, equilibrium output for a monopoly can occur at any point along its long-run average cost curve. Thus, monopoly cannot lay claim to minimization of average total cost and in this respect can be said to be less efficient than perfect competition.

How serious the inefficiency is in practice depends on circumstances. Three cases need to be considered.

1. In the case of a natural monopoly, equilibrium will usually occur at an ourput at which the firm is still experiencing economies of scale. Dividing the industry's total output between two or more firms would mean that each of them would have to operate at an even lower, and hence less efficient, level of output. Thus, although the natural monopoly produces an inefficiently low level of output, it produces that output at the lowest possible cost given the demand and cost curves for the product.
2. Empirical cost studies indicate that many firms experience approximately constant returns to scale after a minimum efficient scale has been reached. If demand for the product is sufficient so that the profit-maximizing equilibrium

output for such a firm is greater than that minimum efficient scale, that output will be produced at the minimum possible cost. This will be so even if the chosen output is smaller than the efficient level, that is, the level that would make price equal to marginal cost.

3. The equilibrium output may lie on the rising portion of the monopolist's average cost curve, where it encounters decreasing returns to scale. Dividing total output among two or more smaller firms would then decrease average total cost. In this case the monopolist not only produces an output that is too small to realize all potential consumer and producer surplus, but also produces that output at an inefficiently high cost.

Failure to minimize average total cost appears to be a problem only when the monopolist experiences diseconomies of scale at the equilibrium output. This can happen only in a closed monopoly. A natural monopoly experiences economies of scale at its equilibrium output. And an open monopoly could not survive in the long run if it operated at a significant cost disadvantage relative to smaller firms entering the market. A limit pricing strategy would not work for such a firm, and a short-run profit-maximizing price would only speed the entry of rivals.

In addition to operating at an inefficient point on its long-run average cost curve, there is another reason that a closed monopolist's costs may be inefficiently high. Earlier we noted that closed monopolists may have to spend heavily on lobbying and legal battles to defend themselves against rent-seeking rivals that want to break down the legal protections the monopoly enjoys. Those costs add little or nothing to output or consumer satisfaction. Loss of the output that the lawyers or lobbyists could have produced if they had worked elsewhere, it can be argued, is another form of deadweight loss from closed monopoly.

For Whom Does Monopoly Promote Inequality?

Cartoonists draw monopolists as fat men with big cigars and long limousines. For good measure, they may sketch in a child in rags watching the limousine drive by. Such cartoons reflect a common view that monopoly promotes inequality. To the extent that noneconomists worry about monopolists at all, they are more likely to dislike them because they are seen as rich and powerful than because they are seen as inefficient.

Sometimes monopoly does confer wealth and power. The "robber barons" who tried to monopolize the oil, steel, and tobacco industries at the turn of the century were a case in point. But aside from such anecdotal evidence, does the theory of monopoly provide any reason to associate the market structure of monopoly with large private fortunes? Not necessarily.

For one thing, we must ask who owns the monopoly. If the monopoly is a giant corporation, much of its stock may be owned by such institutions as insurance companies and union pension funds. If so, the monopoly's profits will benefit widows and orphans as well as fat cats with big cigars. Other monopolies are small operations such as, say, the only gas station or theater in an isolated small town. The owners may barely earn enough to cover costs. In still other cases, monopolies are owned by government—the U.S. Postal Service, the retail liquor monopolies of many states, and the Tennessee Valley Authority's monopoly of electric power in an area covering several states are examples. Any profits made by those monopolies become available to finance other areas of government activity rather than creating private fortunes.

Moreover, as we have seen, there is no guarantee that monopolists will earn pure economic profits in the long run. Competition from substitute products erodes the profits of some monopolies. Closed monopolies may spend potential profits on measures to fend off rent seekers. Open monopolies may limit their profits in order to deter other firms from entering the market.

This is not to say that a market economy does not produce large inequalities of wealth and income. Instead, the point is that monopoly, as a market structure, is neither a necessary nor a sufficient condition for inequality. There are poor monopolists, and there are people who grow rich under oligopoly, monopolistic competition, and even perfect competition.

A Balance Sheet

Taking everything into account, where do we stand on the question of market performance under monopoly? What are its important failures, and what, if any, are its strengths? The material presented in this chapter supports the following conclusions:

1. Simple monopoly can result in market failure by leading to an equilibrium condition in which price exceeds marginal cost. In some circumstances the extent of the market failure can be reduced by means of price discrimination.
2. No monopolist is entirely free of competition from substitute products and potential entrants. In some cases such competition may be sufficient in the long run to eliminate pure economic profit and significantly narrow the gap between price and marginal cost.
3. Closed monopolies pose the most serious threat of market failure. Legal protections shield them, at least partially, from competition by entrants and substitutes, and costs associated with rent seeking may represent additional deadweight losses.
4. Natural monopolies also pose a threat of market failure. Economies of scale protect them from the threat of entry by other firms unless new technology permits efficient small-scale production. Regulation designed to enhance the performance of natural monopolies will be discussed in a future chapter.

5. Open monopolies pose the least serious threat of market failure. The threat of entry by potential competitors limits the ability of firms to earn pure economic profits in the long run. Limit pricing may keep prices close to the level of costs. Inefficiencies resulting from short-run monopoly pricing practices may be offset by a rapid pace of innovation.

Considerably more remains to be said about the relationship between market structure and market performance. To take the next steps, we need to broaden the scope of our discussion to take into account the market structures that lie between perfect competition and monopoly—that is, oligopoly and monopolistic competition. That is the task of the next chapter.

SUMMARY

1. **In what circumstances can monopoly exist?** A monopoly is a firm that is the sole supplier of a product that has no close substitutes. Three classes of monopoly can be distinguished: *closed monopolies,* which are protected by legal restrictions on competition; *natural monopolies,* which are protected by economies of scale; and *open monopolies,* which have no special protections against the entry of potential competitors.
2. **How are the profit-maximizing price and output for a monopoly determined?** A *simple monopoly* (one that does not practice price discrimination) earns a maximum profit by producing the quantity of output that makes marginal cost equal to marginal revenue. The price is determined by the height of the demand curve at the profit-maximizing level. If a monopoly cannot earn a profit in the short run, it will try to keep its loss to a minimum. If the loss-minimizing price is above average variable cost, the firm will continue to operate in the short run. If the loss-minimizing price is below average variable cost, it will shut down.
3. How is long-run equilibrium achieved under monopoly? In the long run, a monopoly that faces no threat of competition maximizes its profit at the level of output for which long-run marginal cost is equal to long-run marginal revenue. Because demand tends to be more elastic in the long run, the long-run profit-maximizing price may be lower than the price that would maximize short-run profit. An open monopoly may discourage other firms from entering the market by charging a price below that which would maximize short-run profit. Such a strategy is known as *limit pricing.*
4. **Why do monopolies and other price-searching firms sometimes engage in price discrimination?** A monopolist or other firm that is not a price taker can practice *price discrimination* if its product cannot be resold by buyers and if it has some way of classifying buyers on the basis of elasticity of demand. Although price discrimination is resented by buyers who must pay higher prices, it may increase efficiency by allowing customers who value the product more than its marginal cost but less than the price that a simple monopolist would charge to buy the product.
5. **How does monopoly affect market performance?** Monopoly can be a source of market failure in that the amount of output it produces is less than the

amount that would make marginal cost equal to the price charged. As a result, some consumers who would be willing to pay a price that is higher than marginal cost are unable to buy from a monopolist. Because some gains from trade (consumer and producer surplus) are not realized under a simple monopoly, there is a *deadweight loss* to the economy. Also, under long-run equilibrium conditions a monopoly does not necessarily produce at the point of minimum long-run average cost.

KEY TERMS

Closed monopoly
Natural monopoly
Open monopoly
Price searcher
Simple monopoly
Limit pricing
Price discrimination
Deadweight loss

PROBLEMS AND TOPICS FOR DISCUSSION

1. **Examining the lead-off case.** "A monopolist can always make a profit because with no competition it can charge any price it likes." Do you think this statement is true? What, if anything, limits the price that a firm like Petrosian can charge for caviar, assuming there are no other sellers of the product?

2. **Short-run shutdown for a monopolist.** Redraw the graph in Figure 8.3, shifting the demand and marginal revenue curves to illustrate the case in which a monopolist will shut down in the short run rather than continue to produce at a loss.

3. **Price discrimination.** Air travelers are sometimes surprised and annoyed to find that the price of a ticket for a short flight may exceed the price for a long flight. For example, a round-trip ticket from Washington, D.C., to Seattle on one airline costs $235, compared with the same airline's price of $278 from Washington, D.C., to Dayton, Ohio. Travelers complain that such prices represent unfair discrimination against the residents of medium-sized cities such as Dayton. They say that airlines should be forced to charge prices that are scaled in proportion to the distance flown. The airlines answer that major city pairs such as Washington, D.C.–Seattle can be served at a lower cost (with larger planes and fewer empty seats) than less frequently traveled city pairs such as Washington, D.C.–Dayton. Discuss the merits of the current price structure and the proposed alternative in terms of fairness and efficiency.

4. **Mass transit pricing and market failure.** Reread the sections of Chapter 4 that deal with market failure and rent seeking. Can it be argued that the market failure theory of government justifies public ownership and subsidy of mass transit systems? What particular types of failure are involved here? What pricing policy would be called for under the market failure theory? Do you think there are any elements of mass transit policy that can be explained under the theory of rent seeking?

CASE FOR DISCUSSION

The Postal Monopoly

The U.S. Post Office was organized in 1789 and immediately began losing money. One of the reasons that it lost money was competition. The post office charged the same price to deliver a letter anywhere in the country, but its costs were not the same in every case. For letters mailed between points in the East, the post office charged more than cost; for letters mailed to points in the West, it charged less than cost.

Competitors flocked to the routes on which costs were low. For example, in the 1840s Henry Wells, who later founded the famous Wells-Fargo Company, set up a mail service between Philadelphia and New York. He charged $.06 for a first-class letter, compared to the post office's rate of $.25. By the early 1840s private firms were carrying at least one-third of the mail in the United States.

To fight off the competition, the post office turned to Congress. In 1845 Congress strengthened the restrictions on private first-class mail service. This saved the post office from extinction and allowed it to continue its policy of uniform rates regardless of the cost of service. This policy remains in force for first-class mail: The cost of mailing a letter to any address in the United States is the same, whatever the distance. However, the cost of delivering a letter clearly is not the same for all addresses. Deliveries to post office boxes are least expensive; deliveries to homes in suburban neighborhoods are a bit more costly; and rural free delivery service is more expensive still.

Source: Based in part on *Economics of Public Policy,* 2nd ed. (Chapter 11), by John C. Goodman and Edwin C. Dolan (St. Paul, MN: West Publishing Company, 1982).

QUESTIONS

1. On the basis of information given in the case, should the postal monopoly on first-class mail be classified as closed, open, or natural? Why?
2. Do you think the practice of charging all customers the same price when costs differ from one customer to another should be viewed as price discrimination? Do you think it has any benefits? Discuss in terms of efficiency and fairness.
3. Although the U.S. Postal Service (USPS) has retained its monopoly on ordinary first-class mail, it allows competition from such firms as United Parcel Service (UPS) and Federal Express (FedEx) in carrying overnight and third-class mail (parcels). In these cases both the USPS and its private competitors charge different prices according to weight and distance and according to whether pickup and delivery services are provided. Why does a policy of charging a single price regardless of cost not work in a market in which competition exists?

END NOTES

1. For a more detailed treatment, see F. M. Schere, *Industrial Market Structure and Economic Performance,* 2nd ed. (Chicago: Rand McNally, 1980).

CHAPTER 9

Industrial Organization, Monopolistic Competition, and Oligopoly

After reading this chapter, you will understand:

1. How the structure of markets in the U.S. economy has changed over time
2. How the interdependence of firms under oligopoly affects price and output decisions
3. Why oligopolistic firms sometimes collude to increase profits, and the problems they encounter as a result
4. The conditions that affect market performance under oligopoly
5. How equilibrium is achieved under monopolistic competition, and how well monopolistically competitive markets perform

Before reading this chapter, make sure you know the meaning of:

1. Consumer and producer surplus
2. Economies of scale
3. Market structure
4. Types of monopoly
5. Limit pricing

CALIFORNIA'S ENERGY CRISIS

In California, public utilities, such as the state's largest utility company, Pacific Gas and Electric (PG&E), purchase electricity from wholesale producers. California's wholesale electricity prices more than doubled between April 1998 and June 2000, reaching an average $143 per megawatt-hour (MWh). State government regulators restricted public utilities from increasing prices charged to customers to fully compensate for higher wholesale prices. As a result, private wholesalers reaped huge profits from high energy prices. While wholesalers compete in private markets, public utilities like PG&E must justify their prices to state and local governments on a regular basis.

Since California's energy crisis, many have accused the wholesale energy providers of colluding to charge higher prices. Since there are relatively few wholesale energy producers, they could have increased their profits through agreements to charge California's public utilities high prices. These agreements, known as cartels, eliminate the competition that could have driven down wholesale electricity prices.

While many factors played into California's energy crisis, including an exceptionally hot summer in 2000 and problems with electric transmission capacity, the electricity market's structure remains an important part of the story. Californians experienced higher electricity bills, but these did not prevent PG&E from filing for bankruptcy in April 2001.

Source: Severin Borenstein, "The Trouble with Electricity Markets," *Journal of Economic Perspectives* (Winter 2002).

CALIFORNIA'S ENERGY CRISIS highlights the fact that the term *competition* has more than one meaning. In the phrase "perfect competition" it refers to *market structure.* A market is perfectly competitive if it has large numbers of small firms, the product is homogeneous, all firms share information equally, and it is easy to enter or leave the market. In contrast, many people think of competition as referring to *business rivalry.* In this sense "rivalry" refers to the activities of entrepreneurs, not just those of business managers who are responding to conditions that they accept as given. The two are related—California's wholesale electricity providers did not act as perfect competitors, eliminating the rivalry that might have mitigated the crisis.

In the market structure of *oligopoly,* to which much of this chapter is devoted, rivalry becomes a central issue. Rivalry is also an important issue for the market structures that border on oligopoly. At one end of the spectrum, oligopoly shades into what we have called open monopoly, a market structure in which a single firm, although it is the sole supplier of a product at the moment, is threatened by the entry of potential rivals. At the other end, oligopoly shades into *monopolistic competition.* In monopolistically competitive markets, rivalry is likely to be strong among firms that are near neighbors. For example, rivalry among vendors on an urban street corner can be as sharp in its way as the rivalry between giant firms in the tobacco or breakfast cereal industry, or the wholesale electricity providers in the case above.

This chapter will take in the whole spectrum of market structures that fall somewhere between the ideal types of monopoly and perfect competition. It will begin with a look at some empirical data on the organization of industry. The next section will take up oligopoly, and the last section will discuss monopolistic competition.

MARKET STRUCTURE IN THE U.S. ECONOMY

The structure of markets has long been of interest not only to economic theorists, but also to those who focus on empirical observation of actual markets. In this section, we will take a look at some data relating to the structure of markets in the United States, today and in the past.

Measures of Market Concentration

Unfortunately, markets do not go around wearing little name tags that identify them as monopolies, oligopolies, monopolistic competitors, and perfect competitors. In place of the theoretical definitions behind those categories, empirical studies of market structure have had to look at the characteristics of markets that are most easily observed. One of these is **market concentration**, the degree to which a market is dominated by one or a few large firms.

Market concentration

The degree to which a market is dominated by a few large firms.

A **concentration ratio** is the simplest measure of market concentration. A concentration ratio gives the percentage of all sales in a market that are accounted for by a specified number of firms in that market. The most commonly used such ratio is the four-firm concentration ratio, which shows the combined market share of the top four firms as a percent of sales in the market as a whole. One set of data for various U.S. industries in the 1970s showed four-firm concentration ratios ranging from 90 percent for automobiles and 85 percent for cigarettes to 15 percent for newspapers and 5 percent for commercial lithographic printing.

Concentration ratio

The percentage of all sales that is accounted for by the four or eight largest firms in a market.

Concentration ratios have a number of limitations. Obviously they do not distinguish between an industry in which a single firm dominates the market and one in which four or more top firms share it more or less equally. A market in which one firm held 77 percent and twenty-three others held 1 percent each would have the same four-firm concentration ratio as one in which five firms each held 20 percent.

A measure of market concentration that overcomes this drawback is the **Herfindahl-Hirschmann index (HHI)**. The HHI of market concentration is calculated by squaring the percentage market shares of each firm in the market and summing the squares. For an industry with n competing firms, the formula is

Herfindahl-Hirschmann index (HHI)

An index of market concentration that is calculated by squaring the percentage market shares of all firms in an industry then summing the squared-values.

$$H = p_1^2 + p_2^2 + \ldots + p_n^2,$$

where p_k is the percentage market share of firm k.

The Herfindahl-Hirschmann index rises as the market becomes more concentrated, reaching a maximum value of 10,000 for a monopoly. Thus, an industry with one hundred equal-sized firms would have a HHI of 100; one with ten equal-sized firms would have an index of 1,000; one with five equal-sized firms would have an index of 2,000; and so on. Unlike concentration ratios, the HHI can distinguish between degrees of concentration in markets with equal numbers of firms. For example, a market with eight firms of equal size has the same eight-firm concentration ratio as one in which one firm has 30 percent and seven others have 10 percent each. But the HHI for the latter market is 1,600 compared with 1,250 for the former. The difference in HHIs for the two markets reflects a widespread view that the presence of one dominant firm in a market makes that market less competitive in the sense that the dominant firm can exercise more influence over price and quantity than other firms in the market. (See Table 9.1.)

The U.S. Department of Justice (DOJ) uses the HHI when evaluating how a merger between two or more companies will affect the industry's competition. As a rule of thumb, mergers within industries that have an HHI value of 1,000 or less are permitted without much intervention from the DOJ. Companies seeking mergers within industries with index values above 1,000 will draw the DOJ's attention. The DOJ then analyzes the market to determine whether the merger will adversely affect competition.

Blending Structural and Behavioral Evidence

Many economists think that structural evidence, such as concentration ratios or the Herfindahl-Hirschmann index, is not enough to judge the competitiveness of a mar-

TABLE 9.1 MARKET CONCENTRATION FOR SELECTED U.S. MANUFACTURING INDUSTRIES

Industry Description	Number of Companies	Share of Sales Accounted for by Largest Companies: 4 Largest	8 Largest	50 Largest	HHI
Wood kitchen cabinets	4,303	19%	25%	46%	156
Book publishing	2,504	23%	38%	77%	251
Petroleum refining	131	30%	49%	97%	414
Meatpacking-plant products	1,296	50%	66%	88%	1,123
Household refrigerators and freezers	52	82%	98%	100%	1,891
Motor vehicles and car bodies	398	84%	91%	99%	2,676

The table above shows manufacturing industry concentration data based on the 1992 U.S. Census. Note that the number of companies is not the only important determinant of the degree of competition in industries. Even though there are only 131 petroleum refiners in the United States, this is a relatively competitive industry. The largest four petroleum refiners account for only 30 percent of all sales in this industry. This is reflected in the low HHI value for petroleum refining. On the other hand, there were almost 400 motor-vehicle and car-body manufacturers in the United States, but more than three-fourths of this industry is dominated by the four largest companies. The top 50 motor-vehicle and car-body companies account for nearly all sales. The high concentration in the motor-vehicle and car-bodies industry is shown by the relatively high HHI value of 2,676.

Source: U.S. Census, *1992 Census—Concentration Ratios in Manufacturing.*

ket. In addition, they say, attention must be paid to the way firms actually behave. Can they block the entry of rivals into the market? Do domestic firms face competition from imports? Do they collude or compete in making pricing decisions? Do they compete vigorously in product innovation and other nonprice areas? Information about such issues should be considered along with structural data in determining competitiveness.

The results of one study that combined structural and behavioral evidence are given in *Applying Economic Ideas 9.1*. That study, conducted by William C. Shepherd, concluded that more than three-quarters of the U.S. economy is "effectively competitive," a category that takes in perfect competition, monopolistic competition, and loose forms of oligopoly. Less than 3 percent of the economy was classified as pure monopoly, with most of that category consisting of public utilities.

Shepherd's results are interesting in that they indicate a strong trend toward increased competitiveness in the U.S. economy from 1958 to 1980. U.S. industries experienced an increase in business consolidation in the 1980s, but this lead to only modest increases in business concentration.[1] The trend toward greater competitiveness has continued, partially because of international pressure. From 1990 to 2002, total imports of goods and services, adjusted for inflation, more than doubled. In addition, many foreign firms entered U.S. markets through purchases of U.S. companies or construction of manufacturing facilities in the United States. Also, 1980 marked the beginning of the trend toward deregulation in transportation, communications, and finance. In structural terms, regulatory reform has decreased concentration in some industries (such as telephone service) while increasing it in others (such as airlines). However, even when reform has been accompanied by numerous mergers of firms, thus increasing the concentration ratio, structural changes have been outweighed by greater freedom to compete, with the result that regulated markets are, on the whole, more competitive than before.

Causes of Market Concentration

Given the evidence that some markets are more concentrated than others, it is natural to ask why. No single theory explains market concentration, but a variety of hypotheses have been proposed. We will discuss these under the headings of economies of scale, barriers to entry, and sunk costs.

ECONOMIES OF SCALE A firm is said to experience economies of scale if its long-run average cost declines as its output increases. At one extreme is the case of natural monopoly, in which economies of scale are so strong that minimum-cost production requires that the entire market supply be produced by a single firm. In less extreme cases, the *minimum efficient scale* for a firm—the point at which the average total cost curve stops falling and begins to flatten out—is so large that only a few firms can efficiently coexist in the market.

APPLYING ECONOMIC IDEAS 9.1

TRENDS IN COMPETITION IN THE U.S. ECONOMY

Economists have followed trends in competition and concentration in the U.S. economy for more than fifty years. In 1982, William C. Shepherd attempted to view all of these studies from a historical perspective. Relying on recent data as well as on older published studies, he classified U.S. markets into four categories for the years 1939, 1958, and 1980. The categories, which combine measurements of market structure with information on the behavior of firms, are as follows:

1. *Pure monopoly:* Market share at or near 100 percent, plus effectively blocked entry, plus evidence of effective monopoly control over the level and structure of prices. In practice, this category includes mainly utilities and patented goods.
2. *Dominant firms:* A market share of 50 percent to over 90 percent, with no close rival. High barriers to entry. Ability to control pricing, set systematic discriminatory prices, influence innovation, and (usually) earn rates of return well above the competitive rate of return.
3. *Tight oligopoly:* Four-firm concentration above 60 percent, with stable market shares. Medium or high barriers to entry. A tendency toward cooperation, shown especially by rigid prices. Excess profits are neither necessary nor sufficient to establish the existence of tight oligopoly.
4. *Effective competition:* Four-firm concentration below 40 percent, with unstable market shares and flexible pricing. Low barriers to entry, little collusion, and low profit rates.

The data in the table below show that the competitiveness of U.S. markets increased slightly from 1939 to 1958 and dramatically from 1958 to 1980. Shepherd attributes the change to three factors: increased international competition, deregulation, and enforcement of antitrust laws. Increased international competition and further deregulation have probably resulted in a continuation of the trend toward competitiveness in the 1980s. Enforcement of antitrust law has played a reduced role in shaping market structure in the 1980s, but it has continued to play an active role in discouraging collusive behavior on the part of rival firms.

Sectors of the Economy	National Income in Each Sector, 1978 ($ billions)[a]	The Share of Each Sector That Was Effectively Competitive		
		1939 (%)	1958 (%)	1980 (%)[a]
Agriculture, Forestry, and Fisheries	54.7	91.6	85.0	86.4
Mining	24.5	87.1	92.2	95.8
Construction	87.6	27.9	55.9	80.2
Manufacturing	459.5	51.5	55.9	69.0
Transportation and Public Utilities	162.3	8.7	26.1	39.1
Wholesale and Retail Trade	261.8	57.8	60.5	93.4
Finance, Insurance, and Real Estate	210.7	61.5	63.8	94.1
Services	245.3	53.9	54.3	77.9
TOTAL	1,506.5	55.0	61.7	79.5

The Share of Each Category in Total National Income	($ billions)	Percentage Shares		
		1939	1958	1980
1. Pure Monopoly	38.2	6.2	3.1	2.5
2. Dominant Firm	42.4	5.0	5.0	2.8
3. Tight Oligopoly	272.1	36.4	35.6	18.0
4. Effectively competitive	1,157.9	52.4	56.3	76.7
TOTAL	1,510.6	100.0	100.0	100.0

[a]1980 figures reflect competitive conditions as of 1980. The industry weights are based on 1978 data for national income, the latest year available.

Source: William G. Shepherd, "Causes of Increased Competition in the U.S. Economy, 1939–1980," *Review of Economics and Statistics* (November 1982), Table 2.

Suppose, for example, that the minimum efficient scale for a single plant producing refrigerators is 15 percent of U.S. consumption. The theoretical minimum four-firm concentration ratio implied by the minimum efficient plant size would then be 60 percent. The industry could not be any less concentrated than this without forcing some firms to use plants that are too small to produce at minimum long-run average cost. However, empirical studies suggest that economies of scale *at the plant level* clearly are not enough to explain the observed degree of market concentration.

Of course, as emphasized previously, there are many sources of economies of scale above the plant level. Operating more than one plant may result in savings in scheduling, transportation, research and development, finance, marketing, and administration costs. In addition to economies of scale in the ordinary sense, which pertain to a plant's rate of output per unit of time, a firm with a larger market share can also carry out longer production runs at an efficient rate of output. To the extent that cost savings can be achieved through "learning by doing," a plant with a large market share benefits from greater accumulated experience with each product than does one with a small market share. These kinds of economies may lie beyond the ability of economists and accountants to measure using the techniques commonly applied in studies of economies of scale.[2]

Even after all such qualifications are taken into account, however, it appears that economies of scale alone do not fully account for the degree of concentration found in U.S. industry. Let's turn, then, to the role of barriers to entry.

Barrier to entry

Any circumstance that prevents a new firm in a market from competing on an equal footing with existing ones.

BARRIERS TO ENTRY For our purposes, a **barrier to entry** may be defined as any circumstance that prevents a new firm from competing on an equal footing with existing firms in a particular market. In a market with neither large economies of scale nor high barriers to entry, growth will tend to occur mainly through the entry of new firms, leading to a decrease in concentration over time. With the presence of barriers to entry, the first firms in the industry may be able to maintain their market shares as the industry grows, even without the help of economies of scale.

Sometimes barriers to entry are deliberately created by federal, state, or local governments. The markets that were referred to as closed monopolies in Chapter 8 are examples, but governments often let more than one firm into a market without opening it to all competitors. For example, to establish a new federally chartered bank, one must obtain permission from a federal agency, the Comptroller of the Currency. One factor that is considered in granting the permit is whether there are already enough banks in the area—in the judgment of the comptroller, not that of the market. The expense of obtaining the permit and the risk that the permit will be denied are significant barriers to competition in the banking industry.

A second kind of barrier to entry is control of a nonreproducible resource. The market for caviar, long controlled by the Soviet Ministry of Fishing, is an example. Ownership of a nonreproducible resource gives existing firms an advantage over new ones and in this way acts as a barrier to entry.

Patents and copyrights, another class of barriers to entry, are important in both oligopoly and monopoly. A patent or copyright can be treated as a restrictive regulation. As an alternative, it can be treated like ownership of any other nonreproducible resource. In either case, patents and copyrights clearly can make entry difficult and contribute to market concentration. For example, patents held by Xerox Corporation slowed (but did not stop) entry of competing firms into the market for office copiers.

As the term is used here, a *barrier to entry* is something that keeps new firms from duplicating the performance of existing ones in terms of cost or product quality. It does not mean that every effort or expense that a firm must undertake to enter a market should be thought of as a barrier to entry. To start a new firm, an entrepreneur must take risks, find investors, recruit workers, attract customers, and so on. All of these activities are hard work—hard enough to discourage some people from making the effort. But the need for hard work is not a barrier to entry in the economic sense. When entrepreneurs are free to buy the building blocks for their new firms on the same terms as existing firms buy them, even huge markets can be penetrated by new entrants. Examples include Honda's entry into the automobile market, starting from the base of its motorcycle business or the entry of Russia's Lukoil brand into the U.S. retail gasoline market via its purchase of Getty Petroleum Marketing.

SUNK COSTS AND CONTESTABILITY OF MARKETS Sunk costs are another consideration that can play a role in determining market structure. Entry into many industries does require substantial sunk costs. The new firm may need to purchase custom-made equipment with little resale value, construct a plant in a place where it would have no other obvious use, or spend heavily on advertising and promotion to establish a new brand name in the minds of consumers.

As we have defined the term, sunk costs are not necessarily barriers to entry provided that firms that are already in the market had to undertake the same expenses when they entered. In a market in which the demand for a product is growing and is expected to remain high enough to enable a new firm with at least the minimum efficient scale to cover all of its opportunity costs, including sunk costs, entry can take place just as it would in an industry in which there are no sunk costs.

However, the situation may be different in markets in which there is a temporary increase in demand. In such a market, sunk costs affect the feasibility of what has been called hit-and-run entry—entry by firms that expect to leave the market again once demand conditions return to normal. A firm will not enter such a market on a temporary basis unless it is sure it can recover its fixed costs when it leaves.

In some cases, firms will not be sure whether changes in demand conditions justify entry. Under conditions of uncertainty, firms will be bolder about entering if sunk costs are low. Low sunk costs encourage firms to "test the water" in a new market. For example, a computer retailer might rent a store in a new shopping center to test demand in that area, knowing that the lease can be terminated if the store turns out to be unprofitable. Another category of retailer might have to build a special building that could not be used for anything else, so it would be more cautious about entering a new market.

Contestable market

A market in which barriers to entry and exit are low.

A market in which there are neither barriers to entry nor sunk costs, and which therefore is open to hit-and-run entry, is known as a **contestable market**. The airline industry is often cited as an example of a contestable market. In that industry, starting a whole new airline may entail sunk costs, but the relevant market is usually considered to be a city pair, such as Baltimore–Miami. Entry into an established city-pair market by a carrier not previously operating there may require little more than renting a few gates and reassigning some airplanes and crews.

THEORY OF OLIGOPOLY: INTERDEPENDENCE AND COLLUSION

Earlier chapters presented simple models of profit maximization for perfect competition and monopoly. Those models were based on the analysis of rational responses of managers to cost and demand constraints. In contrast, there is no single, general model of oligopoly. Instead, the theory of oligopoly consists of some broadly applied generalities plus a collection of more specific models that apply to special cases. This section looks at the general principles; the appendix to the chapter discusses some of the special-case models.

The Constraint of Oligopolistic Interdependence

The chief difficulty in analyzing oligopoly concerns the nature of the constraints the firm faces in a market in which there are just a few rival firms. Those firms, like firms in perfectly competitive and monopolistic markets, face constraints in the form of cost curves and market demand conditions. In addition, however, they face another constraint: the reactions of rival firms. The change in the profit that any one firm realizes as a result of a change in price, output quantity, or product characteristics depends not only on how customers respond (as is the case in the other market structures) but also on how other firms in the market respond. The linkage of each firm's choices to its rivals' reactions is called **oligopolistic interdependence**.

Oligopolistic interdependence

The need to pay close attention to the actions of rival firms in an oligopolistic market when making price or production decisions.

The problem of oligopolistic interdependence can be illustrated by how street vendors operate. Consider a hot-dog vendor named Suzy who sells hot dogs on the corner of 15th and L Streets. If she were the only hot-dog vendor in the market, her profit-maximizing strategy would be based on calculations of marginal cost and marginal revenues—or at least on Suzy's seat-of-the-pants estimates of those variables. If, on the other hand, there were enough firms in the market for perfect competition to exist, each firm would care only about an impersonal market price and would not care about individual rivals' reactions. The price would be treated as a given and output would be adjusted by each firm until the price equaled marginal cost.

Now, consider what happens when Suzy faces competition from only three other vendors. Suppose that, initially, all four vendors charge $2 per hot dog. With only four hot-dog vendors on the corner of 15th and L, however, the pricing decision depends not only on each vendor's estimates of marginal cost and marginal revenue but also on each one's estimates of its rivals' actions. Suzy may decide to raise her price, say to $2.50 instead of $2, banking on the loyalty of her customers. This strategy is based on the hunch that the other vendors will get tired of working so hard for so little profit. before all the customers who are loyal to Suzy's hot-dog cart shift to the cheaper vendors. Another vendor may try to undercut the market, charging $1.75 instead of $2. This vendor's strategy is based on the guess that the $2 customers are not so loyal after all, and that a higher sales volume will allow the low-price seller to earn a profit even at the low price. Thus, the price charged and quantity produced in an oligopoly can change not only as a result of changes in "objective" conditions, such as cost and demand, but also as a result of purely subjective estimates of human traits, such as stubbornness, loyalty, patience, and anger.

An implication of oligopolistic interdependence is that any model of oligopoly must begin by specifying how each firm expects its rivals to react to changing conditions. We can begin with the special case in which the rival firms in a market agree to cooperate in the pursuit of profit.

Cartels

Oligopolistic interdependence may lead to intense rivalry, as in the case of the popcorn vendors, but it can also result in collusion. *Collusion* occurs when the firms in an oligopoly realize that they can jointly increase their profits by raising the product's price and working out an agreement for dividing the market among them. When collusion is open and formal and involves all or most of the producers in the market, the result is called a **cartel**.

Cartel

A group of producers that jointly maximize profits by fixing prices and limiting output.

A simple example will show how cartels work. Imagine an industry made up of one hundred small firms. Assume that the marginal cost of production for all firms in the industry is $1 per unit, regardless of the amount produced. Because marginal cost is the same for all units of output, the marginal cost curve also serves as the long-run average cost curve and the long-run supply curve for the industry. This perfectly elastic long-run supply curve is shown in Figure 9.1, along with a demand curve for the industry.

The industry's equilibrium price and level of output depend on how the market is organized. Initially, suppose that all firms act like perfect competitors. According to the theory set forth in Chapter 7, this will result in an equilibrium in which the market price is $1 per unit (equal to long-run average cost and long-run marginal cost) and 400,000 units of output are produced each month. In that equilibrium, firms earn no economic profit.

Now suppose that one day the heads of the one hundred firms meet to form a cartel. They elect a cartel manager, who is asked to work out a production and marketing plan that will result in the maximum possible total profits for the industry, and to divide them fairly among the members.

The profit-maximizing problem that the cartel manager faces is exactly the same as the one faced by a monopolist. Industry profits are highest at the output level at which marginal revenue equals marginal cost—200,000 units per month. If output is restricted to that quantity, the price can be raised to $2 per unit, which will yield $200,000 per month of pure economic profit.

To divide this profit among all the cartel members, the manager will give each firm an output quota of 2,000 units a month, half as much as each was producing before the cartel was formed. In that way the member firms will reap the benefits of pure monopoly despite their small size and large number.

THE STABILITY PROBLEM Although cartels are good for their members, they are not so good for consumers. For them, cartels mean a smaller supply of goods and higher prices. Fortunately for consumers, cartels have some built-in problems that make them hard to form and unstable over time.

FIGURE 9.1 PROFIT MAXIMIZATION FOR A CARTEL

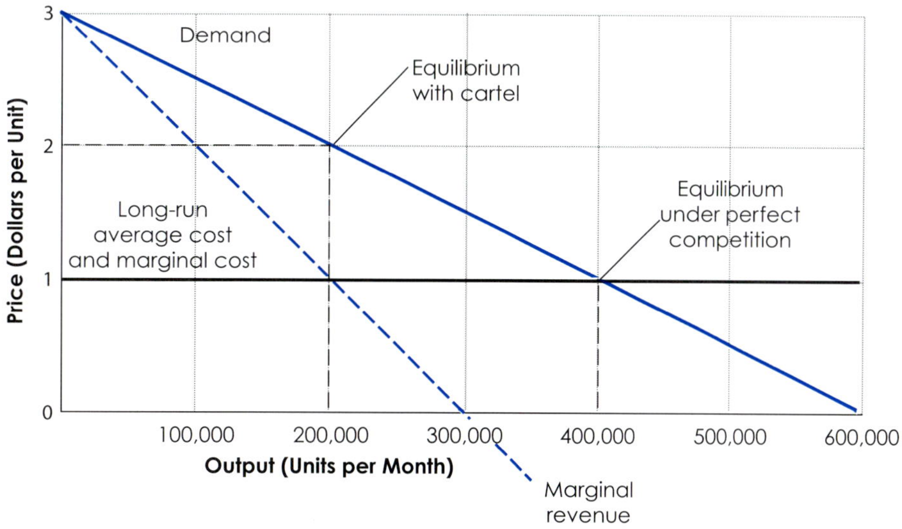

This graph shows an industry made up of one hundred firms, each producing at a constant long-run average and marginal cost. If the firms act like perfect competitors, the industry will be in equilibrium at the point at which the demand and marginal cost curves intersect. If the firms form a cartel, however, they can jointly earn profits by restricting output to the point at which marginal cost equals marginal revenue and raising the price from $1 to $2.

The first problem faced by cartels is control over entry. As we have seen, any industry in which prices are higher than long-run average cost tends to attract new firms. Because the whole point of a cartel is to raise prices above the competitive level, a cartel acts as a magnet for entrepreneurs. But the entry of new firms into the market does not increase the total amount that the cartel can sell at the profit-maximizing price. More firms only mean that the profits must be divided into smaller shares. It is not enough simply to say that new producers cannot join the cartel. If they enter as independent producers, selling outside the framework of the cartel's market sharing agreement, they still depress the cartel's profits. Any cartel, then, needs to find a way to control entry into its market if it is to serve the interests of its founding members.

A second—and even more serious—inherent problem faced by cartels is enforcing output quotas. In a cartel each member has an incentive to cheat. The cheating takes the form of producing output beyond its quota, and the reward, if the cheating is successful, is greater profit. Take the cartel in Figure 9.1. As noted earlier, the quota for each of the one hundred members is 2,000 units per month—just half of what each would produce under perfect competition.

What would happen if one firm cheated on its quota by stepping up its output while the others went on playing by the rules? The answer is simple: Production of an extra 2,000 units per month would have only a small effect on the market price, because it would represent only a 1 percent increase in total industry output. By producing 4,000 units a month, the cheater would double its monthly profit—as long as other firms in the market did not cheat too.

But what if ninety-nine firms cheated and stepped up their output to 4,000 units while the remaining firm stuck to its quota? With industry output at 398,000 units, the price would be forced down toward the competitive level of $1. The firm that played fair would gain nothing for having done so.

The conclusion to which this leads is that every member of a cartel will have an incentive to cheat if it expects other members to play fair—and it will also have an incentive to cheat if it expects others to cheat as well.

CARTELS IN PRACTICE The problems of entry and cheating affect all cartels. The Organization of Petroleum Exporting Countries (OPEC) is a well-known case. In 1973, OPEC controlled about 60 percent of the oil imports of the industrialized countries. Taking advantage of its market power, in the next eight years it increased crude oil prices about tenfold, to a level approaching $40 per barrel (equivalent to over $100 a barrel in 2004 dollars). Output was divided among the cartel's members in proportion to formulas that were agreed upon at meetings of the oil ministers of the various OPEC countries. Saudi Arabia, the largest producer, had the greatest influence and the largest quota.

The price increase brought the OPEC countries fabulous wealth in the short run. However, it also spurred output in non-OPEC areas, such as Alaska, the North Sea, and Mexico. Moreover, the demand for oil proved more elastic in the long run than in the short run as factories installed energy conservation equipment and consumers bought more fuel-efficient cars. As a result of these changes, OPEC lost half of its former market share. Saudi Arabia cut back its own output to less than 25 percent of capacity and tried to persuade smaller member countries to accept lower quotas as well. But cheating in terms of both price and quantity became widespread. By 1986 the OPEC cartel was in disarray; at one point the market price of oil plunged below $10 a barrel.

Since that time, OPEC has had its ups and downs. On the one hand, the pace of new discoveries outside the OPEC countries has slowed, allowing a partial recovery of the cartel's power. Despite a certain degree of control over supply however, OPEC remains highly vulnerable to variations in demand. The Asian financial crisis of 1997 cut world demand by enough to send oil prices to a new record low (measured in constant dollars.) More recently, booming oil demand in China has allowed the cartel to keep oil prices at a level that is below its past peaks, but still quite comfortable for producers.

Because cartels that depend on voluntary cooperation among members run into problems, some cartels have enlisted the government to enforce quotas and restrict entry. In the United States, agricultural cartels known as *marketing orders* are a case in point. However, as can be seen from *Economics in the News 9.1,* even government-assisted cartels may eventually collapse.

Coordination Without Collusion

Formal cartels are not unknown, but they are rare. They are uncommon partly because of their inherent instability, as explained in the preceding section. Also—at least in the United States—most cartels are illegal under the antitrust laws. (Those laws will be described in a later chapter.) But we are left with the question of whether the firms in an oligopoly can, even without open collusion, tacitly coordinate their price and output decisions in a way that will jointly maximize their profit. To put it another way, will an industry in which there are only a few firms but no formal cartel perform more nearly like the model of perfect competition or like that of monopoly?

There have been a number of attempts to answer this question with formal models similar to those of perfect competition and monopoly. Those attempts have not been particularly successful, however, because there is no simple way to handle the problem of oligopolistic interdependence—the dependence of each firm's behavior on its rivals' decisions.

To construct a formal model, one must make a specific assumption about how each firm reacts to what its rivals do and how it expects them to react to what it does. One model, for example, assumes that each firm reacts to its rivals' changes in prices or output but expects them not to respond to changes in its own prices and output. Another model assumes that rivals will always match price cuts but never match

ECONOMICS IN THE NEWS 9.1

BIG TOBACCO, LAWSUITS, AND COMPETITION

The U.S. Department of Justice attempts to monitor industry competitiveness using industry concentration ratios and HHI values. This does not entirely prevent cartels among U.S. producers, especially those protected by regulations dating back to the early twentieth century. For instance, many people know that they are dealing with a cartel when they buy gasoline. But few people realize that for years they were doing the same whenever they bought a pack of cigarettes.

The U.S. tobacco industry is, to a large degree, controlled by the four largest cigarette companies: Altria, R. J. Reynolds, Brown & Williamson, and Lorillard. While not legally permitted to fix prices on tobacco products, these companies have implicitly colluded in the way they have dealt with their recent lawsuit settlements. For years, Big Tobacco fought off lawsuits claiming the companies concealed the true health risks associated with smoking, but a new wave of successful suits led to a large settlement between the big-four companies and state attorneys general in 1998. The settlement required that the companies pay about $200 billion over twenty-five years to cover the states' costs of health care for smokers. If the big four could not be sure of continued high revenues, they would have had a hard time paying these enormous sums, so the settlement enlisted states to support a big-brand cartel that keeps prices high by imposing fees on small rivals not covered by the settlement.

The agreement highlights an important relationship between regulation and competition: the big tobacco producers might not have settled unless the states tried to stop small rivals from undercutting its prices; and the states stood to reap higher payments if the major brands fared well. So, many states passed laws requiring tobacco upstarts to pay the states fees equivalent to—or, after taxes, even more than—what the big four companies pay in the settlement.

The settlement led to new anti-smoking ads, funded by the large tobacco producers themselves. While it appeared to the public a penalty on the big cigarette companies and a coup for state prosecutors, it actually benefits Altria, R. J. Reynolds, Brown & Williamson, and Lorillard. The increased fees paid by smaller tobacco companies make it harder for them to undercut the majors' prices.

Two small tobacco producers have filed a federal lawsuit challenging the settlement, claiming it violates federal antitrust laws. "This is not some bedroom conspiracy to fix prices that we have to prove. It's all there in the settlement," says lawyer David Dobbins, who represented the Las Vegas–based cigarette importer, Freedom Holdings. The big brands' "treble-damage liability is astronomical," he notes. "Eventually this cartel will be abolished and competition will return to the cigarette market."

The settlement may not be working out as well as the states and the big tobacco producers had hoped, however. States expect their settlement fees to fall 16 percent this year to a total $7.8 billion. The reason—entry of cheap, previously unknown brands, whose share has risen to nearly 10 percent of the market, up from 1 percent five years ago. This doesn't come as a surprise: The big brands raised their wholesale price $1.10, to over $3 a pack, several times the sum needed to fund their payments to the states.

Source: Scott Woolley, "A Cozy Cancer Cartel," *Forbes,* January 29, 2004.

price increases. Still another assumes that each firm expects its rivals to do the worst thing possible and plans accordingly.

Several formal models are described in the appendix to this chapter. None of them, however, offers a general solution to the question of how price and output decisions are made under oligopoly. In the absence of a general, formal model, much of the writing on oligopoly deals with informal theories consisting of conjectures about the conditions that tend to make cooperation by oligopolists easier or more difficult. Under conditions that facilitate formal, tacit coordination, price and output may tend to more closely resemble the results of a cartel. Under conditions that make coordination more difficult, price and output may tend to more nearly approximate the result of perfect competition. Some of the most common themes of the informal theories are described next.

NUMBER AND SIZE OF FIRMS There is little doubt that the number and size of the firms in a market make a big difference. Tacit coordination is easier in a market with only two or three large firms of roughly equal size than in a market in which a dozen equal-sized firms control half the market and the rest is controlled by smaller firms. If the number of firms is large enough and the size of the largest firms is sufficiently small, the market ceases to be an oligopoly. With a homogeneous product and easy entry and exit, it becomes perfectly competitive, as discussed in an earlier chapter. With a differentiated product and easy entry and exit, it becomes monopolistically competitive, a case that we will analyze later in this chapter.

The relative size and number of the various firms in the market are considered to be important on the ground that cooperation is easier in an industry in which there is one dominant firm. That firm may be able to act as a price leader. Under the strongest form of **price leadership**, firms are no longer uncertain about how their rivals will react to price changes. The leader knows that the others will follow it, whether it raises or lowers the price. The others know that if they follow the leader others will too, but not if they raise or lower prices on their own. When it works, this arrangement is tantamount to a cartel in that the dominant firm's efforts to maximize its own profit will also maximize the entire industry's profits. U.S. Steel and General Motors are examples of companies that were once thought to play the role of price leaders in their markets, although neither of these firms occupies the dominant position today that it once did.

Price leadership

A situation in which price increases or decreases by a dominant firm in an oligopoly, known as the price leader, are matched by all or most of the other firms in the market.

THE NATURE OF THE PRODUCT The nature of the product also affects the ease or difficulty of coordination. A homogeneous product for which there is a smooth flow of orders tends to make coordination easier; widely used steel products, such as railroad rails and wire, are examples. A variable product for which the flow of orders is irregular tends to make coordination more difficult; the ship building industry is a case in point. In such an industry, there are simply too many things to coordinate. It is not enough that all firms tacitly agree to sell at the same price; they must also agree on a set of price variations based on changes in quality, speed of delivery, size of order, and so on. Under these conditions an agreement to raise the price above the competitive level, even if it can be sustained, is unlikely to lead to higher profits. It is more likely to lead to an outbreak of competition by firms offering higher quality, more convenient scheduling, volume discounts, and so on. These factors will add to the cost of doing business or reduce revenue until excess profits disappear.

GROWTH AND INNOVATION The rates of growth and innovation in a market are another factor that is likely to affect the ease or difficulty of coordination among rival oligopolists. In a market in which product features, production techniques, and buyers' and sellers' personalities do not change from year to year, an agreement among firms, whether it is tacit or overt, will never have to be revised. In a market with rapidly changing elements, any agreement will soon be made obsolete by changing conditions or be disrupted by the entry of new buyers or sellers. Given the uncertainties of tacit agreements and the fact that overt ones are illegal, one would expect that the faster the pace of growth and change, the less successful rival firms will be in coordinating their activities.

EASE OF ENTRY AND EXIT Barriers to entry play an important role in the price and output decisions of an oligopoly. Even if there are only a few firms in the market, the threat of entry by new firms may force existing ones to practice limit pricing to avoid attracting new rivals. Under limit pricing, as explained in Chapter 8, the price is set below the profit-maximizing level implied by short-run demand, marginal revenue, and marginal cost.

Barriers to entry are also important in considering the effect of mergers on price and output decisions in an oligopoly. A merger within an oligopoly reduces the number of firms in the industry and, if the larger members are involved, increases the concentration ratio. Taken in isolation, a reduction in the number and an increase in the size of firms would tend to make coordination easier, perhaps leading to a more cartel-like result. Often, however, new firms quickly enter to fill any gaps left by mergers. The publishing industry is an example of one in which there have been several mergers of leading firms, but also many entries of new small firms, so that the degree of competition remains substantial. Also, as pointed out earlier in the chapter, sunk costs that cannot be recovered when the firm leaves the market can be as important as ease of entry in determining price and output decisions under oligopoly.

Market Performance Under Oligopoly

Neither the formal theories discussed in the appendix to this chapter nor the informal rules of thumb just presented give conclusive answers to the question of market performance under oligopoly. Depending on the situation, some oligopolies may behave much like perfectly competitive markets, with prices equal or close to marginal cost. Others, with or without open collusion, may behave more like a monopoly, with prices higher than marginal cost and a resulting deadweight loss.

When they cannot answer questions about market performance by means of pure theory, economists turn to statistical methods. Ideally, one would like to measure the gap between price and marginal cost at the point of market equilibrium, but it is rarely possible to do so. In the absence of reliable data on marginal cost, an indirect approach can be used. If firms in concentrated industries can be shown, on average, to earn returns that exceed the opportunity cost of capital, one can infer that they are behaving more like monopolists than like perfect competitors. If, on the other hand, firms in concentrated industries earn only "normal profits"—that is, rates of return on capital that are no higher, on average, than those earned by firms in less concentrated industries—one can conclude that oligopolies perform about as well as more competitive industries. Following this reasoning, much of the debate about market performance under oligopoly focuses on rates of return.

The first person to try this approach in a systematic way was University of California professor Joe Bain. In 1951 Bain published the results of a study of forty-two selected industries for the years 1936 to 1940. According to Bain's analysis of the data, industries with concentration ratios of over seventy earned higher profits than less concentrated ones. The link between profits and concentration was neither perfect nor strong, but it did exist.

During the 1950s and 1960s many of Bain's students and followers repeated his studies for other industries and years. Most of them got the same results: a weak but persistent link between profits and concentration. Economists concluded that in general, the more highly concentrated an industry, the more it will tend to perform like a cartel or a monopoly. This would be true even if there were no agreement among rivals to raise prices and divide up markets.

As faith in this idea grew, economists tried as hard as they could to prove it, using the more advanced statistical techniques and better data that became available each year. But the harder they tried, the more elusive the connection became. Some studies showed that if the data are adjusted for the size of firms in different markets, the link between concentration and profits tends to disappear. Others indicated that if the data are adjusted for differences in advertising expenditures, the connection evaporates. Still others suggested that results like Bain's hold only in periods of recession and disappear with the return of prosperity.

Moreover, as the link between concentration and profits was becoming more ambiguous, economists were growing less certain about how such a link should be interpreted even if it could be confirmed. New reasons were found to explain why firms in more concentrated industries might appear to earn higher profits than firms in less concentrated ones. Those reasons had nothing to do with monopoly pricing or tacit coordination. For example, a concentrated industry that was growing rapidly might need to earn high profits to attract capital. Perhaps the high profits of the largest firms in each concentrated industry might simply reflect those firms' superior efficiency relative to smaller firms in the same industry. Finally, the higher profits that some concentrated industries appeared to earn might not be pure economic profits; they might merely reflect the fact that the categories used by accountants to record business transactions do not accurately reflect implicit costs.

THE THEORY OF MONOPOLISTIC COMPETITION

Up to this point we have looked at industries in which many small firms produce a homogeneous product and at others in which a few large firms make products that need not be alike. Those cases leave out a very large class of markets in which there are many small firms, each of which makes a product that differs slightly from those of its competitors. This market structure is known as *monopolistic competition*. Examples include restaurants, service stations, bakeries, some types of publishing companies, and countless others.

Profit Maximization Under Monopolistic Competition

Although there is no general agreement on a formal model for oligopoly, there is a widely accepted model of monopolistic competition. As its name implies, this model, which dates from work done in the 1930s by Edward H. Chamberlin and independently by Joan Robinson, blends monopolistic and competitive aspects. Like a monopolist, the monopolistically competitive firm is a price searcher facing a negatively sloped demand curve. However, like the perfectly competitive firm, the monopolistic competitor is assumed to share the market with many other small firms. For this reason, the model of monopolistic competition ignores oligopolistic interdependence. It assumes that each firm in the market is so small that no one firm is significantly affected by what another one does.

The theory can be understood with the help of Figure 9.2, which shows short- and long-run equilibrium positions for a typical firm under monopolistic competition. The demand curve has a negative slope because each firm's product is a little different from its competitors' products. Each firm therefore can raise its price at least slightly without losing all its customers, because some customers attach more importance than others to the special style, location, or other marketing advantage the firm offers. Given this negatively sloped demand curve, the short-run profit-maximizing position shown in part (a) of the figure is found in the same way as that for a simple monopolist: The output level is determined by the intersection of the marginal cost and marginal revenue curves, and the price charged is determined by the height of the demand curve at that point.

However, this particular short-run equilibrium cannot also be long-run equilibrium under monopolistic competition. The reason is that monopolistically competitive markets are highly contestable, with easy entry and exit. In the short-run position shown in part (a) of Figure 9.2, the firm is earning a pure economic profit; this is shown by the fact that price exceeds average total cost.

But profits attract new firms. As new firms enter the market, two things happen. First, the demand curves of existing firms shift downward. This happens because the new firms' products, although they are not identical to those of the original firms, are substitutes for them. Second, in response to the new competition, firms that are already in the market may step up their advertising, improve their product in some way, or take other steps to win back customers. These efforts cause the firms' average total cost curves to shift upward. The downward shift in the original firms' demand curves, or the upward shift in their cost curves, or both, continue until there are no more profits to attract new firms. The result is the long-run equilibrium position shown in part (b) of Figure 9.2.

FIGURE 9.2 SHORT-RUN AND LONG-RUN EQUILIBRIUM UNDER MONOPOLISTIC COMPETITION

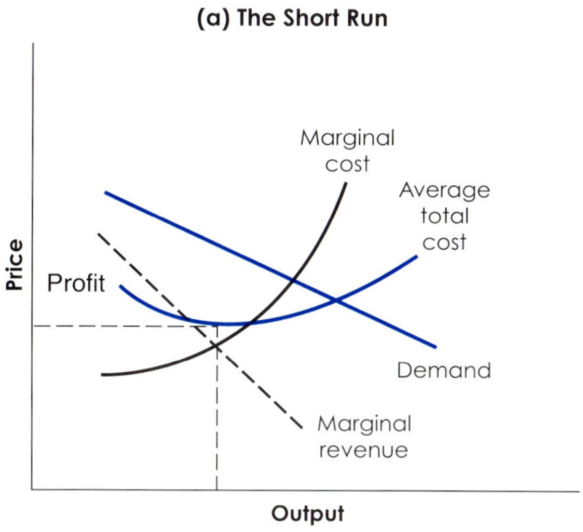

Under monopolistic competition, each firm is a price searcher with a negatively sloped demand curve but there are no barriers to entry by new firms. In the short run, a firm that produces at the point at which marginal cost equals marginal revenue can earn pure economic profits, as shown in part (a). In the long run, however, new firms are attracted to the market. This diverts part of the demand from firms that are already in the market, thus lowering each one's demand curve. Also, those firms may fight to keep their share of the market, using means that will increase their costs. Entry by new firms will continue until a long-run equilibrium is reached in which profits are eliminated, as shown in part (b).

The Performance of Monopolistically Competitive Industries

Some economists have argued that the long-run equilibrium position shown in Figure 9.2 indicates poor performance by monopolistically competitive industries. For one thing, as in the case of pure monopoly, each firm stops short of the output level that would maximize the sum of producer and consumer surplus. Likewise, the gap between price and marginal cost indicates potential added production that would benefit both the firm and its customers. In addition, under monopolistic competition a firm does not operate at the lowest point on its long-run average cost curve. If there were fewer firms, each producing a greater amount of output, the same quantity of goods could be provided at a lower total cost. Following this reasoning, it has been argued that monopolistic competition results in too many gas stations, supermarkets, and restaurants, each operating at less than full capacity and each charging inefficiently high prices. Yet despite the high prices, each earns only the minimum return it needs to stay in business.

The problem with this critique is that it ignores the value of the product variety that is the hallmark of monopolistic competition. It is beside the point to argue that prices would be a little lower if there were fewer barbershops, each somewhat less conveniently located; or fewer supermarkets, each a little more crowded; or fewer ice cream flavors, even if some people could not have their favorite flavor. Would a move in that direction benefit consumers? Not if consumers are willing to pay something for variety.

When all is said and done, the prevailing view is that monopolistic competition and perfect competition are not all that different and that both serve customers reasonably well. Both fall into the category that Shepherd refers to as "effectively competitive." And it is encouraging to consider, as reported earlier in *Applying Economic Ideas 9.1*, that more than three-quarters of the economy fits into this broad category.

SUMMARY

1. **How has the structure of markets in the U.S. economy changed over time?** *Concentration ratios* and the *Herfindahl-Hirschmann index* are two measures of the degree to which a market is dominated by a few firms. They can be used together with information about the behavior of firms to estimate the degree of competition in a market. More than three-quarters of U.S. output is produced in effectively competitive markets. The share of output produced by monopolies, oligopolies with dominant firms, and tight oligopolies appears to be declining.

2. **How does the interdependence of firms under oligopoly affect price and output decisions?** *Oligopolistic interdependence* refers to the need for each firm in an oligopoly to pay close attention to its rivals' actions when making decisions regarding price, output, or product characteristics. Oligopolistic interdependence makes it difficult to construct simple, generally applicable models of oligopoly.

3. **Why do oligopolistic firms sometimes collude to increase profits, and what problems do they encounter as a result?** A group of producers that jointly maximize profits by fixing prices and limiting output is known as a *cartel.* A cartel's profits are maximized by setting output at a level corresponding to the intersection of the marginal cost and marginal revenue curves for the industry as a whole. The chief problems encountered by cartels are controlling entry and preventing members from cheating on prices and output quotas.

4. **What conditions affect market performance under oligopoly?** Among the factors that are thought to affect market performance under oligopoly are the number and size of firms in the market, the presence or absence of *price leadership,* the nature of the product (homogeneous or varied), the pace of growth and innovation, and the ease or difficulty of entry and exit. If barriers to entry and exit are low, a market is said to be *contestable*. Contestable markets are thought to perform well even if they are highly concentrated.

5. **How is equilibrium achieved under monopolistic competition, and how well do such markets perform?** A monopolistic competitor maximizes profit at the output level at which marginal cost equals marginal revenue. In the long run competition in such an industry results in an equilibrium in which price equals average total cost for each firm. In this equilibrium, price does not equal marginal cost and production does not take place at the point of mini-

mum average total cost; nevertheless, consumers enjoy the benefit of product variety.

KEY TERMS

Market concentration	Contestable market
Concentration ratio	Oligopolistic interdependence
Herfindahl-Hirschmann index (HHI)	Cartel
Barrier to entry	Price leadership

PROBLEMS AND TOPICS FOR DISCUSSION

1. **Examining the lead-off case.** Would you classify the market for electricity sold by wholesalers to California public utilities as monopolistically competitive or as oligopolistic? What about the market for energy sold by the utilities to the general public?
2. **Oligopolistic interdependence in action.** Look around your community for a case in which a firm is conducting a special sale or product promotion. To what extent, if at all, is the firm's action a response to something its rivals have done? To what extent, if at all, have its rivals reacted with their own sales or promotions?
3. **Barriers to entry.** "Barriers to entry are lower in the restaurant industry than in the airline industry because a restaurant requires only a few workers and a few thousand dollars in capital, whereas even a small airline requires many workers and millions of dollars in capital." Do you agree? Why or why not?
4. **The market for college education.** What market structure do you think best fits the market for college education? What factors do you believe affect the structure of the college education industry? How important are economies of scale? How important are barriers to entry and exit?
5. **Labor unions as cartels.** In what ways do labor unions resemble cartels? In what ways do they differ from cartels? Do you think labor unions ever suffer from the problems of instability that plague cartels?

CASE FOR DISCUSSION

All Things Begin Small

In 1994, the German automobile maker BMW acquired Rover Group, adding the British Mini Cooper to its collection of cars. In 2001, the Mini Cooper premiered at the Detroit auto show and was available for sale in the U.S. the following year. Despite the phenomenal growth in sport-utility vehicles in the U.S., the compact Mini has been extremely popular.

The rest of the world seems to share this sentiment. In the fall of 2003, BMW was considering plans to increase production of its Mini plant at Oxford to about 200,000 a year to meet growing demand. BMW's chief executive Helmut Panke estimated Mini sales could top 165,000 this year after hitting a record of 144,000 in 2002. By 2003 annual output was about 160,000.

There have been fears that capacity constraints at the Oxford plant could force some Mini production abroad, but Panke said the car would be built only at Oxford, where BMW planned to streamline production to remove bottlenecks. One option being considered is to lengthen workers' shifts from the traditional eight to nine or ten hours.

Panke said that output at BMW car plants could grow by between 40,000 and 50,000 units a year—with minimum investment. Increased output and sales of the Mini are integral to BMW's plans to lift global sales from 1 to 1.4 million between 2003 and 2008.

Panke held up the Mini as "a UK manufacturing success story," destroying the myth that Britain's manufacturing sector would never make a comeback.

Source: Based on David Gow, "BMW to boost production of 'UK success story,'" *Guardian Unlimited*, November 13, 2003.

QUESTIONS

1. How would you best characterize the market in which the Mini is sold: Perfectly competitive, oligopolistic, monopolistically competitive, or oligopoly? Why?
2. If the Mini enjoys strong demand, do you think that will allow BMW to charge a price higher than marginal cost? Why or why not?
3. How might BMW's rivals react to the introduction and success of the Mini? Do you think BMW must take this into account when planning its marketing strategy?
4. What sunk costs does BMW encounter when bringing out a new car like the Mini? What does this say about the degree to which the automobile market is contestable?

END NOTES

1. Julia Porter Liebeskind, Tim C. Opler, and Donald E. Hatfield, "Corporate Restructuring and the Consolidation of US Industry," *The Journal of Industrial Economics* 11(2) (March–April 1996).
2. See John S. McGee, "Efficiency and Economies of Size," in *Industrial Concentration: The New Learning,* eds. Harvey J. Goldschmid, Michael H. Mann, and Fred J. Weston (Boston: Little, Brown, 1974), 55–96.

Appendix to Chapter 9
FORMAL THEORIES OF OLIGOPOLY

Over the years, many economists have proposed formal theories of oligopoly. The goal of such a theory is to determine the equilibrium price and output level for an oligopolistic firm and its industry given aspects of market structure such as number of firms, concentration ratio, cost and technology, and demand curve. No general theory has been developed, but some useful partial theories and interesting analyses of special cases exist. These provide some insight into the broader problem of oligopoly. The three theories discussed in this appendix are a sample from the literature on formal theories of oligopoly.

The Cournot Theory and Its Variations

The oldest attempt to develop a theory of oligopoly began with a work published by Augustin Cournot in 1838. Cournot recognized the problem of oligopolistic interdependence—the need for each firm to take its rivals' behavior into account when deciding on its own market strategy. The way to understand the behavior of rival firms, he thought, was to make a simple assumption about the way each firm would react to its rivals' moves.

In his initial statement of the problem, Cournot assumed that each firm would act as if it did not expect its rivals to change their output levels even if it changed its own. However, later theorists who expanded Cournot's theory usually made price rather than output the crucial variable. In the price-based version of the Cournot theory, each firm is assumed to set its price as though it expects other firms in the industry to leave their prices unchanged.

Figure 9A.1 shows how the price-based Cournot theory might work for an industry with just two firms. Corresponding to each price that its rival may charge, every firm has a price that will yield the maximum profit. These prices are shown in the form of *reaction curves*. For example, firm 1's reaction curve indicates that it will charge $60 if its rival charges $50 (point S). If firm 2 charges $150, firm 1 will charge $130 (point T). In the extreme case, firm 2 may charge so much that it will price itself out of the market, leaving firm 1 with a pure monopoly. In that event, firm 1 will maximize its profits by charging $150, as shown by the broken line labeled "Firm 1's monopoly price." Firm 2's monopoly price is shown in the same way. The two reaction curves can be derived from the two firms' cost and demand curves. The derivation is not given here, but it can be found in many advanced texts.

Given these reaction curves, the behavior of an oligopoly, according to Cournot, can be described somewhat as follows. Imagine that at first firm 1 is the only producer of the good in question. Because it has a pure monopoly, it maximizes profits by setting a price of $150. Then firm 2 enters the market. Under the Cournot theory, firm 2 will set its price as though it expected firm 1 to go on charging $150 indefinitely. Given this assumption, firm 2 sets its price at $125, as shown by point A on firm 2's reaction curve.

At this point, firm 1 begins to notice its rival. Seeing that firm 2 has taken away many of its customers with its much lower price, it moves to point B on its reaction curve, cutting its own price to $115.

FIGURE 9A.1

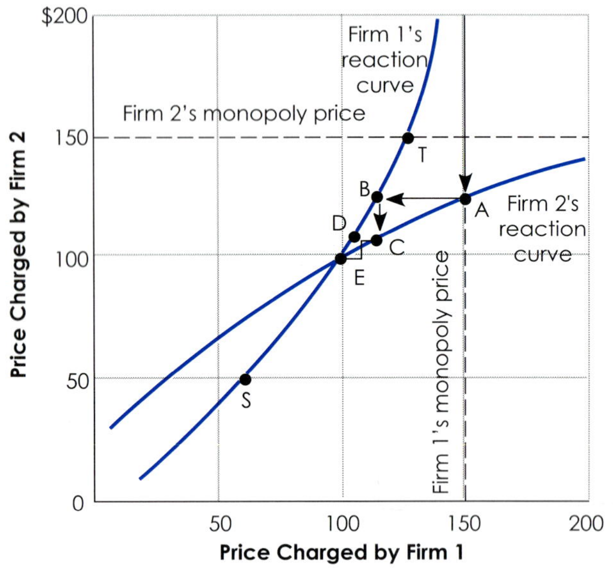

The Cournot theory assumes that each firm will set its price as though it expects its rivals' prices to remain fixed. The reaction curves show the best price for each of two firms given the other's price. For example, point S on firm 1's reaction curve indicates that firm 1 should charge $60 if firm 2 charges $50. If firm 1 has a monopoly, it will set a price of $150. If firm 2 then enters the market, it will touch off a price war, moving the industry step by step to points A, B, C, D, and finally E. Point E is a stable equilibrium.

Firm 2, which entered the market on the assumption that firm 1 would maintain its price at $150, must react next. Given firm 1's $115 price, firm 2 cuts its price to $108 (point C). That sparks a price cut by firm 1, which goes to $107 (point D). After a series of increasingly smaller moves and countermoves, the two firms' prices converge at an equilibrium of $100 at point E.

Two things are appealing about the Cournot theory. First, it gives a stable equilibrium. At prices above the intersection of the two reaction curves, each firm has an incentive to undercut its rival's price. At prices below the intersection, each firm has an incentive to charge more than its rival. Thus, given the assumptions, there is only one price that the market can reach. Second, as the theory is expanded beyond two firms to allow for multifirm oligopolies, it can be shown that the equilibrium price moves steadily away from the monopoly price and toward a price equal to marginal cost. Thus, the Cournot equilibrium for an industry with one firm equals the monopoly price; that for an industry with an infinite number of firms equals the competitive price; and those for oligopolies of various sizes occur along a continuum between these extremes.

Still, there is one feature of the Cournot theory that has always troubled economists. The structure of the theory depends on each firm's assuming that its rivals will not react to its price changes. Yet daily life in the Cournot world proves that assumption to be wrong. In the example in Figure 9A.1, firm 2 enters on the assumption that firm 1 will pay no attention to its entry and capture of a large chunk of firm 1's sales. But firm 1 does react, as does firm 2. Instead of this mindless price war, wouldn't each firm have second thoughts about its price cutting, fearing its rival's reaction? The Cournot theory fails to acknowledge this possibility.

Recently, theorists have explored variations of the Cournot theory in which firms do not base their expectations regarding their rivals' behavior solely on what they did in the previous period. Instead, their expectations are gradually adapted to what the rivals have done over a sequence of previous periods. Under certain circumstances, such models produce outcomes similar to the simple Cournot model—outcomes in which equilibrium is stable and approaches the competitive case as the number of firms increase.

The Kinked Demand Curve Theory

In 1939, a century after Cournot, another major oligopoly theory was proposed. Known as the *kinked demand curve theory,* it was proposed at about the same time by the British economists R. L. Hall and C. J. Hitch and the American economist Paul M. Sweezy. Like the Cournot theory, the kinked demand curve theory begins from a simple assumption about oligopolists' reactions to price changes by rivals: Each firm expects that if it cuts its price, its rivals will match the cut, but that if it raises its price, no other firms will follow.

Figure 9A.2 shows how the market looks to an oligopolist who makes these two assumptions. Let P be the price ($1.70, in this case) that happens to prevail in the market. If the firm cuts its price below P, other firms will lower their prices in turn. Sales in the industry as a whole will expand. The firm in question will keep about the same share of the market and will move down the lower slope of the demand curve. In contrast, if the firm raises its price, the others will not follow suit. Instead of keeping its share of the market, our firm will lose customers to its rivals. As a result, the part of the firm's demand curve above price P is much more elastic than the part below it.

Now bring marginal cost and marginal revenue into the picture. Give the firm a short-run marginal cost curve with the usual positive slope. The marginal revenue curve contains a step that corresponds to the kink in the demand curve. To the left of the step, marginal revenue is very high, showing that revenue will be lost quickly if the firm moves up the very elastic part of the demand curve. To the right of the step, marginal revenue is much lower, indicating that little extra revenue can be obtained by moving down the less elastic part of the demand curve. As drawn, the marginal cost curve cuts the marginal revenue curve right at the step. The prevailing price is an equilibrium price for the firm, because it will be unprofitable to move in either direction.

The kinked demand curve equilibrium for an oligopolist is a very stable kind of equilibrium. Unlike a pure monopolist, the oligopolist with a kinked demand curve will not change its price or output in response to small- or medium-sized changes in cost. The level of marginal cost shown in Figure 9A.2 can move by as much as $.30 in either direction, and the firm will not change its price or output. The marginal cost curve will still cross the marginal revenue curve at the step. Only if marginal cost changes by more than $.30 will the firm break with the prevailing price.

Like the Cournot theory, the kinked demand curve theory is simple and elegant. Its assumptions about the way each oligopolist views its rivals' actions are clearly more plausible than Cournot's. But the kinked demand curve theory has a major limitation of its own. Although it explains why an oligopolist might be reluctant to change its price once it has set

FIGURE 9A.2 THE KINKED DEMAND CURVE THEORY OF OLIGOPOLY

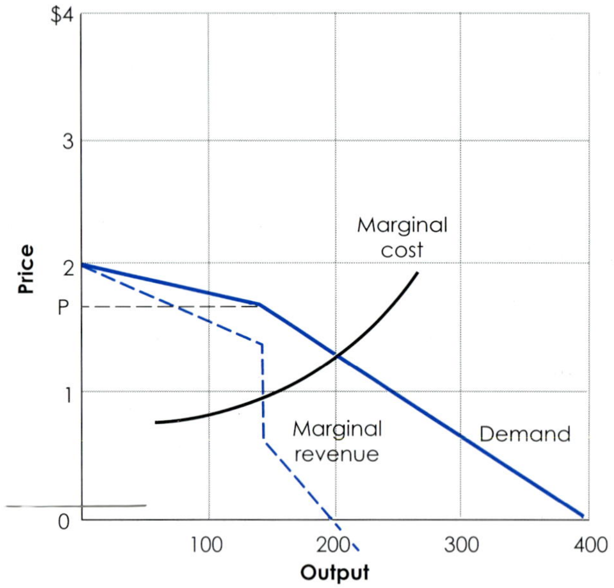

An oligopolist will have a kinked demand curve if its rivals will follow any price decrease it makes but will not follow price increases. There is a sharp step in the marginal revenue curve that corresponds to the kink in the demand curve. Here the marginal cost curve crosses the marginal revenue curve at the step. This makes the equilibrium very stable.

that price, it fails to show how the price comes to be set at any particular level in the first place. The theory thus provides an answer to a question that is not central to the analysis of oligopoly. In addition, some empirical studies have failed to confirm the theory's prediction that prices will be changed less often under oligopoly than under monopoly.

Game Theory and Oligopoly Behavior

It has often been remarked that oligopoly is really a sort of a game—one in which, as in chess or poker, each player must try to guess the opponent's moves, bluffs, counter-moves, and counterbluffs as many moves ahead as possible. Hence, economists who specialize in oligopoly theory were excited by the appearance in 1944 of a thick, highly mathematical book entitled *The Theory of Games and Economic Behavior.*[1] Could it be that the authors, John von Neumann and Oskar Morgenstern, had at last solved the oligopoly puzzle?

Clearly, Neumann and Morgenstern had taken a major step. Instead of starting from some arbitrary assumption about how one firm would react to others' moves, they decided to ask, in effect, what *optimal assumption* each firm should make about its rivals' behavior.

A simple example of an oligopoly game will convey the spirit of the Neumann-Morgenstern approach. Imagine a market in which there are only two firms—Alpha Company

[1] John von Neumann and Oskar Morgenstern, *The Theory of Games and Economic Behavior* (Princeton, N.J.: Princeton University Press, 1944).

and Zed Enterprises. It costs $1 a unit to make their product. If each firm sets its price at $5 a unit, each will sell 100 units per month at a profit of $4 a unit, for a total monthly profit of $400. If each sets its price at $4 a unit, each will sell 120 units at a profit of $3 a unit, for a total profit of $360. Which price will the firms actually set? Clearly, $5 is the price that will maximize their joint profits, but under oligopoly this price may not be a stable equilibrium.

Figure 9A.3 shows why. It presents the pricing strategies available to Alpha Company. Besides the two already mentioned, Alpha must consider two more. One is to cut its price to $4 while Zed holds at $5. That will allow Alpha to take away a lot of Zed's customers and sell 150 units, for a profit of $450. The other is for Alpha to hold its price at $5 while Zed cuts its price to $4. Then Zed will take away many of Alpha's customers and leave Alpha selling only 60 units, for a total profit of $240.

What will happen? One way to seek an answer is to look at the effects of different assumptions that each firm might make about the other's behavior. If Alpha assumes that Zed will charge $5, Alpha will be best off charging $4. If Alpha assumes that Zed will charge $4, it will again be best off charging $4. It looks as though Alpha will be best off charging $4 regardless of what Zed does. Alpha will also be aware that Zed's view of the game is the mirror image of its own. After considering the likely effects of the different assumptions, each firm will see that it is rational to assume the worst. Unless the two firms can agree to keep the price at $5 (and such agreements are assumed to be against the rules of the game as it is played here), $4 is the equilibrium price.

Nash equilibrium

An equilibrium solution to a game in which each player's strategy is optimal given the other players' choice of strategy.

The equilibrium reached in the situation described in Figure 9A.3 is called a **Nash equilibrium** after the American mathematician and game theorist John Nash. In a Nash equilibrium, each player's strategy is optimal given the strategy chosen by its rivals. Thus, neither player has an incentive to change strategies after finding out what strategy the other player

FIGURE 9A.3 A SIMPLE OLIGOPOLY GAME

Alpha's Price Strategy	Zed's Price Strategy $5	Zed's Price Strategy $4
$5	$400	$240
$4	$450	$360

This figure shows the profits Alpha Company would earn under various pricing strategies for itself and its rival, Zed Enterprises. If both firms set their prices at $5 each will earn $400. If both lower their prices to $4, they will continue to split the market and each will earn $360. If Alpha lowers its price while Zed does not, Alpha will steal many of Zed's customers and earn $450. If Zed lowers its price while Alpha's remains at $5, Zed will steal many of Alpha's customers, leaving Alpha with only $240 in profits.

has chosen. The Cournot theory provides another example of a Nash equilibrium. In the Cournot game, at first each firm changes its price as soon as it learns what its rival has done. Gradually, though, the prices converge toward a Nash equilibrium.

As economists and mathematicians have developed more powerful analytical tools, they have explored increasingly complex oligopoly games. The games vary in terms of how much each player knows about what the other is doing, the number of times the game is expected to be repeated, the number of players, and the structure of the payoffs. Consideration has also been given to games in which players pursue "mixed strategies" under which they vary their response to rivals' moves on a random basis. (In sports, an example of a mixed strategy is a baseball pitcher's random use of fastballs, curves, and sinkers to keep the batter guessing.)

The research has led to many interesting results for plausible individual cases, but it has yielded no completely general conclusions. Some games have Nash equilibrium solutions, and some do not. Some converge toward the competitive outcome as the number of firms increase, and some do not. Some produce equilibrium solutions that are efficient (either from the point of view of the players or from that of the market), and some do not. Game theory continues to be an active area of oligopoly research.

CHAPTER 10

Pricing in Resource Markets

After reading this chapter, you will understand:

1. The circumstances that determine demand for productive inputs
2. The circumstances that determine the supply curve for labor
3. The characteristics of equilibrium in a competitive labor market
4. The characteristics of labor market equilibrium with only one or a few employers
5. Why wages are not the same for all labor markets and for all individuals within a labor market

Before reading this chapter, make sure you know the meaning of:

1. Substitutes and complements
2. Elasticity
3. Income and substitution effects
4. Marginal physical product and diminishing returns
5. Perfect competition and price takers
6. Theory of monopoly and price searchers

HELPING WORKERS WORK SMARTER

One of the most dramatic changes in the U.S. labor market over the past three decades has been the decrease in high-paying jobs for workers with modest educational achievement. Once low-skill manufacturing jobs, whether in the automobile, steel, or textile industry, permitted high-school graduates, and even high-school dropouts, to live a middle-class lifestyle. Today this is much less often the case.

For years, U.S. manufacturers have been under pressure to raise productivity in order to remain competitive in world markets. From 1970 to 2002, while manufacturing output held roughly constant as a share of gross domestic product, manufacturing employment plunged from 27 percent of all nonfarm employment to just 13 percent. Meanwhile, employment in service-related industries reached 72 percent by 2000.

So where are all of the low-skill manufacturing jobs going? Overseas. U.S. and multinational corporations have moved production out of the United States into countries where they are able to pay workers lower wages—"outsourcing," this is called. In early 2000, U.S. workers noted an alarming trend—not only were the factory jobs moving abroad, but those in the service industries as well. In July 2003, for instance, U.S. firms shipped 30,000 new service-sector jobs to India while eliminating some 226,000 in this country, according to researchers at the University of California, Berkeley. Forrester Research has estimated that 3.3 million U.S. service-sector jobs will head to foreign countries over the next fifteen years, along with $136 billion in wages.

Why? Simple economics. The U.C. Berkeley research study estimated that computer programming jobs that pay $60,000 to $80,000 per year in the United States can go for as little as $8,952 a year in China, $5,880 in India, or $5,000 in the Russian Federation.

But there is another side to the outsourcing story. *New York Times* columnist Thomas Friedman went to India to do an exposé on outsourcing. He asked the owner of the 24/7 call center, a major outsourcing contractor, how can it be good for America to have Indians doing all these white collar jobs? He was surprised by the answer. "Look around the office," the Indian entrepreneur replied. The computers are from Compaq. The software is from Microsoft. The phones are from Lucent. Even the bottled water is supplied by Coca Cola, a trusted brand name in India. Overall, American exports to India have nearly doubled in the past decade. What goes around, comes around.

Small wonder outsourcing has drawn mixed reactions. On the one hand, by early 2004, eight states had taken up legislation aimed at preventing public dollars from going to companies with workers overseas, according to the National Conference of State Legislatures. On the other hand, Harris Miller, president of the Information Technology Association of America (ITAA), says the issue is overblown. He estimates that less than 2 percent of the 10 million jobs in the information technology industry, including government work, are performed overseas. Miller said that if the government prevents U.S. companies from outsourcing, other countries will retaliate with similar restrictions, "and the big losers are U.S. workers and U.S. industry."

Source: Based in part on Greg Schneider, "Anxious About Outsourcing," *The Washington Post*, January 31, 2004, and Thomas L. Friedman, "What Goes Around . . . ," *The New York Times*, February 26, 2004.

THE ISSUE OF outsourcing draws attention to an important set of markets that we have referred to only indirectly up to this point: the markets in which firms obtain the inputs they need to carry on production. Those markets have traditionally been termed *factor markets* because they provide labor, capital, and natural resources, the basic factors of production. Today, however, economists are just as likely to refer to them as *resource markets* or simply as *markets for inputs*. The more modern terms emphasize the fact that the basic theory applies not just to the three classic factors of production but to inputs of all kinds—everything from the labor of production workers to software for the firm's computers or electric power to light the parking lot.

The first part of this chapter outlines a general theory of demand for inputs. In the second part, attention is focused on markets for labor, which is the most important category of input. In the next chapter we will apply the theory to markets for capital and natural resources.

DEMAND FOR RESOURCES

In many ways resource markets are similar to the product markets we have already studied. The theories of supply and demand and the tools of marginal analysis apply to resource markets just as they do to product markets. However, resource markets differ from product markets in one major respect: In many resource markets, firms are the buyers and households are the sellers rather than the other way around. A theory of the demand for resources therefore must be based on an analysis of profit maximization by firms.

Objectives and Constraints

As in other branches of microeconomic theory, the first step toward a theory of demand for resources is to specify the objectives and constraints faced by firms. We will continue to assume that the objective is profit maximization. Three types of constraints will be considered:

1. *Production technology.* The firm is constrained in part by technology, which determines how inputs can be combined to produce outputs. When one variable input is considered, technological constraints can be represented as marginal physical product curves. Technology with more than one variable input can be represented using the graphical technique explained in the "Cost and Output with Two Variable Inputs" appendix.

2. *Demand for the product.* Firms buy resources not for their own sake but to use them as inputs in producing goods and services for sale. The demand for any input thus is said to be a **derived demand**, because it ultimately reflects demand for the product that the input is used to produce.

Derived demand

Demand for a productive input that stems from the demand for the product the input is used to produce.

3. *Resource cost.* The third constraint that a firm must consider in deciding how much of an input to purchase is the cost of obtaining that input. In competitive input markets that cost is simply the market price of the resource in question. (Imperfectly competitive markets are considered later in the chapter.)

Marginal Physical Product

Previously we defined the *marginal physical product* of a resource as the increase in output that results from a one-unit increase in the input of that resource when the amounts of all other inputs used stay the same. For example, if using one additional worker-hour of labor to cultivate a turnip field yields an additional output of five turnips when no other input to the production process is changed, the marginal physical product of labor in that field is five turnips per labor hour.

As we have seen, the marginal physical product of a resource varies as the amount of it used changes, other things being equal. In particular, as the quantity of a single input increases while the quantities of all other inputs remain fixed, a point will be reached beyond which the marginal physical product of the variable input will decline. This principle is known as the *law of diminishing returns.*

Figure 10.1 shows total and marginal physical product curves for a firm that is subject to the law of diminishing returns over the range from 0 to 20 units of an input. (At this point, it does not matter whether the input in question is labor, a raw material, or something else; the principle is the same for all.) As the amount of this input is increased while the amounts of all other inputs used are held constant, output increases—but at a diminishing rate. The first unit of the input yields a marginal physical product of 20 units of output, the second a marginal physical product of 19 units of output, and so on. After the twentieth unit of input, marginal physical product drops to zero: A ceiling has been reached beyond which adding more of the variable input cannot produce more output unless the amounts of some of the fixed inputs are also increased. For example, if the variable input is labor, adding more than 20 workers may do nothing to increase output unless the amount of machinery available for the workers to use is increased as well. Beyond 20 units of input, where

FIGURE 10.1 TOTAL AND MARGINAL PHYSICAL PRODUCT OF AN INPUT OF PRODUCTION

(a)

Quantity of Input (1)	Total Physical Product (2)	Marginal Physical Product (3)
0	0	
1	20	20
2	39	19
3	57	18
4	74	17
5	90	16
6	105	15
7	119	14
8	132	13
9	144	12
10	155	11
11	165	10
12	174	9
13	182	8
14	189	7
15	195	6
16	200	5
17	204	4
18	207	3
19	209	2
20	210	1

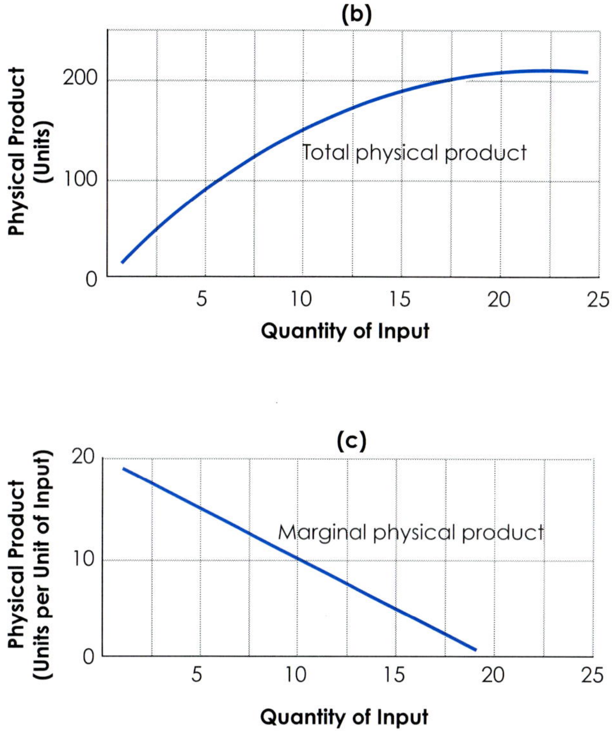

As the quantity of one resource input increases with the quantity of other inputs remaining unchanged, total physical product increases, but at a decreasing rate. As parts (a) and (c) of this figure show, marginal physical product decreases as the quantity of the employed input increases. This decrease is a direct result of the law of diminishing returns.

the marginal physical product of the variable input drops to zero, the total physical product curve becomes horizontal.

Marginal Revenue Product

Marginal revenue product

The change in revenue that results from the sale of the output produced by one additional unit of an input.

Because the demand for a resource of production is a derived demand, the firm must consider the revenue it will earn from the sale of the output produced by an added unit of input as well as the input's marginal physical product. The change in revenue that results from the sale of the added output produced by a one-unit increase in the input of a resource is the **marginal revenue product** of that resource. The relationship of marginal revenue product to demand for the product must be considered separately for firms that are *price takers* and for those that are *price searchers* in their output markets.

MARGINAL REVENUE PRODUCT FOR THE PRICE-TAKING FIRM A firm that is a price taker in its output market faces a perfectly elastic demand curve for the good it produces. The quantity of output it produces has no effect on the price at which its output is sold. Marginal revenue for the competitive firm thus equals the price of the firm's output, which is constant for all quantities of output. For such a firm, then, marginal revenue product equals the **value of marginal product**, that is, marginal physical product times the output's price.

Value of marginal product

Marginal physical product times the product's per-unit price.

Figure 10.2 gives an example. The marginal physical product schedule is the same as that given in Figure 10.1, and a constant price of $1 per unit of output is assumed.

MARGINAL REVENUE PRODUCT FOR THE PRICE-SEARCHING FIRM If the market in which the firm sells its output is not perfectly competitive, the price at which it sells its output will tend to vary as the amount of output changes. As a price searcher, the firm must choose from among a menu of price-quantity combinations given by its negatively sloped demand curve. Because the price per unit decreases as

FIGURE 10.2 MARGINAL REVENUE PRODUCT FOR A TYPICAL PRICE-TAKING FIRM

Quantity of Input (1)	Total Physical Product (2)	Marginal Physical Product (3)	Revenue per Unit (Price) (4)	Marginal Revenue Product (5)
0	0			
		20	$1	$20
1	20			
		19	1	19
2	39			
		18	1	18
3	57			
		17	1	17
4	74			
		16	1	16
5	90			
		15	1	15
6	105			
		14	1	14
7	119			
		13	1	13
8	132			
		12	1	12
9	144			
		11	1	11
10	155			
		10	1	10
11	165			
		9	1	9
12	174			
		8	1	8
13	182			
		7	1	7
14	189			
		6	1	6
15	195			
		5	1	5
16	200			
		4	1	4
17	204			
		3	1	3
18	207			
		2	1	2
19	209			
		1	1	1
20	210			

For a price-taking firm, the marginal revenue product of an input equals the value of marginal product, that is, the input's marginal physical product times the product's price. This figure assumes that the product price is $1 per unit and that marginal physical product is the same as in Figure 10.1.

output increases, marginal revenue per unit of output is always less than price per unit for a price searcher. It follows, then, that the marginal revenue product for such a firm is less than the value of marginal product.

Figure 10.3 shows how marginal revenue product is calculated for a price searcher. The figure uses the same total physical product schedule that is used in Figures 10.1 and 10.2. Column 3 presents the firm's product demand curve, showing that the price at which output can be sold drops from $1.40 per unit at 20 units of output to $.45 at 210 units. Multiplying price by total physical product gives the total revenue that corresponds to each quantity of input, which is shown in column 4.

The differences between successive entries in the total revenue column give the marginal revenue product data, shown in column 5. For example, as input of the

FIGURE 10.3 MARGINAL REVENUE PRODUCT FOR A TOTAL PRICE-TAKING FIRM

Quantity of Input (1)	Total Physical Product (2)	Price of Output (3)	Total Revenue (4)	Marginal Revenue Product (5)	Marginal Physical Product (6)	Marginal Revenue per Unit of Output (7)
0	0	—	0.00			
1	20	$1.40	$ 28.00	$28.00	20	$1.40
2	39	1.31	50.90	22.90	19	1.21
3	57	1.22	69.26	18.36	18	1.02
4	74	1.13	83.62	14.36	17	.84
5	90	1.05	94.50	10.88	16	.68
6	105	.98	102.38	7.88	15	.52
7	119	.91	107.70	5.32	14	.38
8	132	.84	110.88	3.18	13	.24
9	144	.78	112.32	1.44	12	.12
10	155	.73	112.38	.06	11	.01
11	165	.68	111.38	−1.00	10	−.10
12	174	.63	109.62	−1.76	9	−.20
13	182	.59	107.38	−2.24	8	−.28
14	189	.56	104.90	−2.48	7	−.35
15	195	.53	102.38	−2.52	6	−.42
16	200	.50	100.00	−2.38	5	−.47
17	204	.48	97.92	−2.08	4	−.52
18	207	.47	96.26	−1.66	3	−.55
19	209	.46	95.10	−1.16	2	−.58
20	210	.45	94.50	−.60	1	−.60

Note: Figures in columns 3, 4, 5, and 7 are rounded to the nearest cent.

This figure shows how marginal revenue product varies as the quantity of a resource input changes for a firm that faces a negatively sloped demand curve for its product. As column 3 shows, price falls as output increases in accordance with the demand for the firm's product. Total revenue begins to decrease after 10 units of output (the point at which marginal revenue per unit of output becomes negative) even though marginal physical product remains positive. Marginal revenue product can be calculated either as the difference between each entry in the total revenue column or as the product of marginal physical product and marginal revenue per unit of output.

resource increases from 4 to 5 units, total output increases from 74 to 90 units while the price falls from $1.13 to $1.05 per unit. As column 4 shows, total revenue increases from $83.62 when 4 units of the input are used to $94.50 when 5 units of the input are used. This gives a marginal revenue product of $10.88 in the range from 4 to 5 units of input.

It can be verified that this marginal revenue product is less than the value of marginal product (not shown in the figure). The product price is $1.13 when 4 units of the input are used and $1.05 when 5 units of the input are used; thus, it averages $1.09 over the corresponding output range. Multiplying this by the marginal physical product of 16 (column 6 of the figure) gives a value of marginal product of $17.44 at the midpoint of the output range in question, compared with a marginal revenue product of $10.88.

As the price continues to fall, marginal revenue eventually becomes negative. Beyond that point, additional units of the input reduce total revenue even though they increase total physical product. The turning point comes at 10 units of input. Beyond that level, marginal revenue product is negative even though marginal physical product remains positive.

At every level of input, the marginal revenue product of the input equals the marginal physical product times the marginal revenue per unit of output. This relationship is shown in columns 5 through 7 of Figure 10.3. The marginal revenue figures in column 7 are expressed in terms of dollars per unit of output, whereas those in column 5 are expressed in terms of dollars per unit of input.

Marginal Cost Resource

The third constraint that the firm must consider in determining how much of each resource to employ as a productive input is the cost of obtaining each additional unit of that resource, that is, its **marginal resource cost**.

Marginal resource cost

The amount by which a firm's total resource cost must increase for the firm to obtain an additional unit of that resource.

We can begin by considering the case in which the markets where the firm buys its inputs are perfectly competitive, so that the firm is a price taker in those markets. This will be the case if the firm is only one of a large number of firms that are competing to buy a particular resource and if the amount of the resource it uses is only a small fraction of the total used by all firms. For a firm that buys as a price taker, the marginal resource cost equals the market price of that particular input. For example, if the market wage rate for data-entry workers is $7 an hour, the marginal resource cost for data-entry workers' labor is $7 an hour for any firm that is a price taker in the market for data-entry workers.

Profit Maximization

To maximize profits, a firm must use just enough of each input to equalize marginal revenue product and marginal resource cost. If marginal revenue product exceeds marginal resource cost, hiring one more unit of the input will add more to revenue than to cost and, hence, will increase profit. If marginal resource cost exceeds marginal revenue product, *reducing* the amount of that input by one unit will reduce cost by more than revenue and thus increase profit. Only when marginal revenue product and marginal resource cost are equal will it be impossible for any change in the amount of the input to increase profit. In equation form, this rule can be stated as

$$\text{mrc} = \text{mrp},$$

where mrc stands for marginal resource cost and mrp for marginal revenue product. The rule applies both to firms that are price takers in their output markets and to those that are price searchers in their output markets.

Figure 10.4 illustrates the profit maximization rule. Both the table and the corresponding graph assume that the firm is a price taker in the output market and that the market price of the output is $1 per unit, as in Figure 10.2. The firm is also assumed to be a price taker in the resource market, buying inputs of that resource at $5 per unit. Note that profit rises as more of the resource is purchased, up to the 15th unit of input. The firm just breaks even on the purchase of the 16th unit of input, and thereafter profit declines. It is between the 15th and 16th units of input that marginal revenue product becomes exactly equal to marginal resource cost.

Resource Demand Curves

When a firm is a price taker in an input market, whether it is a price taker in the output market or not, its marginal revenue product curve for the input is also its demand curve for the input. A demand curve must indicate the quantity demanded at each price, and it has been shown that the quantity of the input demanded by such a firm will be whatever quantity makes the input's price (and, hence, its marginal resource cost) equal to marginal revenue product.

The same profit-maximizing concept that underlies the demand curves of individual firms for the resource can be extended to all firms hiring a given resource to create a market demand curve for that resource. The resulting curve, like those of the individual firms, is a derived demand curve. As we have seen, the demand for any input ultimately does not stem from the usefulness of the input itself but, rather, from the demand for the products the input is used to produce. The market demand for farmland is derived from the market demand for food, the market demand for typographical workers from the market demand for books, and so on.

Like the demand for outputs, the demand for inputs changes in response to changes in economic conditions. Suppose that demand curve D_0 in Figure 10.5 is the market demand curve for some input. A change in the market price of that input will cause the quantity of the resource demanded to change; this is represented by a *movement along* the demand curve, as shown by the arrow parallel to D_0. Changes in economic conditions other than a change in the input's price can cause a change in the

FIGURE 10.4 PROFIT MAXIMIZATION FOR A PRICE-TAKING FIRM

(a)

Quantity of Input (1)	Marginal Revenue Product (2)	Marginal Input Cost (3)	Total Variable Cost (4)	Fixed Costs (5)	Total Revenue (6)	Total Profit (7)
1			$ 5	$100	$ 20	–$85
2	$19	$5	10	100	39	–71
3	18	5	15	100	57	–58
4	17	5	20	100	74	–46
5	16	5	25	100	90	–35
6	15	5	30	100	105	–25
7	14	5	35	100	119	–16
8	13	5	40	100	132	–8
9	12	5	45	100	144	–1
10	11	5	50	100	155	5
11	10	5	55	100	165	10
12	9	5	60	100	174	14
13	8	5	65	100	182	17
14	7	5	70	100	189	19
15	6	5	75	100	195	20
16	5	5	80	100	200	20
17	4	5	85	100	204	19
18	3	5	90	100	207	17
19	2	5	95	100	209	14
20	1	5	100	100	210	10

(b)

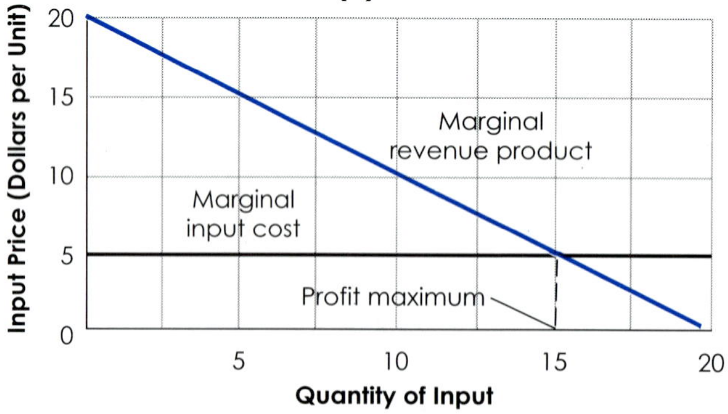

Maximizing profits requires that a firm buy just enough of each resource input to equalize marginal revenue product and marginal resource cost. Here it is assumed that the firm is a price taker, as in Figure 10.2. The point of profit maximization falls between 15 and 16 units of input.

FIGURE 10.5 MOVEMENTS ALONG A RESOURCE DEMAND CURVE AND SHIFTS IN THE CURVE

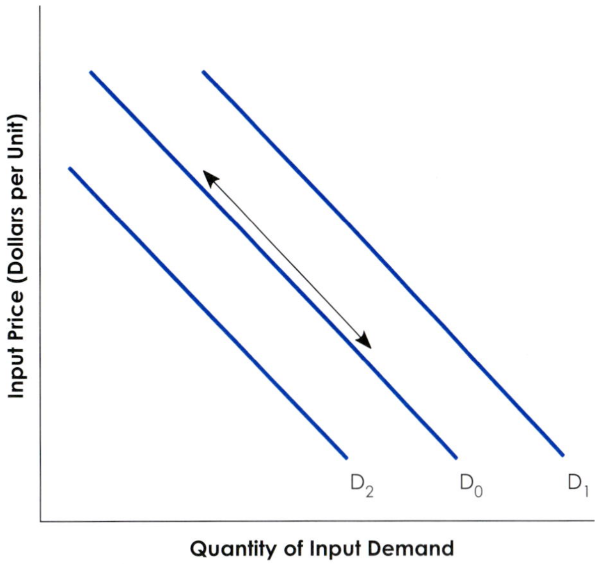

Changes in the price of a resource, other things being equal, will produce movements along a resource demand curve, as shown by the arrow. Other kinds of changes can shift the curve. An increase in demand for the product produced by the input might shift the curve from D_0 to D_1. An increase in the price of another input that is a complement to the given input might shift the curve from D_0 to D_2.

demand for that input; this is shown by a *shift* in the demand curve—say from D_0 to D_1 or from D_0 to D_2. We will first consider the elasticity of demand for inputs in response to changes in their prices, and then examine conditions that can shift resource demand curves.

The Price Elasticity of Resource Demand

The price elasticity of demand for a resource, as for any other good, is the ratio of the percentage change in the quantity demanded of the resource to a given percentage change in its price, other things being equal. The degree of price elasticity of demand for a resource is influenced by several circumstances.

PRICE ELASTICITY OF DEMAND FOR THE PRODUCT Because the demand for any input is derived from the demand for the product it is used to produce, elasticity of demand for an input depends on the elasticity of demand for the product. Suppose, for example, that the demand for taxi services is relatively elastic. If taxi fares are forced up as a result of an increase in drivers' wages, the quantity of taxi service demanded will fall sharply and there will be a correspondingly large effect on the quantity of drivers demanded. On the other hand, suppose that the demand for neurosurgery is relatively inelastic. An increase in the price charged for neurosurgery caused by an increase in neurosurgeons' fees will have relatively little effect on the number of brain operations performed. The increase in fees will consequently have a relatively small effect on the demand for that specialized kind of labor.

THE INPUT'S SHARE IN TOTAL PRODUCTION COSTS Through similar reasoning, we can conclude that a change in the price of an input will have a greater effect on the demand for it the greater its share of total costs, other things being equal. The reason is that a change in the price of an input representing a large share of total costs will have a greater impact on the market price of the product. For example, the cost of coal represents a large share of the cost of generating electricity. Doubling the price of coal therefore will have a big percentage impact on the price of electricity and a correspondingly large effect on the quantity of electricity demanded. The resulting drop in the quantity of electricity demanded will, in turn, cause a substantial drop in the quantity of coal demanded. On the other hand, lubricating oil for a power station's generating equipment accounts for only a trivial share of the total cost of electricity. Doubling the price of lubricating oil would have only a tiny effect on the rates paid by the utility's customers and, thus, only a tiny effect on the quantity of electricity demanded. As a result, doubling the price of lubricating oil will have a smaller percentage impact on the quantity demanded of this input than was the case for the more important input, coal.

SUBSTITUTABILITY AMONG INPUTS Other things being equal, the demand for an input will be more elastic the more easily other inputs can be substituted for it. For example, clowns are an essential part of circus entertainment. If clowns' wages rise, a circus can substitute other inputs, such as trained animal acts, only to a limited degree without disappointing its customers. Thus, a doubling of clowns' wages would have a relatively small percentage effect on the quantity of clowns demanded. On the other hand, automatic elevators are a very satisfactory substitute for the labor of elevator operators. A rise in the wages of operators consequently has a major impact on the number of operators employed. Earlier in the century, as the wages of elevator operators and similar kinds of unskilled labor rose, automatic elevators almost universally replaced manually operated ones.

ELASTICITY OF SUPPLY OF OTHER INPUTS Finally, the elasticity of demand for an input depends not only on the technical substitutability of other inputs but also on the elasticity of supply of other inputs. In the case of elevator operators, automatic elevator equipment, like most manufactured goods, is available under conditions of relatively elastic supply, at least in the long run. In contrast, consider the business of parking cars. It is technically possible to substitute land for labor: The number of attendants used to park a given number of cars can be reduced by spreading a parking lot out over more land so that customers have room to park their own cars. But what is technically possible does not always make sense in economic terms. In small towns, where land for parking is easy to find, self-service lots do predominate. But in urban areas the supply of land is relatively inelastic. A rise in attendants' wages in Manhattan thus cannot practically be offset by an increase in the number of one-level, self-service parking lots. As a result, parking attendants have not gone the way of elevator operators, at least not in big cities.

Changes in Demand for Resources

Let's turn now from price elasticity of demand, which pertains to changes in quantity demanded (that is, to movements along the demand curve), to changes in demand (that is, to shifts in the demand curve). Three kinds of changes are capable of causing shifts in the demand curve for inputs of any productive resource.

A CHANGE IN DEMAND FOR OUTPUT In the case of shifts in the resource demand curve, as in the case of movements along the curve, the principle of derived demand plays a key role. In particular, a change in demand for the product produced by an input (that is, a shift in the product demand curve) will cause a change in demand for the input. The source of changes in product demand can be either microeconomic or macroeconomic in nature. A microeconomic example is the increase in demand for the labor of poultry workers as a result of a shift in consumer tastes from beef to chicken. A macroeconomic example is the rise and fall of the demand for labor as the economy experiences expansions and recessions over the course of the business cycle. Expansion brings tight labor markets and increased overtime work; recessions bring layoffs and unemployment.

A CHANGE IN THE PRICE OF ANOTHER INPUT A second source of shifts in the demand curve for an input is a change in the price of some other input. The notions of *substitutes* and *complements,* which were introduced in an earlier chapter, are applicable here. For example, consider labor and farm machinery, both of which are used to grow corn. In Mexico, where labor is relatively cheap, relatively little machinery is used per bushel of corn produced; more machinery is used in the United States, where labor is relatively expensive. Labor and machinery thus can be viewed as substitutes in the production of corn. On the other hand, consider diesel fuel and the labor of drivers, both of which are used to produce truck transportation. A drop in the price of fuel will lower total costs, increasing the quantity of transportation services demanded. As a result, the number of drivers hired will increase. Thus, labor and fuel are complements in the production of truck transportation.

CHANGES IN TECHNOLOGY Changes in technology are a third condition that affects the demand for inputs. As improving technology shifts firms' cost curves downward, the quantity of inputs needed to produce a *given* quantity of output is affected. Sometimes technology will cause the demand for one input to rise while the demand for another input falls. For example, the introduction of improved crop varieties in developing countries as part of the so-called green revolution has led to a decrease in the amount of land needed per unit of crop yield, but it has required an increase in the amount of chemical fertilizers required per unit of crop yield. Frequently, however, a new technology reduces the quantities of *all* inputs needed to produce a given unit of output. For example, the invention of self-correcting typewriters shortened the time needed to produce a letter. As a result, an office could produce a given quantity of correspondence each day using fewer data-entry workers and fewer computers.

Over time, however, an increase in demand for the product, itself sometimes stimulated by improvements in technology, may more than offset the reduced quantity of an input used per unit of output. The end result of the whole process of technological change and growth may be an increased quantity demanded of a given resource. Consider the relationship between clerical workers and office equipment. In the eighteenth century, firms employed clerks to copy documents laboriously by hand. In the nineteenth century, pen and ink were replaced by the typewriter. In the twentieth century, word processors and photocopiers became available. Each technological innovation vastly reduced the number of clerical-worker hours needed to process a given volume of documents. But at the same time, the quantity of document processing demanded grew dramatically, with the result that the clerical labor force is larger now than at any time in the past.

RESOURCE SUPPLY AND DEMAND: THE LABOR MARKET

Up to this point, we have discussed marginal productivity and demand for resources in general terms that apply to any productive input. When we turn to the supply side of resource markets, however, we cannot be so general because the considerations affecting supply are somewhat different for various factors of production. In this section, we will discuss the supply curve for labor and then see how demand and supply together determine equilibrium in the labor market. A later chapter will take up markets for capital and natural resources.

The Labor Supply Curve

Labor is supplied by the same individuals and households whose role as consumers was analyzed in a previous chapter. A similar approach can be applied here. We begin with the labor supply decision for an individual worker; we then turn to market labor supply curves.

LABOR SUPPLY FOR AN INDIVIDUAL Previously we showed that all consumer choices involve trade-offs. Individuals' decisions regarding how much labor to supply can be analyzed in terms of a trade-off between two "goods": leisure and purchased consumer goods. Leisure is valued for relaxation, recreation, and the completion of household tasks. Time spent at leisure is time taken away from work, however, and hence it is time diverted from earning income that could be used to buy consumer goods. In making the choice between the two, consumers are faced with two key constraints: (1) the limit of a 24-hour day to be divided between income-earning work and leisure, and (2) the wage rate that determines the purchasing power earned per hour of work.

The hourly wage rate can be thought of as the opportunity cost of leisure in that it represents the dollar equivalent of the goods and services that must be sacrificed in order to enjoy an added hour of leisure. As the wage rate increases, the work-versus-leisure decision is affected in two ways:

1. There is a *substitution effect* as the increased wage rate raises the opportunity cost of leisure, providing an incentive to substitute work (and the goods bought with the resulting income) for leisure.
2. The increase in the wage rate has an *income effect* that tends to reduce the number of hours worked. The higher wage rate—assuming that the prices of goods and services remain unchanged—increases workers' real incomes. With higher real incomes, workers tend to consume larger amounts of normal goods and smaller amounts of inferior goods. Leisure is a normal good. Other things being equal, people generally seek more leisure, in the form of shorter working hours and longer vacations, as their incomes rise. Taken by itself, then, the income effect of a wage increase is a reduction in the amount of labor supplied by workers.

As illustrated in Figure 10.6, the net effect of an increase in the wage rate depends on the relative strengths of the substitution and income effects. It is generally believed that for very low wages the substitution effect predominates; therefore, the quantity of labor supplied by an individual initially increases as the wage rises. As the wage rises still more, however, the income effect becomes stronger. People seem to treat leisure as a normal good; after they have assured themselves of a certain material standard of living, they begin to consider "spending" any further wage increases on more time off from work. If such a pattern prevails, the labor supply curve for an individual will have a backward-bending shape like the one shown in Figure 10.6. Over the positively sloped low-wage section, the substitution effect of wage changes predominates; over the negatively sloped high-wage section, the income effect prevails.

MARKET LABOR SUPPLY CURVES Although the labor supply curves for individual workers may bend backward, at least over some range of wages, the supply curve for any given type of labor as a whole is likely to be positively sloped throughout. Consider, for example, the supply of electrical engineers in New York, of

FIGURE 10.6 AN INDIVIDUAL'S LABOR SUPPLY CURVE

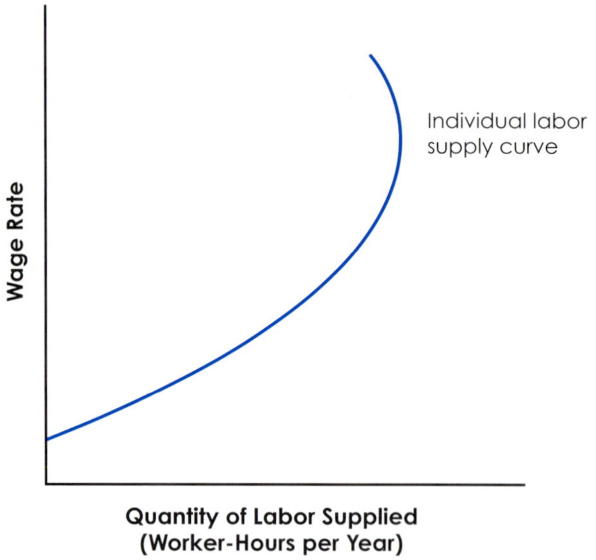

On the one hand, a higher wage tends to increase the amount of work that a person is willing to do, because the extra income compensates for time taken away from leisure pursuits. On the other hand, a higher wage allows a person to take more time off from work and still enjoy a high standard of living. Taken together, the two effects tend to give the individual labor supply curve the backward-bending shape shown here.

data-entry workers in Chicago, or of farm laborers in Texas. Beyond some point, each individual engineer, data-entry worker, or laborer might respond to a wage increase by cutting back on the number of hours worked. For the market as a whole, however, this tendency would be more than offset by the entry of new workers from other occupations or areas. Thus, other things being equal, if the wage rate for electrical engineers in New York rose, more engineering students would take up that specialty; if the wage rate for data-entry workers in Chicago rose, more people would go into such work instead of, say, becoming receptionists; and if the wage rate for farm laborers in Texas rose, workers would be drawn in from Arizona, Florida, and Mexico. As a result, for any discussion of the market for a particular category of labor at a specific time and place, it is reasonable to draw the labor supply curve with the usual positive slope regardless of the shape of the individual labor supply curves underlying it.

Competitive Equilibrium

Determining the wage rate in a labor market that is perfectly competitive on both sides is a simple matter of supply-and-demand analysis. Figure 10.7, for example, shows supply and demand curves for the labor market for data-entry workers in

FIGURE 10.7 DETERMINATION OF THE EQUILIBRIUM WAGE IN A COMPETITIVE LABOR MARKET

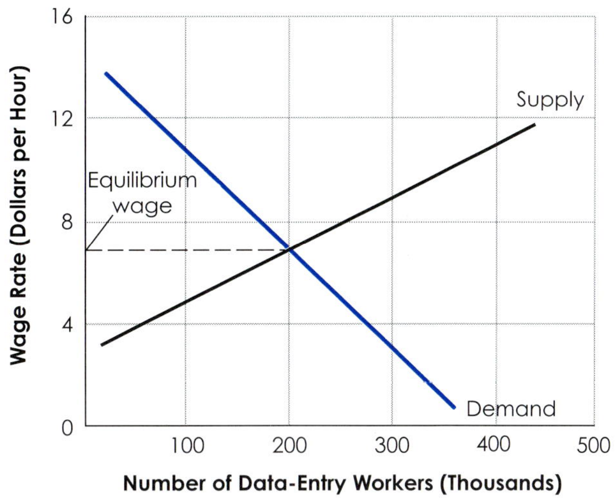

Although each individual worker may have a backward-bending supply curve, the supply curve for data-entry workers in any local market will have the usual positive slope. As the wage rises, people will be drawn into this occupation from other kinds of work or other localities. When both employers and workers are price takers in the labor market, the point of equilibrium is found where the supply and demand curves intersect. Here the equilibrium wage rate is $7 an hour and the equilibrium quantity of labor is 200,000 workers.

Chicago. It assumes that a large number of workers compete for jobs and a large number of employers compete for them so that both are price takers. The market supply curve has a positive slope, and the market demand curve for data-entry workers is derived from the demand curves for individual firms.

Equilibrium in this market requires a wage rate of $7 an hour, with 200,000 workers employed. If the wage rate were lower, there would be a shortage of data-entry workers. Some firms, unable to fill all their job openings, would offer premium wages to workers from other jobs or regions. The wage rate would thus be driven up to the equilibrium level. If, on the other hand, the wage rate were above $7 an hour, there would be a surplus of data-entry workers. Many people would be looking for such jobs and not finding them. After a sufficiently long search, some would be willing to accept work at lower-than-desired wages, thereby pushing the wage rate down toward equilibrium; others would move into other occupations or regions.

In a labor market such as this one—in which both employers and employees are price takers—the equilibrium wage rate equals the marginal revenue product of labor. In the special case in which all employers are price takers (perfect competitors) in the market where they sell their output as well as in the market where they purchase inputs, the equilibrium wage rate also equals the value of marginal product.

The Marginal Productivity Theory of Distribution

Supply and demand determine how much each worker earns as well as how much labor will be used in making each product. When employers are price takers in the markets in which they buy inputs, profit maximization requires that each resource be used up to the point at which its marginal revenue product will equal its price. This reasoning suggests that each unit of each resource receives a reward equal to the contribution it makes to the firm's revenue. The idea that resources are rewarded according to their marginal productivity is known as the **marginal productivity theory of distribution**.

Marginal productivity theory of distribution
A theory of income distribution in which each input of production receives a payment equal to its marginal revenue product.

In an economy in which all markets—output as well as input—are perfectly competitive, the marginal productivity theory applies even more directly. In this case marginal revenue product equals output price times marginal physical product. In such an economy the reward that each unit of each input receives is equal to the value of marginal product. Thus, if an extra hour spent pulling weeds in a cabbage patch increases production by 20 pounds and cabbage sells for $.50 per pound, the equilibrium wage rate must be $10 an hour—no more, no less.

The marginal productivity theory of distribution as we have defined it is a proposition of positive economics. However, some people find this principle of distribution appealing in a normative sense as well, in terms of both efficiency and fairness. Under the marginal productivity principle, the reward of every worker is exactly equal to that worker's contribution to the productive process. If a worker or other resource owner withholds a unit of productive services from the market, that person will suffer a loss of earnings exactly equal to the value of production that is lost to the economy as a whole. The normative version of the marginal productivity theory is, in effect, the old idea of "from each according to ability, to each according to work" restated in the language of neoclassical economics.

Monopsony

Not every input market meets the conditions required for the marginal productivity theory of distribution to apply. In particular, there are cases in which firms are price searchers rather than price takers in input markets. In labor markets, this will tend to occur when one or a few employers dominate the market in a particular location or for a particular skill. It can also happen when workers vary in their perceptions of nonwage characteristics of jobs with different employers. Some people might work for Acme because it is close to their neighborhood; some might prefer Zeus Company because the managers there are friendlier; and so on. Whatever the reason, the employer cannot hire unlimited numbers of workers at a constant wage. The labor supply curve faced by the individual employer is not horizontal as it is in a perfectly competitive labor market.

Monopsony
A situation in which there is only a single buyer in a market; more generally, any situation in which a firm is a price searcher in a market in which it is a buyer.

The extreme case, in which a single employer accounts for 100 percent of the demand in a resource market, is termed **monopsony**. In ancient Greek, from which these terms are derived, *monopsony* means "one buyer" just as *monopoly* means "one seller." In principle, we could also identify the resource market structures of *oligopsony* (a few buyers) and *monopsonistic competition* (many buyers perceived as different by sellers). However, it is common, although not very precise, to apply the term *monopsony* to all markets in which the buyers are price searchers.

In a monopsony labor market, then, the wage rate is not a given. Instead, the employer must choose among a set of price-quantity combinations lying along a positively sloped labor supply curve. As an example, compare the situation of a retail store in Albuquerque that wants to hire a few security guards with the situation of the U.S. government, which wants to hire soldiers for the army. The retail store is a price taker in the market for security guards. If the going wage for such guards is, say, $30,000 a year, it can call an agency or put an ad in the paper and get as many guards as it wants at that price. The situation of the government as the employer of volunteer soldiers is very different. Experience with military recruitment ever since the end of the draft a generation ago has shown that the success of recruitment efforts depends on the level of military pay. At the turn of the twenty-first century, a slack job market made recruitment relatively easy. However, after the U.S. invasion of Iraq, demand for security personnel by private-sector contractors soared, pushing salaries for some security workers over $100,000 per year. Over time, this change in market conditions will inevitably affect the wage the military services will have to offer new recruits.

The Monopsonist's Marginal Resource Cost Curve

In discussing monopoly we distinguished between price-discriminating monopoly and simple monopoly. The latter sells all units at the same price, whereas the former sells to different customers at different prices. The same distinction applies in the labor market. In this chapter we consider only the simple case in which an employer pays the same wage to all workers who do the same job. For example, the employer may have a policy of raising the wages of all workers on the payroll if market conditions make it necessary to pay more for new hires. To pay new workers more than old ones might be bad for morale.

Figure 10.8 shows the supply curve and the marginal resource cost curve faced by a hypothetical simple monopsonist—say, a large insurance company that employs most of the data-entry workers in a small town. The supply schedule for these workers shows that no one will work in this occupation at a wage rate of $3 an hour or less. Above the $3 wage, each extra $.02 per hour will attract one more worker. Suppose that the monopsonistic employer has hired 150 data-entry workers at a rate of $6 an hour, making the total labor cost for a labor force of this size $900 an hour.

Now consider what will happen to the firm's total labor cost per hour if it expands its labor force by one worker. According to the supply curve, hiring 151 data-entry workers requires a wage of $6.02 an hour. That wage must be paid not just to the 151st worker but to all workers. The total cost of a labor force of 151 data-entry workers, then, is \$6.02 times 151, or \$909.02 per hour. The addition of one more worker has raised the total labor cost per hour from \$900 to \$909.02—a marginal resource cost of \$9.02. The result is much the same regardless of the chosen starting point. In every case the monopsonist's marginal resource cost exceeds the resource price (in this case, the wage rate).

FIGURE 10.8 MARGINAL RESOURCE COST UNDER MONOPSONY

(a)

Quantity of Labor Supplied (Number of Workers) (1)	Wage Rate (Dollars per Hour) (2)	Total Resource Cost (Dollars per Hour) (3)	Marginal Resource Cost (Dollars per Hour) (4)
1	\$3.02	\$ 3.02	
2	3.04	6.08	\$ 3.06
3	3.06	9.18	3.10
150	6.00	900.00	
151	6.02	909.02	9.02
152	6.04	918.08	9.06
200	7.00	1,400.00	
201	7.02	1,411.02	11.02
203	7.04	1,422.08	11.06

(b)

Under monopsony, marginal resource cost exceeds factor price. Consider an increase in quantity from 150 to 151 units of labor. The wage rate must be raised from \$6 to \$6.02 not just for the 151st employee but for all the previous 150 as well. Marginal resource cost in this range thus is \$9.02 rather than \$6.02 an hour.

Part (b) of Figure 10.8 shows a marginal resource cost curve based on the marginal resource cost column of the table in part (a). This curve lies above the supply curve at every point. The graph shows that the relationship between the supply curve and the marginal resource cost curve for the monopsonist is similar to that between a monopolist's demand and marginal revenue curves.

Monopsony Equilibrium

Given the monopsonist's marginal resource cost curve, which is derived from the market supply curve for that resource, the equilibrium level of employment for the firm is determined as follows: Figure 10.9 shows the monopsonistic employer's marginal revenue product curve along with the labor supply and marginal resource cost curves from Figure 10.8. Following the general rule that profit is maximized at the quantity of labor for which marginal resource cost equals marginal revenue product, the monopsonist will hire 150 data-entry workers at a wage rate of $6 an hour.

When a labor market is in monopsony equilibrium, the wage rate is lower than both the marginal resource cost and the marginal revenue product of labor. In the example just given, the equilibrium wage rate is $6 an hour (which is equal to the height of the labor supply curve), although the marginal revenue product is $9 an hour at the point at which the marginal revenue product and marginal resource cost curves intersect. Despite the gap between the wage rate and the marginal revenue product, adding to the amount of labor hired would not raise revenue enough to offset

FIGURE 10.9 DETERMINATION OF WAGES UNDER MONOPSONY

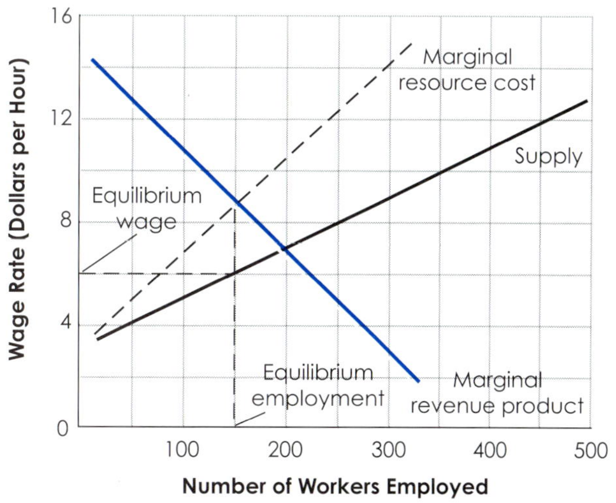

This figure shows the marginal revenue product of labor curve, labor supply curve, and marginal resource cost curve for a monopsonist. The quantity of labor required for maximizing profits is found at the point at which the marginal revenue product and marginal resource cost curves intersect. The equilibrium wage rate does not occur at this point. Instead, it is equal to the height of the supply curve directly below that intersection.

higher labor costs. The reason is that the cost of hiring another worker is not just the $6.02 an hour that must be paid to the 151st worker; instead, it is that sum plus the extra $.02 per hour by which the wages of all 150 previously hired workers must be raised. The complete marginal resource cost for the 151st worker thus is $6.02 + $3.00, or $9.02 an hour.

WHY WAGE RATES DIFFER

According to a widely shared concept of justice, all people are created equal. But if that is so, why do people's earnings in labor markets differ so widely? Why do different people receive different wages within a given labor market, and why do the wage structures of some markets differ markedly from those of others? In this section we look at some extensions of conventional marginal productivity theory that help explain why wage rates differ.

Nonwage Job Characteristics

One reason wage rates differ is that jobs differ in ways other than wages; they differ in such characteristics as safety, prestige, comfort, and challenge, as well. Other things being equal, workers are willing to supply their services at lower wages to employers that offer jobs with more attractive nonwage characteristics. Knowing this, many employers try to make the jobs they offer safe, attractive, and challenging. Employers who must attract workers to jobs that cannot be freed from risk and discomfort often have to pay higher wages. Small wonder wages for private security personnel soared after the U.S. invasion of Iraq! On a more mundane level, employers typically have to pay a wage premium for night work, which relatively few workers find attractive.

But the proposition that employers must pay more to attract workers to jobs with less desirable nonwage characteristics applies only when *other things are equal.* In practice, it turns out that many tedious, unpleasant, and even dangerous jobs pay low wages, while the high-salaried occupants of the executive suite work in air-conditioned comfort and eat lunches served on fine china in special dining rooms. How can this seeming paradox be explained in terms of labor market theory?

Economists see nothing paradoxical in the contrast between the heat and noise of the factory floor and the cool calm of the executive suite. They simply interpret the observed pattern as evidence that comfort on the job is a *normal good.* As people's incomes rise, they want more comfort. An employer must take this into account when offering a package of wage and working conditions to various employees. Suppose that a firm offered a filing clerk a cut in pay from $7 an hour to $6 an hour ($2,000 a year) in return for which it would replace the vinyl tile in the file room with wool carpet and replace the cheap posters on the wall with original artwork. Would it be surprising if the file clerk turned down the offer? But suppose the same firm offered its president a raise from $500,000 a year to $502,000 a year, in exchange for which the carpet in the president's office would be ripped out and its oil paintings replaced with cheap posters. Would it be surprising if the president turned down the offer?

This principle applies on an international scale, as well. Major U.S. multinationals with plants in developing countries are very often regarded as local leaders in terms of the wages and working conditions they offer. Their factories are cleaner, better lit, and safer than those of their small, local competitors. Yet when these overseas plants are compared in terms of working conditions with factories in the United States, they often are denounced as "sweatshops." What is the truth? Are multinational corporations ruthlessly exploiting foreign workers? Or are those workers, who are just making the first steps out of dismal poverty, less willing to trade off hard cash wages for improvements in workplace amenities? There is often no unambiguous answer to such questions.

Human Capital

Differences in the nonwage characteristics of jobs do not fully explain why wages differ. Ability also counts. If the supply of abilities needed for the job of corporate president were as abundant as the supply of abilities needed for the job of file clerk, we would not expect labor markets to give rise to such a big difference in pay to the two occupations.

Some people are born with special abilities, or at least with unusual potential for developing them. The enormous salaries of professional ballplayers, first-rate opera singers, and other superstars are a direct result of the scarcity of those abilities. But the abilities people are born with are only part of the story. Training and education are at least as important as innate ability for most occupations, from lawyers and accountants to glassblowers and hairdressers.

Economists view the costs of training and education as a form of investment. Taking courses to become an accountant, in this view, is much like buying a dump truck in order to go into the gravel-hauling business. In both cases one makes an expenditure now to acquire something that will increase one's future earning power. The main difference is that the dump truck operator acquires capital in the form of a machine, whereas the accountant acquires **human capital**—capital in the form of learned abilities.

Human capital

Capital in the form of learned abilities that have been acquired through formal training or education or through on-the-job experience.

According to human-capital theory, the earnings of each occupation that requires special training must be high enough to make up for the opportunity cost of getting the training. In the case of a person going to college to acquire a degree in accounting, the opportunity cost includes both the costs of getting the degree (tuition, books, and so on) and the income that could have been earned if the college years had been spent working in an occupation that required no college degree (see *Applying Economic Ideas 1.1* from Chapter 1). Other things being equal, we would expect occupations that require longer or more expensive training to pay more than those that require less. Thus, we would expect doctors to earn more than lawyers, lawyers to earn more than hairdressers, and so on—and that is in fact the case.[1]

Of course, the nonwage characteristics of jobs may play a role in people's willingness to invest in various kinds of human capital. If certain occupations are more exciting or prestigious than others, people may be willing to enter them even if the pay alone is not enough to justify the investment in training. For example, the training required to become a ballet dancer may be as long and rigorous as that needed to become, say, an orthodontist, but dancers, on the average, earn less than orthodontists. The difference in pay presumably has something to do with the value placed by would-be dancers on the opportunity for artistic expression.

Formal education is by no means the only way to invest in human capital. As the case at the beginning of the chapter shows, on-the-job training is also important. In

APPLYING ECONOMIC IDEAS 10.1
HENRY FORD'S $5 DAY

The Ford Motor Company was founded in 1903, but it remained small for five years. In 1908 it had 450 employees, most of them skilled craftsmen and machinists. Cars were assembled from parts that were made to low tolerances, requiring much custom machining and fitting. The work was complex, and workers had broad discretion and control over their jobs. In 1908 the firm produced just 10,607 cars.

Over the next five years the company underwent a radical transformation. The Model T was introduced and soon became the only car that Ford made. Ford wanted his cars to be all alike—"just like one pin is like another pin when it comes from the pin factory."

The new car required a new approach to manufacturing. The world's first moving assembly line was introduced. Specialized, single-purpose machine tools replaced conventional multipurpose tools. Parts supplied from outside sources had to be made to tolerances that allowed them to be interchangeable without special fitting.

These changes in production methods were accompanied by a major change in Ford's workforce. By 1913 the number of employees had reached nearly 14,000, almost all unskilled. Three-quarters of the workers were foreign born, and many did not speak English. These unskilled workers did simple, highly subdivided jobs, such as attaching a single nut or bolt. The training required for these jobs was a matter of five or ten minutes in many cases. The company's output rose to 5,000 cars per week.

There were problems, though. One of them was high labor turnover and absenteeism. In 1913 the rate of employee turnover was almost 400 percent, and Ford had to hire 50,000 men to maintain its average workforce of just under 14,000. On any given day, 10 percent of the workers failed to show up for work. The high rates of turnover and absenteeism lowered productivity and were symptoms of other problems, such as arbitrary practices by supervisors.

To cope with these labor problems, a new policy was announced in January 1914. Wages for most male workers aged 22 or older were raised from roughly $2.32 per day to a minimum of $5 per day, and at the same time the workday was cut from nine hours to eight. This was done despite the fact that there had never been a shortage of applicants for available jobs at the old wage.

The results of this program fit the pattern predicted by efficiency wage theory. Productivity rose. From 1913 to 1914 output went up by 15 percent while the workforce shrank by 15 percent and the workday was shortened. The turnover rate fell from 400 percent to 28 percent, and absenteeism also decreased sharply. In the first year of the $5 day, Ford's profit rose by 15 percent, to $30 million, and the following year it rose another 20 percent.

Work at the Ford plant was very hard. As one employee put it, "You've got to work like hell at Ford's. From the time you become a number in the morning until the bell rings for quitting time, you have to keep at it. You can't let up. You've got to get out the production and if you can't get it out, you get out." Nevertheless, after the $5 day was introduced, thousands of men lined up outside the plant, waiting all night in blizzard conditions, to apply for jobs. As for those already inside the plant, "It would almost have required the use of a rifle to separate the average Ford employee from the payroll."

Source: Daniel M. G. Raff and Lawrence H. Summers, "Did Henry Ford Pay Efficiency Wages?" *Journal of Labor Economics*, Vol. 5, no. 4 (October 1987): S57–86.

total, employers may spend as much for on-the-job training as is spent on formal education at all levels. Both employers and employees benefit from this vast investment in human capital. Employers benefit from the ability to fine-tune the skills of their work forces to the physical capital in which they have invested. In that sense, physical capital and human capital are often complementary inputs. At the same time, employees benefit, not only from immediate promotions and higher pay but also because training may broaden their options in the labor market.

Efficiency Wage Theory

Human-capital theory suggests that the ability to perform a job better results in an increase in the wage rate of a worker or group of workers. Another theory suggests that the opposite may also be true—higher pay may itself lead to better on-the-job performance. This line of reasoning is referred to as **efficiency wage theory**.

Efficiency wage theory

The theory that wages above the minimum necessary to attract qualified workers can raise productivity by enough to increase profit.

Efficiency wage theory poses the following question: Why do many firms pay a wage that is higher than necessary to attract workers with the desired minimum qualifications? Anyone who has ever looked for a job has probably had the experience of hearing about an employer who offers a high wage for particular skills and working conditions, only to learn that the employer has hundreds of applications on file and a low turnover rate. According to the simple supply-and-demand model, the profit-maximizing strategy for such a firm would be to lower the wage rate, allowing the backlog of job applications to shrink to just the level necessary to cover turnover. Yet this is not always done.

The explanation offered by efficiency wage theory is that the high wage stimulates increased productivity. Several reasons have been suggested, including improved morale, lower absenteeism, and lower employee turnover. Also, workers at a high-wage firm are likely to be less willing to risk losing their jobs because of poor performance and therefore may work to the best of their abilities with less supervision and monitoring.

Applying Economic Ideas 10.1 discusses an example that is sometimes cited in support of efficiency wage theory: the introduction of the $5 day at Ford Motor Company in 1914. Efficiency wages are not uncommon. For instance, consider the West Coast fast-food restaurant In-N-Out Burger. While most fast-food restaurants often offer starting pay at the minimum wage, In-N-Out's starting wage is $8.25 per hour. It also provides paid vacations, food at work, and an optional 401(k) plan with a company match. Not surprisingly, In-N-Out ranks among the best in food quality and customer service.

SUMMARY

1. **What circumstances determine demand for productive inputs?** For a firm that is a price taker in its output market, the *marginal revenue product* of any input is equal to the input's *value of marginal product*—that is, marginal physical product times the product's price. For a firm that is a price searcher in the output market, it is equal to marginal physical product times marginal revenue and thus is less than the value of marginal product. In both cases the firm makes the maximum profit by buying each input up to the point at which marginal revenue product equals *marginal resource cost*. Hence, the marginal revenue product curve is the resource demand curve for any firm that is a price taker in its input market. The demand for a resource is said to be derived from the demand for the goods it is used to produce.

2. **What circumstances determine the supply curve for labor?** Labor supply curves depend on the trade-off that people make between leisure and the goods and services they can buy with income earned in the labor market. The labor supply curve for an individual worker, and perhaps for the economy as a whole, may bend backward above a certain wage rate. However, the supply curve for a single labor market is positively sloped throughout its length.

3. **What are the characteristics of equilibrium in a competitive labor market?** In a labor market in which employers are price takers, the equilibrium wage rate will be equal to the marginal revenue product of labor, a proposition known as the *marginal productivity theory of distribution*. If employers are also price takers in the output market, the equilibrium wage rate also will be equal to the value of the marginal product.

4. **What are the characteristics of labor market equilibrium with only one or a few employers?** *Monopsony* refers to a situation in which employers are price searchers in the market in which they buy inputs. The marginal resource cost curve for such a firm lies above the supply curve for labor. The equilibrium input is established at the intersection of the marginal resource cost curve and the marginal revenue product curve. In such a market the equilibrium wage is below the marginal revenue product.

5. **Why are wages not the same for all labor markets and for all individuals within a labor market?** Wages differ among markets and among individuals for a variety of reasons. Some wage differences stem from differences in the nonwage characteristics of jobs or from differences in the *human capital* possessed by individuals. According to *efficiency wage theory* some employers pay more than the going wage because doing so results in higher productivity.

KEY TERMS

Derived demand
Marginal revenue product
Value of marginal product
Marginal resource cost
Marginal productivity theory of distribution
Monopsony
Human capital
Efficiency wage theory

PROBLEMS AND TOPICS FOR DISCUSSION

1. **Examining the lead-off case.** How might increased outsourcing affect the quality of the U.S. labor force? If regulations preventing outsourcing were successful, how would this affect U.S. companies? What about consumers buying goods and services from these producers?

2. **Households as buyers in resource markets.** This chapter discusses only resource markets in which the buyers are firms. Are households ever direct buyers of the basic factors of production? For example, are you the direct buyer of a factor of production when you hire someone to type a term paper? How would the theory of resource markets have to be modified to take into account cases in which the buyers of resources are households rather than firms?

3. **A case of backward-bending labor demand?** In his historical novel *Chesapeake* James Michener describes the unsuccessful efforts of early European colonists to run their plantations using hired Native American labor. Among the many factors that led to the breakdown of relationships between the planters and local inhabitants were economic problems. For example, Michener reports the frustration of a planter who finds that an offer of higher wages does not keep Native American workers from quitting their jobs in the fields after a few weeks of work; in fact, the workers seem to quit sooner when their pay is raised. Does what you have learned in this chapter shed any light on this situation? Discuss.

4. **Monopsony and monopoly.** Is a monopsonist always a monopolist, and vice versa? Try to imagine a firm that is a monopsonist in its factor market but a perfect competitor in its product market. Then try to visualize a firm that is a monopolist but not a monopsonist.

5. **The relationship between "how" and "or whom."** Discuss the following statement: "It is a good idea to let resource markets determine how things are produced, but the matter of for whom things are produced should be handled according to need, not according to supply and demand." Is it possible to separate the "how" and "for whom" functions of resource markets?

6. **Trends in the pay of men and women.** The wage gap between men and women has narrowed somewhat in the past ten years and is expected to narrow further. Do you think the narrowing of the wage gap has anything to do with the facts that (a) women are more than proportionately represented in service occupations and (b) demand for services is growing faster than demand for goods? Discuss.

7. **Wages and working conditions in the newly industrialized countries.** Evaluate the following statement: "We probably can't do much about the fact that workers in Korea, Taiwan, and other newly industrialized countries are paid less than U.S. workers doing similar jobs. However, we should not tolerate the fact that those workers are forced to work under conditions that fall far short of U.S. standards for health, safety, comfort, and hours of work. We should either insist on better working conditions or stop importing goods made by workers who are exploited in that way." How would this proposal affect workers in the newly industrialized countries (a) if the threat to cut off trade worked and labor conditions in those countries were brought up to U.S. standards, and (b) if the threat failed and trade with the countries in question were cut off?

CASE FOR DISCUSSION

The Great American Nursing Shortage

Jose Pineda, a doctor in the Philippines, went back to school—to be a nurse. At age 41, Pineda gave up his private practice in 2003 and moved to the United States. "I am not planning for myself anymore," said Pineda. "I am planning for my kids." Pineda makes $50,000 a year as a nurse at St. Mary Medical Center in Long Beach, California—four times what his physician's salary was in the Philippines. Thousands are making the career switch from doctor in the Philippines to nurse in the United States.

Nurses are in such short supply in the United States that hospitals are looking abroad to fill the gap—offering record salaries and signing bonuses. To satisfy the need for more nurses, the U.S. federal government promises priority immigration status. In the Philippines, economic and political uncertainty have many professionals planning to leave.

In this country, Pineda doesn't deliver babies or cure patients. He works in the telemetry ward at St. Mary's, monitoring seriously ill patients. Dr. Alex Leung is one of the few people at St. Mary's who knows his history. "When I talk to Jose, I talk to him like he's a doctor," Leung said. "I tell him, 'Don't call me doctor.' Because he knows more than I do."

One study surveyed 113 nursing students in 2003. Only 6 percent considered nursing an interesting career, and 59 percent said it was degrading to become a nurse. More than three-fourths said money had driven their decisions. "We feel a lot of shame," said 29-year-old Alberto del Pilar, who works the night shift at Western Medical Center in Anaheim, California for $26.22 an hour. "I never imagined myself changing someone's diapers," he said. "It is a real adjustment draining the urine from the urine bags, scratching their backs. Lots of patients like to be scratched."

"Which am I going to choose: to be an RN in America or a surgeon in my own country?" del Pilar asked his father, an engineer. He said, "Son, the opportunity is in America, not here in the Philippines."

Del Pilar plans to make another career switch—to being a doctor again. He spends most afternoons at Starbucks, keeping himself awake with double espressos while studying for the U.S. medical board exams in the hope of eventually practicing medicine in his new country. Many new arrivals come with the same dream, though nursing has proved so lucrative—and the path back to medicine so arduous—that few have time or resources to reinvest in medicine.

Some visas allow foreign physicians to enroll in U.S. medical residency programs, but there are many barriers to entering them. In addition, U.S. physicians have pushed to keep foreign doctors out of practice in America.

A recent federal study estimated that the United States will be 800,000 nurses short of its needs by 2020. Recruitment of nurses abroad has become big business, particularly in California, where nearly a fourth of nurses have received their training overseas. And a new state law mandates higher staffing levels, increasing the demand. Media ads in the Philippines promise high salaries, visa sponsorship, flights to Guam to take the U.S. nursing exams, and moving expenses. The process takes two years.

While paying as much as $10,000 per recruit, American hospitals have discovered that, once recruited, the doctors often save on training costs. For example, it typically takes three months to prepare a nurse for the operating room. "But if you get a surgeon training is shorter," said Manuel Atienza, a Philippine doctor who runs a nurse recruiting business in Las Vegas.

The nursing shortage in the United States may lead to a doctor shortage in the Philippines. The country produces too many nurses and has long been the biggest supplier of foreign-born nurses to the United States. This raises concerns that the country will eventually face a shortage of doctors, especially in rural areas. In the Philippines, it is precisely rural doctors who are most likely to turn to nursing in the United States. The supply of doctors countrywide is already low.

Source: Alan Zarembo, "Physician, Remake Thyself," *Los Angeles Times*, January 10, 2004.

QUESTIONS

1. Analyze the U.S. nursing shortage in terms of supply and demand. Has the demand curve shifted? If so, why? Has the supply curve shifted? If so, why? Do you think market forces will eventually eliminate the shortage? Why or why not?
2. From the point of view of a hospital, one effect of the "prospective payment" system is to raise the opportunity cost of using doctors' labor to provide health care, since the hospital can no longer be certain of reimbursement for unlimited doctors' fees. Why would this cause an increase in demand for nurses' labor? Does the example suggest that doctors' and nurses' labor are substitutes or complements in the production of health care?
3. Jose Pineda says that he quit medicine in the Philippines because of the prospect of higher pay as a nurse in the United States. Would the nursing shortage make hospitals more likely to improve nurses' working conditions? How will the influx of nurses from abroad affect the treatment of existing nurses in the United States? Explain your answer in terms of the theory presented in this chapter.
4. How is the situation in U.S. nursing related to the outsourcing issue in the lead-off case for this chapter? Why might customer service jobs leave the United States, while nursing jobs have remained?

END NOTES

1. Human-capital theory implies that workers with more education tend to be paid more than workers with less education because the knowledge they acquire makes them more productive on the job. This theory has been challenged by some economists, who think that the primary function of education is to help employers screen job candidates for certain desirable traits, such as intelligence and self-discipline, that are not themselves acquired through education.

CHAPTER 11

Markets for Capital and Natural Resources

After reading this chapter, you will understand:

1. How markets determine the rate of return on capital
2. How payments made at different points in time can be compared
3. How supply and demand determine rents for land
4. How markets allocate nonrenewable natural resources

Before reading this chapter, make sure you know the meaning of:

1. Tax incidence
2. Economic rent
3. Law of diminishing returns
4. Marginal revenue product

NEW STEEL

EVTAC Mining Co. received approval today to use its own money to begin rebuilding its Iron Range taconite plant for reopening. EVTAC mines taconite, a rock mined as low-grade iron ore, shipped in the form of pellets to steel manufacturers. The company closed in 2003 due to a lack of pellet orders and would need to spend about $5.9 million to get its mine and processing plant in Minnesota into operating condition for acquisition by Cleveland-Cliffs Inc. and Laiwu Steel Group.

Investing in major repairs would be a strong signal that the taconite plant will reopen. To get the taconite plant ready for operations, about $3 million would be required for a furnace rebuild; $1.1 million for miscellaneous supplies; $975,000 for mine development and maintenance; $600,000 for a shovel rebuild; and $250,000 for a crusher rebuild.

"I don't believe we are going to oppose that $5.9 million being spent on the operation," said Bob Bratulich, United Steelworkers of America District 11 director. "We want those folks to get back to work as soon as possible.

At the end of 2003, EVTAC Mining Co. was renamed United Taconite and reopened. "We are excited about 2004," said John S. Brinzo, chairman and CEO of United Taconite. "Our prospects for this year are solid," he said, noting that United Taconite would need to continue investing in the company to improve the competitive position of its mines.

Sources: Lee Bloomquist, "Duluth, Minn.-Area Iron Mine Seeks Bankruptcy Funding to Prepare for Restart," *Duluth News-Tribune,* October 28, 2003; Lee Bloomquist, "Mine Reopening Costs Help Lower Cleveland-Based Iron Ore Supplier's Earnings," *Duluth News-Tribune,* February 5, 2004.

IN THIS CHAPTER we turn our attention to the other two classical factors of production: capital and natural resources. The example of United Taconite provides a particularly clear example of the way firms coordinate inputs of labor, capital, and natural resources in the production process. The concepts of derived demand and marginal revenue product shape the demand for capital and natural resources, just as they shaped the demand for labor. However, as we will see, markets for capital and natural resources have some special traits on the side of supply that make it worthwhile to give them separate attention.

CAPITAL AND INTEREST

Earlier we defined *capital* as all means of production that are made by people. Some capital takes discrete, tangible forms, such as United Taconite's shovel and crusher. Improvements to land are another form of capital; they include excavations that permit access to mineral deposits, ditches that channel water to fields where crops are grown, and so on. And as we saw in the preceding chapter, skills such as those of a mining engineer, achieved through education and enhanced by experience, are examples of human capital. In this section we look at some features that are shared by all forms of capital.

Capital and Roundabout Production

A fundamental feature that is shared by all forms of capital is a trade-off between the present and the future. To accumulate capital it is necessary to bear opportunity costs now in order to reap a return later. Suppose, for example, that you want to catch fish from a well-stocked pond. You might be able to catch a few fish by wading in and grabbing them with your bare hands. That way you would have some fish today, although not many. But you could also spend the day weaving string into a net and cutting a branch to use as a handle for the net. You would go hungry today, but tomorrow you would be able to catch lots of fish, many more than you could catch with your bare hands. The opportunity cost in the form of forgone meals that you endured to accumulate capital in the form of the net would be repaid by future benefits.

The example of the fishing net shows why economists sometimes refer to production using capital as *roundabout* production. Many other examples could be given. Making cars in an automated factory uses more capital than making them one by one using hand tools. A great quantity of labor and other resources has to go into building the factory before cars start to come off the line, but when they do, more of them are produced at a lower cost per unit. Digging a ditch to lead water to a field is a roundabout method of irrigation compared with carrying water to the field in buckets. Writing a specialized computer program to calculate a company's payroll is a roundabout method compared with working out the numbers each week on a pocket calculator, but the time taken to write the program pays off in time saved later.

The Rate of Return on Capital

Rate of return on capital

The marginal product of capital expressed as an annual percentage rate.

The use of capital as a productive input can be analyzed using a variant on the marginal product technique employed in the preceding chapter. Because capital created today is typically employed over a long period in the future, its marginal product of capital is commonly expressed as a percentage—the **rate of return on capital**. For example, if we say that the rate of return on capital in a certain application is 10 percent per year, this means that adding one dollar to the capital stock will increase output by about $.10 each year in the future. The law of diminishing returns acts to reduce the marginal physical product of capital. Consequently, the demand curve for capital, like the demand curves for other resources, has a negative slope.

The supply curve of capital, on the other hand, can be analyzed in terms of the principle of diminishing marginal utility. To acquire more capital, more present goods must be forgone, raising the marginal utility of the increasingly scarce present goods that remain. At the same time, acquiring more capital makes future goods more abundant, so their marginal utility falls. Thus, the marginal resource cost, or opportunity cost, of capital—the ratio of the marginal utility of present goods forgone to the marginal utility of future goods gained—rises as the quantity of capital invested increases. (In the fishing example, spending more hours on net building means catching fewer fish today. As a result, the increasingly hungry net builder becomes more and more reluctant to make an additional present sacrifice in return for an even larger feast tomorrow.) The rising marginal opportunity cost of capital gives rise to a positively sloped supply curve.

Time Preference

Time preference

The tendency to prefer goods now over goods in the future, other things being equal.

Other things being equal, people prefer goods now to goods in the future. This tendency is referred to as **time preference**. Time preference is revealed in a thousand familiar aspects of human behavior. Young children "can't wait" to open their birthday presents; without time preference, they would attach no more utility to a new bicycle today than to a new bicycle next week. Similarly, teenagers "can't wait" to get a driver's license, grandparents "can't wait" for their first chance to hold their new grandchild, and so on.

But time preference has its limits, because "other things" are not equal. Although we do not want to postpone something now to get something equally good later, we may be persuaded to postpone something good now to get something even better later. Suppose that in our fishing example, a person would be willing to forgo having 10 fish today in order to have 11 fish tomorrow. The *rate of time preference,* expressed in percentage terms per unit of time, would then be 10 percent per day.

If time preference and the marginal productivity of capital are both expressed in percentage terms, a simple relationship emerges: In an equilibrium state in which the optimal quantity of capital is employed, the rate of return on capital and the rate of time preference will be equal.

Interest and the Market for Loanable Funds

Up to this point, the discussion has proceeded entirely in terms of physical units. Our next step—which takes us from the world of an imaginary fisher to that of Wall Street—is to introduce money. Money is a means of payment for goods and services; it is also a store of value that can be used to buy things either now or later. It makes possible another class of transactions involving time: borrowing and lending.

Consider two individuals, A and B. A finds it advantageous to borrow from B whenever A's rate of time preference is higher than B's. The terms of the loan will be mutually beneficial at any interest rate that is higher than B's rate of time preference and lower than A's. Rates of time preference differ in such a way that loans are mutually advantageous for many reasons. Consider some examples:

- One person may simply be more impatient than another. Bill is so eager to go skiing this year that he is willing to borrow the funds, at interest, from Jane.

Jane thinks the interest she will earn is a sufficient inducement to put off skiing until next year.

- People may borrow and lend to smooth out consumption over time. Al, who is just entering the job market, borrows to buy a car. Jose, who has already worked for several years, is saving for retirement. Jose will have even more money after he retires if he lends his savings to Al at interest.
- One person sees better opportunities to use capital than another. Jill thinks that buying a greenhouse in order to start a cut-flower business will result in a rate of return of at least 20 percent. Mike thinks investing to expand his cookie store would result in a return of only 5 percent. It would thus be advantageous for Mike to lend funds to Jill, rather than to invest in his own business, at any interest rate over 5 percent, and it would be advantageous for Jill to borrow, rather than to forgo the business opportunity, at any interest rate less than 20 percent.

Loanable funds market

A general term for the set of markets in which people borrow and lend, for whatever reason.

All the people who borrow and lend, for whatever reason, are participating in a set of markets that economists call the **loanable funds market**. That market is shown in Figure 11.1. The demand curve for loanable funds indicates that, other things being equal, people will borrow more for both investment and consumption if the interest rate is lower. The supply curve for loanable funds indicates that, other things being equal, the higher the rate of interest, the greater a person's willingness to make a loan. The equilibrium interest rate is determined by the intersection of the supply and demand curves for loanable funds.[1]

Ultimately, the equilibrium interest rate in Figure 11.1 is determined by the same forces of time preference and return on capital that were discussed in conjunction with the fishing example. Thus, in a state of equilibrium, the rate of interest on loanable funds will be the same as the equilibrium rate of return on capital and the equilibrium rate of time preference.

Discounting and Investment Decisions

The investment decisions we have used to illustrate the general principles of capital and interest are very abstract. In the real world, business managers are confronted with much more specific situations: Is it worthwhile to build a new warehouse in Tulsa? Would the saving in fuel costs repay the expense of insulating the roof of the warehouse? Should forklifts for the warehouse be bought or leased? Following is a brief look at some of the basic principles that underlie such decisions.

DISCOUNTING Making any kind of investment decision involves comparing expenditures and receipts at different points in time—that is, comparing the cost of

FIGURE 11.1 THE MARKET FOR LOANABLE FUNDS

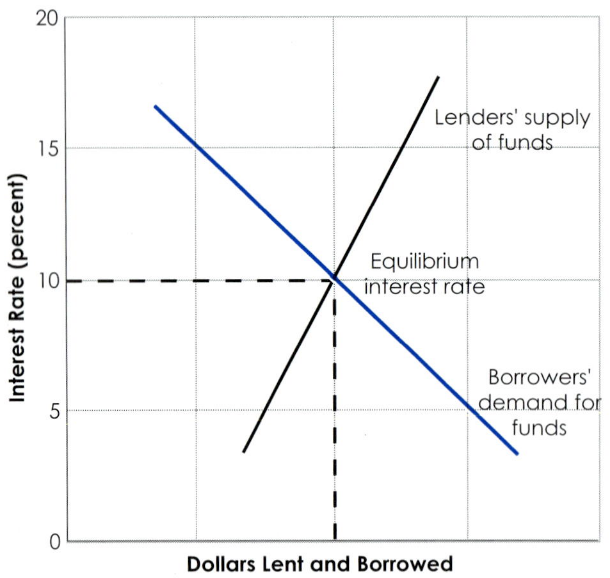

All people who borrow and lend for whatever reason are participants in the market for loanable funds. The demand curve in this market reflects that, other things being equal, people will borrow more for both investment and consumption purposes as the interest rate falls. The supply curve for loanable funds reflects that, other things being equal, people will be more willing to make loans at higher rates of interest. The equilibrium interest rate is determined by the intersection of the two curves.

acquiring an item of capital, which must be borne now, with the return from the capital, which will be received later. The first requirement, then, is a method for comparing the value of sums due at different points in time.

Begin by reflecting that if a firm puts funds to work earning interest by placing them in a bank account, making a loan, or buying a security, the original sum it invests will grow year by year. At 10 percent interest per year, $100 invested today will be worth $110 a year from now; after two years, it will be worth $121; after three years, $133.10; and so on.[2] The $11 gain in the second year reflects interest of $10 on the original principal and $1 interest on the $10 interest earned in the first year. Because interest is paid on previously earned interest, this process is termed *compound interest.*

In a world in which funds can be loaned out at compound interest, it is always advantageous to receive a payment earlier rather than later. The opportunity cost of receiving a sum later rather than sooner is the interest that could have been earned otherwise. Consider, for example, the cost of receiving $100 a year from now rather than today, assuming an interest rate of 10 percent per year. Delaying receipt of the sum would mean forgoing a year's interest. Rather than give up that interest, a firm would be just as well off receiving a smaller sum now as it would be if it received the $100 a year from now. To be precise, it would be just as good to get $91 now as $100 a year from now, because the $91 placed for a year at 10 percent would grow to $100 (give or take a few cents). Similarly, $100 payable two years from now is equivalent to about $83 today assuming 10 percent interest; $100 three years from now is worth about $75 today; and so on.

Present value

The value today of a sum payable in the future. In mathematical terms, the present value of a sum V_p, payable *t* years in the future, discounted at *r* percent interest, would grow to the value V_t in t years; the present value formula is $V_p = V_t/(1 + r)\ t$.

Discounting

The procedure by which the present value of a sum that is payable in the future is calculated.

This kind of example can be generalized to any time period and any interest rate. Let V_p be the sum of money that, if it is invested today at r percent interest, will grow to the sum V_t after t years. V_p is known as the **present value** of the sum V_t, payable t years from now, discounted at r percent per year. **Discounting** is the term for the procedure by which the present value is calculated. The formula for calculating the present value of any future sum is

$$V_p = V_t/(1 + r)^t.$$

APPLYING THE DISCOUNTING FORMULA The discounting formula can be used to determine whether a given item of capital equipment is worth purchasing, given an interest rate and the equipment's purchase price, annual return, and scrap value at the end of its useful life. An example is presented in Table 11.1. It concerns the purchase of a car by a car rental company. The purchase price is $8,000. The car can be rented for $2,000 a year, net of maintenance expenses, for four years. At the end of that time, it will be worth $4,000 in the used-car market. For the sake of simplicity, each year's cash flow is treated as though it takes place on the last day of the year.

Is it worth buying the car? An unsophisticated approach to the question would be to simply add up the lease income from the car plus its resale value, and compare that sum with the car's price. Four years' lease income at $2,000 plus the $4,000 resale value comes to $12,000, compared with the purchase price of $8,000. But before deciding whether the car is worth buying, the firm must discount the various sums to determine their present values.

The required calculations are shown in Table 11.1, assuming first a 10 percent interest rate and then an 18 percent rate. Discounted at 10 percent, the value of the first year's lease income is $1,820 ($2,000 ×.91), the value of the second year's lease income is $1,660, and so on. The $4,000 resale value, which is assumed to be realized at the end of the fourth year, has a present value of $2,720 ($4,000 × .68). Thus, the sum of the present value of all payments that the firm will receive from the car is $9,060, assuming a 10 percent interest rate. This is considerably less than the $12,000 undiscounted sum, but $9,060 still compares favorably with the $8,000 purchase price. If funds for buying the car can be obtained at an interest cost of 10 percent, the firm should add the car to its rental fleet.

Turning to part (b) of Table 11.1, we see the effect of a change in the interest rate from 10 percent to 18 percent. At the higher interest rate, the present value of each

TABLE 11.1 DISCOUNTING AND INVESTMENT DECISION MAKING

(a)
10 Percent Interest Rate

Year	Outlay (–) or Income	Discount Factor	Discounted Outlay (–) or Income
0	–8,000	1.00	–8,000
1	2,000	.91	1,820
2	2,000	.83	1,660
3	2,000	.75	1,500
4	6,000	.68	4,080
	Sum of discounted net cash flows:		$1,060

(b)
18 Percent Interest Rate

Year	Outlay (–) or Income	Discount Factor	Discounted Outlay (–) or Income
0	–8,000	1.00	–8,000
1	2,000	.85	1,700
2	2,000	.72	1,440
3	2,000	.61	1,220
4	6,000	.52	3,120
	Sum of discounted net cash flows:		$–520

These tables illustrate how a car rental agency might evaluate the advisability of purchasing a new car for its fleet. The car is assumed to cost $8,000 initially and to bring in $2,000 a year in lease income for four years. (For simplicity, all the income is assumed to arrive on the last day of each year.) At the end of the fourth year, the car can be sold for $4,000. It will be profitable to buy the car so long as the discounted value of the lease income plus the discounted used-car value exceed the purchase price. As the numbers show, this is the case when the prevailing interest rate is 10 percent but not when it is 18 percent.

future payment is less than it is when discounted at the lower interest rate. This time the sum of the discounted future payments comes to only $7,480, which is less than the purchase price of the car. Thus, at an 18 percent interest rate it will not be worthwhile for the firm to add the car to its fleet.

OTHER APPLICATIONS The preceding example, which concerned the evaluation of investment opportunities by a business, is just one among many applications of the discounting principle. Later in the chapter, we will apply the principle to a rather different problem, conservation of nonrenewable natural resources. Many applications of discounting are found in finance, including methods for valuing securities and calculating insurance premiums. Discounting has even attracted the attention of researchers working in the border area between economics and psychology. *Applying Economic Ideas 11.1* discusses a number of paradoxes related to the way people apply the discounting principle to their daily lives. In short, the concept of discounting is essential to any economic decision involving time, whether it is a matter of high finance or a matter of opening one's birthday presents in the morning rather than after dinner.

APPLYING ECONOMIC IDEAS 11.1
DISCOUNTING IN EVERYDAY LIFE: SOME ANOMALIES

The concept of discounting is central to the way economists formulate problems of rational choice that involve trade-offs between costs and benefits that belong to different time periods. For business decisions, such as whether to borrow at a certain interest rate in order to make an investment yielding a known rate of return, the discounting approach provides a precise solution to the problem of profit maximization: It is worthwhile to borrow if the rate of interest is less than the rate of return on the investment to which the borrowed funds are devoted.

Transferring the same reasoning to the problem of consumer choice, economists often argued that in order to maximize utility over time, people should discount future pleasures and pains at a uniform rate of time preference, which, in equilibrium, should equal the rate of interest applicable to personal borrowing and lending. However, empirical research into the psychology of consumer choice casts doubt on the simple model. In practice, rather than discounting all future pleasures and pains at a uniform rate of time preference, people often apply very different rates of discount to different kinds of future events. For example:

- People tend to have higher rates of time preference over the immediate future than over the more distant future. In a typical experiment, people might be told that they had won $1,000 in a lottery. They would have to wait if they wanted to receive the full amount of the prize, but they could receive the prize sooner if they would accept a reduced amount. If asked whether they would accept $900 now rather than $1,000 a month from now, many people would do so. But given the choice of receiving $900 after twelve months, or instead, the full $1,000 after thirteen months, many of the same people would be willing to wait the extra month for the full amount.
- People tend to display higher rates of time preference when small gains or losses are involved than when large gains or losses are involved. For example, in the case of a lottery, a person might prefer to receive $5 now rather than wait a year for a prize of $10. But the same person might willingly wait a year to receive $10,000 rather than receive $5,000 now.
- People tend to apply higher rates of time preference to rewards than to penalties. For example, a person might not be willing to wait a year to receive a lottery prize unless the amount of the prize were raised from $100 to at least $150. But the same person might be willing to pay a $100 parking fine today if told that the fine would be raised to $125 if payment were delayed by a year.
- People treat nonmonetary rewards and penalties differently than monetary rewards and penalties. They generally prefer to receive monetary rewards sooner and to put off monetary penalties, other things being equal. Sometimes, however, people prefer to delay nonmonetary rewards, as if to savor them. In one experiment, people preferred to delay a free meal in a French restaurant for two weeks rather than take it right away. People also sometimes prefer to suffer nonmonetary penalties immediately rather than to wait in dread of them. Thus, in another experiment, people preferred to suffer a mild electric shock immediately rather than to put it off for three days.

Do experimental results such as these mean that people are irrational? Inconsistent? Or just more complicated than simple economic models make them out to be? You be the judge after thinking about the choices you would make in situations such as those described here.

Source: Based on a variety of experimental results reported in George Loewenstein and Richard H. Thaler, "Intertemporal Choice," *Journal of Economic Perspectives* (Fall 1989): 181–193.

MARKETS FOR NATURAL RESOURCES

We turn now from markets for capital to markets for natural resources. A key natural resource is land—the sites where economic activity takes place. The land that EVTAC uses for its taconite plant is an example. Not all land is alike. Location and physical attributes, such as elevation and climate, make any individual piece of land more suitable for some activities than for others. Some land can be used to grow corn; some is suitable for building houses; still other land is best preserved for its natural beauty.

In the first part of this section, we will focus on the permanent characteristics of land—those that, at least under proper management, are inexhaustible. The discussion will then turn to the special problems posed by nonrenewable natural resources. Oil, natural gas, and metal ores provide familiar examples.

Pure Economic Rent

Economic rent is any income to a factor of production that is greater than its opportunity cost. The theory of rent goes back to the days of the classical economists two centuries ago.

The classical economists thought of land in terms of the natural productive powers of the earth and the locational advantages of particular sites. They considered the supply of land, in this sense, to be perfectly inelastic. No matter how high its rental price, the amount of land is fixed, and no matter how low the price, the land is always there.[3] The income earned by a factor of production whose supply is perfectly inelastic in the long run is referred to as **pure economic rent**. We do not consider artificial improvements to land or reclamation of land—say, by means of drainage—to be part of the supply of land. Instead, such improvements count as capital. To the extent that they raise the lease price of a parcel of land, the added income counts as return on the capital invested, not as rent.

Pure economic rent

The income earned by any resource whose supply is perfectly inelastic with respect to its price.

Capitalized value of a rent

The present value of all future rents that a piece of land or other resource is expected to earn.

The market price paid for land can be expressed either in terms of an annual rental payment, or in terms of its purchase price, when land is bought outright by the user rather than rented. There is a relationship between the value of a piece of land expressed as an annual rent and the price at which that parcel can be sold in the market. The market price of a piece of land is said to be the **capitalized value of a rent**—the present value of all future rents the land is expected to earn.

The relationship among the market price of a piece of land, its annual rent, and the market rate of interest is determined by the discounting formula given in the preceding section. However, in the case of land, the stream of rental income continues into the indefinite future, because the land (as distinct from improvements to it) does not have a finite life. Suppose a given piece of land has an expected annual rental income of R, based on its marginal revenue product. When the discounting formula is applied over an infinite time horizon assuming an interest rate r, the result can be given by the formula R/r. Thus, a piece of land that is expected to produce, say, $5,000 a year rental income for the indefinite future has a capitalized value of $50,000 assuming a 10 percent interest rate, a capitalized value of $100,000 assuming a 5 percent rate, and so on. The formula makes it clear that there are two possible sources of a change in the equilibrium purchase price of a piece of land. One is a change in the land's marginal revenue product or expected rental income. The other is a change in the interest rate according to which the rental income is capitalized.

Differential Rent

The theory of pure economic rent is concerned with land as an abstraction. It implicitly assumes that all land is alike and that it is interchangeable in all uses. In practice, of course, this is far from the case. Land differs in terms of its fertility, its climate, and its locational advantages. It is not all equally suitable for all uses. Land in Kansas has a comparative advantage in producing wheat, land in Cuba for producing sugar cane, and land in France's Rhone valley for growing wine grapes. For that reason, as economists since David Ricardo have recognized, not all land earns the same rent in a competitive market.

Consider Figure 11.2, which shows the marginal cost and average total cost of producing wheat on three different farms with different qualities of land. The costs include all outlays for labor, machinery, fertilizer, and other inputs except the land itself. At a market price of $5 per bushel, farm A will produce 1,200 bushels per year, farm B will produce 1,000 bushels per year, and farm C will not find it worthwhile to grow wheat at all.

Given that market price and those outputs, farm A receives total revenue of $5 per bushel and incurs average total costs of $3 per bushel. The $2 excess of revenue over cost is associated with the superior productivity of the land on farm A. It is a special example of rent that is called **differential rent**.

Differential rent

The rents earned by superior units of a resource in a situation in which units of a resource differ in productivity.

At a market price of $5 a bushel for wheat, farm B just breaks even on its total costs, and earns no differential rent. But what if the market price were to rise to $7 per bushel? In that case, farm C would find it worthwhile to enter the market. Farm B would step up its output to 1,200 bushels per year and earn a differential rent equal to a little under $2 per bushel. And farm A would increase its output to 1,400 bushels, causing its differential rent to rise to $3.50 per bushel.

Differential rents are not unique to land as a factor of production. They can arise in the case of any input that is not homogeneous. Examples can be found in markets for many specialized kinds of labor. For example, in the preceding chapter, the fact that lawyers earn more on the average than truck drivers was attributed to their greater investment in human capital. But strictly speaking, that applies only to the earnings of a lawyer without special aptitudes. Some lawyers have not only the needed education but also a special ability to bewitch jurors and charm judges. Those lawyers earn differential rents over and above the opportunity costs of acquiring their education.

FIGURE 11.2 DIFFERENTIAL RENT

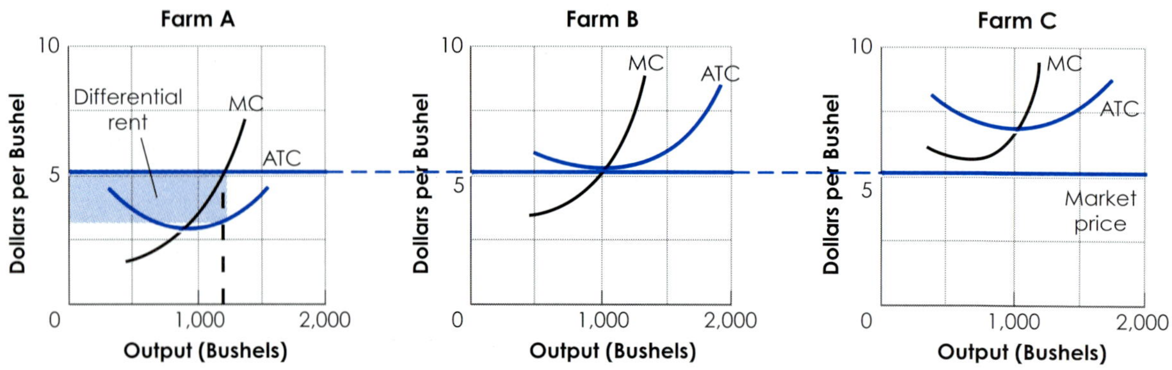

The theory of pure economic rent implicitly assumes that all land is alike. In practice, different pieces of land have different degrees of productivity in various uses. Those differences will affect the rent earned in a particular use. This figure shows marginal and average total cost curves for three wheat farms that differ only in terms of the quality of their land. Given a market price of $5 a bushel for wheat, farm A earns a *differential rent* of $2 per bushel, equal to the difference between the cost of production on its highly productive land and the market rental on land. Farm B just breaks even at $5 per bushel and earns no economic rent, and farm C does not produce at that price. If the price rose to $7, farm C would enter the market, farm B would begin to earn a differential rent, and farm A would earn an even larger differential rent.

Inframarginal Rents

Differential rents arise in markets in which some units of a resource are more productive than others. Another kind of rent can arise in markets in which units are equally productive but differ in terms of the willingness with which they are supplied.

Consider Figure 11.3, which shows hypothetical supply and demand curves for the market for nurses. For the sake of discussion, it is assumed that all nurses, once they have the needed training, are equally productive. However, not everyone is equally willing to be a nurse. In the figure, the first few people would be willing to enter the profession at a wage rate as low as $5 per hour. An increase to $7.50 per hour would attract 500,000 people to the profession, and further increases would draw in even more, as is shown by the supply curve. Given the demand curve, the equilibrium wage rate is $10 per hour, enough to attract 1 million people to the profession.

Why is it that some people are willing to enter the nursing profession at a lower wage than others are? Like other economic choices, a worker's decision regarding whether to enter the nursing profession depends on *objectives* and *constraints* as follows:

1. In part, people who are willing to enter the nursing profession at a relatively low wage rate value the work itself positively. They find that nursing suits

their preferences in terms of flexible hours, opportunities to serve people in need, and so on. A higher wage rate is needed to attract people who dislike the nonwage characteristics of nursing.

2. In part, those who are willing to enter the nursing profession at a low wage do so because of the constraints they face elsewhere in the job market. The better a person's job opportunities in other professions, other things being equal, the higher the wage required to draw the person into nursing.

Inframarginal rents

The difference between the payment made to a unit of resource and the minimum required for that resource to be willingly supplied in a situation in which units of a resource differ in terms of the willingness with which they are supplied.

Whether it is looked at from the viewpoint of objectives or constraints, or both together, the positive slope of the supply curve for labor in a particular profession can be understood as reflecting the differing opportunity costs faced by different workers. In a competitive labor market equilibrium, then, where all workers receive the same wage, all but the marginal worker—the one who is just barely attracted to the profession at the equilibrium wage rate—are paid a wage that is higher than their opportunity costs. In economic terminology, they earn **inframarginal rents** equal to the difference between the equilibrium wage and the minimum they would accept rather than pursue other opportunities.

FIGURE 11.3 INFRAMARGINAL RENT

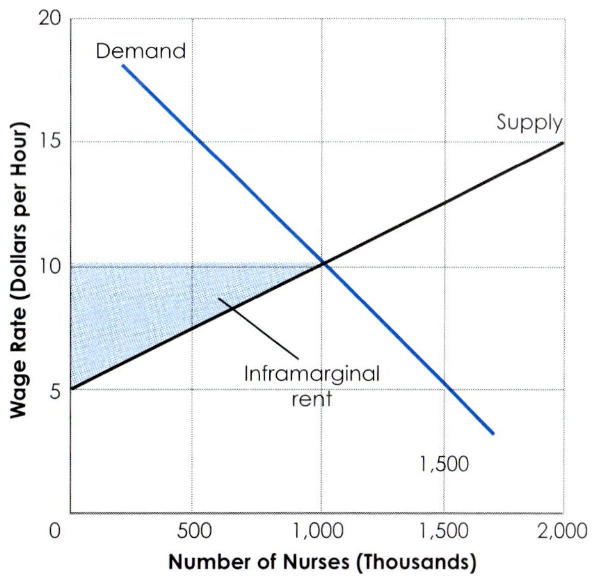

In some markets, units of a resource are equally productive but differ in terms of the willingness with which they are supplied. This figure shows supply and demand curves for nurses. Some people would be willing to work as a nurse for as little as $5 per hour. As the supply curve shows, increasingly higher wage rates must be offered to draw more people into the market. At the equilibrium wage rate of $10 per hour, only the marginal nurse is paid just the wage needed to work in this market. The others earn an *inframarginal rent* equal to the difference between the equilibrium wage and the minimum they would accept rather than pursue other alternatives.

THE ECONOMICS OF NONRENEWABLE RESOURCES

Up to this point, our discussion of natural-resource economics has been confined to the inexhaustible properties of land: location, natural fertility, climate, and so on. However, many natural resources are nonrenewable. An oil field is not like a cornfield. Properly managed, the cornfield can produce forever. But no matter what techniques are used to extract the contents of an oil field, the rate of flow will eventually diminish as the finite quantity of oil in the reservoir is depleted.

The Element of Time

Owners of nonrenewable natural resources, like owners of inexhaustible resources, earn rents. The rent earned by the owner of, say, a taconite mine is the difference between what can be earned from sale of the iron ore, after deducting operating costs, and the opportunity cost of not devoting the site to its best alternative use. When there are differences in the quality of nonrenewable resources or in the costs of extracting them at various sites, owners of superior resources will receive higher differential rents. When stone quarries, oil wells, taconite mines, and the like are sold, the sale price reflects the rents that these resources are capable of generating.

There is one major difference between inexhaustible and nonrenewable resources, however. The owner of an inexhaustible resource—say, a piece of land that is valuable because it offers a spectacular mountain view—incurs no opportunity cost in terms of reduced future value if the view is looked at today. With a nonrenewable resource, the situation is different. The owner faces a constraint on the total quantity available for use over time; what is used today cannot be used tomorrow.

Because of this constraint, the theory of nonrenewable resources, like the theory of capital, focuses on trade-offs between the present and the future. As we saw earlier in the chapter, investment means diverting resources from present consumption in order to obtain greater production (and, hence, potentially greater consumption) in the future. With a nonrenewable resource, there is a similar trade-off: The resource can be used now to produce benefits in the form of increased consumption or investment, or it can be conserved, thereby being made available to produce future benefits.

Both immediate use and conservation have advantages, as follows:

- Immediate use for consumption has the advantage that, because of time preference, present consumption is valued more highly than consumption in the future, other things being equal.
- Immediate use for investment has the advantage of permitting a more rapid increase of capital, which will permit greater production of goods and services in the future, other things being equal.
- Conservation, however, has the offsetting advantage that opportunities for use of the nonrenewable resource may arise in the future that are more

valuable than those available today. In fact, as the resource is used up and becomes scarcer, it is virtually guaranteed that the value future users place on a marginal unit of the resource will rise.

The optimal use of a nonrenewable resource, then, is a matter of balancing the conflicting advantages of immediate use and conservation subject to the constraints that what is used now cannot be used later and what is conserved cannot be used now.

Allocation over Time in a Competitive Market

In a competitive market, the allocation of nonrenewable resources over time is determined by individual resource owners, who make their decisions in response to market prices. Consider the allocation of, say, natural gas. To begin, we will assume a perfectly competitive market, a known quantity of the resource, and zero cost of extraction.

Under these idealized conditions, the owners need not worry about exploration or production technique. Their only decision is whether to extract the gas and sell it now or conserve all or part of it for the future. If the owners are motivated by material self-interest, they can be expected to make the choice that will maximize their total wealth. Keeping the gas in the ground means holding that wealth in the form of a reserve of energy that can be expected to increase in value as scarcity increases the price of gas over time. Extracting the gas and selling it today allows owners to accumulate wealth in the form of capital—production equipment, buildings, and so on. They can make these investments directly, or they can buy corporate stocks or other securities that represent shares in capital investments made elsewhere in the economy.

It follows that the decision of when to sell the gas depends on a comparison of the rate of return on capital with the rate at which the price of gas is expected to increase. Suppose, for example, that the rate of return on capital is 10 percent per year, the price of gas today is $3 per thousand cubic feet (tcf), and the price is expected to rise by 5 percent each year. Selling 1,000 tcf of gas at today's price and investing the proceeds elsewhere at 10 percent will leave the owner of the gas well with $3,300 at the end of a year. On the other hand, leaving the same 1,000 tcf of gas in the ground and selling it a year later at a 5 percent higher price, $3.15 per tcf, will yield a sum of $3,150. Under these assumed conditions, then, owners will be better off if they sell their gas today.

However, there is a limit to how much gas will be sold currently, because today's sales of gas tend to change the conditions that were initially assumed to prevail. For one thing, greater quantities of gas brought to market today will tend to depress the current price below the assumed $3.00 per tcf. In addition, extracting more gas today means that the quantity of gas available in the future will be that much smaller. The smaller future quantity will tend to cause the expected future price to be higher than the $3.15 that was initially assumed. As the current price falls and the expected future price rises, the expected difference between next year's price and this year's also rises. As soon as the expected rate of price increase (which is the return to a person who buys gas and holds it for later sale) becomes equal to the rate of return on the most attractive alternative use of capital, it will cease to be profitable to sell the gas today. Owners who have not yet sold their gas will find it advantageous to conserve their holdings for the future in order to take advantage of the higher expected future price.

In short, when a resource exists in a known, fixed quantity, and the cost of extraction is negligible, a competitive market will allocate that resource over time in a predictable way: The equilibrium market price of the nonrenewable resource will rise over time at a rate equal to the rate of return on capital in the economy as a whole, and as the price rises, other things being equal, the rate of use will fall. If the stated conditions do not hold—if new reserves of the resource can be discovered by investing in exploration or if the cost of extraction is high, the price may rise over time at a rate less than the rate of return on capital. Thus, the preceding argument puts a ceiling on the rate at which the price of a nonrenewable resource will increase and the rate at which it will be used up.

Is Market-Guided Conservation Optimal?

The economics of nonrenewable resources shows that markets contain a built-in conservation mechanism: If the current rate of use exceeds a certain limit, dwindling reserves will create an expectation of higher future prices. The expected higher prices, in turn, provide an incentive for resource owners to invest in conservation rather than sell now and invest the proceeds elsewhere. In that way, the profit motive in a competitive market acts to transform expectations of future scarcity into concrete actions promoting conservation.

Nevertheless, people who are concerned about the welfare of future generations often express distrust of the market mechanism. Are we not, they say, being too greedy at the expense of others not yet born? Even given the market's built-in conservation mechanism, might it not be wise to be still more conservative? Admittedly, such a policy would make our own generation a bit worse off, but should we not make that sacrifice for the benefit of our grandchildren, and our grandchildren's grandchildren?

The question of the present generation's obligation toward the future raises profound ethical questions. Previous generations toiled in mines, fields, and factories, enduring great hardships to accumulate the stock of capital and human knowledge on which our own comparative prosperity depends. Many people today believe that we should do no less for our own descendants. But it is not necessary to resolve all the ethical issues of income distribution among generations in order to answer the narrower question of how rapidly nonrenewable resources should be used up. The reason is that conservation of nonrenewable resources is not purely a question of how much wealth should be left to future generations. It also encompasses the question of the form that wealth should take.

Basically, there are two tangible forms in which wealth may be left to future generations. One form is capital—equipment, structures, highways, the accumulated results of research, and so on. The rate of capital accumulation can be increased very considerably, if people are willing to abstain from present consumption. The other form in which wealth can be left to future generations is in the form of natural resources. Natural resources cannot be created, but they can be conserved. And conservation, like capital accumulation, requires that we abstain from present consumption.

Suppose, then, that the decision has been made to place a certain limit on present consumption in order to leave X amount of wealth to future generations. In what form should that wealth be left? Should we leave the wealth in the ground as coal, iron ore, and natural gas? Or should we extract some of the coal, iron ore, and gas and convert these resources into houses and bridges? Surely, once it has been decided how much wealth to pass along to future generations, it makes sense to adjust the mix of forms in which that wealth is passed on so as to minimize the present sacrifice.

Once the matter is put that way, it becomes possible to determine, at least in principle, the optimum degree of conservation of nonrenewable resources. A dollar's worth of nonrenewable resources should be extracted today and invested in capital goods if and only if the future value of production resulting from the increase in capital is greater than the future value of the resources in their natural state. In other words, future generations will be better off with the given amount of capital rather than the given amount of natural resources as long as the rate of return on capital exceeds the percentage rate of increase in the value of the resources. As we saw earlier, a competitive market operates in such a way as to ensure that this rule will not be violated, given the best available knowledge of what the future will be like. Any decision to conserve more than the market-determined quantity of natural resources at the expense of capital accumulation will make future generations worse off, not better off.

But, say conservationists, what if the owners of natural resources are mistaken? What if they underestimate the future value of natural resources? In that case, we are all in for an unpleasant future surprise.

Economists answer that this is certainly possible. Resource owners are human and can make mistakes. However, even in this case, the market provides incentives that can lead to improved resource allocation over time. If the conservationists are confident that they have better information about the future value of natural resources than do the current owners of those resources, they can take advantage of market institutions to implement their convictions. Specifically, they can begin buying controlling interest in resource companies and use their control to slow the current rate of depletion. Where will they get the funds to do so? They should not have to rely on charitable contributions. If their information about future scarcities is convincing, they should be able to persuade commercial lenders to advance the funds they need for their conservation investments. Over time, the increase in the value of the conserved resources will be more than adequate to pay interest on the loans. That, at any rate, is the logic of the market.

SUMMARY

1. **How do markets determine the rate of return on capital?** The use of capital as a productive resource involves a trade-off between the present and the future. Reducing consumption now makes possible the accumulation of capital, which will increase output in the future. The marginal product of capital, expressed in percentage terms per unit of time, is called the *rate of return on capital.* In a market economy, capital accumulation tends toward an equilibrium rate at which the rate of return on capital just offsets the *time preference*—the tendency to prefer goods now over goods in the future, other things being equal. People differ in terms of their time preference and the investment opportunities they perceive. Their differing preferences and perceptions are accommodated through borrowing and lending in *loanable funds markets.* The equilibrium rate of interest in loanable funds markets tends toward equality with the rate of return on capital and the rate of time preference.

2. **How can payments made at different points in time be compared?** Payments made at different points in time are compared using the process known as *discounting.* The discounting formula is $V_p = V_t/(1 + r)^t$, where V_p is the *present value* of the sum V_t, payable t years in the future and discounted at an annual interest rate of r.

3. **How do supply and demand determine rents for land?** *Pure economic rent* is the income earned by any factor of production whose supply is completely inelastic. Land is the classic example of a factor that earns a pure economic rent. The *capitalized value of a rent* determines the market price of land. Rent can also be said to be earned by other factors whose supply is perfectly inelastic, such as the special talents of athletes or performing artists. Other kinds of rent are possible in markets in which land or other resources are not subject to perfectly inelastic supply. Where various units of a factor differ in terms of productivity, the more productive units are said to earn *differential rents.* Where they differ in terms of the willingness with which they are supplied, those that would be supplied willingly at prices below the equilibrium price are said to earn *inframarginal rents.*

4. **How do markets allocate nonrenewable natural resources?** The allocation of nonrenewable resources is subject to the constraint that what is used today cannot be conserved for use in the future. The use of nonrenewable resources, like the use of capital, therefore involves a trade-off

between the present and the future. In a competitive market, it will be profitable to shift resources from present to future use if the expected rate of price increase exceeds the rate of return on capital. For that reason, the market can be said to include a built-in conservation mechanism.

KEY TERMS

Rate of return on capital	Pure economic rent
Time preference	Capitalized value of a rent
Loanable funds market	Differential rent
Present value	Inframarginal rents
Discounting	

PROBLEMS AND TOPICS FOR DISCUSSION

1. **Examining the lead-off case.** United Taconite's Iron Range taconite plant is not the only source of iron in the United States, but it produces a specific low-grade iron ore. How would the price Cleveland-Cliffs Inc. and Laiwu Steel Group paid for the Iron Range plant in 2003 be related to the value of the rent the mine could potentially earn? How would the price have been affected by the demand for iron ore products at the time of the sale, and how would it have been affected by the demand for such products expected in the future? What would you expect to happen to the price of iron ore over time as the United Taconite's mine is gradually depleted?

2. **Two ways to make bricks.** Suppose that there are two ways to make bricks. One is to form them by hand out of clay scooped from the ground and then bake them over an open fire. Using that method, you can make 100 bricks a month. Another way is to use a whole month's output of bricks to build a kiln in which bricks can be baked. When the kiln is complete, the hotter fire and lower fuel consumption make it possible to make 120 bricks per month with the same labor that was previously used to make 100. Is the kiln an example of capital? Why or why not? If so, what is the rate of return on the investment in the kiln, stated as a percentage per month? Under what circumstances of time preference would it be worth your while to build the kiln?

3. **Capitalized value of an asset.** Suppose you own a professional basketball team. You are negotiating for the services of a certain college basketball star who will soon begin a career as a professional player. You figure that having this player on your team will bring in $1,000,000 a year in added income from ticket sales for five years. After that the player may slow down a bit, but having him on the team will continue to bring in $500,000 in added ticket sales for another ten years. How much will you be willing to pay (in a single, one-time payment) to get the player for your team if the market interest rate is 12 percent per year?

4. **Housing prices and commuting time.** Anyone who has ever lived in or near a large city knows that, other things being equal, the price of a house is inversely related to the length of the commute from the house to the central business district. In the Virginia suburbs of Washington, D.C., for example, a simple three-bedroom house could sell for $700,000 if it were located within walking distance of the Metro in Arlington, fifteen minutes from downtown. Half an hour out, in Fairfax, the same house might go for $550,000. An hour out, in Leesburg, the identical house might go for under $400,000. Assume that the cost of constructing the house is the same in all three locations. Using concepts discussed in this chapter, explain the observed relationship between location and price.

5. **Inframarginal rents and surpluses.** In what ways does the concept of inframarginal rent resemble the concept of consumer surplus? In what ways does inframarginal rent resemble producer surplus? Do you think the area under the demand curve and above the equilibrium price in Figure 11.3 can be considered a "surplus"? If so, what kind of surplus is it?

6. **Snowed in.** Imagine that you are snowed in for the winter in a small cabin in the mountains. Your food supply consists of a sack of potatoes. There are more than enough potatoes to survive on, but less than enough to allow you to eat your fill every day. How will you allocate the potatoes over the winter? Will you eat an equal amount every day? Will you eat more per day at first and gradually taper off to a bare subsistence ration? Will you eat fewer at first and then more toward the end? Explain the logic of your decision in terms of concepts introduced in this chapter.

CASE FOR DISCUSSION

The New Energy Source: Renewable Wind Power

EAST WENATCHEE, Wash.—Mike Sachs lacks the rusted tin pans of a mineral prospector in the Old West.

But the third generation cattleman in north-central Washington is a prospector in his own right —one of a growing number of ranchers hoping to strike gold with the hottest new resource in the Northwest: wind.

"You're trying to find ways to diversify," Sachs said. "Monetarily, you're usually asset rich and cash poor. But we all benefit if we can generate electricity and keep rates down." Wind energy accounts for less than 1 percent of the power generated in the United States annually. Turbines in thirty states produced 6,370 megawatts in 2003—enough power to serve more than 1 million average homes, according to the American Wind Energy Association. California leads the nation with more than 2,000 megawatts of power generated by wind, followed by Texas, Minnesota and Iowa. States in the Northwest trail far behind, but that also means many areas are largely untapped. Utilities, consultants and ranchers are taking note, scattering anemometers across the landscape to prospect for wind.

Dozens of new wind projects are proposed in Washington, Oregon, Idaho, and Montana. "We've got a lot of open space in the Northwest," said Rachel Shimshak, director of the Renewable Northwest Project, which promotes solar, wind, and geothermal energy resources in the Northwest. "Wind power has been a great benefit to rural communities and the rural economy. Never mind that it's helping to provide energy production and clean air," Shimshak said.

Renewable energy also shouldn't be foreign to a region that relies on hydropower—water—for most of its energy, she said. Some call wind energy the perfect complement to dams, because utilities could scale back on one side when the winds pick up and rely more on hydropower when the winds die down.

Wind farms don't come without their share of problems, though. They, too, require a transmission line, which is often unavailable in rural areas. Critics argue wind farms kill too many birds and disrupt wildlife habitats. Even those in the industry sometimes say the cost isn't worth the return. Wind farms require strong and sustained winds—but not too heavy—over time to be productive. Still, some of the most outspoken supporters are ranchers across the West who have been struggling to maintain their rural way of life—and stand to gain from having a wind farm on their property.

"In today's society, you've got to be really creative to make a 2,000-acre dryland wheat operation work," said Ron Lewis, a fifth-generation rancher in rural Douglas County. "I'm going into the past—I'm farming like my great-great-grandpa. I'm going to harness the wind like him, because I'm going to be really productive."

Source: Shannon Dininny, "Ranchers Use Wind to Generate Electricity," *Associated Press*, February 9, 2004.

QUESTIONS

1. On the basis of this article, what can you conclude about the current relationship between the market price of electricity from traditional nonrenewable sources and the cost of harnessing power from wind? How much rent on the wind content of electrical power is currently earned by the owner of a power company?
2. Wind power is the fastest-growing branch of renewable energy sources, such as solar power. Integration of electricity production from wind plants into the world's power systems is not so much a technical but an economic challenge. What prevents power companies from relying on wind power more than they do currently? How do you expect the costs of nonrenewable energy sources to change over time? Will this affect the decision of power companies in the future?
3. On the basis of this article and the theory of nonrenewable resources presented in the chapter, do you think the current market situation is resulting in an efficient allocation of nonrenewable energy sources over time? Why or why not?
4. Suppose you are convinced that a major new demand for electricity will arise early in the next century. You think other people are making a mistake in not recognizing the coming increase in demand. What could you do that would improve the efficiency of wind power over time and, at the same time, earn a large profit for yourself?

END NOTES

1. This account of the loanable funds market is, of course, greatly simplified. It ignores the fact that there is not just one rate of interest but a whole set of interest rates that differ according to the term of the loan and the risk of default. Nothing has been said about the role played by financial intermediaries, such as banks, that collect deposits from savers and lend the funds to borrowers. Nothing has been said about the effect on interest rates of inflation, government policy, and so on. Those details are usually considered the province of macroeconomics.
2. The value V, of $1 invested for t years at a rate of interest of r percent per year is given by the formula $V_t - (1 + r)^t$. At a rate of 10 percent interest compounded annually, the value of $1 after 1 year is $1.10; after two years the value is $(1.10)^2 - (1.10)(1.10) = \$1.21$; and so on.
3. Although the supply of land to the economy as a whole is perfectly inelastic, the same is not true of the supply of land to a particular industry. Any particular industry—say, the parking lot industry—can increase the quantity of land it uses by bidding it away from competing users. Thus, the supply curve of land to a particular use or industry will be positively sloped.

A recent study predicts that by 2009 fully one-third of all music will be delivered through modems, and the CD itself may be obsolete shortly thereafter. This isn't necessarily bad news for the record labels, but it could spell the end for brick-and-mortar stores.

"I tell retailers they need to get out of the plastic business," said Josh Bernoff, the Forrester analyst who wrote the report, titled "From Discs to Downloads." "Two-thirds of the people who currently download say that when it comes to music, it isn't important to them to hold a physical object. They're done with the CD. They just care about the songs." If that's true, the album is doomed and the industry is headed back to its roots in the '40s and '50s, when the single was the most popular format. This could be a glimpse into the future: Hear the song one minute, own it the next.

Hearing music doesn't require a physical transaction at a record store. Consider airline tickets. Thanks to ticketless travel, millions of flyers no longer think of tickets as physical objects that must be printed and brought to the airport. Not surprisingly, travel agencies have suffered. In the past three years, 30 percent of them have closed.

Does online music mean the end for Tower Records and stores like it? Bookstores were supposedly doomed by Amazon not long ago, yet there are still plenty of Borders and Barnes & Noble stores—in part because they started selling CDs—and even independent bookshops around. People like getting out of their homes and mingling more than a lot of tech experts predicted.

Furthermore, most record retailers aren't going quietly, according to Mike Dreese, who runs Newbury Comics, a music chain in Massachusetts. Many are inviting bands for in-store performances and selling other products, including comic books, posters, clothing lines, and DVDs. Larger retailers are launching their own downloadable music stores online to compete with iTunes.

"The music store of the future will have to be an arcade," says Roy Trakin, editor of *Hits* magazine, a music industry tip sheet. "A place where you can try out things, grab legal downloads, see performances."

"There will remain a place for the physical product," Ward predicts. "A good retailer can help people figure out what is new and what is recommended. But we'll offer the chance to buy anywhere people want to buy—

from the home, the office or in a store." Others are less optimistic. "The fat lady is warming up, but she's not exactly singing," says Dreese. "We're five to seven years from a complete meltdown. The only question is whether our death is in seven years or eight. Everybody's lights are out in ten."

Source: David Segal, "Requiem for the Record Store," *The Washington Post*, February 7, 2004.

THE PRECEDING CHAPTERS have discussed business firms as actors in the economy without devoting much attention to what goes on inside the firm. Sometimes this approach can be justified by Ockham's razor—the principle that a theory is stronger when unnecessary details are shaved away. But there are some issues for which knowledge of the internal workings of firms is essential. Understanding the way businesses like Tower Records and Wal-Mart respond to change, and why the response is sometimes slow, is one example. Other examples include policy toward mergers and takeovers, labor market policy, and the comparative economics of capitalism and socialism.

This chapter explores what goes on inside business firms. It begins with a brief survey of the various forms of business organizations found in the United States. The next two sections take up the questions of why firms exist at all and why they do not grow until one huge firm swallows the whole economy. The final section of the chapter deals with issues of corporate control and takeovers.

FORMS OF BUSINESS ORGANIZATION

When discussing the economic role of firms, knowledge about their legal organization is useful. Corporations, such as auto giants GM and Ford, are probably the best-known type of firm, but they are not the most common type. This section covers three major types of profit-making firms and also comments briefly on their not-for-profit cousins.

The Sole Proprietorship

Sole proprietorship

A firm that is owned, and usually operated, by one person, who receives all the profits and is responsible for all the firm's liabilities.

A **sole proprietorship** is a firm that is owned and operated by a single person who receives all of its profits and is personally responsible for all of its liabilities. Sole proprietorships are very common, but they are usually small. Proprietorships are especially common in construction and retail trade. Figure 12.1 shows that nonfarm proprietorships account for 72 percent of all firms submitting tax returns to the federal government, but for only about 5 percent of total receipts reported on those

FIGURE 12.1 FORMS OF BUSINESS ORGANIZATIONS (1998)

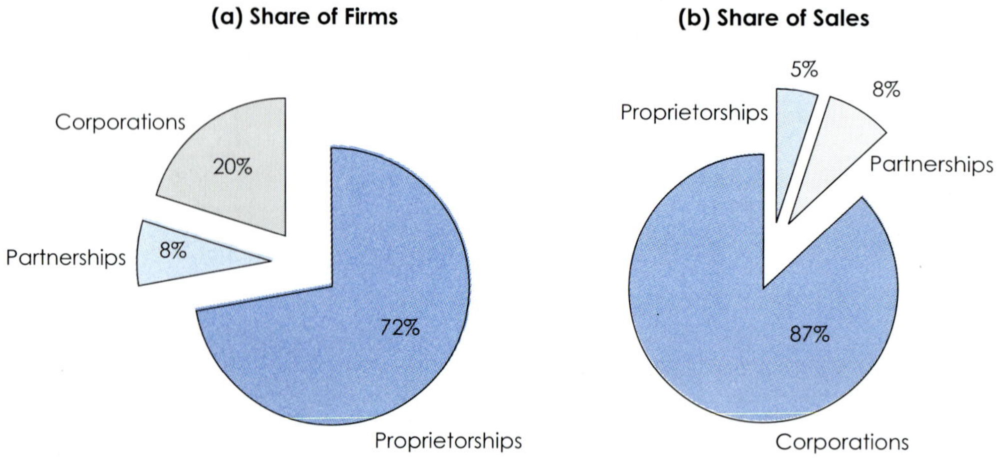

These charts show the relative proportions of corporations, partnerships, and nonfarm proprietorships among firms submitting tax returns to the federal government. Proprietorships are by far the most numerous type of firm even when, as here, farms are excluded. They are also common in retail trade and construction. However, most proprietorships are small; in terms of total receipts, they are overshadowed by corporations. The corporate sector, in turn, is dominated by a small number of firms with reported receipts of $1 million or more, some 892,000 in 1998.

Source: U.S. Department of Commerce, *Statistical Abstract of the United States:* 2001, 121st ed. (Washington, D.C.: Government Printing Office, 2001), Table 710.

returns. A great many farms are also organized as proprietorships; these are not included in data reported in the figure.

The sole proprietorship has a number of advantages that make this business form well suited to small firms. Perhaps the biggest advantage is that it is easy to start the business. Starting a proprietorship requires little more than registering the firm's name. Proprietorships are also easy to dissolve: The owner simply stops doing business, and the firm ceases to exist.

A second advantage of the proprietorship is that its owner receives all the profits (if any) directly. Income from a proprietorship is usually subject only to the personal income tax.

Finally, proprietors have the advantage of working for themselves without being accountable to employers or other owners. Many people value this independence so highly that they are willing to run their own businesses in return for lower incomes than they could earn working for someone else.

Proprietorships, however, have certain drawbacks that limit their usefulness for large ventures. One is the owner's unlimited financial liability. Just as the owner receives all the profits, he or she must bear any losses. Any liabilities that the firm incurs, such as business debts, lawsuits, or damages for breach of contract, are borne by the proprietor. Thus, a bankrupt proprietorship means a bankrupt owner.

The fact that a proprietorship cannot be separated from its owner is another drawback. In order to expand, the firm may require more capital than the owner can purchase with his or her own funds, and it is difficult for a proprietorship to tap outside sources of funds. Also, the legal life of a proprietorship comes to an end upon the death of the proprietor.

The Partnership

Partnership

An association of two or more people who operate a business as co-owners under a voluntary legal agreement.

A **partnership** is an association of two or more people who operate a business as co-owners. Partnerships are the least common of the three major forms of business organization. They account for only about 8 percent of all U.S. firms and 8 percent of all business receipts. Partnerships are most often found in professions, such as law, medicine, and accounting. In these fields state laws restrict the use of the corporate form of organization by groups of professionals. Some of these laws have been relaxed in recent years, however, and professional corporations are becoming more common.

Partnerships have some advantages over proprietorships. Forming a partnership is one way for a proprietorship to grow. Two or more partners can pool their skills and financial resources to create a firm that is larger and stronger than either could become alone. Also, partnerships sometimes have tax advantages over corporations, as we will see shortly when we discuss the way corporate income is taxed.

Offsetting these advantages are some serious drawbacks. One is the partners' unlimited liability. In terms of liability, a partner is worse off than a proprietor because he or she bears the liabilities of the entire firm. If the firm fails, a partner can lose far more than he or she put into it. A partner in a professional partnership may even be held liable for damages awarded in suits against other members of the firm.

Continuity is another serious problem for partnerships. Partnership agreements must be carefully drafted to allow the organization to survive the death of a partner. Withdrawal by a partner, or refusal of a partner to withdraw in case of irreconcilable conflicts, can also create problems.

For some purposes, such as real estate ventures, a special kind of partnership called a *limited partnership* is used to avoid the problem of unlimited liability. A limited partnership includes one or more general partners, who are in charge of running the firm and have much the same status as the co-owners of an ordinary partnership. It also includes one or more limited partners, who put in funds and share profits but whose liability can never exceed the amount they have invested. A limited partnership has many of the advantages of a corporation in terms of raising funds with which to acquire capital. At the same time, it retains the tax advantages of a partnership.

Corporation

A firm that takes the form of an independent legal entity with ownership divided into equal shares and each owner's liability limited to his or her investment in the firm.

The Corporation

The **corporation** is the third major form of business organization. A corporation is a business that is organized as an independent legal entity, with ownership divided into shares. The corporation is the dominant form of organization for large firms. Only about 20 percent of all U.S. firms are corporations, but they account for about 87 percent of all business receipts. Small corporations are also common, however; roughly one-quarter of all corporations report receipts of less than $25,000 a year.

The usefulness of the corporate form of organization for large businesses stems from two facts: (1) the corporation is a legal entity apart from its owners, and (2) the owners have limited liability.

The legal independence of the corporation makes it stable and long-lived. Stockholders can enter or leave the firm at will. Creditors and customers have only one legal entity to deal with, rather than a number of partners. Further, the firm can own property and enter into contracts in its own name rather than just in the names of its owners.

There is no practical limit to the number of stockholders in a corporation. In some, there are only a few stockholders, and they manage the corporation themselves. Other corporations have thousands or even millions of stockholders. The stockholders elect a board of directors, who in turn appoint managers to run the corporation. The stockholders and their elected directors retain ultimate control.

Limited liability means that stockholders cannot suffer a loss greater than the sum they have invested in the business. This is the stockholder's most important protection. A person can own shares in dozens of corporations without ever facing the risks that a partner or proprietor must face. Together, legal independence and limited liability make the corporation ideal for raising large sums from many small investors.

Corporations also have some disadvantages—if they did not, every firm would be a corporation. One disadvantage is the relative cost and difficulty of forming or dissolving a corporation. Although each state has its own laws in this area, forming a corporation usually requires the services of a lawyer and the payment of fees. These costs make the corporate form of organization poorly suited to many small or temporary business ventures.

Corporations also have a major tax disadvantage in that corporate income is taxed twice. When it is earned, it is subject to corporate income taxes; when it is paid out to stockholders as dividends, it is subject to the personal income tax. This double taxation can be very costly. For example, if state and federal corporate taxes take 40 percent of a firm's profit when it is earned and personal income taxes take 33 percent of the remainder when it is paid out as dividends, the firm's owners receive only $.40 of each dollar earned by the firm.

Not-for-Profit Firms

In addition to profit-seeking proprietorships, partnerships, and corporations, the private sector contains many *not-for-profit firms*. These include churches, colleges, hospitals, charities, labor unions, country clubs, and other organizations. Like profit-seeking firms, these organizations participate in markets, produce goods and services, and provide jobs.

Most not-for-profit firms have the legal form of corporations. Unlike profit-seeking corporations, however, they have no stockholders. They are run by independent boards of trustees whose members are chosen under rules set forth in the organization's bylaws. In a typical private college, for example, the trustees are elected by alumni, faculty, and sometimes students.

Some not-for-profit firms depend on donations for their income. Many also receive income from fees and sales of goods and services; examples include not-for-profit hospitals, publishers, and theater groups. If a not-for-profit firm takes in more donations and sales revenues than it spends, it is required by law to invest the surplus back into the business.

Cooperatives are closely related to not-for-profit firms. They are formed by consumers, farmers, and sometimes factory workers to run a business for their mutual benefit. Unlike not-for-profit firms, however, cooperatives may distribute any surplus they earn to their members. For example, the surplus of a co-op supermarket might be distributed to members at the end of the year on the basis of each member's total purchases during that period.

Unlike ordinary corporations, however, cooperatives do not always have profits as their main goal. Other benefits of forming a cooperative include consumers' opportunity to pool their purchasing power to buy goods at wholesale prices and farmers' opportunity to control the marketing of their crops.

FIRMS AS COORDINATORS

As was pointed out previously, there are two principal means of coordinating economic activity. The first is *spontaneous order,* in which independent agents adjust their actions in response to information and incentives from their immediate environment. Markets, in which decisions are adjusted in response to changing prices, are the leading economic example of spontaneous order. The second means of coordination is *hierarchy,* in which individual actions are guided by instructions from a central authority. The internal operation of firms, within which employees act in accordance with instructions from supervisors and managers, is a leading example of hierarchy. Units of government also operate according to the principle of hierarchy, although they are not discussed in this chapter.

More than fifty years ago, Ronald Coase wrote a pioneering article on the nature of the firm[1] (see *Who Said It? Who Did It? 12.1*). In that article he posed the following questions: If markets work so well, why do we need to use the hierarchical principle of organization even within firms? Why is all economic activity, including that of office workers and assembly line workers, not coordinated according to the principle of spontaneous order in response to market prices? Why, in short, do workers need

WHO SAID IT? WHO DID IT? 12.1
RONALD COASE: INTERPRETER OF ECONOMIC INSTITUTIONS

Economists are sometimes accused of expressing their models in such abstract mathematical or graphical forms that they lose all touch with real-world economic institutions. But not Ronald Coase. Through his own writings and his work as editor of the *Journal of Law and Economics*, Coase has fostered a lively interplay between analytic and institutional economics. In the approach that Coase favors, one selects an economic institution and asks two related questions about that institution:

1. What are the effects of this particular institution on the allocation of resources?
2. How can one account for the evolution and continued existence of the institution in terms of an analysis of its effects on resource allocation?

Coase, who was born in London, began his studies of economic institutions early in his career. His paper on the nature of the firm was published in 1937 and brought him international recognition. He came to the United States in 1951 to teach, first at the University of Buffalo, then at the University of Virginia, and finally at the University of Chicago. In 1961 his most famous paper, "The Problem of Social Cost," appeared in the *Journal of Law and Economics*. At that time the journal was new and the study of law and economics hardly existed as an independent specialty within either profession. Coase's probing analysis of the nature of the law as an economic institution sparked so much interest among both economists and lawyers that the economic analysis of law soon became an exciting field of study.

Within a little over a decade, all leading law schools had economists on their staffs and were offering courses in the new approach. In 1991, the ultimate professional recognition arrived when Coase was awarded the Nobel Memorial Prize in Economics.

bosses? On the other hand, if hierarchy is a better way of coordinating activities, why do we need markets at all? Why is the whole economy not organized as one big firm, with everyone taking orders from one central boss?

Observing that the actual economy consists of a mixture of hierarchical coordination within firms and market coordination among firms, Coase concluded that each coordinating principle must have its advantages. Markets predominate where they are the more efficient means of coordination, and firms predominate where they do the job better. In the decades since Coase's original article, many other economists have addressed the questions he raised.[2] This section and the next one outline some of their most important conclusions.

Transaction Costs

Transaction costs

The costs, other than production costs, of carrying out a transaction.

The cost of any economic task is made up of two components: production costs and **transaction costs**. Production costs were discussed in detail in a previous chapter. Transaction costs, which have not received much attention up to this point, are the costs, other than production costs, of carrying out a transaction. They include costs of identifying participants, negotiating an agreement, monitoring performance, enforcing compliance, and adapting to change.

Both production costs and transaction costs help determine how a task should be organized. If spontaneous coordination through markets minimizes the sum of production and transaction costs for a certain task, it will tend to be organized through markets. If hierarchical organization within a firm minimizes the sum of production and transaction costs, the task will tend to be organized within a firm.

Organization of Simple Transactions

For simple, repetitive transactions that involve no commitment of specialized resources, the transaction costs of market coordination tend to be low. Think of buying an apple. Finding a supermarket or a fruit stand willing to sell the apple is easy. The price, set by supply and demand in a competitive market, normally is not a matter for negotiation. Monitoring performance, enforcing compliance, and adapting to change usually are not problems either. If you are dissatisfied with the apple or the store you buy it from, you just go elsewhere for your next apple.

Conceivably, the task of buying apples could be organized hierarchically within a firm. For example, a group of consumers could form a company called Apple Eaters, Inc. The firm could buy land for an orchard, hire employees to plant and harvest the crop, and hire a dietary specialist to provide advice about various types of apples. But the transaction costs of setting up such a firm and running it would be substantial, and what would consumers really gain in return?

Costs of Complex Transactions

Not all transactions are as simple as buying apples, however. Many are complex and involve long-term commitments of specialized resources. In such cases it is not always obvious which aspects of the task should be organized through markets and which aspects should be organized through the formation of firms. Transaction costs play a major role in determining which means of coordination is used.

For example, suppose that you want to assemble a team of computer programmers to write a package of accounting software to sell to small-business customers. You estimate that the job will keep five programmers busy for two years. How will you go about organizing this task?

One way would be to work entirely through the market. You would find five freelance programmers, divide the task among them, and negotiate a separate contract with each one specifying a delivery date for each part of the work. Or instead, you could form a firm, Small Business Software, Inc. The firm would hire the five programmers and pay them salaries. You, the firm's manager, would supervise their work and coordinate their activities. When the task was completed, you would find something else for the programmers to do.

Which alternative you choose will depend in large part on transaction costs, not only those of setting up the team but also those of supervising it. The transaction costs of organizing a complex task such as assembling a team of programmers are greater than those of a simple task such as buying an apple. This is so for three reasons:

1. There is a commitment of specialized resources.
2. There must be safeguards against opportunism.
3. There must be a way of dealing with unexpected circumstances.

Let us take a closer look at each of these points.

COMMITMENT OF SPECIALIZED RESOURCES The programming project entails a commitment of specialized resources both by you and by the programmers who will work for you. The commitment takes the form of developing the special skills and knowledge needed for the project, in addition to the general skills that the programmers have before you hire them. Once you have invested in developing the special skills, it becomes costly for either you or the programmers to walk away from the agreement. If they leave your team to find other work, they cannot use the special skills elsewhere. Similarly, if you replace them, you will incur new costs to train the replacements.

Such a commitment of specialized resources is characteristic of many complex transactions. Sometimes specialized skills or human resources are involved, as in our example. In other cases specialized tools or facilities are needed. A manufacturing firm may need special dies to fill a certain customer's order. A railroad may construct a new branch line to serve a certain mine or power plant. In each case, once the commitment has been made, it is no longer costless to switch one's business to a new trading partner (unlike the case of buying apples).

Opportunism

An attempt by one party to an agreement to seek an advantage at the expense of another party to the agreement.

SAFEGUARDS AGAINST OPPORTUNISM **Opportunism** refers to any attempt by one party to an agreement to seek an advantage at the expense of the other party. Opportunism can take the form of outright cheating on the terms of the agreement, but it is not limited to cheating. Forms of opportunism that stop short of outright cheating include taking advantage of information that is available to one party but not the other; concealing one's true preferences during bargaining; selective interpretation of ambiguities in an agreement; and so on.

Any complex, ongoing transaction needs to include safeguards against opportunism. Take the case of the team of programmers. If you are paying them by the hour as employees, you need to guard against the possibility that they will loaf on the job. If you are paying them a fixed price for the job as freelancers, you need to guard against hasty work that produces a poor-quality product. If you are paying them as freelancers on the basis of the costs they incur plus a percentage for profit, you need to guard against the possibility that they will "gold plate" the product by adding expensive features that are not really necessary.

In short, whatever the details, each party to a complex agreement needs to *monitor* the other parties' fulfillment of the agreement. The costs of monitoring, which may take the form of keeping records, hiring supervisors, conducting audits, and so on, are a major transaction cost of accomplishing the task at hand.

DEALING WITH UNEXPECTED CIRCUMSTANCES UNDER BOUNDED RATIONALITY Despite one's best efforts, one can never anticipate all the circumstances that will arise as a transaction is carried out. This is so because of *bounded rationality*, which we defined previously to mean that people intend to make choices that best serve their objectives, but they have only limited ability to acquire and process information. A discussion of transaction costs must assume bounded rather than full rationality, because the costs of acquiring information, reaching decisions, and making errors are among the most important costs of this type.

Under conditions of full rationality, unexpected circumstances would never arise, because all conceivable circumstances could be taken into account at the time of the original agreement. In the case of the programming team, a fully rational agreement would spell out what was to be done in case competing products appeared on the market, in case technical glitches of various types arose, and so on. But in a world of bounded rationality people must commit themselves to complex, ongoing agreements without being able to plan for every possible contingency. They must adapt to unexpected circumstances one by one as they occur, whether those circumstances arise from omissions or mistakes in the original agreement or from external changes beyond the control of the parties.

Transaction Costs and Changing Circumstances

The three features of complex tasks that we have just listed all tend to increase the transaction costs of market coordination, especially when it becomes necessary to adapt to changing circumstances.

To begin with, once specialized resources have been committed, it becomes costly for parties to switch business partners. Unless they want to abandon the investments they have made in specialized skills or equipment, they must continue to work together. But markets can adapt to change most successfully when buyers have a choice among sellers and sellers have a choice among buyers.

In addition, the need to guard against opportunism increases the difficulty of adapting to change. If the parties could trust one another fully, they could adapt to change through a "general clause" in their initial agreement to the effect that any unexpected profits or losses will be shared among the parties in an agreed-upon ratio. But taking opportunism into account, each party will want to invest in auditing and monitoring to make sure the others are not presenting distorted information in order to gain an unfair advantage when unexpected profits or losses occur.

Finally, bounded rationality limits the extent to which the parties can agree in advance on how to handle changes. To be sure, some major possibilities can be handled by contingency clauses. For example, a contract with a computer programmer might specify what action could be taken if the programmer became unable to complete the job because of illness, or what penalty would be paid if a delivery deadline were missed.

To the extent that such contingencies can be anticipated, transaction costs are minimized by dealing with them at the time of the original contract negotiations, before the parties have locked themselves in through the commitment of specialized resources. But because of bounded rationality, it is never possible to anticipate every eventuality. When the unexpected does occur, it may prove costly to resolve disputes. For example, if a crucial deadline is missed, the parties might become embroiled in a lawsuit over who was responsible for the problem and how the resulting losses were to be borne.

The Firm as a Means of Economizing on Transaction Costs

As increasing complexity raises the transaction costs of organizing a task via the market, hierarchical organization within a firm becomes more attractive. Although forming a corporation for the simple task of buying apples might be absurd, forming one for the complex task of writing a software package might make sense. Consider the following advantages of organizing the transaction within a firm:

1. The need to commit specialized resources means that the parties will to some extent be bound to one another until the task is complete, no matter how it is organized. That being the case, formalizing the commitment by establishing a firm may reduce transaction costs rather than increase them.
2. One way or another, the issue of opportunism must be confronted. The firm provides a framework within which supervisors can be hired and record-keeping systems instituted; these will minimize the organizational friction caused by the temptation to behave in opportunistic ways.
3. Circumstances may change unexpectedly. In a relationship between independent contractors, costly disputes may arise over how to adapt to change. It is often easier to adapt to change within the context of a firm because the firm's employees agree, in return for a fixed salary, to follow the employer's instructions, whatever they might be.

Forming a firm does not eliminate transaction costs. On the contrary, a firm incurs significant costs in setting up a legal framework, hiring monitors and supervisors, and reassigning tasks among employees to meet changed circumstances. But for many complex tasks the transaction costs of hierarchical organization within a firm are lower than the corresponding transaction costs of organization through markets. That was Ronald Coase's explanation of the existence of firms fifty years ago, and, with some refinements, it remains the dominant explanation today.

LIMITS OF THE FIRM

In explaining the existence of firms as a means of economizing on transaction costs, we have answered one of Coase's questions. Next we need to explain why the entire economy is not organized as one big firm, that is, as a single enormous hierarchy. To be specific, suppose that you are the owner of Small Business Software, Inc. (SBS), a company that writes computer programs for various applications, and I am the owner of Big Business Hardware, Inc. (BBH). In the past, my company has purchased operating systems from your company. What would be gained and what would be lost by expanding the scope of operations by merging the two firms?

Gains from Expansion

It is not hard to think of possible gains. First, the merged firm would provide a stable framework within which long-term, specialized commitments could be made. Suppose, for example, that you can reduce the cost of producing your software and improve its quality by tailoring it to run only on my BBH computers, rather than making it compatible with all computers. You re-equip your firm with all-new BBH machines, train your programmers in the peculiarities of the new hardware, and so on. If our two firms dealt with each other only through the market, such a commitment would be too risky. One party might terminate the agreement, leaving the other to absorb substantial sunk costs.

Second, some aspects of the problem of opportunism would be reduced by the merger. For example, it is sometimes difficult for independent firms to negotiate a fair price for a new product. The seller tries to justify a high price by showing data that indicate a high cost of developing the product. The buyer tries to justify a low price by showing data that minimize the product's benefits. A lot of "smoke and mirrors" may go into the competing sets of data as each side maneuvers for an advantage. If the firms are merged, so that the parties become divisions of one large firm, the problem disappears. Each division's books are open to the other. Each party's knowledge of costs and benefits is fully shared with the other.

Third, it may be easier for the merged firm to adapt to unexpected changes. Suppose that BBH has to discontinue a certain model of computer because a competitor's machine has made it obsolete. SBS, Inc., is halfway through development of a new software package for the discontinued machine. If the two firms deal in the market, this unexpected development could give rise to mistrust, lawsuits, and lengthy negotiations. But if SBS and BBH are two divisions of the same firm, the firm's president simply calls in the two division managers, explains the situation, and gives each division a new assignment. Everyone continues to draw full salary, and everyone is happy.

In short, the potential gains from merging two firms into one are similar, in terms of their effects on transaction costs, to those of forming a firm in the first place.[3]

Costs of Expansion

The potential gains from merging two firms are offset by certain disadvantages. Total costs will not automatically be reduced by merging two firms with a supplier-customer relationship. This is so for several reasons.

ECONOMIES OF SCALE For one thing, an independent supplier may be able to realize economies of scale by serving a number of customers. As an independent firm, SBS could sell to a number of customers, including hardware manufacturers that compete with BBH. BBH may not have a large enough demand for programming services to keep SBS fully occupied at its optimal scale of production.

BUREAUCRATIZATION Hierarchical coordination within a firm avoids certain transaction costs of market coordination, but it creates new transaction costs of its own. For example, not everyone in a hierarchical firm needs to know the reason for a change in procedures. It is enough for some central manager to know the reasons, make a decision, and tell everyone else what to do. This is one of the reasons that a hierarchy can sometimes adapt quickly to changed circumstances. However, there is an offsetting disadvantage. Often new information first becomes available to people at the lowest operating level of the hierarchy. Before it can be used, it must be passed up the line to higher levels of management, and when a decision is made, instructions must be passed back down the line. This process is time consuming and can introduce errors.

As a hierarchy grows, the cost of transmitting information up and down the hierarchy grows and the danger of errors increases. If the organization expands by assigning more subordinates to each manager, the attention that can be devoted to each subordinate is decreased. If it grows by adding more layers of management, information must pass along a longer chain to get to the top, which means more delays and a greater possibility of error. In short, the larger the organization, the more it becomes *bureaucratized*. Whether this term is applied to a government agency or to a large corporation, the implications of sluggishness, rigidity, and error are the same.

HIGH-POWER INCENTIVES AND ENTREPRENEURSHIP Finally, when coordination of a task is taken out of the market and placed within a firm's internal hierarchy, the organization loses the advantage of **high-power incentives**—incentives that take the form of a claim to all of the pure economic profit resulting from a task, combined with bearing the full risk of any loss.

High-power incentives

Incentives that take the form of a claim to the residual profit resulting from a task, combined with bearing the risk of any loss.

For example, suppose that SBS enters into a contract with a freelance programmer. Under the terms of the contract a product is to be delivered by a specified date at a fixed price. The freelancer is subject to a high-power incentive. The fewer hours the job takes, the greater the profit it will yield. But if the job is done carelessly so that the product does not work and is rejected by the buyer, the freelancer bears the entire loss. If the freelancer becomes a salaried employee of SBS, the situation changes. The firm will provide **low-power incentives**, such as promises of promotion for good work and reprimands for errors, but the pressure to perform is significantly reduced.

Low-power incentives

Incentives that take such forms as promotion for work well done or reprimands for errors.

High-power incentives have some drawbacks. When such incentives are involved, the problem of fair distribution of unexpected profits and losses can stand in the way of adjustment to change and create additional problems of opportunism.

But high-power incentives have advantages, too. Because they discourage slacking, they reduce the costs of monitoring. Above all, high-power incentives are vital as a stimulus to entrepreneurship. Slack work habits and loss of entrepreneurial initiative can be problems for large firms.

The Paradox of Selective Intervention

The preceding section listed a number of disadvantages of excessive expansion. However, as Oliver Williamson has pointed out, problems with economies of scale, bureaucratization, and loss of high-power incentives can sometimes be overcome through *selective intervention.*[4] By this he means intervening in the decisions of a newly acquired division when it is helpful to do so, but letting the division operate independently when intervention would be harmful. In particular:

- If the parent firm does not have enough demand for the division's product to permit it to operate at an optimal scale, the division can increase its output and lower its costs per unit by selling to outsiders.
- To avoid bureaucratization, the division can make most day-to-day decisions for itself. Central managers intervene only selectively, for example, to adapt the division's operations to changes in overall corporate strategy.
- To avoid loss of high-power incentives, the division can be treated as an independent "profit center." Costs and revenues for such a division are kept in separate accounts, so that its profits can be calculated separately from the corporation as a whole. The division's managers retain a share of those profits, after paying appropriate fees for use of capital equipment owned by the parent corporation.

In practice, multidivisional firms do follow policies of selective intervention. But there is a paradox: *If selective intervention were fully possible, there would once again be no limit to the growth of firms.* A large firm could then always match the performance of a number of independent firms (if the central manager did not intervene at all), and in some respects it could do better through selective intervention.

But, says Williamson, a large multidivisional firm cannot really duplicate the performance of a collection of smaller independent firms. The reasons can be illustrated with a variation on our earlier example in which my firm, BBH, acquires your firm, SBS, with the intention of allowing it to operate as a fully independent profit center. What are the limitations of such an arrangement?

First, as manager of the SBS division, you are no longer the actual owner of the capital equipment that your division uses. Instead, the equipment is owned by the parent firm. A charge is assessed against your division by the parent firm to represent the opportunity cost of capital. This being the case, there is a subtle change in the incentives you face. What if you decide to reduce costs by using capital equipment more intensively and cutting back on maintenance? The equipment will wear out faster, but so what? It's not your equipment any more. To avoid opportunistic abuse of capital equipment, the head office will have to monitor your maintenance practices. But as soon as it does that, it has introduced new transaction costs that were not present when SBS was a truly independent firm.

Second, as manager of the SBS division, you are free to fill your order books by selling to outsiders. But what price will you charge? Your division will have some costs, such as the costs of office staff, telephones, and so on, that are hard to attribute to any given unit of output. What if you subtly shift some of the costs from your outside customers to the parent firm (for example, by undercharging the outside customers for overhead costs) in order to boost your profits on outside sales? To prevent such opportunistic abuse, the parent firm will have to monitor your dealings with outside customers. But again, doing so introduces new transaction costs.

Finally, as manager of the SBS division, you are supposed to retain high-power incentives. In particular, you are supposed to retain a strong incentive to innovate. As a fully independent firm, you could be sure of reaping the full net benefits of any innovation (and also of bearing the full risk of investment in an innovation that flops). But as a division of a large firm, your situation is different.

- Your only source of equity capital is the parent firm. If its managers do not like your idea, you cannot finance it through sales of stock to outside investors, as you could if you were independent.
- The parent firm is probably your only customer for the improved product, or at least it will have the right of first refusal. Can you be sure you will be offered the best price for your innovation, as you would be if you could play many independent bidders off against one another?
- What if your innovation is not a product but a cost-cutting change in the design of equipment? The equipment now belongs to the parent firm, which will demand a share of the savings in costs.
- The innovation may take years to pay off. As manager of a division, how do you know you will still have your job when the payoff comes? What if you retire? As an independent owner, you could sell your firm at a price that reflected the future benefits of the innovation. As a division manager, you cannot sell your job.

In short, a large, multidivisional firm can never meet the ideal of selective intervention. Merging with an independent firm inevitably creates new occasions for opportunism. These must be countered with increased monitoring, thereby raising costs and reducing the division's independence. High-powered incentives never work quite as well within a multidivisional firm as within a fully independent firm, because the central firm remains the owner of each division's capital. Innovation is a particularly sticky problem. A few huge firms claim to have successfully institutionalized the process of innovation, but many have not done so.

There are, then, limits to the firm after all. One big firm cannot do everything that a collection of small firms can.

Scale, Scope, Transaction Costs, and Neoclassical Theory

The neoclassical theory of the firm addresses the issue of the size of firms in a limited way. Production costs play a critical role in neoclassical theory. In perfectly competitive markets, each firm must produce at the scale corresponding to the minimum point on its long-run average cost curve. Economies of scale also help determine the size of firms and the structure of industries under monopoly, oligopoly, and monopolistic competition. But production costs do not provide a complete explanation of the size of firms.

The new transaction cost approach emphasizes that the optimal size of firms is determined jointly by production costs and transaction costs. It suggests that for many industries, unit transaction costs may continue to decline beyond the point where economies of scale in production are exhausted, but that beyond a point, unit transaction costs will again begin to rise as hierarchical coordination within the firm becomes less efficient. Thus, the optimal scale of operation is determined by a long-run average cost curve that includes both production costs and transaction costs.

What is more, the transaction cost approach provides an explanation for the size of firms that encompasses not only *scale* (the volume of output in each product line) but also *scope* (the number of different activities or product lines). It offers specific hypotheses regarding which inputs or production stages a firm is likely to handle internally and which it is likely to acquire through the market from independent suppliers. Among these hypotheses are the following:

- If the firm's demand for the input is not sufficient to occupy a supplier operating at the minimum efficient scale, the input is more likely to be acquired through the market. For example, newspaper publishers often own their own printing presses and delivery trucks, whereas book publishers obtain the needed services from independent firms.
- If production of the input requires a long-term commitment of specialized resources by the supplier, the input is more likely to be produced within the firm. For example, a fine French restaurant might hire a specialist to make cakes and pastries, whereas a simple family restaurant might buy these from an independent bakery.
- How important are high-powered incentives? If originality and innovation are important, or if monitoring of product quality is difficult, the input is likely to be acquired through the market to preserve high-power incentives. For example, even very large firms hire outside agencies to create advertising campaigns, rather than rely on their own employees.

CORPORATE CONTROL AND THE TAKEOVER GAME

Control over large corporations is a complex issue. Decision-making powers are shared by stockholders, directors, and managers. This raises the questions of who is really in control and whose interests are being served.

To complicate matters further, U.S. industry has undergone extensive restructuring in recent years. The restructuring has included huge mergers as well as the selling of parts of corporate empires. These mergers and divestitures have often sparked fierce debate. Who wins? Who loses? Are managers getting rich at the expense of stockholders? Are stockholders getting rich at the expense of the public? Are Wall Street merger wizards getting rich at everyone's expense? Or is the whole process just a way of adapting to change that keeps U.S. industry dynamic and efficient?

Transaction cost theory suggests that mergers and divestitures can improve industrial efficiency under certain conditions. But sometimes there may be more at stake in corporate restructuring than minimizing production and transaction costs. This section presents a brief overview of the issues behind the headlines.

Stockholder's Rights

We can begin by looking more closely at the rights of corporate stockholders, which were mentioned briefly in the first section of the chapter. In a corporation the stockholders are the *principals* in whose interest the firm is supposed to be run. The directors are their *agents,* whose primary function is to monitor the performance of the firm's operating managers. The directors have a legal duty to serve the stockholders' interests, particularly their interest in earning a return on the funds they have invested.

In many corporations, however, stockholders exercise little day-to-day power over the firm's policies, especially when ownership is fragmented. Typically, stockholders own shares in many different corporations. If they disapprove of the policies of one firm's managers, they simply sell that stock and buy the stock of another company, rather than voicing their concerns via shareholder meetings and election of directors.

If this is the case, what guarantee is there that directors will uphold the stockholders' interests? It is not just that directors may be slack in their monitoring, allowing managers to get away with things that they would not approve of. Directors may forget whose agents they are, identifying more strongly with the interests of managers than with those of stockholders, especially in corporations where operating managers are themselves directors. In such cases, what will keep directors and managers from turning corporations into private fiefdoms in which they occupy lavish suites, gad about in corporate jets, and pay themselves extravagant bonuses while the business goes from bad to worse?

Incentives and Bonuses

One way to keep manager-agents working in the interests of their stockholder-principals is to cut them in on high-power incentives tied to the firm's profitability. A common type of incentive is the stock option, which gives a manager the right to buy a certain number of shares of the firm's stock at a set price before a specified date. Suppose that in July 2000 a manager is given the option to buy 10,000 shares of the firm's stock at any time until 2005 at the 2000 price of $25. If the manager does a good job of running the firm, the price of the stock is likely to rise. If it rises to, say, $45 by 2005, the option to buy 10,000 shares at $25 is worth $200,000. That is a nice reward for a job well done. But if the company is poorly managed and the stock's price falls below $25, the option will be worthless.

In part because they are thought to make managers concerned about the interests of ordinary stockholders, stock options have been the fastest-growing segment of executive pay. This created serious problems during the dot-com boom of the 1990s. Many Internet start-up companies compensated their employees with stock options, which allowed these companies to hide their costs in the immediate term. Also, as these businesses were successful, stock prices rose, giving employees the impression that they were wealthier because they had access to stock options. Many of these companies collapsed, leaving the employees with worthless stock options, yet to be exercised.

Takeovers

There are other mechanisms besides bonuses and stock options that affect the principal-agent relationship between stockholders and managers, however. In corporations where stock ownership is widely dispersed, the threat of a *takeover* may be the strongest incentive for managers to work in the stockholders' interests.

We have noted that when stockholders do not like a firm's policies, they are likely to sell their shares and buy stock in another firm. If many stockholders decide to sell at the same time, the price of the stock is driven down. The firm may then be subject to a takeover bid, that is, an offer by a new owner to buy a block of shares that is large enough to control the election of the firm's directors.

Sometimes takeovers are friendly; an example is Ford's acquisition of Volvo in 1999. In such cases, managers believe the merger will serve the interests of both of the original firms. But other takeovers are not friendly. If the price of its stock sags, a firm may face the prospect of a hostile takeover, in which the buyer—if successful—will replace the present management team with its own.

A hostile takeover bid may be made by an individual, a group, or, most often, another corporation. One tactic is to make a *tender offer,* meaning an offer to stockholders at large to buy a controlling interest in the firm's stock at a stated price that is usually well above its current market price. Another tactic is to ask stockholders for *proxies,* that is, promises to vote for a new board of directors at the next stockholder meeting. Often the takeover may be *leveraged*. This means that the takeover group or corporation pays for the stock of the acquired company largely with borrowed funds. In any case, if the takeover succeeds, the new management will do its best to raise profits. When investors realize this, the price of the firm's stock will be driven up and the takeover group will reap handsome gains.

Management Buyouts

When a company is not as profitable as it could be, the market price of its shares on the stock exchange falls. Under such circumstances, managers may see a takeover as a threat to their security. However, managers may also see the situation as an opportunity. They can buy a controlling interest in the company themselves. They can then make changes, such as firing excess corporate staff or selling off nonperforming divisions, that raise the firm's profits. When that has been done, they can then sell some of their shares to the public at a higher price than they paid for them.

A takeover of ownership of a corporation by its own managers is called a *management buyout*. If the managers purchase the corporation's stock largely with borrowed money, it is called a *leveraged management buyout*.

Takeovers and management buyouts are a subject of lively debate among economists and other observers of the corporate scene. Some see them as a means of enhancing the economic performance of the business corporations. Others are skeptical of such claims.

Recent research has improved economists' understanding of the effects of takeovers and buyouts. One of the relatively settled points is that the shareholders of firms that are taken over or bought out tend to come out winners. On the average, takeovers raise the value of their shares by several percentage points. This fact suggests that legislation aiming to provide more protection for takeover targets may be misguided, at least to the extent it is viewed as protecting the interest of the target firm's shareholders.

Evidence regarding the effect on share prices of the *acquiring* firm after a takeover or buyout is less clear cut. Some studies have suggested that the price of acquiring firms' shares tends to drop, on the average, after takeover bids are made. No one seems to understand fully why this is so. One hypothesis is the "winner's curse": The winner when several firms make competing takeover bids tends to be whatever firm overestimates the value of the target most. Another interpretation is that managers of acquiring firms are indulging their empire-building fantasies at the expense of their own shareholders.

Other research focusing on companies that have been bought out by their managers indicates an improvement in performance. Such findings are consistent with the notion that owner-managers have a stronger incentive to maximize profits than managers of firms in which ownership is widely dispersed. To the extent that this is true, the tendency of management buyouts to replace passive, dispersed owners with active owners involved in day-to-day management is a positive development.

Whatever the net effect of takeovers and buyouts on the economy as a whole, they clearly produce both losers and winners among those immediately involved. And that, says analyst John C. Coffee, Jr., is natural. "Loss is a basic fact of economic life. Four out of five new restaurants that open in Manhattan this year will probably fail within two years; yet we do not ban new restaurants. We generally believe that social gain accrues when people take entrepreneurial risks, even if some individuals incur losses. The same applies to takeovers."[5]

SUMMARY

1. **Why do business firms exist in so many different sizes and organizational forms?** Different forms of business organization suit different firms, depending on their size and scope of operations. The most common type of firm is the *sole proprietorship*. Small firms often choose this form because of its flexibility and the complete control it gives the owner. However, limited liability and continuity make the *corporation* a more suitable form of organization for large firms. Some firms, especially those in the professions, use the *partnership* form of organization.

2. **How do firms improve the coordination of economic activity?** Economic activity can be coordinated either via markets or via hierarchies. The choice between the two alternatives depends on which one will minimize the sum of production costs and *transaction costs*—the costs of identifying participants, negotiating an agreement, monitoring performance, enforcing compliance, and adapting to change. For simple tasks, the market is usually the best means of coordination. For complex tasks that require long-term commitment of specialized resources, hierarchical organization within a firm may significantly reduce transaction costs, especially when *opportunism* and bounded rationality are taken into account.

3. **What factors limit the size and scope of firms?** Expanding the scope of a firm by adding additional functions or product lines can sometimes increase rather than decrease transaction costs. The larger firm may not be able to operate all its divisions at an optimal scale. It may suffer from bureaucratization. And it may experience a loss of *high-power incentives*. These problems can sometimes, but not always, be reduced through selective intervention. In short, a large firm cannot always do everything that a collection of small firms can.

4. **What are the forces underlying corporate control and takeovers?** Stockholders have the legal power to control the corporations they own. Their main channel of control is the right to elect the firm's board of directors. However, in practice managers have considerable day-to-day independence from stockholders. Stockholders become involved in corporate control in a major way only when the firm is faced with a takeover bid. The extent to which takeover activity improves economic performance is a controversial issue.

KEY TERMS

Sole proprietorship
Partnership
Corporation
Transaction costs
Opportunism
High-power incentives
Low-power incentives

PROBLEMS AND TOPICS FOR DISCUSSION

1. **Examining the lead-off case.** Why might Tower Records' "inside" directors have interests that differ from those of "outside" managers? What does this have to do with the "clubby" atmosphere that prevailed before the 1990s? What approaches to executive compensation can help combat such problems?

2. **Forms of business organization.** Look around your community for businesses organized as proprietorships, partnerships, corporations, and not-for-profit firms. Do you think each firm has chosen the most appropriate form of organization? Why or why not?

3. **Spontaneous order and hierarchy on sports teams.** Do you play or are you a regular spectator of any team sport? To what extent are the team's actions on the field organized by hierarchical principles? To what extent are they organized through spontaneous order, with each member reacting independently to what is happening in his or her immediate environment? Would it be possible to change the mix of hierarchy and spontaneous order? Would the team play more or less effectively as a result? Discuss.

4. **Transaction costs in studying economics.** Learning economics requires a coordinated effort by you and your teacher. List some transaction costs of achieving the needed coordination. What kinds of safeguards against opportunism (on the part of the student, the professor, or both) must be implemented to ensure the effective teaching and learning of economics? Can you think of any teaching situations in which opportunism is not a problem?

5. **The taxi business.** In some cities taxi service is provided by a fleet of cabs belonging to one big firm or to a few large firms. In others, taxi service is provided largely by owner-drivers. What do you think the advantages and disadvantages of each system are?

6. **Transaction costs of marriage.** Human reproduction is a task that requires at least a minimum of cooperative action. In most societies reproduction is organized within stable family units, which can, in a sense, be thought of as "firms." However, there is no legal or technological reason not to organize reproduction entirely via the market. Women can use the services of sperm banks; men can hire surrogate mothers to bear their children; men or women can hire child-care services. To what extent, if any, do you think transaction costs affect the predominance of the family in human society? Is it necessary to commit specialized resources in forming a family? Are safeguards against opportunism needed? Is there a need to adapt to change under conditions of bounded rationality? Or do you think it is silly even to try to discuss an institution such as the family in terms of economics?

7. **Mergers and acquisitions in the news.** Scan recent issues of business magazines such as *Business Week*, *Fortune*, or *Forbes* for a story about a merger or management buyout that has recently taken place or is being considered. What reasons are given for the action? Do you think it makes sense in terms of the theories discussed in this chapter? Is this a "friendly" merger or management buyout in which the acquired company's current management is participating, or is it a

hostile takeover that management is trying to resist? What controlling role, if any, do you think the acquired firm's stockholders are expected to play in the merger?

CASE FOR DISCUSSION

Is Big Still Beautiful?

Big corporations, cornerstones of the U.S. economy for generations, are undergoing wrenching transformations. Famous old names such as International Harvester, American Can, and Pan American Airlines are gone forever. Firms from *Fortune* magazine's list of the 500 largest industrial corporations account for a smaller share of employment and total output today than they did in 1954, when the list was first introduced. Sixty percent of new jobs created in the 1980s were in firms of 500 employees or fewer.

But changes in the size of corporations alone does not explain all that has been happening. Corporations are changing their shape as well as their size. For one thing, there has been a tendency for firms to concentrate on a single core business that they can do best. Often this happened because earlier conglomerate mergers, which combined firms in very different lines of business, were undone. An example is Sears' divestiture of its financial service and real estate operations in order to concentrate on its core retailing business.

Perhaps partly because they have slimmed down and concentrated on their core businesses, the Fortune 500 companies have remained profitable. In fact, they may have had the last laugh watching small Internet start-up companies fail in the late 1990s.

The effects on individual workers have been mixed. In some cases, they have benefited from stabilization of the companies they work for. In other cases, employees have suffered as firms have contracted out work previously done "in house." Working for a big corporation is often like being a member of a family, with job security and generous fringe benefits being the reward for loyalty. Workers in the entrepreneurial sector sometimes have to shift for themselves when it comes to fringe benefits.

Eli Ginzberg, professor emeritus at Columbia University, calls this a "core and peripheral employment system." The peripheral firms fight to keep costs low by doing without dental insurance, company picnics, and expense account lunches. The core firms survive, but with less total employment.

Sources: Walter Guzzardi, "Big Can Still Be Beautiful," *Fortune*, April 25, 1988, 50–64; Amanda Bennet, "As Big Firms Continue to Trim Their Staffs, Two-Tier Setup Emerges," *The Wall Street Journal*, May 4, 1987, 1; Jean Saddler, "Fears Mount That Small-Business Sector Is in a State of Permanent Retrenchment," *The Wall Street Journal*, February 14, 1992, B1; and Frank Lichtenberg, "Dediversification and Its Consequences for Productivity," National Bureau of Economic Research, working paper No. 3231, 1990.

QUESTIONS

1. What concepts presented in this chapter help explain why large firms might sometimes benefit by concentrating on the basics and contracting work out to independent suppliers?
2. The case notes that Fortune 500 corporations now account for a smaller share of total employment but a larger share of total corporate profits than formerly. Does the trend toward a core-and-peripheral employment system help explain that observation? Discuss.
3. Evaluate the core-and-peripheral system in normative terms, from the employer's point of view. How does the trend affect efficiency? Equity?

END NOTES

1. Ronald H. Coase, "The Nature of the Firm," *Economica* (November 1937): 386–405.
2. An article by Armen Alchien and Harold Demsetz, "Production, Information Costs, and Economic Organization," *American Economic Review* (December 1972): 777–795, is considered a landmark contribution to the literature on the nature of the

firm. Oliver E. Williamson is another key contributor to the field. His book *The Economic Institutions of Capitalism* (New York: Free Press, 1985) provides a thorough summary of research, from which this chapter draws extensively.

3. This discussion focuses on a merger of firms that previously had a buyer-seller relationship. It ignores gains in the form of potential monopoly profits that could arise from the merger of two or more firms that previously competed as sellers in the same market.
4. Williamson, *Economic Institutions*, Chapter 6.
5. Coffee et al., "Corporate Takeovers," 25.

CHAPTER 13

The Economics of Information and Uncertainty

After reading this chapter, you will understand:

1. How insurance helps protect people from the consequences of risk
2. The information problems faced by the insurance business
3. Why speculators willingly accept risk
4. The socially useful purposes served by speculation
5. The role of auctions in the economy

Before reading this chapter, make sure you know the meaning of:

1. Diminishing marginal utility
2. Perfect competition
3. Economics of nonrenewable resources
4. Transaction costs
5. Opportunism

THE HUSTLER

The poolroom hustler makes his living by betting against his opponents in different types of pool or billiard games, and as part of the playing and betting process he engages in various deceitful practices. The terms "hustler" for such a person and "hustling" for his occupation have been in poolroom argot for decades, antedating their application to prostitutes. . . .

The structure of a gambling game determines what methods of deception, if any, may be used in it. In many games (dice, cards, etc.) one can deceive opponents by various cheating techniques. Pool and billiard games are so structured that this method is virtually impossible. Every move is completely visible, easily watched by opponents and by spectators; nor is it possible to achieve anything via tampering with the equipment.

However, one structural feature of pool or billiards readily lends itself to deceit: On each shot, the difference between success and failure is a matter of a small fraction of an inch. In pool or billiards it is peculiarly easy, even for the average player, to miss one's shot deliberately and still look good. The hustler exploits this fact so as to deceive his opponent as to his (the hustler's) true level of skill (true "speed").

As the foregoing indicates, the hustler's cardinal rule is, *don't show your real speed*. . . . It might be thought that once a hustler has engaged an opponent, a bet has been agreed upon, the stake money put up, and the game has started, the hustler might safely let out all the stops. This would be terribly shortsighted.

In the first place, the typical nonhustler bets only a small amount on the game. The hustler's only hope of making real money, therefore, is to extend the first game into a series of games, entice his opponent into doubling up when he is behind, etc. If the hustler does this well, the opponent will hang on for a long time, may even come back after the first session to play him on another day, turn into a real "fish" (the poolroom term for an inferior opponent who doesn't catch on that he's outclassed and keeps coming back for more).

Secondly, there are spectators to take into account. Some of them are potential opponents. . . .

The sooner everyone in the poolroom knows the hustler's true speed, the sooner he exhausts the real hustling possibilities among the room's regular players. Such a situation constitutes one of the career crises that every hustler has to face. When it occurs, either he must move on to a poolroom where he's less known or, if he stays in the room, he has to take games he shouldn't or else restrict his pickings to strangers who wander in.

Source: Ned Polsky, *Hustlers, Beats, and Others* (Garden City, N.Y.: Doubleday Anchor Books, 1969), Ch. 1. Originally published by Aldine, 1967.

Information asymmetry

A situation in which some parties to a transaction possess relevant information that other parties do not possess.

POOLROOM HUSTLING ILLUSTRATES the importance of information and uncertainty as factors shaping economic activities and institutions. The hustler's game depends on the "fish's" uncertainty regarding the hustler's "true speed." As soon as that information becomes known to everyone in the poolroom, it's time for the hustler to move on. Economists use the term **information asymmetry** to refer to situations in which some parties to a transaction possess relevant information that others do not.

Economists have long recognized the importance of information in determining how resources are used to meet people's wants. More than forty years ago Friedrich von Hayek maintained that efficient use of knowledge is the central economic problem facing society (see *Who Said It? Who Did It? 13.1*). Hayek concluded that the success of markets as an economic institution can be traced to the effectiveness of market prices as a mechanism for creating and transmitting information.

Previously we extended the traditional neoclassical analysis of markets by introducing transaction costs, which include the costs of exchanging information. According to transaction cost theory, the exchange of information, which is distributed asymmetrically to begin with, is hampered by the fact that potential buyers and sellers may opportunistically hide what they know as they maneuver to gain an advantage.

This chapter introduces a number of other extensions of the neoclassical analysis. Their common element is the treatment of uncertainty as a barrier to efficient resource use and the treatment of information as a scarce resource. Buyers and sellers are seen as uncertain about the future state of the world and about each others' intentions. Information is often asymmetrically distributed, so that some people know things that others do not.

INSURANCE AND RISK POOLING

One aspect of imperfect information is lack of knowledge about what the future will bring. Will there be enough rain for the corn crop? How good a job offer will I get if I major in economics instead of accounting? Whenever people are uncertain about what will happen in the future, we say that they face *risk*.[1]

Attitudes Toward Risk

Expected value

For a set of possible outcomes, the sum of the probability of each outcome multiplied by the value of that outcome.

People's attitudes toward risk vary according to their personalities and the circumstances in which they find themselves. Suppose, for example, that I owe you a dollar, and instead of simply paying, I offer you double-or-nothing on the flip of a coin. Heads, I pay you $2; tails, I pay you nothing. What I offer you is a fair gamble, inasmuch as the **expected value** of the outcome is the same as the $1 I owe you to begin

WHO SAID IT? WHO DID IT? 13.1

FRIEDRICH VON HAYEK ON MARKETS AND INFORMATION

Friedrich von Hayek, a recipient of the Nobel Memorial Prize for economics, was a pioneer in monetary theory and made fundamental contributions to many other branches of economics as well. Born and educated in Vienna, he is considered a key contributor to the approach to economics known as the *Austrian school.* With such books as *The Road to Serfdom* and *The Constitution of Liberty,* he also gained a reputation as a political philosopher.

A distinguishing feature of the Austrian school is its focus on the process through which markets adjust to changing circumstances. In Hayek's view, the role of markets as creators and transmitters of information is a key to understand the market process. In 1945, Hayek presented his views on this matter in a classic article, "The Use of Knowledge in Society."

Suppose, says Hayek, that a major new use for tin arises. It may be in manufacturing, electronics, medicine—it does not matter. The exact nature of the new use does not matter, either. All the users of tin really need to know is that the opportunity cost of using tin has gone up—that is, some of the tin they used previously can now be used more profitably elsewhere—and, as a consequence, they must economize on tin. The great majority of them need not know what the new use is. They need only know that there is some new, more urgent use. If only some of them know the nature of the new use and switch resources over to it, they will create a gap between the quantities supplied and demanded at the originally prevailing price. People who are aware of the resulting gap will fill it with new supplies, and the effect will spread rapidly. It will influence the uses not only of tin but also of its substitutes and of substitutes for the substitutes. It will affect the supply of all things made of tin, the supply of all things made of its substitutes, and so on. All of this will happen with the great majority of those involved unaware of the exact cause of the original disturbance.

How will people be notified of the change in the tin market? The means of communication that Hayek has in mind are not television, newspapers, or government directives but the market price of tin. It is a rise in the price of tin that will notify each user that a more urgent use has arisen elsewhere.

Prices are an efficient means of communicating this information because they allow each user to concentrate on the details of the particular work for which tin is needed in each case. No one needs to know about all uses of tin. Prices give just enough information about opportunity costs to guide decisions in the right direction. As Hayek puts it, "The whole acts as one market not because any of its members survey the whole field, but because their limited individual fields of vision sufficiently overlap so that through many intermediaries the relevant information is communicated to all."

In recent years there has been a resurgence of interest in the economics of information. A common theme in the literature of this topic is the need to understand that markets are more than curves crossing on a graph. They are the nerve fibers along which messages pass from one part of the economic organism to another, thereby allowing the whole to adapt to a constantly changing environment. Hayek's 1945 article is frequently cited as a seminal contribution to the economics of information.

Source: *Friedrich von Hayek on Markets and Information* adapted from F. A. von Hayek, "The Use of Knowledge in Society," *American Economic Review* (September 1945): 519–530. Reprinted by permission of the *American Economic Review.*

with. (Expected value is calculated as the sum of the values of each outcome times the probability of that outcome. See *Applying Economic Ideas 13.1.*)

Will you take the offer of double-or-nothing? If you prefer a risk-free outcome with a certain value over a set of risky outcomes with the same expected value, you are said to display **risk aversion**. A risk-averse person would turn down the double-or-nothing offer. If you prefer the risky outcome with the same expected value as the risk-free outcome, you are said to display **risk preference**. A person with risk preference would accept the double-or-nothing offer. And if you are indifferent between risky and risk-free outcomes with the same expected value, you are said to display **risk neutrality**.

Risk aversion

A preference for a certain outcome with a given value over a set of risky outcomes with the same expected value.

There is a good reason, grounded in the theory of consumer behavior, to expect most people to be risk averse most of the time. This can be explained with the aid of the concept of *utility.* It is sometimes useful to imagine that utility can be measured in

Risk preference

A preference for a set of risky outcomes with a given expected value over a certain outcome with the same expected value.

Risk neutrality

Indifference between a certain outcome with a given value and a set of risky outcomes with the same expected value.

units called "utils," even though in practice it is impossible to measure utility. If you were able to measure the utility, not of just one good, but of a person's total wealth, in utils, you could draw a graph similar to the one in Figure 13.1. The graph shows that starting from zero, adding $1,000 to your total wealth would give you 200 utils. Another $1,000 would add 100 more utils, a third $1,000 would add 40 more, and a fourth $1,000 would add just 20 more.

The fact that each equal addition to your wealth increases your utility by less than the previous addition reflects the principle of *diminishing marginal utility.* On a total utility graph such as that in Figure 13.1, the marginal utility of wealth is equal to the slope of the total utility curve. Thus, as wealth increases, the slope of the total utility curve decreases, indicating a diminishing increment to utility for each equal increment of wealth.

To see the link between risk aversion and diminishing marginal utility, suppose you start with a total wealth of $2,000, and I offer to bet you $1,000 on the flip of a coin. Heads, I pay you $1,000; tails, you pay me $1,000. If you win, your total wealth will rise to $3,000. If you lose, you will be down to $1,000. In terms of money, it is a fair bet. Your expected value is zero, because the probability of a $1,000 gain is equal to that of a $1,000 loss. But in terms of utility the bet does not look so attractive. If

FIGURE 13.1 RISK AVERSION, UTILITY, AND WEALTH

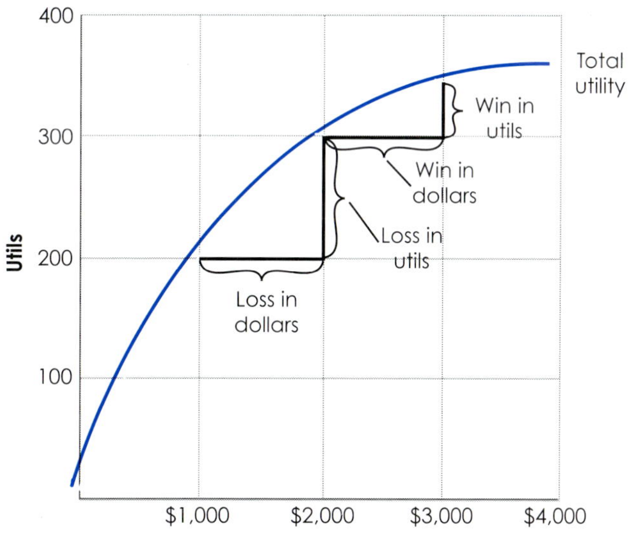

The total utility curve shown here is drawn on the assumption that utility can be measured in units called "utils." As you acquire more wealth, your total utility increases, but each added $1,000 adds less to total utility than the previous $1,000—an example of the principle of diminishing marginal utility. Suppose that you initially have a total wealth of $2,000, equivalent to 300 utils on the arbitrary utility scale. A decrease in wealth of $1,000 would decrease your utility by 100 utils, but an increase in wealth of $1,000 would increase your utility by just 40 utils. That being the case, you would not find it attractive to wager $1,000 on the flip of a coin. The wager would have an expected value of –30 stated in utils, even though it would be a fair wager (zero expected value) in terms of dollars. This reasoning shows that a person who is subject to diminishing marginal utility of wealth will tend to be *risk averse*.

APPLYING ECONOMIC IDEAS 13.1

EXPECTED VALUE

The expected value of a set of possible outcomes is equal to the sum of the probability of each outcome multiplied by the value of each outcome. This concept has numerous applications in economics, statistics, games, and elsewhere.

Suppose, for example, that you hold one of 50 tickets in a lottery. The winner of the lottery will receive a prize worth $100. The expected value of a ticket is calculated as follows:

Probability of winning: .02
Value of winning outcome: $100
Probability of not winning: .98
Value of nonwinning outcome: 0
Expected value: (.02 x $100) + (.98 x 0) = $2.00

Sometimes some of the outcomes in the set under consideration have negative values. For example, suppose that you have a bright idea for a new Christmas toy. You will have to invest $100,000 to bring the toy to market. If it is successful you will recover the $100,000 you have invested and earn a profit of $500,000 besides. If the toy is a flop, you will lose your entire investment. Your experience in the toy business tells you that your idea has about one chance in five of succeeding. You calculate the expected value of your investment as follows:

Probability of failure: .8
Loss in case of failure: $100,000
Probability of success: .2
Profit in case of success: $500,000
Expected value of project:
(.8 x –$100,000) + (.2 x $500,000)
= –$80,000 + $100,000
= +20,000

Conclusion: Although bringing out the new toy is a risky venture, it does have a positive expected value.

you lose, your utility level will drop by 100 utils, from 300 to 200. If you win, it will rise by just 40 utils, from 300 to 340. The expected value *in utils* of flipping the coin is $(-100 \times 0.5) + (40 \times 0.5) = -30$. Your *expected utility* drops by 30 utils if you accept the coin toss. You therefore decide to keep your $2,000 rather than flip the coin. Diminishing marginal utility makes you risk averse.[2]

The Principle of Risk Pooling

Risk is part of life. No amount of human ingenuity can eliminate it. However, there are ways to soften the effects of risk. One way to do so is to share risks among several people so that the impact of an undesirable outcome on any one of them is small. This technique is called **risk pooling**.

Risk pooling
A technique in which the risk of loss is shared among many people so that the impact of a loss on any one of them is small.

Many examples of risk pooling can be found in financial markets. Suppose, for example, that you have $5,000 that you would like to invest in the stock market. Because stock is usually sold in units of 100 shares, with only $5,000 to invest, you would probably end up putting all your eggs in one basket. Over time the average return on stocks of major U.S. corporations has been very good, but any company can run into trouble. If you were unlucky, a big chunk of your $5,000 could be wiped out by a drop in the price of your chosen stock.

Risk pooling offers a solution to this problem for small investors. Suppose that you put your $5,000 together with similar amounts that 1,000 other people want to invest. This would give you a pool of $5 million, which you could invest in the stock of dozens or hundreds of different companies. You and your fellow investors would share equally in the profits and losses earned on stocks in the pool. Your pool would be called a *mutual fund*.

Now and then one of the companies represented in the pool of stocks would have a run of bad luck, but that would very likely be offset by the unusual good fortune of another company. Your investment in the mutual fund would be largely shielded against fluctuations in value caused by changes in the fortunes of individual companies. Of course, a problem such as a recession or severe inflation in the economy as a whole could affect all companies at once and could still cause a loss for the fund. Pooling cannot eliminate all risk, but it can help.

Application of Risk Pooling to Insurance

Financial risks such as changes in stock prices are not the only ones that people face. There are many risks in everyday life as well, such as the risks of being in an automobile accident, being robbed, or becoming ill. People can protect themselves against the consequences of these risks through risk pooling in the form of *insurance*.

Suppose, for example, that you live in a house valued at $100,000. There is one chance in a thousand that your house will burn down in any given year. The expected dollar value of your loss from a fire is $100 per year. However, your expected loss in utility from a fire is much greater than the marginal utility of $100 cash, because, although a fire is not likely, if one happened it would push you far down along the steep portion of your utility curve. What should you do?

One solution is to join with a group of your neighbors to form a mutual insurance fund. Suppose there are 1,000 members in the group. Each time a member's house burned down, that person would be compensated with $100,000 from the fund, and the members would kick in $100 each to cover the expense. On the average, you would have to pay just one claim for loss each year. If no houses burned down, you would pay nothing; if two burned down, you would pay $200; and so on. By adding more members—tens of thousands or even millions—the risk of variation in your annual contribution would become very small, so that an annual contribution very close to $100 would be a virtual certainty.

By forming the mutual insurance society, you and your neighbors convert a small risk of a catastrophic loss into a highly likely small loss. Risk pooling through insurance does not change the expected value of loss in dollar terms, but for risk-averse people it produces a big benefit in terms of expected utility. This is the fundamental principle underlying all forms of insurance.

Asymmetrical Information, Opportunism, and Transaction Costs of Insurance

In the real world, policyholders must pay premiums that exceed the expected value of claims, because their premiums have to cover the costs of organizing and operating the insurance companies as well as the cost of claims. Costs other than claims accounted for about 23 percent of each premium dollar for property insurers and about 16 percent for life insurers as of 1980. Such costs include the clerical costs of keeping the books and mailing out bills. In addition, they include transaction costs associated with problems of asymmetrical information and opportunism. Two of these, *adverse selection* and *moral hazard*, are of particular interest.

Adverse selection

The tendency of people facing the greatest risk of loss to be most likely to seek insurance.

ADVERSE SELECTION

Adverse selection refers to the tendency of people who face the greatest risk of loss to be most likely to seek insurance. The people closest to a river are most likely to buy flood insurance; those who live in bad neighborhoods are most likely to buy theft insurance; and so on.

If measures are not taken to control adverse selection, insurance can become unavailable to many people. Suppose, for example, that there are two neighborhoods in a city, one of which is closer to a river than the other. Residents in the Riverside neighborhood face an expected loss from flood of $10,000 per year. Those in the Highlands neighborhood face an expected loss of just $1,000 per year.

If equal numbers of people from each neighborhood sign up for flood insurance, the average expected loss will be $5,500 per year. A premium set at that level (plus an allowance for clerical costs) would just allow the company to break even over time. However, residents of Highlands would quickly recognize that it is not worth their while to sign up. Seeing that the premium far outweighs the expected loss, they would start dropping out. As they did so, the average expected loss of those remaining in the insurance plan would rise, as would the premium required for the company to break even. Eventually all the Highlanders would drop out, the premium would rise to $10,000 per year, and insurance would be purchased only by the Riversiders.

To generalize, if adverse selection is not controlled, insurance will be available only at rates corresponding to the worst risk category. To control this tendency, firms employ *underwriters* whose job is to select and classify applicants into risk groups so that the company can calculate an appropriate premium for each group.

In the flood insurance example, the underwriter's job would be easy. Residents of Highlands are placed in a low-risk class and pay a premium of $1,000 per year, and residents of Riverside are placed in a high-risk class and pay a $10,000 premium. But it is not always so easy to classify applicants into risk groups, because some of the relevant information may be known only to the insured.

Take life insurance, for example. Insurance companies ask life insurance applicants a lot of questions to try to classify them into risk groups. How old are they? Do they smoke? Are they overweight? What is the family's health history? Even so, the companies do not learn everything they need to know.

For one thing, some applicants may opportunistically conceal information to try to qualify for a lower premium. They may lie about their drinking habits. They may "forget" to mention that Uncle Fred died of a heart attack at age thirty-five. By slipping through the underwriting process, such people gain an advantage at the expense of other policyholders, whose premiums are pushed up accordingly.

In addition, legal or ethical restraints limit the kinds of information that insurance underwriters can take into account. Information about race is one example. In the past, life insurance companies took race into account in their underwriting. They then charged blacks more than whites for equivalent policies for the statistically valid reason that life expectancy is lower in the black population than in the white population. Today, even though it remains true that life expectancy is lower for the black population than for the white population, it is no longer ethically (or legally) acceptable to use race as a factor in setting insurance premiums.

Insurance is not the only area of business in which adverse selection occurs, although it was the first in which the problem was clearly recognized. Adverse selection can occur any time that sellers are unable to classify customers according to the cost of serving them. Adverse selection can also occur when buyers are unable to distinguish among sellers offering different qualities of service (see *Applying Economic Ideas 13.2*). In short, adverse selection must be counted as a pervasive phenomenon that boosts transaction costs in a world in which information is not universally available or willingly disclosed by those who possess it.

Moral hazard

Behavior that increases the risk of loss, yet is undertaken in the knowledge that losses will be covered by insurance.

MORAL HAZARD The term **moral hazard** refers to behavior that increases the risk of loss yet is undertaken in the knowledge that losses will be covered by insurance. Sometimes a simple lack of care is involved: A driver whose car is insured against theft might be less careful about locking it when it is parked. In other cases there is actual dishonesty, as, for example, if a landlord sets fire to a building to collect the insurance.[3]

Insurance companies take whatever measures they can to control moral hazard. Sometimes they insist on certain precautions as a condition for insurance. Thus, a hotel might be required to install a sprinkler system to qualify for fire insurance. To protect against fraud, insurance companies hire specialists to investigate the circumstances of suspicious claims. Finally, insurance companies try to prevent people from overinsuring. Selling someone $10,000 of theft insurance on a car that is worth only $5,000 is an invitation to a real or faked theft.

But like efforts to control adverse selection, efforts to control moral hazard are never completely successful. Again, information asymmetry is a reason. Many kinds of opportunistic behavior simply cannot be observed by the insurer. As a result, moral hazard makes insurance premiums higher than they would otherwise be, and the careless and dishonest benefit at the expense of the careful and upright.

Speculation

Buying something at a low price in the hope of selling it later at a higher price.

SPECULATION AND ITS ROLE IN THE ECONOMY

The whole point of insurance is to avoid risk, but there are occasions when people voluntarily take on risk. **Speculation**—the activity of buying something at a low

APPLYING ECONOMIC IDEAS 13.2
THE ECONOMICS OF "LEMONS"

In 1970 George A. Akerlof caused a minor sensation in the economics profession with an article entitled "The Market for Lemons." The subject of the article was the market for used cars—more specifically, the market for bad used cars, or lemons. The article drew attention to a potential source of market failure that had previously received little attention. This article, and related work, was later to win Akerlof the 2001 Nobel Prize in economics.

Akerlof's argument can be restated as follows. Suppose that there are two kinds of used 1985 Ford Escorts. Some have been maintained lovingly and driven carefully. Owners would not part with them for less than $2,000, and potential buyers would be willing to pay up to $2,400 for them. The other 1985 Escorts have been hot-rodded around, have never had their oil changed, and cannot be counted on for reliable service. They are lemons. Owners would be happy to unload them for anything over $1,000, and buyers, if they knew what they were getting, would not pay more than $1,200.

If there were separate markets for good cars and lemons, there would be no problem, but, says Akerlof, there is a catch: Sellers know whether or not a car is a lemon, but buyers have no way to tell. Sellers of lemons will opportunistically misrepresent the quality of the cars, and the true quality of the cars cannot be observed.

Asymmetrical information strikes again. Not knowing which cars are which, buyers have to take their chances. If equal numbers of good cars and lemons were sold, buyers would have a 50-50 chance of getting one or the other. The maximum they would pay for a car of unknown quality would be $1,800, the average of the value to them of the two types of cars. However, owners of good cars would not sell them for $1,800. They would rather go on driving them. That would leave only lemons on the market. Buyers would pay up to $1,200 for a lemon, a price at which owners would willingly sell. In the end, lemons would drive good cars out of the market altogether even though potential buyers value the good cars more than sellers do. That would be a clear case of market failure.

As economists discussed the issue, it became clear that the lemons problem was not a completely new form of market failure but, rather, the old problem of adverse selection in a new guise. The tendency of lemons to drive good cars out of the market is much the same as the tendency of bad risks to drive good risks out of the insurance market. The difference is that the insurance example involves adverse selection among buyers, whereas the lemons problem involves adverse selection among sellers.

When the problem is recognized as one of adverse selection, the path to resolving it is clear, Buyers must find some way to penetrate the information asymmetry. In the case of cars, they have several options. They can ask to see service records. They can (for a fee) take the car to an expert mechanic who may be able to detect signs of mistreatment. Or they can buy used cars only through reputable dealers who hope to get repeat business from satisfied customers and those customers' friends. The process will never be perfect. A few lemons will slip through (just as a few people with weak hearts may slip through the qualifying procedures for life insurance). But if buyers can form at least a rough idea of the quality of used cars, it will be possible to maintain a market in both good and bad cars.

Source: George A. Akerlof, "The Market for Lemons: Qualitative Uncertainty and the Market Mechanism," *Quarterly Journal of Economics* (August 1970): 488–500. Copyright 1970 The MIT Press. Reprinted by permission.

price in the hope of selling it later at a higher price—is an important example. Speculators can be found in many markets, including those for stocks, bonds, agricultural commodities, precious metals, foreign currency, and real estate, to name just a few.

Speculation and Risk

Speculation is inherently risky. Suppose I buy stock in ExxonMobil at $40 a share in the hope that rising world oil prices will boost the firm's profits, allowing me to sell the stock for $60 a share next year. Instead, the discovery of huge new oil reserves in Kazakhstan sends world oil prices tumbling, and ExxonMobil stock falls to $20. *C'est la vie;* it is all in a day's work for a speculator.

Why would I want to take such a risk? One explanation would be that unlike the majority of people, who are risk adverse, I actually prefer risk. But economists like to avoid explaining behavior in terms of preferences alone when other explanations are available. In this case there is such an explanation. Even though I am risk averse and would not speculate on ExxonMobil stock if I thought there was an equal chance that its price would rise or fall, I might do it if I thought there was a greater chance of an increase than of a decrease. For example, suppose that I think there is a 75 percent chance of an increase to $60 a share and just a 25 percent chance of a fall to $20 a share. In that case the expected value of the stock a year from now would be $50 ([.75 x $50] + [.25 x $20] = $50). If I bought the stock now at $40, my expected gain would be $10 a share. That expected gain could well be enough to overcome my aversion to risk.

But this account of speculation raises another question: If the expected value of the stock next year is $50, why would anyone sell it for $40 today? Here there are two possible answers. One is that other people are even more risk averse than I am. The 25 percent chance of a loss so terrifies them that they will pass up the expected $10-per-share gain. The other answer is information asymmetry: Other people have not yet discovered the information I have that leads me to think world oil prices are significantly more likely to rise than to fall.

In practice, both factors may be at work. A smaller-than-normal degree of risk aversion probably explains why some people become professional speculators. But their success as speculators depends on being the first to learn new information, whether through organized research or simply by keeping their ears to the ground.

Futures Contracts and Options

In the preceding example, speculation took the form of buying ExxonMobil stock today and holding it for resale a year from now. Two other methods of speculation involve *futures contracts* and *options.*

Futures contract

An agreement to exchange something at a specified date in the future at a price that is agreed upon now.

Spot price

The price at which a good is offered for immediate sale.

A **futures contract** is an agreement to exchange something at a specified future date at a price that is agreed on now. Suppose that I find another trader who expects the *spot price* for ExxonMobil stock a year from now to be $40, the same as today's spot price. (The **spot price** is the price at which a good is offered for immediate sale at any given time.) I could enter into a futures contract with that trader under which I would buy 10,000 shares of ExxonMobil stock a year from now at $40. If the spot price rises to $60 by then (as I think there is a 75 percent probability that it will), I will make a killing because I can immediately resell the shares for $20 more than I paid for them under the terms of the futures contract. Of course, there is a risk (which I put at 25 percent) that the spot price will fall to $20. In that case I am still bound by the futures contract to purchase the stock at $40 a share, $20 over its spot price at that time.

Win or lose, from my point of view as a speculator the futures contract has an advantage over buying the stock at today's spot price and holding it for a year. The advantage is that I do not have to tie up my own funds by actually holding the stock. All the buying and selling is done a year from now on the date specified by the contract.

Options

Contracts under which one party obtains the right (but not the obligation) to buy something at a specified date in the future at a price that is agreed upon now.

Options are a variation on the idea of agreeing now on the terms of a transaction to be completed later. If I enter into an options contract to buy ExxonMobil stock from you at $40 a share a year from now, you have the obligation to sell the stock to me at that price if I still want it, but if I change my mind, I have the right not to exercise the option. If the spot price goes up to $60, I make the purchase and profit from it. If the spot price falls below $20, I say, "Thanks but no thanks." Of course, you would not enter into such a "heads I win, tails I break even" deal unless there were some compensation to you. The compensation is in the form of an up-front fee of, say, $2 a share for accepting the options contract. If I exercise the options contract at a loss to you, the $2 fee helps you offset the loss. If I do not exercise the option, the $2 is a profit for you.

The Social Usefulness of Speculation

In terms of popularity and social respect, speculators rank about as high as poolroom hustlers. In fact, though, speculators perform a number of socially useful functions.

HEDGING Although speculation itself involves the calculated acceptance of risks, speculators also make it possible for other traders to avoid risk. This is done through **hedging**, an operation that uses futures or options markets to offset one risk with another.

Hedging

An operation in which futures markets or options markets are used to offset one risk with another.

Suppose, for example, that you are a baker. You enter into a contract to sell 10 million loaves of bread to the Army at $.50 a loaf over the course of the next year. Your bid is based on the current price of flour, which, in turn, depends on the price of wheat. The price of wheat is currently $6 per bushel and is expected to stay at that level over the next year, but no one is sure what will actually happen. If the price of wheat unexpectedly goes up during the year, flour will become more expensive; that would wipe out your profit on the bread contract. What can you do to avoid this risk?

The answer is that you can enter into a futures contract at $6 a bushel to buy a quantity of wheat equivalent to the flour needed to make the bread. If the spot price of wheat rises, you will make a profit on your wheat futures contract that will offset the impact of a higher wheat price on your bread profits. If the spot price of wheat falls, you will make a loss on the wheat futures contract, but cheaper flour will allow you to make a greater profit than you expected on the bread contract. Through hedging you have shifted the risk of gain or loss on wheat prices to a speculator. You can tend to your own specialty, which is baking bread.

TRANSMISSION OF INFORMATION A second socially useful function of speculation is transmission of information about future economic developments to the general public. This might seem paradoxical at first. Speculators clearly have an incentive to acquire information. They therefore acquaint themselves with the details of a business, hire research staffs, construct computer models, and so on. But our earlier example showed that speculators' profits depend on knowing information that other people do not know. Why would they share the results of their research with others?

The answer is that they cannot help doing so. Consider the example of oil prices and the prices of oil-company stocks. If my research indicates that the price of oil is likely to rise, I can profit by buying oil-company stock today (or trading in futures contracts or options, which amounts to the same thing). But as soon as I and my fellow speculators start buying the stock, we bid up its market price. Other people look at the movement of the stock's price and say to themselves, "Somebody must think oil prices are going to rise. In fact, they must be sure enough of it to put their money on their information." The secret is out.

SPECULATION AND CONSERVATION A final socially useful function of speculation is to promote conservation by smoothing out trends in the use of scarce resources over time. Recall the discussion of nonrenewable resources earlier in this book. Suppose that something—say, natural gas—will become increasingly scarce in the future as reserves are depleted. Optimal use of the resource over time requires that conservation efforts begin now, but the lower the current spot price, the less incentive there will be to conserve gas.

Enter the speculator. Anticipating future shortages, speculators buy up gas wells and cap them, hoping to sell later when the price is higher. By doing so they reduce the flow of gas to the market today, thereby driving up the current price. This is the signal that is needed to spur conservation.

In sum, economists tend to view speculation as a socially useful activity. Of course, speculators have been known to make mistakes. When they do so, they may destabilize prices and send false signals of scarcity to other market participants. But speculators who make mistakes also make losses. A process of market selection thus favors the speculators who are most skilled at their job of discovering new information and putting it to use.

THE ECONOMICS OF AUCTIONS[4]

In most of the markets we have discussed up to this point, sellers inform buyers in advance of the prices they will charge. Buyers are offered the opportunity to buy as much or as little of the good as they want at that price, or not to buy at all.

For some goods, however, it is not feasible to announce prices in advance. Instead, the price is established at the actual moment when the transaction takes place. Several examples come to mind. One is markets for unique items that are bought and sold only rarely, such as works of art. Another is markets for perishable goods such as fish or cut flowers in which inventories cannot be carried over; prices change from moment to moment in such markets to keep quantities supplied and demanded closely in balance. Markets for such goods as race horses or tobacco, which vary in quality from one unit to the next, are still another example.

When a price is not established until a transaction actually takes place, how do buyers and sellers get the information and incentives they need to use resources efficiently? How can the market ensure that scarce resources will move to their most highly valued uses? Auctions are one institution used to deal with these issues. This section examines the economics of auctions, with special emphasis on the way they handle information.

Types of Auctions

Reservation price

The maximum price that a buyer is willing to pay for a good or the minimum price at which a seller is willing to offer it.

An auction always begins from a situation of asymmetric information. Suppose I want to sell a painting. I know my **reservation price** (the minimum I would accept to part with the painting), but I do not know the reservation prices of potential buyers (the maximum that they are willing to pay). Information is asymmetric on the buyers' side, too. Buyers know their own reservation prices, but they do not know that of the seller or those of other buyers. Needless to say, both buyers and sellers in an auction expect others to behave opportunistically. Each side seeks to gain an advantage while revealing as little as possible about its own reservation price.

The preceding paragraph describes an auction that is organized and conducted by the seller, who accepts bids from buyers. We can call these *sellers' auctions*. In other cases, the auction is organized by a buyer, who solicits bids from a number of potential sellers. We can call these *buyers' auctions*. For example, I might seek bids from a number of construction contractors to build a house. In such a case I know my reservation price (the maximum I am willing to pay) but not the reservation price (the minimum acceptable bid) of potential contractors. Also, the contractors do not know the minimum acceptable bids of other contractors.

English auction

An auction in which bidding starts low and proceeds until the good is sold to the highest bidder.

Dutch auction

An auction that begins with a high bid, which is lowered until a buyer is found.

Sealed-bid auction

An auction in which all buyers submit bids at the same time, and the item is sold to the highest bidder (or bought from the lowest bidder).

Three types of auctions are common. The sellers' versions are described here, but buyers' versions of each also exist.

1. In an **English auction**, the bidding starts low and competing buyers successively call out higher bids until only one buyer is left. The object is then sold to the high bidder.
2. In a **Dutch auction**, the bidding starts high and the auctioneer calls out successively lower bids until one is accepted. In this case, the object is sold to the first buyer who accepts a bid.
3. In a **sealed-bid auction**, all buyers submit bids simultaneously, and the object is sold to the highest bidder.

English auctions are probably the most familiar type. They are frequently used for artwork, livestock, and charity fundraisers. Sealed-bid auctions are most often seen in the buyer's version, in which competing contractors submit bids to build houses, pave roads, develop weapons systems, and so on. The U.S. Treasury also sells certain securities through sealed-bid auctions. Formal Dutch auctions are not as common, although they are used in the Netherlands to sell fresh flowers. An informal version of the Dutch auction is often used to sell houses, used cars, and other items. The item is first advertised at a price that reflects the seller's most optimistic hopes. If there is no response, the price is gradually lowered until a buyer is found.

The Revenue-Equivalence Theorem

Which type of auction works best? Which will yield the highest price to the seller when there are many buyers? Which will elicit the lowest bid for the buyer when there are many sellers? The surprising answer is that under certain broad conditions the three types of auctions can be expected to produce very nearly the same results on the average. This is known as the **revenue-equivalence theorem**.

Revenue-equivalence theorem

The proposition that under certain general circumstances English, Dutch, and sealed-bid auctions can be expected to produce approximately the same winning bid.

The essence of the revenue-equivalence theorem can be understood by means of an example. Suppose that I am selling a 1988 Ford Escort at a wholesale auction to a group of experienced used-car dealers who plan to offer the car for resale. On the basis of an estimate of the resale value, each buyer mentally sets a reservation price for the car—a price at which the resale transaction would just break even. Because the buyers are uncertain exactly how much they can get for the car, the reservation prices for a given car will differ from one buyer to another.

To begin with the simplest case, suppose that I use an English auction. The bidding starts at $1,000 and quickly moves to a point at which only two bidders, Henry and George, are left. Henry bids $2,400, and George answers with $2,450. Finally Henry bids $2,500 and George does not respond. Sold, to Henry, for $2,500. What have I learned? I have learned that George's reservation price was a little less than $2,500, while Henry's reservation price is at least $2,500. To generalize, an English auction will result in a sale at a price a little higher than the *second-highest* reservation price among the competing buyers.

Now consider the Dutch auction. I start the auction at $5,000, expecting no immediate takers, and there are none. At $3,000 I hit Henry's reservation price. Will Henry immediately jump in? No, because at $3,000 he would be buying the car for exactly the amount he thinks he will get when he resells it. There would be no profit. So Henry puts on a poker face and keeps quiet. Behind the poker face, he is putting all his experience to work to estimate the reservation price of the *second-highest* bidder at such an auction. He guesses that it will be somewhere near $2,500. Just as the bid drops to that level, Henry raises his hand and buys the car. Sometimes Henry will guess wrong, and George or Gladys or someone else will get the car before he has a chance to bid. But all the buyers are professionals. Their guesses will tend to be correct on the average. As a result, the average selling price at a Dutch auction will again be close to the reservation price of the second-highest bidder.

Finally, suppose that the auction is conducted by means of sealed bids. Henry's reasoning will be almost the same as in the Dutch auction. He certainly will not bid his reservation price of $3,000—that would guarantee that he would not make a profit. His profit-maximizing strategy in a sealed-bid auction such as this one is to submit a bid close to his estimate of the reservation price of the second-highest bidder. With this strategy, he stands a good chance of getting the car for $2,500.

Under certain general conditions, then, the expected winning bid will be about the same for all three types of auction: close to the second-highest reservation price among the bidders. There are exceptions, however. Sometimes special characteristics of the product or the information available to buyers or sellers will make one type of auction work better than another. Presumably, buyers and sellers in various markets develop a feel for such things over time, so that when a particular type of auction would make a difference, that type is chosen.

All in all, auctions are a reasonably efficient solution to the problem of pricing unique goods under conditions of asymmetric information and opportunism. In sellers' auctions, goods tend to end up in the hands of those who value them most; in buyers' auctions, the winners tend to be those who can supply the goods at the lowest cost. Adequate incentives are maintained in both types of auctions to call forth a supply of the goods and services that are demanded.

The Winner's Curse

Winner's curse

The tendency for winners of an auction to pay more for a good or service than it is worth (or to offer to sell at a price below the cost of providing the good or service).

Despite a generally favorable assessment of auctions, a number of observers have identified a potential market failure known as the **winner's curse**. This term refers to an alleged tendency for the winners of auctions to pay more than the item is worth or, in the case of buyers' auctions, to bid less than the cost of supplying the item.

The winner's curse is associated with a certain class of auctions known as *common-value* auctions. In such auctions, the item to be sold has the same actual value to all buyers, but the buyers do not know the exact value of the item when they submit bids. In a classic classroom demonstration, students are asked to bid on a jar of coins. Their bids are based on a guess regarding how many coins are in the jar. Bidding for oil drilling rights on government land is a real-world example. No one knows how much oil will be found on a given tract until a well is drilled, so bids must be based on estimates derived from indirect geological information.

Suppose that in a common-value auction each bidder's estimate is based on a method that on average accurately reflects the actual value of the item. For example, bids on a jar containing $10 worth of coins might range from $5 to $15, centered on an average value of $10. Under these conditions the winner of the auction will be the bidder who had the bad luck to most overestimate the value of the item being sold. Someone will end up paying $15 for $10 in coins, or $15 million for drilling rights worth $10 million, or whatever. In a buyers' auction the curse would take the form of a winning bid to supply an item that failed to cover the supplier's costs, for example, a bid of $250,000 to pave a stretch of road that cannot be completed for less than $300,000.

Various writers have claimed to observe the winner's curse at work. Oil companies have been said to overpay for the value of offshore drilling rights. Publishers have been said to overpay for the rights to best sellers. Nevertheless, many economists doubt that the curse is widespread. They reason that people would not participate in auctions year after year knowing that the auctions were cursed. Instead, they think that bidders learn how to protect themselves by submitting bids that are lower than their reservation prices—lower, that is, than their actual estimates of the value of the item.[5]

SUMMARY

1. **How does insurance help protect people from the consequences of risk?** Most people are *risk averse,* meaning that they would prefer a certain outcome with a given value over a set of risky outcomes with the same expected value. Risk-averse individuals can protect themselves through *risk pooling,* a technique in which losses are shared among the members of a large group so that each faces the certainty of a small loss rather than a small risk of a large loss. Mutual funds and insurance are examples of risk pooling.

2. **What information problems are faced by the insurance business?** The insurance business faces two problems arising from *asymmetrical information*. The first, *adverse selection,* refers to the tendency of individuals facing the greatest risk to be most likely to seek insurance. The second problem, *moral hazard,* refers to behavior that increases the risk of loss, yet is undertaken in the knowledge that losses will be covered by insurance. Adverse selection and moral hazard, and efforts to control them, raise the transaction costs of providing insurance.

3. **Why do speculators willingly accept risk?** *Speculation,* the activity of buying at a low price in the hope of reselling at a higher price, is inherently risky. Risk-averse people will find speculation attractive only if they think they possess better information about future market conditions than other market participants do. Speculation can take the form of buying something in the *spot market,* holding it, and reselling in the spot market at a later date. Alternatively, speculators can use *futures contracts* or *options* to profit from expected changes in prices of goods that they do not currently own.

4. **What socially useful purposes are served by speculation?** Speculators make it possible for others to avoid risk by *hedging*—an operation that uses futures markets or options to offset one risk with another. A second socially useful function is the transmission of information about future economic developments via price changes that take place when speculators trade in spot, futures, or options markets. A third socially useful function of speculation is to promote conservation by smoothing out trends in the use of scarce resources over time.

5. **What is the role of auctions in the economy?** Auctions are a method of trading in markets in which prices are subject to variation with every transaction. Auctions are possible with one seller and many buyers, one buyer and many sellers, or sometimes many of each. In the *English auction,* bidding starts low and proceeds until one high bidder remains. A *Dutch auction* begins with a high bid, which is lowered until a buyer is found. In a *sealed-bid auction,* all buyers submit bids at the same time. The *revenue-equivalence theorem* states that under certain general conditions the expected winning bid is the same for all three types of auctions, although special circumstances may make one type work better than others for some purposes. An auction is said to be subject to a *winner's curse* if the winning bidder typically pays more than the item is worth (or bids less than the cost of supplying it, in a buyer's auction).

KEY TERMS

Information asymmetry	Spot price
Expected value	Options
Risk aversion	Hedging
Risk preference	Reservation price
Risk neutrality	English auction
Risk pooling	Dutch auction
Adverse selection	Sealed-bid auction
Moral hazard	Revenue-equivalence theorem
Speculation	
Futures contract	Winner's curse

PROBLEMS AND TOPICS FOR DISCUSSION

1. **Examining the lead-off case.** Evaluate the following argument: The ordinary pool player of average skills wants to play for even odds against another player of equal skill, or against a slightly better player at odds that make the game a fair match. Hustlers thwart this desire. They disguise themselves as average players and, in order to get games, offer odds that are more attractive than ordinary players can afford to give. The result is an equilibrium in which hustlers drive ordinary players from the poolroom, leaving only hustlers and "fish" at the tables.

   What parallels do you see between this argument and the "lemons" problem discussed in *Applying Economic Ideas 13.2?* What conditions are necessary for ordinary players to survive in the poolroom and successfully enter into games with one another?

2. **Expected value.** You are offered a chance to invest $5,000 in the production of a Broadway play. There is one chance in ten that the play will be a success. If it is a success, your share of the profit will be $50,000. If the play is a flop, you will get nothing back on your investment. What is the expected value of the investment? Bonus question: Under what conditions, if any, would you be willing to make the investment?

3. **Nuclear war insurance.** Home insurance policies often exclude coverage for damage caused by nuclear war. Why does the principle of risk pooling not work in the case of nuclear war? Can you think of any similar examples?

4. **Speculation.** The Black Knight has laid siege to Fairie Towne. As soon as he hears the news, Trader Sharp runs to the market in Fairie Towne and begins to buy all the wheat, corn, and potatoes he can get his hands on. Other citizens complain to the sheriff that Sharp is driving up the price of foodstuffs. The sheriff arrests Sharp and issues a decree that no merchant is allowed to raise the price of wheat, corn, or potatoes above the price that prevailed on the day before the siege.

Which person's actions contribute more to helping Fairie Towne survive the siege as long as possible—Sharp's or the sheriff's? Discuss.

5. **Silent auctions.** St. John's Church decides to hold a "silent auction" to raise funds for new choir robes. Parishioners contribute quilts, jars of jam, and other items to be auctioned. The goods are put on display, with a box beside each item. People put slips of paper into the boxes with their names and the amounts they bid for various items. At the end of the evening, the winning bids are read off and the winning bidders pay for the items. All the proceeds go to the choir fund. In several cases the winning bidder turns out to be the person who donated the item in the first place. Some people think this is cheating. Next time, they say, there should be a rule that people should not be allowed to bid on their own contributions. Other people think that no such rule is needed, but that people were stupid to buy their own items. If they were going to do that, why not simply contribute cash to the choir fund? What do you think?

6. **The winner's curse.** Fill some jars of different shapes and sizes with coins and auction them off by the sealed-bid method in your economics class. Do the results show evidence of a winner's curse? Discuss the results.

CASE FOR DISCUSSION

Insurance and the Crisis in Health Care

A widespread perception has developed that the U.S. system for financing health care is in crisis.

In part the perception of a crisis comes from the rapid growth in the percentage of gross national product devoted to health care. In the 1950s, health care expenditures amounted to 5.3 percent of U.S. spending. By the 2003, that share had risen to about 12 percent. Several countries that spend less on health care have better health statistics, as measured by such indicators as life expectancy and infant mortality.

Some economists see overly generous insurance coverage as one reason for high health-care spending. People who have "first dollar" coverage, that is, who pay nothing to see a doctor or enter the hospital, are more likely to seek medical help for relatively trivial problems. Those whose policies include a "coinsurance" clause, under which they have to pay a set percentage of their medical bills, spend less. A study by economist Willard C. Manning indicated that people with first-dollar coverage spend 40 to 50 percent more on health care than those with a 33 percent coinsurance rate. Yet U.S. tax law, which makes employer-provided health insurance fully tax deductable, encourages big companies to provide first-dollar coverage.

What is more, there is a perception that health care has become not only increasingly expensive but also less equitably distributed. For the most part, people working for the government and large corporations still receive full health insurance coverage. But some 40 million people have no health insurance. Those who are uninsured include not just the poor but millions of self-employed people and employees of small businesses.

Part of the problem stems from the reluctance of health insurance companies to insure those who need insurance the most. Instead, the companies try to estimate each person's likelihood of becoming ill, and set their premiums accordingly. People who have suffered illnesses in the past, or who are genetically predisposed to illness, may find it altogether impossible to buy private insurance.

Small employers are disproportionately hit. Large firms can obtain low premiums by spreading the risk of illness among hundreds or thousands of employees. But a small firm that hires even one employee in a high risk group may see its health-insurance premiums jump to prohibitive levels. As methods for early detection of illness are perfected, the problem becomes more and more severe.

During the 2004 presidential campaign, all candidates promised to do something about the health insurance crisis. Details of their plans differed, but they had certain elements in common: reducing administrative costs, encouraging greater risk-spreading, and making health insurance universally accessible.

Given the widespread agreement as to the need for change, it is likely that major changes in the U.S. health-insurance system lie ahead.

Sources: Williard G. Manning, et al., "Health Insurance and the Demand for Medical Care: Evidence from a Randomized Experiment," *American Economic Review* (June 1987): 251–277; Joseph P. Newhouse, "Medical Care Costs: How Much Welfare Loss?" *Journal of Economic Perspectives* (Summer 1992): 3–21; Kathleen Day, "Health Insurer's Catch 22: The Ill Need Not Apply," *The Washington Post,* October 4, 1992, H1; *Health Insurance Coverage: 2002*, Current Population Survey, U.S. Census Bureau, September 30, 2003; and *National Product and Income Accounts,* Bureau of Economic Analysis, January 2004.

QUESTIONS

1. Does this case provide any evidence that a problem of moral hazard lies behind the health insurance crisis, at least in part? What about a problem of adverse selection?
2. Why does traditional insurance coverage tend to break down in cases of illnesses that can be predicted far in advance, such as illnesses with genetic causes, or those, like AIDS, for which infection precedes actual illness by a long period?
3. Review recent news stories for health-care proposals put forward in Congress or by the White House. What aspects of the insurance crisis do these proposals appear designed to address?

END NOTES

1. Sometimes a distinction is made between *uncertainty,* meaning lack of information about the probabilities of future events, and *risk,* meaning a situation in which people do not know exactly what will happen but do know the mathematical probability of various possible outcomes. In this introductory discussion, however, we use the terms *risk* and *uncertainty* interchangeably.
2. If diminishing marginal utility implies risk aversion, why do people ever gamble? Economists have puzzled over this question for years. One hypothesis is that some people experience increasing marginal utility over some ranges of their utility function. (Imagine a utility graph that has several humps in it, like a playground slide.) A second hypothesis is that people overestimate the likelihood of winning. (That is what the poolroom hustler counts on.) A third hypothesis is that people get pleasure out of the act of gambling itself. (That seems to fit people who play poker for small stakes but would be bored playing for matches.) Take your pick.
3. Some insurance experts distinguish between *moral hazard,* meaning dishonest behavior on the part of the insured, and *morale hazard,* meaning merely careless behavior. Economists usually combine both types of behavior under the heading of moral hazard.
4. This section draws on an excellent review of the literature on auctions by R. Preston McAfee and John McMillan, "Auctions and Bidding," *Journal of Economic Literature* (June 1987): 699–738. For a shorter summary, see Paul Milgrom, "Auctions and Bidding: A Primer," *Journal of Economic Perspectives* (Summer 1989): 3–22.
5. For an excellent discussion of the winner's curse, see Richard H. Thaler, "The Winner's Curse," *Journal of Economic Perspectives* (Winter 1988): 191–202.

CHAPTER 14

Entrepreneurship and the Market Process

After reading this chapter, you will understand:

1. The role played by entrepreneurship in the market process
2. How economists view the area of business activity known as marketing
3. How advertising affects market performance
4. How market structure affects efficiency in both a static and a dynamic sense

Before reading this chapter, make sure you know the meaning of:

1. Entrepreneurship
2. Spontaneous order
3. Market structure
4. High-powered incentives
5. Risk preference and risk aversion

RESTORATION JOE'S

A new kind of chain store has emerged to cater to affluent, practical 30- and 40-somethings. It is a store that takes everyday items and buffs them up just enough that they seem like luxury items and yet manages to keep prices low.

One such store is Restoration Hardware, started in 1980 by Stephen Gordon, who was restoring a Queen Anne-style house in Eureka, California. Gordon had difficulty finding the period-style fixtures he wanted, so he began selling them himself. The phenomenon is not only catering to the baby boomers and former Gen X'ers, but to younger audiences as well. Urban Outfitters turns its stores into theatrical sets to draw in teenage shoppers.

These chains excel at a new style of retailing. While marketing themselves as practicality stores, you'd never visit them to buy more socks for the kids or a bolt to hang a new lamp. Rather, they invite consumers to question the underlying assumptions behind their everyday needs and to reorder those needs.

The trend has filtered to food stores as well. While Trader Joe's sells food, it isn't really a grocery store. "The traditional grocery store handles between 25,000 and 40,000 items," says Trader Joe's spokeswoman Michele Gorski. "We handle between 1,500 and 2,000." But Trader Joe's isn't a gourmet food store either. It's bigger and less pricey than most gourmet shops, noted for its inexpensive wines, tasty frozen meals, and variety of imported foods. In fact, when the prices are high the store makes fun of itself, as it does with its private label, "Really Expensive Authentic Handcrafted" frozen chicken burrito, which sells for $2.19.

The process of turning counterculture rebellion into profit-making opportunity isn't really new. American consumers saw it before with products such as Nike (which used William S. Burroughs to sell sneakers) and the films of Quentin Tarantino ("always hip but scrupulously content-free"). In the case of Restoration Hardware and Trader Joe's, the dissent is a bit more subtle, drawing on baby-boomer nostalgia for simpler times while appealing to practicality.

Source: Timothy Noah, "Restoration Joe's," *Slate,* January 2, 1999.

RESTORATION HARDWARE, TRADER Joe's, and Urban Outfitters are examples of entrepreneurship, which we defined earlier as the activity of looking for new possibilities, making use of new ways of doing things, being alert to new opportunities, and overcoming old limits. In this case, the opportunity lay in the affluent baby boomer population in the United States. Stephen Gordon found the need for period fixtures when restoring his home. Trader Joe's spotted a niche for unique food and wine products at a low price.

In this chapter, we look at entrepreneurship in more detail than we have done up to this point. The chapter continues the process of extending the traditional boundaries of neoclassical models. We will use some of the ideas introduced earlier to explore the conditions of market disequilibrium in which the activity of entrepreneurship takes place.

ENTREPRENEURSHIP AND THE MARKET PROCESS

A key trait of some of the models of market structure that we have looked at previously is their focus on *equilibrium*. The notion of equilibrium is one of the most powerful metaphors of neoclassical economics. It conveys the idea that buyers and sellers will stop seeking gains from trade only when the possible gains have been exhausted. It shows how two separate sets of considerations—those that govern consumers' choices and those that govern producers' choices—interact to determine market prices.

However, as has been mentioned several times in earlier chapters, the neoclassical equilibrium models have their limitations. One is their tendency to treat the conditions that determine cost and demand as givens. They are not well suited to situations in which entrepreneurs seek to shift cost curves through innovations in organization and technology, or seek to shift demand curves, or create new products for which demand curves previously did not exist at all. In short, although the neoclassical models can help us understand the factors that determine the equilibrium price of period fixtures and international food products, they are of little use in explaining the sudden appearance of Restoration Hardware and Trader Joe's as competitors to the other stores where fixtures and groceries have always been sold.

Although neoclassical economics has treated entrepreneurship as a side issue, another school of thought—the Austrian school—has made it a focal point. The Austrian school traces its origins to Karl Menger, Friedrich von Wieser, and Eugen von Böhm-Bawerk, who worked in Vienna in the latter part of the nineteenth century. In the twentieth century, the Austrian tradition was brought to the United States by Ludwig von Mises and Friedrich von Hayek, among others. Today the Austrian school continues to have a strong following in the United States.

Like the neoclassicists, economists of the Austrian school treat the market economy as a system of spontaneous order. However, in the view of the Austrian economists, the spontaneous order of the marketplace is best viewed not in terms of an equilibrium that exists at a given moment but in terms of a *market process* that takes place continuously. The central player in the market process is the entrepreneur. It is the entrepreneur's efforts to move resources from less valued to more valued uses (making a profit in doing so) that make the process an orderly one. Success in these efforts requires (1) willingness to bear risks; (2) alertness to opportunities presented by the marketplace; and (3) the creation of new opportunities through innovation. Let us look at each of these factors in turn.[1]

Entrepreneurship and Risk

Entrepreneurship and risk taking are often seen as nearly synonymous. The reason might seem self-evident: Because entrepreneurship involves new ideas and new ways of doing things, no one can be sure how they will work out. Unexpected technical problems may crop up. Customers may not like a new product. Market conditions can change for reasons that are beyond the entrepreneur's control. If new ideas are to be tried, then, someone must be persuaded to bear the unavoidable risks. How can this be accomplished?

One possibility is for the entrepreneur to share the risk or shift it to someone else. For example, we have seen how the techniques of risk pooling, insurance, and hedging can be used to protect against risk. Entrepreneurs, like anyone else, can be expected to use those techniques where they are applicable. However, they are not applicable to many of the risks faced by entrepreneurs.

For example, insurance is normally available only in cases in which many people are exposed to similar risks, so that underwriters can calculate exact probabilities of loss. But entrepreneurs often face new kinds of risk that no one has ever experienced before. Futures markets in which hedging can take place exist only for homogeneous commodities, such as wheat or gold, and for widely traded securities, such as the stocks of major corporations. Entrepreneurs, however, often deal with new and unique products for which no futures markets exist.

Another way for an entrepreneur to share risk is to join with other owners to start a business. Partnerships and corporations are business structures that can help an individual business owner attract additional capital to a firm. These forms of organization can also be viewed as a way of sharing risks. Some individuals, known as *venture capitalists,* make a specialty of seeking out entrepreneurs with good ideas but inadequate funds with whom they can share risks and potential profits.

Despite the advantages of sharing risks, the classic image of the entrepreneur as owner-manager of an independent firm is far from dead. Such firms offer some unique advantages as a way of implementing entrepreneurial ideas.

One reason that an entrepreneur may want to go it alone has to do with information asymmetry. By definition, entrepreneurs are engaged in putting *new* ideas to work. They are operating on the basis of information that they are the first to uncover. To persuade someone else to bear the risk of implementing the idea, entrepreneurs would have to share the information. Doing so might be difficult. Their ideas might not be completely formulated; they might be based partly on hunches and guesses that others would find unconvincing. There is also the danger that the ideas might be stolen by those with whom they are shared. For these reasons, entrepreneurs may have no choice but to implement their ideas themselves if they are to be implemented at all.

Another advantage of the independent firm is its unique ability to mobilize high-power incentives in the form of a claim to the firm's entire profit. An entrepreneur who is motivated by profit and loss does not require supervision to call forth maximum effort, does not require outside auditing to guarantee careful control of costs, and can adapt quickly to changing conditions without the need for lengthy internal negotiations.

In sum, whatever the institutional context, risk is an unavoidable part of entrepreneurship. For the most part, entrepreneurs, like other people, are risk averse. This means that they will not be willing to bear risks without the expectation of a reward. The greater the risk, the greater the reward. Sometimes the risk can be shared, at least in part, with others, but doing so will also require sharing the rewards. The reward for bearing risk thus is a key part of the profits earned by entrepreneurs.

Entrepreneurship and Arbitrage

Willingness to bear risks is just one requirement of a successful entrepreneur. No less important is the ability to recognize risks that are worth taking. To be successful, then, an entrepreneur must be alert to market opportunities that no one else has recognized yet.

A key concept in understanding how entrepreneurs take advantage of opportunities is **arbitrage**—the activity of buying something at a low price in one market and reselling it at a higher price in another. Unlike speculation, which involves buying at one time and reselling at a later time in the same market, arbitrage depends on a difference in prices for the same good at the same time in different markets.

Arbitrage

The activity of earning a profit by buying something at a low price in one market and reselling it at a higher price in another.

When markets are in equilibrium, opportunities for arbitrage tend to disappear as the flow of goods from the low-price market to the high-price market equalizes prices. Opportunities for arbitrage arise when circumstances change, throwing plans out of alignment and markets out of equilibrium.

Arbitrage can be seen in its purest form in certain organized markets for agricultural commodities, precious metals, and securities. In these markets, a trader peering at a computer screen might learn that platinum is trading at a slightly higher price in the London market than in the Chicago market. An order to buy platinum in Chicago and sell it in London will earn the trader a quick profit. The profit-seeking activities of arbitrageurs, together with those of other buyers and sellers of platinum, contribute to the efficiency of the world economy by sending signals, in the form of price changes, about changes in the opportunity cost of using that metal.

Arbitrage is not limited to organized commodity exchanges. To take a broader example, any type of international trade that follows the principle of comparative advantage can be considered an example of arbitrage. In this case entrepreneurs—who may be selling agents for a manufacturer, purchasing agents for a retailer, or independent brokers—compare the prices at which some good can be bought and sold in various countries. The prices indicate the opportunity costs of production in one place or another. By buying each good in the country in which its domestic opportunity cost is low and selling it where its domestic opportunity cost is higher, international arbitrageurs make a profit. They also—albeit unintentionally—contribute to the efficiency of resource allocation in the world economy.

In securities markets, the purchase and sale of stocks, bonds, and other securities by arbitrageurs tend to move these instruments into the hands of those who place the highest estimates on their values. This kind of arbitrage is especially important in the case of common stock because ownership of common stock carries the right to vote on corporate control. Thus, one aspect of financial arbitrage in the stock market is the takeover process, through which more effective management replaces less effective management.

As mentioned earlier, arbitrage can take place only when markets are in a state of disequilibrium. However, disequilibrium in a market does not mean disorder. The reason is that arbitrage does not cause prices to move at random; it causes them to move in the direction of equilibrium. To take a simple case, suppose that a construction boom in the Northeast has raised the wages of construction workers there, while a slump in the Southwest has lowered construction workers' wages in that region. Building contractors, playing the role of arbitrageur, will place ads in southwestern newspapers and send agents to the region to hire workers, perhaps offering to pay their moving expenses. As workers move away from the Southwest, the supply of labor there will decrease, and wages will move back toward the national average. Similarly, as workers move into the Northeast, the supply of labor there will increase, and wages will fall toward the national average. The market will move toward a new equilibrium in which departures of wages from the national average reflect only differences in cost of living, climate preferences, and so on.

In practice, circumstances often change before the new equilibrium is reached. Austrian economist Murray Rothbard compared this aspect of the market process to what goes on at a racetrack where a mechanical rabbit is used to urge dogs to run. In Rothbard's view, equilibrium is "like the mechanical rabbit being chased by the dog. It is never reached in practice, and it is always changing, but it explains the direction in which the dog is moving."[2]

Arbitrage is normally conceived of as buying a good in one market and selling it unchanged in a different market. However, Israel Kirzner has pointed out that there is an element of arbitrage in all profit-making transactions, even those that involve a transformation of inputs into outputs through some production process.[3] Consider the entrepreneur-owner of, say, a shoe factory. This entrepreneur buys inputs in one set of markets at the lowest possible prices and, after combining the inputs to form finished shoes, sells the product in another market at the highest possible price. If all markets were in perfectly competitive long-run equilibrium, it would be no more possible to make an economic profit by buying labor and leather and selling shoes than it would be to make a profit by buying gold in Hong Kong and reselling it in London. In a state of universal equilibrium, the price of the leather and labor would be bid up and the price of the shoes would be bid down to the point at which revenue was just equal to total cost. When markets are not in equilibrium, however, entrepreneurs can find many profit opportunities that involve moving goods and factor services indirectly as well as directly from one market to another.

Entrepreneurship and Innovation

Arbitrage depends on alertness to changes stemming from forces beyond the entrepreneur's control. However, entrepreneurs do not always wait for things to happen and then react. They also *make* things happen—that is, they *innovate*.

The first firm to come out with a new product or to introduce a new cost-saving production method is able, at least for a time, to sell its product at a price that is higher than its opportunity cost. Before long, competitors will react. As other suppliers pick up the innovation, the forces of supply and demand will once again drive the price toward the level of opportunity cost. But by that time, with a little hard work, another innovation will be ready to be brought to market.

The personality traits of creativity and innovative ability are not distributed evenly among the population. Harvard Medical School researchers Ruth Richards and Dennis Kinney developed a scale broad enough to encompass a range of traits from artistic creativity to entrepreneurship in the world of business.[4] They found that only about 1 percent of people have "exceptional" creativity—the kind associated with widely recognized entrepreneurial achievement or outstanding artistic achievement. Another 10 percent have "high" creativity on Richards and Kinney's scale. That does not mean that the rest of the population has no innovative flair, however. Another 60 percent of people surveyed by Richards and Kinney have "moderate" or "some" creativity. Creating situations in which creativity can flourish is a key to promoting economic innovation and entrepreneurship just as much as to promoting artistic achievement.

There are some things government can do to promote innovation. Investment in education is one possibility. Government funding of scientific research is also seen by some as important. Patents and copyrights are policies that aim to encourage innovation by granting innovators exclusive rights to new products and processes for a specified period.

More important than all the positive programs government can undertake to promote innovation, however, is the willingness of governments to stand aside and let market incentives work. All the money government could spend on education and science may be wasted if entrepreneurs have to fight their way through a thicket of government restrictions, bureaucracy, and red tape to bring their ideas to fruition.

Governments are not the only organizations that must be concerned with fostering innovation. Despite many well-known examples of inventors and innovators working on their own, many people who come up with ideas for new products and processes are employees of large corporations. For a corporation as a whole to be a successful innovator, it must learn to take advantage of the creative abilities of such individuals.

Intrapreneurship

Entrepreneurial activity carried out within a large business organization.

Entrepreneurial activity that takes place in a corporate setting has been called **intrapreneurship**. Successful corporations have discovered that promoting intrapreneurship involves more than just providing a generous research and development budget. It must also include an appropriate pattern of rewards and incentives for innovators, and it must ensure that corporate bureaucracies do not stifle creative impulses.

The Market Process as a Process of Selection

Risk bearing, arbitrage, and innovation complement one another as parts of the market process. An innovation is introduced—for example, the compact disk player, fluidized-bed combustion for electric power plants, or the limited partnership for real estate ventures. The innovation disrupts the old equilibrium, creating a profit opportunity for the first firm to introduce it and very likely threatening competitors with a loss. Buyers' and sellers' plans no longer mesh at the old set of prices, not only in the market in which output is sold but also in input markets, markets for substitutes and complements, and so on. For example, the introduction of compact disk players disrupted equilibrium in the markets for computer chips (used as a component in the players) and in the market for conventional stereos. Arbitrageurs set to work to exploit the profit opportunities that the innovation has created, and the effects ripple throughout the economy.

We have already seen that this process tends to move the market toward a new equilibrium (although the new equilibrium may move before it is reached, like the rabbit chased by the dog). To complete the picture, however, we now bring in risk. Because entrepreneurs cannot be sure how their ideas will work out, they often make mistakes. A corporate marketing staff may bring out a product that seemed to be a good idea but is not accepted by the marketplace. In such cases the entrepreneurs that made the initial move suffer a loss.

Losses and profits are the mechanisms through which the market economy selects superior ways of doing things and rejects inferior ways. When a firm makes a profit, its capital grows and its power to influence the market increases. When a firm suffers a loss, its capital shrinks and its influence wanes. Nineteenth-century economists thought they saw a similarity between this economic selection process and the process of natural selection that Charles Darwin identified as the driving force in the evolution of plant and animal species. Entrepreneurial innovation produces many small variations in products and production processes just as genetic processes produce small variations in the size, color, and other features of plant and animal species. Profit and loss determine the variations that survive in the market in somewhat the same way suitability to environmental conditions determines which variants survive in the biological realm.

MARKETING AS A FORM OF ENTREPRENEURSHIP

Marketing

The process of finding out what customers want and channeling a flow of goods and services to meet those wants.

One of the most fruitful places to look for examples of entrepreneurship is in **marketing**—the process of finding out what customers want and channeling a flow of goods and services to meet those wants. Marketing is a topic that is often neglected by economists. For example, the models of the firm examined in previous chapters assume, for the most part, that the problem of marketing has been solved before the analysis begins. They are set in a world in which both firms and consumers are assumed to know what kinds of goods and services will meet their wants and how they will be made available. The only function performed by the market in those models is that of providing a forum in which buyers and sellers can agree on the price of each good and the quantity to be sold. We have already seen some problems that require extensions of the standard neoclassical models. This section introduces additional extensions that focus on entrepreneurship.

To organize the discussion, we will follow a traditional scheme in which marketing is divided into four activities. The first is creating a *product* that will meet consumer needs. The second is getting the product to a *place* where consumers can conveniently buy it—an activity that includes not only physical transportation but also the whole process of wholesale and retail trade. The third is *promoting* the product through advertising, personal selling, and other means. The fourth—the one that economists have not neglected—is putting the right *price* on the product. These four activities are often called the "four Ps" of marketing. As Figure 14.1 shows, the costs of the four Ps account for about half of the costs of all consumer goods sold in the United States.

Competition and Product

In the model of perfect competition, the product is thought of as given. But in most markets, shaping the product to fit consumer needs is a key element of competition.

Innovation is one major aspect of product competition. Consider the case of recorded music. At one time, what customers mostly wanted was music in their living rooms that sounded like a live performance. Although the ideal has never quite been reached, long-playing records, metal-oxide cassette tapes, Dolby noise suppression systems, and compact disks each represented a step closer toward this goal.

FIGURE 14.1 MARKETING COSTS AND CONSUMER SPENDING

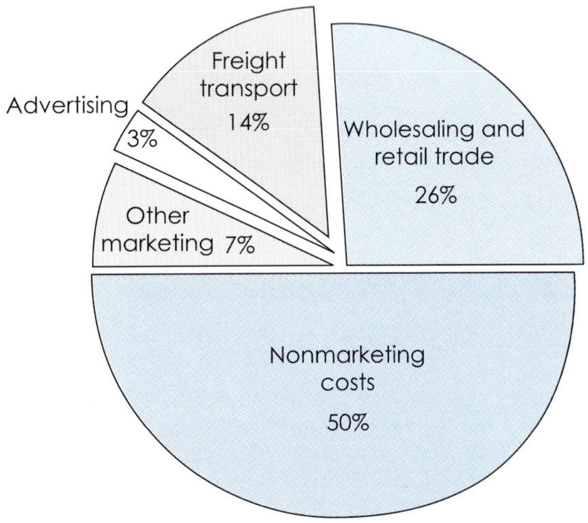

As this chart shows, marketing costs account for about half of the cost of all consumer goods sold. The costs and profits of wholesale and retail trade are the largest single item, followed by freight transportation. Advertising, although the most visible of marketing activities, accounts for only about 3 percent of the cost of consumer goods and services. All aspects of marketing are important to the process of competition.

More recently, consumers have wanted music they can take with them wherever they go. The famous Sony Walkman was a first step toward satisfying this market niche. Today players that are hardly bigger than a credit card can be loaded with hundreds of songs in a variety of digital formats. In all these cases, the first competitor to take each step was able to take at least a temporary advantage.

Diversity is another aspect of product competition. Consumers have different needs and tastes. Economists talk about "the market" for cars, but that market is really composed of many segments: the markets for economy cars, for sports cars, for SUVs, and so on. Competition ensures that products will be made that will meet the needs of consumers in each segment; a neglected segment will soon attract a firm in search of profits.

Quality is yet another dimension of product competition—one that has recently received more attention. The quality of many U.S.-made goods has been improving for years. Tires last longer; fabrics are easier to wash; contact lenses give better vision. However, the demand for quality seems to have risen even more rapidly than the supply. European and Asian firms have gained a competitive advantage in many markets by being the first to respond to this demand. As U.S. firms scramble to catch up, consumers, who are offered higher quality products from both domestic and foreign sources, are the winners.

Nevertheless, economists have sometimes challenged the notion that innovation, diversity, and improved quality are always beneficial to consumers. One line of reasoning is that actions taken by a firm to distinguish its product more clearly from those of its rivals have the effect of making the firms' products less close substitutes, in the eyes of consumers. The demand curve for the product of the firm making the innovation thus becomes less elastic. The less elastic the demand curve, the greater the gap between price and marginal cost in equilibrium and, hence, the less efficient the market.

This argument has been used in comparing monopolistic competition with perfect competition. The defense of monopolistic competition turns, in part, on the notion that diversity itself is a good that benefits consumers even if they must pay more to get it. But this notion has its detractors, too.

The problem, it is said, is that some kinds of diversity add no objective value to the product. To be sure, it is good for consumers to be offered a choice between gas stoves and electric stoves, because each may suit some consumers better, depending on objective factors such as cooking habits, fuel prices, and so on. But what about something such as the changes in pharmaceutical company advertising, described in *Economics in the News 14.1*? Is it not blatant exploitation of consumers to make them pay more than before for the same product, or buy a product they might not otherwise need, just because it is advertised differently?

Those who see product diversity as beneficial commonly answer that even such silly product innovations as toothpaste pumps and upside-down tubes should be judged in the light of the principle of consumer sovereignty. So long as plain, boring

ECONOMICS IN THE NEWS 14.1

RISING HEALTH CARE COSTS AND TV ADS

In 2003, it was hard to turn on the television without seeing an add for a prescription drug. These ads often portray people rock climbing, swinging beneath a tree, or playing touch football with friends and family. While conveying the message that the drug is good for you, they are often short on specifics. What is the drug supposed to do? The commercials typically tell consumer to "ask your doctor about (fill in the drug's name here)." Do people actually do this?

"I think the commercials definitely affect what patients do," said Dr. Janet Pregler, associate professor of medicine at the University of California Medical Center and director of the Iris Cantor UCLA Women's Health Center. "However I've found in my practice that patients really are pretty sophisticated when it comes to advertising and often they won't come in and say 'I saw drug X on television, give it to me,' but rather, the ad will raise some questions in their mind."

The vagueness in prescription drug advertising is fairly recent. Prior to 1999, it was assumed that if pharmaceutical companies informed physicians about potential risks of a medication, they were protected against personal injury suits and tort law. "There was not also the necessity that they would inform consumers when they were advertising," Pregler said.

A 1999 lawsuit in which Wyeth laboratories was sued over a contraceptive drug known as Norplant. The women in the case said that because Wyeth marketed directly to consumers, they also had the responsibility to tell consumers about the risks associated with the drug. The New Jersey Supreme Court agreed. According to Pregler, this "may have had an effect on the type of advertising that you're seeing today."

So what are the pros and cons of pharmaceutical advertising? For one, it may help to educate the public about illness such as high cholesterol and depression. Drug companies are in a much better position to fund television and radio ads, compared with public health entities.

But, Pregler said, there is a cost. Pharmaceutical companies dedicate enormous financial resources toward advertising to consumers and doctors. "If they weren't spending that money to advertise, the cost of those drugs could be lowered by 10, or 20, or even 30%." This has become an issue in prescription drug coverage for Medicare and states. "Many people who look at our health care system as a whole find that advertising in particular may be a wasteful use of our resources," Pregler said.

Source: Madeleine Brand, "Pharmaceutical Ads and the Cost of Health Care," *Day to Day*, National Public Radio, November 12, 2003.

old tubes share drugstore shelves with fun, fancy new packages, consumers are not being exploited. Never mind that toothpaste pumps add nothing to the objective value of the product—in this case, its tooth-cleaning power. In a free market, the prices at which goods change hands reflect the subjective values that consumers place on them. Thus, fancy toothpaste packaging must be adding subjective value for at least some consumers or they would not be purchased, given their higher price.

Competition in Distribution

The second of the four Ps of marketing—place—refers to all the activities involved in getting a product to consumers. It includes transportation and other aspects of physical distribution and, even more important, the services of wholesale and retail firms.

Innovation and diversity affect distribution systems as much as they affect products themselves. Tried-and-true methods of retailing, such as supermarkets, which were radical innovations by entrepreneurs of the past, are now undergoing a new wave of change, as can be seen in the case of Restoration Hardware, Trader Joe's, and Urban

Outfitters. At the same time that some retailers are offering extra services, other stores with minimal service are making inroads among budget-conscious consumers.

However, the patterns of distribution that arise in a competitive economy also have their critics. As Figure 14.1 shows, wholesale and retail trade—even when the transportation aspect of distribution is excluded—account for some $.26 out of every dollar's worth of consumer goods produced. What do people get in return for all they spend to support wholesale and retail trade?

The answer is that consumers are buying services with that $.26. Frills such as the food samples at Trader Joe's or the youthful atmosphere at Urban Outfitters are only a small part of those services. Provision of information is a more important one—visiting a car dealer or a department store is often the most efficient way for a consumer to learn about product availability and characteristics. And convenience—a chance to economize on the opportunity cost of time—is the main service provided by many branches of retailing. It is the reason that many people buy motor oil a quart at a time at the gas station instead of buying it by the case at a discount store and servicing their own cars in their driveways.

Consumers are not forced to buy the services that conventional retailers offer. In an economy characterized by consumer sovereignty, there are low-cost, low-service options for buying almost any good. Clothing, toys, and groceries can be bought at off-price stores, where there are few clerks and incomplete selections but very low prices. And Internet retailing has brought a revolution that strongly favors price-conscious buyers. Computers, tools, and books, not to mention more specialized products like veterinary supplies and used auto parts can be bought from many competing suppliers. Entrepreneurial Web sites have sprung up that help buyers search automatically for the lowest price. Although this approach entails some waiting and the goods cannot be examined in advance, prices are much lower than in local stores. In some communities, consumer cooperatives have been formed for buying goods in bulk and reselling them to members at reduced prices. Even with all these low-price alternatives, however, many people prefer to pay the extra $.26 on the dollar for the additional services they get at department stores and convenience markets, just as people often choose to eat in restaurants rather than preparing meals more cheaply at home.

Competition in Promotion

Advertising, together with other promotional activities, such as personal selling, store displays, and public relations, is the communication link between producers and their customers. It is the most visible aspect of competition in many markets—so visible, in fact, that many people are surprised to find that it accounts for only $.03 of each consumer dollar, as shown in Figure 14.1.

A major purpose of advertising and other aspects of promotion is to spread information. Information is a scarce resource and, as such, cannot be obtained without cost. One way in which consumers can get information is by reading such publications as *Consumer Reports* or visiting the Web sites of this and similar publications. Doing so entails an opportunity cost to the consumer in the form of the time taken to read them. Advertising, personal selling, and other promotional activities are another channel through which consumers can learn about prices, product features, and where to buy desired goods and services. These too have an opportunity cost, which consumers pay in the form of higher prices for advertised brands.

The marketplace allows for competition among these sources of information. It offers consumers a choice between well-known, nationally advertised brands and lower-priced local brands or unbranded "generic" products. It offers a choice between stores with many sales clerks and those with few. The fact that some firms find heavy spending on promotion profitable can be taken as an indication that advertising, personal selling, and other forms of promotion are—at least in some cases—an efficient means of providing information.

Advertising and Its Critics

Advertising does more than just inform consumers; it also shapes their tastes and perceptions. This aspect of marketing is also a subject of controversy.

According to one line of argument, popularized by economist John Kenneth Galbraith in *The Affluent Society,* a best-selling book published in the 1950s, a distinction should be made between true wants and those created by advertising. In Galbraith's view, advertising that goes beyond a simple statement of the facts about a product is at best a waste and at worst harmful to consumer welfare. Advertising aimed at persuading people to buy toothpaste pumps would be a typical object of Galbraith's criticism.

Other economists, however, doubt that there are such things as true or natural wants other than the very basic needs for food, security, affection, self-esteem, and so on. Advertising may affect which goods people choose to satisfy these needs. It may cause them to choose round-toed rather than square-toed boots to keep their feet dry, but that does no harm. Economists who take this point of view believe that efforts to limit the choices open to consumers in the name of giving people what they "truly" want pose a greater threat to consumer sovereignty than advertising does.

In addition to creating false wants in consumers' minds, advertising and other promotional activities lead to reduced market performance, according to some critics. Advertising appears chiefly in oligopoly and monopolistic competition, market structures that have been criticized for poor performance. Like product differentiation, advertising is said to make things worse because it increases the perceived differences among the products of various firms. This, in turn, makes each firm's demand curve less elastic than it otherwise would be and, under conditions of equilibrium, increases the gap between price and marginal cost.

Moreover, in the case of oligopoly, advertising is seen as a barrier to entry by new firms and, hence, as a force that leads to high levels of market concentration—and concentration, as we have seen, is sometimes said to be linked with poor market performance. The way in which advertising is thought to act as a barrier to entry is by creating brand loyalties. Consumers who might otherwise treat all cola drinks as close substitutes are divided into opposing camps, some fiercely loyal to one brand, others to its rival. If brand loyalty were strong enough, each firm could raise its price with little fear that its action would cause customers to go elsewhere. Further, no firm would have to worry about the resulting high profits attracting new firms to the market, because the new firms not only would have to spend money to build plants and hire workers but also would have to mount expensive advertising campaigns.

However, other economists see advertising as a tool used by entrepreneurs to penetrate new markets and break down barriers to entry. For example, Yale Brozen notes that firms aim their advertising less at increasing loyalty among their own customers than at getting their rivals' customers to try their products.[5] The real way to create a barrier to entry and protect existing firms, in his view, would be to ban advertising. Then it would be far harder for a new firm to enter a market.

Advertising and Market Performance

The debate over the benefits of advertising and other marketing techniques seems to turn on two opposing views of the world. Would a world without advertising be one in which consumers treat all sources of supply as homogeneous and move freely among them in response to small changes in price? Or would it be one in which lack of information causes consumers to cling to familiar sources of supply, giving each firm a monopoly with regard to its own customers? Further, does advertising set up barriers among firms, thereby adding to their monopoly power, or does it break down barriers, thus destroying that power? Several kinds of evidence might help answer these questions.

Some studies, such as that described in the *Case for Discussion* in this chapter, suggest that brand loyalty can arise even in the absence of advertising. Other studies show that new products are advertised more heavily than old ones. This may indicate that makers of old products tend to depend on consumer loyalty and that advertising is a way of breaking down that loyalty. Still other studies show that consumers in markets in which advertising is heavy are less loyal to one brand than those in markets with light advertising. This, too, might indicate that advertising helps make consumers more willing to try substitute products.[6]

Perhaps most interesting of all, real-life experiments have been done in which advertising was introduced into a market in which it had been prohibited before. The market for legal services, discussed in *Economics in the News 14.2,* is one such case. There the introduction of advertising seems to have spurred a wave of entrepreneurial activity by lawyers and, ultimately, to have improved market performance.

Economics in the News 14.2

THE PRACTICE OF LAW ENTERS THE ADVERTISING AGE

AUTO ACCIDENTS! PERSONAL INJURY! No Recovery, No Fee!

BANKRUPTCY!
Stop Foreclosure
Stop Lawsuits
Stop Creditor Calls

Free Telephone Consultation!

Turn to the *Yellow Pages* in any big-city phone book under the heading "lawyers," and you will find dozens of ads like these. Yet until the Supreme Court handed down a revolutionary decision in 1977, all such ads were forbidden.

Arguing that for lawyers to compete in "the hustle of the marketplace" would "tarnish the dignified public image of the profession," the bar associations of all fifty states formerly banned all advertising by lawyers. Even *Yellow Page* entries could give no more than a name and telephone number.

Nonsense, said economists, The ban, they said, had nothing to do with the dignity of profession. It had to do with competition. Competition which, if permitted, would erode high fees jealously protected by the cartel-like bar associations.

The challenge to the old system came from two young lawyers in Phoenix, John Bates and Van O'Steen. They published a modest ad in the newspaper that said, modestly, "Need a lawyer? Legal services at very reasonable rates."

The Arizona bar association tried to stop the ad, but the Supreme Court upheld the young lawyers. Since then, the practice of law has changed.

Some say it has become more cutthroat. And some ads really do seem to undermine the dignity of the profession. Consider the Florida ad that said "Holiday Special—Give that spouse of yours something he or she has been wanting for a long time—a divorce."

But a majority of observers agree that advertising has benefited consumers. A 1983 Federal Trade Commission study concluded that advertising had cut fees 5 to 13 percent. And in some markets the discounts are greater than that. Manhattan law firm Jacoby & Meyers, which used to charge $1,500 for an uncontested divorce, reduced the fee to $500 after advertising was legalized.

Source: Based in part on Ruth Marcus, "Practicing Law in the Advertising Age," *The Washington Post,* June 30, 1987, A6.

Price as a Marketing Tool

This brings us to price, the central tool of competition in neoclassical models. How do marketing theorists view this last of the four Ps? Does it fade to insignificance compared with product, place, and promotion, or does it have a key role to play?

Writers on marketing agree with economists that good pricing decisions are vital to a firm's success. But in the real world, they say, the right price cannot be found by picking a point on a graph. Pricing decisions are entrepreneurial in nature; they require judgment as well as calculation, they involve risks, and they must be coordinated with other marketing decisions to enable the firm to satisfy consumer wants as effectively as possible.

Take quality and variety, for example. Some consumers are willing to pay top price for top quality, while others would prefer less than top quality at a lower price. That is why premium-quality brands can be found next to standard-quality "house" labels on supermarket shelves. Some consumers are willing to pay high prices to satisfy unusual tastes; others prefer to save by following the crowd. Thus, for example, the few people who buy books of poetry pay more for their books than do people who prefer mass-market crime or romance novels.

Pricing is a key factor in distribution, too. Often the same goods are available at different prices in swanky boutiques and barnlike off-price outlets or over the Internet. Some consumers prefer one, some the other.

Finally, price and promotion interact. Although some consumers will pay extra for advertised brands, others prefer low-priced generic goods.

In sum, when all aspects of marketing are taken into account, competition begins to look like a much more complex process than it appears to be on a graph where price and quantity are the only variables. It is much less a matter of calculating a maximum on the basis of given conditions and much more an issue of entrepreneurship—of looking for new possibilities, utilizing new ways of doing things, being alert to new opportunities, and overcoming old limits.

ENTREPRENEURSHIP, EFFICIENCY, AND MARKET DYNAMICS

Static efficiency

The ability of an economy to get the greatest degree of consumer satisfaction from given amounts of resources and technology.

Dynamic efficiency

The ability of an economy to increase consumer satisfaction through innovation and technological change.

Up to this point, our discussions of economic performance have concentrated on **static efficiency**—the ability of an economy to get the greatest possible amount of consumer satisfaction with given amounts of resources and technology. Static efficiency measures how well the economy performs at a given time with given resources and technology. Here we will focus on the economy's **dynamic efficiency**—its success in increasing the rate of output per unit of resources. Dynamic efficiency is a measure of the rate at which the production possibility frontier shifts outward over time as a result of innovation and technological change. As we will see, dynamic efficiency is closely linked to entrepreneurship.

Of the two kinds of efficiency, dynamic efficiency is much more important in the long run. In the past, the most important single factor in U.S. economic growth was innovation and technological change. The remaining economic growth is due to capital accumulation, population growth, increased education, and other factors. The contribution of innovation and technological change is very large compared to the loss in static efficiency caused by monopolistic and oligopolistic market structures.

The Schumpeter Hypothesis

If every policy that promotes static efficiency also contributed to dynamic efficiency, the distinction between the two would hardly matter. However, there are reasons to think that this may not necessarily be the case. One key issue is the relationship between market structure and market performance. In earlier chapters we saw that neoclassical models imply that perfectly competitive markets are the most efficient in the static sense and monopoly is the least efficient. However, when efficiency is viewed in dynamic terms, the superiority of perfect competition is not so clear. It has been argued that the traditional categories of market structure are largely irrelevant to market performance measured in dynamic terms. This view is often referred to as the *Schumpeter hypothesis*, after the Austrian-born economist Joseph Schumpeter, who first brought it to widespread attention (see *Who Said It? Who Did It? 14.1*). Schumpeter and others suggested that in some cases large, oligopolistic firms may outperform small, perfectly competitive firms in dynamic terms.

According to Schumpeter, the source of innovation and technological change is competition—but competition among entrepreneurs, not the kind found in perfectly competitive markets. He saw two ways in which entrepreneurial competition promotes dynamic efficiency even when it leads, at least temporarily, to some degree of monopoly power.

First, Schumpeter points out, the hope of achieving monopoly power is often the entrepreneur's chief incentive for competition. The first firm to obtain new knowledge and put it to use is able to make pure economic profits because its new discovery gives it a temporary monopoly. If each new product had to be brought out at a price that just covered cost, or if each cost-reducing innovation had to be followed by a matching reduction in price, there would be little reason to innovate at all. If the first firm to adjust to changing conditions were unable to increase the gap between costs and revenues by doing so, there would be no incentive to be first. Competition among entrepreneurs is competition for monopoly power, at least in the short run. In this sense, monopoly is not the opposite of competition but a normal result of it.

Second, monopoly power acts to spur competition. This is true in the sense that an industry in which monopoly profits are being made tends to attract entrepreneurs from the outside. This applies both to the entry of new firms and to indirect competi-

WHO SAID IT? WHO DID IT? 14.1
JOSEPH SCHUMPETER ON COMPETITION AND ENTREPRENEURSHIP

Joseph Schumpeter was born in Austria in 1883. He studied law at the University of Vienna and attended lectures by the leading economists of the day, including some of the founders of the Austrian school. He served briefly as minister of finance after World War I. In 1932, he left Austria for Harvard University, where he wrote most of the works for which he is known today.

Schumpeter had little use for the kind of economics that reduces everything to graphs and equations. He thought economic theories paid too little attention to the role of the entrepreneur. He saw competition among entrepreneurs, rather than the abstract notion of perfect competition, as the source of economic progress. As he wrote in *Capitalism, Socialism, and Democracy*:

> *The competition that counts is competition from the new commodity, the new technology, the new source of supply, the new type of organization (the largest scale unit of control, for instance)—competition which commands a decisive cost or quality advantage and which strikes not at the margins of the profits and the outputs of the existing firms, but at their foundations and their very lives. This kind of competition is as much more effective than the other as a bombardment is in comparison with forcing a door, and so much more important that it becomes a matter of comparative indifference whether competition in the ordinary sense functions more or less promptly; the powerful lever that in the long run expands output and brings down prices is in any case made of other stuff.*

"In this respect," Schumpeter added, "perfect competition is not only impossible but inferior, and has not title to being set up as a model of ideal efficiency."

Source: Joseph Schumpeter, *Capitalism, Socialism, and Democracy* (New York: Harper & Row, 1942, 1942k), 84–85, 105.

tion by substitutes. For example, in the 1970s, OPEC's attempts to exploit its monopoly power led to a speedup in the rate of oil exploration and also to innovations in alternative energy sources and conservation techniques. In this sense, monopoly is an impetus to competition.

Empirical Evidence on the Schumpeter Hypothesis

Not surprisingly, Schumpeter's provocative hypothesis has inspired a number of attempts at confirmation or refutation on the basis of empirical evidence regarding economic growth, market concentration, and innovation. To date, however, the results have been inconclusive.[7]

The main problem in testing the Schumpeter hypothesis lies in measuring innovation. Schumpeter had in mind a fairly broad view of innovation. Inventing new products or techniques, figuring out how to apply new inventions, working out new forms of business organization, finding new ways of financing investment, and creating new methods of marketing and distribution all were, to Schumpeter, major sources of dynamic efficiency. But most of them clearly can be measured only indirectly, and some not at all.

Perhaps the safest conclusion is that innovation—in Schumpeter's sense—is simply too complex to be subjected to quantitative analysis. Under favorable conditions, firms of all sizes in markets with all degrees of concentration are able to contribute to the dynamic efficiency of the economy as a whole. This implies that neither a policy of breaking up large firms into smaller ones nor one of welding small firms into larger ones can be counted on to speed the pace of innovation. The ability of large corporations to assign R&D teams to solve tough technical problems is important, but so is the flash of insight that may come to a solitary inventor. In short, for all we know, the present mix of large-firm intrapreneurship and small-firm entrepreneurship may be about right from the standpoint of dynamic efficiency.

SUMMARY

1. **What role does entrepreneurship play in the market process?** Economists of the Austrian school view the market as a place in which spontaneous order is maintained even when the market is not in equilibrium. The activities of entrepreneurs are crucial to the market process through which this order is maintained. Successful entrepreneurship requires willingness to bear risk, alertness to opportunities for *arbitrage,* and the creation of new opportunities through innovation. A process of selection through losses and profits enhances the likelihood that successful entrepreneurs will survive.

2. **How do economists view the area of business activity known as marketing?** Many examples of entrepreneurship can be found in marketing. *Marketing* means finding out what customers want

and channeling a flow of goods and services to meet those wants. It consists of four activities: making a product that will meet consumer needs; getting it to a place where consumers can buy it conveniently; promoting it through advertising, personal selling, and other means; and putting the right price on it.

3. **How does advertising affect market performance?** Some economists view advertising as a barrier to the entry of new firms into a market and a source of monopoly profits. Others dispute these claims, contending that advertising is used more by entrepreneurs entering a market than by existing firms.
4. **How does market structure affect efficiency in both a static and a dynamic sense?** *Static efficiency* means the ability of an economy to get the greatest amount of consumer satisfaction from given amounts of resources and technology. *Dynamic efficiency* means increasing consumer satisfaction over time through innovations and technological changes that raise output per unit of resources. Joseph Schumpeter suggested that market structure, as conventionally understood, may have little to do with dynamic efficiency and that, at least in some cases, relatively concentrated markets may actually be more dynamically efficient than perfectly competitive ones.

KEY TERMS

Arbitrage
Intrapreneurship
Marketing
Static efficiency
Dynamic efficiency

PROBLEMS AND TOPICS FOR DISCUSSION

1. **Examining the lead-off case.** What illustrations of risk taking, arbitrage, and innovation are illustrated in this case? Which of the "four Ps" of marketing are illustrated? How does the case bear on the issue of large versus small firms as a source of innovation?
2. **Drug company ads.** How does the example of pharmaceutical ads illustrate entrepreneurship and what economists of the Austrian school call the market process? How does the case illustrate marketing? Do you think prescription drugs cater to "true" or "false" consumer needs, or is this distinction invalid?
3. **The "four Ps" of marketing.** Look through recent issues of business magazines such as *Fortune, Forbes,* and *BusinessWeek* for articles illustrating each of the "four Ps" of marketing. Do the examples bear out the notion that advertising is an entrepreneurial activity?
4. **Advertising and its critics.** Critics of advertising often claim that it causes consumers to buy things that they do not "really" want or need. Can you think of an example of something that you buy because of advertising but do not really want or need? If so, why do you buy it? If not, do you think that you are an exception—that advertising has no adverse effect on you but does on other people? Discuss.

CASE FOR DISCUSSION

Brand Loyalty Without Brands

In a study of brand loyalty, a random sample of 60 beer drinkers was drawn from Stanford University students living in married-student housing. The subjects were told that they were taking part in a marketing test of three types of beer produced by a local brewer.

Once a week the subjects were presented, in their homes, with a chance to choose among three bottles labeled "M," "L," and "P." They were told that brand M was a high-priced beer, brand L a medium-priced beer, and brand P a bargain-priced beer. The subjects did not have to pay for their beer; but to make the price difference more realistic, the medium-priced beer had a $.02 "refund" taped to the bottle while the low-priced beer had a $.05 "refund." The subjects could keep the refunds.

In point of fact, the three brands of beer all came from the same production run at the brewery; only the labels differed. However, this did not prevent the development of fierce brand loyalty by many of the subjects. (Subjects were considered to be brand loyal if they chose the same brand four times in a row.) Although at first the subjects experimented with the three brands, by the end of 24 trials, 57 of the 60 subjects had developed brand loyalty. Of those 57, 26 chose brand M, 12 brand L, and 19 brand P.

Since the beer was all the same, it is surprising how firmly set in their opinions some of the subjects became. One subject reported, "M is a good, strong, malty beer, but I like L because it is lighter. Mmm!!! P would poison me—make me ill." Another subject, who developed a strong taste for P, once tried a bottle of M and reported, "Worst I've ever had; you couldn't give it away."

Source: J. Douglass McConnell, "The Development of Brand Loyalty: An Experimental Study," *Journal of Marketing Research* (February 1968): 53–19.

QUESTIONS

1. Critics of advertising blame it for creating brand loyalty. This, in turn, is said to create barriers to entry in oligopolistic industries and to make the demand curves of firms in monopolistically competitive industries less elastic than they would otherwise be. In both cases advertising is thought to contribute to poor market performance. What does this case suggest about the connection between advertising and brand loyalty? Does it support a policy of setting limits on advertising as a means of improving market performance in the beer industry?
2. Economies of scale have led to a high degree of concentration in the brewing industry. That industry is now an oligopoly dominated by a few major brewers. Yet those brewers still produce a great many brands of beer. If one looked only at the number of brand names displayed in a typical store, one would think brewing is an example of monopolistic competition. What does brand loyalty have to do with this type of market structure? Do you think market performance would be improved by limiting each large firm to just one brand?

END NOTES

1. For another discussion based on the same classification of entrepreneurial traits, see Carl P. Kaiser, "Entrepreneurship and Resource Allocation," *Eastern Economic Journal* (January–March), 1990.
2. Murray Rothbard, *Man, Economy, and State* (Los Angeles: Nash, 1962), 250. As quoted by Jack High, "Equilibration and Disequilibration in the Market Process," in *Subjectivism, Intelligibility, and Economic Understanding,* ed. Israel M. Kirzner (New York: New York University Press, 1986), 112.
3. See Israel Kirzner, *Competition and Entrepreneurship* (Chicago: University of Chicago Press, 1974).
4. Richards and Kinney's work is described in Daniel Goleman, "A New Index That Illuminates the Creative Life," *The New York Times,* September 13,1988, Cl.
5. For a representative exposition of Brozen's views, see Yale Brozen, "Entry Barriers: Advertising and Product Differentiation," in *Industrial Concentration: The New Learning,* eds. Harvey J. Goldschmid, H. Michael Mann, and J. Fred Weston (Boston: Little, Brown, 1974), 115–137.
6. The article by Brozen cited in footnote 5 discusses and provides the references to these and similar studies.
7. For a survey of these efforts, see Jesse W. Markham, "Concentration: A Stimulus or Retardant to Innovation?" in *Industrial Concentration: The New Learning,* eds. Harvey J. Goldschmid, H. Michael Mann, and J. Fred Weston (Boston: Little, Brown, 1974), 247–272.

CHAPTER 15

The Theory of Public Choice

After reading this chapter, you will understand:

1. How economic theory can be applied to government
2. The role of self-interest in the theory of public choice
3. How public expenditures are determined under direct democracy
4. How representative democracy differs from direct democracy
5. The similarities and differences between private firms and government agencies
6. The reasons for the privatization of some government activities

Before reading this chapter, make sure you know the meaning of:

1. Public goods
2. Market failure
3. Political rent seeking
4. Transaction costs and the firm

NATIONAL PARK SERVICE

Death Valley National Monument includes sites with names like the Funeral Mountains, Coffin Peak, Hell's Gate, Starvation Canyon, and Dead Man Pass. This is a place with a bad history, reflecting the troubles and misfortunes endured by the pioneers who first traversed, inhabited, and mined the region during the end of the last century. The area may have had a foreboding reputation, but visitors today enjoy the amazing beauty with many colorful rocks and canyons, miles of pristine sand dunes, unique evaporative salt features and even a diverse range of wildlife.

Now Death Valley is struggling again. The weather-beaten roof of the visitor center there was so dilapidated that a ceiling tile recently fell and struck a woman standing in the gift shop. With relatively few park rangers available to patrol the massive desert and salt flats, thieves routinely steal priceless Indian rock art and remnants of historic ghost towns.

"Every park staff is struggling with operational issues—not having enough staff and funds to do what we know we need to protect the parks and serve the users," said James T. Reynolds, superintendent of Death Valley, the largest national park in the contiguous United States. He is not the only one worried. Park officials, conservationists, and lawmakers are troubled by the declining state of many of the 385 national parks and sites.

At Yellowstone National Park repeated spills from worn-out water treatment plants have dumped untreated waste into the pristine waters of Yellowstone Lake, the Firehole River, and other park waterways. Acadia National Park in Maine lacks the staff to adequately patrol the park's complex, 115-mile boundary—leaving miles of roads and trails vulnerable to damage from illegal snowmobile and all-terrain vehicle use, trail cutting, and poaching.

"We all wish we lived in an ideal world where we can get to every single one of those problems," said Donald Murphy, deputy director of the National Park Service (NPS). "The fact is, if we don't manage well and if we don't take care of the maintenance backlog . . . the system will have deteriorated to the point where we won't ever be able to catch up."

California's Death Valley National Monument is a case in point. A sharp growth in the number of visitors and increased park acreage have strained resources, forcing the NPS to put off tens of millions of dollars of necessary improvements. In addition, inadequate staffing has made it virtually impossible to patrol the park's large area closely. The number of park patrol rangers has been cut almost in half.

Some say the national parks' real problems center on the relationship between politics and funding. In the last thirty years, the number of NPS park sites has risen, with the vast majority of these new parks established by Congress members seeking a park for their home districts. Congress channels funding to those activities which generate the highest political return, such as to the creation of new, and often expensive, parks that serve as local economic development projects.

As a consequence, they neglect less visible, but necessary, park maintenance and operations. The NPS has deemed that many of these "park pork" projects are either unnecessary or too expensive, but has little power to change the way Congress allocates funds. For instance, Senator Robert Byrd pushed for $2.5 million to renovate a train station and establish a visitor's center for an old mining boomtown in Thurmond, West Virginia. The train doesn't stop at Thurmond because the town only has seven residents.

Source: Excerpts from Eric Pianin, "National Parks Suffering From Lack of Funds," *Washington Post*, April 14, 200; and Richard J. Ansson, "Our National Parks—Overcrowded, Underfunded, and Besieged with a Myriad of Vexing Problems," *Journal of Land Use & Environmental Law*, 1996.

IN AN EARLIER chapter we introduced two theories of government. According to the first theory, government should play a limited role in the economy. Whatever the market can do well should be left to the market; the government should step in only in cases of *market failure*—for example, in cases of externalities, public goods, or insufficient competition. According to the second theory, government programs are better explained in terms of the ways in which people use government institutions to promote private ends, a process we have termed *political rent seeking*.

The case of the National Park Service in some respects fits both theories. It could be argued that key historical sites are public goods, inasmuch as their preservation serves a sense of national pride for all citizens, even those who never visit. But when one compares the difficulty of finding adequate funding for the Death Valley visitor's center with the generous funding for that in Thurmond, West Virginia, political rent seeking seems like the better explanation.

Public choice theory
The study of how people use the institutions of government to promote private ends.

Explanations of government policies in terms of the ways in which people use the institutions of government to promote private ends have drawn increasing attention from economists in recent years. This area of economics, known as **public choice theory**, received particular recognition in 1987 when its foremost practitioner, James Buchanan of George Mason University, was awarded the Nobel Memorial Prize in economics for his work (see *Who Said It? Who Did It? 15.1*).

THE SELF-INTEREST ASSUMPTION OF PUBLIC CHOICE THEORY

A basic principle of public choice theory is that people act in the same way in both public and private roles. They are the same people all day long as they eat, shop, drive cars, enter the voting booth, go to work in a government bureau, or rise to speak on the floor of the Senate. In analyzing people's private choices, economists have long assumed that people act in rational pursuit of self-interest. As consumers, they maximize utility; as entrepreneurs, they maximize profit; and so on. Thus, public choice theorists assume that the actions and choices of people in public roles are guided by self-interest as well.

Some people protest that this assumption of self-interested behavior is cynical and unrealistic; when properly understood, however, it is neither. The self-interest assumption must be understood as a working hypothesis, not as an unqualified assertion that applies to every person in every instance. In this respect, the self-interest assumption of public choice theory may be compared with the rationality assumption as applied to consumer choice. Using the rationality assumption as a tool for understanding consumer behavior does not mean denying that people sometimes behave altruistically or that they sometimes make choices that are inconsistent with their stated goals. Reasonable conclusions may be drawn on the basis of the rationality assumption, such as the prediction that lowering the price of donuts will increase

WHO SAID IT? WHO DID IT? 15.1

JAMES BUCHANAN AND PUBLIC CHOICE THEORY

James Buchanan, founder of the public choice theory, grew up on a farm in Murfreesboro, Tennessee. He initially planned a career in law and politics, but eventually settled on economics. He received a doctorate in economics from the University of Chicago and taught at Florida State University, the University of Virginia, UCLA, and Virginia Polytechnic Institute. He now heads the Center for the Study of Public Choice at George Mason University.

Buchanan traces his thinking on public choice issues to an obscure dissertation on the economic theory of government written in 1896 by the Swedish economist Knut Wicksell. *The Calculus of Consent*, which Buchanan wrote in 1962 with Gordon Tullock, explains how public choice theory differs from traditional political theory. Traditional analysis, the authors write, has

> *often been grounded on the implicit assumption that the representative individual seeks not to maximize his own utility, but to find the "public interest" or "common good." Moreover, a significant factor in the popular support for socialism throughout the centuries has been the underlying faith that the shift of an activity from the realm of private to that of social choice involves the replacement of the motive of private gain by that of social good.*

Buchanan and his colleagues, in contrast, believe that people do not change when they move from the marketplace into the political arena. In both realms they seek to use existing institutions in their own best interests. Any analysis of political institutions that ignores the rational pursuit of self-interest on the part of individual citizens and government officials is subject to serious error.

In his *Demand and Supply of Public Goods* (1968), Buchanan made a pioneering contribution to the positive theory of public spending. Instead of asking how much of a public good the government ought to supply, as earlier writers on public goods had done, Buchanan sought to develop a theory of the political marketplace analogous to the theory of the economic market. He strove to learn who decides, and on what basis, how much of each good and service to provide and how the costs are to be shared. Says Buchanan,

> *In order to get better government policy, we'd better look not to electing better people, but to changing the structure of the rules which constrain them. The ordinary man has always had a sort of common-sense wisdom about politics and government—especially early on in the history of this country. This isn't far from what public choice distills in an informal way.*

Sources: Quoted passages are from James Buchanan and Gordon Tullock, *The Calculus of Consent* (Ann Arbor: University of Michigan Press, 1962), and Paula Odin, "Nobel Laureate," *George Mason Magazine*, Fall 1986, 2.

sales of donuts. But common sense must be used, too. Naive application of the rationality assumption might lead to the prediction that people will take money out of the collection plate when it is passed around in church rather than putting money into it; however, that prediction turns out to be false for the most part.

In the same way, the self-interest assumption is applied to public choice as a working hypothesis. For example, public choice theorists do not assert that all politicians are corrupt vote sellers. Nevertheless, they notice that lobbyists spend a lot of money for campaign contributions, travel, honoraria for making speeches, and so on in their efforts to influence congressional votes. It would not be rational for these lobbyists to spend so much year after year unless they thought they were getting something in return. When public choice theorists observe that legislators who receive contributions from a given industry are more likely to vote for projects favored by that industry, they consider this finding to be consistent with the self-interest hypothesis.

PUBLIC CHOICE IN A DIRECT DEMOCRACY

We will return to the issue of the self-interested behavior of elected representatives later in the chapter. For a first illustration of public choice theory, we will turn to the simpler case of direct democracy.

A *direct democracy* is a democracy in which the people affected by public policies—taxation, public works projects, regulations, and so forth—have the right to vote in person on each policy. This form of organization is used in some government units in the United States, such as traditional New England town meetings, and is often used in small not-for-profit organizations, such as clubs.

How Much Should Be Spent?

Public choice theory can be applied to any decision made by government. To take a specific example, we will begin with the question of how much government ought to spend on the provision of a given good or service. One way to approach this question is to ask whether the benefits the public receives from a government program are great enough to justify its costs.

Figure 15.1 gives an example of a benefit-cost analysis for the project of providing streetlighting in a small community that has only three citizens, whom we will call Smith, Jones, and Brown. All three would get some benefit from streetlights. However, they would not all benefit equally because of where they live, how often they go out at night, and so on. For the sake of the example, we will assume that Smith gets 50 percent of the total benefit of the streetlights, Jones 30 percent, and Brown 20 percent.

The more lights are provided, the greater the total benefits to the community. However, the added benefit of each additional light—that is, the *marginal benefit*—is greatest with the first few lights. As more and more lights are added, each additional light yields a smaller marginal benefit to the community. Part (a) of Figure 15.1 provides information

FIGURE 15.1 A BENEFIT-COST ANALYSIS OF STREETLIGHTING

(a)

(1) Number of Lights	(2) Community Total Benefit	(3) Community Marginal Benefit	Individual Marginal Benefit to: (4) Smith 50%	(5) Jones 30%	(6) Brown 20%
1	$ 900				
		$800	$400	$240	$160
2	1,700				
		700	350	210	140
3	2,400				
		600	300	180	120
4	3,000				
		500	250	150	100
5	3,500				
		400	200	120	80
6	3,900				
		300	150	90	60
7	4,200				
		200	100	60	40
8	4,400				

(b)

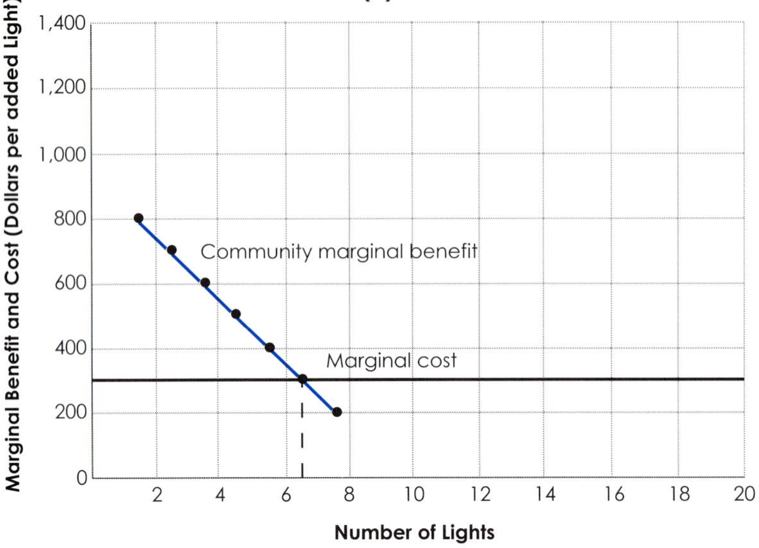

This figure shows the costs and benefits of streetlighting in a small community inhabited by three people—Smith, Jones, and Brown. Columns 2 and 3 of part (a) show total and marginal benefits of lighting to the community as a whole. Because of where they live and how often they go out at night, benefits are not distributed equally. Smith is assumed to get 50 percent of the total benefits, Jones 30 percent, and Brown 20 percent. The individual shares of marginal benefits are shown in columns 4 through 6. Part (b) compares marginal costs with community marginal benefits. Streetlights are assumed to cost $300 each. The efficient number of streetlights in this town is seven. Beyond that point the added benefits of another light are less than the added cost.

about the benefits of lighting. Column 2 shows the total benefit to the community of various levels of lighting. Column 3 shows the added benefit to the community as a whole of each additional light; this is termed the *community marginal benefit.* The numbers in the community marginal benefit column are the differences between successive entries in the community total benefit column. Finally, columns 4 through 6 show the *individual marginal benefits* to Smith, Jones, and Brown. These are 50, 30, and 20 percent, respectively, of the corresponding community marginal benefits.

Part (b) of Figure 15.1 represents the streetlighting problem in graphical terms. The negatively sloped line, which represents the community marginal benefits of streetlighting, is based on column 3 of part (a). In addition, a horizontal line is added to show the marginal cost of the streetlighting program, assuming that lights cost a constant $300 per unit.

The data given in the figure are all we need for a benefit-cost analysis of the streetlighting program. The rule for efficient streetlighting is to add lights up to the point at which the benefit of the last light added (that is, the community marginal benefit) just equals the cost of the last light (that is, the marginal cost). This means putting in seven lights Smith gets $150 in benefits from the last light added, Jones gets $90, and Brown gets $60, for a total of $300. That is enough to justify the $300 cost of the last light. An eighth light would give them only $200 more in benefits—not enough to justify the cost.

How Much Will Be Spent?

Now that we know how much *should* be spent using the benefit-cost standard, we move on to the question of how much *will* be spent. According to public choice theory, the amount spent depends on the self-interests of citizens and on the political structure within which they make choices. We have already specified one key feature of the political structure, namely, the fact that choices are made by a majority vote of all citizens. Now let's look at the effect of another feature of the political structure: the way in which the costs of public activities are shared among members of the community.

COSTS SHARED IN PROPORTION TO BENEFITS RECEIVED First we will examine the case in which costs are shared in proportion to the benefits received. In our example this means that for each dollar of taxes raised, Smith pays $.50, Jones $.30, and Brown $.20.

Under these conditions the town meeting will vote unanimously for the first six lights, because each voter's share of total costs exceeds his or her share of total benefits. The meeting may very well also approve the seventh light, for which costs are equal to benefits. However, none will vote for an eighth light, for which their individual shares of the cost exceed their individual shares of the benefits.

We can conclude, then, that in a direct democracy in which taxes are shared in exact proportion to the benefits of public programs, an efficient amount of spending will take place if everyone votes according to his or her own self-interest.

COSTS SHARED EQUALLY Next let us suppose that costs are shared equally but benefits are not. In our example, this means that Smith, Jones, and Brown will each pay $100 of the $300 cost of each light.

Given this distribution of benefits, the town meeting goes a bit differently. The proposal for a fifth light is still passed by a unanimous vote, but just barely. Smith is looking at a $250 individual marginal benefit to offset his $100 share of the marginal costs; Jones sees a $150 benefit and $100 in costs; and Brown sees a $100 benefit and $100 in costs. The proposal for a sixth light passes by a vote of 2 to 1. This time Brown is looking at an $80 individual marginal benefit and $100 as his share of marginal costs. If he votes in his own self-interest (as public choice theorists assume), he will vote no. If a seventh light is proposed, the proposal will fail by a 1-to-2 vote. Smith will see $150 in benefits and $100 in costs; Jones $90 in benefits and $100 in costs; and Brown $60 in benefits and $100 in costs.

Conclusion: In a direct democracy, when the costs of a program are distributed evenly but the benefits are not, there will be a tendency to spend less than the efficient amount on each government program.

BENEFITS EQUAL, COSTS SHARED UNEQUALLY Finally, suppose that the benefits of the streetlights are distributed equally but the costs are shared unequally: Smith now pays 60 percent of total taxes while Jones and Brown pay 20 percent each.

By now the reasoning is familiar, although the results differ. Smith drops out on the vote for the fifth light, because his share of the marginal benefit ($166) now falls short of his share of the marginal cost ($180). Lights 6 and 7 also pass by 2-to-1 votes. Then the eighth light comes up for a vote. The community marginal benefit of light 8 is just $200—less than the cost. But Jones's and Brown's share of that benefit is $66—more than their $60 share of the cost. Thus, eight lights—one more than the efficient number—are approved.

Conclusion: In a direct democracy, when the benefits of a program are spread evenly but the costs are shared unequally, there will be a tendency to spend more than the efficient amount on each government program.

Real-world examples can be found to fit each of the three cases we have just reviewed. Highway construction can be compared with the example in which costs and benefits fall equally on each citizen in that much of the cost of highway construction is paid for by gasoline taxes and other road-use taxes. Other things being equal, this method of financing highway construction therefore would tend to move expenditures toward the optimal level.

For an example in which costs are spread equally but benefits are not, think of a town in which there are many retired people but only a few young families. Such a town is likely to be stingy with its school budget, spending less than analysis of total costs and benefits, regardless of the way these costs and benefits are distributed, would call for.

Finally, for an example in which benefits are spread equally but costs are shared unequally, picture a country that provides for its defense needs by maintaining an army of draftees. All citizens benefit from national defense, whereas the burden of the draft falls disproportionately on young people who are a minority of voters. Public choice theory would predict that, other things being equal, a country that uses a draft will tend to maintain a larger standing army than one that relies on a volunteer army, which must be paid competitive market wages financed by a tax imposed on the citizenry as a whole.

The Median Voter Model

In addition to the conclusions that have just been drawn, the streetlighting example can be used to bring out another point. Unless costs are distributed exactly in proportion to benefits, the person whose preferences lie in the middle of the scale—Jones, in the example—plays a crucial role in the voting. Jones always gets her way. When Jones wants more lights, she allies herself with Smith, who favors streetlighting more strongly than she does. When Jones does not want another light, she allies herself with Brown, who is less enthusiastic about lighting than she is.

Generalizing, we can say that in a direct democracy that operates by simple majority vote, the decision made by the community will tend to correspond to the interests of the *median voter*—the voter whose preferences lie in the middle of the community scale. This is called the **median voter model**. If the issue is streetlights, the number of lights voted will not be the number preferred by the people who want the most lights or the least, but the number wanted by the median voter. If the issue is how much to spend on the school budget, the outcome will correspond not to the wishes of the families with the most children nor to the wishes of those with no children, but rather to the wishes of median-size families who hold the balance of votes needed for a majority.

Median voter model

A model showing that there is a tendency for decisions in a direct democracy to correspond to the interests of voters whose preferences lie near the middle of the community scale.

The tendency to follow the preferences of the median voter often keeps democratic decisions from going to extremes, and avoiding extremes is often a virtue. However, the median voter model does not guarantee that the decision made is an efficient one. As we have shown, depending on the way costs and benefits are distributed, the level of expenditures preferred by the median voter can lie either above or below the optimum as determined by benefit-cost analysis.

PUBLIC CHOICE AND RENT SEEKING IN A REPRESENTATIVE DEMOCRACY

Our analysis of spending for public goods in a direct democracy is only a starting point. In this section we will shift our focus from direct democracy to representative democracy. In a representative democracy citizens vote periodically to elect representatives to Congress, state legislatures, city councils, and the like. The representatives, in turn, vote on specific issues. This two-stage procedure has the advantage of specialization. Citizens can go about their daily lives without having to worry about the details of thousands of government programs. But this approach also changes the kinds of decisions the government makes.

In a representative democracy one encounters many decisions that do not fit the median voter model. For example, in a direct democracy one would not normally see programs that benefit a small group of workers and industrialists at the expense of the vast majority of the population, such as import restrictions on shoes, shirts, and other widely purchased consumer goods. Nor would one see votes for tax loopholes (for example, special depreciation allowances for racehorse owners) that excuse a small group of citizens from bearing their proportionate share of the costs of programs that benefit all citizens equally. Yet such decisions are made routinely in Congress, state legislatures, and city councils. The ability of small groups of political rent seekers to obtain decisions favorable to special-interest groups stems largely from certain features of representative democracy that are not found in the simpler form of government examined in the preceding section.

Lobbying, Information, and the Costs of Political Expression

In representative democracy, as in direct democracy, voting is an important channel of political expression. The act of voting is sometimes compared to that of purchasing goods in a market economy, inasmuch as people are said to exercise "consumer sovereignty" by "voting with dollars." In the "political marketplace" they use many of the same advertising, promotion, and public relations tools that business firms use. However, there is an important difference as well.

In the marketplace consumers can pick and choose among a wide variety of goods to suit their individual preferences, whereas in an election voters must choose among a few candidates who offer "package deals" covering a broad range of issues. In a supermarket a shopper may choose separately what to have for breakfast, lunch, and dinner, but at election time it is not possible to choose one person as a representative for foreign policy issues, another for civil rights issues, and a third for economic issues.

But voting is not the only channel of political expression in a representative democracy. People who want to influence the outcome of particular legislative decisions can also engage in **lobbying**. We use this term in a broad sense to mean any method of communicating with elected officials to advocate a particular policy.

Lobbying

Any method of communicating with elected officials to advocate a particular policy.

Like all human activities, lobbying has opportunity costs. First, people must become informed about the issues and decide what decisions they want the government to make. Information has an opportunity cost in terms of time, money, or both. Second, voters must communicate with their representatives. Expressing oneself through letters, telegrams, newspaper ads, or professional lobbyists in Washington or the state capital also costs time and money. Few voters feel that they have enough at stake in any one issue to repay the effort of even writing a letter.

However, groups of people with shared interests are in a different situation. They can share the costs both of keeping informed and of making their views known to their representatives. They can hire full-time lobbyists. As a result, their influence may be much greater than would be possible if each member acted alone.

The disproportionate strength of small, well-organized groups works in favor of some groups that seek what they see as the general good of all citizens. But it also applies to groups of rent seekers who have narrow self-interests in mind. Consider the case of price supports for milk, discussed in the beginning of the text. Many more voters are milk consumers than dairy farmers. Yet for most consumers the price of milk is a minor issue, whereas for dairy farmers it is central. As experience indicates, the small, intensely interested group of dairy farmers is able to mount a more effective lobbying campaign.

Logrolling

As mentioned earlier, in a representative democracy citizens do not vote often, and few of them meet for political purposes between elections. Representatives, on the other hand, vote on hundreds of issues during every congressional session and meet daily. This gives them an opportunity to engage in vote trading, or **logrolling**, as the practice is often called.

Logrolling
The practice of trading votes among members of a legislative body.

The idea of logrolling is simple. Each member of Congress selects a few issues that are important to the voters in his or her home state or district. In exchange for votes on those issues, the member promises to vote for or against legislation that is important to other members.

Logrolling leads to the passage of certain kinds of programs that would never be approved in a direct democracy. These are programs that generate rents for a few people while dispersing costs widely among taxpayers or consumers in general. Often this means that logrolling promotes local interests at the expense of national interests, because local issues are what affect voters most. Thus, it may make sense for a representative to trade away his or her votes on weighty national issues—the budget deficit, a Supreme Court nomination, a treaty—in order to win the votes of others on a narrow issue such as a defense contract or a protective tariff that would benefit a local employer.

A variant of vote trading is the *pork barrel*. This is a bill that consists largely or entirely of a series of small, local projects (parks, highways, post offices, harbor dredging) that produce benefits for local interests at the expense of taxpayers in general. Political entrepreneurs in Congress add more pork to the barrel until it commands a majority of votes; they then submit the whole package as a single bill. The bill passes even though none of its components would command a majority vote or pass a benefit-cost test individually. The introductory case at the beginning of this chapter provides an example of the use of pork barrels. Some parks, such as the old mining boomtown in West Virginia, have faired will because of pork barrels, but many are now under neglect due to a disproportionate allocation of funds.

Despite many examples in which logrolling leads to wasteful spending, public choice theorists are quick to point out that the practice is inherently neutral—it does not favor either "good" or "bad" policy. Rather, its function is to give expression to preferences that are strongly favored by a minority and treated indifferently or mildly opposed by a majority. These may include pork-barrel spending and special tax loopholes, but they may also include such issues as civil rights for racial and ethnic groups, freedom for small religious groups, and protection of whales. It is far from certain that representative government would be better without vote trading.

The Self-Interest of Representatives

One additional difference between representative and direct democracies lies in the fact that representatives have interests of their own that do not always match those of the voters who elect them. For a politician, reelection usually has a high priority. Whether representatives want to promote voters' interests, fight for a cause, gain power and prestige, or simply have a job, getting reelected is a must.

But getting reelected costs money. Therefore, the representative must become a political entrepreneur. Sources of campaign contributions must be found. Lobbyists for rent-seeking special-interest groups are one of the richest sources of contributions for political candidates. Although few members of Congress would accept an outright cash payment specifically in return for casting a vote, campaign contributions do buy time on representatives' crowded schedules. Often the side that gets the time to present its views most fully is the side that wins.

Constitutional Choice: Voting on the Rules

The discussion of voting as a resource allocation mechanism has revealed two principles:

1. Voting cannot always be counted on to produce an optimal level of public spending on each project. On only some occasions is just the right amount spent: Sometimes too much is spent, and sometimes too little.
2. The outcome of the democratic process depends on the particular rules by which decisions are made. Thus, for example, the decisions made in a representative democracy differ in some ways from those that would be expected in a direct democracy.

Together, these two principles suggest the possibility of choosing the democratic rules that can be expected to produce the fairest and most efficient outcomes, at least on the average. The choice of rules for democratic decision making is often referred to as **constitutional choice**.

Constitutional choice

A choice among various sets of rules for democratic government that is intended to produce desirable outcomes when applied to future situations whose details are not known.

The drafting of the U.S. Constitution provides one example of constitutional choice. The delegates who met in a hot room in Philadelphia two centuries ago argued long and hard about such issues as direct or indirect election of the president, equal representation by states or representation in proportion to population, and the balance of power among the government's legislative, executive, and judicial branches. In many cases they were guided by a sound, intuitive understanding of the ways in which different rules would affect outcomes.

Students of constitutional choice often emphasize that the prospects for choosing a fair and efficient set of rules are best when the people who make the rules do not know any details of the particular decisions to which those rules will be applied. Thus, for example, the framers of the U.S. Constitution debated the powers of the Supreme Court without knowing who the justices of the Court would be or exactly

ECONOMICS IN THE NEWS 15.1

CONGRESS CLOSES EIGHTY-SIX BASES

It is not often that an economics professor gets to carry out a massive, real-world test of theory. U.S. Representative Richard Armey, a former college economics teacher, is one of the few to have that opportunity.

The problem for which Armey devised a solution was that of closing unneeded military bases. Virtually everyone agreed that the U.S. government had more bases than it needed. But no one could agree on which ones to close. As soon as the Pentagon would draw up a list of bases it no longer wanted, representatives from the affected districts would form a coalition to block all of the closings. The result: congressional stalemate.

Armey's solution was based on the theory of constitutional choice, a branch of public choice theory. In the first step, Congress would pass a law authorizing a commission to designate a list of bases to close. Then as a second step, it would accept or reject the whole list, with no possibility for change. If it did not reject the list, it would automatically go into effect. Even if Congress did vote to reject the list, the rejection could be nullified by presidential veto.

The objective: arrange things so that no individual member could be blamed for closing any particular base.

In a triumph of applied economics, the plan worked. The commission was appointed, and in December 1988 duly reported its plan. Eighty-six bases were slated for closure, saving the Pentagon $693 million annually. Naturally, when the list became known, there were howls of protest. If normal logrolling procedures had been allowed, blocs of legislators would have pulled bases off the list a few at a time until none were left. But the rules did not permit this to be done. A vote to override the commission's recommendations failed to muster a majority, and the closings went into effect.

Source: John J. Fialka and John E. Yang, "Panel Backs Closing 86 Bases in Biggest Realignment since 1940s," *The Wall Street Journal,* December 30, 1988, A3. Copyright 1988 Dow Jones & Company, Inc. Reprinted by permission of *The Wall Street Journal.* All Rights Reserved Worldwide.

what cases would be brought before it. The greatest difficulties faced by the Constitutional Convention arose in cases in which everyone knew exactly whom the rules would affect and how. Thus, the convention came closest to breaking down over such questions as the rights of large versus small states and the issue of slavery.

But we do not have to go back two hundred years to see the principle of constitutional choice in action. Many issues arise that can be resolved by an appropriate change in the rules. *Economics in the News 15.1* provides a case in point. For years Congress had been unable to find a formula for closing unneeded military bases. Each time it tried, the logic of logrolling and the pork barrel defeated the effort. Finally a workable formula was found under which a vote to close unneeded bases could be taken without the members knowing in advance exactly which bases would be closed. Although there were protests when the final list was announced, the procedure worked, resulting in a considerable saving to taxpayers.

THE ECONOMICS OF BUREAUCRACY

Up to this point our discussion of public choice theory has focused on the choices made by voters and elected representatives. However, the actual work of government at all levels is accomplished in the multitude of departments, agencies, and bureaus that are collectively known as "the bureaucracy."

Similarities Between Government Bureaus and Firms

Government bureaus have an obvious resemblance to private firms. Both bureaus and firms use the hierarchical principle: They are made up of individuals who are bound together in a long-term contractual relationship, and they use hierarchical principles of internal organization. As a means of carrying out complex tasks, they share the advantages of private firms that were noted in the chapter on business structure. Those advantages are as follows:

1. Bureaus, like firms, provide a stable context within which people can make long-term commitments of specialized resources, including investment in specialized human capital through formal training and on-the-job experience.
2. Bureaus, like firms, provide an organizational framework within which opportunistic behavior can be controlled through monitoring, supervision, and record keeping.
3. Bureaus, like firms, are able to adapt to change by means of instructions issued by managers to subordinates, without the need for costly renegotiation of contractual relationships.

At the same time, government bureaus are subject to two disadvantages that also limit the expansion of private firms:

1. As they expand, bureaus, like firms, suffer from a tendency for communication to slow down and become error-prone as information is passed up and down through more and more layers of the hierarchy.
2. In their internal operations, bureaus, like firms, must rely primarily on low-power incentives rather than on the high-power incentives of market relationships. As a result, as they grow, they encounter increased monitoring costs, increased slacking by members, and decreased entrepreneurial initiative.

Differences Between Government Bureaus and Firms

Despite these similarities, government bureaus are not entirely equivalent to private firms. In many respects they are less able to exploit the advantages of the hierarchical form of organization, and at the same time they suffer more from its disadvantages. The reasons can be examined under the headings of monitoring, competition, and the self-interest of bureaucrats.

WHO MONITORS THE MONITOR? In any hierarchical organization, subordinates must be monitored to ensure that they will do their jobs. Marine Corps drill sergeants monitor privates to make sure they do their push-ups; the head teller in a bank monitors the transactions made by junior tellers; school principals monitor teachers. But the question always arises: Who monitors the monitor? Who is ultimately responsible for ensuring that the organization does the best possible job of performing its function?

In private firms, the ultimate monitors are the firms' owners. In a previous chapter we discussed problems related to the control of firms by their owners, especially in large corporations in which ownership is dispersed among many stockholders. In such cases the solution to the problem of monitoring the monitors is for stockholders to elect a board of directors to oversee the activities of the firm's managers. The system is far from perfect. Both managers and directors sometimes behave opportunistically, pursuing their own aims of wealth, comfort, security, or empire building at the expense of stockholders' interest in earning a maximum profit. They are able to do so because individual shareholders are neither willing nor able to monitor directors or managers on a day-to-day basis.

In a government bureau, elected legislators are the closest equivalent of a corporation's board of directors. One of their jobs is to oversee the activities of government bureaus and, together with elected executive officers, to appoint top management. The U.S. Congress also uses a special government agency, the Government Accounting Office, to monitor activities of other federal agencies. Management analysts have often written of the imperfections of control in private corporations, especially the failure of managers, in some cases, to act in the interest of shareholders. However, by comparison, control of government bureaus by voters and their responsiveness to the needs of citizens is even more imperfect.

One reason is that legislators, unlike corporate directors, are not elected for the specific purpose of monitoring a particular agency. Instead, as was pointed out earlier, voters must elect them on the basis of a "package deal," which means that their skill as monitors of the bureaucracy must be weighed together with their views on all sorts of other issues ranging from taxes to civil rights. Thus, a legislator's skill as a monitor may play a minor role, if any, in determining the outcome of an election.

A second reason is that shareholders in a corporation have an important means of keeping directors and managers in line that voters do not have: By proxy or by selling their shares, they can transfer their votes to someone who is willing to keep informed, to fulfill the monitoring function, and to take action when necessary. There is nothing in the political realm comparable to a takeover by stock acquisition. As a result, government bureau chiefs often have more freedom to pursue their own self-interest than corporate managers have.

LACK OF COMPETITION In addition to differences between the ways in which firms and government bureaus relate to their owners, there are differences between the ways in which they relate to their customers. These differences stem largely from the fact that government bureaus are less subject to the pressures of competition than are private firms.

As a case in point, consider the difference between the procedures for renewing a driver's license and making a bank deposit. Both transactions require only a minute or two of clerical time on the part of the agency providing the service, but renewing a driver's license often involves far more time on the part of the customer. If the transaction is done in person, one quickly finds that motor vehicle offices are fewer in number, less conveniently located, open for shorter periods, and plagued with longer lines than banks. If the transaction is done by mail, the license application takes longer to be processed.

Why the difference in customer service? Primarily because a customer who finds the lines in a bank too long can go to another bank, whereas there is only one agency that issues driver's licenses in any given state.

Of course, there are areas of private business in which competition is lacking. Private monopolies, especially closed monopolies such as electric utilities, can also be difficult for customers to deal with. And there are some areas in which governments face competition. For example, suburban communities sometimes compete with one another to offer better schools and roads as a means of attracting new development and tax dollars. All in all, though, the discipline of competition tends to be weaker in the public sector than in the private sector.

THE SELF-INTEREST OF BUREAUCRATS We have suggested that problems of monitoring and lack of competition give bureaucrats more leeway than business managers have to pursue their self-interest at the expense of the interests of their principals. If so, what are the self-interests of bureaucrats? Observers of bureaucracy have identified several.

One often-noted interest of heads of government bureaus is the expansion of their organizations. Salary, perquisites such as office space and travel, prestige, and possibilities for promotion all tend to increase as the size of the organization that a manager directs increases. Thus, agency directors actively lobby Congress and the administration for increases in their budgets and responsibilities. It is rare to see an agency argue that some function it now performs could perhaps better be performed elsewhere in government. It is virtually unknown for an agency to return unspent funds to the treasury; something can always be found to spend the money on—new furniture, a trip to a conference, or whatever.

A consequence is that agencies often tend to grow larger than Congress originally intended. Congress originally sets up an agency in response to lobbying pressure from an interested group of voters. But after the agency has been set up, pressure for its expansion comes from two directions—the interested voters and the agency itself.

A second aspect of self-interest of bureaucrats stems from the "revolving door" that cycles managers from private firms to related government agencies and back again. Take the regulation of financial markets by the Securities and Exchange Commission, for example. The agency cannot do its job unless at least some of its decision makers have a good knowledge of financial markets. The only way to get such knowledgeable people is by recruiting them from the ranks of financial managers. At the same time, financial markets cannot operate effectively unless at least some of their managers have good knowledge of government financial regulations. The best way to get such people is by recruiting them from the ranks of regulators.

The speed at which the door revolves is greatly increased by the fact that senior managers in industry are often paid five to ten times as much as their counterparts in government. A stint in government service thus is an investment in human capital that can be made to pay off only when the manager leaves government for a job in industry.

Sometimes the revolving door creates a tendency for government regulators to be sympathetic to the industries they regulate. For example, the SEC chairperson might treat markets sympathetically in the expectation of getting a better job later as a financial market executive. At other times, however, the opposite effect can occur. For example, lawyers for the antitrust division of the Department of Justice might try to increase the complexity of regulations restricting corporate mergers. Doing so will create a greater demand among private firms for experts on merger law, thereby improving the lawyers' future job prospects.

Finally, some observers think that bureaucrats, by comparison with managers in the private sector, have a bias against risk taking and innovation. The Food and Drug Administration (FDA), which is responsible for approving new therapeutic drugs, is sometimes cited as an example. Suppose a private firm has developed a new ulcer treatment, which it calls XYZ. If the drug is successful, the company will reap huge profits. If it turns out to be harmful, the company will be hit with damage suits and suffer huge losses. The firm will weigh the potential profits against the risks in deciding whether to seek approval for the drug. The FDA official, however, is in a somewhat different position. If the drug is effective, the official who approves it will get no share of the profit. If it is effective and the official turns it down, no one outside the industry will likely notice. But if the official approves a drug that turns out to be harmful, woe betide. There will be reprimands, Congressional hearings, television coverage—in short, a disaster. The safe thing to do is to consider only the risks and ignore the benefits—turn down the application for introduction of XYZ.

In each of the cases just described, the self-interest of bureaucrats appears to lead them to act against the public interest. Public choice theorists caution that this does not mean that government officials never serve the public interest. Many, because of pride and a sense of professionalism, do what they think is right for the public even when it might be in their own self-interest to act otherwise. But the theorists caution that pride and professionalism cannot always be expected to prevail. Self-interest is a steady wind that produces a gentle but constant pressure on bureaucratic decision making.

Privatization

The size and scope of private firms depend on the relative transaction costs of organizing any given task within a firm or through the market. Over time, the size and scope of firms adjust to changing circumstances in a way that tends to minimize total production plus transaction costs. Within the private sector, then, the boundary between activities organized within firms and those organized directly through markets tends to be drawn in a way that promotes efficiency.

No comparable mechanism, however, guarantees that the boundary between government bureaus and private firms will be drawn in a cost-minimizing manner. Just as a democratic government sometimes spends too much on the projects it undertakes, it may sometimes move activities into the public sector that would best be left in the private sector. In principle, a democracy might also sometimes leave tasks to the private sector that could be accomplished more efficiently by government. However, a number of economists think that political rent seeking has created a bias toward governmental efforts to perform activities that the private sector could handle more efficiently. The conviction that governments are trying to do too much has led to increased interest in **privatization**—the turning over of government functions to the private sector.

Privatization

The turning over of government functions to the private sector.

Privatization can take various forms. Sometimes it involves outright sale of government-owned enterprises. The sales of British Telecom, British Airways, and British Gas in the United Kingdom provide examples of this approach. In other cases privatization is done by turning over operation of a public enterprise to the private sector under a management contract, as in the case of the Indianapolis airport. Sometimes just a part of a public organization, such as food service, is privatized under contract.

The perceived benefits of privatization vary from one case to another. Among the most frequently cited benefits are improved administration through the introduction of high-power incentives, increased competition through elimination of closed monopolies, and reduced opportunities for rent seeking.

However, despite the many successes of privatization, government participation in the economy is not likely to disappear soon. Privatization has some inherent limitations.

In some cases, where public goods or externalities are involved, turning a government activity over entirely to the private sector is difficult, as in the case of national defense. In other cases, the government has taken on businesses that are too unprofitable to attract private buyers. Finally, although privatization can limit rent seeking, it does not always eliminate it. For example, the U.S. government, unlike many others, relies almost exclusively on private firms to supply weapons to the armed forces. However, defense contracting remains a notorious arena for political rent seeking, as various examples in this chapter have illustrated.

Ultimately, drawing the line between the activities that are best undertaken by government and those that are best left to the private sector remains a judgment call. Nevertheless, public choice theory provides grounds for caution in expanding the economic role of government. In particular, it suggests that governmental efforts to correct market failures will not necessarily improve matters. One reason is that government bureaus are subject to administrative inefficiencies and are often shielded from competition. Another is that the powers that government needs to be granted in order to deal with market failures can be—and often are—used to serve the interests of political rent seekers. Thus, the ever-present possibility of government failure must be balanced against the losses that could result from market failure in the absence of government action. Despite the best intentions of the designers of government programs, the market, for all its imperfections, often produces better results.

SUMMARY

1. **How can economic theory be applied to government?** *Public choice theory* examines how people use the institutions of government to promote private ends. It allows for the possibility that government programs will be used in the service of rent seeking as well as to correct market failures.
2. **What is the role of self-interest in the theory of public choice?** Public choice theory seeks to explain government policies in terms of the interaction between the self-interest of individuals and the rules of the political process. However, the assumption of self-interest should be properly interpreted as a working hypothesis rather than as an absolute statement that allows no exceptions.
3. **How are public expenditures determined under direct democracy?** Under direct democracy, the level of public expenditure on any given program is determined by the way in which costs and benefits are distributed among voters. According to the *median voter model* there is a tendency for governmental decisions to reflect the preferences of voters in the center of the political spectrum.
4. **How does representative democracy differ from direct democracy?** Three features of representative democracy make it possible for programs to be instituted that will benefit rent-seeking minority interests at the expense of the majority. The first is the ability of small, well-organized interest groups to share the costs of information and political expression, and thus to be more effective at *lobbying*. The second is the practice of vote trading, or *logrolling*. The third is the tendency of representatives to act in their own interests rather than those of their constituents.
5. **What are some similarities and differences between private firms and government bureaus?** As hierarchical organizations for carrying out economic tasks, government bureaus share three advantages of private firms: They provide a stable context for long-term commitments of specialized resources; they control opportunistic behavior through monitoring; and they provide a means of adapting to change. They also share some disadvantages of firms: As they expand, internal communication and decision making slow down, and they are unable to make use of high-power incentives. However, bureaus tend to partake in the advantages to a smaller degree and the disadvantages to a greater degree than private firms. The reasons are found in the limited monitoring ability of voters, the lack of competitive discipline in government bureaus, and the self-interest of bureaucrats.
6. **What are the reasons for the privatization of some government activities?** The belief that government has in some cases taken on tasks that could be accomplished more efficiently in the private sector has led to increased interest in

privatization, the turning over of government functions to the private sector. Anticipated advantages of privatization include improved administration, increased competition, suppression of rent seeking, and improved services.

KEY TERMS

Public choice theory	Logrolling
Median voter model	Constitutional choice
Lobbying	Privatization

PROBLEMS AND TOPICS FOR DISCUSSION

1. **Examining the lead-off case.** How do the examples given illustrate the principles of *logrolling* and the *pork barrel?* Do you think the allocation of funds among various national parks is efficient from the point of view of a cost-benefit standard? How might the outcome of the appropriation process differ if decisions to finance parks were made under direct, rather than representative democracy? Would the outcome necessarily be more efficient? Why or why not?

2. **Political expression.** Have you ever tried to influence the outcome of a political decision by writing to or otherwise communicating with a government official? Do you belong to any groups that try to influence legislative decisions? What lobbying actions do those groups undertake?

3. **Farm subsidies.** Farm subsidies are often defended on the ground that without them, some small, low-income farmers would be driven out of business. Yet, because subsidies raise prices both for large, efficient farms and for small, high-cost farms, most subsidies go to relatively prosperous farmers who would survive without them. Can you explain, in terms of public choice theory, why farm subsidies are not limited exclusively to small, high-cost farms?

4. **Bureaucracy.** As discussed previously, stockholders of private firms often use devices such as stock options to provide directors and top managers of their firms with high-power incentives oriented toward profit maximization. Could or should similar incentives be provided to the heads of government bureaus? How does the presence or absence of high-power incentives for top managers bear on the relative efficiency of private firms and government bureaus?

CASE FOR DISCUSSION

Mexico's Privatization Drive, In Reverse

President Carlos Salinas was determined to move the Mexican economy into the world mainstream. Privatization was a key element of his plan to do so.

In 1982, when Salinas was secretary of budget and planning, Mexico had 1,155 state-owned enterprises. A decade later, the number had fallen to just 269, and was still decreasing. Some enterprises, which engaged in no real productive activities, were merged or liquidated. A few, such as the giant, money-losing steel mill, Fundidora de Monterrey, were simply closed. But a great number of firms have successfully made the transition to private ownership, including two airlines, the National Hotel Group, the telephone company, and nineteen sugar mills.

Privatization has helped in several ways. Perhaps the most immediate payoff is freeing the government budget of subsidies previously paid to unprofitable state entities. This has helped touch off a "virtuous cycle" of debt renegotiation, foreign investment, and capital repatriation that is fueling rapid growth of the

Mexican economy. But the long-term success of privatization will be judged by the profitability of companies under their new ownership.

Turning a sluggish state-owned giant into a dynamic, private firm is not always easy. Consider the somewhat different experiences of Mexico's two airlines, Mexicana and Aeromexico, both now privatized.

In its first three years after privatization, Aeromexico underwent a huge turnaround. Delays and inefficiency were replaced by world-class service. The airline's fleet is now one of the newest in the business. Aeromexico airline earned more than $5 million in profits over this period. Quite a turnaround for an airline which, according to its president, Guillermo Heredia, used to be a "feudal" organization. It was the tool of a government structure where resources were incredibly wasted," he says.

Things have not gone so smoothly at the larger Mexicana, Latin America's second-largest airline. Founded in 1929, Mexicana has a proud history. However, after nationalization in 1982, government officials used the airline almost as a plaything. Employees were badly trained and poorly paid, the fleet was old, and the whole enterprise was gripped by bureaucracy.

Mexicana's new owners, including Chase Manhattan Corp. and Drexel Lambert Inc.'s Americas Development Fund, face a tough task, especially in dealing with the aging fleet of planes.

Millions of dollars spent on cosmetic treatment in the first years of private operation may have been wasted. In 1990, the airline suffered a $10 million loss.

In February 2002, Vincente Fox ended the ruling party's seventy-year control of Mexico's presidency in the national election. President Fox promised a better future for Mexico's citizens through improved immigration policy with the United States and by reversing many of the policies implemented by the Salinas administration. In September 2001, the Mexican government renationalized twenty-seven indebted sugar mills to save them from bankruptcy.

Sources: Guillermo Ortiz, "Mexico's Been Bitten by the Privatization Bug," *The Wall Street Journal,* September 15, 1989, A1; and Andrea Dabrowski, "Mexico's Privatization Plan under Pressure," *The Washington Post,* September 3, 1991, El.

QUESTIONS

1. Would nationalization of Mexico's airlines be better explained by a market failure theory or a rent-seeking theory of government? Discuss.
2. In what ways would pressures for efficiency and cost reduction differ for the airlines under public and private ownership? Do you agree with the policies of Salinas or Fox?
3. Some critics have said that newly privatized firms will not be efficient because they face too little competition within the relatively small Mexican economy. Is this a valid criticism? If so, what might be done to counter it?

PART IV

Issues in Microeconomic Policy

CHAPTER 16

Antitrust and Regulation

After reading this chapter, you will understand:

1. Which business practices are illegal under the antitrust laws
2. How economists' views on antitrust policy have changed over time
3. How natural monopolies are regulated and what problems are posed by regulation
4. Why some industries are regulated despite their inherently competitive structure
5. The effects of regulatory reform
6. Current trends in health and safety regulation

Before reading this chapter, make sure you know the meaning of:

1. Political rent seeking
2. Market failure
3. Public choice theory
4. Natural monopoly
5. Herfindahl index and concentration ratios
6. Transaction costs

JUSTICE DEPARTMENT FOILS IVY LEAGUE CONSPIRACY

Suppose that the presidents of General Motors, Ford, DaimlerChrysler, Toyota, Nissan, and Honda were to meet each December to discuss topics of mutual interest. Suppose that among the topics on the agenda were the raises they planned to give their workers, the prices they planned to charge for their cars, and the rebates they would give to selected buyers. Suppose that pressures were brought to bear on members who got out of line to lower wages or raise prices in concert with the others. And suppose that members of the group, angered by Korean automakers' refusal to join it, organized a secret plan to recruit them.

Would anyone think for a minute that such practices would be anything but a conspiracy against the public interest? Anything but a brazen attempt to create a cartel that would control not only the market for the firms' outputs but the market for their inputs as well? Would anyone imagine that such meetings, if they did take place, would be held in anything but the utmost secrecy?

Yet for years, the presidents of Harvard, Yale, Columbia, Brown, Cornell, and Princeton Universities, together with those of the University of Pennsylvania, Dartmouth College, and MIT, held exactly such meetings and discussed exactly such subjects. And they did it openly.

For example, when the group met on December 3, 1986, they learned that Dartmouth planned to raise faculty salaries by 8.5 percent. The other schools wanted to hold the line to a range of 5 to 6.5 percent. Dartmouth caved in.

Another time the discussion turned acrimonious when Harvard and Yale accused Princeton of undercutting the cartel by offering excessively generous scholarships to top students. As if Merit Scholars were football players!

Still another time, the group organized a secret plan, "Operation Highstick," to try to drag uncooperative Stanford into the cartel, and stop it from skimming the cream of Eastern prep schools.

Finally the Justice Department's antitrust division said enough is enough. A cartel is a cartel. Cut it out.

The presidents feigned shock. "Who, us? But we are doing it for the good of the country, providing quality education for all!" According to the Justice Department, that was as if the automakers were to justify their cartel by pointing to the investments they made in pollution control.

The Ivy League quickly capitulated. In 1991 the eight schools signed a consent order, according to which, without admitting or denying guilt, they agreed to stop most, if not all, of their consultations.

MIT refused to sign the consent order. It pursued the case all the way to the Supreme Court, which, in 1992, said the law applies to all, even the colleges of the elite.

Source: Gary Putka, "Ivy League Discussions on Finances Extended to Tuition and Salaries," *The Wall Street Journal*, May 8, 1992, A1, and Peter Passell, "Tuition Price-Fixing Case Isn't Academic for MIT," *The International Herald Tribune*, May 14, 1992, 11.

Antitrust laws

A set of laws, including the Sherman Act and the Clayton Act, that seek to control market structure and the competitive behavior of firms.

IN EARLIER CHAPTERS we discussed the market failure and public choice theories of policy in general terms. Now we turn our attention to two specific areas of government policy to which these theories can be applied. We begin with a discussion of **antitrust laws**—a set of laws that seek to improve market performance by regulating the competitive behavior of firms. The price-fixing activities of the Ivy League universities, although involving an unusual product, are in many ways a typical example of antitrust law in action. Later in the chapter we turn to other regulatory policies that also attempt to influence the competitive behavior of firms and the performance of markets.

ANTITRUST LAWS AND POLICIES

The antitrust laws are a complex group of statutes, court decisions, and regulatory rulings that have developed over the past century. What they have in common is the aim of regulating competitive practices that are deemed unfair, inefficient, or otherwise harmful to the public interest. We can begin our discussion of the antitrust laws with a brief review of the major statutes in this area.

The Sherman Antitrust Act

The Sherman Antitrust Act of 1890 forms the core of antitrust policy in the United States. It outlaws "every contract, combination in the form of a trust or otherwise, or conspiracy in restraint of commerce among the several States, or with foreign nations." It also declares that "every person who shall monopolize, or attempt to monopolize, or combine or conspire with any other person or persons, to monopolize any part of the trade or commerce among the several States, or with foreign nations, shall be deemed guilty of a misdemeanor." (In 1974 the act was amended so that violations of its provisions would be treated as felonies.)

The government can sue firms that violate the provisions of the Sherman Act and ask for any of several types of penalties. It can request fines or jail sentences. (The latter, once rare in antitrust cases, have become much more common now that violations constitute felonies.) It can also obtain an *injunction* (a court order that bars the offending firm from continuing an action that is in violation of the act). In extreme cases it can ask the court to order the offending firm to be broken up into smaller units that would compete with one another, as was done in the case of the AT&T telephone monopoly.

In addition, private parties who claim to have been harmed by violations of the Sherman Act can bring suits of their own. If they win, they can obtain damages equal to three times the value of any loss they can prove to have suffered. Private antitrust suits are quite common today.

The Clayton Act and the Federal Trade Commission Act

Antitrust officials of the federal government won some notable early victories under the Sherman Act; the most dramatic of these were the breakups of Standard Oil and American Tobacco in 1911. Nevertheless, many people felt that the Sherman Act was not enough. Their concerns led to the Clayton Act of 1914, which has four major provisions: (1) It outlaws certain forms of price discrimination; (2) it limits *tying contracts* (contracts for the sale of a firm's products that include an agreement prohibiting the purchaser from using or dealing in a competitor's products); (3) it restricts mergers achieved through purchase of stocks when the effect is to reduce competition substantially; and (4) it restricts *interlocking directorates* (situations in which the same person is on the boards of directors of two or more firms).

In the same year that it passed the Clayton Act, Congress passed the Federal Trade Commission Act, which supplements the former. This act declares broadly that "unfair methods of competition in commerce are illegal." It leaves the decision as to what constitutes an unfair method to the Federal Trade Commission (FTC), which was formed by the act as an independent agency with the purpose of attacking unfair practices.

Antitrust Policy

In practice, U.S. antitrust policy is not determined by the antitrust statutes alone. The laws are written in broad terms. Congress left to the courts the questions of what constitutes an "attempt to monopolize," a "substantial lessening of competition," and an "unfair method of competition." The government's two major antitrust agencies—the Federal Trade Commission and the Antitrust Division of the Department of Justice—also have a great deal of discretion in setting antitrust policy. Within the framework of the laws and prior court decisions, it is their job to decide precisely what kinds of business conduct should be viewed as anticompetitive.

This section outlines the growth of antitrust policy over the years with respect to the subjects of price fixing, mergers, so-called vertical restraints, and price discrimination.

Price fixing
Any attempt by two or more firms to cooperate in setting prices.

PRICE FIXING Whatever else the Sherman Act may do, no one denies that it outlaws **price fixing**. Competing firms must make their pricing decisions on their own;

they cannot cooperate to set prices that are more to their liking than those resulting from independent action. The recent tendency of the courts and antitrust officials has been to treat price fixing as a per se violation of the law—which means that only the fact of a price-fixing agreement need be proven in order to win a conviction. Thus, in a case such as the one discussed at the beginning of the chapter, it is not necessary to prove that the price-fixing attempt was successful or that the prices set were unreasonable. Also, accused price fixers cannot defend themselves on the ground that their action might have had beneficial effects.

Besides making price fixing illegal, the law has been interpreted as applying to other forms of cooperative conduct that might affect prices indirectly. For example, certain practices that cartels engage in, such as agreeing to restrict output or divide markets, have been treated just as severely as agreements on prices.

MERGERS The Clayton Act includes provisions designed to discourage mergers, but initially these provisions did not prove to be very effective. Not until the Clayton Act was amended by the Celler-Kefauver Act in 1950 did control of mergers become a major part of antitrust law enforcement. After that time the courts and antitrust agencies moved in a direction that brought virtually any merger under scrutiny. Besides opposing **horizontal mergers** (mergers of firms that compete in the same market), the government often challenged **vertical mergers** (mergers of firms with a supplier-customer relationship, such as an automaker and a spark plug manufacturer). **Conglomerate mergers** (mergers of firms in unrelated markets, for example, an oil company and a retail chain) were also frequent targets of antitrust enforcement. In some cases, the Court acted despite the fact that the companies involved had relatively small market shares. It viewed its mission as one of stopping anticompetitive trends before they could start.

Horizontal mergers
Mergers of firms that compete in the same market.

Vertical mergers
Mergers of firms with a supplier-purchaser relationship.

Conglomerate mergers
Mergers of firms in unrelated markets.

CURRENT POLICY ON MERGERS Although the Celler-Kefauver Act remains on the books, federal policy on mergers tends to be much less strict than it was in the 1960s. The more permissive policy stems partly from trends in economic theory. For several reasons, economists are less certain that increased market concentration leads to poor performance than they were a few years ago.

First, economists now have a broader understanding of the potential gains in efficiency that might result from a merger. Such gains were once viewed narrowly, in terms of economies of scale in manufacturing operations. Now, as explained previously, economists believe that redrawing the boundaries of firms through mergers may produce savings in transaction costs as well as in production costs; also, mergers may improve market performance in entrepreneurial respects as well as in terms of static efficiency. Second, mergers are now widely seen as an important mechanism through which shareholders are able to discipline corporate directors and managers. And third, whereas merger policy once focused exclusively on the domestic economy, today international competition is often taken into account. For example, the merger of Chrysler and American Motors reduced the number of U.S. auto makers by one, but created a company more able to compete with Japanese rivals.

Today horizontal mergers, even between large firms, may be permitted if there is "clear and convincing" evidence that the merger would result in increased efficiency in production or nonproduction operations, or if one of the firms is in danger of failing if the merger does not take place. For example, the government did not challenge the 1987 merger of Chrysler and American Motors, despite a Herfindahl index of well over 2,000 for the industry with the combined firm, in part because of considerations of international competition, as mentioned previously, but in part also because American Motors was viewed as a failing firm. Later, as reported in the *Economics in the News 16.1,* the government approved a further merger between Chrysler and Germany's Daimler motors. But not all such mergers are approved. In the same year that Chrysler merged with American Motors, the government blocked the proposed merger of Coca-Cola with Dr Pepper, seeing no mitigating circumstances in that case.

In most cases vertical and conglomerate mergers are less likely to be challenged than horizontal mergers by firms of equal size. However, several factors could cause the Justice Department to object to such mergers, including the elimination of potential market entrants, the creation of barriers to entry, a tendency to facilitate collusion, or the elimination of a firm that has not "played along" with tacit cooperative arrangements in the past.

VERTICAL RESTRAINTS Like vertical mergers, vertical restraints on trade involve agreements between a supplier and a customer. They are distinct from horizontal restraints, such as the price-fixing case discussed at the beginning of the chapter, which involve agreements between direct competitors. Many kinds of vertical restraints have been attacked under the antitrust laws, though not always successfully. Among the kinds that have been challenged most often are resale price maintenance agreements, territorial restrictions, tying agreements, and exclusive dealing.

Under *resale price maintenance agreements,* retailers agree not to sell a good below a price set by the manufacturer. Such agreements have been held to be unlawful restraints on trade because they limit price competition among the retailers that carry the manufacturer's product. In practice, the prohibition on resale price maintenance has never been watertight; some agreements that indirectly achieve the same thing have survived court tests.

Manufacturer-imposed limits on the area in which a retailer can sell a product also reduce competition at the retail level. Antitrust officials have viewed such *territorial restrictions* with suspicion; but, as in the case of resale price maintenance, the ban on such restrictions has not been complete.

The Clayton Act outlaws *tying agreements* when their effect is to substantially limit competition. These include agreements under which a buyer is required to purchase one product in order to purchase another, for example, to buy a company's sup-

ECONOMICS IN THE NEWS 16.1

DAIMLER-CHRYSLER CONFIRM MERGER

May 7, 1996—The German industrial giant Daimler-Benz and U.S. car manufacturer Chrysler have agreed to merge in a multi-billion pound (£) deal that will spark a revolution in the world's motor industry.

The deal, which took analysts by surprise, will create a company that by the end of this year will be valued at around $92 billion, with annual sales of $130 billion. It is the world's biggest industrial merger. Although Daimler will control 57 percent of the new company, to be called Daimler-Chrysler, it described the agreement as a merger of two equals and said the two companies were "a perfect match."

The new company will be led jointly by Daimler chairman, Jurgen Schrempp, and Chrysler chief, Robert Eaton. Schrempp said: "This is a historic merger that will change the face of the automotive industry."

The third biggest U.S. car maker, Chrysler has 94,300 U.S. employees and a 16 percent share of new vehicle sales in the United States this year. Only General Motors and Ford sell more, with shares of 31 percent and 24 percent respectively.

In addition to cars, Daimler, which is Germany's largest industrial group, is also involved in aerospace, defense and financial services.

Driving the merger plans are Chrysler's desire to build up its presence in Europe, where it is overshadowed by its American rivals as well as European and Japanese makes, and Daimler-Benz's ambitions to expand on the other side of the Atlantic.

It marks a major turnaround for Chrysler which as recently as 1979 was on the brink of going bust. Since then, Chrysler has turned itself into the lowest cost car producer in the United States, specializing in sport-utility vehicles and low-priced cars. Through its Mercedes subsidiary, Daimler-Benz has a major foothold in the opposite end of the car market, in high-priced luxury models.

Industry analysts believe the fact that there is so little overlap between the two companies makes the deal a good fit, but some have been skeptical about whether they can bridge the cultural gap between the respective boardrooms. However, they agree that other top motor companies will now be forced to consider pooling their resources in the face of competition from a new world force.

Source: "Daimler, Chrysler Confirm Merger," *BBC News*, May 7, 1998. Reprinted with minor editorial changes.

plies if it buys its equipment. The Supreme Court has found that "tying arrangements serve hardly any purpose beyond the suppression of competition."[1]

One of the biggest antitrust actions to focus on competitive practices was the government's case against Microsoft, settled in 2002. Among the issues in that case was Microsoft's practice of "bundling" free versions of its web browser and media software with its Windows operating system. Competitors offering free-standing versions of such software saw Microsoft's policies as unfair and illegal. In a settlement in 2002, Microsoft agreed to modify some of its practices, but the issues in the case were so complex that there is disagreement about the importance of the precedent that was set.

In an *exclusive-dealing agreement*, a manufacturer obtains from a retailer a promise that the latter will not deal in products supplied by the manufacturer's competitors. Many exclusive-dealing agreements have been overturned by the courts, although the practice of exclusive dealing has survived in some industries.

Although many vertical restraints remain illegal under the Clayton Act, antitrust authorities are less inclined than formerly to pursue such cases vigorously. A major reason is the now widely held view that some vertical restraints have the desirable effect of reducing transaction costs and controlling opportunistic behavior.

For example, a computer manufacturer might want to impose retail price maintenance requirements to encourage retailers to provide high-quality presale consulting services to potential customers. If retailers were free to compete on the basis of price, some would choose to skimp on service in order to sell at deeply discounted prices. Customers could turn to the full-service dealers for presale consultation but make the actual purchase from a discounter. Such opportunistic behavior could eventually drive full-service dealers out of the market, leaving nothing but discounters.

The current thinking is that customers do not need to fear agreements between manufacturers and retailers as long as there are competing manufacturers. In such industries some manufacturers may adopt a high-price, high-service marketing strategy while others use a low-price, minimal-service strategy. This pattern, which can be seen in industries ranging from computers to designer clothes, gives consumers a wide range of choices.

PRICE DISCRIMINATION In the original Clayton Act, price discrimination was listed as an illegal practice, but that section was not widely enforced at first. Things changed in 1936. In that year the Clayton Act was amended by the Robinson-Patman Act, which greatly strengthened the law against price discrimination. Although the Robinson-Patman Act is complex, its basic purpose is to prevent price discrimination by sellers of goods (but not services). To this end it prevents sellers from offering different prices to different buyers unless it can be shown that any discounts reflect cost savings or are efforts to meet competition.

The Robinson-Patman Act has been criticized by economists for the ease with which it can be turned from a tool for promoting competition into a means by which a firm can shield itself from competition by its rivals. *Applying Economic Ideas 16.1* shows what can go wrong under the Robinson-Patman Act.

Partly because of the tendency of the Robinson-Patman Act to produce bizarre results, the government has sharply cut back its enforcement efforts in recent years.

THE NEW ECONOMICS OF ANTITRUST

For many years vigorous enforcement of antitrust laws enjoyed widespread support among economists. The need for antitrust policy seemed to follow naturally from traditional neoclassical economics, in which any departure from perfect competition is seen as a potential source of market failure. F. M. Scherer expressed the traditional view when he wrote in 1980 that "the enforcement of antitrust laws is one of the more important weapons wielded by government in its effort to harmonize the profit-seeking behavior of private enterprises with the public interest."[2]

However, that view of antitrust action no longer predominates. Today many economists are increasingly skeptical of antitrust policy, at least as practiced in the past. The critics include reformers, who think that a revised antitrust policy can still contribute to the defense of the public interest; public choice theorists, who see

APPLYING ECONOMIC IDEAS 16.1

THE UTAH PIE CASE

In 1958 Utah Pie Company, a local bakery in Salt Lake City, built a new frozen-pie plant. The frozen-pie market in that city was growing rapidly; in fact, it more than quadrupled in size between 1958 and 1961. Through an aggressive campaign stressing low prices, Utah Pie was able to capture a full two-thirds of this market soon after building its plant.

Utah Pie's main competitors were three national food product companies—Pet Milk Company, Carnation Milk Company, and Continental Baking Company. Nowhere else had these firms faced the kind of competition that Utah Pie was giving them. But rather than pulling out of the Salt Lake City market, they decided to fight back. By cutting prices on their own pies and making special deals with supermarkets to sell their pies under house brands, they succeeded in cutting Utah Pie's slice of the market back to 45 percent by 1961. (In absolute terms, Utah Pie's sales grew steadily throughout the period because the size of the market as a whole was growing.)

Angered by the actions of the three outside companies, Utah Pie sued them under the Robinson-Patman Act. Its lawyers claimed that Pet, Carnation, and Continental were engaging in illegal price discrimination by selling pies at lower prices in Salt Lake City than elsewhere. When the case reached the Supreme Court, it was decided in favor of Utah Pie. In the words of the Court, Pet, Carnation, and Continental "contributed to what proved to be a deteriorating price structure over the period covered by this suit," thereby harming the local firm. And that, said the Court, was just the sort of action the Robinson-Patman Act was designed to prevent.

Economist Ward Bowman has sharply criticized the Court's decision. Initially, Bowman points out, Utah Pie had a virtual monopoly over its local market. Then Pet, Carnation, and Continental moved in, with the result that consumers benefited from lower prices and more pies, although prices stayed high enough to give all four companies a profit. True, the three national companies did engage in price discrimination—they sold their pies more cheaply in Salt Lake City than elsewhere. But if that was a sign that something was wrong, the solution surely should have been to encourage more competition in the other markets, not less competition in Salt Lake City.

Sources: Ward S. Bowman, "Restraint of Trade by the Supreme Court: The Utah Pie Case," *Yale Law Journal* 77 (1967): 70–85; and *Utah Pie v. Continental Baking Co.*, 386 U.S. 685 (1967).

antitrust policy as a tool of political rent seekers; and members of the Austrian school, who argue for outright repeal of the antitrust laws.

The Antitrust Reformers

Antitrust reformers share the traditional view that government should intervene in the economy where necessary to correct market failures. In their view, the flaws in past policy stem from its failure to take into account such considerations as transaction costs and the scarcity value of information. When interpreted in terms of the new extensions of neoclassical economics, many business practices that once seemed harmful now appear benign. The reformers propose that future antitrust efforts be guided by the following principles:

1. Consumer welfare should be the touchstone of antitrust policy. The potential benefits of any action in terms of efficiency of production or distribution should be weighed against possible anticompetitive effects in judging consumer welfare.
2. The main enforcement targets should be conspiracies to fix prices or divide markets, horizontal mergers that would create very large market shares, and

predatory actions aimed at harming competitors (with predation carefully distinguished from active competition).

3. Enforcement actions should not overemphasize vertical restraints, nor should they be directed at small horizontal mergers or any vertical or conglomerate merger or at price discrimination.

In setting forth a similar program for antitrust policy, Robert Bork wrote in 1978 that these are "not prescriptions for the nonenforcement of the antitrust laws, but rather for their enforcement in a way that advances, rather than retards, competition and consumer welfare."[3] Beginning about that time, a number of academic critics of traditional antitrust policy left their universities for government posts. Among them were William Baxter, who headed the antitrust division of the Department of Justice during the first term of the Reagan administration, and James C. Miller III, who headed the Federal Trade Commission. Other critics, including Bork, Richard Posner, and Ralph Winter, were appointed to federal judgeships.

Meanwhile, trends in legal education were also having an effect on the thinking of antitrust lawyers. Legal education has long stressed learning from past cases and judicial opinions. Today, however, this aspect of legal training is often supplemented with formal training in economics. As a result, students of antitrust law are encouraged to focus more closely on the questions of efficiency and consumer welfare raised by the cases with which they deal.

Antitrust and Public Choice Theory

Public choice theorists look at antitrust policy from a different perspective. As in other areas of government policy, they reject the notion that government policy is driven primarily by pursuit of the general public interest. Instead, they see antitrust policy as rooted in the private interests of voters, lobbyists, legislators, and bureaucrats.

The history of antitrust policy offers more than a little support for such a view. At the time that the Sherman Antitrust Act was passed, neoclassical economics, with its concepts of efficiency and market failure, barely existed. Americans were hostile toward "trusts," as they called the large firms of their day, not because they were inefficient but because they were rich and powerful. If they were efficient as well, that made them still richer and more powerful. Consider the viewpoint reflected in the following passage from an 1897 Supreme Court decision:

> *[Large firms] may even temporarily, or perhaps permanently, reduce the price of the article traded in or manufactured, by reducing the expense inseparable from the running of many different companies for the same purpose. Trade or commerce under those circumstances may nevertheless be badly and unfortunately restrained by driving out of business the small dealers and worthy men whose lives have been spent therein and who might be unable to readjust themselves to their altered surroundings. Mere reduction in the price of the commodity dealt in might be dearly paid for by the ruin of such a class.*[4]

Modern public choice theorists believe that today, as in the past, antitrust policy is shaped by the interests of "small dealers and worthy men." The essence of the antitrust laws, they say, is to transfer rights from large economic entities to small ones.[5] The mechanism that brings this about can be described as follows.

First, it is said, small-business interests, which are expressed through community leaders in every congressional district, exercise substantial influence. Lawmakers accommodate those interests through broad measures such as antitrust laws while keeping their big-business constituents happy through more narrowly focused benefits such as corporate tax loopholes and military contracts. Having passed a set of broadly written antitrust laws, the legislatures turn enforcement over to the bureaucracy.

The second force shaping antitrust policy, then, is the self-interest of the enforcement agencies. These agencies, like other bureaus, seek to maximize their budgets, the size of their staffs, and the number of cases brought by the agencies. In the opinion of some observers, these universal bureaucratic tendencies have been sharpened by the unusual arrangement under which antitrust enforcement is divided between two competing federal agencies, the FTC and the Justice Department. The cases brought by these agencies, some say, have little if anything to do with the public interest. Rather, as Richard Posner once put it, they are undertaken "at the behest of corporations, trade associations, and trade unions whose motivation is at best to shift the costs of their private litigation to the taxpayer and at worst to harass competitors."[6] Thus, the bureaucratic interests of the enforcement agencies in creating more litigation dovetail neatly with those of political rent seekers in the business community.

From the perspective of public choice theory, such cases as *Utah Pie* are not products of mistaken economic theory or misinterpretations of the public interest by prosecutors and judges. Rather, they are a natural outcome of the political process that created the antitrust laws in the first place.

The Austrian Critique of Antitrust

Economists of the modern Austrian school constitute a third group of critics of antitrust laws. D. T. Armentano of the University of Hartford, a leader in developing the Austrian position, sees two fundamental problems with antitrust policy.[7]

First, the antitrust laws, by their very nature, prevent freely contracting parties from making, or refusing to make, certain agreements that they perceive as being in their mutual interest. Among these are agreements involving product prices, marketing arrangements, mergers, and other areas that come under antitrust scrutiny. Mutually beneficial voluntary agreements are the fundamental mechanism of coordination in a market economy. In the view of the Austrian school, any interference with such agreements is not only inconsistent with liberty and justice but also likely to do more harm than good on a practical level.

Second, Armentano and other members of the Austrian school see the neoclassical notion of efficiency underlying conventional antitrust theory as far too narrow.

They favor a broader view of the market process, one in which all voluntary agreements, including restrictive ones, are consistent with efficiency in that they aim to bring the plans of both parties into closer coordination. An efficient market is seen as an open one in which individuals have the widest possible access to information and the widest scope for private planning. In short, the modern Austrian school economists see rivalry and cooperation not as opposites, but simply as different elements in an entrepreneurial process through which coordination is achieved.

The Future of Antitrust Policy

As the discussion in the preceding section made clear, reformers succeeded in making a number of important changes in antitrust policy during the 1980s. In many respects, their once-radical ideas have become the new conventional wisdom. Does this mean that antitrust policy will play a permanently reduced role in economic affairs, with possible repeal of some of the more restrictive statutes? Perhaps, but perhaps not.

For one thing, outside the economics profession the old populist view of antitrust action remains alive. As one critic of recent reforms has put it, "antitrust [law] was intended also to further a social and moral vision of America. At the core of that vision was a conviction that the past greatness, and future potential, of the country depended on the kind of character—resourceful, practical, and determined—that only competitive individualism would foster."[8] (Consumer activist and former FTC Chairman Michael Pertschuk puts it more simply, characterizing the proper focus of antitrust policy as a "Jeffersonian preference for dispersed power" applied not only to the dispersion of power among various branches of government but also to the dispersion of economic power among a multitude of relatively small firms.)

At the same time, public choice theorists were skeptical as to whether the changes brought about by the reformers of the 1980s would last, given no change in the underlying constitutional arrangements and the influence of special-interest groups. For example, Robert Tollison characterized the idea that "better people make better government" as "tried and true nonsense." Government, he said, "cranks along by an internal logic of its own."[9] Tollison, it should be noted, was himself a top staff economist on the FTC under the chairmanship of reformer James Miller, so perhaps he knows whereof he speaks.

REGULATION OF NATURAL MONOPOLY

The aim of antitrust policy is to prevent one firm, or a few firms acting in concert, from gaining control of a market. However, there are some cases, known as natural monopolies, in which there is no practical way to avoid the dominance of one firm. In this section we examine policies intended to improve the performance of these markets.

The Policy Problem

A *natural monopoly* is an industry in which total costs are kept to a minimum by having just one producer serve the whole market. Local telephone service is often cited as a natural monopoly; gas, electric, cable TV, and water services are other examples. It is easy for one such utility to hook up more customers once it has run its lines into their neighborhood, but it is wasteful and costly for a number of different companies to run lines down the same street.

The policy problem raised by a natural monopoly is how to keep the firm from taking advantage of its position to raise prices and restrict output. Consider the example shown in Figure 16.1. That firm, an electric utility, has constant marginal costs and a negatively sloped long-run average cost curve. The demand curve intersects the long-run average cost curve at quantity Q_1, not far from the minimum efficient scale of production. If this output were divided between two firms, each of which produced half of quantity Q_1, the cost per unit would be a lot higher—and still more so if there were more than two firms.

If one unregulated firm operates in a market, it can be expected to act like a pure monopolist. Instead of producing Q_1 it will produce Q_2, which corresponds to the intersection of the firm's marginal revenue and marginal cost curves. The price that corresponds to this output is P_2, which is far above marginal cost. This is too small an output and too high a price to permit efficient production.

FIGURE 16.1 REGULATION OF A NATURAL MONOPOLY

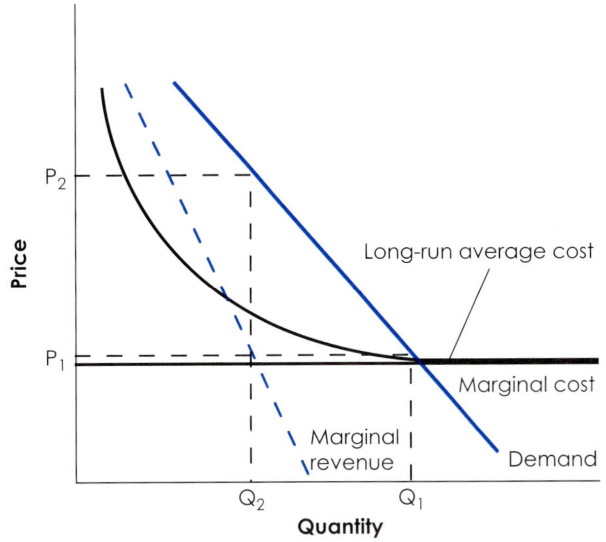

This graph shows the cost and demand curves for a natural monopoly such as an electric utility. As an unregulated monopolist, the firm would make the maximum profit by charging price P_2 and selling quantity Q_2. If regulators impose a maximum price of P_1, the firm will find it worthwhile to produce quantity Q_1.

The Regulatory Solution

It appears, then, that in a natural monopoly competition by two or more firms is inefficient, as is monopoly pricing by a single firm. The traditional solution is to allow just one firm to operate but to regulate the price at which it can sell its output. For example, the firm may be limited to a price of no more than P_1, the price at which the demand curve intersects the long-run average cost curve in Figure 16.1 With this price ceiling in force, the firm becomes a price taker for output levels up to Q_1, because even if it kept output below that level, it would be prevented from further raising the price. The maximum profit is earned under the regulated price by producing Q_1 units of output. This is a lower price and a greater quantity than would result either from an unregulated pure monopoly or from production by two or more competing firms.

For the market to be perfectly efficient, the price would have to be reduced to the level of marginal cost, which is slightly lower than P_1. At any price lower than P_1, however, the firm would suffer a loss. It could survive in the long run only if it were subsidized. By allowing the firm to charge price P_1, which is high enough to just cover all costs, the regulators would avoid the need for a subsidy while giving up only a small degree of efficiency.

Rate of return

A firm's accounting profit expressed as a percentage of its net worth.

RATE OF RETURN AS A FOCUS OF REGULATION The correct regulated price in Figure 16.1 is easy to identify because the shapes and positions of the demand and cost curves are right there on the page. In the real world, however, regulators do not have complete information about demand and cost. Lacking this information, they set the regulated price indirectly by focusing on the rate of return earned by the firm. The **rate of return** is the firm's accounting profit expressed as a percentage of its net worth.

To see why the rate of return is a useful focus of regulatory policy, consider the implications of setting various prices. If the price is set equal to average total cost, the firm will earn a "normal profit," that is, a rate of return equal to the opportunity cost of capital. If the price is higher than average total cost, the firm will earn more than a normal profit, that is, enough to cover the opportunity cost of capital with some left over as economic profit. If the price is set below average total cost, the firm will earn less than a normal profit. Because revenue is insufficient to meet all opportunity costs, including that of capital, the firm will suffer an economic loss.

Armed with this reasoning, the regulators proceed in five steps:

1. They measure the value of the firm's capital—say, $1.2 million. This is called the *rate base*.
2. They measure the average rate of return for the economy, that is, the normal rate of profit. Suppose this turns out to be 15 percent per year. (In practice, steps 1 and 2 are more difficult than they sound, but for our purposes the regulators can be given the benefit of the doubt.)

3. They multiply the rate base by the permitted rate of return to calculate a total cost of capital for the firm—in this case, $180,000 per year. This sum should be enough both to make interest payments on the portion of the firm's capital that was acquired by borrowing and to yield an accounting profit high enough to compensate the owners for their investment in the firm.
4. They ask the firm to propose a price or set of prices that it thinks will allow it to meet its capital costs.
5. As time goes by, they keep track of the firm's actual rate of return, cutting the price if it rises above the normal level and allowing it to rise if returns fall below the normal level.

LIMITATIONS OF RATE-OF-RETURN REGULATION For a number of reasons, rate-of-return regulation may not always achieve its goals of lower prices and greater output. One possible reason is that regulators may be influenced by political rent seekers. This may occur, for example, if regulated firms "capture" the regulatory agency by gaining control over the appointment of regulators, or if regulators follow lax policies in the hope of finding well-paid jobs in the industry after their terms as regulators expire. On the other hand, regulatory agencies in some areas have been "captured" by groups that represent consumers. They seek the short-run gains that come from keeping rates low without regard for the regulated firms' long-run need to attract capital in order to maintain capacity and service quality.

Another possible problem is that regulators may not know enough about the industry to control its rate of return. It is by no means easy to measure such factors as the regulated firm's stock of capital, its actual rate of return, and the opportunity cost of capital. The more regulators must rely on guesswork, the less likely they are to be effective.

Finally, by allowing the firm to charge a price equal to its costs plus a normal profit, regulation distorts incentives. If a firm is allowed to earn revenues that exceed its cost by a certain maximum amount, why should it try to minimize its costs at all? Minimizing costs is hard work for managers. Why not relax and take things easy? Why not take Wednesday mornings off for golf? Install new carpeting in the boardroom? Give the president's nephew a job? There is no incentive to try to keep costs down.

DISTORTIONS CAUSED BY THE WRONG RATE OF RETURN For several reasons, then, regulators may set rates of return that are either higher or lower than the opportunity cost of capital. Either case will cause problems. For example, a study by Harvey Averch and Leland Johnson suggested that in the 1950s and 1960s regulated rates for electricity tended to be too high.[10] They allowed utilities to achieve a rate of return that was higher than the opportunity cost of capital. This gave the utilities' stockholders an indirect way of taking advantage of their monopoly position. They could raise capital to build new plants whether they were needed or not, and then add the plants into their rate base. The regulators then would allow them to raise their rates enough not only to pass along the costs of the new plants but to earn a pure economic profit as well. The outcome—now known as the *A-J effect*—was that too high a rate of return led to wasteful overinvestment in the regulated industry.

By the 1980s the situation had changed. Some economists came to fear that rates of return had fallen too low. If this were so, it would cause the A-J effect to operate in reverse. Utilities would avoid investing in new plants even when the plants would be justified from the consumer's point of view. Such a policy of "rate suppression" might keep rates low for consumers for many years before problems become apparent. But as old plants wear out, the quality of service falls. Some writers predict serious shortages of electric power in the future if rate suppression continues.

Not all economists agree that rate suppression is widespread. It is no easier for outside observers to know whether a utility is charging just the right rates than it is for regulators to make this judgment. It is widely agreed, however, that the A-J effect cuts both ways: Either too high or too low an allowed rate of return is harmful. Thus, in their search for efficiency regulators must walk a narrow line between two kinds of errors.

REGULATION OF COMPETITIVE INDUSTRIES

Natural monopolies are not the only industries to come under regulation. There are many others—transportation, banking, finance, and communications, to name just a few—that have long been regulated even though their market structures, in the absence of regulation, are oligopolistic, monopolistically competitive, and in some cases, close to perfectly competitive. In this section we look at the regulation of competitive behavior in such industries.

Historical Origins

Railroads first came under regulation in the late nineteenth century, but the big surge in regulation came in the 1930s. One tends to think of the Great Depression mainly in terms of high unemployment; however, another major feature of the Depression was low prices. Between 1929 and 1933 the consumer price index dropped about 25 percent. Today most economists would explain both the high unemployment and the falling prices in macroeconomic terms, blaming them on low aggregate demand, inappropriate monetary policy, and so on. At the time, however, people tended to blame the high unemployment levels on low prices. If only prices could be raised, business leaders said, it would be possible to put more workers on the payroll.

It is not surprising that competition, which tends to keep prices low in certain markets, was not popular during the Depression. In fact, too much competition was seen as a barrier to economic recovery. In 1933 Congress passed the National Recovery Act, which encouraged firms to use cartel-like methods to prop up prices. That act was declared unconstitutional by the Supreme Court, but other legislation that applied only to specific industries survived. Two of the most important industries that were regulated in order to limit competition were trucking, which was brought under the control of the Interstate Commerce Commission (ICC) in 1935, and airlines, which came under the regulation of the Civil Aeronautics Board (CAB) in 1938. As discussed in an earlier chapter, agricultural marketing orders, another way of limiting competition, date from the same period.

Rate and Entry Regulations in Transportation

The case of transportation regulation reveals some key differences between the regulation of competitive industries and that of natural monopolies. Two of these differences were a focus on controlling entry by new firms and a tendency to set minimum rather than maximum prices. The traditional argument for regulation of natural monopolies was that without regulation prices would rise too high. In the case of airlines and trucking, the concern was that without regulation prices would fall too low.

It is generally agreed that regulation of trucking and airlines achieved the goal of raising prices and limiting the number of firms in those industries. As the years passed, however, many economists began to have second thoughts as to whether high prices and limited competition were the proper goals of government policy. With the advent of high inflation rates in the 1970s, the doubts about regulation grew stronger, and economists turned almost unanimously against the regulation of entry and the setting of minimum rates in competitive industries.

Regulation and Political Rent Seeking

Critics of transportation regulation tended to view this area of policy as an example of political rent seeking. They saw regulation as a device that permits rival firms to form cartels, which enable them to raise prices above opportunity costs and earn profits in excess of those that would be possible in a more competitive environment.

REGULATED INDUSTRIES AS CARTELS It is easy to see why this theory developed. In an earlier chapter we saw that two major weaknesses of most cartels are inability to control competition by nonmembers and inability to keep members from cheating on price agreements. The laws that gave the ICC and the CAB authority over trucking and airlines were directed at these problems. Both agencies became highly restrictive in terms of entry by new firms. (The CAB did not let in a single new major airline for forty years, and the ICC was only slightly less restrictive.) Further, both agencies were granted, and used, the authority to prevent carriers from cutting prices below specified minimum levels, as well as the authority to regulate maximum rates.

A number of studies carried out in the 1960s and 1970s seemed to support the cartel theory of regulation. Many of them were based on comparisons of regulated and unregulated markets. One study, for example, showed that unregulated intrastate airline fares in California and Texas were only about half of regulated interstate fares for similar distances. Other studies compared regulated freight rates for industrial goods with those for agricultural produce, which had been exempted from regulation. Again the regulated rates seemed substantially higher.

IMPERFECTIONS IN THE CARTELS But certain aspects of regulation did not support the notion that regulators acted as cartel managers aiming solely to maximize the profits of regulated firms. For example, despite the CAB's best efforts, regulated airlines were not always able to earn high profits. In the trucking industry, the major users of freight service, which should have been hurt most by high rates, rarely complained—in fact, they tended to praise regulation for bringing about a high level of service.

In trying to explain these puzzling facts, economists began to pay more attention to imperfections in the cartels allegedly created by regulation. The most glaring of these was the fact that although airline and trucking regulations controlled *price* competition, they did not control *nonprice* competition. Both trucking firms and airlines were free to compete for customers by offering more frequent and convenient service, advertising more heavily, and engaging in active personal selling. This nonprice competition was very costly. In the case of airlines, for example, adding more flights every day meant that each flight would carry fewer passengers. Nonprice competition thus pushed up the cost per passenger to a level so high that no matter what level of fares the CAB allowed, no more than a normal rate of return could be earned—and sometimes not even that.

As some of these effects of regulation became better understood, economists began to see that regulation could not be thought of simply in terms of a transfer of rents from users to producers. The effects of regulation were much more complicated than that. Some producers no doubt were sometimes able to earn higher profits than they otherwise would have. But most of the rents resulting from high fares went elsewhere.

Unionized workers were one group that seemed to benefit from regulation. Controls on entry reduced competition by nonunionized firms and made it possible for teamsters and airline pilots to bargain for higher wages. (Both of these unions strongly favored regulation.) Because nonprice competition sometimes put more planes in the sky and more trucks on the road than were actually needed, suppliers of trucks and planes may have enjoyed higher sales than they otherwise would have. Also, at least some customers were able to benefit from nonprice competition by getting a higher level of service than would have been likely without regulation. In particular, small shippers at out-of-the-way points may have benefited in that their rates did not always reflect the higher cost of their service compared with the cost of serving larger customers on heavily used routes.

Regulatory Reform

In the late 1970s long-standing criticisms of transportation regulation began to be translated into policy. Through legislation and the appointment of reform-minded regulators, restrictions on competition were eased for passenger airlines, air freight, trucking, and intercity bus service. There was also extensive deregulation of railroad rates and a relaxation of barriers to competition between railroads and motor freight. The CAB was abolished, and a few of its former powers were granted to the Federal Aviation Administration (FAA), whose main concern is air safety. The ICC stayed in business with a reduced staff and much more limited functions.

In addition to the reform of regulation in the transportation industries, there were significant regulatory reforms in other industries. In financial industries, banks were freed from regulations that had barred them from competing by offering higher interest rates and new services. In communications, the breakup of AT&T brought competition to the telephone industry, and the Federal Communications Commission changed the regulatory atmosphere in radio and television broadcasting.

Certain results can be identified in nearly every industry in which regulatory reform has taken place. These include the following:

- Prices have fallen on the average, although not for all customers.
- A greater variety of services became available, including many low-price, no-frills choices that had not been offered under regulation.
- Many new firms entered the industries, and there were many mergers and business failures among firms that were not able to adapt to increased competition.

Applying Economic Ideas 16.2 illustrates these effects in the case of the airline industry.

Despite these generally positive outcomes, it would be an exaggeration to characterize the deregulatory efforts of the early 1980s as unqualified successes. In several cases, policies were flawed by the fact that some elements of government intervention in markets were relaxed while others remained in force. For example, passenger fares and route selection by airlines were almost completely deregulated. However, two other elements of the air transportation system—air traffic control and airports—remained under government control. Friction between the private and government parts of the system often led to overcrowding and poor service. Also, internal airline markets within the United States remained almost totally shielded from international competition.

Another example of the harmful effects of partial deregulation can be found in the banking industry. At the beginning of the 1980s, banks' policies regarding lending and deposits were substantially deregulated. However, one important element of the regulatory system—deposit insurance—remained untouched. This allowed some unscrupulous bankers to take a "free ride" on the government insurance scheme, and use depositors' money for excessively risky loans. This was one of the factors leading

APPLYING ECONOMIC IDEAS 16.2

REGULATORY REFORM IN THE AIRLINE INDUSTRY

Airlines were the first major transportation industry to experience regulatory reform. The results, in terms of prices, service, and industry structure, have in many ways been typical of the experience of other industries undergoing regulatory reform.

Regulatory reform of the industry began in 1979. Since that time, average fares have declined and passenger volume has risen dramatically. Revenue per passenger mile, the broadest measure of air fares, declined from 4.5 cents per mile to 3.5 cents per mile on an inflation-adjusted basis. Over approximately the same period, passenger volume increased by 60 percent. The fact that the 60 percent increase in passenger volume was accompanied by just a 25 percent increase in takeoffs indicates that better utilization of equipment was a major source of savings.

Compared with the situation in the 1970s, air travelers today have a wider variety of options, ranging from ultra-discount tickets with severe restrictions on refunds and travel times to full-fare tickets with no restrictions. New entrants to the industry have offered everything from no-frills, brown-bag service to all-first-class flights. However, despite many new entries, mergers of existing carriers left the market dominated by a relatively few "supercarriers" by the 1990s.

The airline situation is complicated by the fact that one part of the air travel system—the airlines—was deregulated and made more competitive, while two other parts—the air traffic control system and the airport—remained government monopolies. The growth in air traffic has placed great strains on air traffic control and the airports, leading to more flight delays and increased concern about safety. Despite legitimate safety concerns, however, the actual safety record remained superior to the record prior to 1980s deregulation, as shown in the accompanying chart.

The terrorist attacks on September 11, 2001, set off a *re-regulation* of the airline industry, this time with a focus on airport security. By 2004, the federal government assumed control of baggage screening and required random searches of individuals boarding planes. Also, the government took an active role in supporting the airlines financially. The combination of the terrorist threat and the inconvenience caused by added airport security discouraged many individuals from traveling by air. Increased security requirements not only meant longer lines at security checkpoints, but it increased costs for the airlines. They needed to fund additional training for pilots and flight attendants and pay for added security features such as locks on cockpit doors. The supercarriers that emerged from the deregulation in 1980 began cutting perks, such as free meals and movies in flight, making it difficult for them to compete with low-price, no-frills carriers such as Southwest Airlines.

The re-regulation of the air travel industry highlights an important issue: Is there a tradeoff between safety and airline ticket prices?

Source: President's Council of Economic Advisers, *Economic Report of the President* (Washington, D.C.: Government Printing Office, 1988), Ch. 6.

Airline Accident Rate (1983–2002)

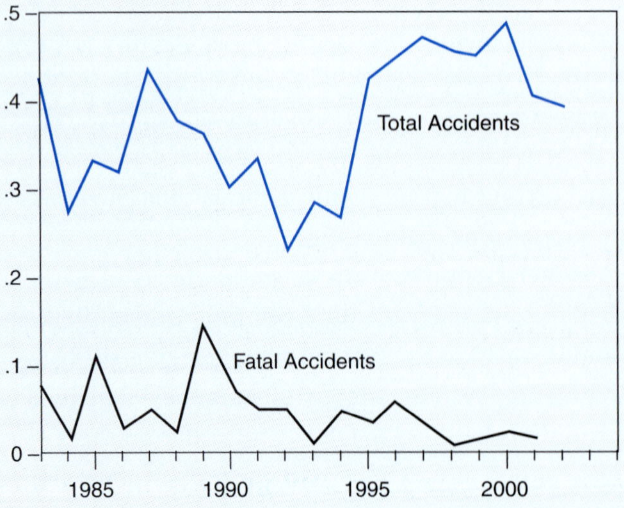

to the savings and loan crisis, in which many institutions failed, and taxpayers had to rescue the government deposit insurance agency to keep it from failing.

Finally, changes in regulatory laws were not, in every case, followed up by vigorous enforcement. In some cases, the rent-seeking interests that had opposed deregulation in the first place were able to undermine the implementation of the new laws.

Finally, it must be said that even at the height of the deregulation movement, there was a trend toward increased regulation in the areas of health, safety, and the environment. Health and safety regulation is examined in the next section, and environmental regulation is discussed in the following chapter.

HEALTH AND SAFETY REGULATION

At the same time that regulatory reform was reducing the economic role of old-line regulatory agencies such as the ICC and the CAB, other areas of regulation were expanding. Among the agencies reflecting this trend are the Occupational Safety and Health Administration (OSHA), the Consumer Product Safety Commission (CPSC), the National Highway and Traffic Safety Administration (NHTSA), and the Environmental Protection Agency (EPA). In addition, some older agencies, such as the Food and Drug Administration (FDA), have become much more active than before. These agencies are not directly concerned with prices and competition; rather, their focus is on the kinds of goods that are produced and how they are produced. Let us take a look at what economists have to say about health and safety regulation, an issue that has provoked much debate.

Normative Issues

The goal of health and safety regulation is to make the world a safer, healthier, more pleasant place in which to live. Because this is a goal that no one can argue with, why are regulations designed to achieve it a matter of debate? Part of the answer is that even when goals are agreed upon, there can be disagreements about the best ways to pursue those goals. Such disagreements, which belong to the realm of positive economics, will be discussed shortly. Other major sources of controversy are normative. Although almost everyone believes that health and safety are good in themselves, there are disagreements about their relationship to other worthwhile goals. Two such normative disagreements often threaten to overshadow any consideration of the positive economics of health and safety regulation. They are the question of valuing health and safety and that of deciding whose values should shape policy when values differ.

CAN HEALTH AND SAFETY BE ASSIGNED AN ECONOMIC VALUE? The first issue is whether one should even consider trade-offs between human health and safety on the one hand and material well-being on the other. Many supporters of strong, strictly enforced health and safety regulations argue that there is no way to measure the value of human life. Regulations therefore should be set without regard to economic trade-offs or cost-benefit ratios of any kind.

Others, however, do not share this view. They do not belittle the value of human life; rather, they see no point in condemning something that people do every day—and people do sacrifice their own health and safety in favor of other goals daily. They choose the convenience of car travel over the discomforts of bus travel, even though buses are known to be many times safer than cars. They take high-paying jobs in cities rather than low-paying jobs in the country, even though city air is known to be much less healthful than country air. They have medical checkups once a year but not twice a year or once a month because the gain in terms of health is not worth the sacrifice in terms of time and money.

WHOSE VALUES? The second normative question remains to be answered even if one concedes that cost-benefit analysis can be reasonably applied in the areas of health and safety. That is the question of whose values should govern any trade-offs made between health and safety on the one hand and economic costs on the other. Should policy be guided by the values of the people who receive the benefits and bear the costs, or should it be left to the judgment of experts? In practical terms, this comes down to the question of when people should simply be warned about health and safety hazards and when they should be forced to be safe and healthy whether they want to or not.

Strictly speaking, economics as a science has nothing to say about these normative issues. Nevertheless, economists often strongly believe that it is reasonable to consider economic costs and benefits in making health and safety decisions and to allow well-informed people to make those choices for themselves whenever possible. When such an economist discusses health and safety regulation with someone who believes in health and safety at any cost, what is likely to take place is a fight rather than a rational debate. This is unfortunate, because there are some things that economics as a science—that is, positive economics—can contribute to the controversy over health and safety regulation.

Positive Issues

One area of positive economics on which economists and regulators should be able to agree is ensuring that regulatory goals, once chosen, are achieved at the lowest cost. Consider the matter of giving local decision makers the greatest possible leeway in choosing the lowest-cost means of complying with regulation. One way to do this is to issue regulations in the form of performance standards rather than engineering controls. *Performance standards* are rules that specify the results to be achieved, whereas *engineering controls* are rules that specify particular techniques to be used or equipment to be installed.

Another issue on which positive economics can focus is evaluating the benefits of a proposed regulation relative to its costs. For example, in 1984 the EPA issued a study that showed that banning lead in gasoline would have benefits totaling $1.8 billion. In the EPA's view, this would more than offset the cost, which it estimated at about $.02 per gallon of gasoline. Ethyl Corporation, which produced the lead additive that the EPA sought to ban, said that the agency had left out a major cost. According to Ethyl, banning lead would mean that older cars (which had been designed before lead-free gasoline was widely available) would need valve repairs much more often. In Ethyl's estimate, the cost of these repairs would be $18 billion per year, far more than the benefits. The point of this case is not that cost-benefit analysis ended the dispute over the proposed ban on leaded gasoline; it is that the grounds of the dispute were narrowed and shifted to the plane of positive economics, where some progress could be made toward agreement.

Still another area of regulation in which positive economics can be helpful is tracing the unintended consequences of regulation. For example, in an earlier chapter we discussed the cases of auto safety regulation and safety caps on aspirin bottles. Auto safety regulation turned out to have the unintended effect of increasing hazards to pedestrians and bicyclists. Safety caps on aspirin bottles had the unintended effect of making it more likely that people would leave the caps off altogether. A study by Richard L. Stroup and John C. Goodman detailed dozens of other cases in which well-intentioned health and safety regulations have had unintended effects that endanger health and safety.[11]

Looking Ahead

This chapter has covered a lot of ground, from traditional antitrust policy to health and safety regulation. Everywhere it has turned, however, it has encountered a constant theme: Economists tend to be skeptical of government attempts to improve market performance through regulation. The economic case against regulation can be stated in the form of three basic propositions.

The first proposition is that, in practice, regulation tends to be dominated by questions of political rent seeking and income distribution rather than efficiency. In some cases, the goal may be to keep the owners of regulated firms from earning monopoly profits. In others, it may be to prevent such firms from competing so intensely that none of them can earn a profit. The goal may be to favor one group of customers or suppliers at the expense of others. It may be to give workers higher wages than they otherwise would earn or to give them a different balance between wages and a safe workplace. Economists do not argue with any of these goals; their complaint is that regulation is an inefficient way of benefiting one group at the expense of another. Many dollars in costs are incurred for every dollar in benefits gained by those whom the regulation is intended to help.

The second proposition is that regulation is less efficient than the market as a means for making decisions and using information. Regulators fail to keep prices down because they know too little about the cost and demand conditions under which firms operate. They try to second-guess the market in deciding which firms should be allowed to serve which markets. In this way they end up raising costs for everyone. They leave too little room for innovation and local initiatives aimed at satisfying special needs or suiting unique circumstances.

Third, regulations intended to serve the public interest often have unintended consequences. Sometimes those consequences can be traced to political rent seeking by special interests, as when antitrust laws are used by firms to harass their competitors, or when regulatory agencies are "captured" by the industries they are intended to regulate. In other cases the unintended consequences are simply a result of failure to think things through according to sound economic principles. Whatever the case, the unintended consequences of regulation have costs that tend to offset the intended benefits.

As we turn to other areas of microeconomic policy in the remaining chapters, we will encounter these themes again. They affect government policies in the areas of environment, labor markets, poverty, and international trade just as they do in the areas of antitrust and regulation examined in this chapter.

SUMMARY

1. **Which business practices are illegal under the antitrust laws?** *Antitrust laws* seek to control market structure and the competitive behavior of firms. The oldest of the antitrust laws is the Sherman Act of 1890, which outlaws combinations and conspiracies in restraint of trade and makes any attempt to monopolize a market illegal. The Clayton and Federal Trade Commission Acts of 1914 seek to control unfair trade practices. The Clayton Act, together with the Celler-Kefauver Act of 1950, controls mergers. The Robinson-Patman Act of 1935 regulates price discrimination.

2. **How have economists' views on antitrust policy changed over time?** For many years vigorous enforcement of antitrust laws had widespread support among economists. Recently, however, economists' views have changed. Reformers, armed with new views about the efficiency effects of business practices, urge greater consideration for consumer welfare, fewer restrictions on all but the largest horizontal mergers, and less attention to vertical restraints and price discrimination. Public choice theorists see antitrust laws in terms of political rent seeking by small economic entities at the expense of large ones. Economists of the modern Austrian school see antitrust laws as injurious to economic freedom and justice and damaging to the entrepreneurial market process.

3. **How are natural monopolies regulated, and what problems are posed by regulation?** Natural

monopolies, such as electric utilities, are subject to regulation that aims to prevent excessive *rates of return*. Regulation does not always work smoothly, however. If too high or too low a rate of return is set, the regulated firm's investment incentives will be distorted.

4. **Why are some industries regulated despite their inherently competitive structure?** Many industries have been regulated even though they are not natural monopolies. Some economists have seen such regulation as a form of rent seeking. In effect, regulation amounts to government imposition of a cartel. The rents generated by regulatory "cartels" are shared among firms, their workers, and their customers. Efficiency does not seem to be a major reason for the regulation of such industries.

5. **What are the effects of regulatory reform?** A great deal of regulatory reform has taken place in airlines, air freight, trucking, intercity bus service, and railroads as well as in some areas of banking and communications. The results are lower prices, though not for all customers; increased competition, with many new entrants and some failures of established firms; and greater variety in the products and services offered to consumers.

6. **What are the current trends in health and safety regulation?** Regulation has been growing in the areas of health and safety at the same time that it has been decreasing in such industries as transportation, communication, and financial services. Disputes in these areas of regulation raise both normative and positive issues. The normative issues include the question of whether one can place an economic value on health and safety, as well as the issue of whose values should guide regulatory policy. The positive issues include finding ways to keep down the costs of regulation, compare its costs and benefits, and trace its unintended consequences.

KEY TERMS

Antitrust laws
Price fixing
Horizontal mergers
Vertical mergers
Conglomerate mergers
Rate of return

PROBLEMS AND TOPICS FOR DISCUSSION

1. **Examining the lead-off case.** In your opinion, which students would have benefited from the efforts of Ivy League schools to coordinate scholarship policy? Which students would have been harmed? How would faculty at the schools have been affected? Do you agree or disagree that not-for-profit firms, dedicated to service of the public good, should be exempt from the antitrust laws? Discuss.

2. **Antitrust laws and economic rights.** "Everyone should have the unrestricted right both to sell goods and services in any market and to withhold goods or services from sale." Are the antitrust laws consistent with this statement? Why or why not?

3. **Public ownership of utilities.** In some cities utilities such as electric companies and gas distribution companies are owned by the city government. What do you think are the advantages and disadvantages of public ownership of a natural monopoly compared with regulated private ownership? With unregulated private ownership?

4. **Value of trucking permits.** Before 1980 the ICC limited the number of trucking firms that could serve any given route. Often the only way a new firm could get permission to serve a route was to buy the "certificate" (permit) of a firm that already served that route. Some of those permits were worth hundreds of thousands of dollars.

Why were the permits worth so much? After deregulation the value of such permits fell to zero. Why do you think this happened?

5. **Regulation of taxis.** How are taxis regulated in the area where you live? Is there free entry into the market? Are minimum or maximum fares set? How easy is it to get a cab if you need one? Would you suggest any changes in regulatory policy for your area?

6. **Highway speed limits.** In 1987 states were given the option of raising the speed limit on rural interstate highways from 55 to 65 miles per hour. The move was controversial, because it was feared that the rate of highway fatalities would increase as a result of higher speeds. How would you go about judging whether a change in the speed limit is a good idea? Discuss both positive and normative aspects of the question.

CASE FOR DISCUSSION

Tipping the Balance

The growing popularity of sport utility vehicles (SUVs) and the widely publicized rollover deaths in Ford Explorers using Firestone tires in the 1990s have drawn the critical eye of government regulators. After the Ford-Firestone incident, Congress required the National Highway Traffic Safety Administration (NHTSA) to test automobiles on a track. Prior to the increased fear of rollovers, the NHTSA used a mathematical formula to estimate a vehicle's star rating. For instance, a five-star rating meant that an automobile has a less than 10 percent chance of rollover in a single accident.

The NHTSA track tests were incorporated into safety ratings beginning with the 2004 models. Compared with prior years, the 2004 results showed improvement for a few SUVs. This added fuel to lobbyists' arguments against increased regulations targeting the SUV, such as gas mileage restrictions and subsidies for promoting the development of hybrids. "SUV Rollover Hysteria Appears Misplaced," said a news release from the lobbyist group Sport Utility Vehicle Owners of America.

Others remained unconvinced. "I think there are many SUVs, probably a majority of SUVs that have stability issues," said Brian O'Neill, president of the Insurance Institute for Highway Safety. "What consumers really need to know, if they're bound and determined to buy an SUV, is which ones are more stable than others." People often equate the size of SUVs with increased safety, but their high center of gravity makes them more prone to rollover compared with other automobiles.

"You don't have to get the C.G. [center of gravity] very high to get the vehicle to a point where it's unstable," said Paul Mercurio, an engineer for Bosch. Bosch makes stability control technology that helps reduce rollovers in cars and trucks.

Are rollovers common? The SUV industry lobbyists often cite that only 2.5 percent of accidents involve a rollover. However, among drivers and passengers involved in a rollover accident, one-third of them die as a result of the accident. So, while rollovers are rare, the chances of surviving are less than comforting. According to statistics from the Insurance Institute for Highway Safety, SUVs had higher fatality rates compared with cars. Between 2000 and 2001, 1997–1999 model year cars weighing between 3,500 and 3,999 pounds had a fatality rate of 87 accidents per million registered vehicles. This compares with a fatality rate of 160 for SUVs in the same weight class and model years.

"Personally, I believe a minivan is as functional as an SUV without the handling questions," he said. "It's typically a less-expensive vehicle. It's just not trendy."

Source: Information from Danny Hakim, "The Tipping Point for Safety," *The New York Times*, February 22, 2004.

QUESTIONS

1. Suppose that Ford and Firestone offered to pay $1 million per fatal accident in the Ford Explorer. Is this a reasonable figure? To put it in human terms, consider the following two ways of looking at the offer:
   a. Imagine yourself in a hospital following a fatal rollover accident. A representative of the Ford Motor Company enters the room and offers you a choice:

      You can either have $1 million or be restored to health. Which option would you take?
   b. Imagine that you are about to buy an SUV and that a stability control system is optional rather than required equipment. You expect to drive the car 100,000 miles before junking it. If the car has no stability control, your chances of being killed in a rollover accident over that period are about 16 in 10,000. If it has a stability control system and you use it regularly, your chances of being killed over the same period are about 2 in 10,000. If you value your life at $1 million, you should be willing to pay up to $1,000 for the stability control system. What is the maximum you would actually be willing to pay?
2. Setting aside the issue of whether $1 million is the "right" value for a human life, do you agree in principle that a cost-benefit formula is the proper framework for making the decision about modifying the stability design of SUVs? Or do you feel that cost doesn't really matter? If you were an SUV manufacturer, would you install stability-control safeguards at a cost of say $400 per vehicle? If you were a consumer rather than a manufacturer, how much would you pay for an optional, stability package that would prevent a rollover accident? More than $400? Less?

END NOTES

1. *Standard Oil Co. of California and Standard Stations, Inc,* v. *United States,* 337 U.S. 293, 305 (1949).
2. F. M. Scherer, *Industrial Market Structure and Economic Performance* (Chicago: Rand McNally, 1980), 491.
3. See Robert H. Bork, *The Antitrust Paradox* (New York: Basic Books, 1978), 405–406.
4. *United States* v. *Trans-Missouri Freight Ass'n.,* 166 U.S. 323 (1897).
5. See Bruce L. Benson, M. L. Greenhut, and Randall G. Holcombe, "Interest Groups and the Antitrust Paradox," *Cato Journal* (Winter 1987): 801–817.
6. Richard Posner, "The Federal Trade Commission," University of Chicago *Law Review* 37 (1969): 87.
7. For a short exposition of Armentano's views, see "Efficiency, Liberty, and Antitrust Policy," *Cato Journal* (Winter 1985): 925–931. Those views are developed at greater length in *Antitrust and Monopoly: Anatomy of a Policy Failure* (New York: Wiley, 1982).
8. Robert A. Katzman, "The Attenuation of Antitrust," *Brookings Review* (Summer 1984): 24.
9. Robert D. Tollison, "Public Choice and Antitrust," *Cato Journal* (Winter 1985): 905–906.
10. Harvey A. Averch and L. L. Johnson, "Behavior of the Firm under Regulatory Constraint," *American Economic Review* (December 1962): 1052–1069.
11. Richard L. Stroup and John C. Goodman, "Making the World Less Safe: The Unhealthy Trend in Health, Safety, and Environmental Regulation," National Center for Policy Analysis Policy Report no. 137, April 1989.

CHAPTER 17

Externalities and Environmental Policy

After reading this chapter, you will understand:

1. How the problem of pollution can be understood in terms of the economics of resource markets
2. How externalities can be controlled through voluntary exchange
3. The policies used by the government to control pollution
4. Alternatives to governmental regulation of pollution
5. How public choice theory can be applied to environmental issues

Before reading this chapter, make sure you know the meaning of:

1. Externalities
2. Property rights
3. Market failure and government failure
4. Supply and demand in resource markets
5. Transaction costs
6. Public choice theory

LIMITING MERCURY POLLUTION IS THE SUBJECT OF HOT DEBATE

WILSONVILLE, Ala.—Larry Monroe pointed to a set of eight manhole cover-size plates mounted on the exhaust vent to limit mercury emissions from Gaston 3, a coal-burning power plant that feeds electricity to a half-dozen southern states. Mobil Oil Corporation would also like to help keep the California economy humming, but the oil giant faces much the same problem as Sundance: how to reconcile its production plans with the need for clean air.

Gaston 3 and plants like it, the backbone of the U.S. power industry, are the focus of a furious debate over mercury pollution—how much and how fast the nation should move to regulate a toxic metal capable of causing severe neurological damage, especially to fetuses and young children.

Each of the plates at Gaston 3 houses an injector that squirts activated carbon dust into Gaston 3's flue gas. Particles of mercury cling to the carbon, which is then trapped by filters and discarded as toxic waste.

When the impetus to regulate mercury arose in 2000, the EPA eventually concluded that every power plant should be required to reduce mercury emissions to the level achieved by the cleanest 12 percent. This would require overall reductions of 90 to 95 percent by 2007.

Experts at first were optimistic about making the deadline. By the end of 2002, however, a first round of experiments sponsored by the Department of Energy and the industry had shown that a one-size-fits-all approach would not work. Technology to remove SOx [sulfur dioxide] and NOx [nitrogen oxides] extracted one type of mercury—the ionized form in compounds such as mercury chloride or mercury oxide—but was useless in removing elemental mercury—the vaporized metal itself. Power plants emit both pollutants in varying proportions depending on coal type, flue-gas temperature, and plant configuration.

After consulting with industry, the EPA in December backed away from the strict standard, instead using another section of the Clean Air Act to propose a "cap-and-trade" program whereby companies could either control their own mercury emissions or buy "credits" from other companies that have already done so. That proposal requires that overall emissions be trimmed by 70 percent by 2018, with each plant cutting mercury by 29 percent by 2007.

Industry representatives argue that market forces make cap-and-trade a superior method of achieving greater mercury reductions faster. Advocates do not necessarily disagree, but say cap-and-trade is meaningless with such low targets.

"There is no market with these phony control levels," said David Hawkins, director of the Natural Resources Defense Council's Climate

Center. "They've rigged the game by setting the levels so low that most plants won't have to do anything to reach compliance in 2007. Cap-and-trade is an excuse to do nothing."

Source: "Limiting Mercury Pollution is the Subject of Hot Debate," By Guy Gugliotta *Washington Post* Staff Writer, Monday, March 15, 2004; Page A03.

PREVIOUSLY WE INTRODUCED the term *externality* to refer to effects of production or consumption that have an impact on third parties. Pollution is a leading example. In addition, as noted in our earlier discussion, externalities are a potential source of market failure. They hinder the efficient operation of the price system inasmuch as uncompensated costs imposed on pollution victims are not reflected in market prices. As a result, users of the product that causes the pollution receive a false signal that tells them to use more of the product than they should, given its true opportunity costs. This chapter takes a closer look at this problem and at potential solutions, such as the "cap-and-trade" method, that attempt to restore market signals where they would otherwise be missing.

POLLUTION ABATEMENT AS A PROBLEM IN RESOURCE ECONOMICS

Pollution, says the *American Heritage Dictionary,* is "the contamination of soil, water, or the atmosphere by noxious substances." That is a fine definition—from the victim's point of view. But an understanding of pollution as an economic problem must take into account the polluter's point of view as well. Seen from its source, pollution could better be defined as "the use of soil, water, or the atmosphere to provide valuable waste-disposal services." When both perspectives are taken into account, pollution can be understood as a problem of resource economics and analyzed in terms of the concepts presented in the chapter on pricing in resource markets.

The Benefits of Waste Discharge and the Costs of Pollution Abatement

Most of the types of pollution that dominate the news have their origins in the productive activities of business firms. They arise because noxious gases, toxic chemicals, and bulky solids are side effects of many production activities. Wastes must be disposed of so that workers will not be smothered and production equipment will not disappear under heaps of ashes, scraps, and wastepaper.

There are many methods of waste disposal. One is the discharge of unprocessed wastes into the environment. This method uses up natural resources in quantity but typically requires little labor and a minimum of capital—just a smokestack, a pipe to the nearest river, or a dumptruck. Other methods—incineration, composting, compacting, reprocessing, recycling—reduce inputs of natural resources but require greater inputs of labor and capital. As far as the firm is concerned, determining the mix of productive inputs used in waste disposal is subject to the same economic principles as the use of other productive inputs: The value to the firm of a marginal unit of the input decreases as the quantity of the input used increases.

Pollution abatement

Reduction of the quantity of waste discharged into the environment.

The marginal value of a one-unit increase in waste discharge is the avoided cost of disposing of the same unit of waste in a nonpolluting manner, that is, the marginal cost of **pollution abatement**. The marginal value of waste discharge decreases as the quantity discharged increases because the marginal cost of pollution abatement decreases as the amount of discharge increases.

Figure 17.1 illustrates this principle with the example of sulfur dioxide emissions from a coal-burning power plant. If the plant discharges all of its waste into the atmosphere through a simple smokestack, it will emit 75,000 tons of sulfur dioxide (SO_2) per year. The cheapest method of pollution abatement is to switch to cleaner coal from a slightly more distant mine. That would cut total discharge to 60,000 tons per year at a cost of $250 per ton of SO_2. In the range of 60,000 to 75,000 tons, then, we can say that the marginal cost of pollution abatement is $250 per ton of SO_2. Or we can say that within that range the marginal value of waste discharge is $250 per

FIGURE 17.1 VALUE OF WASTE DISCHARGE AND COST OF POLLUTION ABATEMENT

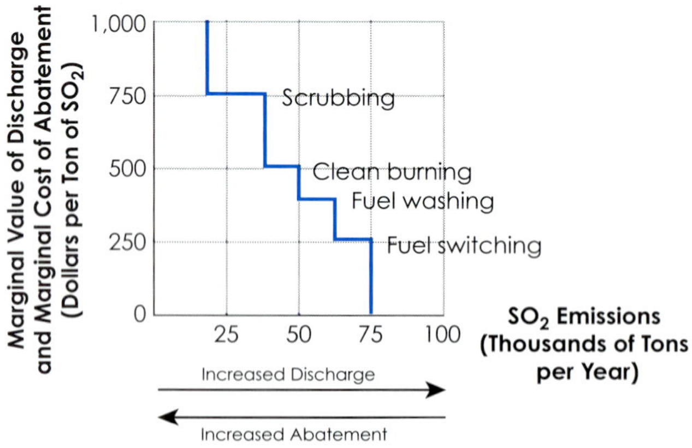

This graph shows the marginal value of waste discharge and marginal cost of pollution abatement for the case of sulfur dioxide emitted by a coal-fired electric power plant. With no pollution control, the plant would emit 75,000 tons of SO_2 per year. The cheapest method of pollution abatement, switching to low-sulfur coal, costs $250 per ton of SO_2 eliminated. The marginal value of waste discharge over the range of 60,000 to 75,000 tons is equal to this avoided cost of pollution abatement. As pollution is progressively reduced, more and more expensive abatement technologies must be introduced. For that reason, as the amount of discharge decreases, the marginal value of waste discharge and the marginal cost of abatement Increase.

ton, because that is how much the firm would avoid in abatement costs by burning the cheaper, dirty coal and discharging the waste into the atmosphere.

To reduce SO_2 emissions still more, the firm must invest in increasingly complex pollution abatement equipment and hire the labor to operate it. Equipment to remove part of the sulfur content of the fuel by "washing" it before it is burned would permit another 10,000 tons of abatement at $400 per ton. Buying an improved furnace to burn the coal more cleanly would cut another 10,000 tons of SO_2 at a cost of $500 per ton. Adding stack scrubbers to remove half the remaining SO_2 from combustion gases as they leave the plant would make possible a further 20,000 tons of abatement at a cost of $750 per ton. No further reduction of emissions would be possible without closing down the plant.

When read from right to left, the stair-step curve in Figure 17.1 represents the increasing marginal cost of pollution abatement. When read from left to right, it represents the diminishing marginal value of waste discharge. Each ton of waste discharge has a marginal value to the firm of $750 in the range of 20,000 to 40,000 tons; $500 in the range of 40,000 to 50,000 tons; and so on. Of course, it is not necessary for the curve to have a stair-step shape as in this example. In many cases marginal abatement costs would vary continuously, so that the curve would have a smooth slope.

The Marginal Social Cost of Pollution

We turn now from the benefits polluters receive from the discharge of wastes to the costs they impose on others. The total of the additional costs borne by all members of society as a result of an added unit of pollution can be termed the *marginal social cost of pollution*.

Each type of pollution has its own particular characteristics. In some cases pollution up to a certain threshold may do no harm at all, after which further increases become harmful. For example, in some locations naturally alkaline soils "buffer" the effects of acid rain. Lakes and streams are not damaged until a threshold of acidity is reached that exhausts the soil's buffering capacity. On the other hand, some pristine ecosystems are sensitive to very small amounts of pollution. In Siberia, the unique wildlife of Lake Baikal is threatened by the pollution from a single paper mill. If that one mill is enough to kill off the lake's native species, it could be argued that once they were gone a second or third mill would do comparatively little additional harm.

Extreme examples aside, the marginal social cost of pollution likely increases as the level of pollution increases. If it were measured accurately, however, the marginal social cost curves for particular types of pollution might well be full of flat spots, steps, dips, and discontinuities.

The Optimal Quantity of Pollution

Figure 17.2 shows a positively sloped curve representing the marginal social cost of pollution together with a negatively sloped curve representing the marginal value of

FIGURE 17.2 THE OPTIMAL QUANTITY OF POLLUTION

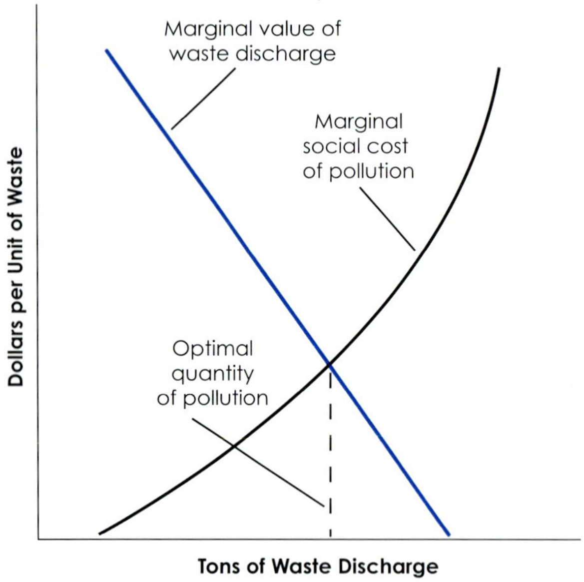

This figure shows a positively sloped curve representing the marginal social cost of pollution together with a negatively sloped curve representing the marginal value of waste discharge. (The marginal value of discharge is equal to the avoided marginal cost of pollution abatement.) The point where the two curves intersect is the optimal quantity of pollution. To the right of that point, the harm done by pollution exceeds the value to the firm of waste discharge. To the left of that point, the value of waste discharge exceeds the harm done by pollution.

waste discharge. The resulting figure makes it possible to identify the point—the intersection of the two curves—at which the marginal value of discharge (which is also the marginal cost of abatement) equals the marginal social cost of pollution. This is the economically optimal quantity of pollution.

If pollution is allowed to exceed this amount, the harm done by additional pollution will exceed the benefits of additional waste discharge. To the right of the intersection in Figure 17.2, then, a reduction in pollution would be worthwhile. The marginal cost of abatement practices (cleaner fuel, recycling, or whatever) would be more than justified by reduced social costs (better health, cleaner recreation facilities, and so on).

To the left of the intersection, however, the marginal value of waste discharge exceeds the marginal social cost of pollution. In that region further pollution abatement is not economically justified. The relatively small harm done by pollution is not enough to make it worth diverting scarce resources from other uses. Direct discharge of wastes into the environment is the most cost-effective means of waste disposal, even when all harm done to everyone is taken into account.

Criticisms of the Optimal-Pollution Concept

To economists, the logic of the optimal quantity of pollution is no different from that underlying the choice of the least-cost method of producing running shoes or the choice of the optimal balance of oil and vinegar in making a salad dressing. No one denies that cleaning up the environment entails costs and trade-offs. Few people would advocate choosing either of the extremes—the whole world as an uninhabitable sewer or the whole world as a pristine but deserted wilderness. Therefore, say the economists, there must be an optimal point between the two extremes.

Yet some observers reject the optimal-pollution concept as a guide to public policy. The criticisms are of two types, some focusing on problems of measurement and some on problems of rights.

PROBLEMS OF MEASUREMENT Attempts to measure the social cost of pollution usually focus on such factors as damage to property, health costs (measured in terms of medical expenses and time lost from work), and the value of wildlife and crops killed. These attempts encounter a number of problems. First, data on the costs of pollution are limited at best, and the many gaps must be filled by guesswork. Second, it is difficult to account for purely subjective costs, such as damage to natural beauty and discomforts that do not result in actual damage to health. Finally, estimates of the social costs of pollution rarely give more than the average cost figures, even though marginal cost data, which are much more difficult to obtain, are more important in making pollution policy decisions.

Data on abatement costs tend to be easier to come by. The processes are localized and the engineering is often well understood. The result, say critics, is that studies of the costs and benefits of pollution control tend to list dollars-and-cents data on the cost side against vague, subjective claims on the benefit side. This tends to stack the deck against pollution control. Economists often warn policy makers that the problems of measuring the social costs of pollution do not mean that those costs are small. Even so, the fear that benefit-cost studies tend to be biased in favor of pollution has given the whole idea of an optimal quantity of pollution a bad name among many environmentalists.

PROBLEMS OF RIGHTS The optimal-pollution concept also encounters a quite different criticism. Environmental policy, it is said, must respect certain basic rights and should not be guided by economic trade-offs alone.

The idea here is that pollution should be viewed as a form of "invasive coercion" similar to the crimes of theft, vandalism, or rape. Suppose that a vandal breaks into a person's home and smashes a valuable statue. How should a court decide the case? Should it listen to testimony from the owner about the statue's value, then hear testimony from the vandal about the thrills of smashing it, and make its decision by weighing the vandal's marginal utility against the owner's? Most people would be outraged by such an approach. They would say that the vandal violated the owner's right to enjoy the statue and that the vandal's benefit from the smashing should count for nothing in deciding the case.

CONTROLLING EXTERNALITIES THROUGH VOLUNTARY EXCHANGE

At several points we have characterized markets as mechanisms for achieving coordination of plans among producers and consumers. We have seen that under proper conditions markets can be counted on to provide us with such things as shoes, cars, Wheaties, and manicure services in something close to the optimal quantities, and to use scarce labor, capital, and natural resources efficiently in the process. The question we take up here is under what conditions, if any, voluntary exchange in a market context will result in efficient waste disposal and an optimal quantity of pollution.

Markets Without Transaction Costs

We can begin by seeing how voluntary exchange would handle the problem of pollution in a world without transaction costs. In that world, technical information about the causes and effects of pollution is available to everyone at no cost. Also, people do not behave opportunistically. They honestly share information about how much they suffer from pollution or how much it would be worth to them to escape its effects, and they voluntarily abide by any agreements they reach.

Suppose that in our hypothetical world there is a forest owned by Joan Forester and, upwind from it, a steel mill owned by John Miller. Noxious fumes from the steel mill are killing the trees in the forest. (For simplicity, we assume that no one else is harmed by the pollution.) What will be done?

PROPERTY RIGHTS To know how the situation will be handled, we first need to know Miller's and Forester's property rights. There are two possibilities. One is that ownership of the forest includes a right to exclude pollution from the air above it. The other is that ownership of the mill includes a right to emit wastes into the air regardless of where they end up. Let us consider each of these possibilities in turn.

First suppose that the air rights belong to Forester. Acting on the basis of these rights, she approaches Miller to inform him of the damage being done to her trees by pollution from his mill. He recognizes an obligation to do something. After an open and honest discussion, they reach one of several possible agreements:

1. Miller agrees to stop the pollution. He accomplishes this either by installing pollution-control equipment or by shutting down the mill, whichever is less costly to him.
2. Miller agrees to compensate Forester for the value of the trees killed by pollution. This alternative will be better for both parties than a reduction of pollution if the value of the trees killed by the pollution is less than the cost of pollution abatement.
3. Miller agrees to buy the forest at a price acceptable to Forester. He then manages the combined steel and forestry enterprise in a profit-maximizing man-

ner, installing whatever pollution control equipment, if any, is deemed cost-effective.

Suppose instead that the air rights belong to Miller. In that case, when Forester approaches him to discuss the pollution damage, he is under no obligation to do anything. In this case there is a different set of possible outcomes for their negotiations:

1. Forester pays Miller an agreed-upon amount to stop the pollution either by installing control equipment or shutting down the mill, whichever is less costly.
2. Forester buys the mill at a price acceptable to Miller and then manages the combined enterprise in a profit-maximizing manner.
3. The parties agree that the value of the trees killed by the pollution is less than the cost of pollution abatement, in which case no action is taken.

THE COASE THEOREM Several aspects of the example of the forest and the steel mill are worth noting. First, negotiations between the parties will always result in an optimal quantity of pollution; pollution will be reduced if and only if the cost of abatement is less than the damage it does to the trees. Second, if pollution is to be reduced, the most efficient means of abatement—installing control equipment, shutting the mill, or whatever—will be used. Finally, these results will be achieved regardless of the initial assignment of property rights. Whether the air rights initially belong to the owner of the forest or to the owner of the steel mill will determine who must compensate whom, but will not affect the degree of pollution abatement or the means used to achieve it. Thus, for example, if it is cost-effective to install control equipment on the mill, the initial determination of property rights will determine whether Forester or Miller bears the cost of the equipment, but in either case it will be installed.

The proposition that, in the absence of transaction costs, problems of externalities will be efficiently resolved by private agreement regardless of the initial assignment of property rights is known as the **Coase theorem** after Ronald A. Coase, who first stated it in 1960.[1]

Coase theorem

The proposition that problems of externalities will be resolved efficiently through private exchange, regardless of the initial assignment of property rights, provided that there are no transaction costs.

Market Resolution of Externalities in Practice

Transaction costs are never zero in the real world. They are sometimes low enough, however, to permit externality issues to be resolved through voluntary exchange.

One common example is the use of restrictive covenants in real estate development—legally binding agreements that limit what owners can do on their property. Left to their own devices, people do many things that annoy their neighbors. They hold loud parties, leave bright outdoor lights on all night, park boats or junked cars in their front yards, and leave garbage uncollected. Real estate developers have found that many people will pay a premium price for a home in a neighborhood where they know their neighbors will not do those things. Accordingly, when they subdivide a tract of land for a new neighborhood, they add restrictive covenants to the deeds.

When home buyers sign the deeds, they agree to a list of restrictions on loud parties, lights, boats, garbage, and so on. In most cases neighbors comply with the covenants voluntarily because they find it mutually beneficial to do so, but the covenants can be enforced in court if necessary.

Another example of the use of markets to handle externalities concerns the pollination of crops by honey bees. Although most of the examples discussed in this chapter concern harmful externalities, this one concerns a beneficial externality. In this case, farmers pay fees to beekeepers to bring their hives by truck to locations near their apple orchards, blueberry farms, or whatever. Such fees total more than $40 million a year in the United States. The fees the farmers pay are more than compensated by the increase in crop yield. Beekeepers, in turn, gain a second source of revenue.

Without such a market, beekeepers would limit the number of hives to the quantity at which the marginal cost just equals the marginal revenue derived from the sale of honey. The external benefit to fruit growers would not enter into their calculations. When they can earn extra revenue by selling pollination services, they expand the number of hives. Doing so benefits not only beekeepers and fruit growers but also consumers, who get more of both honey and fruit.

Transaction Costs as Barriers to Voluntary Resolution of Externalities

Unfortunately, there are many cases in which private negotiations are unable to resolve problems of externalities. The reason: high transaction costs. Three sources of high transaction costs are particularly troublesome. The case of acid rain, one of the most publicized pollution problems, will serve to illustrate all three.

SCIENTIFIC AND TECHNICAL UNCERTAINTIES To resolve a pollution dispute through private negotiations, one must know the source of the pollution and the nature of the damage. Acquiring such knowledge is often expensive and sometimes impossible.

In the case of acid rain, intensive study has led to agreement that the phenomenon results from chemical reactions in the atmosphere involving sulfur dioxide and oxides of nitrogen, and that acid soils and water can sometimes be harmful to trees and aquatic wildlife, and possibly to cause other forms of damage as well. Beyond these general facts, however, major uncertainties remain.

First, patterns of atmospheric transportation of pollutants are poorly understood. As a result, it is not currently possible to trace the acid rain falling on any one area to any particular source. Victims of acid rain therefore do not know whom to negotiate with.

Second, the mechanisms of environmental damage are not known in detail. Reducing sulfur and nitrogen oxide emissions might or might not result in a proportional reduction in the acidity of rain in downwind areas. Thus, the environmental damage that would be avoided by any given reduction in emissions is not clear.

LEGAL UNCERTAINTIES The Coase theorem suggests that voluntary agreements can resolve externalities regardless of the initial assignment of property rights. However, this assumes that all parties to the dispute agree on the initial property rights. In practice, environmental property rights are often open to dispute.

The acid-rain controversy again provides an illustration. Environmentalists typically assume that inhabitants of eastern states have a right to clean air. If so, they are in a position to demand action from midwestern pollution sources.

However, owners of midwestern pollution sources, such as electric utilities, assert certain legal rights of their own. They argue, for example, that their factories and power plants were built in accordance with all state and federal pollution standards that were applicable at the time. They claim that those regulations, in establishing certain limits, amounted to the grant of a right to discharge wastes up to those limits. If the limits are lowered, they ought to be compensated for the resulting loss of profits.

INHERENT COSTS OF NEGOTIATION Even if all scientific and legal uncertainties were resolved, the process of negotiating and enforcing an agreement to resolve an externality might be prohibitively expensive. One problem is the sheer number of parties involved in many important environmental disputes. In the case of acid rain, the parties include tens of millions of inhabitants of the eastern states, on the one hand, and thousands of midwestern pollution sources, on the other. It is hard to imagine private negotiations taking place on such a scale.

In sum, private negotiations within a market framework cannot always resolve large-scale environmental problems, however useful they may be on a local scale. Externalities plus high transaction costs lead to market failure. The next question, then, is whether public policies can overcome these market failures without falling victim to the alternative problem of government failure.

GOVERNMENT POLICIES FOR CONTROLLING EXTERNALITIES

Awareness of environmental problems in the United States has increased greatly over the past few decades. Many of the problems that have been identified appear to be beyond resolution through voluntary exchange. As a result, pressures for governmental action have increased. This section examines both what the government has done to bring environmental externalities under control and what it might do to make its efforts more efficient and effective. Four approaches to pollution control are examined: command and control, tort law, pollution charges, and marketable pollution permits.

Command and Control

To date, most pollution-control efforts, like the health and safety regulations discussed in the preceding chapter, have taken the command-and-control approach. This strategy, as embodied in the original Clean Air Act, the Clean Water Act, the National Environmental Policy Act, the Noise Control Act, and several other laws enacted during the 1970s, relies on engineering controls and pollution ceilings. Such laws often state that a specific pollution control method must be used, without considering its cost compared with alternative methods. In other cases a quantitative goal, such as 90 percent cleanup, is set. Sometimes, in areas in which pollution is especially bad, new pollution sources are banned entirely. (See *Economics in the News 17.1*.)

The command-and-control strategy has scored some successes. However, in many cases this approach pays too little attention to efficiency. In the past, it was thought that regulators could find a safe threshold level for each type of pollutant, a level below which pollution would be harmless and above which it would be extremely dangerous. The prevailing view today, however, is that there are few identifiable thresholds. At least for many pollutants, cleaner is always safer. The scientific or engineering question of finding a threshold thus has been replaced by the economic question of how much safety people want to pay for. At the same time, requirements to use specific cleanup methods reduce the incentive to discover new, lower-cost techniques. If no attempt is made to balance the marginal social costs of various kinds of pollutants, the result is that the most serious problems are not always attacked first. Moreover, different plants are subject to quite different cleanup standards, depending on their age and location.

The high costs and uneven achievements of past policies have created pressure to cut back on pollution-control efforts. Economists see this as the wrong response to the problem. Instead, for years they have argued that the cost-effectiveness of pollution control can be greatly increased by using approaches other than command and control to achieve environmental quality. Three frequently discussed possibilities are making increased use of tort law, imposing emission charges, and emissions trading.

Private Litigation and Tort Law

Tort law is a long-established area of civil law that is concerned with harms ("torts") done by one person to another. Lawsuits involving accidental personal injury, product defects, and damage to property through negligence are familiar examples of tort litigation.

The areas of tort law that touch most directly on pollution are *nuisance* and *trespass*. The law of nuisance can be used for protection against externalities such as a neighbor's noisy parties or a firm's malodorous manufacturing processes. Trespass traditionally covers one person's entry onto another person's land, but it has been extended to include harmful invasions by smoke, chemical leakage, and so on. Pollution often raises issues of both nuisance and trespass.

Advocates of a rights-based approach to pollution, including many economists of the modern Austrian school, believe that tort law should play an important role in pollution control.[2] They see several advantages to this approach. First, it fits well

ECONOMICS IN THE NEWS 17.1

ELECTRIC TRACTORS

California's San Joaquin Valley is known for yielding large quantities of high-quality agricultural products. In addition to crops, the land of milk and honey produces something else: heavy air pollution. The summer harvest season is when it's most noticeable. Diesel farming equipment, dust, and organic matter combined with the region's growing number of automobiles have resulted in poor air quality for California's central valley.

According to the American Lung Association's "State of the Air, 2003" report, three major metropolitan areas located in the San Joaquin Valley—Fresno, Bakersfield, and Visalia-Tulare-Porterville—were behind only the Los Angeles-Riverside-Orange County area in worst air quality. The ALA's annual report looks at ozone levels across the country. Ozone, one of the toxic components of smog, is a form of oxygen that even at low levels can cause health problems such as shortness of breath, coughing, and wheezing.

To help cure air pollution, state Senator Dean Florez wants to lower growers' electricity bills, enticing them to make the voluntary switch and spare the sky a hefty dose of pollution. Farmers say the charges can total as much as 40 percent of their electricity bills, even when the pumps are rarely used, leading many to choose cheaper, but dirtier, diesel fuel.

According to the California Air Resources Board, eliminating approximately 8,200 agricultural diesel pump engines in use statewide (about 4,500 of which are in the San Joaquin Valley) would prevent 1,000 tons of small bits of dust and chemicals from entering the air each year. It also would cut about 13,200 tons of smog-forming nitrogen oxide and volatile organic compounds.

"We'd like to see more and more of these be electric," said Dave Jones, planning director for the San Joaquin Valley Air Pollution Control District.

Keith Nilmeier, a central valley farmer, said that most farmers prefer diesel power because it's less expensive than electricity. He started converting his irrigation pumps to diesel from electricity about fifteen years ago to save money. "Diesel fuel was very cheap at the time," Nilmeier said. "We sat down and put a pencil to it and saw what we could save in our own operation." Nilmeier estimates that he saves about 35 percent by moving water with a diesel-powered pump instead of one powered by electricity.

Florez proposes to raise or use a chunk of a surcharge already built into utility bills to pay farmers' standby charges. The surcharge—called the public goods charge—accounts for about 1 percent of each customer's electricity bill for a total of about $540 million statewide. Opponents of Florez's bill have argued it is unfair for all electricity users to pay for an agriculture subsidy.

"Energy costs are already high," said state Assembly Member Sarah Reyes. "I don't know of any ratepayer who is willing to pay for one industry's problem, because that will just increase their energy bills."

Source: Jennifer M. Fitzenberger, "Taking diesel out of farm air," *Sacramento Bee*, January 25, 2004.

with the philosophical view that people have a right to enjoy their property free of pollution and the right to self-defense if their property is invaded. Second, the threat of nuisance or trespass suits by a victim of pollution can encourage negotiated agreements leading to efficient resolution of the problem. And third, the tort law approach gives victims of pollution a right to do something on their own initiative, without depending on bureaucrats or legislators to take action on their behalf.

Unfortunately, wider use of tort law for the defense of pollution victims stumbles over many of the same problems of information asymmetries and transaction costs that impede the private resolution of externalities in general. One problem is scientific uncertainty, which may prevent a victim from proving his or her case in court: Was a plaintiff's cancer caused by hazardous wastes from a nearby chemical plant or by something else? Another problem is the difficulty of establishing legal liability when a person is victimized by pollution from more than one source. Still another is inability to collect damages for past pollution from a company that has

- Coal-mining interests in the high-sulfur areas of Ohio, Illinois, and elsewhere that wanted to strengthen demand for their product. These factions, including both mine owners and unions, were afraid that changing fuels would result in the loss of coal production jobs.
- Industrial and political interests from eastern and midwestern states that wanted to protect profits by stopping the flight of industry to western and southern states. By focusing control efforts on newly built plants, the Clean Air Act gives old, dirty plants a few more years of life. Moreover, by focusing on scrubbing rather than changing fuels, the act ensures that coal-burning plants in the South and West are unable to exploit the cost advantage of a location close to sources of low-sulfur coal.
- Environmentalists, who were unable to obtain a majority in Congress by themselves and were willing to enter an unholy alliance on the theory that any pollution control measures were better than none.

After the passage of the 1977 Clean Air amendments, environmentalists became dissatisfied with the deal that had been made. The degree of pollution reduction was less than had been hoped, partly because scrubbers are not always reliable and partly because the regulations slowed the replacement of old, dirty facilities with new, cleaner ones. Thus, important elements of the coalition changed by the time the 1990 amendments were under consideration. This time, environmentalists broke with the midwestern coal and industrial interests, and supported wider experimentation with marketable permits.

The Influence of Special Interests

In a previous chapter we noted that small, well-organized interest groups tend to have proportionately more influence than larger, less well-organized groups, in part because of their superior ability to make use of information and communication resources. The power of high-sulfur coal interests to influence clean-air legislation could be considered an example of this tendency. In other cases special-interest groups have done more than just weaken measures intended to preserve the environment. They have won the implementation of policies that are actively destructive to the environment.

Western water policy provides an example. According to Marc Riesner, a historian of water use in the West, agriculture causes more environmental damage than any other single activity in that area.[5] Riesner blames much of the problem on the Bureau of Reclamation, which sells water to ranchers and farmers at "astoundingly subsidized rates, often as little as a quarter of a cent per ton." The Bureau began its life as an organization that would aid farmers through sales of water at rates that would recoup all costs for dams and irrigation systems, but the concept of self-financing has long since been abandoned. Most of the water goes for such crops as cattle feed that could be produced more economically elsewhere in the country.

Logging in national forests provides another example of a policy that is destructive to the environment. In Alaska's rain forests and other areas of the West, the U.S. Forest Service subsidizes logging by constructing access roads and making other investments for which loggers are not charged. Often the value of the timber is below what the government spends building roads to get it out. Well-organized logging interests benefit while the environment is destroyed and taxpayers are burdened.

SUMMARY

1. **How can the problem of pollution be understood in terms of the economics of resource markets?** Pollution occurs when firms (or sometimes consumers) discharge wastes into soil, water, or the atmosphere. The marginal value to a firm of resources used for waste discharge is equal to the avoided cost of disposing of the wastes in a nonpolluting manner; that is, it is equal to the marginal cost of *pollution abatement*. The optimal quantity of pollution is the quantity beyond which the marginal social cost of pollution exceeds the marginal value of waste disposal.

2. **How can externalities be controlled through voluntary exchange?** In a world without transaction costs, problems of externalities would be resolved through voluntary exchange. For this to happen, all parties would need complete information and there would have to be no opportunistic behavior. According to the *Coase theorem*, voluntary exchange would result in efficient resource allocation regardless of the initial assignment of property rights, provided that the rights were clearly defined.

3. **What policies has the government used to control pollution?** To date, most pollution control policy in the United States has followed the command-and-control approach. This approach has been successful in reducing the levels of some, but not all, pollutants. Economists have criticized the command-and-control approach for poor performance in terms of efficiency. Current regulations often do not take marginal abatement costs into account and do not provide incentives to employ the least-cost control technology.

4. **What alternatives to governmental regulation of pollution arc available?** One alternative to the command-and-control approach is the use of tort law, under which pollution is equated with nuisance or trespass. A second is the imposition of emission charges, which would require pollution sources to pay a per-unit fee for the discharge of wastes into the environment. A third is a system of emissions trading based on marketable waste-discharge permits. Economists favor these approaches because they include incentives to meet a given pollution control target in an efficient manner.

5. **How can public choice theory be applied to environmental issues?** Public choice economics can help explain why the pollution control policies adopted by government are not always the most efficient ones. Often those policies reflect the use of logrolling to build majority coalitions. In addition, small, well-organized interest groups, such as loggers and ranchers, sometimes persuade the government to undertake policies that are destructive to the environment. Environmental policy thus provides many examples of government failure as well as market failure.

KEY TERMS

Pollution abatement

Coase theorem

PROBLEMS AND TOPICS FOR DISCUSSION

1. **Examining the lead-off case.** Why were plants unable to meet the goal of reducing mercury emissions to the level achieved by the cleanest 12 percent? Explain why buying credits from other companies, as described in the case, will help reduce total mercury emissions. Why did some experts feel that the "cap-and-trade" policy was meaningless?

2. **Environmental rights.** Where do you stand on the issue of environmental rights? Do you think people (or other species) have some environmental rights that ought to be upheld regardless of the economic cost of doing so? Discuss.

3. **Beneficial externalities and property rights.** Beekeepers need flowers to produce honey, and farmers need bees to pollinate crops. At present, beekeepers have the right to place hives where their bees will fly onto neighbors' property, and the neighbors do not have the right to exclude the bees. Suppose instead that invasion by bees was considered a form of trespass, so that property owners could sue beekeepers who allowed the insects to fly onto their land without permission. How would this alter the economic relations between farmers and beekeepers? Do you think that it might lead to a situation in which beekeepers have to pay farmers for access to the blossoms of their crops? Discuss in terms of the Coase theorem and the Miller-Forester example.

4. **Smoking in restaurants.** Smoking results in externalities that are unpleasant for nonsmokers. Given this fact, why would a restaurant find it profitable to establish smoking and nonsmoking areas? Do you think that the problem of smoking in restaurants is adequately resolved by voluntary market incentives, or should there be a government policy mandating (or preventing) designated smoking areas in restaurants? Do you think that the same conclusions apply to smoking on airplanes? In a government office? Discuss.

5. **Automobile pollution.** At present, automobile pollution is controlled by the addition of catalytic converters and other devices to cars so that they do not exceed a certain quantity of pollution per mile driven. For comparison, imagine a system in which drivers had to pay an annual tax based on the total pollution emitted by their cars. The tax would be calculated by measuring the quantity of pollution per mile, using a testing device such as those now used for vehicle inspections, and multiplying that figure by the number of miles per year shown on the car's odometer. People could choose to buy catalytic converters, more expensive and effective devices, or no control devices at all. What considerations would determine the type of pollution control device purchased? Do you think that the tax system would be more efficient than the current command-and-control system? Would it be as effective in reducing pollution? Would it be as fair? Discuss.

CASE FOR DISCUSSION

Save the Forests—Sell the Trees

The rhetoric of environmentalists is heavy with condemnations of private greed and single-minded pursuit of profits at the expense of environmental values. Yet cases abound in which the profit motive and private property serve to protect the environment.

Take the case of the scimitar-horned oryx, for example. This antelope-like creature is nearly extinct in its native African habitat. Yet 29 of the 31 remaining oryx bloodlines survive, not in the wild, not in a public zoo, but on a private "game ranch" in Texas. David Bramberger, owner of the ranch, along with 450 other members of the Exotic Wildlife Association, have bred more than 200,000 individuals of 125 species. Their object: a stock of animals that can be hunted, for profit. A cruel business, no doubt. But it has saved a species from extinction for the simple reason that no one will pay to hunt an animal that no longer exists.

Turning from wild animals to forests, similar results are found. Trees are treated better where they grow on private land for profit than where they grow on public land under the control of politicians.

All over the world, private woodlands are treated better than public ones. In fact, governments in many countries are infuriated by the refusal of private owners to cut as much timber as they would like.

Ontario's government accuses owners of 10 million acres of forest—often farmers, retirees, and professionals—of an "indifferent" attitude toward their land. Why? Because they are interested in cross-country skiing, birdwatching, hunting or simply the pleasure of looking at—rather than cutting—trees.

Sweden has more standing forests today than it has had since Viking times. Is the government happy? No. It accuses small woodlot owners of selfishly letting their trees stand, at a time when the country has become an importer of wood products. The situation is similar in neighboring Finland, where logging interests rail against the "ignorance" of small woodlot owners who want to leave their trees alone.

The United States has many private forests, but it has many public ones, too. It is the public forests that are most often devastated. A major culprit: logging operations on Forest Service lands that exist only because of low-cost leases, government construction of access roads, and other subsidies. Many such operations could nor earn a profit if carried out on private lands.

Source: Lawrence Solomon, "Save the Forests—Sell the Trees," *The Wall Street Journal*, August 25, 1989, A8. Reprinted by permission of Lawrence Solomon, Environment Probe, Toronto, Ontario, Canada.

QUESTIONS

1. Washington State has recently closed its borders to the import of nonnative wildlife and banned private owners of nonnative species from breeding their animals. Is this an effective means of protecting the species in question? Discuss.
2. What externalities are produced by maintaining a well-managed woodlot? What externalities are produced by clear-cutting such a lot? Are the externalities beneficial or harmful?
3. Economic theory suggests that when an activity produces a beneficial externality, there will be a market failure in the sense that private owners will engage in too little of the activity. Do you think that this happens in the case of forestry? Why or why not?
4. Is government management of forests an example of government action that successfully corrects a market failure? Or is it an example of government failure?
5. Looking at the matter from the point of view of public choice theory, why do you think governments tend to cut more timber from their forests than private owners?

END NOTES

1. Ronald Coase, "The Problem of Social Cost," *Journal of Law and Economics* (October 1960): 1–44. This is the same Ronald Coase who is known for work on the theory of the firm.
2. See Murray Rothbard, "Law, Property Rights, and Air Pollution," *Cato Journal* (Spring 1982): 55–100. Several other papers in a symposium on pollution in the same volume also discuss pollution-engendered torts.
3. This list of suggestions is taken from Richard L. Stroup, "Environmental Policy," *Regulation* (1988) no. 3, 48.
4. These programs are discussed in Robert W. Hahn, "Economic Prescriptions for Environmental Problems: How the Patient

Followed the Doctor's Orders," *Journal of Economic Perspectives* (Spring 1989): 104–107.

5. Marc Riesner, "No Country on Earth Has Misused Water as Extravagantly as We Have," *The New York Times*, October 30, 1988, 4E, cited in "Using Private Property Rights to Conserve Water Resources and End Pork-Barrel Projects," *FREE Perspectives on Economics and the Environment* (February 22, 1989): 6–13.

CHAPTER 18

Public Policy and Labor Markets: Unions, Discrimination, and Equal Pay

After reading this chapter, you will understand:

1. How labor unions have evolved over time in the United States
2. The main provisions of U.S. labor law
3. How wage rates are determined in unionized markets
4. What unions do in addition to bargaining over wages and benefits
5. How labor markets are affected by discrimination
6. The nature of the controversy over equal pay for men and women

Before reading this chapter, make sure you know the meaning of:

1. Monopsony
2. Human capital
3. Efficiency wage theory
4. Inframarginal rent
5. Transaction costs
6. Opportunism
7. Asymmetric information
8. Median voter model

UNIONS STRUGGLE TO SURVIVE IN CHANGING LABOR MARKET

Negotiations between 70,000 unionized grocery store employees and three major supermarket chains broke down in October 2003. Feeling pressure from nonunion, low-cost competitors, the supermarkets sought to cut costs by reducing wages and benefits. Albertsons, Ralphs, and Vons proposed a two-tiered wage system that would pay newly hired employees less and wanted to require all workers to share in health-insurance costs.

"I'm a single parent, I have two children," said a Ralphs employee Oscar, who declined to give his last name. "I'm concerned about medical benefits. I'm concerned about our wages," he continued. "We're the real Ralphs, that's how I feel."

The United Food & Commercial Workers Union (UFCWU) voted to strike when it was unable to reach an agreement with the supermarkets. Workers set up picket lines that remained standing four months later.

According to Vons spokeswoman Sandra Calderon, the combination of higher health-care costs and falling pension-fund values make "this negotiation more difficult than negotiations in the past."

Despite union benefits falling to as low as $100 per week, and the loss of health-insurance coverage, the employees are determined to force a compromise with the supermarket chains.

"A lot of people are looking at us as an example," said Yvonne Gapasen, a 14-year employee of Vons supermarket. She said that other unions would lose bargaining power with their employers if the UFCWU strike was unsuccessful.

George Waylan, a retail management consultant, points out that grocery chains, especially those in California, are heavily unionized with a well-paid workforce.

Waylan said traditional supermarkets have "a very different way of doing business, offering lots of selection and lots of service." Vons, Ralphs, and Albertsons have to respond to the low-cost threat of retailers like Wal-Mart. "You have a competitor come in and sell essentially the same kind of merchandise for substantially less because their costs are less, then you have to do something to compete with that," he said.

Sources: Eric Anderson, "California Grocery Workers on Strike," *Morning Edition*, National Public Radio, October 13, 2003; Carrie Kahn, "Grocery Strike Talks Recommence," *All Things Considered*, National Public Radio, February 11, 2004.

OUR EARLIER DISCUSSION of labor markets took a fairly abstract approach to the relations between workers and employers. As is the case with other sectors of the economy, however, models of supply and demand do not give a complete picture of labor markets. This chapter takes a look at some of the important institutions and public policies that are also at work in U.S. labor markets.

LABOR UNIONS AND PUBLIC POLICY

Craft union

A union of skilled workers who all practice the same trade.

Unions had their start in the United States toward the end of the eighteenth century. The earliest labor groups, called **craft unions**, were organizations of skilled workers who worked at the same trade. Their shared interests made it relatively easy for them to work together in union activities and gave their organizations some degree of monopoly power in dealings with employers.

However, most of the early local craft unions were short-lived and faced legal as well as economic problems. It was not until 1842 that the courts recognized unions as legal. Even after that date, the courts were often unfriendly. Moreover, few of the early local unions were strong enough to survive the frequent business downturns of that period.

The First Successful Unions

Unionism did not take root on a wide scale until after the Civil War. At that time the first successful national organization appeared—the Noble Order of the Knights of Labor. The Knights reached their peak membership of more than 700,000 workers in 1886.

Many local unions of skilled craft workers were affiliated with the Knights of Labor, but the Knights were much more than an association of craft unions. They welcomed anyone who worked for a living, including farmers, farm workers, and unskilled laborers.

After 1886, the Knights of Labor lost ground to the American Federation of Labor, which had been founded in 1881. The AFL's founders included independent craft unions and some local craft unions affiliated with the Knights that felt that the bargaining power of skilled craft workers would be wasted in efforts to win benefits for unskilled workers.

The AFL found strong leadership under Samuel Gompers, its president for all but one year from 1886 until his death in 1924. Gompers sought to avoid the mistakes that had led to the downfall of the Knights of Labor. Under his leadership, the AFL reached a membership of 2 million by 1904. The federation owed its success largely to three features of its organization and philosophy:

1. *Craft unionism.* The AFL's leaders thought that the dangers of economic depressions and employer opposition could be overcome only by relying on skilled workers who could not easily be replaced during strikes.
2. *Business unionism.* The AFL's member unions devoted most of their energies to pay and working conditions. Unlike many European labor unions, they did not seek the overthrow of private property or the establishment of socialism.

3. *A limited political role.* Again in contrast to European labor movements, the AFL did not found a labor party. Gompers believed that political involvement would weaken the organization's ability to achieve economic goals.

Although the AFL dominated the union scene around the turn of the century, the principle of craft unionism was not accepted everywhere. In some places there were notable early successes in organizing **industrial unions**—unions that included workers of all crafts and skill levels within a given industry. Brewery workers were organized in 1886; the United Mine Workers union was organized in 1890. During the same years, however, industrial unionism suffered some major failures. Strikes by steel and railway workers were broken after clashes involving Pinkerton detectives, state troopers, and hired strikebreakers. A number of labor leaders were jailed.

Industrial union

A union of all the workers in an industry, including both skilled and unskilled workers in all trades.

Unions and Public Policy During the Great Depression

In the 1920s unionism waned. One reason was the renewed hostility of the courts. Beginning in 1908, the Sherman Antitrust Act was applied to restrict union activities, on the grounds that they were conspiracies to restrain trade. Employers were able to obtain *injunctions* (court orders) barring striking, picketing, and many other union activities.

During the Great Depression of the 1930s, the decline was reversed. With unemployment high and wages falling, public sympathy toward unions increased. This sympathy was reflected in two landmark pieces of legislation. The Norris–La Guardia Act of 1932 gave workers the right to strike and picket. It was followed in 1935 by the Wagner Act, which for the first time put the government squarely on the side of unions.

The Wagner Act declared that "employees shall have the right to self-organization, to form, join, or assist labor organizations, to bargain collectively through representatives of their own choosing, and to engage in concerted activities, for the purpose of collective bargaining or other mutual aid or protection." The law created its own enforcement agency, a three-member National Labor Relations Board. This board was to oversee enforcement of the act, arrange for representative elections, and serve as judge and jury whenever the act was violated.

The Wagner Act also outlawed a specific list of "unfair employer labor practices." Employers could no longer use lockouts, intimidation, blacklists, or spying. They could no longer force employees to sign contracts that made nonmembership in a union a condition of employment. In some cases, employers were even barred from speaking against unions.

During the Depression the nation saw renewed efforts to organize mass-production industries where earlier attempts had failed. This led to serious conflicts within the AFL, whose old-line craft unionists did not believe that stable unions could be formed in those industries. As a result of this dispute, an opposition group formed within the AFL; it was led by John L. Lewis of the United Mine Workers. In 1938 the group was expelled from the AFL and became the rival Congress of Industrial Organizations. The CIO scored some major successes during the 1930s, notably the unionization of the steel, rubber, automobile, electrical, meatpacking, and textile industries. By the end of 1938, its membership of 4 million exceeded the AFL's membership of 2.9 million.

The CIO's successes clearly showed that craft unionism was not the only workable recipe for labor organization. They also contributed to a rapid growth in total union membership—although the AFL also grew quickly during that period. By 1939 union membership had risen to 29 percent of nonagricultural employees—more than double the figure of just four years earlier. In 1945 union membership reached a peak; over one-third of nonagricultural workers were organized into unions.

World War II to Present

After World War II, unions faced more difficulties. The political and legislative climate began to turn against them. In 1947 a Republican Congress passed the Taft-Hartley Act, which moved the government back toward a neutral position on labor issues. It created a list of unfair union practices to go with the Wagner Act's list of unfair management practices. It also restricted the conditions under which unions could form a "closed shop," in which union membership was a condition of employment, and it allowed for emergency federal intervention in labor disputes.

Unionization drives in the South, which had been expected to yield millions of new members, were relatively unsuccessful. In 1955, in an effort to strengthen the labor movement, the AFL and the CIO merged. The decline in union membership has continued to the present day, however. Many factors have contributed to that decline. For one thing, blue-collar workers, traditionally the easiest to organize, now make up a much smaller percentage of the labor force than in the past. Women, who account for an increasing portion of the labor force, have never belonged to unions in proportion to their numbers. Moreover, unions have not successfully followed the shift of jobs from the industrial Northeast and Midwest to the Sunbelt states. Finally, some observers believe that younger workers do not consider unions important to their well-being. Despite some success in the organization of state and local government employees and agricultural workers, the prognosis for unionism is one of continued gradual decline. As of 2003, only 14 percent of employed individuals were represented by unions.

ECONOMIC ANALYSIS OF UNIONS

Partly because of the varied roles unions perform for their members, economists have interpreted unions in various ways. On the one hand, unions can be seen as attempts to exercise monopoly power in order to raise members' wages. On the other, they can be regarded as the collective voice of workers bargaining for safety, democracy, and dignity in the workplace. This section looks at both aspects of unions.

Unions as Monopolistic Maximizers

One approach to understanding labor unions is to treat them as maximizing organizations that operate in much the same way as firms and households. This approach emphasizes the monopoly power that union members achieve by presenting employers with a united front. Consider, for example, the case of a union that was formed in a competitive market and now seeks higher wages through the threat of a strike.

Figure 18.1 shows a labor market in which the competitive equilibrium wage rate is $8 an hour and the equilibrium level of employment is 300,000 worker-hours per year (point E_1). Now suppose that the newly organized workers tell employers that they want $10 an hour or else they will go on strike. The strike threat is shown in the graph by a change in the shape of the supply curve. Initially the supply curve had the usual positively sloped shape. After the strike threat, employers face a supply curve that contains a kink. The horizontal left-hand branch of the kinked supply curve shows that if the employers do not pay at least $10 an hour, no workers will be available. Up to 400,000 worker-hours will be supplied at $10 an hour. To hire

FIGURE 18.1 EFFECT OF UNIONIZATION IN A COMPETITIVE LABOR MARKET

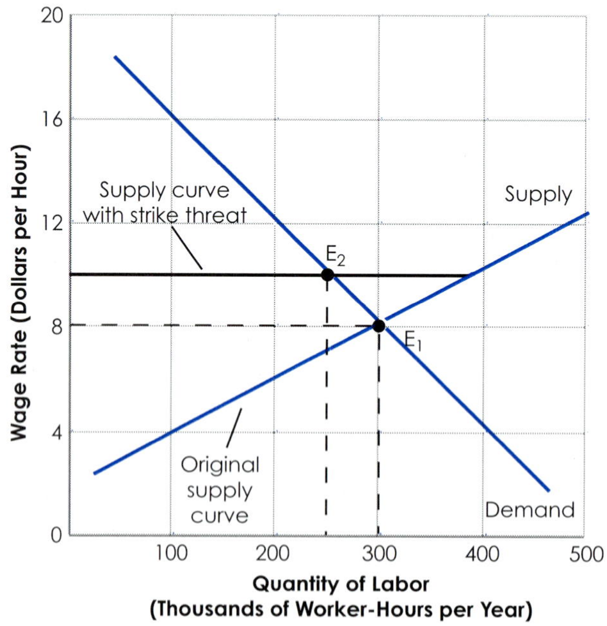

A union formed in a competitive labor market can use a strike threat to bargain for higher wages. Here the union threatens to strike unless the wage is raised from its competitive level of $8 an hour ($E_1$) to $10 an hour. At that point, the supply curve for labor becomes horizontal at $10 an hour up to 400,000 worker-hours per year. A new equilibrium is reached at E_2, where the new supply curve intersects the demand curve. The wage is higher than before, but the quantity of labor employed is smaller.

more labor than that, the employers will have to raise the wage above what the union is demanding.

If the employers accept the union's demand, they will react by shifting to a new equilibrium at point E_2, where the demand curve and the horizontal part of the new supply curve intersect. There they will hire 250,000 worker-hours per year at $10 an hour. The union will have succeeded in raising its members' wages, but only at the cost of reducing the amount of work available from 300,000 to 250,000 worker-hours per year.

In this example the union can win a higher wage rate, but only at the expense of jobs for its members. This trade-off raises the question of what unions try to maximize. How far up the demand curve should they try to move in attempting to serve their members' interests? Over the years economists have proposed a number of answers, none of which apply to all cases. Several of those answers are illustrated in Figure 18.2.

MAXIMUM EMPLOYMENT One possibility is for a union to maximize the number of jobs open to its members. In Figure 18.2, this will require a wage of $8 an hour, as shown by the intersection of the supply and demand curves. At that wage, 300,000 worker-hours per year will be employed. At any higher wage, employers will be unwilling to use so much labor. At any lower wage, workers will not be available. However, $8 an hour is the same as the wage that would prevail in a competitive market without a union. Thus, an employment-maximizing union might represent workers politically or might provide social benefits, but it would not affect the wage rate.[1]

MAXIMUM WAGE BILL Another suggestion is that unions seek to maximize the *total wage bill*—that is, the product of the wage rate and the number of hours worked per year. As Figure 18.2 shows, the wage bill is maximized at $10 an hour—the point at which the elasticity of labor demand is equal to 1. Keeping the wage at this level, however, creates an excess supply of labor. Workers will be willing to supply 400,000 hours per year, but only 250,000 will be required. The union can simply allow workers to compete for jobs on a first-come, first-served basis and not worry about who can get a job. Alternatively, it can try to divide up the available work among all the workers who want jobs in the industry. Each worker will be able to put in only a limited number of hours. Whatever route is taken, the union must be able to prevent nonunion workers from undercutting it by offering their services as strikebreakers.

MAXIMUM INFRAMARGINAL RENTS The positively sloped supply curve for workers in a given industry can be understood as reflecting the opportunity costs faced by different workers. Workers at the low end of the supply curve perceive opportunities in other industries as relatively unattractive, so they are willing to work in the given industry for a relatively low wage. Higher portions of the supply

FIGURE 18.2 MAXIMIZING MODELS OF UNION BEHAVIOR

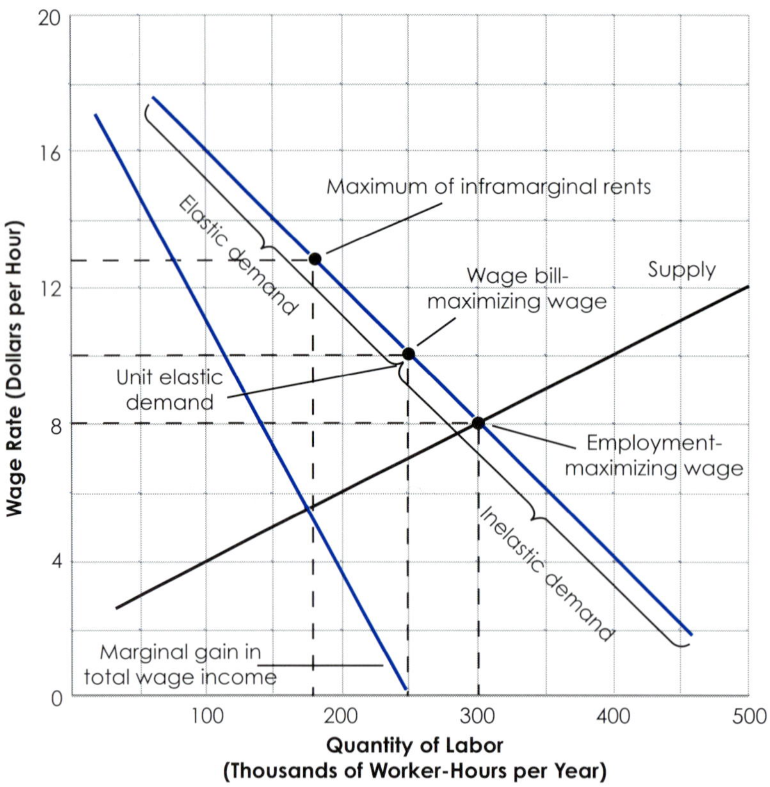

Unions in industries in which employers are price takers may choose various ways of dealing with the wage-job trade-off. If the union's goal is to maximize employment, it will not bargain for a wage higher than the competitive equilibrium. If the labor demand curve is inelastic at the competitive equilibrium point, the total income of union members can be increased by raising the wage to the point at which the demand curve becomes unit elastic. If unions take workers' opportunity costs into account, they may want to raise wages to the level that will maximize inframarginal rents.

curve represent workers who perceive relatively more attractive opportunities elsewhere and, hence, need a greater inducement to enter the given industry.

The difference between the equilibrium wage and the minimum that a given worker would accept to work in this industry is that worker's *inframarginal rent*. For example, in Figure 18.2 worker 200,000 would be willing to work in the industry for \$6 per hour. If the equilibrium wage were \$8 per hour, that worker would receive an inframarginal rent of \$2 per hour.

Some economists have reasoned that rather than trying to maximize the total wage bill, unions should try to maximize inframarginal rents. To do this, they should permit employment to expand only to the point at which the marginal gain in total wage income for their members will begin to fall below the opportunity cost of supplying the marginal unit of labor. The marginal gain in total wage income for members can be represented by a line that is related to the labor demand curve in the same way that, in the product market, a firm's marginal revenue curve is related to the demand curve for its product. Such a line is drawn in Figure 18.2. The point at which this line intersects the labor supply curve (which represents the opportunity cost of supplying labor) is the point at which inframarginal rents are maximized.

Whether or not one accepts the idea that unions consciously maximize inframarginal rents, the notion of inframarginal rent is useful in understanding differences in people's attitudes toward their jobs and their unions. Some people do not feel strong attachments to their jobs. They work for a while and then switch to another employer or drop out of the labor force altogether. If they were let go from their current job, they would shrug and find another with no great sense of loss. These are the attitudes of workers earning small inframarginal rents.

On the other hand, some people identify strongly with a given job. They stay with a single employer for their entire careers. Losing those jobs would be disastrous for them. They would see little prospect of finding new jobs equally suited to their needs. These are the attitudes of workers earning high inframarginal rents. Workers with high inframarginal rents are often the ones who have the strongest attachment to unions.

Unions as Political Entities

Models of unions as maximizers treat labor organizations as though they were firms. In those models, unions are seen as single-mindedly pursuing some goal just as a firm pursues the goal of profits. However, the maximizing models have been criticized for glossing over a crucial difference between a labor union and a business firm: Union members have no common interest that unites them in the way that profits unite a firm's owners.

Consider a corporation that is trying to decide whether to increase output of its product. It compares marginal cost with marginal revenue. If marginal revenue exceeds marginal cost, increasing output will increase profit, and the added profit will be shared among all the owners—the partners in a partnership or the stockholders in a corporation. Thus, if the marginal cost–marginal revenue calculations are favorable, owners can be expected to agree unanimously to the increase in output; if the calculations are unfavorable, they will unanimously reject the increase.

The situation of a union bargaining for an increase in the wage rate is fundamentally different. Depending on circumstances, the increase in the wage rate may, as was shown earlier, increase the total wage bill, total inframarginal rents, or both, but the gain will not be shared among all union members. Instead, some will lose their jobs as the employer is forced up and to the left along the labor demand curve, while those who remain on the job will reap all the gains.

It follows that each worker's "maximizing" wage is different from every other's. Whether a given worker will favor a given wage increase will depend on whether he or she fears being laid off as a result. If, as is often the case, layoffs are made in reverse order of seniority, the more senior the worker, the higher the wage he or she favors.

THE MEDIAN WORKER MODEL Faced with the diversity of interests among union members, some labor economists have borrowed concepts from public choice theory to analyze union behavior. For example, Bruce E. Kaufman has suggested using a variant of the median voter model. If union leadership is responsive to the wishes of a majority of members, he says, the target wage rate will correspond to the interests of the *median worker*—the one in the middle of the seniority scale. The idea is that the median worker plus all more-senior workers form a majority voting bloc within the union. This bloc can, in principle, override the interests of less-senior workers, who are most threatened by layoffs.[2]

However, as Kaufman and others who take this approach recognize, the median worker model has some curious implications. Taken at face value, it suggests that 50 percent of the union plus one member would force through a wage increase that would get the rest of the membership laid off; the next year, half of those left would force through another such wage increase; and so on until only one worker remained on the payroll.

INTERESTS OF UNION LEADERS In practice, other factors offset the tendency for unions to shrink to the vanishing point, as would happen in the pure form of the median worker model. One is the fact that unions are complex representative structures that are influenced by the interests of union leaders as well as those of the rank and file. Union leaders have an interest in keeping the union membership large to enhance their own power, income, and prestige. They may also be subject to pressures from community leaders, such as city council members and newspaper editors, to behave in a "responsible" manner. If so, union leaders will balance the interests of their members against those of local government officials, merchants, and others who do not want labor-management conflict to threaten the survival of the employer.

Whatever the specifics, the point remains that once unions are viewed as political entities, no simple maximizing model analogous to the profit-maximizing model of the firm can do justice to the process of collective bargaining. Rather, like governments, unions must be treated as instruments for reconciling the divergent interests of their members. And, as in the case of government, there can be no guarantee that the outcome will optimize or maximize any particular definition of those interests.

What Else Unions Do

To focus entirely on unions effects on wages would be misleading; unions do many other things besides bargain over wages. This has been true from the earliest days of unionism, when the Knights of Labor campaigned for worker education and self-improvement, to the present, when unions provide social activities, help members with personal and family problems, and serve as a channel for participation in national politics. Some of the things that unions do reach beyond the scope of economics. But even on the economic level, unions affect more than wages.

THE UNION VOICE IN THE WORKPLACE Most important, unions give workers a voice in how the workplace is run. They bargain with employers over health and safety conditions in the workplace. They help settle workers' grievances in matters ranging from job assignments to company policy to conflicts with supervisors. They bargain over issues of fairness, such as the role of seniority in layoffs and recalls. In many plants, unions and management also cooperate to elicit ideas from the work force that can lead to improvements in production processes and product design.

The role of unions within the firm reflects the more general role of firms in the market economy. Firms exist because they reduce the cost of organizing complex transactions, especially those in which the parties must make a long-term commitment of specialized resources. Through their internal governing structures, firms facilitate coordination, control tendencies toward opportunistic behavior, and adapt to changes in the business environment. Unions contribute to the accomplishment of these tasks. Consider the following points in particular:

1. Workers often make commitments of specialized resources, such as acquiring firm-specific job skills or moving to a location where few alternative jobs are available. Those commitments bind the firm and the workers to each other and make separations more costly for both sides. Unions can potentially reduce the transaction costs of managing such long-term relationships.
2. Both workers and managers face temptations to behave opportunistically. Supervisors and line managers are needed to prevent shirking by workers. At the same time, union shop stewards and grievance procedures are needed to prevent arbitrary behavior by supervisors, increases in workload beyond the agreed-upon level, and so on. Without a framework for resolving such problems, worker morale would drop and turnover would rise. Unions are one way of providing such a framework.
3. Circumstances may change unexpectedly for better or worse. If a firm prospers, workers will want to claim a share of the rewards. If it falters, workers may have to share hardships to ensure the firm's survival. New technologies may sharply change working conditions and require new skills. Collective bargaining often provides a way of making the necessary adjustments to change.

FIRMS WITHOUT UNIONS But, it is fair to ask, if unions are so helpful in facilitating coordination and cutting transaction costs, why has union membership been falling for nearly half a century? Three answers can be given.

First, some researchers think that U.S. unions have simply priced themselves out of the market. During the 1950s and 1960s, unions gained wage differentials some 20–25 percent above labor market rates for nonunionized workers. Economists David Blanchflower and Richard Freeman conclude that such differentials were "probably economically justified when the United States was the clear world economic leader," but that today, in a more competitive world economy, they have become "a major liability to the development of unionism in the country. They note that differentials over market rates earned by workers in other countries are significantly smaller, which may explain the fact that union membership has not declined elsewhere as it has in the United States.[3]

Second, although unions are sometimes partners with management in improving quality and raising productivity, there is a darker side to unions' voice in company affairs. Sometimes unions fight new technologies that they fear will eliminate jobs; they may try to prevent women, members of minority groups, and immigrants from gaining access to jobs that have traditionally been reserved for white males; they may stir up worker hostility to make themselves seem more needed; and they may battle competition by nonunion workers with threats and violence. These aspects of unionism reduce labor-management cooperation and economic efficiency.

Third, managers have discovered that harmonious and productive labor relations can be achieved without unions. In the earlier part of the century, workers were often treated as robots. Management attitudes of that period created a fertile climate for the growth of unions. Today, top nonunion firms often go out of their way to give workers a voice in company affairs. *Applying Economic Ideas 18.1* contrasts management practices then and now. The fact that some top nonunion firms are willing to pay high wages to a highly productive work force is consistent with efficiency wage theory as discussed in an earlier chapter.

MINORITIES AND WOMEN IN THE LABOR FORCE

As we have seen, workers have been attracted to unions not just by the hope of higher wages but also by the ideals of justice and equality in the workplace. However, neither unions nor market forces have succeeded in eliminating inequality and perceived injustices.

Persistent differences in earnings between whites and nonwhite minorities and between men and women are a particular focus of concern. On average, as of 1998, black men who were employed full-time on a year-round basis earned only about 72 percent of what non-hispanic white men earned. Black women earned about 88 percent of what was earned by non-hispanic white women. Among both races, women earned less than men, but the gap was much larger for white women (69 percent of earnings of white men) than for black women (84 percent of earnings of black men). True, there has been some progress. Fifty years ago, black men earned less than half as much as white men. Black women, who earned barely more than a third as much as white women 50 years ago, have closed the gap even more. But the remaining gaps are large.

In part, the wage gaps can be explained by the different human-capital endowments of men, women, and minorities. Among these are differences in years of formal

APPLYING ECONOMIC IDEAS 18.1

LABOR-MANAGEMENT RELATIONS

Bob Stinson remembers what labor-management relations were like in the automobile industry before the advent of unions.

"I started working at Fisher Body in 1917 and retired in 1962, with 45 and 8/10 years service," he says. "Until 1933, no unions, no rules: You were at the mercy of your foreman.

"I left the plants so many nights hostile. If I were a fella big and strong, I think I'd a picked a fight with the first fella I met on the corner. It was lousy. Degraded. You might call yourself a man if you was on the street, but as soon as you went through the door and punched your card, you was nothing more or less than a robot. Do this, go there, do that. You'd do it."

Today the "do this, go there, do that" style of management is out at top U.S. nonunion companies such as Black & Decker, Eli Lilly, Gillette, Grumman, IBM, and Polaroid. According to a study by Fred. K. Foulkes, these firms see the main advantage of operating in a nonunion environment as higher productivity, not lower wages. The higher productivity comes partly from lower employee turnover and less absenteeism, partly from greater worker loyalty, and partly from wider acceptance of new technology.

Foulkes found that managers of the companies he studies made special efforts to give workers a voice in company affairs and to improve the quality of work life. For example:

- Managers work hard to create a sense of equality. Executive status symbols, such as exclusive dining rooms, and country clubs, are avoided. In many firms, managers and workers park in the same parking lots and eat in the same cafeterias.
- Many firms do everything they can to avoid layoffs. Instead, they handle slack periods by reducing hours or producing goods to be stored for later sale. They respond to peak demands by employing part-time or recently retired workers rather than hiring workers who would have to be laid off when the peak had passed.
- The firms tend to promote from within. They post notices of job openings in their plants and offer training to workers who want to upgrade their skills.
- Many firms offer wages and fringe benefits that are competitive with those in unionized firms. (Exceptions can be found in such industries as steel, airlines, and trucking, where union wage scales are unusually high.) They also tend to pay blue-collar workers monthly salaries rather than hourly wages.
- Managers are good listeners and keep their office doors open. They are very careful about the handling of grievances and pay attention to workers' suggestions as well as complaints.

Should these practices be viewed as evidence that unions are not really necessary in a well-managed firm? Or should they be considered evidence that the threat of unionization causes nonunion firms to treat their workers better? You be the judge.

Sources: The Stinson quotes are from an interview in Studs Terkel, *Hard Times: An Oral History of the Great Depression* (New York: Pantheon Books, 1970), 129. The material on management practices today is based on Fred K. Foulkes, "How Top Nonunion Companies manage Employees," *Harvard Business Review* (September–October 1981): 90–96.

education, years of job experience, amount of on-the-job training, and time spent out of the labor force after completion of schooling. Some of those differences reflect discrimination that takes place outside the labor market, and some may reflect cultural differences or differences in preferences. Such indexes of human capital account for about half of the wage gap—the exact numbers vary from one group to another and from one study to another. The remaining half cannot be explained in terms of human capital or other easily observable economic factors. This section is concerned with this unexplained part of the wage gap, which is widely suspected to be a result of discrimination in labor markets, and with policies designed to correct the effects of discrimination.

An Economic Model of Discrimination

Labor market discrimination

A situation in which employers are unwilling to hire members of a disfavored group at the same wage rate that they pay to equally productive members of a more favored group.

Employers can be said to practice **labor market discrimination** against a group of workers if they are unwilling to hire members of that group at the same wage rate that they pay to equally productive members of a more favored group.

Figure 18.3 shows the effects of discrimination by employers. Part (a) shows the supply and demand curves for workers in the favored group. This demand curve, as usual, is the marginal revenue product curve. Part (b) shows the supply and demand curves for workers in the disfavored group. In this market the demand curve is shifted to the left relative to the marginal revenue product curve. This indicates that employers will hire members of the disfavored group only if they are more productive than members of the favored group or if they are equally productive but will work for less.

EQUILIBRIUM UNDER DISCRIMINATION Two types of equilibrium are possible under discrimination.

FIGURE 18.3 EFFECTS OF DISCRIMINATION ON WAGE RATES AND HOURS WORKED

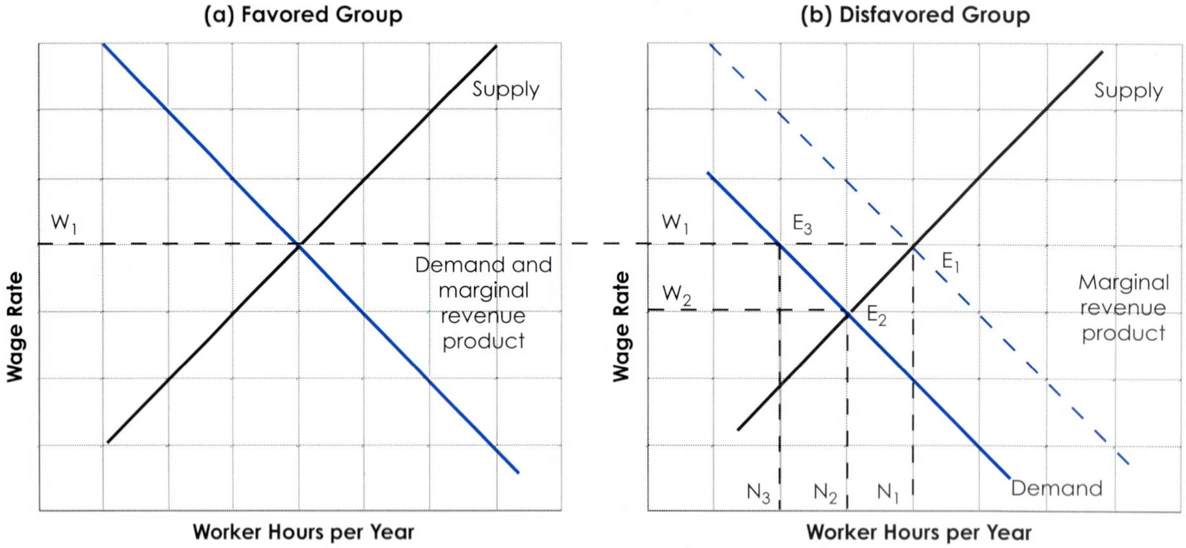

This figure shows the effect of discrimination in a labor market that can be divided into a group of workers who are favored by employers and a group of workers who are disfavored. The two groups are assumed to be equal in terms of productivity, but the demand curve for the disfavored group is shifted to the left of the corresponding marginal revenue product curve. If there are no equal-pay laws, the disfavored group's pay will fall to W_2, below the level of W_1 received by members of the favored group. If the law requires equal pay, both groups will receive wage W_1, but fewer members of the disfavored group will be employed. Many members of the disfavored group who would be willing to work in this occupation at wage W_1 will be forced into other, less attractive sectors of the job market or into unemployment. With or without the equal-pay law, then, discrimination is harmful to the disfavored group.

First, let us assume that there are no legal restrictions on discrimination. In this case, the wage rate for the disfavored group in Figure 18.3 will fall to W_2 compared with a rate of W_1 for the favored group. Workers from the two groups will then work side by side, doing the same job, but will receive different pay. All members of the disfavored group who want to work at wage W_2 will be able to find jobs in this market.

In the second case, we assume that the law prohibits paying different wages to members of different groups for doing the same work. In this case, employers must pay wage W_1 to members of both the favored and the disfavored groups. As a result, they will employ only N_3 worker-hours per year from the disfavored group.

The effect of the equal-pay law on members of the disfavored group is mixed. On the one hand, members of that group who are employed in this market are paid more than they would be without the law. On the other hand, fewer workers from the disfavored group get jobs at wage W_1. Those who do not get jobs in this market either remain unemployed or are crowded into some other sector of the labor market, possibly one in which employers do not discriminate. However, whether employers in those markets discriminate or not, wages there will be pushed down by the increased supply of workers who are unable to find jobs in the market shown in Figure 18.3. In the end, then, discrimination lowers the average wage of members of the disfavored group even when the law requires equal pay for all workers doing a given job and there are some markets in which employers do not discriminate.

COMPETITION AND DISCRIMINATION Now that we have examined the effects of discrimination on workers, we turn to the effect on employers. At first it might seem that employers gain from discrimination in that it pushes down the wages of members of disfavored groups. However, this is true only to the extent that employers are united in their desire to discriminate. Looking at the matter from the viewpoint of a single employer, there is an incentive not to discriminate.

Consider the case in which there is no equal-pay law. In that situation the wage rate for workers from the disfavored group is lower than that for workers from the favored group. Employers who set aside their prejudices and hire only workers from the disfavored group will have a cost advantage over employers who discriminate. This cost advantage potentially allows them to undercut their competitors' prices, either driving them out of the market or forcing them to change their hiring practices. In the long run, competition will tend to erode both the practice of discrimination and the pay gap.

All in all, the situation of discrimination in the labor market is somewhat like that of a cartel. Discriminating employers or cartel members can gain as long as they are united. But in practice each has an incentive to cheat on the system. Just as cartel members are pulled by the profit motive to undercut their fellow members, so are employers pulled by the profit motive to abandon established patterns of discrimination. *Applying Economic Ideas 18.2* looks at these forces in the South during the Jim

Crow era. In that case competition and the profit motive undermined discrimination to such an extent that states passed laws fostering employer discrimination.

SOME QUALIFICATIONS Although competition is a force that tends to break down labor market discrimination, it does not necessarily eliminate discrimination in all cases. One possible case is that of employers that are monopsonists in the markets in which they hire labor. An employer that faces a positively sloped supply curve in the labor market can be compared with a seller that faces a negatively sloped demand curve in the product market. It is profitable for a seller to practice price discrimination provided that the market can be divided into two or more segments with different price elasticities of demand. A higher price is then charged in the market in

APPLYING ECONOMIC IDEAS 18.2

DISCRIMINATION AND THE LAW IN THE JIM CROW SOUTH

In the southern United States in the Jim Crow era (the 1890s through the early 1950s), there was no lack of discrimination against black workers. Especially in the early part of the period, the economy was dominated by white plantation owners who employed large numbers of blacks As a group, they had an interest in holding down the wages of black farmworkers, both to boost their own profits and to maintain the dominant position of the white race.

There was one problem, however. The greed of many white employers overcame racial solidarity. Despite warnings in newspapers that "white men must stick together," the employers competed for black labor. Black workers often left their jobs for higher-paying ones, especially at harvest time, when labor was in short supply. In addition, labor recruiters from the North would appear in the South to entice black workers to come to work in the North's growing industries at wages that, while low by today's standards, were still better than those paid by the southern planters. Something had to be done to protect the traditional system of exploitation against erosion by market forces. The solution was the following set of labor laws, which were passed in most southern states between 1890 and 1910.

- *Enticement laws,* which made it a crime for white employers to "entice" a worker who had a contract with another employer. The aim was to prevent competition for workers that might bid up wages.
- *Contract enforcement laws,* which made it a crime for a black worker to break a labor contract with a white employer in order to seek work elsewhere. The standard contract period was one year. The aim was to prevent competition at harvest time, when the demand for labor was strongest.
- *Vagrancy laws,* which made it a crime for any person who was able to work to "wander or stroll in idleness." The aim was to keep black workers in the labor force and to prevent them from spending time between jobs shopping around for the best wage offer.
- *Emigrant-agent laws,* which curbed the activities of labor recruiters from other states or even other counties. For example, a law passed by the city of Montgomery, Alabama, imposed a $100 fine or six months in jail on anyone who printed, published, wrote, delivered, posted, or distributed any advertisement that tried to persuade people to leave the city to seek work elsewhere.
- The *convict lease system,* which allowed black prisoners, including those who had been imprisoned for violating contract or vagrancy laws, to be leased to private employers. Being on the chain gang was worse than being a slave: Since the lease was short term, the employer, unlike a slave owner, did not even have an interest in preserving the worker's health.

In a study of the Jim Crow labor laws, economist Jennifer Roback finds that they were effective in keeping wages down and limiting migration. She concludes that without the laws, competition would have undermined racial exploitation of workers.

Source: Jennifer Roback, "Exploitation in the Jim Crow South: The Market or the Law?" *Regulation* (September–December 1984): 37–44. A longer version of the article appears in the *University of Chicago Law Review* (Fall 1984).

which the elasticity of demand is lower. In labor markets, a monopsonistic employer can discriminate if groups can be identified according to their elasticity of supply. The profit-maximizing strategy is to pay a lower wage to the groups with the least elastic supply. Those will be the groups that have the least attractive alternative employment opportunities—namely, women and minorities.

In other cases, competition may fail to eliminate discrimination because the discrimination originates with customers or fellow employees rather than with the employer. If customers do not want to be served by members of a minority group, they will take their business to employers who do not hire minority-group members. The discriminating employers may then be at a competitive advantage overall even if they have to pay somewhat higher wages, as the theory set forth earlier indicates that they will. On the other hand, workers from dominant groups may not want to work side by side with minority-group members. In that case, an employer who wants to hire a mixed labor force may have to pay higher wages to members of the dominant group than one who hires only members of the dominant group. Again, this could give the discriminating employer an advantage over the nondiscriminating employer, despite the considerations discussed earlier.

Finally, there are cases in which employers are shielded from market forces altogether. Government employers are an example. It is no accident that some of the major targets of the drive for equal pay for women have been city and state governments. In addition, some economists have argued that managers of large corporations do not always share their stockholders' interest in maximum profits. If the white male managers of such a corporation like to hire only other white males even when more highly qualified women or minority candidates are available, they may be able to get away with doing so, at least for a time, even if the firm's profits suffer as a result.

Discrimination and Asymmetrical Information

The preceding discussion assumes that someone *wants* to discriminate—that employers, fellow workers, or customers prefer not to deal on an equal basis with members of the other gender or other racial groups. It is possible, however, that discrimination can occur even when, other things being equal, all parties would prefer not to discriminate. This can happen when employers wrongly ascribe to an individual member of a certain group characteristics that may be statistically valid for the group as a whole, but are not true of that individual—a phenomenon sometimes termed *statistical discrimination*.

One commonly cited example concerns the tendency of women, on the average, to spend more time out of the labor force than men. It is not disputed that the number of years a person spends in the labor force has a positive effect on productivity and wages. Given these circumstances, suppose that I am an employer looking for entry-level workers to train for career positions, and that I am convinced that women and men who spend equal years with my firm will turn out to be equally productive in their jobs. I have just interviewed two young, unmarried candidates who are alike in all respects except that one is a woman. Which do I hire?

If I am a rational profit maximizer (and if I am constrained to offer the same wage to both candidates), I hire the man. I have no way of knowing how many years each candidate will remain in the job, but the statistical probability is that the man will stay longer. Suppose, though, that you are the woman who is passed over for the job. *You know* that you are career bound, that you, unlike many women, will not drop out of the labor force to raise children. *You know* that you will therefore be just as productive as the male candidate. You feel discriminated against, and you are right to feel that way.

The problem here is one of asymmetric information: I do not know as much about your future employment plans as you do, and I have no way of finding out. Can I ask? No. First of all, it is illegal for me to do so; even to ask about your family intentions is considered evidence of discrimination. Moreover, it would be pointless to ask. You might simply change your mind. Even if you intended to drop out of the labor force the minute you got married, there would be no reason for you to tell the truth. Asymmetric information and opportunism compound each other. In this case, they prevent me, the employer, from learning what I would like to know about you, the employee, in order to make a decision that is in all ways fair and efficient.

Now the story just told contains some implicit assumptions that make it a worst-case scenario. In many cases there are other sources of information available to an employer who is not lazy or prejudiced. For example, if a job requires math skills, it would be ridiculous for an employer to exclude women on the basis of a belief that "women are not good at math." The generalization is not valid to begin with, and even if it were, the employer can determine an individual candidate's math skills by testing, looking at high school and college transcripts, and so on.

Also, the story assumes that employers cannot arrange contracts in a way that protects them against employees who leave their jobs before the employer reaps the full benefits of their on-the-job training. Seniority-based salary scales, bonus systems, and deferred compensation in the form of pensions and other devices can protect the employer against employees of either gender who leave for any reason.

Empirical studies suggest that the problem of asymmetric information does not always prevent employers from rewarding women and men equally when they are equal in terms of labor force attachment. One study showed, for example, that men who never marry and women who never marry have comparable labor force histories, whereas married women spend fewer than half as many years in the labor force as never-married women. Within the category of never-marrieds, women earn 99 percent as much as men, even though married women earn substantially less than married men. Another study focusing on college professors showed that never-married women actually did better in terms of salary and promotions than never-married men.[4]

Such studies suggest that labor markets—like markets for other goods and services—find ways of at least partially overcoming the problem of asymmetric information. Nevertheless, it is likely that at least some cases of perceived labor market discrimination are due to information asymmetry.

Federal Antidiscrimination Policies

Since the 1960s, the federal government has instituted a number of policies designed to combat discrimination in the labor market. The first of these was the Equal Pay Act of 1963. As explained earlier, however, mandating equal pay for members of different groups within the labor force is not enough by itself to protect disfavored groups against the effects of discrimination. In the face of employer discrimination, an equal-pay requirement alone may only reduce the number of workers hired from the disfavored group.

A more direct attack on employment discrimination was made by the Civil Rights Act of 1964. Title VII of that act outlaws discrimination of any kind based on race, color, religion, sex, or national origin. The law applies to firms with fifteen or more employees and also to labor unions. In the years since passage of the act, there has been much debate and litigation about what constitutes discrimination. The current interpretation is that any practice is suspect if it has a "disparate impact" on various groups. A practice with a disparate impact can be justified only if an employer proves that it is related to job performance. Thus, the requirement of a minimum height for employees holding a certain job could be challenged on the ground that it has a disparate effect on women. The requirement would be upheld if the employer could prove, say, that only a person over the minimum height could safely operate a certain piece of equipment.

A third important federal policy is Executive Order 11246, which was signed by President Johnson in 1965. This order sets antidiscrimination standards for all companies doing business with the federal government; it therefore covers most major firms. A key feature of the executive order is that major federal contractors must file *affirmative-action programs*. Under an affirmative-action program, a firm pledges to do more than simply not discriminate: it conducts a statistical analysis of its work force and takes concrete steps, through recruitment, training programs, and the like, to hire women and members of minority groups for jobs in which those groups are currently underrepresented. Federal law explicitly forbids the establishment of numerical quotas for hiring on the ground that they constitute discrimination against white males. However, affirmative-action measures are often criticized as constituting de facto quotas.

A number of empirical studies have attempted to determine the effectiveness of federal antidiscrimination policy. They have focused on reductions in the wage gaps among various groups before and after passage of the key civil rights acts. These studies have found federal policy to have had a modest, but measurable, favorable impact on the earnings of minority men. They appear to have had a strong effect in helping to close the wage gap between black and white women. Their effects on the earnings of white women have been negligible, however. In some cases affirmative action has caused white women to be displaced by minority-group members of both genders.[5]

The Comparable-Worth Controversy

In many respects, theory and policy issues having to do with discrimination by race and gender are similar, but there are some notable differences. One of the differences concerns segregation by occupation. Occupational segregation by gender is much stronger than segregation by race. For example, there are black and white truck drivers and black and white secretaries, but the truck drivers, whatever their race, tend to be men, whereas the secretaries tend to be women.

Duncan index of dissimilarity

For a set of occupations in which both men and women are employed, the percentage of men (or women) who would have to change occupations to equalize the numbers of men and women in each occupation.

MEASURING OCCUPATIONAL SEGREGATION A common measure of occupational segregation is the **Duncan index of dissimilarity**. This measures the percentage of either group alone that would have to change occupations to equalize the numbers of men and women in each occupation. The index is 100 if occupations are completely segregated and 0 if each group is equally represented in each occupation. For example, suppose that the labor force consists of 100 men and 100 women. Of the women, 75 are secretaries and 25 are truck drivers, while 25 of the men are secretaries and 75 are truck drivers. The Duncan index in this case would be 50. Occupational segregation could be eliminated if 50 of the male truck drivers (half of all male workers) became secretaries, or if 50 of the female secretaries (half of all female workers) became truck drivers.[6]

The Duncan index of gender segregation for the U.S. labor force was 57 in 1980. This implies that more than half of all men (or women) would have to change jobs to equalize representation by occupation. By contrast, the Duncan index for occupational segregation by race was 33 for men and just 28 for women. Moreover, occupational segregation by gender is changing less rapidly than segregation by race. Between 1960 and 1980 the index of occupational segregation by race fell by 17 points for men and by 28 points for women. Over the same period the index of gender dissimilarity fell by 14 points for blacks and by just 5 points for whites. The index of occupational segregation by gender is over 50 for all age groups; this is also true for all educational groups except people with graduate degrees, for whom it is 43.[7]

The occupational segregation of men and women would be of little consequence if the occupations dominated by women were paid as well as those dominated by men, but that is not the case. Instead, occupations dominated by women have significantly lower average pay levels than those dominated by men.

Occupational differences in pay contribute strongly to the gender gap in earnings. As we saw earlier, about half of that gap can be explained by differences in human capital. Nearly all of the remaining half can be explained by occupation. To put it in more concrete terms, male and female truck drivers with equal training and experience get paid about the same. So do male and female secretaries with equal training and experience. But the average pay of all truck drivers, most of whom are men, is higher than that of all secretaries, most of whom are women.

The policy implications of this situation are substantial. In the case of race, where there is relatively little occupational segregation, much progress toward equality can be made by ensuring that blacks and whites are placed on the same pay scales and have equal opportunities for promotion within their occupation. Those are the chief goals of the major civil rights legislation of the 1960s. In the case of gender, where there is much more occupational segregation, those measures will not by themselves equalize pay without either a change in the relative pay of various occupations or a major shift of genders among occupations.

ORIGINS OF OCCUPATIONAL SEGREGATION The source of occupational segregation by gender is one of the most controversial topics in labor market economics. There are two very different views on this matter.

According to one view, occupational segregation reflects choices made by women, choices that have both cultural and economic origins. Cultural factors might lead women into nurturing occupations such as teaching and nursing and men into more physical occupations such as construction or mining. (As cultural images change, occupational choices change, too. For example, the idea of women as doctors and lawyers seemed strange to many people a generation ago, but today, one-quarter to one-third of new graduates in these professions are women.) Economic choices leading women into certain occupations are said to reflect women's greater role in child care. That role causes women to favor occupations in which they can work in residential areas, arrange for flexible working hours, and move into and out of the labor force with relative ease. In return for these desired job characteristics, women are willing to accept lower pay.

According to the opposite view, occupational segregation reflects choices made by men. In this model, men choose first. They decide which occupations they would like, leaving the rest for women. Economist Barbara Bergman conjectures that the earmarking of jobs by sex has its origin in social systems that decree that women are and should be inferior in status to men. The result is that men feel uncomfortable when working side by side with women as equals, and even more so when working under the supervision of women. To avoid this discomfort, men confine women to a limited set of job categories.[8]

In both views, wages are set by supply and demand within each occupation, and it is supply and demand that determines the pay gap. The disagreement is over why the supply of women in certain occupations is as great as it is despite low pay. In the one view, women choose those occupations voluntarily because they have attractive nonwage characteristics. In the other view, men leave women no other place to go.

THE COMPARABLE-WORTH REMEDY The different views on the origins of occupational segregation by gender have very different policy implications. Those who see occupational segregation as a product of women's choices see no need for any remedy beyond those already on the books. Those measures prohibit paying different wages to men and women doing the same work and, through affirmative action, grant women access to nontraditional occupations. But those who see occupational segregation as male dominance of labor markets want more. They want equal pay for women now, without waiting for massive cultural and occupational shifts to occur.

No one claims that all occupations deserve exactly equal pay, because not all occupations are comparable. Some require more skills or education than others. Some are dirty and distasteful, others comfortable and pleasant. Some are boring, others exciting; some routine, others challenging. What the advocates of pay equity want is equal pay for work of *comparable worth*.

To measure the value of different occupations, such as those of secretary and truck driver, advocates of comparable worth propose the use of *job evaluation techniques* similar to those used by many large employers in setting internal pay scales. These techniques begin by identifying a number of traits that are relevant to the pay received by a worker, such as initiative, physical demand, and responsibility for equipment. Each job is assigned points for each trait, and total points are plugged into a formula that can be used to arrive at a pay recommendation. Such job evaluation techniques consistently identify traditionally female-dominated occupations as underpaid relative to traditionally male-dominated occupations.

Under a comparable-worth policy, job evaluations would be used to spotlight wage scales that, on the face of things, appear to be discriminatory. Not even the most enthusiastic advocates of comparable worth suggest rigid application of job evaluations as wage-setting formulas throughout the economy. Rather, they suggest that they be applied directly to wage setting in the public sector and indirectly as guidelines for wage setting in the private sector. Comparable-worth guidelines, like affirmative-action requirements, might be required for federal contractors and voluntary for other firms. Also, they might play a legally valid role in employee lawsuits, in conjunction with other indications of discrimination.

OBJECTIONS TO COMPARABLE WORTH Opponents of comparable worth see the concept not only as unnecessary (because they assume that current wage differences reflect voluntary choice) but as actively harmful, for several reasons.

First, they say, job evaluations fail to take supply and demand into account. Suppose that petroleum engineers and lawyers receive equal job evaluation points and hence are assigned equal pay. Then, during a boom in the oil industry, firms would have no way of bidding up wages to attract the extra engineers they need, and positions would go unfilled. And during a downturn in the industry, petroleum engineers would have to be laid off rather than be offered the option of continued employment at reduced pay.

Second, job evaluation techniques are inherently subjective. Different point scales and different evaluators produce different relative values for the same pair of jobs. Some scales use as few as four factors, some a dozen or more. Some evaluators might give a secretary more points for "responsibility for equipment" than a truck driver; others might give the secretary fewer points. For these reasons, private firms that now use such scales use them only as one factor among many in setting wages.

Finally, the critics point out that raising wages in traditionally female-dominated jobs would cause firms to cut back on employment in those occupations. Hospitals would use more automated monitoring equipment in order to economize on nurses. Insurance companies would substitute computers for clerical workers. The reduced employment opportunities would offset the wage gains for women in the affected occupations.

Advocates of comparable worth acknowledge that job evaluation techniques are imperfect. They agree that assigning every wage decision in the country to a federal bureaucracy would be a bad idea, and they deny that this is their intention. They claim that comparable-worth policies in other countries have had small if any employment effects. The debate over this issue is likely to continue for the foreseeable future.

SUMMARY

1. **How have labor unions evolved over time in the United States?** The earliest labor unions in the United States were *craft unions*—unions of skilled workers who practiced the same trade. The modern labor movement dates from 1881, when the American Federation of Labor, an association of craft unions, was founded. *Industrial* unions—which include all the workers in an industry regardless of their trade—were a later development. Union membership reached its peak in 1945 at about one-third of the labor force.

2. **What are the main provisions of U.S. labor law?** Before 1930 the courts were generally hostile to unions, limiting the goals they could pursue and the means they could employ. The Norris–La Guardia Act of 1932 was intended to place the government in a neutral position with respect to unions. Three years later the Wagner Act swung the power of government to the union side. This act created the National Labor Relations Board, set procedures under which workers could form unions, and limited the antiunion tactics that employers could use. The Taft-Hartley Act of 1947 limited the powers of unions somewhat and gave the government the power to intervene in strikes that threatened the national interest.

3. **How are wage rates determined in unionized markets?** In a competitive labor market, any increase in the wage brought about by unionization tends to reduce employment. Some models of unionization emphasize maximization of employment, the wage bill, or inframarginal rents. Other models view unions as political structures, applying concepts borrowed from public choice theory.

4. **What do unions do in addition to bargaining over wages and benefits?** Besides affecting wages, unions give workers a voice in how the workplace

is run. In this regard, unions can be viewed as part of the mechanisms by which firms coordinate complex transactions under conditions of long-term commitment of specialized resources, opportunism, and change. Managers of top nonunion firms recognize that productivity is enhanced when workers are allowed a voice in company affairs.

5. **How are labor markets affected by discrimination?** A firm is said to practice *labor market discrimination* against a group of workers if it is unwilling to hire members of that group at the same wage rate that is paid to equally productive members of a more favored group. Discrimination by employers will reduce the wages of members of the disfavored group if there are no legal restrictions, and it will reduce employment of members of the disfavored group even if the law requires equal pay for equal work. Competition tends to erode discrimination by employers but not discrimination by customers or fellow workers. Where there is asymmetric information about worker characteristics, discrimination can occur even though employers would prefer not to discriminate, other things being equal.

6. **What is the nature of the controversy over equal pay for men and women?** The degree of occupational segregation is much greater by gender than by race, and occupations that have traditionally been dominated by women are less well paid than those that have traditionally been dominated by men. To correct this situation, some have proposed that the equal-pay principle be extended so that workers performing jobs of comparable worth receive equal pay.

KEY TERMS

Craft union
Industrial union
Labor market discrimination
Duncan index of dissimilarity

PROBLEMS AND TOPICS FOR DISCUSSION

1. **Examining the lead-off case.** What, if anything, can unions do to help make workers' lives better without threatening job security? How can unions in grocery stores such as Vons and Albertsons deal with the fact that these stores have to compete with competition such as Wal-Mart, which has lower costs and can sell its products for much less?

2. **Unions and monopsony.** Turn to Figure 10.9, which shows supply, demand, and marginal resource cost curves for a monopsonist. The equilibrium wage under monopsony is $6 per hour. Suppose now that the workers threaten to go on strike unless they are paid at least $8 per hour, and the employer is forced to accept this demand. What happens to the supply curve of labor, given the union's wage demand? What happens to the marginal resource cost curve? Compared with the initial equilibrium, what happens to the wage rate? To the number of workers? Is this an exception to the rule that a union can raise wages only if it is willing to accept a reduction in jobs? Is there a limit to how high this union can raise wages without sacrificing the jobs of members? If so, what is the limit?

3. **Unionization on campus.** Is the nonteaching staff of your university unionized? Is the teaching faculty unionized? Are any efforts under way to unionize either of these groups? Interview one member of the nonteaching staff and one member of the faculty to learn their attitudes toward unionization.

4. **Labor unions and cartels.** Review the section on cartels in Chapter 9. In what ways do unions resemble cartels? How do they differ from cartels? Do you think that public policy should treat unions and producer cartels differently? Discuss.

5. **Labor unions in the news.** Examine recent copies of *The Wall Street Journal, Fortune, Forbes, Business Week,* and other business publications for news about labor unions and collective bargaining. Have recent rounds of bargaining centered on issues of wages and benefits or on such matters as job security and productivity? Give examples.

6. **Discrimination at Hertz.** In 1981 two women who had worked as automobile rental agents at Hertz Corporation filed a suit saying that they had been discriminated against when they had applied repeatedly for jobs as station manager and had been passed over in favor of male candidates. Although most rental agents were women, few had ever been promoted to the position of station manager. Hertz's city manager in the city where the women worked had told them that a woman should not be given the job of station manager because she cannot go away for training and because, in the manager's view, "a woman's place is in the kitchen." The judge in the case decided in favor of the women. Do you think that the judge's decision was a proper one? Would it have been better to wait for competition to eliminate the discrimination? Or do you think there was no real discrimination? Discuss.

7. **The Duncan index of dissimilarity.** A company employs 200 men and 200 women as clerks and managers. Of the managers, 160 are men and 40 are women. Of the clerks, 40 are men and 160 are women. What is the Duncan index of occupational dissimilarity by gender for this firm?

CASE FOR DISCUSSION

Productivity Often Overshadows Wages in Collective Bargaining

The big issue in collective bargaining used to be wages. Confrontations over dollars per hour often took the form of high-profile, industry-wide negotiations, such as those of the United Auto Workers with General Motors, Ford, and Chrysler. Today, the negotiations that determine workers' and companies' futures often center on work rules and cooperative measures to increase productivity. Such negotiations are more likely to take place on a local than a national scale. Consider some examples:

- In Columbus, Ohio, UAW Local 969 signed an agreement with a GM plant that cut production costs by $17 million by changing seniority provisions. The act saved some 770 jobs in the firm's aluminum mouldings department.
- Donnelly Corporation of Holland, Michigan, maker of mirrors and other auto parts, has seen its work force grow from 200 to 1,000 workers since 1975. Among the secrets of its success: cooperative labor-management committees that aim to draw the best from every worker. At Donnelly, even the company president serves on such a committee.
- In Flint, Michigan, members of UAW Local 659 are engaged in a wide variety of cooperative measures with their employer, GM, from running their floor operations without foremen to helping decide the speed of the production line. The result: turning the plant from one of the least efficient engine plants in the GM system into one of the most efficient.

But not all workers are happy with the new cooperative approach. Jerry Tucker, leader of a group of UAW dissidents, thinks quality circles and work teams are just a trick to co-opt workers into following an agenda set by management.

"You have 17 people on a very productive work team and the management says, 'Next week there will be only 16 on the team, but I want the same productivity,' " says Tucker.

Archaic labor law rules also sometimes get in the way of cooperative union-management efforts.

Decades ago, labor laws were passed to prohibit management from forming tame internal unions as a means of combating union organizing efforts. Today, these same rules sometimes constrain the ability of firms to form quality circles and other labor-management groupings.

Sources: Jacob M. Schlesing, "Plant-Level Talks Rise Quickly in Importance; Big Issue: Work Rules," *The Wall Street Journal*, March 16, 1987, 1; Frank Swoboda, "Labor Management Cooperation at GM Produces Success, Dissent," *The Washington Post*, December 7, 1989, A3; and Steve Gunderson, "Archaic Rules Foul Innovative Labor Solutions," *The Wall Street Journal*, October 21, 1991, A18.

QUESTIONS

1. Many union work rules, such as those that prevent workers from moving from one job to another within a plant or specify minimum crew sizes larger than the number actually needed to operate equipment, initially were established in an attempt to preserve jobs. Now these restrictive work rules are being eliminated in the name of job security. Why?
2. What factors do you think explain whether a given local union chapter will be willing to accept a certain work rule change? Do you think such decisions could be characterized better in terms of a maximizing model or in terms of a model that emphasizes political processes within the union?
3. What do you think is the relationship between the downward trend in union membership and the current trend toward cooperation with management? Could the decline in union membership be related to restrictive work rules at unionized plants?

END NOTES

1. A possible exception is the situation in which the employer is a monopsonist. See the second item in "Problems and Topics for Discussion" at the end of the chapter.
2. Bruce E. Kaufman, *The Economics of Labor Markets and Labor Relations* (Hinsdale, IL: Dryden Press, 1986), 461–463.
3. David Blanchflower and Richard Freeman, "Going Different Ways: Unionism in the United States and Other Advanced OECD Countries," NBER Working Paper No. 3342, 1992.
4. These and other studies are discussed in Walter Williams, *Explaining the Economic Gender Gap* (Dallas: National Center for Policy Analysis, 1983).
5. For a brief summary of the empirical literature, see Kaufman, *Economics of Labor Markets*, 392–393.
6. Mathematically, the Duncan index is found by summing across occupations the absolute value of the differences between the percentages of the two groups employed in each occupation and dividing that sum by two. If M1 is the percentage of one group in occupation i and Ni is the percentage of the other group in occupation i, then the index, D, is found by the formula

$$\sum_i \frac{|M_i - N_i|}{2}$$

7. See Victor R. Fuchs, "Women's Quest for Equality," *Journal of Economic Perspectives* (Winter 1989), Table 1.
8. See Barbara Bergman, "Does the Marker for Women's Labor Need Fixing?" *Journal of Economic Perspectives* (Winter 1989): 43–60.

CHAPTER 19

Income Distribution, Poverty, and Government Assistance

After reading this chapter, you will understand:

1. What poverty is and how it can be measured
2. How social insurance differs from public assistance
3. Why poor households are often subject to higher net tax rates at the margin than nonpoor households
4. How poverty can be attacked through programs that encourage self-sufficiency

Before reading this chapter, make sure you know the meaning of:

1. Income and substitution effects
2. Human capital
3. Public choice theory
4. Economics of discrimination

FRUSTRATED INNER-CITY RESIDENTS TURN TO SELF-HELP

September, 1991—After years of frustration with deteriorating neighborhood conditions, crime, and underfunded or ineffective government programs, many frustrated inner-city residents are turning to self-help.

In Pittsburgh's Homewood area, banker Mulugetta Birru, once an official in Ethiopia's Marxist government, is practicing urban renewal, capitalist style. As head of the Homewood-Brushton Revitalization and Development Corp., he targets deteriorated housing for rehabilitation, campaigns to attract new businesses to empty storefronts, and scrapes together financing from a variety of government, commercial, and private charitable sources. He sees parallels between the problems of Homewood and those in the third world—inhospitable conditions for the development of markets, low self-esteem, distrust of outsiders. But the efforts of local businesses and residents working together are paying off.

Best of all, according to Sara Trower, owner of a dry cleaning establishment and a member of Homewood-Brushton's board of directors, "We're dancing to our own tune, and nobody else's."

Other self-help efforts take very different forms. In Atlanta, Dottie Burns stands in the kitchen of a shabby apartment used as a "shooting gallery" by drug addicts. She quietly warns of the dangers of drug use, and hands out bleach (for cleaning needles), condoms, and literature on AIDS.

She is listened to because the people here know her. "I used to come here and do dope myself," she says. "I care for you and I don't want you to die."

The organization Burns now works for, Outreach, Inc., was started by another Atlanta resident, Sandra McDonald. McDonald's inspiration, in turn, comes in part from her maternal grandmother, who lived and worked in a black community where the motto was "Don't wait for anyone to do it for you—do it yourself."

Baltimore resident Richard Rowe considers himself lucky to have escaped some of the traumas and deprivation experienced by Burns and others. A college graduate, he grew up in a stable home with supportive parents. Understanding how important his own father's influence had been, he founded the African American Men's Leadership Council, which matches black youths aged 11 to 14 with black male adults who act as role models.

Rowe's effort drew "some resistance" initially from the Urban League, a well-established civil rights organization for which Rowe formerly worked. But his efforts are paying off. Inspired by Rowe's program, students at a local high school have started their own effort to encourage positive behavior among their peers.

The new self-help activists do not reject government assistance. Community development programs, educational efforts, and others receive government as well as private assistance. But, says U.S. Representative Kweisi Mfume, a Democrat from Maryland, "government is not the generator, it's the facilitator."

Sources: Joseph N. Boyce, "More Blacks Embrace Self-Help Programs to Fight Urban Ills," *The Wall Street Journal*, July 26, 1990, A1; and Alex Kotlowitz, "Community Groups Quietly Make Strides in Inner-City Housing," *The Wall Street Journal*, September 17, 1991.

THIS CHAPTER EXAMINES a growing problem in the U.S. economy—the poor. Despite the United States' status as one of the richest countries in the world, the disparity between the wealthy and the poor remains a problem. The poor command limited resources as consumers. Their attachment to the labor market is marginal at best. They are often dependent on others not only for money income but also for health insurance, housing, job training, and other basic goods and services that a majority of U.S. households obtain for themselves though the labor market. This chapter examines the nature and origins of poverty in the United States and potential solutions to the problems of the poor, ranging from nationwide government programs to local self-help efforts like those of Birru, McDonald, Rowe, and thousands of others.

INCOME DISTRIBUTION AND POVERTY

The Distribution of Income

Resource markets help determine not only how goods and services are produced but also for whom they are produced. Workers and owners of capital and natural resources are rewarded according to the productivity of the factors of production they contribute. Entrepreneurs earn profits or losses according to their degree of success in finding and taking advantage of new opportunities. But not everyone starts from the same position when entering the labor market. People are born with different skills and talents. They grow up in different school districts, control different amounts of capital and natural resources, and encounter different prejudices. These differences by themselves are enough to cause incomes to vary, and as people go through life, the decisions they make and the entrepreneurial risks they take cause incomes to vary still more. As a result, some earn little or nothing, while others earn millions of dollars a year.

In addition to what people earn in factor markets, taxes and government income transfers introduce further variations in the distribution of income. Each year federal, state, and local governments pay out over $1.3 trillion through a wide variety of transfer programs. Cash payments to the poor account for a large portion of total government transfer payments. Part of the rest goes to providing services for the poor, such as training and child-care benefits. Another large part, however, is targeted at middle-class and even wealthy people, for example, social security and Medicare.

As a result, even when transfers are taken into account, there is a great deal of income inequality. In 2001, the poorest one-fifth of the U.S. population earned an annual income of $10,136 on average, receiving less than 5 percent of all income. In contrast, the richest fifth has an annual average income of $145,940, accounting for roughly 50 percent of total income in the U.S.[1]

Lorenz curve

A graph that represents the degree of income inequality in an economy.

Figure 19.1 shows how the distribution of income can be summarized using a diagram called a **Lorenz curve**. The Lorenz curve gives only a static picture of income distribution: One's interpretation of the existing distribution depends not only on the degree of inequality at a given time, but also on comparisons with other times and places. It appears that income distribution tends to become somewhat more equal over time as countries grow more prosperous. For example, one study found that Switzerland, by some measures the country with the highest per capita income in the world, is the most egalitarian country, with the United States not far behind.[2] The study found that the level of a country's per capita income had more

FIGURE 19.1 A LORENZ CURVE FOR THE U.S. ECONOMY

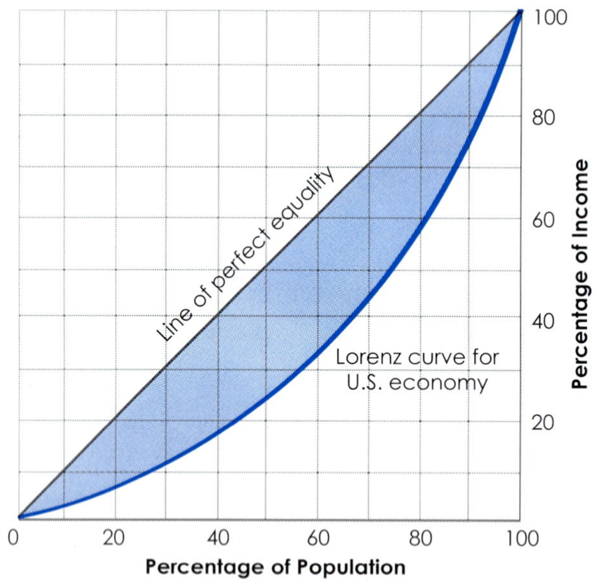

A Lorenz curve can be used to represent the degree of inequality in an economy. Such a diagram is drawn in a square, with the horizontal axis representing the percentage of the population and the vertical axis the percentage of all income earned by those at or below each population percentile. In an economy in which income was distributed equally, the poorest 20 percent of the population would earn 20 percent of all income, the poorest 40 percent would earn 40 percent of all income, and so on. In that case, the Lorenz curve would be a straight line from one corner of the box to the other. In the U.S. economy, where the poorest 20 percent of the population earns just 3.5 percent of all income and the richest 20 percent earns 50.1 percent, the Lorenz curve sags toward the lower right-hand corner of the box. The degree of inequality can be measured by the shaded area between the Lorenz curve and the line of perfect equality.

Source: U.S. Bureau of the Census, Table IE-1: Selected Measures of Household Income Dispersion: 1967 to 2001.

influence on income distribution than its social system. Before reunification, for example, West Germany appeared to be more egalitarian than East Germany, and South Korea appears to be more egalitarian than North Korea.

Many people have questioned whether the United States of the 1990s fits this pattern, despite record-setting economic expansion during that decade. In the 1990s, the percentage of total income received by the lowest fifth of all families fell from 4.6 percent in 1990 to 4.3 percent by 2000, while the percentage received by the highest fifth rose from to 43.3 percent to 47.7 percent during the same period. In fact, families in the highest 5 percent accounted for 17.1 percent of national income in 1990. That number has grown to over 20 percent as of 2000. The growth of inequality was particularly pronounced among men. Those with only a high school education or less fared especially poorly.

Yet not all the news was bad. Much, if not all, of the decreased share of all income received by families on the bottom of the income scale is a result of a decrease in the average size of such families. Income per family member has not shown a corresponding decline. And some of the increase in incomes at the upper end of the scale is not really a matter of "the rich getting richer," but rather, the rich reporting a higher percentage of their income in response to reduced income tax rates.

The Concept of Poverty

The focus of this chapter is not so much on inequality as on poverty. Although the two concepts are related, the relationship is not a simple one. Just how low an income must a household have to be considered poor?

A poverty-level income may be defined in absolute terms or relative to the incomes of other members of the society. For example, some suggest that a poverty-level family income should be defined as one that is less than half of the median income for all similar families. As of 2001, the median income for all families was $51,407, and the median income for a family of four was $63,278. A little over 20 percent of all families had cash incomes of less than half the median.

The official measure of poverty in the United States is not defined in terms of the median income, however. Instead, it is based on a more direct attempt to estimate the income needed to provide a minimum standard of living. It begins with an economy food plan devised by the Department of Agriculture. The plan is supposed to provide a balanced diet at the lowest possible cost given prevailing market prices. By itself, a total income equal to the cost of the economy food plan is not enough to keep a family out of poverty. To take other needs into account, the government sets the low-income level—the dividing line between the poor and the nonpoor—at three times the cost of the economy food plan. In 2003 the low-income level was $18,660 for a family of four, about 30 percent of the median income for such families. Below that level, it is assumed that the pressure of a family's needs for shelter, clothing, and other necessities tends to become so great that the family will forgo the needed food to get other things. However, the government's 3-to-1 ratio was based on a study done in 1961. More recent surveys suggest that poor families typically spend less than a quarter of their income on food. Thus, some have suggested that the poverty "multiplier" should be raised to 4 or even to 5.

To keep things in perspective, various measures of the poverty threshold in the United States should be compared to poverty around the globe. *Applying Economic Ideas 19.1* gives some indications of the dimensions of the world-wide poverty problem.

How Many Poor?

One reason for the attempt to establish an official definition of poverty was to provide a benchmark against which to measure progress toward eliminating the problem. As officially defined, the incidence of poverty fell rapidly during the 1960s, both before and after President Johnson's 1964 declaration of a "war on poverty." As shown in Figure 19.2, 22 percent of the population was officially classified as poor in 1960; by 1973, the figure had fallen to 11.1 percent. During the mid-1970s, however, the official poverty rate stopped falling, and in the late 1970s it began to move up. In 1983 the poverty rate reached 15.3 percent, its highest level since 1965. When the

APPLYING ECONOMIC IDEAS 19.1

MEASURING POVERTY AROUND THE GLOBE

Poverty in the United States is undeniably a serious problem that merits serious attention by economists and policy makers. Nonetheless, to place things in perspective, it is worth keeping in mind that even low-income families in the United States are incomparably richer than the poor in many regions of the world.

The World Bank often uses incomes of $1 or $2 per person per day as a measure of global poverty. Two dollars per day, or $2,920 per year for a family of four, is just 16% of the U.S. government's official poverty threshold. By these measures, 2.8 billion people, or 56% of the world population, live on less than $2 per day, and 1.2 billion people, or 23 percent of the world's population, live on less than $1 per day. Sub-Saharan Africa is the poorest region of the world, where half of all people get by on $1 a day or less. In Ethiopia, four out of five people fall below this threshold.

World Bank data do show some limited good news. Globally, poverty is falling. World Bank projections estimate that in the quarter century from 1990 to 2015, poverty, measured by the $2 per day threshold, will decline from 62% of the world population to 38%. Even taking population growth into account, there will be 15% fewer total poor people in 2015. But in Sub-Saharan Africa, the picture is bleak. The percent of the population in poverty will fall only from 76 to 70 percent over the period. Because of rapid population growth in the poorest African countries, the absolute number of poor people is projected to rise by nearly 60%.

Some people in the United States have a hard time understanding what it means to live on less than $1 per day. Numbers alone fail to paint a clear picture. To help understand the nature of global poverty, try answering yes or no to the following questions:

1. Yes/No: Do you own more than one change of underwear?
2. Yes/No: Do you own a pair of shoes?
3. Yes/No: Do you have access to transportation other than walking (e.g., car, bicycle, or public transportation system)?
4. Yes/No: Do you have more than one choice of food for your dinner tonight?

If you answer "yes" to three or more of these questions, you are wealthier than 80 percent of the world's population.

FIGURE 19.2 OFFICIAL POVERTY RATE, 1959–2002

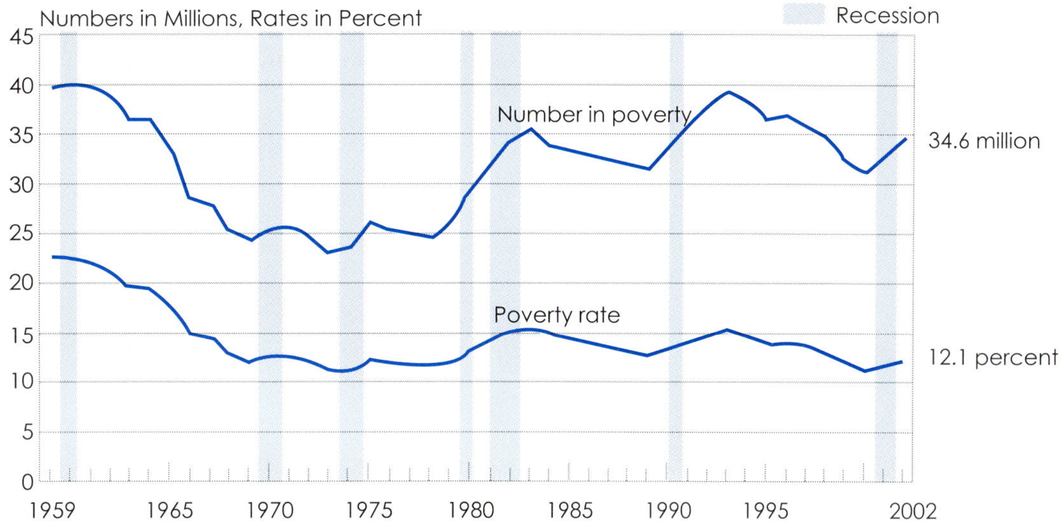

The official poverty rate is computed by comparing a household's census income (cash income from all sources) with a poverty line that is adjusted each year for changes in the cost of living. During the 1960s, the poverty rate fell steadily. In the 1970s, the decline leveled out. The poverty rate increased during the back-to-back recessions of the early 1980s, and then fell somewhat as economic growth resumed. The poverty rate fell beginning in the mid-1990s, but rose during the 2001 recession.

economy had recovered from the back-to-back recessions of 1980 and 1981–1982, the poverty rate fell somewhat. But even by 1988, the sixth consecutive year of economic growth, the official poverty rate had fallen to only 13.1 percent—well above the levels of the 1970s. And predictably, the poverty rate rose again during the 1990–1991 recession. The poverty rate and the number of people in poverty declined through the mid- to late 1990s following the recession, but rose again in 2000.

In some ways the official data on poverty give an incomplete picture, however. The official data can be adjusted in a number of ways that shed additional light on the problem.

Census income

Cash income from all sources, including earned income and cash transfer payments.

Pretransfer poverty

A measure of how many people would be poor on the basis of their private sources of income alone.

PRETRANSFER POVERTY One problem with the official data is that they are based on a household's **census income**—its cash income from all sources, including wages and salaries, property income, pension benefits, social security benefits, and cash welfare benefits. For some purposes, it would be useful to know how many people would be poor if only their private sources of income are taken into account, excluding government transfer payments. Households that would be poor without government transfers are said to experience **pretransfer poverty** even if social security, welfare, or some other form of government aid raises their census income above the poverty threshold.

The Bureau of the Census now reports data on the pretransfer poverty as a supplement to its official poverty series. The bureau's measure of pretransfer poverty is calculated by subtracting all government transfer payments from census income. For example in 1999, a year of relative prosperity, when the official poverty rate stood at 11.9 percent of all persons, the pretransfer poverty rate was estimated to be 19.4 percent.

The Bureau of the Census began publishing pretransfer poverty rates in 1979, but private research has addressed the question of historical pretransfer poverty rates. A study by Sheldon Danziger and Robert Plotnick estimated the pretransfer poverty rate at 21.3 percent for 1965 and 20.5 percent for 1979.[3] Comparing these estimates with the data presented in Figure 19.2 suggests that almost all of the six-percentage-point reduction in poverty as officially measured between 1965 and 1979 is attributable to an increase in government cash transfer programs rather than to increases in private income.

Useful though these measures of pretransfer poverty are, they should be interpreted cautiously. The pretransfer poverty estimates given here show what percentage of families would be poor on the basis of their observed private income and living arrangements. That is not necessarily the same as the percentage that would be poor if government transfer programs did not exist. As we will explain later in the chapter, government programs can in some cases affect decisions regarding family arrangements and labor force participation. For example, an elderly person living alone whose income is above the poverty line thanks to social security benefits might be counted among the pretransfer poor, whereas if there were no social security program, that person might be living in the household of a nonpoor child. The pretransfer poverty rate thus should be regarded as an upper boundary of the poverty rate that would prevail in the absence of government transfers.

ACCOUNTING FOR IN-KIND TRANSFERS The discussion of pretransfer poverty suggests another kind of adjustment that might usefully be made in the official poverty data: If we want a measure of the number of people who remain poor even with the benefit of government transfer payments, **in-kind transfers** should be taken into account. In-kind transfers include all aid given to the poor in the form of free or below-cost goods and services rather than cash. Medicaid, food stamps, and housing assistance are examples.

In-kind transfers

Transfer payments in the form of goods or services, such as food, housing, or medical care, rather than cash.

Adding the cash value of in-kind transfers to census income raises the income of some families enough to lift them above the poverty line. Bureau of the Census estimates indicate that adding cash value of in-kind transfers to census income lowers the poverty rate by more than 2 percentage points.

Accounting for in-kind transfers is particularly important when interpreting poverty trends over time. If in-kind transfers simply added a constant percentage to census income, the official poverty data would overstate the percentage of the population living in poverty, but the pattern over time would not be seriously distorted.

TRANSFER PROGRAMS TO AID THE POOR

We have seen that poverty is a complex phenomenon not easily captured in a single number. Neither is it easily overcome by any one policy. This section and the next examine a variety of policies and programs intended to aid the poor.

The antipoverty policies of federal, state, and local governments can be grouped into one of two broad categories. One consists of transfer payments, whose purpose is to allow poor households to achieve an adequate standard of living despite inadequate earned income. The other category consists of programs designed to encourage self-sufficiency, whose purpose is to enable poor households to earn enough to escape poverty on their own.

Social Insurance Versus Public Assistance

Social insurance

Programs under which transfers are made available to everyone, regardless of income, upon the occurrence of a specified event such as retirement, unemployment, or disability.

Public assistance

Programs under which transfers are made to people who meet some specified low-income standard.

Transfer programs can be further divided into two groups. The first, **social insurance**, includes programs in which transfers are made available to everyone, regardless of income, upon the occurrence of a specified event such as retirement, unemployment, or disability. The second category, **public assistance**, includes programs that are available to people who meet some specified low-income standard. Public assistance programs are also known as *means-tested programs* or *welfare*.

Social Security and Related Programs

The Social Security Act of 1935 set up what has become the largest single income transfer program of the U.S. government. Social security is one of the most popular, and in some ways one of the most successful, programs of the federal government. As we have seen, this is especially true when one views the program as a way of reducing poverty among the elderly.

Despite its accomplishments, social security is the target of many criticisms. It is worth looking at some of them.

FAIRNESS Although social security has made a major contribution to reducing poverty among the elderly, many critics see it as unfair in certain respects. One problem concerns the type of tax used to finance it. Social security benefits are financed by a special payroll tax, half of which is deducted from employees' gross pay and half of which is paid by employers. However, most economists believe that all or most of the true incidence of the tax is on employees' wages and salaries. Because the tax is levied only on earnings below a certain threshold ($87,900 as of 2004) and on wage and salary income, lower- and middle-income households pay taxes that are higher in relation to their incomes than the taxes paid by higher-income households. Thus, the tax used to finance social security adds to income inequality, partly offsetting the effect of the benefits paid out under the program.

Some critics think that the distribution of benefits is unfair with regard to the treatment of women and minorities. One problem concerns working wives; both working and nonworking wives receive a benefit equal to 50 percent of their husband's benefits. If a married woman earns enough to qualify for social security in her own right, she must forgo that benefit. Thus, women whose earnings are low relative to those of their husbands often gain nothing in return for the social security taxes they pay.

Some observers also see the system as unfair to blacks and other minorities. Because minority-group members have shorter life expectancies than whites, they can expect to receive less, on the average, in retirement benefits. According to one calculation, a white male entering the labor market in the mid-1980s could expect to receive 74 percent more in retirement benefits than a black male earning the same wage.[4] Changes in the system that aim to ease its financial problems by raising the retirement age above 65 are likely to be devastating to blacks given current mortality rates.

FINANCIAL PROBLEMS For the moment, the social security system is financially sound because the large "baby boom" generation born in the 1940s and 1950s is paying for the retirement of a much smaller previous generation. This situation will change dramatically in the near future, however. Today there are about five workers paying taxes into the system for each retiree receiving benefits. By the middle of this century, that ratio will fall to between 1.5 and 2.5 workers per retiree.[5] Given the lower figure, the social security tax would have to rise to 38 percent of the national payroll to keep the system solvent. Given the likelihood that such a tax burden would provoke a political backlash, it is small wonder that two-thirds of workers under thirty polled by *The Washington Post* believed that social security would not exist by the time they were ready to retire.[6] Massive federal government budget deficits and an expected increase in retirement benefits from the baby-boom generation pose a serious threat to the viability of social security.

Other Social-Insurance Programs

The second-largest social-insurance program is Medicare. This adjunct to the social security program provides in-kind medical benefits to the elderly. The sources of financing for Medicare parallel those of the rest of the social security system, and some of the same criticisms have been leveled against it as a result. The remaining social-insurance programs are smaller and tend to channel a smaller percentage of their benefits to the poor. For both reasons, then, they do less to alleviate poverty.

Public Assistance

In addition to social security and other transfer programs keyed to specific events, the federal government operates a number of means-tested transfer programs. The most important of these are listed below.

TEMPORARY ASSISTANCE FOR NEEDY FAMILIES (TANF) To most people, "welfare" means TANF—the monthly cash assistance program for poor families with children under age 18. A family of three (mother and two children) may qualify for TANF if their gross income is below a specified level. There is a four-year lifetime limit on cash assistance. Work is a major component of TANF; adult recipients with a child over age one year are required to participate in a work activity. These work activities are intended to help recipients gain the experience needed to find a job and become self-sufficient.

This program originated in the 1930s as part of the social security program and was later called Aid to Families with Dependent Children (AFDC). It was intended to help a relatively small number of poor widows raise young children at home. Its coverage grew over time with most of its beneficiaries being households headed by women who are divorced, separated, or never married. In several states, TANF is also available to two-parent households with unemployed fathers.

The actual level of welfare benefits and the terms of eligibility vary from one state to another. In the 1970s, the median welfare benefit was about two-thirds of the poverty level, but today it has fallen to about two-fifths of the poverty level, and is no more than half of the poverty level even in the most generous states. *Economics in the News 19.1* discusses recent reforms to AFDC.

SUPPLEMENTAL SECURITY INCOME Supplemental security income is the second largest cash public-assistance program. It includes grants intended to provide a minimum standard of living to the aged, blind, and disabled. About 84 percent of these payments are estimated to go to people who would be poor if they did not receive government benefits.

MEDICAID Medical assistance to low-income people under the Medicaid program is the largest in-kind transfer program. TANF families qualify for Medicaid in all states, and in some states families with somewhat higher incomes are also eligible. Medicaid coverage is not universal; for one reason or another, a substantial percentage of poor people do not qualify for this program.

FOOD BENEFITS Food stamps are the largest component of in-kind nutritional benefits for the poor. Available to low-income families to be spent in grocery stores to purchase food items, these coupons and electronic benefit transfer cards (EBT) account for about two-thirds of all food benefits. Other nutritional assistance includes subsidized school lunches, special nutritional programs for mothers and infants, and other smaller programs.

Income Transfers and Incentives

Despite these social insurance and public assistance programs, poverty remains a problem in the United States. How is it that poverty rates have grown?

ECONOMICS IN THE NEWS 19.1

WELFARE AS WE KNEW IT BEFORE REFORM

July 13, 1996—Aid to Families with Dependent Children is the safety net for the poorest American families with children. In 1994, AFDC provided cash assistance to about 4.2 million single mothers and their children and about 335,000 two-parent families through the AFDC-Unemployed Parent program. AFDC costs the federal government about $14 billion a year and states another $12 billion. Add other federal expenditure for AFDC families—food stamps ($12 billion), Medicaid ($17 billion, with another $13 billion in state spending), and harder-to-calculate expenditures for housing, child care, social services, and so forth—and total federal expenditure for AFDC families exceeds $50 billion a year, or roughly 4 percent of federal outlays.

About one in seven American children is now on AFDC. Of the 9.4 million children on AFDC in 1994, about 38 percent were African American, 21 percent Hispanic, and 33 percent non-Hispanic white. This means that about four of every ten black children were on AFDC, as were about three out of ten Hispanic children, and about 7 percent of white children.

Never-married mothers now head more than half of all AFDC households. When AFDC started in the 1930s, two-thirds of children on welfare were there because of the death or incapacitation of a parent. By 1975, children of divorced or separated parents accounted for the majority of cases (about 56 percent), while the children of never-married mothers made up another third. By 1994, children of never-married mothers accounted for almost two-thirds of the caseload, compared with only 30 percent for children of divorced or separated parents, and 2 percent for the children of widows.

Long-term welfare dependency is a serious problem. According to estimates by the Urban Institute's Ladonna Pavetti, 62 percent of recipients at any given time are in the midst of welfare spells that eventually will last nine or more years. Many mothers, mainly divorced ones, spend a relatively short period of time on welfare—leaving as soon as they can get a job. But many others, especially unwed mothers who had their first baby as teens and either dropped out of high school or have little work experience, find it much more difficult to work their way off welfare. Thus, the increasing percentage of never-married mothers on welfare probably has increased the length of time the average welfare mother stays on the rolls.

More immigrants are receiving welfare benefits. Illegal immigrants are not eligible for AFDC, although their U.S.-born children are. Legal immigrants are eligible, but during their first three years in the country they are presumed to receive some assistance from their sponsor if they have one. Immigration has not had a big effect on the AFDC caseloads of most communities, although it has a substantial impact in places like California, where non-citizens account for about 15 percent of all persons on the program. Immigration also has increased federal spending for the indigent elderly and disabled under the Supplemental Security Income Program. Between 1982 and 1993, the number of aliens getting SSI benefits jumped from 128,000 (3 percent of recipients) to 786,000 (12 percent of recipients), at a cost of more than $3 billion a year. Eighty-five percent of these non-citizen recipients come from three areas—Latin America (39 percent), Asia (37 percent), and the former Soviet Republics (10 percent).

Over the last three years, 44 states have begun reforming their welfare programs using "waivers" from the Clinton administration. The most common provisions allow recipients who go to work or get married to keep more of their earnings or stay on Medicaid longer. Other common reforms reduce benefits if welfare mothers don't send their children to school, don't keep their children's immunizations up-to-date, and so forth. In recent months, however, 25 states have received waivers that go to the very heart of the program: They end the absolute and unconditional entitlement to long-term benefits. Five more states have similar waivers pending. About half completely terminate cash benefits and about half trigger a work requirement after a specific period on the rolls, usually 24 months or 36 months. Three others terminate benefits after a period of mandatory work. States making these fundamental changes include some with the largest welfare caseloads in the country—California, Illinois, Ohio, and Texas. New York will probably join the list soon. In fact, time limits already cover over 60 percent of the nation's welfare caseload.

Many waiver requests submitted by states initially proposed an absolute termination of benefits after the time limit. So far, however, the Clinton administration has insisted that there be some sort of protection for long-term recipients. The most common safety-net provisions exempt families from the time limit for personal hardship (14 states), inability to find a job (13 states), the caretaker's age (10 states), and the child's age (9 states).

After rising 32 percent under George Bush (from 1989 to 1993), AFDC caseloads are now declining. Between January 1994 and February 1996, the number of families on welfare nationwide fell by 8.5 percent. President Clinton already is claiming credit for this decline. He may be right, but the bite of these new rules will not be felt for many years. Have recipients really changed their behavior in anticipation of future penalties? Another explanation is the stronger labor market for low-skilled workers. The decline in AFDC rolls started in 1994, when, for example, the poverty rate among African-Americans declined from 33.1 percent to 30.6 percent.

Source: Douglas J. Besharov, "Welfare As We Know It," *Slate*, July 13, 1996. Reprinted with permission.

The persistence of poverty despite the large sums spent on transfer programs has led many critics to suggest that antipoverty policy needs a major restructuring if it is going to accomplish its goals. The most widespread objection to current income transfer programs is the presence of incentives that conflict with the goal of encouraging self-reliance. Some critics go so far as to charge that TANF and related programs amount to little more than "paying people to be poor."[7] What truth, if any, is there in this charge?

In one way or another, all income transfer programs affect the incentive to work by imposing either explicit or implicit taxes on earned income. The social security payroll tax is an example of an explicit tax. As noted earlier, this tax applies to the first dollar earned by the lowest-paid workers, but (as of 2004) not to earnings over $87,900 per year. As an example of an implicit tax, consider the food stamp program, under which a recipient's benefits are reduced by $.25 for each added dollar of earned income. The reduction in a program's benefits as a result of increased income is known as that program's **benefit reduction rate**.

Benefit reduction rate

The reduction in the benefits of a transfer program that results from a $1 increase in the beneficiary's earned income.

Putting the two together, the percentage of each additional dollar of earned income that a household loses through either explicit taxes or benefit reductions can be termed the **net marginal tax rate** for that household. Marginal tax rates and benefit reduction rates are *additive* in their effects on the net marginal tax rate. For example, a family facing a 7 percent marginal tax rate for the social security payroll tax and a 25 percent benefit reduction rate under the food stamp program is subject to a 32 percent net marginal tax rate. If school lunch benefits are reduced at a rate of 5 percent, the total benefit reduction rate for the family rises to 37 percent, and so on.

Net marginal tax rate

The sum of the marginal tax rate for all taxes paid by a household plus the benefit reduction rates of all transfer programs from which the household benefits.

All means-tested transfers are subject to some kind of benefit reduction as income increases. Not all are subject to a simple percentage benefit reduction as in the food stamp program, however. The benefit reduction provisions of the TANF program are a case in point. On paper, before 1968 and after 1981 benefits were supposed to be reduced by $1 for each $1 of earned income, resulting in a 100 percent benefit reduction rate. From 1968 through 1980, the benefit reduction rate was lowered to 67 percent. However, caseworkers have always had some leeway in applying the program's rules. Through favorable interpretations of rules regarding child-care expenses, transportation, and other items, beneficiaries were allowed to retain more of their earnings than indicated by the nominal benefit reduction rate.

The benefit reduction provision of Medicaid is still another story. Families either are eligible for this program or are not, with eligibility often linked to TANF. Until a family's income rises to the threshold beyond which it is no longer eligible for TANF, there is no percentage benefit reduction; once the threshold is crossed, the entire Medicaid benefit is lost.

Applying Economic Ideas 19.2 shows how the effects of various programs combine to create net marginal tax rates that can exceed 100 percent for households in certain income ranges. The taxes paid by low-income families are, of course, lower than those paid by higher-income families, but when benefit reduction rates are taken into

APPLYING ECONOMIC IDEAS 19.2

NET MARGINAL TAX RATES FOR A LOS ANGELES FAMILY

Poor families are often subject to extremely high net marginal tax rates, as shown by the data in the accompanying table. The data show how taxes and reductions in benefits affect the monthly disposable income of an inner-city family of four in Los Angeles at various levels of gross monthly wages. Gross monthly wages are the cost of labor to the employer and include both employer and employee contributions to social security. The data on disposable income reflect all payroll and income taxes and assume that the family makes use of the maximum city, county, state, and federal welfare benefits to which it is entitled.

The net marginal tax rate is the sum of the marginal tax rates and benefit reduction rates to which the family is subject. The disincentive effects of benefit reductions and taxes reach a peak just above and below the poverty threshold ($833 a month, based on an official poverty line of about $10,000 a year for a family of four at the time). Note that as the family's gross wages increase from $700 a month to $1,200 a month, its disposable income falls from $1,423 to $1,215. This reflects the loss of $385 in welfare benefits; the loss of $9 in food stamps; a reduction of $23 in the family's housing subsidy; an estimated reduction of $130 in the value of its medical benefits; an $8 increase in state income and disability insurance taxes; $68 in payroll taxes; and $85 in federal income taxes.

Source, Arthur Laffer, "The Tightening Grip of the Poverty Trap," Cato Institute Policy Analysis No. 41, August 30, 1984. Reprinted with permission.

Monthly Gross Wages (Dollars)	Monthly Family Disposable Income (Dollars)	Change in Disposable Income (Dollars)	Net Marginal Tax Rage (Percent)
0	1,261	NA	NA
100	1,304	43	57
200	1,341	37	63
300	1,366	25	75
400	1,391	25	75
500	1,419	28	72
600	1,429	10	90
700	1,423	–5	105
800	1,418	–5	105
900	1,420	2	98
1,000	1,432	12	89
1,100	1,253	–178	278
1,200	1,215	–39	139
1,300	1,217	2	98
1,400	1,296	39	61
1,500	1,294	38	62
1,600	1,330	37	63

NA = Not available

account, the net marginal tax rates for low-income families are actually higher than those for high-income ones.

The elderly, including in some cases those living below the poverty line, also face exceedingly high net marginal tax rates. A complex set of rules subject some social security benefits to federal, state, and local income taxes and also reduce benefits by $.50 for each added dollar of earned income above a certain threshold. When all the complexities are taken into account, the net marginal tax rate on the elderly can exceed 100 percent. For example, John C. Goodman and A. James Meigs of the National Center for Policy Analysis calculate that an elderly widow earning $13,400 per year would see her annual income reduced by $27 if she received a $1,500 raise, and a married man earning just $8,800 would lose $18 in total income if his wages rose by $1,000.[8]

The "Negative Income Tax" Proposal

Many economists see high net marginal tax rates as a disturbing feature of current transfer programs. At best they reduce work incentives. And when net marginal tax rates exceed 100 percent, as they sometimes do, the charge that people are being "paid to be poor" is not so far fetched. As a solution to this problem, many economists have suggested "cashing out" all in-kind transfers and combining them, along with all existing cash transfers, into a single program with a benefit reduction rate well below 100 percent. In this way work incentives would be maintained for households at all income levels.

Negative income tax

A plan under which all transfer programs would be combined into a single program that pays cash benefits according to a household's income level.

Among the first to advance this idea was University of Chicago economist Milton Friedman.[9] He termed his proposal a **negative income tax**, a term that is now often applied not only to Friedman's approach but to any similar scheme. The basic idea is simple. Under a positive income tax, people pay the government an amount that varies according to how much they earn. A negative income tax puts the same principle to work in reverse: It requires that the government pay individuals an amount that varies inversely with their earnings.

Figure 19.3 compares a negative income tax to a conventional income-replacement program such as TANF. The horizontal axis of the graph measures the income a household earns; the vertical axis measures what it actually receives after payments from or to the government. The 45-degree line ABFC represents the amount of total income households would have if there were no taxes or transfers of any kind.

The conventional program limits benefits to households whose earned income is below the poverty level and incorporates a 100 percent benefit reduction rate. The benefit level is set equal to the poverty line, here assumed to be $10,000 per year. Households above the poverty line are assumed to pay a conventional income tax at a 20 percent marginal rate. The benefit schedule for the conventional program thus is represented by the line segment DB, and the after-tax earnings of nonpoor households are represented by the line segment BE.

Under the negative income tax, the minimum benefit is also just equal to the poverty level of $10,000. A minimum benefit of that amount is necessary if the goal is to eliminate poverty even among households with no earned income at all. Starting from that point, however, benefits are reduced by just $.50 for each dollar earned. The benefit schedule under the negative income tax thus is the line segment DF. When earned incomes reach a level equal to twice the low-income level, a breakeven

FIGURE 19.3 A NEGATIVE INCOME TAX

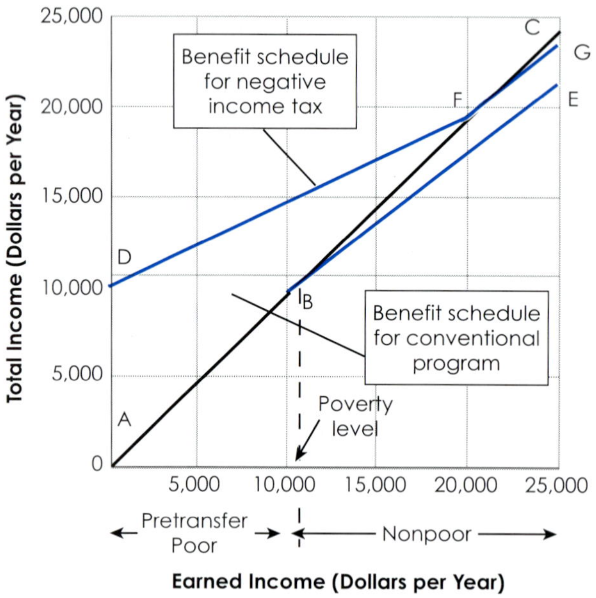

A negative income tax would replace all transfer programs with a single cash transfer based on income. This chart assumes a poverty level of $10,000 for a family of four. A family with no earned income receives $10,000 in benefits from the negative income tax. From $0 to $10,000, benefits are reduced by $.50 for each $1 of additional earned income. When earned income exceeds $20,000, benefits fall to zero and the family begins to pay income tax at a rate of 20 percent. The benefit schedule for such a program is the line DFG. By comparison, a conventional income-replacement program with a 100 percent benefit reduction rate is represented by the line DBE.

point is reached at which no more benefits are received. After that, households begin to pay the 20 percent tax on earned income, as shown by the line segment FG.

The effects of the two programs on work effort can be expressed in terms of the concepts of income and substitution effects that were applied to labor supply in a previous chapter. Here the income effect takes the form of a tendency for an increase in income to reduce work effort, other things being equal and assuming that leisure is a normal good. The substitution effect takes the form of a tendency for an increase in the net marginal tax rate, other things being equal, to discourage work effort because it raises the opportunity cost of a dollar of earned income, measured in terms of hours of forgone leisure.

If a negative income tax replaces a conventional income-replacement program as illustrated in Figure 19.3, the effects can be analyzed as follows:

1. For households with earned incomes below $10,000, the net marginal tax rate is cut from 100 percent to 50 percent. The resulting substitution effect tends to encourage work effort. However, total income for all but the poorest of such families is increased. There is therefore an offsetting income effect that tends to discourage work effort. The net effect on work effort for families with earned incomes below the poverty level may be positive, but is not certain to be so.

2. For households with earned incomes of $10,000 to $20,000, the net marginal tax rate increases from 20 percent to 50 percent, and total incomes also increase. Both the income and substitution effects thus tend to discourage work effort in this range.

It follows that the overall effects on work effort of a negative income tax cannot be predicted from theory alone. They depend on the relative strength of the income and substitution effects and on the distribution of households between income brackets where the net effects of the program encourage or discourage work effort. A number of attempts have been made to resolve the issue through empirical research. Some studies have compared the effects of programs with different benefit formulas in various states. In addition, in the late 1960s and early 1970s, the federal government sponsored negative income tax experiments in several cities. Empirical evidence from both types of studies suggests that the income and substitution effects of transfer programs operate in the expected directions but are small. Thus, they do not provide much basis for expecting that replacing current programs with a negative income tax would have a major overall effect on work effort one way or the other.[10]

After thirty years of discussion and study, the concept of a negative income tax retains many advocates among economists, but it has never gained wide support outside that profession. In part, this may be because economists cannot point to persuasive evidence that a negative income tax would really produce a major increase in work effort by low-income households. The whole concept also has a serious political liability inasmuch as voters have never shown much enthusiasm for public-assistance programs that pay substantial benefits to households whose earned incomes are already above the poverty level. For these and other reasons, then, efforts to encourage self-sufficiency among the poor have taken other directions over the years. Some of these efforts are discussed in the next section.

PROGRAMS TO ENCOURAGE SELF-SUFFICIENCY

Conventional transfer programs are based on the notion that combating poverty is primarily a matter of income replacement. They are often based on the implicit notion that the poor can be divided into a "deserving" category who, because of age or disability, have no possibility of achieving self-sufficiency, and an "undeserving" category who are capable of self-sufficiency and therefore should be left to fend for themselves. This was the motivation behind welfare reforms implemented at both the state and federal level in the late 1990s. The Personal Responsibility and Work Opportunity Reconciliation Act of 1996, also know as the welfare reform bill, sought to address problems with social insurance and public assistance programs. Reforms were designed to reduce long-term dependence on welfare, through work training and time limits on the receipt of benefits such as TANF.

In practice, it is not so easy to distinguish between the "deserving" and the "undeserving" poor. For one thing, social expectations regarding self-sufficiency have changed dramatically over time. Half a century ago, it was accepted as a matter of course that the aged, the disabled, and mothers of young children could not and should not be expected to participate in the labor market. Today, it is widely felt that many people in these categories have not only a potential to become self-sufficient, but also a definite right to do so. It is no longer considered odd, as it would have been a generation or two ago, to see a business executive roll into a boardroom in a wheelchair, to find a seventy-year-old teacher still teaching classes although eligible for social security, or to see a single mother drop off an infant at a day care center on her way to work.

Moreover, the notion of "factors beyond a person's control" turns out to be inadequate as a basis for categorizing the poor. It is not that anyone would deny that there are some such factors that affect people's potential for self-sufficiency. Physical or mental disabilities acquired through accident or genetic inheritance are examples. People also do not choose their gender or their ethnicity, factors that can affect income when there is discrimination in labor markets. And people do not choose their place of birth, a factor that is important in view of wide regional variations in economic opportunities. However, leaving aside extreme cases of physical or mental disability, these factors determine whether people will be economically self-sufficient only in conjunction with other factors that are to one degree or another matters of individual choice. Characterization of the poor as helpless victims of circumstances, or, on the other hand, as moral reprobates who deserve what they get only interfere with understanding the economic nature of poverty.

Instead, it is more fruitful to look at poverty in terms of the same categories of preferences, constraints on opportunities, and choices that provide insights into other areas of economic behavior. Life outcomes are jointly the product of circumstances and choices made in response to those circumstances. Policies that ignore this fact are all too likely to fall victim to the law of unintended consequences. Three especially critical areas in which circumstances and choice interact are education, family status, and work experience. Let us consider each of these together with policies designed to encourage self-sufficiency within each of these areas.

Education

As Figure 19.4 shows, education has a strong effect on economic status. People who have not completed high school experience poverty rates more than twice as high as the rate for those who completed only high school, and nearly five times as high as the rate for people who earned a four-year college degree.

A person's educational achievement is determined in part by the education opportunities available, that is, by such circumstances as the quality of public schools in the local community and the availability of financial aid for college. However, achievement also depends to a substantial degree on the extent to which individuals

FIGURE 19.4 POVERTY RATES FOR PEOPLE WITH DIFFERENT EDUCATION LEVELS

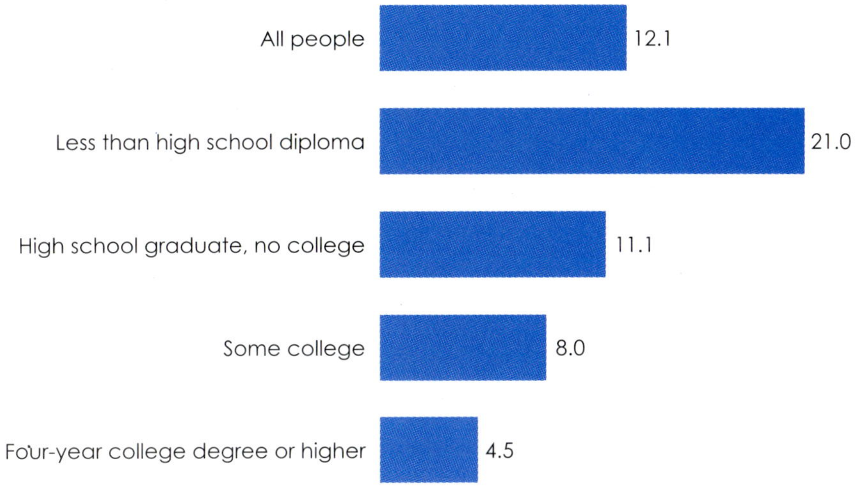

Poverty rates among individuals vary widely according to education level. This figure shows that the greater the education, the less the chance that the individual will be poor.

Source: Bureau of the Census, *Poverty in the United States: 2002*, Table POV29 (published October 2003).

take advantage of the available opportunities. For example, graduates of even the worst high schools fare better than people who do not graduate from high school at all. Similarly, students who graduate from less expensive community colleges or state universities have lifetime incomes only a few percent below those of graduates of the best Ivy League institutions, if allowance is made for grades and fields of study. For example, a forty-year-old mechanical engineer with a 3.5 grade point average and a degree from MIT might earn $85,000 a year, compared to $82,000 a year for a similarly trained engineer with identical grades and a degree from Texas A&M.

To put matters in economic terms, educational choices are shaped both by constraints on opportunities and by the individual preferences, values, and motivations that determine the choices made from among those available. Programs to encourage self-sufficiency through education must address both sets of elements. The following, for example, are programs that emphasize removing constraints and broadening opportunities:

- Head Start and other preschool programs that aim to ensure that all children start school ready to learn.
- Conventional programs of every kind that aim to upgrade the quality of public schools through better funding of programs, rewards for effective teaching, better laboratory facilities, and so on.
- Programs giving students and parents a choice of schools. These include the use of magnet schools with special programs and policies that allow students

to choose among public schools within a town or city. An even broader range of choice can be achieved by giving parents "education vouchers" that can be spent for education at either public or private schools.

- Programs that give dropouts a second chance to earn a high school equivalency degree or practical job and communication skills.
- At the college level, programs of direct aid and loan programs that permit students to pay part of their costs out of the enhanced future earnings that result from education.

Programs that emphasize preferences, values, and motivations are harder to capture in simple formulas. Nevertheless, the following approaches show definite promise:

- Parental involvement in the educational process is a key element in motivating educational achievement. Some experiments go far beyond the traditional Parent-Teacher Association. For example, in Chicago parents vote for school administrators and participate directly in the administration of schools on a neighborhood-by-neighborhood basis.
- The returns to education for minority youth are very high, yet the benefits of education may be invisible if individuals who achieve an education flee their home communities. Leaders in such communities frequently call for successful minority-group members to become more involved in schools as mentors and role models. Richard Rowe's mentoring program for minority youth in Baltimore, mentioned at the beginning of this chapter, is an example.
- Negative peer pressure deters some students from taking advantage of educational opportunities. Students who earn good grades and improve communication skills are sometimes ridiculed and made to feel that they are "not one of the group." Such pressures are not easy to deal with, but educators increasingly recognize the need to break down negative stereotypes and inculcate positive educational values. The student-run program at St. Frances Charles Hall High School in Baltimore uses this approach.

Some of these programs call for money, others call for little more than willingness to try new solutions to old problems. But it is hard to imagine any really effective antipoverty effort that does not include education as an element. As *Washington Post* columnist William Raspberry puts it, "Too many of our children are leaving school as dropouts, premature parents or criminals, not merely because they are cheated of opportunity but also because we have not made them understand the extent to which the future is in their own hands."[11]

Family Status

A second major determinant of economic success is the type of household to which an individual belongs. As Figure 19.5 shows, families headed by married couples

FIGURE 19.5 POVERTY RATES FOR FAMILIES WITH SELECTED CHARACTERISTICS, 2002

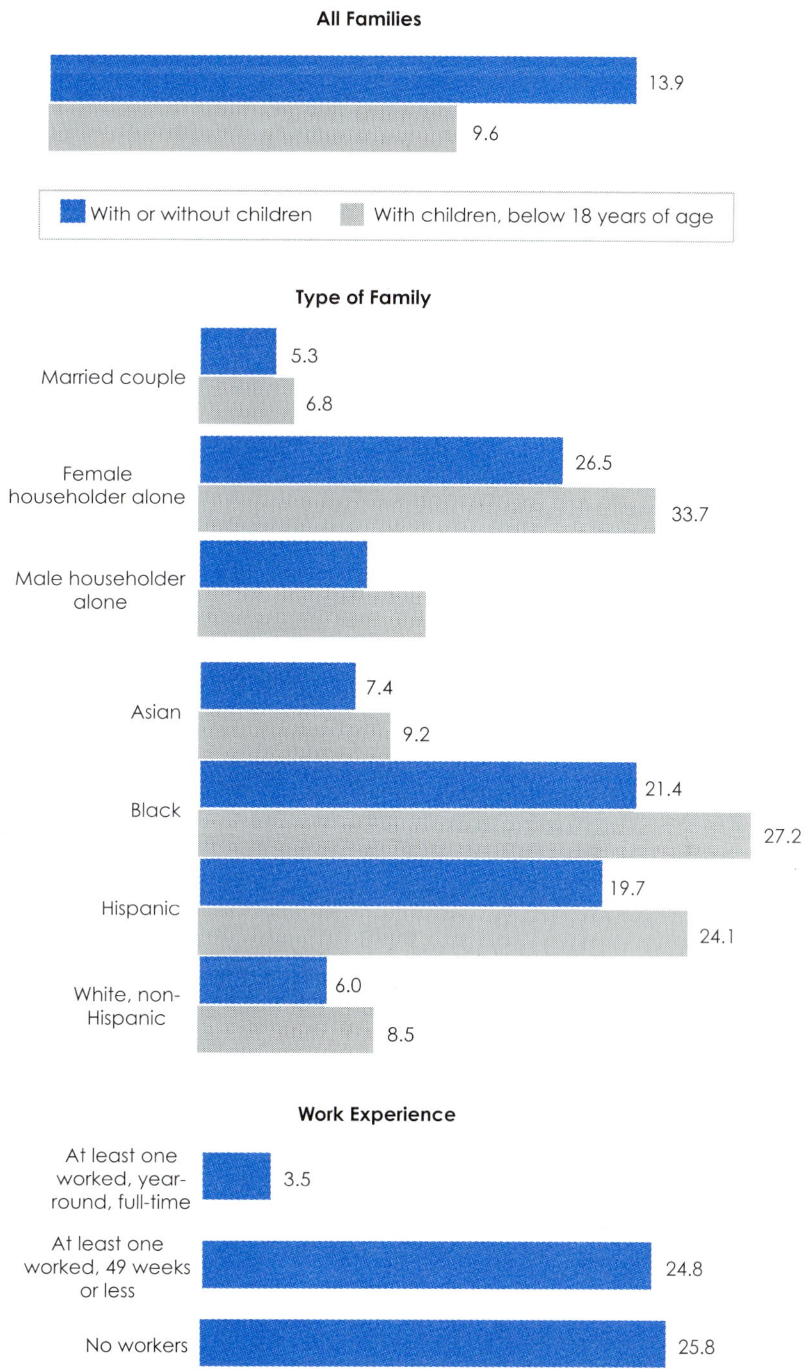

Poverty rates of families vary widely depending on characteristics of the family head and type of family. This figure shows that the greater the work experience of the family head, the less the chance that the family will be poor. It also shows that families headed by women with no spouse present are more likely to be poor than other types of families. Families with children are more likely to be impoverished, regardless of the characteristics of the head of household or type of family. The figure also reveals higher poverty rates among Hispanics and African Americans.

Source: Bureau of the Census, *Historical Poverty Tables,* Table 4 (published October 2003).

experience the lowest poverty rates, while those headed by women with no spouse present experience the highest rates. The poverty rate for unrelated individuals (those living alone or with nonrelatives) is also substantially above the average for families.

On the face of it, one might conclude that antipoverty policy should encourage the formation and maintenance of married-couple families and discourage childbearing outside of marriage. However, those are not only difficult but perhaps inappropriate objectives of government policy. Moreover, there is no simple, causal link between marriage and economic self-sufficiency. Instead, there are a number of factors that are jointly damaging to economic self-sufficiency and family stability. These include alcohol and drug abuse, low educational achievement, and unemployment. Programs that successfully addressed these problems would, presumably, both lower poverty rates and encourage family stability.

Although anything that can be done to encourage family stability is probably for the good, the strong association between family status and poverty suggests a need for programs that aim to overcome constraints that particularly limit the opportunities of families headed by women. For example:

- Under present circumstances, divorce tends to be much more economically damaging to mothers with dependent children than to the fathers of those children. In response to this fact, many states have, with some success, redoubled efforts to enforce payment of child support by absent fathers.
- Many poor families are headed by women who have never married and who first became mothers as teenagers. Many such mothers have not completed high school and have virtually no work experience. Programs designed to meet the needs of such families by providing prenatal and neonatal medical care, educational opportunities, child care, and other services have expanded in recent years but are still far from meeting all needs.
- Although it may not be the responsibility of government to actively encourage marriage, many observers think that public policy should at least be neutral with respect to family status. For example, the old AFDC program was often perceived as rewarding family breakup, because a woman with dependent children may be eligible for benefits that are not available to a family with a husband present.[12] The expansion of the welfare benefits to cover households with unemployed fathers represents an attempt to deal with this problem, but only half of all states currently offer this variant of the program.

Employment

Figure 19.5 suggests that work is one of the most effective avenues to economic self-sufficiency. The poverty rate for families with a full-time worker was only 3.5 percent. For this reason, programs focusing on improving labor market opportunities for the poor have long been seen as an important element of antipoverty policy.

ANTIDISCRIMINATION PROGRAMS Antidiscrimination programs are one example. Previously we showed how discrimination can lower the incomes of people in a disfavored group. In the absence of prohibiting it, discrimination is likely to lead to a situation in which workers from different racial or ethnic groups receive different pay for the same work. Today equal-pay laws prohibit this practice.

However, equal-pay laws by themselves do not benefit all members of a disfavored group if employers' discriminatory attitudes are not changed. Instead, they tend to replace low wages with limited job opportunities. In fact, equal-pay laws by themselves can even increase the degree to which minority workers are crowded into low-paying, "dead end" jobs. To combat this danger, the equal-pay laws are often supplemented by affirmative-action programs intended to ensure that minority-group members are given equal treatment in filling job openings as well as in pay.

PUBLIC EMPLOYMENT Another traditional job market strategy for aiding the poor is to have the government itself become an employer of last resort. The U.S. government has experimented with various types of public-employment programs for more than fifty years.

However, public-employment programs have some drawbacks. One of the most frequent problems is that the jobs the government can create most easily are those that require little capital investment, such as park maintenance. Such jobs do not provide the skills and training needed to qualify people for jobs in the mainstream of the private economy. To get around this problem, some economists favor subsidies to private employers that create jobs for the poor in place of employment in the public sector itself.

THE MINIMUM WAGE Minimum-wage laws are another approach that is often seen as a poverty-fighting measure. Some jobs pay such low wages that even a full-time job held by the head of a household does not bring in enough income to raise the household above the poverty level.

A seemingly simple way to raise the working poor to a more comfortable standard of living would be to legislate a higher minimum wage. The first federal minimum-wage law was passed in 1938 and required employers to pay $.25 per hour. Since then the federal minimum wage has been raised several times. As of 2004, the minimum wage was $5.15 per hour, with several states and a few cities mandating a wage above that rate. For instance, Washington has a state minimum wage of $7.16. As of January 2004, the city of San Francisco required an $8.50 per hour wage.

Many economists doubt the effectiveness of the minimum wage as an antipoverty program, however. Although raising the minimum wage does make some low-skilled workers better off, it reduces the quantity of such workers demanded. Each increase in the minimum wage therefore means that some people lose their jobs—restaurants remain open fewer hours, automated gates replace parking lot attendants, and so on. Moreover, over half of all workers at the minimum-wage level come from households in the top half of the national income distribution.[13] These workers include students working part time and living with their families, low-paid spouses in households in which both husband and wife work, and so on. At the same time, low-income households get less than 14 percent of their total income from low-wage jobs. Most low-income households depend more on income from pensions, disability payments, welfare, and other nonwage sources.

New Directions in Antipoverty Policy

Antipoverty policy always sparks intense debate. Conservatives deplore programs that allegedly create a permanent, welfare-dependent underclass. Liberals blame the stubbornly high official poverty rate on everything from me-first greed on the part of the "baby boom" generation to cuts in welfare benefits by the Republican presidential administrations. Sometimes the debates generate more heat than light. But out of the debates have emerged certain elements on which liberals and conservatives often agree. These elements combine a "safety net" of conventional transfer programs with new initiatives that focus on education, opportunity, personal responsibility, and self-sufficiency.

One common element in this new generation of antipoverty programs characterized by the Personal Responsibility and Work Opportunity Reconciliation Act of 1996, also known as the welfare reform bill, is a recognition that many welfare recipients lack literacy and basic money-handling skills. Building those skills is a time-consuming process. Past programs often failed because they focused on short-term training programs lasting only a few weeks or a few months. To be effective, programs must be based on the recognition that if welfare clients had high motivation and high self-esteem, they would not be poor to begin with.

A second element of the new approaches is an attempt to overcome the disincentives built into the present welfare system, through the "welfare to work" idea and benefit time limits imposed on TANF recipients. As *Applying Economic Ideas 19.2* illustrated, even a job that pays well above the minimum wage may not be an attractive alternative to welfare in short-run monetary terms. The negative income tax concept attempts to overcome disincentives by manipulating benefit reduction rates, but many of the new programs do not take this approach. Instead, they attempt to ease the transition into the labor market through continued assistance in the areas of medical care, child care, transportation, and housing, as well as conventional education and job training. This has been a criticism of TANF—many single-parent households are forced to leave their children unattended after school.

Third, many new programs that aim to encourage self-sufficiency view the relationship between the beneficiary and society as a contract in which each side takes on certain obligations. In return for aid, the recipient is implicitly, and often explicitly, expected to make the necessary effort to achieve personal and financial independence. Depending on circumstances, the effort may consist of completing a high-school equivalency program, entering job training, or actually taking a job.

In these regards, the new approaches move far beyond the older notion of "workfare" as primarily a means of eliminating from the welfare rolls "cheats" who are capable of working but prefer not to. Such programs not only were grounded in questionable notions regarding the "deserving" and "undeserving" poor, but also emphasized the notion that the poor are disinclined to work in contrast to the idea that constraints on opportunities shape the labor market choices of the poor. "Workfare" programs that have been introduced as a quick way to cut welfare budgets have produced disappointing results. The current tendency is to view job and education programs as investments. In the short run, the funds spent on training, subsidized child care, and casework may mean that there are no immediate budgetary savings. But every time a former welfare client can be brought to the point at which he or she can see new opportunities or say, "I'm a different person," the investment pays off.

SUMMARY

1. **What is poverty and how can it be measured?** The U.S. government measures poverty in relation to an income equal to three times the cost of an economy food plan. The official measure is based on *census income,* that is, earned income plus cash transfer payments. There are other ways to measure poverty as well. One approach measures *pretransfer poverty,* taking into account only income from private sources. Another approach adjusts the official measure of poverty to take into account the value of in-kind transfers. However it is measured, poverty in the United States decreased during the 1960s and 1970s. Since 1980, the poverty rate has risen during recessions and fallen during expansions, with somewhat of a lag in timing.

2. **How does social insurance differ from public assistance?** The term *social insurance* refers to transfer programs to which everyone is entitled regardless of income. Social security is the largest such program; veterans' benefits and Medicare are other examples. *Public-assistance* programs are those to which people are entitled only if they meet a specific low-income standard. Temporary Assistance for Needy Families (TANF) is one of the largest public-assistance programs that pays benefits in cash; Medicaid, food stamps, and housing assistance are programs that provide benefits in kind.

3. **Why are poor households often subject to higher net tax rates at the margin than nonpoor households?** The *benefit reduction rate* of a transfer program is the amount of benefits lost per $1 increase in earned income. A household's net *marginal tax rate* is the sum of its marginal tax rate for taxes paid plus the benefit reduction rates of all transfer programs to which it is entitled. In

the United States net marginal tax rates are higher for low-income households than for high-income ones, and higher for the elderly than for the young. Many economists believe that high net marginal tax rates provide a major incentive not to work. A *negative income tax* would convert all transfer programs into cash and subject them to a uniform net marginal tax rate that is lower than the rate currently imposed on poor families.

4. **How can poverty be attacked through programs that encourage self-sufficiency?** Poverty can be viewed as the outcome both of circumstances beyond people's control and of the choices people make in response to those circumstances. Many antipoverty programs aim to encourage self-sufficiency by removing constraints on opportunities. Examples include programs designed to improve educational opportunities, provide greater opportunities to individuals regardless of family structure, and improve job opportunities.

KEY TERMS

Lorenz curve	Public assistance
Census income	Benefit reduction rate
Pretransfer poverty	Net marginal tax rate
In-kind transfers	Negative income tax
Social insurance	

PROBLEMS AND TOPICS FOR DISCUSSION

1. **Examining the lead-off case.** Of the self-help projects mentioned in this case, which ones focus on changing constraints on opportunities and which ones focus on values and preferences? (Some may do both.) In your opinion, are such programs better viewed as complements or substitutes for government antipoverty efforts? What, if anything, could government do to encourage the spread of self-help programs?

2. **Cash versus in-kind transfers.** What are the relative merits of cash and in-kind transfers? Review Chapter 5, paying particular attention to the concepts of marginal utility and consumer equilibrium. Suppose that program A gives a family a \$1,000 cash benefit and program B gives it \$1,000 worth of goods in kind, but in proportions that are not chosen by the family itself. Which program would be likely to give the family greater utility? *Bonus question:* If you read the appendix to Chapter 5, illustrate these two programs for the case of an economy in which there are just two consumer goods: food and clothing.

3. **Social insurance versus public assistance.** Suppose that an effective negative income tax was in force and poverty, as defined by the Bureau of the Census, had been eliminated. Would you then be willing to see social-insurance programs such as social security, Medicare, and unemployment compensation abolished? Why or why not?

4. **Transfer payments and the nonpoor.** Discussions of "waste" in poverty programs often focus on the fact that some benefits go to families whose incomes are above the poverty line. After reading this chapter, do you agree that it is wasteful to pay benefits to some nonpoor families? Would you favor a program that cut off all benefits when the poverty line was reached? In what ways might such a program itself be wasteful? Discuss.

5. **Fight Poverty—Get a Job.** A popular bumper sticker reads "Fight Poverty—Get a Job!" This slogan is presumably intended to do more than call attention to the fact that those who work are less likely to be poor. Rather, its purpose seems to be to evoke a set of normative judgments related to "deserving" versus "undeserving" poor, will-

ingness to work versus opportunity as reasons for not working, and so on. What is your position on these issues? Discuss.

CASE FOR DISCUSSION

Two Steps Forward, One Step Back

The Sacramento City Council adopted a "living wage" ordinance that took effect on January 1, 2004. "This is a great day," said Chris Jones, chairman of the Sacramento chapter of the Association of Community Organizations for Reform Now. Jones added, however, that it is "just the beginning" of city efforts to improve pay for the region's low-wage workers.

The ordinance will increase wages to $9.00 an hour for private employees on city contracts, if the company provides health benefits. If the company does not provide benefits, the hourly wage will be $10.50 an hour. The living wage rises to $9.50 in 2005 and to $10 in 2006, with an additional $1.50 for companies that don't provide health coverage.

All that glitters is not gold, though. According to a city-funded report, when low-wage workers earn higher income, they no longer qualify for the same federal and state public assistance and social insurance benefits. For instance, a single parent with two children would receive $2,533.20 in annual food stamps if he/she earned minimum wage. With a living wage of $8.50/hr., that benefit falls to $1,273.20. Living-wage workers also receive less from the federal Earned Income Tax Credit, the state disability insurance fund, and pay more in federal and state taxes.

Even with reduced federal and state-funded aid, the living wage does improve disposable income for prior minimum-wage workers. For households with two children, disposable annual income including transfer payments would rise by $1,553.65 with a $8.50/hr. living wage, and by roughly $2,700 with a $10.00/hr. living wage.

Who pays the bill? The cost of the living wage will be shared by city government, taxpayers, and employers. With higher wages, employers will not only pay more to their workers, but to social security taxes as well. Also, if the $9.00 living wage chases away potential contractors for the City of Sacramento, the remaining vendors may be able to bargain for more costly contracts to offset higher labor cost.

Source: Suzanne O'Keefe and Stephen Perez, "A Living Wage for Sacramento," CSUS Regional Development Initiative, September 2002; Andy Furillo, "City Living-Wage Plan Gets Final Approval," *Sacramento Bee*, December 10, 2003.

QUESTIONS

1. What do you think is the motivation for the additional $1.50 per hour to be paid to workers who do not receive health benefits? Is there a social insurance program this worker might have turned to before?
2. How does the living wage help to reduce poverty? Suppose a household with two children earns an additional $2,000 per year in annual gross income as a result of Sacramento's living wage. Will this household take home $2,000 in disposable income? Why or why not?
3. How does the living wage change the nature of public assistance in Sacramento? Who bears the cost of helping the poor now that the city has imposed the living wage? Who bore this cost before?

END NOTES

1. U.S. Bureau of the Census, Table IE-1: Selected Measures of Household Income Dispersion: 1967 to 2001.
2. Thomas Dye and Harmon Ziegler, "Socialism and Equality in Cross-National Perspective," *Political Science and Politics* (Winter 1988).
3. Sheldon Danziger and Robert D. Plotnick, "Poverty and Policy: Lessons of the Last Two Decades," March 1985, unpublished.

4. The impact of social security on racial minorities is detailed in National Center for Policy Analysis, "Social Security and Race," Policy Report No. 528, June 1987.
5. The future financing problems of social security are discussed in National Center for Policy Analysis, "Social Security: Who Gains, Who Loses?" Policy Report No. 127, May 1987.
6. ABC/Washington Post Poll, January 11–16, 1985, reprinted in *Public Opinion* (April–May 1985): 22.
7. See, for example, Lowell Gallaway and Richard Vedder, "Paying People to Be Poor," National Center for Policy Analysis, Policy Report No. 121, February 1986.
8. John C. Goodman and A. James Meigs, "The Elderly: People the Supply Side Revolution Forgot," National Center for Policy Analysis, Policy Report No. 135, February 1989.
9. Milton Friedman, *Capitalism and Freedom* (Chicago: University of Chicago, 1962), Chapter 12.
10. The empirical evidence is discussed briefly in Gary Burtless, "The Economist's Lament: Public Assistance in America," *Journal of Economic Perspectives* (Winter 1990): 57–78. The article also gives references to more detailed discussions of the issue.
11. William Raspberry, "Teach for the Future," *The Washington Post*, February 28, 1989, A23.
12. The empirical evidence regarding the effect of welfare programs on family composition is not entirely conclusive, but it is probably safe to say that popular perceptions of the problem are exaggerated. Burtless cites several studies that show negligible or small effects of welfare on family breakup. Gallaway and Vedder estimate that each $1 billion in added welfare spending adds 5,000 to the number of households headed by women. Even this estimate, which lies at the high end of the range, is not terribly large. Given total public-assistance spending of about $130 billion in 1986, it implies that perhaps 650,000 out of a total of 10 million poor households headed by women were formed in response to incentives provided by the welfare program.
13. William R. Johnson and Edgar K. Browning, "The Distributional and Efficiency Effects of Increasing the Minimum Wage: A Simulation," *American Economic Review* (March 1983): 204–211.

CHAPTER 20

International Trade and Trade Policy

After reading this chapter, you will understand:

1. How the principle of comparative advantage can be applied to international trade
2. How the notion of competitiveness is related to that of comparative advantage
3. The general trend of international trade policy during the post–World War II period
4. How international trade affects income distribution within each country
5. How protectionist policies can be understood in terms of public choice theory and rent seeking

Before reading this chapter, make sure you know the meaning of:

1. Comparative advantage
2. Political rent seeking
3. Human capital
4. Public choice theory

NAFTA

In 1994, Mexico, Canada, and the United States entered into the North American Free Trade Agreement (NAFTA). Ten years later, in the 2004 presidential election, NAFTA remained a hot-button issue.

NAFTA has brought some obvious positive results. Between 1993 and 2003, trade within NAFTA countries doubled. Mexico replaced Japan as America's second largest trading partner behind Canada. Early winners included U.S. export powerhouses like Caterpillar, Inc. The construction equipment giant saw its exports to Mexico triple in the five years before NAFTA was initiated, and captured the lion's share of future growth in this market. A key reason: NAFTA resulted in elimination of Mexico's 20 percent import tariff on U.S. construction equipment, while leaving the tariff in place on equipment made by Japanese rivals.

For U.S. firms, the opening of the Mexican market meant building new plants south of the border. Hoover Company, for example, started building hand-held vacuum cleaners in Ciudad Juarez, just across the border from El Paso, Texas. Hoover previously manufactured these machines in Asia, but believed it would be more economical to move the work to Mexico.

The free trade agreement is not limited to manufacturing. It will create significant opportunities for U.S. service industries, as well. Southwestern Bell Corporation helped to rebuild Mexico's creaky telephone system. Bank of America, which already has branches in every U.S. state along the Mexican border, expanded into Mexico itself as barriers to international banking were relaxed.

Not all results of NAFTA have been as positive as had been hoped by those who conceived and negotiated the pact in the 1990s. In particular, effects on Mexican labor markets have been mixed. More than half a million new manufacturing jobs have been created, but NAFTA has opened Mexico's farm sector to competition from efficient and often subsidized U.S. producers. The result: more farm jobs have been lost than were gained in the factory sector. Also, although there have been huge gains in productivity growth due to foreign investment in Mexico, this has not fed through to the labor force in the form of higher real wages.

"NAFTA has had positive effects in Mexico but they could have been better," said David de Ferranti, World Bank Vice President for Latin America and the Caribbean, summarizing his organization's report on the first ten years of NAFTA. "Free trade definitely brings new economic opportunities, but the lessons from NAFTA for other countries negotiating with the U.S. are that free trade alone is not enough without significant policy and institutional reforms."

Source: Daniel Lederman, Louis Maloney, and Louis Serven, *Lessons from NAFTA*, World Bank, 2003; John J. Audley and Demetrios Papademetriou, Sandra Polaski, and Scott Vaugh, *NAFTA's Promise and Reality*, Carnegie Endowment for World Peace, 2003.

As shown by the publicity received by the tenth anniversary of NAFTA, U.S. competitiveness, U.S. firms are at the center of the action in world trade. The United States now accounts for a larger share of exports than any other economy, having overtaken even Germany in the 1980s. Since 1980, the real volume of U.S. exports more than quadrupled while the economy as a whole doubled in size. Moreover, the activities of many U.S. companies do not show up in conventional trade statistics. For example, in 2002 import-export data showed that the United States imported $121.4 billion worth of goods made in Japan while exporting only $49.7 billion worth of U.S.-made goods to Japan.

THE THEORY OF COMPARATIVE ADVANTAGE: REVIEW AND EXTENSIONS

The theory of international trade begins with the concept of *comparative advantage*, which we introduced in the beginning of this text. Although it can be applied to the division of labor within the economy of a single country, the concept was originally developed by David Ricardo as an explanation of trade between countries. We will begin our discussion of international trade by reviewing this theory, first using a numerical example and then applying a graphical approach.

Numerical Approach

For illustrative purposes, imagine a world with just two countries—Norway and Spain. Both have farms and offshore fishing grounds, but Spain's moderate climate makes both the farms and the fishing grounds there more productive. A ton of fish can be produced in Spain with 4 hours of labor and a ton of grain with 2 hours of labor. In Norway, 5 labor hours are required to produce a ton of fish and 5 labor hours to produce a ton of grain. We will consider only labor costs in this example; other costs can be assumed to be proportional to labor costs. Also, we will assume constant per-unit labor costs for all output levels.

Because it takes fewer labor hours to produce both fish and grain in Spain, Spain can be said to have an **absolute advantage** in the production of both goods. However, absolute cost differences do not matter for international trade; it is the difference in opportunity costs between the two countries that matters. In Norway, producing a ton of fish means forgoing the opportunity to use 5 labor hours in the fields. A ton of fish thus has an opportunity cost of 1 ton of grain there. In Spain, producing a ton of fish means giving up the opportunity to produce 2 tons of grain. In terms of opportunity costs, then, fish is cheaper in Norway than in Spain and grain is cheaper in Spain than in Norway. The country in which the opportunity cost of a good is lower is said to have a *comparative advantage* in producing that good.

Absolute advantage
The ability of a country to produce a good at a lower cost, in terms of quantity of factor inputs, than the cost at which the good can be produced by its trading partners.

Considering only labor costs, mutually beneficial trade between Spain and Norway might not seem possible. Norwegians might like to get their hands on some of those cheap Spanish goods, but why would the Spanish be interested? After all, couldn't they produce everything at home more cheaply than it could be produced abroad? If that is the case, how could they gain from trade? A closer analysis shows that this view is incorrect and that absolute advantage is unimportant in determining patterns of trade; only comparative advantage matters.

To see the possibilities for trade between the two countries, imagine that a Norwegian fishing boat decides to sail into a Spanish port with a ton of fish. Before the Norwegians' arrival, Spanish merchants in the port will be used to exchanging 2 tons of locally produced grain for a ton of fish, while the Norwegians will be accustomed to getting only 1 ton of Norwegian grain for each ton of Norwegian fish. Thus, any exchange ratio between 1 and 2 tons of grain per ton of fish will seem attractive to both parties. For instance, a trade of 1.5 tons of grain for a ton of fish will make both the Spanish merchants and the Norwegian fishers better off than they would be if they traded only with others from their own country.

The profits made by the first boatload of traders are only the beginning of the story. The more significant benefits come as each country begins to specialize in producing the good in which it has a comparative advantage. In Norway, farmers will discover that instead of working 5 hours to raise a ton of grain from their own rocky soil, they can fish for 5 hours and trade their catch to the Spaniards for 1.5 tons of grain. In Spain, people will find that it is no longer worth their while to spend 4 hours catching a ton of fish. Instead, they can work just 3 hours in the fields, and the 1.5 tons of grain that they grow will get them a ton of fish from the Norwegians. In short, the Norwegians will find it worthwhile to specialize in fish, and the Spaniards will find it advantageous to specialize in grain.

Now suppose that trade continues at the rate of 1.5 tons of grain per ton of fish until both countries have become completely specialized. Spain no longer produces any fish, and Norway no longer produces any grain. Norwegians catch 200 tons of fish, half of which are exported to Spain. The Spanish grow 500 tons of grain, 150 tons of which are exported to Norway. Table 20.1 compares this situation with a nonspecialized, pretrade situation in which each country produces some of both products. The comparison reveals three things. First, the Norwegians are better off than before; they have just as much fish to eat and 50 tons more grain than in the pretrade equilibrium. Second, the Spaniards are also better off; they have just as much grain to consume as ever-and more fish. Finally, total world output of both grain and fish has risen as a result of trade. Everyone is better off, and no one is worse off.

Graphical Presentation

Comparative advantage can be illustrated graphically using a set of production possibility frontiers based on the example just given. This is done in Figure 20.1, which shows three production possibility frontiers.

TABLE 20.1 EFFECTS OF TRADE ON PRODUCTION AND CONSUMPTION

	Spain	Norway	World Total
Before Trade			
Fish			
Production	75	100	175
Consumption	75	100	175
Grain			
Production	350	100	450
Consumption	350	100	450
After Trade			
Fish			
Production	0	200	200
Consumption	100	100	200
Grain			
Production	500	0	500
Consumption	350	150	500

All figures represent tons produced or consumed

This table shows production and consumption of fish and grain in Spain, Norway, and the world as a whole before and after trade. It is assumed that each country specializes in the product in which it has a comparative advantage and that fish are traded for grain at the rate of 1.5 tons of grain per ton of fish.

Part (a) is the production possibility frontier for Spain. Given 1,000 available labor hours and a cost of 2 labor hours per ton of grain, Spain can produce up to 500 tons of grain per year if it produces no fish (point B). If it produces no grain, up to 250 tons of fish per year can be caught at a cost of 4 hours per ton of fish (point D). The combinations of grain and fish that Spain can produce are represented by the line running from B to D.

Part (b) shows the production possibility frontier for Norway. In Norway, fish and grain both take 5 labor hours per ton to produce. If Norwegians devote all their time to fishing, they can catch up to 200 tons of fish per year (point B^1). If they devote all their time to farming, they can grow up to 200 tons of grain (point D^1). The line between B^1 and D^1 represents Norway's production possibility frontier.

According to the example summarized in Figure 20.1, before trade begins, Spain produces and consumes 350 tons of grain and 75 tons of fish. This is shown as point A on Spain's production possibility frontier. Norway is assumed to produce and consume 100 tons each of fish and grain. This is shown by point A^1 on Norway's frontier.

FIGURE 20.1 A GRAPHIC ILLUSTRATION OF COMPARATIVE ADVANTAGE

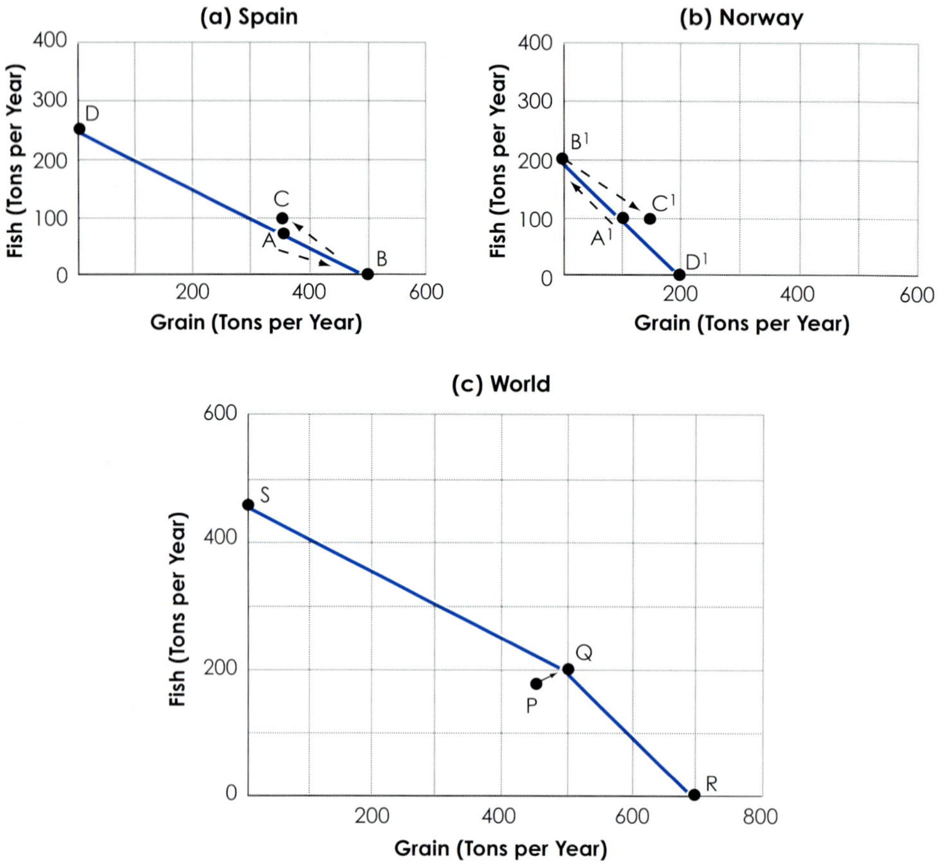

This figure shows production possibility frontiers for Spain, Norway, and the two countries combined. Before trade, Spain produces and consumes at point A and Norway at point A. Together these correspond to world consumption point P, which is inside the world production possibility frontier. After trade begins, Spain specializes in producing grain (point B) and trades part of the grain for fish, moving to consumption point C. Norway specializes in producing fish (point B^1) and reaches consumption point C^1 through trade. As a result, world efficiency is improved and point Q on the world production possibility frontier is reached.

The World Production Possibility Frontier

A production possibility frontier for the world as a whole (consisting of just these two countries in our example) can be constructed as shown in part (c) of Figure 20.1. First, assume that both countries devote all their labor to grain. That results in 500 tons of grain from Spain plus 200 from Norway, or 700 tons of grain in all (point R in part (c) of Figure 20.1). Starting from there, assume that the world output of fish is to be increased. For the sake of efficiency, Norwegian farmers should be the first to switch to fishing, because the opportunity cost of fish is lower in Norway (1 ton of grain per ton of fish) than in Spain (2 tons of grain per ton of fish). As Norwegians switch to fishing, then, world production moves upward and to the left along the line segment RQ.

When all Norwegians have abandoned farming for fishing, the world will have arrived at point Q—500 tons of grain (all Spanish) and 200 tons of fish (all Norwegian). From that point on, the only way to get more fish is to have Spanish farmers switch to fishing. At the opportunity cost of 2 tons of grain per ton of fish, this moves the economy along the line segment QS. When all Spanish farmers are fishing, the world arrives at point S, where 450 tons of fish and no grain are produced. The production possibility frontier for the world as a whole, then, is the kinked line RQS.

Effects of Trade

The pretrade production point for the world as a whole lies inside the world production possibility frontier. Adding together the quantities of fish and grain from A and A^1, we arrive at point P in part (c) of Figure 20.1—450 tons of grain and 175 tons of fish. This is inefficient; the world economy as a whole could produce more of both goods. To increase efficiency, both countries must specialize.

Suppose that Spain shifts its production from 350 tons of grain and 75 tons of fish (point A) to 500 tons of grain and no fish (point B). It then trades the extra 150 tons of grain for 100 tons of Norwegian fish. Spain's consumption thus ends up at point C, while its production remains at B. At the same time, Norway shifts its production from A^1 to B^1, that is, it specializes entirely in fish. The extra 100 tons of fish are traded for the 150 tons of Spanish grain, moving Norwegian consumption to point C^1.

As a result of specialization plus trade, then, both Spain and Norway have moved to points that lie outside their own production possibility frontiers. As they do so, the world as a whole moves from point P inside its production possibility frontier to point Q on the frontier. Thus, specialization improves the efficiency of the world economy as a whole, increases production of both goods, and leaves both countries better off than they would be if they did not trade.

Empirical Evidence on Comparative Advantage

Ricardo's theory of comparative advantage suggests that each country will export goods for which its labor is relatively productive compared with that of its trading partners. A number of economists have put this simple version of the theory to empirical tests.

One of the first to do so was G.D.A. MacDougal. In 1951 MacDougal published a study of U.S.-British trade, using data from 1937.[1] He compared a number of industries in terms of relative labor productivity in the two countries with the ratio of their exports of the products of those industries. The results strongly supported the Ricardian theory. Labor productivity was higher in the United States than in the United

Kingdom for all of the industries studied, indicating that the United States had a Ricardian absolute advantage in all of the products. As predicted by the theory, however, the United Kingdom was relatively successful in exporting the goods in which its labor productivity disadvantage was lowest. British exports were greater than U.S. exports for all the industries studied in which British labor was more than half as productive as U.S. labor (for example, woolen cloth, footwear, hosiery). U.S. exports exceeded British exports for all the industries in which U.S. labor was more than twice as productive as British labor. Later studies using different sets of data have tended to confirm this result.

Comparative Advantage with Multiple Factors of Production

The Ricardian model of comparative advantage focused on a single factor of production: labor. Studies such as MacDougal's indicate that the single-factor version of the theory has considerable explanatory power. However, it can also be extended to take multiple factors of production into account.

THE HECKSCHER-OHLIN THEOREM Early in the twentieth century two Swedish economists, Eli Heckscher and Bertil Ohlin, developed a model that took into account two factors of production: capital and labor. They reasoned that countries with abundant supplies of labor and little capital would have a comparative advantage in labor-intensive goods, whereas countries with abundant capital and relatively less labor would have a comparative advantage in capital-intensive goods. The proposition that countries would tend to export products that use their relatively more abundant factor more intensively has come to be known as the **Heckscher-Ohlin theorem**. An illustration of this theorem is the pattern in which the United States exports capital-intensive aircraft and computers to China in exchange for labor-intensive clothing and handicrafts.

Heckscher-Ohlin theorem

The proposition that countries tend to export goods that make intensive use of the factors of production that the country possesses in relative abundance.

The Importance of Demand

Both single-factor and multiple-factor versions of the theory of comparative advantage focus on supply conditions as the explanation of trade patterns. They implicitly assume that the consumer tastes that underlie the demand for goods and services are identical in all countries. In practice, however, patterns of trade contain some features that can be explained only by taking demand into account.

One such feature is the tendency of countries to trade most heavily with others at a similar level of economic development. This is not predicted by the simple Ricardian theory, which suggests that trade would be most profitable between countries that differ from each other as much as possible. For example, simple comparative advantage would suggest that the United States would have more trade with Mexico, a very different economy, than with Canada, which not only has a much smaller population than Mexico, but also is more similar in many ways to the United States. However, Canada turns out to be the largest U.S. trading partner, and several distant countries, including Germany and Japan, rank close to nearby Mexico.

A closely related puzzle is the fact that countries both import and export the products of many industries. The United States is both a major importer and exporter of motor vehicles, textiles, computers, foodstuffs, and footwear, to name just a few examples.

Comparative advantage can explain these trade patterns only at the expense of trivializing the concept—by saying, for example, that Germany has a comparative advantage in producing BMWs and the United States has a comparative advantage in producing Fords. A better explanation is that such trade patterns reflect the influence of demand and tastes. Firms in developed countries sell where the demand for their products is greatest—in other developed countries. Cross-trade within product categories reflects patterns of tastes: Although U.S. automakers pattern their cars to fit the tastes of a majority of domestic consumers, some domestic buyers share European tastes for Saabs and BMWs. These demand-side influences are not taken into account by the Ricardian theory and its modern variants, which look only at production costs.

Comparative Advantage and "Competitiveness"

As noted at the beginning of the chapter, U.S. involvement in world trade has grown greatly in recent decades. However, as U.S. exports have set records, imports have grown even more rapidly. In the first decade of the twenty-first century, the *trade deficit*—the amount by which imports exceed exports—reached an all-time high. This became a major cause of national concern. News reporters, editorialists, and politicians feared that the United States was no longer "competitive" in the world economy. Competitiveness means different things to different people, but at the heart of it is a concern that foreign workers work harder and foreign business managers have become smarter than their U.S. counterparts. "Soon the Japanese, the Koreans, and the Europeans will be better at everything than we are," people have said. "Eventually we won't be able to export anything at all!"

Certainly trends in trade after the 1980s had some worrisome aspects because U.S. exports did not grow as quickly as the amount that the U.S. imports from abroad. However, the theory of comparative advantage casts doubt on the notion that a country can reach a point at which it imports everything and exports nothing. In fact, classical trade theory, as embodied in the Spain-Norway example presented earlier, maintains that a country always has a comparative advantage in producing something even when it has an absolute disadvantage (in terms of labor hours or other factor inputs) for all goods. In terms of comparative advantage, then, a country must always be "competitive" in producing something.

However, comparative advantage does not guarantee an exact match between the value of a country's exports and the value of its imports. The numerical examples given earlier, which suggest that this must be the case, omit two important details. First, they leave out international financial transactions, including purchases and sales of corporate stocks, government bonds, and other securities, as well as several kinds of international banking transactions. Second, they assume that trade takes the form of barter, whereas in practice most international trade uses money as a means of payment. Let us look briefly at the implications of each of these considerations for comparative advantage and competitiveness.

FINANCIAL TRANSACTIONS AND THE BALANCE OF TRADE International financial transactions are important because they allow a country to import more goods and services than it exports, or to export more than it imports, in a given year. To take a very simple case, suppose that U.S. consumers decide to buy $100 million worth of television sets from Korean firms. What will the Korean firms do with the $100 million they receive? They can use it to buy airliners built in the United States, in which case trade in goods between the United States and Korea will balance. However, they can instead use it to buy U.S. government bonds or make deposits in U.S. banks. In that case, no U.S. goods will be exported in the current year to balance the imports. The Korean owners of the bonds or bank deposits have a claim on future exports from the United States; they can cash in their financial assets and spend them any time they like. But meanwhile, despite the U.S. comparative advantage in producing airliners, the U.S. trade accounts will not be balanced.

Could we say, then, that the U.S. balance-of-trade deficit after the 1980s reflects a comparative advantage for the United States in the production of financial assets? That would certainly be one way to look at it. We could also say that Korean buyers simply prefer future U.S. airliners over current ones. Either way, we should be cautious about assuming that the imbalance in merchandise trade reflects a loss of "competitiveness" in the sense of lost comparative advantage.

EXCHANGE RATES AND COMPETITIVENESS To understand international trade fully, we must also take into account the fact that it is conducted in terms of money. However, there is no "world money"; each country has its own currency. Thus, before one can buy goods, services, or financial instruments from abroad, one must first visit the *foreign-exchange markets,* in which one currency can be traded for another. The windows at international airports where tourists can use dollars to buy French euros or British pounds are a tiny part of these markets. Larger exchanges of currency are carried out through major banks in New York, London, Tokyo, and other world financial centers.

The rates at which two currencies are exchanged are determined by the forces of supply and demand. These vary greatly from day to day and from year to year. For example, in early 2000 a U.S. dollar was worth 1.10 euros; one year later it was worth only

0.80 euros. As exchange rates vary, so do the prices of countries' imports and exports. At 1.10 euros to a dollar, an American firm need spend only $50 to import a 55-euro bottle of French wine. At 0.80 euros to the dollar, it takes $62.50 to buy the same 55-euro bottle. Similarly, at 1.10 euros to the dollar, a French buyer would have to lay out 2,200 euros to buy a $2,000 IBM computer made in the United States. At 0.80 euros to the dollar, the price to the French buyer would be much less—only 1,600 euros.

We see, then, that the ability of U.S. exporters to compete in world markets—and the ability of U.S. firms to compete against imports in their home markets—depends not only on Ricardian considerations of factor productivity but also on exchange rates. In fact, the troubles U.S. exporters faced in the first half of the 1980s and the growing appetite of U.S. consumers for imported goods in that period were caused mainly by a steady rise in the dollar's exchange value from 1980 to early 1985. It is not necessary to cite declining management skills, technological leadership, or marketing ability to explain the loss of "competitiveness" of U.S. industry during this period. Indeed, the success of U.S. multinational companies with operations outside the United States—ranging from Kentucky Fried Chicken to Caterpillar Tractor—suggests that there has been no such decline.[2]

In contrast, during 2003, the U.S. dollar's exchange value fell dramatically, benefiting U.S. exporters. Not all U.S. firms benefit though. Those relying on parts and services imported from abroad saw an increase in cost, because these U.S. companies need to pay more for items shipped from abroad.

Similarly, changes in "competitiveness" caused by exchange rate fluctuations do not reflect a loss of comparative advantage. Exchange rates do affect a country's balance of trade and have a strong impact on the flow of international financial transactions. But whether exchange rates are high or low, whether there is a trade deficit or a trade surplus, the goods that a country exports still are those that it can produce at a comparatively low opportunity cost, and those that it imports are the ones that can be produced at a relatively low opportunity cost abroad.

TRADE POLICY AND PROTECTIONISM

Up to this point we have not mentioned governmental policy regarding international trade. We have pictured a world in which Norwegian fishers and Spanish farmers are free to trade as dictated by comparative advantage. In practice, however, governments are deeply involved in the regulation and promotion of trade. In this section we examine government's role in international trade.

Moves Toward Freer Trade Since World War II

The post–World War II period saw a broad movement toward freer trade aided by several new international organizations. The International Monetary Fund was created in

Protectionism

Any policy that is intended to shield domestic industries from import competition.

Tariff

A tax on imported goods.

Import quotas

A limit on the quantity of a good that can be imported over a given period.

1944 to maintain a stable financial climate for trade. The General Agreement on Tariffs and Trade (GATT) was founded in an attempt to prevent a return of **protectionism**—policies designed to shield domestic industries from competition by imports—which was common in the 1930s. In 1995, GATT was replaced by the World Trade Organization (WTO), which is now the world's principal authority overseeing international trade.

WTO rules permit taxes on imports, known as **tariffs**, but restrict their use. Under the so-called most-favored-nation principle, WTO member nations are supposed to charge the same tariff rates for imports from all WTO countries. A series of multinational negotiations sponsored by WTO succeeded in lowering the average level of tariffs from 40 percent at the end of World War II to less than 10 percent today. Throughout this period, the volume of world trade grew consistently faster than the volume of world output. Also, WTO has tried, with far from complete success, to discourage the use of **import quotas**—restrictions on the quantity of a good that can be imported during a given period.

REGIONAL TRADING BLOCS In addition to the activities of WTO, there have been efforts to set up regional trading blocs in several parts of the world. The best known of these is the European Union (EU). A key aim of the EU has been to eliminate all barriers to trade among the major European countries, eventually leading to a situation in which trade among these countries is nearly as free as trade among the states of the United States.

Not all goals of the EU have been achieved in full. Differences in levels of economic development among the countries of the EC, which are greater than those among the states of the United States, have been a recurring source of problems. Also, the goal of a single currency for Europe has proved more difficult to achieve than many had hoped. Nonetheless, after its expansion to 25 countries in 2004, the EU, with a population of 450 million, can fairly be considered the world's largest unified economic zone in most respects.

On the other side of the Atlantic, progress was under way toward the formation of an even larger trading bloc. Its foundations were laid when the United States reached an agreement with Canada, its largest trading partner, to eliminate almost all trade barriers over a ten-year period beginning in 1989. (The U.S.-Canada treaty does allow for con-tinued use of quotas on some farm, forest, and fishery products, and in some other re-spects falls short of the free-trade ideal.) This was soon followed by the North Ameri-can Free Trade Agreement (NAFTA), discussed in the opening case of this chapter.

Still another regional trading bloc, formed in late 1992, unites six countries of the Association of Southeast Asian Nations in the ASEAN Free Trade Area (AFTA). The member countries—Thailand, Philippines, Malaysia, Brunei, Singapore, and Indone-sia—have a total population of 320 million people.

There is a downside to regional free trade blocs, however. That is the tendency of such blocs to raise protectionist barriers against outsiders. Thus, NAFTA contains provisions protecting North American (mainly U.S.) firms against competition from Asian and European rivals. The EU is notorious for shielding its farmers from outside competition. Serious worries remain about the possibility of open trade war between the blocs. The AFTA, on the other hand, is composed of relatively poor nations that cannot afford to cut themselves off from world trade. Their bloc is based on the principle of "open regionalism" that will lower barriers within the group without raising them against outsiders.

Countertrends: The New Protectionism

Spurred by the strengthening of free-trade institutions, the volume of world trade has increased greatly in the past four decades. However, protectionism is far from dead. In addition to the continued use of traditional tariffs, a "new protectionism" has sprung up, resulting in the imposition of additional restrictions on international trade. The new protectionism consists in part of devices such as "orderly marketing agreements" and "voluntary export restraints." These involve the use of political pressure—usually backed by the threat of a tariff or quota—to restrain trade in a particular good.

A leading example of the new protectionism is the so-called Multifiber Agreement (MFA). This agreement, which began as a temporary restriction on imports of Japanese cotton textiles into the United States, has grown into a vast web of quotas that all major trading countries use to manage trade in all types of textiles and apparel. The agreement is a major violation of WTO principles, not only in its emphasis on quotas, but also in its open discrimination among exporting nations. By imposing much more stringent limits on imports from developing countries than from industrialized exporters in the EC and elsewhere, the MFA undermines not only the principles of WTO, but also the stated U.S. policy of promoting economic development in low-income countries.[3] Several developing countries have complained about unfair treatment because of the MFA restrictions, which cost them as much as 20 million jobs each year.[4] The new protectionism not only applies to preventing the import of foreign goods, but to preventing the export of jobs. Many companies in the United States and other countries have shifted their operations away from the high-wage environment at home to one with cheaper labor to lower their costs of production. This practice of shifting jobs from one country to another is known as outsourcing. As discussed in *Economics in the News 20.1*, countries such as China and India are the most common locales for outsourcing everything from customer service centers to city government administrative services. In 2004, the backlash against the foreign outsourcing of U.S. jobs grew in state legislatures around the country. Bills aimed at curbing the outflow of jobs were introduced in several states.

Most required that state contracts go only to companies that certify the work will be done inside the United States.

Although these new protectionist agreements are referred to as voluntary, their effects on consumers scarcely differ from those of a compulsory tariff or quota. Prices go up and reductions in efficiency occur as production moves against the direction of comparative advantage. For example, the cost of the Multifiber Agreement to U.S. consumers was estimated at more than $20 billion per year, or about $238 per U.S. household as of 1986.

Antidumping rules are another aspect of the new protectionism. A country is said to be "dumping" its goods when it sells them in a foreign market for less than the price at which it sells them at home or for less than the cost of producing them. Under certain provisions of U.S. law, domestic producers facing competition from imports that have been "dumped" on the U.S. market can seek tariffs. Steel is one of the industries that have sought this type of protection. Application of antidumping rules has been a constant source of friction between the United States and the EU. The WTO has ruled against the United States in several recent antidumping cases, including an attempt by President George W. Bush to impose antidumping tariffs on steel imports.

Advocates of free trade object to antidumping laws on two grounds. First, they point out that in times of slack world demand for a product, efficiency requires that firms temporarily sell that product at prices below average total costs. Second, they claim that "dumped" imports, like all other imports, produce benefits for consumers that must be weighed against the harm done to producers.

In recent years, some economists have argued that the traditional case for free trade relies too much on the model of perfect competition. They say that in an era of global oligopolies, such as electronics and airline industries, countries can sometimes gain, at the expense of their trading partners, from "strategic" use of new protectionist policies. However, the case for the new strategic protectionism has many of the weaknesses of the case for the old protectionism: Retaliation by trading partners pursuing their own strategies may lead to a situation in which everyone is left worse off than under free trade. And rent seeking by special interest groups is likely to steer trade policies toward strategies that make one group better off at the expense of others within the country, rather than at the expense of foreign competitors.[5] For example, U.S. manufacturers of flat display screens for laptop computers have recently sought protection against competing screens made in Asia. But among the biggest losers from such a trade restriction would be U.S. firms manufacturing laptop computers (many for export) using screens made in Asia.

Understanding Protectionism: Impacts of Trade on Income Distribution

Why is it that protectionist measures are so widely used, despite the potential economic efficiency to be gained from free trade? To understand the sources of protec-

ECONOMICS IN THE NEWS 20.1
OUTSOURCING

Shifting U.S. jobs overseas has become a hot-button political issue. But the bottom line for companies is that outsourcing saves them a lot of money.

Early in 2004, Gregory Mankiw, chairman President Bush's Council of Economic Advisers, took a lot of heat from both sides of the political aisle for suggesting that outsourcing to India and other countries is a win-win for both sides. Democratic presidential candidate John Kerry and Republican House Speaker Dennis Hastert sharply criticized the senior Bush aide, saying jobs should stay in the United States. Kerry said offshoring is done by "Benedict Arnold CEOs."

Just as China is the top low-cost manufacturer, India is the equivalent in business services. India exported nearly $10 billion in tech services in 2003, mostly to the United States. The volume is said to be growing more than 30 percent a year. Some big changes in the past decade are driving this growth. India has opened itself to trade and eased business restrictions. Plus, communications advances have made it far easier to have operations around the world. That $10 billion makes up less than 3 percent of global spending on IT services, says Ashish Thadhani, senior vice president of Brean Murray & Co. "So there's lots of room to grow," he said.

Putting a stop to such growth now won't be easy. Savings are a big draw, with quality of work a close second. "The rule of thumb is that each employee in India translates into annual savings of $20,000 to $30,000," said Thadhani. "General Electric is saving well over $300 million doing captive in-house business process outsourcing in India. Recently IBM indicated its savings (in information technology services) could be more than $150 million a year," he said.

GE spokesman Peter Stack, echoing Mankiw's win-win sentiment, says savings are only part of the allure. "The abilities of (developing) countries to rapidly grow middle classes and well-compensated work forces benefits us tremendously. They create markets for us to sell into," he said. "It's about global competitiveness."

Since entering India in 1997, GE's work force there has swelled to over 20,000. Stack says jobs done in India are increasingly sophisticated and include pure science research and development.

China and India have a seemingly endless supply of lower cost workers. India's 1.1 billion population is second only to China's 1.3 billion. But India has a steady stream of high-caliber professionals. They are English-speaking engineers, software technicians, and other high-tech specialists. They're also call-center personnel trained to modify their Raj-rooted Anglo-Indian accents and speak like Americans. "The Indian education system places strong emphasis on technical and quantitative skills, English proficiency and a diligent work ethic," Thadhani said.

Source: Marilyn Alva, "U.S. Firms' Outsourcing To India Reaps Big Savings, Political Heat," *Investor's Business Daily*, February 20, 2004. Portions reprinted with permission.

tionism, we can begin by considering the effects of trade on the distribution of income within each country. A modification of the Spain-Norway example to take into account more than one factor of production will illustrate some basic principles.

Suppose that fishing requires a relatively large capital investment per worker, in the form of expensive boats, nets, and navigation equipment, while farming requires a relatively small investment in tractors and plows. Fishing can then be said to be capital intensive and farming to be labor intensive. Also assume, as before, that in the absence of trade the opportunity cost of fish will be higher in Spain than in Norway, so that Spain has a comparative advantage in grain and Norway has a comparative advantage in fish. As in the single-factor example, international trade will still make it possible for total world production of both fish and grain to increase. It will still enable the quantities of both goods available in both countries to rise. Now, however, a new question arises:

How will the gains from trade be distributed within each country?

To answer this question, we must look at what happens in factor markets as trade brings about increasing specialization in each country. In Norway, production shifts from farming to fishing. As grain production is phased out, large quantities of labor and relatively small quantities of capital are released. The shift in production thus creates a surplus of labor and a shortage of capital. Factor markets can return to equilibrium only when wages fall relative to the rate of return on capital. Only then will fisheries adopt more labor-intensive production methods. Meanwhile the opposite process occurs in Spain: The shift from fishing to farming depresses the rate of return on capital and increases the wage rate.

These changes in relative factor prices determine how the gains from trade are distributed among the people of each country. Spanish workers and Norwegian boat owners will gain doubly from trade: first because trade increases the size of the pie (the total quantity of goods) and second because the shifts in factor prices give them a larger slice of that pie. For Norwegian workers and Spanish owners of agricultural capital, in contrast, one of these effects works against the other. These groups still benefit from the growth of the pie, but they get a smaller piece of it than before. They may or may not end up better off as a result of the trade.

Suppose that the comparative advantage in the pretrade situation is large and the difference in factor intensity between the two countries is small. Norwegian workers and owners of Spanish farms will still gain from trade in an absolute sense, even though they will lose ground relative to others in their own country. If conditions are less favorable, however, they can end up worse off than they were before trade began. Who gains and who loses depends partly on the degree of specialization of factors of production.

So far we have looked at matters only in terms of broadly defined labor, as if workers could move from job to job without cost. However, suppose instead that we think not in terms of labor in general but in terms of people with farming skills and people with fishing skills, or auto workers and textile workers. When specialized skills and locational factors are taken into account, the effects of trade include not only changes in relative wages, but also periods of unemployment, costs of retraining, and moving expenses.[6] The uneven impact of changes in trade patterns on the lives and jobs of specific categories of workers turns out to be one of the main sources of political support for protectionism, as we will see in the next section.

Protectionism and Public Choice

International competition, like other forms of competition, tends to drive wages and returns to other factors of production toward the level of opportunity costs. Protection against foreign competition relieves the pressure and permits the protected firms and workers to earn rents, that is, profits and wages in excess of opportunity costs. Thus, the political process that results in trade restrictions can be analyzed in terms of public choice theory and rent seeking.

As a specific example, consider the quotas that were imposed on U.S. imports of automobiles from Japan beginning in 1981. *Applying Economic Ideas 20.1* describes those quotas and their effects. According to the research cited there, the quotas imposed high costs on U.S. consumers, substantially boosted the profits of both U.S. and Japanese auto companies, and resulted in wage increases for workers, with either a small job gain or a small job loss. Virtually all economists who have investigated the quotas agree that the total costs to U.S. consumers exceeded the gain in profits and wages to U.S. firms and workers. Public choice theory suggests how this policy could have won approval in the representative democracy of the United States despite its unfavorable ratio of benefits to costs.

First, consider consumers. According to Mannering and Winston's estimates, the 20 percent increase in the prices of Japanese autos and the 8 percent increase in those of U.S. autos cost consumers $14 billion in 1984 alone. However, some 77 million U.S. households owned cars that year. Thus, the cost of the quotas per car-owning household averaged less than $200 per year. According to public choice theory, benefits or costs that are shared among large numbers of people tend to have relatively little political impact.

Next, consider producers. Three major U.S. producers shared some $9 billion in rents in 1984 alone as a result of the quotas. Those three ranked first, third, and eleventh in size among all U.S. corporations. Large benefits concentrated on a few visible and politically active parties tend to have a more than proportionate influence in a representative democracy.

The situation with respect to workers is more complex. The United Auto Workers (UAW) strongly supported the quotas, arguing that they would protect jobs for American workers. Estimates by Robert Crandall showed some gain in jobs for U.S. autoworkers, though at a very high cost per job. Unionized workers fit the pattern of a well-organized group on whom benefits are concentrated. Such a group would tend to have more political clout in proportion to its size than would more numerous but less organized consumers. However, what can we make of Mannering and Winston's estimates, which showed an actual loss of jobs in the United States as a result of the quotas? If these estimates are valid, do they imply that the UAW behaved irrationally in supporting quotas? Not necessarily, because the principles of public choice also apply to internal union politics. According to the median worker model of union behavior, the least senior workers tend to have relatively little influence on union policy. Yet it is those workers who would have borne the brunt of the layoffs resulting from the quotas. The median autoworker would support quotas in the expectation of sharing increased industry rents via higher wages.

Finally, consider the Japanese automakers. According to Mannering and Winston's estimates, the 20 percent rise in the prices of Japanese cars more than offset the reduction in sales of those cars, leading to a $3 billion gain in revenue. (This would perhaps be shared in part by Japanese autoworkers.) It is not surprising, then, that the Japanese agreed to the quotas—and even decided to continue them after they were abandoned

APPLYING ECONOMIC IDEAS 20.1

BENEFITS AND COSTS OF AUTOMOBILE IMPORT QUOTAS

The early 1980s were hard times for the U.S. auto industry. A combination of soaring gasoline prices and back-to-back recessions cut demand. Sales of fuel-hungry U.S.-built cars were especially hard hit, falling from 9 million units per year in 1978 to an average of just under 6 million units in 1980 through 1982. Meanwhile, the profits of U.S. automakers, which had been well above the average of all industries, turned into losses in the 1980s. It took a government bailout to save Chrysler, one of the Big Three U.S. automakers, from bankruptcy.

As the market share of foreign producers soared from around 15 percent in the mid-1970s to nearly 30 percent in the early 1980s, the automakers, the United Auto Workers, and politicians from car-producing states joined forces to demand protection. The Reagan administration's response was an agreement with the Japanese government to limit U.S. imports of Japanese cars to 1.68 million units in the year beginning April 1981. This quota was extended for the next two years at the same level and for the following year at a level of 1.85 million units.

The effects of the quotas were dramatic. As the economy recovered from recession in 1983 and 1984, a frantic seller's market developed. Waiting lists for popular models grew. Dealer markups of hundreds and even thousands of dollars replaced the rebates and low-interest loans of previous years. The quotas, which had been quietly accepted as a way of saving American jobs during the recession, became a subject of widespread debate.

Were the gains in terms of profits and jobs saved worth the cost of the quotas to consumers? Probably not, according to studies of the effects of the quotas.

First, it is necessary to estimate the impact of the quotas on car prices. The claims were conflicting. The automakers themselves said that any increase in prices had resulted from consumers' tendency to switch to larger cars after fuel prices started to fall in 1982 and 1983. A study by Robert Crandall of the Brookings Institution used three different statistical approaches to separate the effects of the quotas from those of changes in the size and other features of cars sold. All three methods led to similar conclusions. In the 1981 to 1983 period, the quotas raised the prices of U.S.-made cars by about $400 per unit and those of Japanese cars by about $1,000 per unit. The total cost to U.S. consumers in 1983 was about $4.3 billion. Fred Mannering and Clifford Winston, also of Brookings, extended the study to 1984 when the effects of the quotas were even stronger. In that year they found prices of Japanese costs were raised by 20 percent and those of U.S.-made cars by 8 percent for a total cost to consumers of $14 billion.

What were the gains to workers? Crandall estimated that for 1983 about 26,000 autoworker jobs were saved out of a base of 600,000, at a cost of $160,000 per job saved. Using a somewhat different method, Mannering and Winston estimated that there was an actual loss of U.S. autoworker jobs as a result of the quotas; the loss peaked at 30,000 jobs in 1984. This job loss occurred because U.S. automakers, shielded from Japanese competition, cut back their output in order to raise prices and profits. However, although jobs may have been lost, the average industry wage was estimated to have risen by about 10 percent as automakers shared some of their increased profits with their employees.

Mannering and Winston estimated that the quotas boosted the profits of U.S. automakers by $8.9 billion in 1984. Japanese automakers also gained. The 20 percent increase in the price of their cars more than offset the decrease in volume sold, increasing the profits of Japanese firms by an estimated $3 billion.

In effect the quotas amounted to an international automobile cartel organized and enforced by the U.S. and Japanese governments. The Japanese were so pleased with the results of this cartel that they decided to continue it unilaterally by limiting their automobile exports to 2.25 million units per year after the United States withdrew from the quota agreement in 1985.

Sources: Robert W. Crandall, "Import Quotas and the Automobile Industry: The Costs of Protectionism," *Brookings Review* (Summer 1984): 8–16; Clifford Winston and associates, *Blind Intersection: Policy and the Automobile Industry* (Washington, D.C.: Brookings Institution, 1987), Chapter 4.

by the United States. Why, though, should the United States have preferred quotas to a tariff increase? A 20 percent tariff would have cut Japanese sales by just as much while raising revenue for the U.S. Treasury rather than for the Japanese automakers.

Again the answer is found in public choice theory. U.S. taxpayers are a large but poorly organized group. They have no effective means of lobbying for a tariff rather than a quota. The Japanese government, by contrast, maintains an effective political presence in Washington, and the Japanese auto industry, in turn, is an influential lobbying force within the Japanese political system. Thus, it is no surprise to find that the Japanese earned a generous slice of the rents generated by the quotas.

This analysis could be repeated for any protected market. For example, the cost to consumers of each job saved in the apparel industry is estimated at $46,000 per year, compared with average earnings of just $11,000 per year for textile workers.[7] Studies of tariffs and quotas on sugar, peanuts, books, ceramic tile, and other products give similar results. In each case economic investigators have found that total gains to producers fall short of total costs to consumers; however, the benefits are concentrated on compact, politically active groups while the costs are spread among millions of households.

The Rhetoric of Protectionism

Although protectionist policies can be explained in terms of the theory of rent seeking, advocates of such policies are often reluctant to speak the language of self-interest, at least in public; rather, they prefer to present their policies as consistent with the general interest. They rarely invoke positive economic analysis, which, with its focus on benefits and costs, tends to favor free trade. Instead, they tend to play on normative themes.

Nationalism is one such theme. Economic strength is often equated with a country's ability to produce all of the goods its own consumers demand. The desire to buy foreign goods simply because they are cheaper or better is depicted as selfish and unpatriotic. At the same time, protectionists routinely treat jobs for American workers as the only jobs that matter and ignore the damage done by protectionist policies to workers abroad. In such cases as the MFA's textile quotas, which are much tighter for developing countries than for industrialized countries, this aspect of protectionist rhetoric borders on open racism. It calls to mind the efforts of white workers in earlier times to protect their jobs against competition by minority workers within the United States.

In other cases, rather than scorning foreign workers the protectionists pose as their allies. Foreign workers who earn lower wages than U.S. workers are characterized as "exploited," implying that those workers would somehow be better off if we stopped buying the products they make. However, this proposition is hard to support in terms of positive economics. If foreign workers earn less than U.S. workers, it is not necessarily because they are exploited but because their countries are poorly endowed with human and physical capital. Injecting capital into their economies through foreign investment and adding to the demand for their labor by importing the goods they make is far more likely to benefit those workers than to harm them.

The notion of "creating a level playing field" is another rhetorical device employed by protectionists. Other countries do not follow the rules of free trade. They impose tariff and nontariff barriers on *our* exports; therefore, we should retaliate by refusing to buy *their* exports. But a distinction must be drawn between the use of tariffs and quotas as bargaining tools through which to win freer trade and the notion that retaliatory trade restrictions are beneficial in themselves. Free traders offer an analogy of their own. Suppose, they say, that you are in a lifeboat and one of your fellow passengers shoots a hole in it. That is a stupid thing to do—but is it smart to retaliate by shooting another hole in the boat yourself?

There is no reason to expect the war of words over trade policy to end soon. There is also no indication that firms and workers will stop using the machinery of representative democracy to pursue their own economic interests, sometimes at the expense of their neighbors. But an understanding of the economics of international trade can help in evaluating the claims made by the various participants in this ongoing debate.

SUMMARY

1. **How can the principle of comparative advantage be applied to international trade?** A country is said to have a comparative advantage in the production of a good if it can produce it at a lower opportunity cost than its trading partner can. Trade is based on the principle that if each country exports goods in which it has a comparative advantage, total world production of all goods and services can increase and boost total consumption in each trading country. The *Heckscher-Ohlin theorem* proposes that countries will tend to have a comparative advantage in goods that make intensive use of the factors of production that are relatively abundant in that country.

2. **How is the notion of competitiveness related to that of comparative advantage?** In the first half of the 1980s, U.S. imports expanded more rapidly than exports, leaving the country with a record trade deficit. Some observers interpreted this situation as indicating a loss of competitiveness, implying that U.S. firms were no longer capable of producing goods that other countries wanted. However, the principle of comparative advantage holds that a country must always have some goods that can be exported profitably. International financial transactions and exchange rates rather than failures on the part of U.S. workers or managers, seem to explain much of the apparent loss of competitiveness by the United States in the 1980s.

3. **What was the general trend of international trade policy during the post–World War II period?** The general trend in international trade policy has been toward a reduction of traditional *tariff* and *quota* barriers to trade. However, recent years have seen increased use of *protectionist* devices such as orderly marketing agreements, voluntary quotas, antidumping laws, and restrictive product standards.

4. **How does international trade affect income distribution within each country?** In a world with two or more factors of production, trade

tends to increase the demand for factors that are used relatively intensively in producing goods for export and to decrease the demand for factors that are used relatively intensively in producing goods that compete with imported goods. Thus, although trade benefits a country as a whole, it may not benefit owners of factors that are specialized for producing goods that compete with imports.

5. **How can protectionist policies be understood in terms of public choice theory and rent seeking?** Because protectionist policies shield firms and factor owners from international competition, they allow rents—that is, payments in excess of opportunity costs—to be earned. Often those who benefit from these rents are small, well-organized groups that have political influence out of proportion to their numbers. Although the overall costs of protectionism tend to outweigh the benefits, the costs are spread widely among consumers, each of whom is affected less than producers by any given trade barrier.

KEY TERMS

Absolute advantage	Protectionism
Heckscher-Ohlin theorem	Tariff
	Import quotas

PROBLEMS AND TOPICS FOR DISCUSSION

1. **Examining the lead-off case.** What does the example suggest about U.S. versus Mexican comparative advantage in the production of construction equipment? Of vacuum cleaners? Do these examples suggest a pattern of trade that would be consistent with the Heckscher-Ohlin theorem? What are the potential benefits and costs of NAFTA for U.S. and Mexican workers? Consumers? Owners of productive resources other than labor?

2. **A change in costs and comparative advantage.** Suppose that new, high-yield grains are introduced in Norway and that the number of labor hours needed to grow a ton of grain there is cut from 5 hours to 2.5 hours. What will happen to trade between Norway and Spain? If the number of labor hours needed to grow a ton of grain in Norway falls all the way to 2, what will happen to the pattern of trade?

3. **Competitiveness.** Consider the following statement: "The United States may still be number one, but I don't think we will be much longer. The European Union, Japan, all areas of the world are catching up. Soon it will no longer be economical for us to produce anything." On the basis of what you have learned about the principle of comparative advantage, do you think it is possible to reach a point at which it is no longer worthwhile to produce anything—that is, a point at which it becomes economical to import all goods? Discuss.

4. **Trade bargaining.** If you were a strong supporter of free trade and in charge of U.S. international trade policy, would you cut tariffs and quotas or would you negotiate with the nation's trading partners, maintaining trade barriers unless they lowered theirs too? Discuss.

5. **Protectionism in the news.** Scan several issues of a business publication, such as *The Wall Street Journal, Fortune, Forbes,* or *BusinessWeek,* looking for articles on trade restrictions. Are the restrictions discussed imposed by other nations on U.S. goods or by the United States on imports from abroad? Do the restrictions take the form of tariffs, quotas, or "new protectionist" measures? What arguments are mentioned in favor of or against the restrictions? Who gains and who loses from them?

CASE FOR DISCUSSION

WTO Ruling in Cotton Subsidy Case Makes U.S. Farmers Nervous

A ruling by the World Trade Organization condemning U.S. subsidies to cotton producers could open the door to similar cases, perhaps forcing advanced countries to agree to deeper cuts in their subsidies, say trade officials and agricultural experts.

The WTO ruled in a confidential decision that the U.S. had fallen foul of its WTO obligations by providing subsidies of $12.5 billion to U.S. cotton growers between 1999 and 2002, boosting U.S. exports and depressing prices at the expense of Brazilian cotton growers and other producers.

Under its left-leaning president, Luis Inacio Lula da Silva, Brazil has taken a lead among emerging countries in pushing for reductions of agricultural subsidies in the developed world.

The threat of further cases should help strengthen the bargaining position of agricultural exporting countries. Farm exporters are pressing for big cuts in domestic supports for rich-country producers, but the U.S. and European Union say developing countries must also make concessions, for instance, by cutting tariffs on agricultural and industrial goods.

U.S. farmers are nervous that the ruling could set a broad precedent. Payments similar to the cotton subsidies are made for other U.S. commodities such as soybeans, rice, and wheat.

Source: Jonathan Wheatley, Edward Alden, and Frances Williams, "Brazil Victory Could Prompt Subsidies Cases," *Financial Times*, April 28, 2004, p. 8..

QUESTIONS

1. A subsidy on exports is, in a sense, the opposite of a tariff on imports. If a tariff lowers efficiency, would you expect a subsidy to increase efficiency, or also lower it? How do tariffs and subsidies compare in the way they distort trade according to comparative advantage?
2. Who gains and who loses from U.S. cotton subsidies? Consider each of the following groups: U.S. producers, U.S. taxpayers, Brazilian producers, consumers in both countries? Do you think total gains exceed or fall short of total losses?
3. How could you explain the expenditure of billions of taxpayer dollars to subsidize a relatively few, highly prosperous U.S. cotton producers? Do the categories of public choice theory help here?

END NOTES

1. G. D. A. MacDougal, "British and American Exports: A Study Suggested by the Theory of Comparative Costs," *Economic Journal* (December 1951).
2. A study by Robert E. Lipsey and Irving B. Kravis showed that in the two decades following 1966, U.S.-based multinationals have held a steady 7.7 percent share of world exports. See "The Competitiveness and Comparative Advantage of U.S. Multinationals, 1957–1983" National Bureau of Economic Research Working Paper No. 2051, October 1987.
3. For a thorough discussion of the MFA, see Thomas Grennes, "The Multifiber Arrangement and the Management of International Textile Trade," *Cato Journal* (Spring/Summer 1989): 107–131.
4. Kevin Watkins, "The High Cost in Lives from Broken Promises on Trade," *International Herald Tribune*, November 16, 2002.
5. For a good summary of the literature on strategic use of new protectionist devices, see Robert E. Baldwin, "Are Economists' Traditional Trade Policies Still Valid?" *Journal of Economic Literature* (June 1992): 804–829.
6. Data cited by Grennes give some idea of the size of these impacts. Between the 1950s and the 1980s, employment in the U.S. apparel industry decreased from more than 9 percent of manufacturing employment to less than 6 percent, and wages fell from 82 percent of average manufacturing earnings to 60 percent. These changes can be attributed at least in part to the increases in apparel imports that took place despite MFA quotas. The average apparel worker displaced from a job by imports was unemployed for 24 weeks before finding a job elsewhere. Without the MFA, the declines in

the wages and jobs of apparel workers would have been even greater. Total employment in the U.S. apparel industry is estimated to be some 200,000 or more higher than it would be without the MFA.

7. See Grennes. The comparison of consumers' costs to workers' wages actually understates the true cost-benefit ratio, because the MFA's cost to consumers continues year after year, whereas displaced apparel workers are out of work less than six months, on the average. Taking this fact into account, it has been estimated that consumers bear $31 in costs through higher apparel prices for each $1 benefit to apparel workers.

GLOSSARY

Absolute advantage The ability of a country to produce a good at a lower cost, in terms of quantity of factor inputs, than the cost at which the good can be produced by its trading partners.

Accounting profit Total revenue minus explicit costs.

Adverse selection The tendency of people facing the greatest risk of loss to be most likely to seek insurance.

Antitrust laws A set of laws, including the Sherman Act and the Clayton Act, that seek to control market structure and the competitive behavior of firms.

Arbitrage The activity of earning a profit by buying something at a low price in one market and reselling it at a higher price in another.

Barrier to entry Any circumstance that prevents a new firm in a market from competing on an equal footing with existing ones.

Benefit reduction rate The reduction in the benefits of a transfer program that results from a $1 increase in the beneficiary's earned income.

Bounded rationality The assumption that people intend to make choices that best serve their objectives, but have limited ability to acquire and process information.

Capital All means of production that are created by people, including tools, industrial equipment, and structures.

Capitalized value of a rent The present value of all future rents that a piece of land or other resource is expected to earn.

Cartel A group of producers that jointly maximize profits by fixing prices and limiting output.

Census income Cash income from all sources, including earned income and cash transfer payments

Change in demand A change in the quantity of a good that buyers are willing and able to purchase that results from a change in some condition other than the price of that good; shown by a shift in the demand curve.

Change in quantity demanded A change in the quantity of a good that buyers are willing and able to purchase that results from a change in the good's price, other things being equal; shown by a movement from one point to another along a demand curve.

Change in quantity supplied A change in the quantity of a good that suppliers are willing and able to sell that results from a change in the good's price, other things being equal; shown by a movement along a supply curve.

Change in supply A change in the quantity of a good that suppliers are willing and able to sell that results from a change in some condition other than the good's price; shown by a shift in the supply curve.

Closed monopoly A monopoly that is protected by legal restrictions on competition.

Coase theorem The proposition that problems of externalities will be resolved efficiently through private exchange, regardless of the initial assignment of property rights, provided that there are no transaction costs.

Comparative advantage The ability to produce a good or service at a relatively lower opportunity cost than someone else.

Complementary goods A pair of goods for which an increase in the price of one results in a decrease in demand for the other.

Concentration ratio The percentage of all sales that is accounted for by the four or eight largest firms in a market.

Conditional forecast A prediction of future economic events in the form "If A, then B, other things being equal."

Conglomerate mergers Mergers of firms in unrelated markets.

Constant returns to scale A situation in which there are neither economies nor diseconomies of scale.

Constitutional choice A choice among various sets of rules for democratic government that is intended to produce desirable outcomes when applied to future situations whose details are not known.

Consumer equilibrium A state of affairs in which a consumer cannot increase the total utility gained from a given budget by spending less on one good and more on another.

Consumer surplus The difference between the maximum that a consumer would be willing to pay for a unit of a good and the amount that he or she actually pays.

Contestable market A market in which barriers to entry and exit are low.

Corporation A firm that takes the form of an independent legal entity with ownership divided into equal shares and each owner's liability limited to his/her investment in the firm.

Craft union A union of skilled workers who all practice the same trade.

Cross-elasticity of demand The ratio of the percentage change in the quantity of a good demanded to a given percentage change in the price of some other good, other things being equal.

Deadweight loss A loss of consumer or producer surplus that is not balanced by a gain to someone else.

Demand The willingness and ability of buyers to purchase goods.

Demand curve A graphical representation of the relationship between the price of a good and the quantity of that good that buyers demand.

Derived demand Demand for a productive input that stems from the demand for the product the input is used to produce.

Differential rent The rents earned by superior units of a resource in a situation in which units of a resource differ in productivity.

Discounting The procedure by which the present value of a sum that is payable in the future is calculated.

Diseconomies of scale A situation in which long-run average cost increases as output increases.

Duncan index of dissimilarity For a set of occupations in which both men and women are employed, the percentage of men (or women) who would have to change occupations to equalize the numbers of men and women in each occupation.

Dutch auction An auction that begins with a high bid, which is lowered until a buyer is found.

Dynamic efficiency The ability of an economy to increase consumer satisfaction through innovation and technological change.

Econometrics The statistical analysis of empirical economic data.

Economic efficiency A state of affairs in which it is impossible to make any change that satisfies one person's wants more fully without causing some other person's wants to be satisfied less fully.

Economic rent Any payment to a factor of production in excess of its opportunity cost.

Economics The social science that seeks to understand the choices people make in using scarce resources to meet their wants.

Economies of scale A situation in which long-run average cost decreases as output increases.

Efficiency in distribution A situation in which it is not possible, by redistributing existing supplies of goods, to satisfy one person's wants more fully without causing some other person's wants to be satisfied less fully.

Efficiency in production A situation in which it is not possible, given available knowledge and productive resources, to produce more of one good without forgoing the opportunity to produce some of another good.

Efficiency wage theory The theory that wages above the minimum necessary to attract qualified workers can raise productivity by enough to increase profit.

Elastic demand A situation in which quantity demanded changes by a larger percentage than price, so that total revenue increases as price decreases.

Elasticity A measure of the response of one variable to a change in another, stated as a ratio of the percentage change in one variable to the associated percentage change in another variable.

Empirical Based on experience or observation.

English auction An auction in which bidding starts low and proceeds until the good is sold to the highest bidder.

Entrepreneurship The process of looking for new possibilities—making use of new ways of doing things, being alert to new opportunities, and overcoming old limits.

Equilibrium A condition in which buyers' and sellers' plans exactly mesh in the marketplace, so that the quantity supplied exactly equals the quantity demanded at a given price.

Excess burden of the tax The part of the economic burden of a tax that takes the form of consumer and producer surplus that is lost because the tax reduces the equilibrium quantity sold.

Excess quantity demanded (shortage) A condition in which the quantity of a good demanded at a given price exceeds the quantity supplied.

Excess quantity supplied (surplus) A condition in which the quantity of a good supplied at a given price exceeds the quantity demanded.

Expected value For a set of possible outcomes, the sum of the probability of each outcome multiplied by the value of that outcome.

Explicit costs Opportunity costs that take the form of explicit payments to suppliers of factors of production and intermediate goods.

Externalities The effects of producing or consuming a good whose impact on third parties other than buyers and sellers of the good is not reflected in the good's price.

Factors of production The basic inputs of labor, capital, and natural resources used in producing all goods and services.

Fixed costs The explicit and implicit opportunity costs associated with providing fixed inputs.

Fixed inputs Inputs that cannot be increased or decreased in a short time in order to increase or decrease output.

Full rationality The assumption that people make full use of all available information in calculating how best to meet their objectives.

Futures contract An agreement to exchange something at a specified date in the future at a price that is agreed upon now.

Giffen good An inferior good accounting for a large share of a consumer's budget that has a positively sloped demand curve because the income effect of a price change outweighs the substitution effect.

Government failure A situation in which a government policy causes inefficient use of resources.

Heckscher-Ohlin theorem The proposition that countries tend to export goods that make intensive use of the factors of production that the country possesses in relative abundance.

Hedging An operation in which futures markets or options markets are used to offset one risk with another.

Herfindahl-Hirschmann index (HHI) An index of market concentration that is calculated by squaring the percentage market shares of all firms in an industry then summing the squared-values.

High-power incentives Incentives that take the form of a claim to the residual profit resulting from a task, combined with bearing the risk of any loss.

Horizontal mergers Mergers of firms that compete in the same market.

Human capital Capital in the form of learned abilities that have been acquired through formal training or education or through on-the-job experience.

Import quotas A limit on the quantity of a good that can be imported over a given period.

Implicit costs Opportunity costs of using resources contributed by the firm's owners (or owned by the firm itself as a legal entity) that are not obtained in exchange for explicit payments.

Income effect The part of the change in quantity demanded of a good whose price has fallen that is caused by the increase in real income resulting from the price change.

Income elasticity of demand The ratio of the percentage change in the quantity of a good demanded to a given percentage change in consumer incomes, other things being equal.

Industrial union A union of all the workers in an industry, including both skilled and unskilled workers in all trades.

Inelastic demand A situation in which quantity demanded changes by a smaller percentage than price, so that total revenue decreases as price decreases.

Inferior good A good for which an increase in consumer incomes results in a decrease in demand.

Information asymmetry A situation in which some parties to a transaction possess relevant information that other parties do not possess.

Inframarginal rents The difference between the payment made to a unit of resource and the minimum required for that resource to be willingly supplied in a situation in which units of a resource differ in terms of the willingness with which they are supplied.

In-kind transfers Transfer payments in the form of goods or services, such as food, housing, or medical care, rather than cash.

Intrapreneurship Entrepreneurial activity carried out within a large business organization.

Inventory A stock of a finished good awaiting sale or use.

Investment The act of increasing the economy's stock of capital—that is, its supply of means of production made by people.

Labor The contributions to production made by people working with their minds and muscles.

Labor market discrimination A situation in which employers are unwilling to hire members of a disfavored group at the same wage rate that they pay to equally productive members of a more favored group.

Law of demand The principle that an inverse relationship exists between the price of a good and the quantity of that good that buyers demand, other things being equal.

Law of diminishing returns The principle that as one variable input is increased while all others remain fixed, a point will be reached beyond which the marginal physical product of the variable input will begin to decrease.

Limit pricing A strategy in which the dominant firm in a market charges less than the short-run profit-maximizing price in order to limit the likelihood of entry by new competitors.

Loanable funds market A general term for the set of markets in which people borrow and lend, for whatever reason.

Lobbying Any method of communicating with elected officials to advocate a particular policy.

Logrolling The practice of trading votes among members of a legislative body.

Long run A time horizon that is long enough to permit changes in both fixed and variable inputs.

Lorenz curve A graph that represents the degree of inequality in an economy.

Low-power incentives Incentives that take such forms as promotion for work well done or reprimands for errors.

Macroeconomics The branch of economics that studies large-scale economic phenomena, particularly inflation, unemployment, and economic growth.

Marginal-average rule The rule that marginal cost must equal average cost when average cost is at its minimum.

Marginal cost The increase in cost required to raise the output of some good or service by one unit.

Marginal physical product The increase in output, expressed in physical units, produced by each added unit of one variable input, other things being equal.

Marginal productivity theory of distribution A theory of income distribution in which each input of production receives a payment equal to its marginal revenue product.

Marginal resource cost The amount by which a firm's total resource cost must increase for the firm to obtain an additional unit of that resource.

Marginal revenue The amount by which total revenue changes as a result of a one-unit increase in quantity sold.

Marginal revenue product The change in revenue that results from the sale of the output produced by one additional unit of an input.

Marginal utility The amount of added utility gained from a one-unit increase in consumption of a good, other things being equal.

Market Any arrangement people have for trading with one another.

Market concentration The degree to which a market is dominated by a few large firms.

Market failure A situation in which a market fails to coordinate choices in a way that achieves efficient use of resources.

Marketing The process of finding out what customers want and channeling a flow of goods and services to meet those wants.

Market performance The degree to which markets work efficiently in providing arrangements for mutually beneficial trade.

Market structure The key traits of a market, including the number and size of firms, the extent to which the products of various firms are different or similar, ease of entry and exit, and availability of information.

Median voter model A model showing that there is a tendency for decisions in a direct democracy to correspond to the interests of voters whose preferences lie near the middle of the community scale.

Microeconomics The branch of economics that studies the choices of individuals, including households, business firms, and government agencies.

Minimum efficient scale The output level at which economies of scale cease.

Model A synonym for theory; in economics, often applied to theories that are stated in graphical or mathematical form.

Monopolistic competition A market structure in which there are many small firms, a differentiated product, and easy entry and exit.

Monopoly A situation in which there is only a single seller of a good or service.

Monopsony A situation in which there is only a single buyer in a market; more generally, any situation in which a firm is a price searcher in a market in which it is a buyer.

Moral hazard Behavior that increases the risk of loss, yet is undertaken in the knowledge that losses will be covered by insurance.

Natural monopoly An industry in which long-run average cost is minimized when only one firm serves the market.

Natural resources Anything that can be used as a productive input in its natural state, such as farmland, building sites, forests, and mineral deposits.

Negative income tax A plan under which all transfer programs would be combined into a single program that pays cash benefits according to a household's income level.

Net marginal tax rate The sum of the marginal tax rate for all taxes paid by a household plus the benefit reduction rates of all transfer programs from which the household benefits.

Normal good A good for which an increase in consumer incomes results in an increase in demand.

Normal profit (normal return on capital) The implicit opportunity cost of capital contributed by the firm's owners (equity capital).

Normal return on capital *See Normal profit.*

Normative economics The area of economics that is devoted to judgments about whether economic policies or conditions are good or bad.

Ockham's razor The principle that simpler theories are to be preferred to more complex ones when both are consistent with given observations.

Oligopolistic interdependence The need to pay close attention to the actions of rival firms in an oligopolistic market when making price or production decisions.

Oligopoly A market structure in which there are a few firms, at least some of which are large in relation to the size of the market.

Open monopoly A monopoly in which one firm is, at least for a time, the sole supplier of a product but has no special protection from competition.

Opportunism An attempt by one party to an agreement to seek an advantage at the expense of another party to the agreement.

Opportunity cost The cost of a good or service measured in terms of the forgone opportunity to pursue the best possible alternative activity with the same time or resources.

Options Contracts under which one party obtains the right (but not the obligation) to buy something at a specified date in the future at a price that is agreed upon now.

Partnership An association of two or more people who operate a business as co-owners under a voluntary legal agreement.

Perfect competition A market structure that is characterized by a large number of small firms, a homogeneous product, freedom of entry and exit, and equal access to information.

Perfectly elastic demand A situation in which the demand curve is a horizontal line.

Perfectly inelastic demand A situation in which the demand curve is a vertical line.

Political rent seeking (rent seeking) The process of seeking and defending economic rents through the political process.

Pollution abatement Reduction of the quantity of waste discharged into the environment.

Positive economics The area of economics that is concerned with facts and the relationships among them.

Present value The value today of a sum payable in the future. In mathematical terms, the present value of a sum V_p, payable t years in the future, discounted at r percent interest, would grow to the value V_t in t years; the present value formula is $V_p = V_t/(1 + r)\ t$.

Pretransfer poverty A measure of how many people would be poor on the basis of their private sources of income alone.

Price discrimination The practice of charging different prices for various units of a single product when the price differences are not justified by differences in cost.

Price elasticity of demand The ratio of the percentage change in the quantity of a good demanded to a given percentage change in its price, other things being equal.

Price elasticity of supply The ratio of the percentage change in the quantity of a good supplied to a given percentage change in its price, other things being equal.

Price fixing Any attempt by two or more firms to cooperate in setting prices.

Price leadership A situation in which price increases or decreases by a dominant firm in an oligopoly, known as the price leader, are matched by all or most of the other firms in the market.

Price searcher Any firm that faces a negatively sloped demand curve for its product.

Price taker A firm that sells its output at prices that are determined by forces beyond its control.

Principle of diminishing marginal utility The principle that the greater the consumption of some good, the smaller the increase in utility from a one-unit increase in consumption of that good.

Privatization The turning over of government functions to the private sector.

Producer surplus The difference between what producers receive for a unit of a good and the minimum they would be willing to accept.

Production possibility frontier A graph that shows possible combinations of goods that can be produced by an economy given available knowledge and factors of production.

Property rights Legal rules that establish what things a person may use or control, and the conditions under which such use or control may be exercised.

Protectionism Any policy that is intended to shield domestic industries from import competition.

Public assistance Programs under which transfers are made to people who meet some specified low-income standard.

Public choice theory The branch of economics that studies how people use the institutions of government in pursuit of their own interests.

Public goods Goods that (1) cannot be provided for one person without also being provided for others and (2) when provided for one person can be provided for others at zero additional sum.

Pure economic profit The sum that remains when both explicit and implicit costs are subtracted from total revenue.

Pure economic rent The income earned by any resource whose supply is perfectly inelastic with respect to its price.

Rate of return A firm's accounting profit expressed as a percentage of its net worth.

Rate of return on capital The marginal product of capital expressed as an annual percentage rate.

Rationality Acting purposefully to achieve an objective, given constraints on the opportunities that are available.

Rent seeking *See Political rent seeking.*

Reservation price The maximum price that a buyer is willing to pay for a good or the minimum price at which a seller is willing to offer it.

Revenue Price times quantity sold.

Revenue-equivalence theorem The proposition that under certain general circumstances English, Dutch, and sealed-bid auctions can be expected to produce approximately the same winning bid.

Risk aversion A preference for a certain outcome with a given value over a set of risky outcomes with the same expected value.

Risk neutrality Indifference between a certain outcome with a given value and a set of risky outcomes with the same expected value.

Risk pooling A technique in which the risk of loss is shared among many people so that the impact of a loss on any one of them is small.

Risk preference A preference for a set of risky outcomes with a given expected value over a certain outcome with the same expected value.

Scarcity A situation in which there is not enough of a resource to meet all of everyone's wants.

Sealed-bid auction An auction in which all buyers submit bids at the same time, and the item is sold to the highest bidder (or bought from the lowest bidder)

Short run A time horizon within which output can be adjusted only by changing the amounts of variable inputs used while fixed inputs remain unchanged.

Simple monopoly A monopoly that, at any given time, sells its product at a single price that is uniform for all customers.

Social insurance Programs under which transfers are made available to everyone, regardless of income, upon the occurrence of a specified event such as retirement, unemployment, or disability.

Sole proprietorship A firm that is owned, and usually operated, by one person, who receives all the profits and is responsible for all the firm's liabilities.

Speculation Buying something at a low price in the hope of selling it later at a higher price.

Spot price The price at which a good is offered for immediate sale.

Static efficiency The ability of an economy to get the greatest degree of consumer satisfaction from given amounts of resources and technology

Substitute goods A pair of goods for which an increase in the price of one causes an increase in demand for the other.

Substitution effect The part of the increase in quantity demanded of a good whose price has fallen that is caused by substitution of that good for others that are now relatively more costly.

Supply The willingness and ability of sellers to provide goods for sale in a market.

Supply curve A graphical representation of the relationship between the price of a good and the quantity of that good that sellers are willing to supply.

Sunk costs Once-and-for-all costs that, once incurred, cannot be recovered.

Tariff A tax on imported goods.

Tax incidence The distribution of the economic burden of a tax.

Theory A representation of the way in which facts are related to one another.

Time preference The tendency to prefer goods now over goods in the future, other things being equal.

Total physical product The total output of a firm, measured in physical units.

Transaction costs The costs, other than production costs, of carrying out a transaction.

Unit elastic demand A situation in which price and quantity demanded change by the same percentage, so that total revenue remains unchanged as price changes.

Utility The pleasure, satisfaction, or need fulfillment that people obtain from the consumption of goods and services.

Value of marginal product Marginal physical product times the product's per-unit price.

Variable costs The explicit and implicit costs of providing variable inputs.

Variable inputs Inputs that can be varied within a short time in order to increase or decrease output.

Vertical mergers Mergers of firms with a supplier-purchaser relationship.

Winner's curse The tendency for winners of an auction to pay more for a good or service than it is worth (or to offer to sell at a price below the cost of providing the good or service).

INDEX